Portraits of Medieval and Renaissance Living

Portraits of Medieval and Renaissance Living
Essays in Memory of David Herlihy

Edited by
Samuel K. Cohn Jr.
Steven A. Epstein

Ann Arbor

THE UNIVERSITY OF MICHIGAN PRESS

Copyright © by the University of Michigan 1996
All rights reserved
Published in the United States of America by
The University of Michigan Press
Manufactured in the United States of America
⊛ Printed on acid-free paper

1999   1998   1997   1996   4   3   2   1

A CIP catalog record for this book is available from the British Library.

Library of Congress Cataloging-in-Publication Data

Portraits of Medieval and Renaissance living : essays in memory of
   David Herlihy / edited by Samuel K. Cohn, Jr., Steven A. Epstein.
     p.   cm.
   Includes bibliographical references and index.
   ISBN 0-472-10671-6
   1. Civilization, Medieval. I. Cohn, Samuel Kline. II. Epstein,
Steven, 1952– . III. Herlihy, David.
CB351.P67 1996
940.1—dc20   96-5360
                                                CIP

Contents

Part 2
Power and Patronage in the Middle Ages and the Renaissance: Local History

Part 3
Power and Patronage in the Middle Ages and the Renaissance: Social History in Town and Countryside

Introduction

Samuel K. Cohn Jr. and Steven A. Epstein

Portraits of Medieval and Renaissance Living commemorates the work and influence of David Herlihy. The title of this collection of essays comes from a book Herlihy was planning but did not live to complete. Written by his students, colleagues, and friends, these essays demonstrate the unusual breadth of his influence on Medieval and Renaissance history. Today, because of the tremendous achievement of his last three books, *Medieval Households, Opera muliebria,* and *Les Toscans et leurs familles* (in collaboration with Christiane Klapisch-Zuber), David Herlihy is probably best remembered as a historian of the family and, predominantly, the Renaissance family. Yet, surprising for a historian of the postwar period, when specialization increasingly hemmed in all academic disciplines, his intellectual journeys and publications cover a remarkably wide canvas in terms of method, subject matter, chronology, and geography.

His doctoral dissertation, completed under the direction of Robert S. Lopez at Yale University— an archival study of notarial charters in late medieval Pisa— expanded the methodological practices of his teacher by means of an early reckoning with quantitative reasoning. In the preface to the book developed from this dissertation, *Pisa in the Early Renaissance* (1958), Herlihy expressed his fascination with and enthusiasm for the sheer mass of early contracts and other notarial records, which had formerly been the preserve of legal historians and philologists. His insight that these and other medieval cartularies could be scrutinized statistically (and ultimately with the aid of mechanical calculators and computers) led him from the archives of Pisa to explore more broadly social and economic patterns across Western Europe and across the Middle Ages from the seventh century through the High Middle Ages. These scholarly adventures of the late 1950s and early 1960s led him to questions and practices of numismatics, the history of the church, agriculture, law, and technology. It was in this period that Herlihy began to train large numbers of graduate students, first at Bryn Mawr and then at the University of Wisconsin, Madison. The research—its methods and conclusions—gleaned from this systematic analysis of large numbers of medieval contracts (the cartulary) lives on not only in Herlihy's many articles, now collected in two books, but in the work of his students and colleagues, as can be attested in this memorial volume. Indeed, the majority of these essays find stimulus in this period of Herlihy's pioneering work with medieval cartularies (Rosenwein, White, Kreutz, Epstein, Weinberger, Venarde, Given, Miller, Callahan, and Dameron).

From the broad sweep of time and space represented in his studies of property and the church, Herlihy returned to Italy in the mid-1960s and turned his attention again to the particular. This time it was Florence and, at least initially, a single year, 1427. Again, Herlihy had an eye for the remarkable document and the new vistas of the past that could be realized through a quantitative approach. He seized upon the unusual characteristics of the Florentine tax called the Catasto of 1427 and had the imagination to realize that with the assistance of rapidly advancing computer technology—only recently utilized by fellow social scientists and then almost unknown in historians' circles—the historian could reconstruct the economic and demographic characteristics of a territorial state with a degree of detail and sophistication unknown for any city, state, or territory before at least the nineteenth century. With the collaboration of Christiane Klapisch-Zuber such a work was published as *Les Toscans et leurs familles* in 1978. Ever since, it has become a standard source not only for historians of Florence but more broadly for scholars of demography and the family across disciplines, periods, and countries. In the present volume, the impact of this work is attested in the essays of Klapisch-Zuber, Cohn, and Molho and his colleagues.

Since 1978, Herlihy's work fanned in two directions. He continued to plough through archival *fondi* from Florence and other Italian cities, pumping into his computer thousands of electoral registers, *Tratte,* and guild matriculation lists. Unfortunately, his untimely death has robbed the historical community of the major fruit of this endeavor, a collective biography of the Florentine ruling class from the late fourteenth century to the fall of the Republic in 1530.[1] At the same time, analyzing a wide

---

1. At least two essays have been published from this work, and Professor Burr Litchfield at Brown University is now engaged in converting these computer files from Herlihy's Fortran programs to standard ASCII files that will be accessible to a general scholarly community.

array of sources as varied as medieval polyptychs, Icelandic sagas, and saints' lives, Herlihy continued to explore questions of the family. In keeping with the accordion dialogue that had structured his intellectual quests since graduate school, he once again moved from the particulars of the individual Italian city-state to test his hypotheses across the large horizons of Europe and the Middle Ages. With these studies, *Medieval Households, Opera Muliebria,* and numerous articles, Herlihy continued his pioneering role in the burgeoning field of medieval women's history. Herlihy revitalized the study of women in the Middle Ages with quantitative approaches, suggested as early as 1972 in his Smith History Lecture "Women in Medieval Society." The last heritage of David Herlihy as a teacher and historian—the family—is reflected in almost all the essays dedicated to his memory here and is the starting point of the book. We begin with his own words, his last public lecture, the presidential address delivered to the American Historical Association in 1990.

Writing a preface to commemorative essays for David Herlihy is a sad and difficult task. Reasonable hopes encouraged his students and friends to believe that they had all the time in the world in which to plan something, but such proved to be not the case. We have tried to put together a volume that honors the man, and, a harder task, to shape a book he would have enjoyed reading. Herlihy wrote more than his share of essays, especially early in his career, and he contributed unstintingly to all sorts of collections. But any reader of Herlihy's books knows that he did not cite with any frequency what he may have regarded as ephemera—articles. A striking feature of this collection of essays on medieval and Renaissance social history is that the articles all address big questions, just as Herlihy always did in his own work. One of his enduring legacies to us all is his exemplary hard work that never lost sight of the historian's obligation to ask questions that matter, not just to fill some proverbial gap in the literature or to add a brick to the edifice of learning. Herlihy's writings on the family, children, the status of women, and Florence are so good because he cared about these subjects, cared enough to ask serious and penetrating questions.

A tedious introduction summarizing what the reader is impatient to judge for him- or herself would have bored David Herlihy, so here is a brief menu. The essays in this book comprise a collective response to Herlihy's wide range of research and interests. Herlihy's presidential address on the family to the American Historical Association reveals his final thoughts on the subject that had been at the center of his work for most of his career. Christiane Klapisch-Zuber's eloquent tribute describes the genesis of their famous study of the Florentine Catasto of 1427, and it also places Herlihy's career in the context of European and American historiography since World War II.

Part 1 collects the essays that pick up the theme of the medieval family. Anthony Molho and his Italian colleagues continue the project of exploiting fresh sources on Florentine and Italian marriage in the Renaissance. Lisa Bitel explores similar questions, with a sharp eye on the family's economic functions in Ireland, a place always dear to Herlihy's heart. Barbara Rosenwein and Stephen White continue the theme of the early Middle Ages by looking at family politics and dynastic feuding in Lombard Italy and Merovingian France. Barbara Kreutz, also working on early medieval Italy, closely examines how Roman law and Lombard customs shaped marriage and the exchange of marital gifts. Steven Epstein concludes this section by selecting some insights from Herlihy's work and examining the problematic side of family life.

In Part 2 the essays concern another enduring aspect of Herlihy's work—his serious, respectful, but not uncritical analysis of religion and power in medieval society. Stephen Weinberger uses early charters from Provence to illuminate the roles literacy and memory played in determining property rights. Bruce Venarde, studying the charters of Fontevraud, finds abbesses working hard as skilled managers of monastic estates. James B. Given explores how people inside and outside the church used the Inquisition's power to enforce orthodoxy and settle scores. Maureen Miller uses evidence from medieval Verona to recast the chronology of church reform and the ways urban growth helped to change the church. Daniel Callahan looks at the spiritual power surrounding St. Martial of Limoges and the ways in which Ademar of Chabannes fostered this cult to suggest and intensify apocalyptic fears around the millennium. George Dameron shows how the power of the Florentine church helped to shape property relations in the Tuscan contado. Giovanni Ciappelli also looks at Florence, and the local cult of Andrea Corsini.

Part 3 contains the essays concerning social history, Herlihy's favorite subject, but in the specific venues of town and countryside. Giles Constable provides an overview of a central question for both places by looking at the sources for defining a medieval middle class. Lorraine Attreed and María Jesús Fuente examine how taxing towns in England and Castile caused internal stresses and changed relationships to outside powers. James Powell achieves a broader understanding of the ways the law developed in a social and religious framework by examining the career of the thirteenth-century lawyer Albertanus of Brescia. Samuel K. Cohn Jr. challenges Fernand Braudel's portrayal of mountain peoples in the Mediterranean by looking at how Florentine tax policies coerced mountaineers and may have caused other social responses to their urban-centered state. Giorgio Chittolini takes up the problem of the relationship between city and contado by searching for the reasons why northern Italian cities came to control certain rural areas and smaller cities. John Martin concludes this section by bringing social history back to one of Herlihy's favorite types of sources, a contemporary witness, by analyzing the ways in which Tommaso Garzoni attempted to construct for readers the social world of work in the late sixteenth century.

The book ends with a bibliography, compiled by Maureen Miller, of David Herlihy's published work from 1951 to 1992. The extraordinary range, quality, and importance of this forty years of scholarship remind us of Herlihy's many legacies to his students, colleagues, and friends.

Steven Epstein wishes to thank Shona Kelly Wray for translating Chittolini's article. Natalia Lozovsky helped to make the corrections in Herlihy's article that he undoubtedly would have made had his health permitted. Benjamin Ladd assisted in translating Klapisch-Zuber's contribution. Patricia Murphy provided invaluable assistance in preparing the manuscript and tables.

We want to express our deep gratitude to Ellen Bauerle of the University of Michigan Press, because her interest in and support of this project made it possible for us to make our hopes a reality. Nancy Vlahakis expertly steered the project past many obstacles on its way to publication. Finally, we thank Patricia Herlihy for inspiring us to press on, and for being our friend.

Family

David Herlihy

The word *family* in modern languages carries many resonances, not all of them harmonious. In the view of some, the family is an instrument of social oppression; it imprisons adults and ruins children. "Families, I hate you," French novelist André Gide exclaimed in 1897 and reiterated in 1933.[1] American social critic Paul Goodman declared that "the family is the ultimate American fascism."[2] British poet Philip Larkin had this to say concerning family life.

> Get out as early as you can
> And don't have any kids yourself.[3]

But to others the family is a haven in a hostile world. To be treated "like family" in common parlance means to be loved and supported. A justice of the Rhode Island Supreme Court, in upholding an ordinance against domestic picketing in January 1990, described the home as "the one retreat to which men and women can repair to escape the tribulations of

This essay is a slightly corrected version of Herlihy's speech published in the *American Historical Review* 96 (1991): 1–16. The changes here are almost all in the notes and concern small matters and slips David would have certainly corrected had his health permitted.

1. André Gide, *Nourritures terrestres*, vol. 4:1, cited in *Dictionnaire alphabétique et analogique de la langue française*, ed. Paul Robert (Paris, 1966), 10:830. He later explained, "Sans doute, j'écrivais un jour: 'Families, je vous hais,' mais il s'agit d'institutions, non de personnes, et ce n'est pas du tout la même chose" (*Journal*, 1168, cited in *Trésor de la langue française* [Paris, 1980], 8:635). See also *A History of Private Life*, ed. Philippe Ariès and Georges Duby, vol. 4: *From the Fires of Revolution to the Great War*, ed. Michelle Perrot (Cambridge, Mass., 1990), 241.

2. Paul Goodman, cited in Jon Winokur, *The Portable Curmudgeon* (New York, 1987), 98.

3. Quoted from Philip Larkin, "This Be the Verse," in *High Windows* (New York, 1974), 30.

their daily pursuits." It was, in his estimation, "the last citadel of the tired, the weary and the sick."[4]

Here I want to explore the distant origins of this double vision: of the family as loving and of the outer world as loveless. Put another way, I want to examine the emergence of the family in the West as a moral unit and a moral universe: a unit in the sense that it is sharply differentiated from the larger associations of kin and community, and a universe in the sense that human relations within it are very different from human relations outside its limits. The epoch of our interest, late antiquity and the Middle Ages, is admittedly remote, but it is also a formative period in the history of Western domestic culture. The writings we shall explore are legal, philosophical, and theological texts. Historians of law have systematically analyzed the legal codes of antiquity and the Middle Ages bearing on the family, but their goals have been much different from my own.[5] Philosophical and theological tracts have been, in contrast, rarely scrutinized for purposes of social history; the materials in them seemed too speculative and abstract, too far removed from quotidian experience.

We must first attempt brief definitions of crucial terms. What did the ancient and medieval writers call the family? Curiously, the ancients had no exact equivalent to our modern word *family*. This fault of terminology suggests that they came only slowly to conceive of the domestic community as sharply separated from the larger society.

The English word *family* is a direct borrowing from the Latin *familia,* which also supplies a common word for family to most other modern European languages, including German and Polish. It appeared very early in the Romance languages, from at least the twelfth century; it entered English by the fifteenth and German only in the sixteenth.[6] In

---

4. Cited in *The Providence Journal,* January 24, 1990, 1. The author of the decision was Justice Thomas F. Kelleher.

5. See most recently the remarkable survey of medieval canon law bearing on sexual and marital issues by James A. Brundage, *Love, Sex, and Christian Society in Medieval Europe* (Chicago, 1987).

6. *The Oxford English Dictionary,* 2d ed., vol. 5 (Oxford, 1989), 707, cites its use in ca. 1400 in the sense of servants. Compare its use in Scottish dialect as a community of consumers in *Bernardus de cura rei famuliaris with Some Early Scottish Prophecies, etc.,* ed. J. Rawson Lumby (London, 1870), 4: "Fede nocht thi famel with costly victuale." The translation is of the fifteenth century. *Altfranzösisches Wörterbuch,* ed. A. Tobler and E. Lormatzsch (Berlin, 1925–), 3.2 (1952), col. 1,622, cites its appearance in the poems of Gilles li Muisis and in Statutes of Lille from the fourteenth century. *Deutsches Wörterbuch* (Berlin, 1940), 2:289, notes an appearance (in the form *Familien*) in 1564, but it does not become common until at least a century later.

classical Latin, *familia* carried several meanings.[7] As the ancients themselves noted, the word could refer to both persons and property.[8] Both
ancient and medieval grammarians believed, correctly it seems, that the
Romans had borrowed the word from a neighboring people, the Oscans.
The Oscan root, *famel,* meant "slave," and the word also supplied Latin
with a common name for slave, *famulus.*[9] *Familia* thus originally meant
a band of slaves. "Fifteen freemen make a people," wrote the second-
century novelist Apuleius, "fifteen slaves make a family, and fifteen prisoners make a jail."[10] The word in its original sense thus implied an
authoritarian structure and hierarchical order, founded on but not limited to relations of marriage and parenthood. In a related way, the Latin
word for father, *pater,* designated in its original sense not a biological
parent but the holder of authority. The biological male parent was *geni-
tor.* Authority, in sum, and not consanguinity, not even marriage, was at
the core of the ancient concept of family. Even an unmarried male could
be a *paterfamilias.* Moreover, in early Roman law, the father's authority,
the *patria potestas,* was absolute, including even the *ius necis,* the right to
put to death members of his family.

Familia long held this meaning of a band of slaves. "We are accustomed to call staffs of slaves families," the jurist Ulpian observed in the
second century A.D.[11] Even when slavery waned in late antiquity and the
Middle Ages, the term continued to be used to designate servants or serfs.
Pope Gregory the Great at the end of the sixth century compared the

7. On the word's origins, see R. Henrion, "Des origines du mot *Familia*," *L'An-
tiquité classique,* vol. 10 (1941): 37–69; vol. 11 (1942): 253–90. See also M. R. Leon-
hard, "Familia," *Paulys Realencyclopädie der classischen Altertumswissenschaft,* vol.
6, ed. Georg Wissowa (Stuttgart, 1909), cols. 1,980–85.
8. See the comment by Ulpian, in *Digest,* 50.16.195. See also *The Digest of Justinian: Latin Text Edited by Theodor Mommsen with the Aid of Paul Krueger,* trans.
and ed. Thomas Watson (Philadelphia, 1985), 4:949: "Familiae appellatio . . . varie
accepta est: nam et in res et in personas deducitur." The Codex Justinianus (6.38.5)
states "we discern that the name of the family has the following force: parents and
children and all relatives and property, freedmen also and their patrons and likewise
slaves are identified with this word" (*Corpus Iuris Civilis,* ed. Paul Krüger, Theodor
Mommsen, Rudolf Schoell, and Wilhelm Kroll, 3 vols. [Berlin, 1928], 2:571).
9. Sexti Pompei Festi, *De verborum significatu quae supersunt cum Pauli Epi-
tome,* ed. W. M. Lindsay (Leipzig, 1933), 77, ll. 11–12: "Famuli origo ab Oscis depen-
det, apud quos servus famel nominabatur, unde et familia vocata."
10. Apuleius, *Pro se magia liber (apologia),* ed. Rudolf Helm (Leipzig, 1959),
47.437: "XV liberi homines populus est, totidem serui familia, totidem uincti ergas-
tulum."
11. Ulpian, *Digest,* 50.16.195: "servitutium quoque solemus appellare familias."

human mind to a family. Our separate thoughts are like numerous servant girls, who gossip and neglect their chores, until their mistress, reason, shushes them and sets them to their tasks, imposing order on our
mental *familia*.[12] Elsewhere, Gregory applied the word to the *coloni*, or
peasants, who worked on the papal estates.[13] The staffs of both lay and
ecclesiastical officials in the Middle Ages were routinely referred to as
"families." Still, in the nineteenth century, the entire papal bureaucracy,
including hundreds of functionaries from clerks to cardinals, was known
as the *famiglia pontificia*, the pontifical family.[14]

From slaves subject to a master, the word was easily extended to all
persons—wives and children, natural or adopted—who were under the
patria potestas. "In strict law," explained Ulpian, "we call a family the
several persons who by nature or law are placed under the authority of a
single person."[15] Even the clients or retainers of a powerful person,
though not fully subject to the *patria potestas*, were reckoned to be part
of the great man's family. The ancient family in this sense could reach
colossal size. Julius Caesar, in his *Gallic War*, related how the Helvetian
chief Orgetorix, when put on trial by his tribe, "gathered from every
quarter to the place of judgement all his family, to the number of some
ten thousand men."[16]

By further extension, the word applied to groups of people possessing
some organization, or at least some similarity, in their styles of life. In
classical Latin literature, under the name of *family*, there appear prosti-
tutes in a brothel; publicans or tax collectors, moneyers; military units;
schools of philosophers; and, in Christian usage, demons, monks, and the
clergy generally.[17] St. Augustine of Hippo referred to the entire Christian

---

12. *S. Gregorii Magni Moralia in Job Libri I–X*, ed. Marcus Adrizen (Turnhout,
1979), 1.3: "Multam nimis familiam possidemus cum cogitationes innumeras sub
mentis dominatione restringimus, ne ipsa sui multitudine animum superent."
    13. *Gregorii I Papae Registrum epistolarum*, 1.42 (Munich, 1978), 1:64: "si quis
ex familia [colonis] culpam fecerit."
    14. *Dizionario di erudizione storico-ecclesiastica*, ed. Gaetano Moroni (Venice,
1843), 23:27 ff., entry under "Famiglia pontificia."
    15. Ulpian, *Digest*, 50.16.195: "iure proprio familiam dicimus plures personas,
quae sunt sub unius potestate aut natura aut iure subiectae."
    16. Julius Caesar, *De bello Gallico*, i.4, *The Gallic War*, trans. H. J. Edwards
(Cambridge, Mass., 1979), 9: "Orgetorix ad iudicium omnem suam familiam, ad
hominum milia X, undique coegit et omnes clientes obaeratosque suos . . . eodem con-
duxit." Edwards translates *familiam* as "retainers."
    17. See numerous examples in the *Thesaurus linguae Latinae*, vol. 4, pt. 1 (Leipzig,
1892–1926), cols. 234–46. For the *familia ecclesiastica*, see Gregory the Great, *Regis-
tum epistolarum*, 1.42 (May 591) (1.67): "Si vero ex familia ecclesiastica sacer-

church as the *family of Christ* or the *family of God*.[18] The Christian author Lactantius, in his diatribe *On the Death of Persecutors,* gave the word an even larger sweep. Lactantius was condemning the cruelty of the pagan emperor Galerius. The wicked Galerius, wrote Lactantius, like the Persian kings before him, treated the entire empire *tamquam familia,* "like a family," that is, a limitless aggregation of sullen slaves all suffering under his tyrannous power.[19] This use of the word *family* to designate a huge community of the cowed rings strange to modern ears, but it is consistent with the term's core meaning, an aggregation of slaves.

Did the ancients even recognize the domestic unit to be a distinct social entity separate from the outside world? They certainly had a developed sense of what was public and what was private. In the second century A.D., the moralist Aulus Gellius posed the question whether a father was obligated to give up his seat of honor to a magistrate son.[20] He replied that "in public places and functions," magisterial authority prevailed over paternal authority, and the father must defer to his magistrate son. Within the domestic sphere, however, "public honors cease and the natural honors conferred by birth are recognized." Here, the magistrate son must yield place of honor to the father. The ancients did draw a firm line between the *res publica* and the *res domestica.* In the public realm, the state commanded; in the domestic, the father. On the other hand, the father's authority could extend well beyond the coresidential unit, to slaves working elsewhere, to freedmen likely to be living elsewhere, to

dotes vel levitae vel monachi vel clerici vel quilibet alii lapsi fuerint." For the sense of descent group, compare Bede, *Historia ecclesiastica gentis Anglorum,* 1.7, *Opera historica,* trans. J. E. King (Loeb Classical Library; Cambridge, Mass., 1963), 1:38: "Cuius, inquit, familiae vel generis es?"

18. St. Augustine of Hippo, *De civitate Dei,* i.29, *The City of God against the Pagans,* trans. George E. McCracken (Loeb Classical Library; Cambridge, Mass., 1981), 1:122: "Quid familia Christi respondere debant infidelibus . . . Habet itaque omnis familia summi et veri Dei."

19. Lucii Caecilii De mortibus persecutorum Liber vulgo Lactantio tributus, *L. Caeli Firmiani Lactanti Opera omnia,* ed. Samuel Brandt and Georgius Laubmann (Prague, Vienna, and Leipzig, 1897), cap. 21 (p. 196): "nam post deuictos Persas, quorum hic ritus, hic mos est, ut regibus suis in seruitium se addicant et reges populo suo tamquam familia utantur, hunc morem nefarius homo in Romanam terram uoluit inducere." There is an English translation of this work in Lactantius, *The Minor Works,* trans. Mary Francis McDonald, O.P. (Washington, D.C., 1965), 117–203.

20. Aulus Gellius, *Noctes Atticae,* 2.2.9, ed. P. K. Marshall, 2 vols. (Oxford, 1968), 1:86: "sed cum extra rem publicam in domestica re atque uita sedeatur, ambuletur, in conuiuio quoque familiari discumbatur, tum inter filium magistratum et patrem priuatum publicos honores cessare, naturales et genuinos exoriri."

absent but unemancipated sons such as those serving in the army. The ancient *familia* was therefore not coterminous with the household.

As Ulpian noted, the second principal meaning of *familia* was property. This usage seems to have represented an extension from its original meaning of "vocal" property—that is, slaves—to the master's other possessions. In the word's earliest attestation in the Roman Law of the Twelve Tables (fifth century B.C.), it carries the sense of "inheritance." The Justinian code in the sixth century A.D. affirms that in certain instances "the word family should be understood as property, because it designates slaves and other things in a person's patrimony."[21] This understanding also persisted in medieval usage. The Venerable Bede, in his *Ecclesiastical History of the English People* in the early eighth century, used *familia* in the sense of peasant farm or peasant inheritance.[22] This meaning may have been reinforced with the revival of Roman legal studies in the West from the twelfth century. A fourteenth-century Italian author, Paolo da Certaldo, used the Italian word *famiglia* with the sense of patrimony. "[I]n order that the *famiglia* may grow," he counseled his readers, "it is desirable to save and to put aside in just measure as much as you can."[23]

Among the master's possessions, the *domus,* the house or domicile, held a special importance, and *domus,* too, is often used in classical Latin to identify the domestic unit.[24] A girl, in marrying, wrote Aulus Gellius, leaves the *domus* of her parents in order to join the *familia* of her husband.[25] St. Augustine instructed in a sermon: "The residents of a house are called a house. . . . [We here call] a house not walls and rooms, but

21. *Corpus Justianum,* 6.38.5.3, edn. Krüger, Mommsen, Schoell, and Kroll, 2:571: "In aliis autem casibus nomen familiae pro substantia oportet intellegi, quia et servi et aliae res in patrimonio uniuscuiusque esse putantur."

22. See, for example, Bede, *Historia ecclesiastica,* 1.2, *Opera historica,* trans. J. E. King (London, 1930), 1:108, in relation to the Isle of Thanet: "magnitudinis iuxta consuetudinem aestimationis Anglorum, familiarum sexcentarum." Compare 4.23, "locum unius familiae," 2:128.

23. Paolo da Certaldo, *Libro di buoni costumi,* no. 142, in *Mercanti scrittori: Ricordi nella Firenze tra Medioevo e Rinascimento,* ed. Vittore Branca, 2d ed. (Milan, 1986), 31–32: "E anche, perché la famiglia sempre cresce, però si vuole avanzare e mettere innanzi quanto puoi con giusto modo."

24. For examples of the word's many meanings, see the entry *domus* in the *Thesaurus Linguae Latine* (Leipzig, 1909–34), 5:1, cols. 1949–87.

25. Aulus Gellius, *Noctes Atticae,* 13.10.3, ed. P. K. Marshall (Oxford, 1968) 2:392: "Soror," inquit, "appellata est, quod quasi seorsum nascitur separaturque ab ea domo, in qua nata est, et in aliam familiam transgreditur."

the residents themselves."[26] But *domus,* like *familia,* had many derivative meanings and could be applied to much larger groups than the domestic unit. The seventh-century Spanish encyclopedist Isidore of Seville explained: "The house is a residence of a single family, just as the city is the residence of a single people, just as the world is the residence of the entire human race. 'House' is also the kindred, family or the union of man and wife. It begins from two persons, and is a Greek word."[27] It could be applied, in other words, to descent groups, tribes, and entire nations, such as the "House of Israel," that claimed to be based on blood relations. Later, in medieval usage, it would be equally applied to religious communities and representative assemblies such as the houses of parliament.

To identify the domestic unit, ancient and medieval writers usually combined *domus* and *familia,* as did Isidore. When, in the thirteenth century, Thomas Aquinas wished to identify the household, he used such terms as *familia domestica* or *domus vel familia,* "house or family."[28]

The laws and institutions governing the domestic community changed profoundly from early Roman times into the Middle Ages. The Roman father soon lost his powers of life and death over family members, if, indeed, he had ever really used them. In medieval law, the father could discipline for just cause his wards, including his wife, but not to the point of maiming them.[29] Even his authority over family property or its patrimony weakened. He could not consume that property arbitrarily but had to accept responsibility for the support of wife and children. We do not follow these diverse evolutions here. But, in one respect, the ancient understanding of the family survived. The family continued to be viewed

---

26. Augustine Sermo, 170.4, *Patrologia Latina,* ed. J. P. Migne (Paris, 1861), 38, col. 929: "Quomodo dicitur domus habitatores domus . . . domum appellans non parietes et receptacula corporum, sed ipsos habitatores."

27. Isidore of Seville, *Isidori hispalensis episcopi etymologiarum sive originum libri XX,* ed. W. M. Lindsay, 2 vols. (Oxford, 1911), 9.4.3: "Domus unius familae habitaculum est, sicut urbs unius populi, sicut orbis domicilium totius generis humani. Est enim domus genus, familia sive coniunctio viri et uxoris. Incipit autem a duobus, et est nomen Graecum."

28. Thomas Aquinas, *Summa Theologica* (hereafter, *ST*), 2.2.2, *Opera omnia* (Rome, 1897), 9:81: "Pater autem et dominus, qui praesunt familiae domesticae"; and 2.2.47, *Opera omnia* (Rome, 1895), 8:359: "oeconomica, quae est de his quae pertinent ad bonum commune domus vel familiae."

29. See, for example, Aquinas, *ST,* 2.2.2, *Opera omnia,* 9:81: "Pater autem et dominus, qui praesunt familiae domesticae, quae est imperfecta communitas, habent imperfectam potestatem coercendi secundum leviores poenas, quae non inferunt irreparabile nocumentum. Et huiusmodi est verberatio."

as an organized and stable community, what the medieval doctors called a *multitudo ordinata,* set within another organized community, the state itself.[30]

And the family was, in Aquinas's phrase, a "communion of domestic persons" or a "domestic communion," that is, a community that acquired and shared the resources, especially food and shelter, needed to sustain the lives of its members.[31]

The progressive weakening of paternal authority allowed for, and perhaps even made necessary, the strengthening of another form of bonding that gave cohesion to the household: domestic affection. The ancient writers often mention, even if they are slow to emphasize, love within the household, the *amor* or *amicitia, caritas* or *dilectio,* shared by family members. Cicero in the first century B.C. alluded to that special *caritas* joining parents and children, which cannot be destroyed except by a heinous crime.[32] Emperor Caligula in the first century A.D. is said to have imposed a special oath on his soldiers and functionaries. Those taking the oath swore not to hold themselves and their children dearer than Caligula and his sisters.[33] Clearly, for Caligula, the love of parents for children was the supreme measure of devotion.

Even more than their pagan predecessors, Christian writers in the late imperial period commented extensively on love, in its social as well as religious dimensions. *Caritas* bonded together individuals and communities, marriages and households. In his "Commentary on Genesis," Augustine raises the question of why Adam obeyed Eve's bidding to eat the forbidden fruit.[34] He was not prompted by lust, which in the state of innocence did not rule his members; he was not maneuvering to seduce

---

30. Aquinas, *ST*, 3.8.1, 2d 2, *Opera omnia* (Rome, 1903), 11:127: "aliqua multitudo ordinata, est pars alterius multitudinis. Et ideo paterfamilias, qui est caput multitudinis domesticae, habet super se caput rectorem civitatis."

31. Aquinas, *ST*, 1.2.105.4, *Opera omnia* (Rome, 1892), 7:271.

32. Cicero, *Laelius de amicitia,* 8.27, *De senectute, De amicitia, De divinatione,* trans. William A. Falconer (Loeb Classical Library; Cambridge, Mass., 1964), 138: "Quod in homine multo est evidentius, primum ex ea caritate quae est inter natos et parentes, quae dirimi sisi detestabili scelere non potest."

33. Suetonius, Caligula, *De vita Caesarum,* 4.15.3, *Suetonius,* trans. J. C. Rolfe (Loeb Classical Library; Cambridge, Mass., 1970), 1:425: "He caused the names of his sisters to be included in all oaths: 'And I will not hold myself and my children dearer than I do Gaius and his sisters.'"

34. Augustine, *De genesi ad litteram,* 11.42, ed. Joseph Zucha (Prague, Vienna, and Leipzig, 1894), 378: "[Adam] noluit eam contristare . . . non quidem carnis uictus concupiscentia, quam nondum senserat in resistente lege membrorum legi mentis suae, sed amicali quadam beniuolentia, qua plerumque fit, ut offendatur deus, ne

her. And he was much too intelligent to believe the devil's ruse—that the
shared and eaten fruit would change him and his mate into gods. He
obeyed her simply because he loved her and wished to please her. He
acted, in Augustine's phrase, out of loving goodwill. Many, Augustine
reflected, like Adam, offend God in order to please their friend. *Amicitia*
in marriage, in Augustine's view, was present from the time of Creation.

Even earlier, around 230 A.D., Tertullian detected in families a "common spirit," although he was limiting his observations exclusively to his
fellow Christians.[35] These families share emotional experiences; they feel,
in his words, "common hope, fear, joy, pain and suffering." Emotional
communion linked together, in his phrase, "brothers and fellow slaves,"
by which he seems to have meant family members who served one
another. In a discourse written for his wife, he stated that between him
and her there was "no difference of soul or body."

In more general terms, "love," Augustine affirmed, "ties men together
in a knot of unity."[36] "Many souls," he wrote elsewhere, "are made one
soul through loving."[37] In a famous passage in the *City of God,* he
stated that "two loves have made two cities," the one Jerusalem, the
other Babylon, the one oriented toward Heaven, the other toward Earth,
the both embracing all humanity and active throughout history.[38] In

homo ex amico fiat inimicus." See also Augustine, *De civitate Dei,* 14.11, *The City of
God against the Pagans,* trans. Philip Levine (Loeb Classical Library; Cambridge,
Mass., 1966), 4:330. Adam obeyed for reason of friendship, "sociale necessitudine."
There is an English translation, *The Literal Meaning of Genesis,* trans. John Ham-
mond Taylor (New York, 1982).

35. Tertullian, *De paenitentia,* 10.4, ed. J. G. Ph. Borleffs (Turnhout, 1954), 1:337:
"Inter fratres atque conservos, ubi communis spes, metus, gaudium, dolor, passio,
quia communis spiritus de communi domino et patre, quid tu hos aliud quam te
opinaris." Elsewhere Tertullian used "fratres et conservos" to refer to himself and his
wife (*Ad uxorem,* 2.7, ed. A. Kroymann [Turnhout, 1954]), 1:393: "quale iugum
fidelium duorum unius spei, unius uoti, unius disciplinae, eiusdem servitutis! Ambo
fratres, ambo conserui, nulla spiritus carnisue discretio."

36. Augustine, *De doctrina Christiana,* Prooemium, 6, ed. Joseph Martin, in *Aure-
lii Augustini opera,* 4.1 (Turnhout, 1962), 4: "Deinde ipsa caritas, quae sibi homines
inuicem nodo unitatis adstringit, non haberet aditum refundendorum et quasi miscen-
dorum sibimet animorum, si homines per homines nihil discerent."

37. Augustine, *In Iohannis . . . evangelium tractatus CXXIV,* ed. R. Willems,
O.S.B. (Turnhout, 1984), 348: "multae animae per charitatem una anima est et multa
corda unum cor." There is an English translation, *Lectures or Tractates on the Gospel
According to John,* trans. Marcus Dods, D.D., 2 vols. (Edinburgh, 1873).

38. Augustine, *De civitate Dei,* 14.28, *The City of God,* trans. Levine, 4:404,
"Fecerunt itaque civitates duas amores duo." See also in his "Commentary on the
Psalms," 64.2, *Patrologia Latina,* edn. Migne, 36, col. 773: "Duas istas civitates faci-
unt duo amores: Jerusalem facit amor Dei; Babyloniam facit amor saeculi."

patristic thought, *caritas* in the community functions as an essential cohesive force, much as *potestas,* or power, had served in pagan conceptions of society.

But *caritas* could work mischief, too, as Adam's fall confirmed. Christians were supposed to love everyone, but were they required to love everyone equally? Could they love some persons more, others less? The theologian who launched a tradition of speculation on degrees of affection was Origen of Alexandria, active in the early third century, one of the most original minds of the early church. Origen wrote extensive commentaries on the books of the Old and New Testaments and made fundamental contributions to the methods of biblical exegesis. Our interests here are in a commentary and two homilies he devoted to the Old Testament "Canticle of Canticles," or "Song of Songs." This erotic text perplexed ascetically minded Christian exegetes as it had Jewish commentators before them. Origen's commentary and homilies do not survive in the original Greek, but they are extant in Latin translations, by Jerome and by Rufinus, respectively.[39] Authors of the High Middle Ages commonly attributed these works to Ambrose of Milan, and this association with one of the four Latin fathers gave them added authority.

The crucial passage was canticle 2.4, in which the maiden says of her king-lover, "he has ordered me in love." Inspired by this statement, Origen affirms that "saints" or the "perfect" would not love everyone equally but in ordered degrees. Love was, to be sure, a universal human experience. "Without doubt," he stated, "all men love something, and there is no one who arrives at an age when he can love who does not love."[40] But we do not and should not love equally. First and foremost, we are to love God. After God, we love in order our parents, our children, and our "domestics," by which Origen seems to mean both coresidential relatives and servants. Finally, we love our neighbors—those out-

---

39. The standard edition of the commentary and the two homilies is Origen, *Homilien zu Samuel I zum Hohelied und an den Propheten: Kommentar zu Hohelied in Rufins und Hieronymus Uebersetzungen,* ed. W. A. Baehrens (Leipzig, 1925). The two homilies, which seem to have circulated more widely than the commentary, are printed in Latin with a French translation in Origen, *Homélies sur le Cantique des Cantiques: Introduction, traduction et notes,* by Dom Olivier Rousseau, O.S.B., 2d ed. (Paris, 1966). There is an English translation of these works in Origen, *The Song of Songs: Commentary and Homilies,* trans. R. P. Lawson (Westminister, Md., and London, 1957).

40. In Cant. Cantic. Liber 3, *Homilien,* edn. Baehrens, 186: "Omnes homines amant sine dubio aliquid et nullus est, qui ad id aetatis venerit, ut amare iam possit, et non aliquid amet."

side our homes.[41] Origen assigned no formal place to love of self, and he did not in this ranking mention love of spouse or siblings. In another passage, however, he proposed a parallel order of affection in regard to women: we should love first our mothers, who also deserve the highest reverence; then our sisters but not with the same honor; then wives in a special fashion; and then all other women, both relatives and neighbors, according to their merit but always chastely.[42] Origen, in sum, was not rigid or rigidly consistent in the order or orders he proposed. But, quite clearly, in the force field of affection, the persons presumably living with us—parents, children, and domestics—were at the center. Fondness, on the other hand, fades with distance.

Biblical commentators and theologians of late antiquity received Origen's notion of an *ordo caritatis* with enthusiasm.[43] Augustine provided a dynamic version of the same model.[44] Love, Augustine explained, is like a fire that first consumes the objects close to it, then those more distant. Your brother is closest to you, and he is first to be warmed by your love. Then love should be extended to neighbors, and then to strangers who do not wish you ill. "Go beyond even these," he urged his readers, "reach the point that you love even enemies."[45] Love for those closest to us is thus a school of sentiment, from which all other loves are learned. Moreover, this notion of an *ordo caritatis* explained several discomfiting passages in the New Testament, in which the founder of Christianity apparently condemns familial affection. In Matthew 10.37, Jesus asserted, "He that loveth father or mother more than me is not worthy of

41. Origenes, in Cant. Cantic. Homilia 2.8, *Homilien*, edn. Baehrens, 52: "Ut autem post Deum etiam inter nos ordo ponatur, primum mandatum est, ut 'diligamus' parentes, secundum ut filios, tertium ut domesticos nostros."

42. In Cant. Cantic. Liber 3, 188–89: "Et maiore quidem cum honorificentia matri deferenda dilectio est, sequenti vero gradu cum quadam nihilominus reverentia etiam sororibus. Proprio vero quodam et sequestrato ab his more caritas coniugibus exhibenda. Post has vero personas pro meritis etiam et causis uniquique in omni, ut supradiximus, castitate deferenda dilectio est. Secundum haec vero etiam de patre vel fratre atque aliis propinquis observabimus."

43. See Hélène Pétré, *Caritas: Etude sur le vocabulaire latin de la charité chrétienne* (Louvain, 1948).

44. Most particularly in Augustine, *In epistolam Iohannis ad Parthos tractatus decem*, 8.10, translated as *Commentaire de la première épître de S. Jean*, trans. Paul Agaëss, S.J. (Paris, 1961). See Jacques Gallay, *La Charité fraternelle selon les "Tractatus in Primam Johannis" de St. Augustin* (Lyon, 1953).

45. Augustine, *In epistolam Iohannis*, 8.4, p. 346: "Transcende et ipsos; perveni, ut diligas inimicos." Earlier, he stated, "Qui usque ad inimicos pervenit, non transilit fratres" (Who reaches enemies does not skip brothers).

me, and he that loveth son or daughter more than me is not worthy of me."[46] Still stronger are his words in Luke 14.26: "If any man come to me and hate not his father, and mother, and wife, and children, and brethren, and sisters, yea, and his own life also, he cannot be my disciple."[47] These passages, concluded the commentators, were not a condemnation of familial love or of self-love but rather of disordered love. The good person should love parents, wife, and children, and even himself, but only after God.

The ancient sages, in sum, both pagan and Christian, recognized in the household a community of especially strong affection. Moreover, they saw within it a place of psychological solace or refreshment. Cicero contrasted the relaxation and enjoyment deriving from domestic activities with the vexing labors of public life.[48] Augustine went so far as to compare the *requies temporalis,* "which you find when you enter your home," with the *requies sempiterna,* the "eternal rest," to be expected in the house of God.[49] He seems to make of the home a terrestrial analog to heaven.

Much has been written in recent years about the loving or affective family as a modern, even a recent formation, about the coldness, indifference, or insensitivity that allegedly characterized domestic ties in the distant past.[50] But what, then, are we to make of these sentimental pas-

46. The Vulgate text of Mt. 10.37 is: "Qui amat patrem et matrem plus quam me, non est me dignus; qui amat filium aut filiam super me, non est me dignus."
47. Lk. 14.26: "Si quis venit ad me, et non odit patrem suum, et matrem, et uxorem, et filios, et fratres, et sorores, adhuc autem et animam suam, non potest meus esse discipulus."
48. Cicero, *M. Tulli Ciceronis epistulae,* vol. 3: *Epistulae ad Atticum,* ed. L. C. Purser (Oxford, 1958), 9.10.3: "et, ut verum loquar, aetas iam a diuturnis laboribus devexa ad otium domesticarum me rerum delectatione mollivit."
49. Augustine, *In epistolam Iohannis tractatus decem,* 10.9: "Domum tuam intras propter requiem temporalem, domum Dei intras propter requiem sempiternam. Si ergo in domo tua, ne quid peruersum fiat satagis, in domo Dei ubi salus proposita est et requies sine fine, debes pati quantum in te est, si quid forte peruersum videris?"
50. On this alleged "sentimentalizing," see Edward Shorter, *The Making of the Modern Family* (New York, 1975). On the "affective" family, see also Lawrence Stone, *The Family, Sex, and Marriage in England, 1500–1800* (New York, 1977). A recent statement of this view may be found in *A History of Private Life,* ed. Philippe Ariès and Georges Duby, vol. 3: *The Passions of the Renaissance,* ed. Roger Chartier (Cambridge, Mass., 1989), 8: "Ultimately [in the eighteenth century] the family became the focus of private life. . . . It became something it had never been: a refuge, to which people fled in order to escape the scrutiny of outsiders; an emotional center; and a place where, for better or for worse, children were the focus of attention." For the most recent of many criticisms of Ariès's thesis on the supposed failure in the past

sages, and of many others that could be cited, from ancient authors? Unmistakably, these authors assume that persons who live together will normally love together and that this love is the first to be learned and the last to be relinquished.

I ought not to imply that a modern set of familial sentiments emerged fully formed out of ancient Mediterranean waters. As suggested by the lack of a single name to identify it, the coresidential unit still did not show clear boundaries with or against the larger society. Augustine, for example, in his "Commentary on John," was very vague in distinguishing the circles of *fratres, proximi, ignoti,* and *inimici;* in this instance, he made no mention at all of the family or domestic unit. There is little sense of polarity, still less of hostility, between the domestic and the public realms. Only the intensity, not the nature of affection, changes as one moves beyond the domestic circle. Neighbors and strangers are not viewed as heartless and menacing, only as persons whom we are justified in loving less.

Medieval commentators and theologians were equally attracted by Origen's seminal concept of the *ordo caritatis.*[51] In the twelfth century, in one of the earliest systematic works of medieval theology, Hugh of St. Victor proposed a simple ranking: one loved God above all, then one's self, then "others."[52] This would be a standard ordering. If the high ranking given one's self seems odd to us, it was because the salvation of one's soul outranked every other value; one could not sin, for example, to aid a neighbor. Hugh's student Richard of St. Victor, writing sometime between 1152 and 1173, distinguished four degrees of what he called "violent," meaning passionate, love. His chief interest was in the psychological states of love and not its objects. He did, however, affirm that, in the domain of human relationships, conjugal love dominates all other affective ties. It unites the married couple in "chains of peace" and makes their union "pleasing and joyous."[53]

---

to recognize children as children, see Shulamith Shahar, *Childhood in the Middle Ages* (London, 1990).

51. Pierre Rousselot, *Pour l'histoire du problème de l'amour au Moyen Age* (Münster, 1908). Rousselot found a distinction in the medieval authors between "physical" (that is, natural) and "ecstatic" (mystical) love. His chief interest was in the latter.

52. Hugh of St. Victor, "Summa Sententiarum Tract.," 4.2., cap. 7, in *Patrologia Latina,* ed. J.D. Migne (Paris, 1880), 176, col. 126: "Et in hoc etiam potest ordo charitatis considerari; quia Deum prae omnibus diligere debemus . . . post ipsum nos ipsos, tertio loco alios." This tract is traditionally attributed to Hugh.

53. Richard of St. Victor, *Epître à Severin sur la charité, par Ives; Les Quatre degrés de la violente charité: Texte critique avec introduction, traduction et notes,*

For our purposes, the most influential of all twelfth-century commentators on love and its objects was Master Peter Lombard, bishop of Paris. Probably between 1155 and 1160, he published the *Four Books of Sentences,* which was destined to become the standard textbook of medieval Christian theology.[54] Subsequently, too, it attracted numerous commentaries.[55] The *Sentences* included an entire chapter entitled "The Order of Loving, What Should Come Before and What After."[56] Peter first examined the opinion of the ancients as to the proper ranking. His own conclusion is the following: "From the foregoing it is clearly to be concluded that a distinction is to be made in loving, so that we love different persons with a differing, not equal, affection; above all we love God, ourselves in second place, in third our parents, then our children and siblings, then domestics, finally enemies."[57] The master's dependence on pseudo-Ambrose, really Origen, is clear, but he also departed from him in one striking way. Origen had made clear distinctions between neighbors, whom we must love "with our whole heart," and enemies, whom we only have to love and not hate.[58] Master Peter, on the other hand, called all those beyond the domestic circle *inimici,* "enemies." We must still love these unfriendly outsiders, but his words strongly imply that they do not love us.

---

ed. Gervais Dumeige (Paris, 1955), 145: "Mutuus namque intimi amoris affectus inter federatos pacis vincula adstringit, et indissolubilem illam perpetuandam que societatem gratam et jocundam reddit." This passage is from the "De IV gradibus violentae caritatis." According to Gervais, Bernard of Clairvaux is more likely than Richard to have been the author of the letter to Severinus. Other twelfth-century theologians who commented extensively on love were William of St.-Thierry and Peter of Blois, but their interests tended to be again in the psychological stages of love and not in its different objects. See also Gervais Dumeige, *Richard de Saint-Victor et l'idée chrétienne de l'amour* (Paris, 1952).

54. Peter Lombard, *Magistri Petri Lombardi Sententiae in IV Libris distinctae* (Rome, 1981).

55. For an inventory, see F. Stegmüller, *Repertorium commentariorum in Sententias Petri Lombardi,* 2 vols. (Würzburg, 1947).

56. "De ordine diligendi: quid prius, quid post"; *Sententiae,* 2.171.

57. *Sententiae,* 2.174: "Ecce ex praemissis aperte insinuatur quae in affectu haritatis distinctio sit habenda: ut differenti affectu, non pari, homines diligamus, et ante omnia Deum; secundo nos ipsos, tertio parentes, inde filios et fratres, post domesticos, demum inimicos diligamus. Sed inquunt illi quae de ordine dilectionis supra dicuntur, esse referenda ad operum exhibitionem, quae differenter proximis exhibenda sunt. Primo parentibus, inde filiis, post domesticos, demum inimicis."

58. Origen, *Homélies,* trans. Rousseau, 94: "nec dicit 'diligite inimicos vestros' ut vosmet ipsos, sed tantum: 'diligite inimicos vestros.' Sufficit eis quod eos 'diligimus' et odio non habemus."

Lombard's assumption, that all beyond the domestic circle were enemies, bothered his commentators. For example, in 1245, Albert the Great
argued, "Between the domestic and the enemy, there are many degrees of
love, as for in-laws, fellow citizens, godparents, and the like."[59] In his
view, Master Peter must have been using the term *domestics* in a
metaphorical sense to signify the entire church. By this strained interpretation, the *inimici* become not all those outside our households but all
those outside the church. But was this really the master's intent?

Thomas Aquinas, in his own "Commentary on the Sentences" and in
his *Summa Theologica,* seems not to discuss the question whether all persons outside the household can be called enemies.[60] But he did have much
to say about the "order of loving" and devoted to it an entire "Questio"
of his *Summa Theologica.*[61] He developed several distinctions between
the love owed to one's closest relatives and the love owed to neighbors.
Like many commentators before him, Thomas affirmed that domestic
love is marked by greater intensity, while *caritas* cools with distance, like
heat emanating from a fire.[62] Thomas further affirmed, as his predecessors seemingly had not, that love of those close to us differed in its origins
from love for outsiders. Origen wrote about love among the "saints,"
that is, those moved by grace. Aquinas, in a manner typical of thirteenth-
century Scholasticism, stressed instead nature and the natural wellsprings
of human behavior. In this view, our love for those joined to us by blood
relationships was founded on nature and was therefore stable and
durable; in contrast, our love for those unrelated to us was based on con-
vention and was unstable and shifting.[63] Finally, the love that joins us to

---

59. Albert the Great, *B. Alberti Magni . . . Opera omnia,* ed. St. C. A. Borgnet
(Paris, 1894), 28:547: "Inter domesticum et inimicum sunt multi gradus, scilicet
affinis, concivis, et compaternalis, et hujusmodi." Albert further observed that the circle of loved ones up to domestics constituted a *societas ex convictu,* a community of
those eating together, a *domus* or household.

60. See Thomas Aquinas, *S Thomae Aquinatis Scriptum super Sententiis,* ed. M. F.
Moos, O.P. (Paris, 1956), 3:918–49, for his comment on book 3, question 39, of the
"Sentences." For comment on Thomas's views, see Louis Bertrand Geiger, *Le Prob-
lème de l'amour chez saint Thomas d'Aquin* (Montreal, 1952).

61. Aquinas, *ST,* 2.2.q.26, *Opera omnia* (Rome, 1895), 8:209–23.

62. Aquinas, *ST,* 2.2.q.27, a.7, *Opera omnia,* 8:230: "Ergo diligere amicum est
magis meritorium quam diligere inimicum . . . Sed sicut idem ignis in propinquiora
fortius agit quam in remotiora, ita etiam caritas ferventius diligit coniunctos quam
remotos."

63. Aquinas, *ST,* 9.2b, a.8, 8:218: "Si autem comparemus coniunctionem ad coniunctionem, constat quod coniunctio naturalis originis est prior et immobilior: quia est
secundum id quod pertinet ad substantiam; aliae autem coniunctiones sunt superve-

our closest relatives has many modes. We may count, as Thomas did not explicitly do, the ways of loving: these are the *amicitia* due to friends regarded as other selves, the sympathy from shared experiences that Tertullian noted, parental commitment to children, conjugal love, filial respect for parents, and so on. The love for neighbors, simple *amor caritatis* in Thomas's phrase, is single stranded and necessarily weak.

Thomas did not here draw explicit distinctions between coresidential and nonresidential kin, but elsewhere he showed a clear picture of the *domus* as the constituent element of society. "It is manifest," he wrote, "that the *domus* holds an intermediate position between the individual and the city or the kingdom; for just as a single person is part of the *domus,* so each *domus* is part of the city or kingdom."[64] The *domus* is in turn based on three sets of relationships: lord to servant, husband to wife, and father to child, all of which Thomas explored.[65]

Thomas further attempted to determine the order of loving among household members, although his efforts sometimes seem exercises in futility. Do parents love their children more or less than children love their parents? Parents love their children more, he concluded, for two reasons. Parents have greater certainty of who their children are than children have of who their parents are. And parents are conscious of their children for a longer time than children are conscious of their parents, and time strengthens love.

Are parents or spouses loved the more? By "reason of the good" they have wrought, parents merit greater affection, as we owe them our being. But, "by reason of the tie," spouses are more loved, as the conjugal pair are two in one flesh; to love one's spouse is therefore equivalent to loving oneself. Parents, however, deserve the greater honor. Is the father or the mother to be loved more? Thomas seems uncertain here, as personal qualities enter so strongly. However, other things being equal, fathers are to be loved more, since, in the ancient and Scholastic view of procreation,

nientes, et removeri possunt. Et ideo amicitia consanguineorum est stabilior. . . . Amicitia tamen consanguineorum est stabilior, ut pote naturalior existere: et praevalet in his quae ad naturam spectant."

64. Aquinas, *ST,* 2.2.50.3, *Opera omnia,* 8:376: "Manifestum est autem quod domus medio modo se habet inter unam singularem personam et civitatem vel regnum: nam sicut una singularis persona est pars domus, ita una domus est pars civitatis vel regni."

65. Aquinas, *ST,* 1.2.105.4, *Opera omnia,* 7:271: "Sic igitur in domestica communione sunt tres combinationes: scilicet domini ad servum, viri ad uxorem, patris ad filium."

fathers supplied the active element in conception. Quaint though his arguments may be, Thomas clearly thought of the household as a community of affection. Moreover, the love within it is intense, natural, complex, and lasting.

If Thomas presented a rather static and detached model of society and family, his approach may mirror the relatively stable state of medieval society in the placid thirteenth century. In contrast, over the fourteenth and fifteenth centuries, plagues, famines, wars, and social unrest shook the equilibrium of the medieval world and undermined the serene outlook of its thinkers. The greatest sages in that disturbed epoch tried not so much to construct abstract models of the natural order as to offer moral guidance to perplexed individuals living amid tumultuous surroundings. One theologian sensitive to moral issues was Antoninus, archbishop of Florence in the middle fifteenth century, shepherd to a large, rich, and troubled flock of merchants, bankers, and artisans. In his own *Summa Theologica,* Antoninus included a chapter called "De amore" (On love). In it, he examined love of God, love of self, love of children, and love of wife. Antoninus saw no need to exhort his readers to love children or spouse. Rather, he warned them repeatedly against excessive attachment to offspring, husband, or wife. Here is his denunciation of parents.

> Oh how many are the parents, who because of disordered love for their children, earn damnation! Oh how many are they, who serve their children like idols! . . . [Making] idols of their children, they accumulate wealth by fair means or foul in order to leave them wealthy, and they are unconcerned about going to hell.[66]

Antoninus also condemned the tyranny of parents who prevent their children from entering the religious life. He gave expression to a long-standing ecclesiastical suspicion of parental power.

There was danger, too, in conjugal love; it was not that spouses lacked affection but, in Antoninus's view, they often loved not wisely but too

---

66. Antoninus, *Summa Theologica,* tit. 5, cap. 2, "De amore" (1:432): "O quot sunt parentes, qui propter inordinatum amorem ad filios, damnationem incurrunt! O quot sunt, qui eis quasi idolis inserviunt! Et nota, quod idololatria habuit initium ab inordinato amore parentum in filios, et e converso. Nam Ninus, qui aedificavit Ninivem, mortuo Bello patre suo, . . . Sic multi faciunt de filiis idola. Nam, ut dimittant eos divites, congregant per fas et nefas, nec curant ire ad infernum."

well. He cited from Augustine the salutary example of Adam who, at Eve's request, ate the forbidden fruit "lest he displease and sadden his companion."[67] The church gave no blanket endorsement to familial sentiments.

Did these speculations of schoolmen reflect deeper changes in late medieval society? We can look for evidence of shifting attitudes toward the family to movements of popular piety. A cult of paramount interest here is that of St. Joseph, the foster father of Christ. Late ancient and early medieval piety had largely ignored Joseph. In contrast, in the late Middle Ages, he attracted considerable attention, even in lay and vernacular poetry. In the fourteenth century, French poet Eustache Deschamps composed a ballad in praise of Joseph. The poem observes that Joseph had guarded his wife and child "in great fear" and "never in this world had a holiday."[68] Eustache says to fathers everywhere that

You who serve wife and infants
Ever have Joseph in your remembrance.[69]

Closely related to the veneration of Joseph is the cult of the Holy Family. The words *Sancta Familia* seem totally absent in the voluminous devotional literature antedating the fourteenth century. Artistic representations of the Holy Family also seem to date only from the fourteenth century. Eustache Deschamps reported that he had seen in many churches representations of the flight into Egypt.[70]

How can we explain the growing veneration of these domestic images, of the solicitous father and the small family forced to flee into a foreign land? Could it have been that many small families in the late Middle Ages felt themselves isolated and harassed, beleaguered by plague, famines,

---

67. Antoninus, *Summa Theologica*, 1:434: "non quia credidit se per hoc similem Deo futurum, sed ne displiceret et contristaret sociam, ductus non amore concupiscentiae, quae adhuc non erat in eo, sed amore sociali, quo timet quias non offendere amicum suum, ut dicit Augustinus."

68. *Oeuvres complètes de Eustaches Deschamps,* ed. Le Marquis de Queux de Saint-Hilaire (Paris, 1878), 1:277–78 (no. 150): "Mere et enfant garda en grant doubtance . . . Et si n'ot oncq feste en ce monde ci." The allusion to a holiday may reflect the efforts of such prominent churchmen as Jean Gerson, chancellor of the University of Paris, to have Joseph honored by a major feast day in the church calendar.

69. *Oeuvres de Deschamps:* "Vous qui servez a femme et a enfans / Aiez Joseph toudis en remembrance."

70. *Oeuvres de Deschamps:* "En pluseurs lieux est figuré ainsi, Lez un mulet, pour leur fair plaisance."

wars, and social uncertainties? The Holy Family according to its legend survived amid hostile and dangerous surroundings. For families facing similar uncertainties, perhaps its image offered a model of behavior and a promise of help.

In the late Middle Ages, this sense of an order in loving found expression in secular as well as religious writings. Lay people are, to be sure, slow to acquire voices in medieval cultural history. One place where they precociously learned to speak was Florence, capital of a new lay learning that was to culminate in humanism. In both domestic memoirs and formal treatises, Florentine writers commented extensively on the family and the sentiments associated with it. About 1360, a layman named Paolo da Certaldo included in his "Book of Good Customs" a passage on the four "greatest loves" in life. The greatest of all was love of one's own soul, followed by love for one's children, then for one's wife, and finally for one's friend. He did not mention love of God, but his ranking seems an expression in secular terms of the order proclaimed by theologians since Origen's time.[71] About 1393, an unnamed townsman of Paris instructed his wife on how she should order her affections: "you ought to be very loving and privy towards your husband above all other living creatures, moderately loving and privy towards your good and near kinsfolk in the flesh and your husband's kinsfolk, and very distant with all other men."[72] The ancient concept of degrees of loving extended beyond the ranks of the erudite.

The abundant domestic literature of late medieval Florence further indicates a sharpening division between the family's inner circle and the surrounding society. Giovanni Morelli, a Florentine writing in the years 1393 to 1403, instructed his descendants on how to counter the dangers of the world. One such danger was the plague. The defensive perimeter he drew up encircles the family. The family also was to be taken to a safe locale and given the proper food. The family also had to be treated to the proper cultural diversions to maintain morale, even if they were costly.

---

71. Paolo da Certaldo, *Libro di buoni costumi*, cap. 156, edn. Branca, 37: "I maggiori amori che sieno si sono quattro: il primo se è quello de l'anima tua, il secondo si è quello de' tuoi figliuoli, il terzo si è quello de la tua donna, cioè della buona moglie, lo quarto si è da l'uno amico a l'altro."

72. Anon., *The Goodman of Paris (Le Ménagier de Paris): A Treatise on the Moral and Domestic Economy by a Citizen of Paris (c. 1393)*, trans. Eileen Power (London, 1928), 107.

"Hold your family," Morelli recommended, "in pleasure and delight, and seek together with them the good and healthy life."[73]

Although the menace of plague threatened the family from the outer world, there were other dangers, too. The government's insatiable appetite for taxes and the machinations of dishonest neighbors could rain ruin on the family if these intrusions were not countered by appropriate measures. In describing those methods, Morelli warned against trust in anyone outside the household, even seeming friends, even close relatives. "Strangers I call them," he pronounced, "since where money is involved or any property, there can be found neither relative nor friend who loves you more than he does himself.[74] He continued, "A relative or friend will remain for as long as your property and status shall last, whence he thinks to gain some profit."[75] Morelli would have agreed with Peter Lombard's blunt assessment that, beyond the domestic circle, there are only enemies.

But, if the Florentine family felt threatened by disease, taxes, and pervasive dishonesty, its members seem to have developed a stronger sense of internal cohesion and seem to have found, or hoped to find, in their companionship essential rest and refreshment. Giannozzo Alberti, the sage who dominates the third book of Leon Battista Alberti's *Four Books on the Family,* urged the young Alberti males to eschew public office and government honors. "My children," he advised, "let us remain happy with our little family."[76] He uses here the diminutive form, *famigliola,* clearly implying affection. This seems a novel usage. The Latin equivalent of the word, *familiola,* meant in classical times only a small band of slaves. Alberti means by it a dear and loving group of parents and children clearly separated from the outer world and emotionally independent of it.

---

73. Giovanni Morelli, *Ricordi,* ed. V. Branca (Florence, 1969), 213–14: "tieni in diletto e in piacere la tua famiglia e fa con loro insieme buona e sana vita."

74. Morelli, *Ricordi,* 173: "Istrani gli chiamo, perché dove giuoca pecunia o alcuno bene proprio, né parente né amico si truova che voglia meglio a te che a sé, disposta la buona coscienza da parte."

75. Morelli, *Ricordi,* 173: "Peró che tanto basta il parente e l'amico quanto ti basterà l'avere e lo stato dove e' penserà trarre utilità."

76. Leon Battista Alberti, *Opera omnia,* ed. Cecil Grayson (Bari, 1960), 1:1982, 182: "Figliuoli miei, stiamoci in sul piano, e diamo opera d'essere buoni e giusti massai. Stiànci lieti colla famigliuola nostra, godiànci quelli beni ci largisce la fortuna faccendone parte alli amici nostri, ché assai si truova onorato chi vive senza vizio e senza disonestà."

What explains the new and wide division between household and society evident in these Florentine texts? The real change, as I see it, was less in the family itself—always thought to be a community of affection—than in the apprehension of external society as hostile and demanding. Governments were becoming better organized, more powerful, and, through their taxes and policies, more intrusive than ever into the domestic realm. The family itself was coming to rely more and more for its support on cash transactions. Contractual obligations and cash connections now linked households within the larger society. But loan oft loses friend, and so might every other type of monetary transaction.

The unnamed citizen of Paris told of a couple who drew up a nuptial agreement, stipulating their separate rights and duties.[77] One day, the husband fell into a river and called upon his wife to save him from drowning. The wife consulted the agreement and found no clause obligating her to rescue a drowning spouse. She let him sink, though others finally saved him. The moral here seems clear: contract and cash, which govern relationships in the outer world, should not do so within the family. By the end of the Middle Ages, at least in certain areas and certain classes of European society, the family had become a moral unity and a moral universe in the sense I have defined.

Of course, the evolution of family structures and cultures continued after the Middle Ages ended. Styles of domesticity, and the set of values and expectations associated with it, have changed across modern times even as lifestyles change. The tension between the family and the greater society has also waxed and waned according to shifting patterns of politics and modes of private behavior. Many of these fluctuations in modern family history have been studied in what is now a vast literature.[78]

Nonetheless, the ancient and medieval origins of many contemporary attitudes toward the family need to be recognized. Still today, the family

---

77. *The Goodman of Paris*, 138.

78. The recent, collaborative *History of Private Life*, vol. 4: *From the Fires of Revolution to the Great War*, is devoted almost entirely to the family, especially in France. Also see Michael Mitterauer and Reinhold Sieder, *The European Family*, trans. Karla Osterveen and Manfred Hörzinger (Oxford, 1982); and *Histoire de la famille*, ed. André Burgière, Christiane Klapisch-Zuber, Martine Segalen, and Françoise Zonabend, vol. 1: *Mondes lointains, mondes anciens*, and vol. 2: *Le Choc des modernités* (Paris, 1986). For relations of the family with kin and community, see Peter Laslett, "Family, Kinship and Collectivity as Systems of Support in Pre-Industrial Europe: A Consideration of the 'Nuclear-Hardship' Hypothesis," *Continuity and Change* 3 (1988): 153–75.

seems to some a prison. For them, it preserves its ancient meaning as a band of slaves; it continues to reflect the emphasis on authority written into its distant past. To others, it seems a haven, a refuge in which the furious pace of getting and spending is slackened, the burden of affairs is lightened, tensions are eased, enmities forgotten. For these, as for Augustine long ago, the family is *requies*. Still others argue that the traditional family, based on monogamy and child-rearing, does not meet their own emotional needs, that other forms of domestic partnership should be accepted. They question only the universal applicability of one definition of the family, not the value of the supportive and recreative functions the small domestic community has long provided. The cult and culture of the modern family, and its problems, too, have traces running deep into ancient and medieval history, which here in part I have tried to follow.

David Herlihy and the
Florentine Catasto

Christiane Klapisch-Zuber

In the autumn of 1966, Emmanuel Le Roy Ladurie returned from a symposium in Italy and said to me, "I've just met again an American colleague who has begun some extraordinary research. Would you like to work with him? Fernand Braudel is enthusiastic about this project and will find the necessary means to establish a collaboration."

That American scholar was David Herlihy. Emmanuel and David knew each other from a famous conference on climatology held in Aspen, Colorado, four years earlier.[1] I knew his name from two articles on agrarian history and a book on Pisa, which I had read with admiration over the course of my own research for my dissertation on the trade in marble from Carrara. I was still a beginner and had no reason to think that David had read any of my small scholarly output. I accepted the offer and met David several weeks later in an icy villa in the Florentine hills where he had found shelter after a major flood in Florence. That meeting in November 1966 began a collaboration that would last for more than 10 years. It obliged us to raise teams of researchers and direct their work; to familiarize myself (and, for David, to master) the languages that would allow us to converse with "those monsters" (as computers were called in those days); to punch, correct, transfer, store, and analyze tens of thousands of punch cards; to exchange hundreds of letters and cross the Atlantic ourselves several times for intensive work sessions; and finally to write together a big book of 700 pages, in spite of the language barrier and stylistic differences.

---

1. David Herlihy gave a talk there entitled "Some References to Weather in Eleventh Century Chroniclers," and he prepared the data that were published in the *Annales, E.S.C.* in 1963.

I don't want to linger in a nostalgic evocation of a time of intense research and intellectual exchange. Rather, it is to the encounter of two different types of historiographical formation and culture that I will devote this essay. David, as an American historian, was the heir of a great school of historians of the medieval economy and humanism founded primarily by refugees from Nazi or fascist Europe. He was especially influenced by Robert Lopez, one of those Europeans who was able to transplant Italian historiographical traditions and approaches into the fertile ground of American universities where it left a deeply rooted and enduring fascination with Mediterranean Renaissance culture. Lopez aroused in David an interest in the Commercial Revolution of the late Middle Ages, which he discusses in his book on Pisa.

As for myself, I began my research career in 1962 under the direction of disciples and friends of Fernand Braudel. Until the sixties, the first cohorts of students, mainly foreigners who had gravitated toward the Centre des Recherches Historiques (CRH), created in 1947 and directed by Braudel, dedicated most of their efforts to the history of commerce and monetary flows. Their research, synthesized from gigantic quantities of data centered on Mediterranean trade, was financially supported by the CRH and naturally came to be published first in the center's collections. The CRH acted as a publisher of scholarly research in certain specialized fields rather than a true research center with a program and a permanent staff. Many scholars had an association with the center but were not members, and rarely was a collective project undertaken by a fixed group of researchers.

Still, in the midst of this wave of studies on commerce and the economy of the Mediterranean world, I enrolled as a participant in a project on "Byzantium and the Western Mediterranean." I immersed myself in the records of Genoese notaries of the twelfth and thirteenth centuries, so magnificently edited by historians of the American school, and especially in the work of Robert Lopez. Soon after, Ruggiero Romano suggested to me as a thesis subject "The Trade of Marble from Carrara," which he thought fit solidly into the tradition of research on commercial flow and economic exchange. Here also I encountered work by Lopez, and I could not help but be struck by his investigation of the relationship between the depression at the end of the Middle Ages and "the investment in culture."[2] So, without our knowledge, the attraction of Lopez had both David and I revolving in similar spheres of research.

---

2. Robert Lopez, "Hard Times and Investment in Culture," in W. K. Ferguson, ed. *The Renaissance: Six Essays* (New York, Harper and Row, 1962), 29–54. R. S. Lopez and H. A.

After 1960, however, soon after I began working at the CRH, everything, from topics and methods to personnel, began to change at the center. The first group of historians gathered by Braudel was being succeeded by a large group of young French recruits who had been influenced by Ernest Labrousse as much as by Braudel himself. In addition, there was a new influence emanating from Polish historians and archaeologists—remember at this time, at least among historians, Braudel was said to be the "king" of Poland—which had widened Braudel's interests in the analysis of material life of past times. This provided a foundation for a more concrete social and economic history. At the same time, Braudel also encouraged and promoted a parallel but not contradictory search for a "real social science," which would benefit from models built by economists and demographers.

The decline in attention paid to trade and monetary history came as a result of this change in Braudel's objectives as well as the influx of young *Annales* historians who joined the VIth Section of the Ecole Pratique des Hautes Etudes at this time. The books published by the center were more and more devoted to social, agrarian, and demographic history during the sixties and early seventies. Even the bonds with the Mediterranean world and culture were vanishing. Historians' energies turned back to the French hexagon, and *grandes thèses* explored all the dimensions of the social life of every province of France. However, the *Annales* historians and the French historical school as a whole were not closed to debates coming from abroad. Clearly, the international debate begun by Michael Postan and his neo-Malthusian students brought a new impulse to French regional studies, as Le Roy Ladurie's thesis on Languedoc reveals.[3]

This debate also invigorated David's research on Pistoia just before 1965. Chapter 5 of his book, published in 1967, examines, successively, "the impact of natural disasters, the influence of overpopulation, and the role of births." The central thrust of his argument is a discussion of neo-Malthusian theses.[4] Far from aligning himself with a mechanistic vision

Miskimin, "The Economic Depression of the Renaissance," *Economic History Review*, 2d ser., 14, no. 3 (April 1962): 408–26; Carlo M. Cipolla, Robert S. Lopez, and Harry A. Miskimin, "The Economic Depression of the Renaissance?" *Economic History Review*, 2d ser., 16, no. 3 (April 1964): 519–29.

3. Emmanuel Le Roy Ladurie, *The Peasants of Languedoc*, trans. John Day (Urbana: University of Illinois Press, 1974).

4. David Herlihy, *Medieval and Renaissance Pistoia: The Social History of an Italian Town, 1200–1430* (New Haven: Yale University Press, 1967), 104.

of a population adapting to resources at hand, David liberated the role of natality. He based his conclusions on observations from the great Florentine census of 1427, the Catasto, and strongly suggested that economic and cultural factors influenced the birthrate.

David's first investigation of the Catasto convinced him that this massive document was a treasure. Thus, he conceived the project of analyzing the whole document in order to test the hypotheses he had posed about the small city of Pistoia and its surroundings and generalize them on a larger scale that would encompass all of Tuscany. This project entailed not only the collection of basic social and economic data on families in Tuscany from every social milieu but also the collection of data on individuals, especially their sex and age. Handling such a vast corpus of data was possible only with the computer, a new, powerful tool capable of holding, comparing, and processing amazing amounts of statistical data.

In this period, the computer was a novelty that was viewed by most French historians with respectful awe. The first regular exchanges between the CRH and American universities, in particular the University of Michigan, Ann Arbor, persuaded men like François Furet and Le Roy Ladurie that historians would greatly benefit from adopting the use of computers to accomplish their most ambitious research tasks. No longer would historians be forced to fall back on the tradition of publishing raw data; they would be able to present processed information. In 1966, the center began an association with the Centre National de la Recherche Scientifique (CNRS) on a program of collective research, using large staffs of research assistants to gather and prepare immense data sets for the computer. The computer now occupied the key role in the design and execution of these large-scale projects. The prestige associated with new technology would also confirm the center's and the Braudelian school's leadership of French historians. David's project anticipated the center's undertaking and could only please them with its large regional and social coverage, the quality and variety of information prepared for cross-analysis, the ambition to use technological means toward well-defined ends, and, last but not least, the employment of an international team of researchers in the Braudelian tradition.

David was not daunted by the size of the task he had assigned himself, and because he was such a strenuous worker I have no doubt he could have finished it alone. Nevertheless, after a year passed in the Florentine archives (1965–66), he had to consider the mass of registers remaining to be scrutinized. (Note that no historian at that time, nor any contemporary of the census, had determined the exact Tuscan population. The only way to estimate it was by examining every register.) He therefore welcomed the help offered by Braudel and Le Roy Ladurie, knowing that it would considerably shorten the duration of the work.

Things did not exactly happen that way, because soon I met Louis Henry, the founder and leader of historical demography in France. Henry at first glance saw the main advantage of the Catasto: it opens for the historian a way to penetrate deeply into the intimate family structure of the period. Louis Henry advised us not to overlook such a historiographical godsend and to add not only the data regarding marital status but also the position of every member of the household vis-à-vis the head. We could thus expect to understand the household's composition and the relationships that ensured its cohesion and development. The sharp eye of Louis Henry enabled us to greatly enrich our analysis by broadening it to include the links between family structure, economic production, and available resources. Unfortunately, it obliged David to revise data that had already been encoded, and both of us had to proceed more slowly than before.

I do not relate these episodes out of a love for anecdotes. Rather, to me, they seem typical of the directions of research at that time and of ways of doing research in two different countries.

As to the directions of research, when Louis Henry became interested in the information the Catasto could provide, I ask myself now if he had any awareness of where his intuition would take us. At that time, J. Hajnal's famous paper, which posited a wide interpretation of European models of marriage, was just published (1965), and we may assume that Henry knew it.[5] However, except for some banal and endlessly repeated phrases, familial or domestic structures were not considered by historians or even by demographers of past societies. They relegated to marginal status the work of a historian like Philippe Ariès or of a sociologist like William Goode; they did not imagine that these structures might vary from one culture or era to another.[6] I do not think that in those days

---

5. See J. Hajnal, "Age at Marriage and Proportions Marrying," *Population Studies* 7 (1953): 111–36, and "European Marriage Patterns in Perspective," in *Population in History*, ed. D. V. Glass and D. E. C. Eversley (London: E. Arnold, 1965), 101–43.

6. P. Ariès, *Histoire des populations françaises et de leurs attitudes devant la vie depuis le XVIIIe siècle* (Paris: Editions du Seuil 1971 [1948]); P. Ariès, *L'enfant et la vie familiale sous l'Ancien Régime* (Paris: Editions du Seuil; 1970 [1960]);

Louis Henry had more in mind than the possibility of verifying, in a rather imprecise way, the apparent fertility of Florentine couples. I do not remember him suggesting a framework for the analysis of medieval households different from the categories used in modern French censuses or from the family forms he had created in order to measure fertility rates and compare them over time. His interest in the Catasto was probably excited only by the hope that indirect measures of mortality and fertility could apply to a large set of households distributed according to their size.

The rapid takeoff of family history in France dates from the beginning of the seventies. It was accelerated by the first encounters with Peter Laslett's Cambridge Group and by the receptiveness of the *Annales* historians to social anthropology. They became aware of the implications for their own discipline of the variety of familial forms across human societies. The diffusion of working concepts such as the "domestic cycle of development," borrowed from sociology by historians like Lutz Berkner and Hans Medick,[7] allowed historians to leave behind their rigid and external description of family life and to converse usefully with sociologists and anthropologists. Without knowing the full import of his suggestion, Henry had urged us to distinguish the continuity that lay beneath the snapshots taken by the census and to reconstitute the domestic cycles in Tuscany from the census forms in which they were preserved. His idea also gave us an indication of the connections between the domestic world and wider kin relationships, a topic that was not included in the original demographic project.

In the mid-sixties, though, these developments were still to come.

W. Goode, *World Revolution and Family Patterns* (Glencoe: Collier-Macmillan, 1963). Cf. M. Segalen, *Sociologie de la famille* (Paris: A. Colin, 1987 [1981]).

7. See the following articles by Lutz K. Berkner: "The Stem Family and the Development Cycle of the Peasant Household: An Eighteenth Century Austrian Example," *American Historical Review* 77, no. 2 (April 1972): 398–418; "Rural Family Organization in Europe," *Peasant Studies Newsletter* 1 (1972): 145–55; "Recent Research on the History of the Family in Western Europe," *Journal of Marriage and the Family* 35, no. 3 (August 1973): 395–405; "The Use and Misuse of Census Data for the Historical Analysis of Family Structure," *Journal of Interdisciplinary History* 5 (Spring 1975): 721–38; "Inheritance, Land Tenure and Peasant Family Structure: A German Regional Comparison," in *Family and Inheritance*, ed. Jack Goody et al., 71–95 (Cambridge and London: Cambridge University Press, 1976); and "Peasant Household Organization and Demographic Change in Lower Saxony (1689–1766)," in *Population Patterns in the Past*, ed. Ronald Demos Lee, 53–69 (New York: Academic Press, 1977).

Then the purpose of our research was an overall description of the specific traits in various social and professional groupings and a study of the social dimension of certain demographic variables. Actually, we tended toward a historical sociology of medieval populations. Such a project fitted perfectly with the other programs of quantitative description promoted by the CRH, which were grouped under the title "An Anthropology of the French people in traditional society."[8] Today, as I reflect on the intentions and historical interests of both parties, I wonder whether the French participation in David's enterprise mixed antagonistically with his own modes of thinking and whether the flourishing French themes concealed the more frankly "medieval" aim of his original vision. Perhaps the French influence limited the place given to the debate over Malthusian reactions to the depression, which has marginal status in the subsequent book, but it seems to me to have been at the very core of David's reflections at that time.

Let me make another observation: the variety of methods in the analysis and the presentation of results in the book also express the diversity of individual orientations and national habits. David's primary goal was to reveal historical change, and he considered correlation analysis to be the best means not only of detecting and explaining relations between phenomena but also of exploring the path of that historical change. As for me, I still carried the baggage of geography that all French historians of my generation acquired in the course of their studies. I certainly benefited from the know-how of the Ecole's cartography specialists, who developed and enriched the tradition of historical geography. Because of them, I became interested in identifying spatial relations between phenomena, and I also gained facility in communicating them visually. But, again, I think David was more profoundly a historian than I will ever be.

In conclusion, let me return one final time to the differences in approach among historians. A historian at an American university expects to find there, or through one of the great national public or private foundations, the means of pursuing his or her research. This system encourages him or her to submit fundamentally individualistic projects to individual publications, which are then evaluated and either rise or fall in

---

8. The project included these investigations: "Archives militaires du recrutement du 19e siècle," "Statistique Générale de la France (19e s.)" (with the University of Michigan), and "Apostolat mendiant et fait urbain dans la France médiévale." Cf. Lutz Raphael, "Le Centre de Recherches Historiques de 1949 a 1975," *Cahiers du Centre de Recherches Historiques* 10 (April 1993): 1–70.

value in the market of academic work. In France, a professor cannot be fired from a position, but a career advances only in predetermined stages, and research can only modestly affect its progression. It is well known that Braudel, first as the president of the VIth Section, and then of the Ecole des Hautes Etudes en Sciences Sociales (EHESS), proposed to French historians a very different approach to research. He conceived of the CRH as a true laboratory, like those found in the natural sciences, a place where people work together daily, share common aims and ideas, and write and publish collectively.

His plan for perfect collaboration never fully came to fruition. Paradoxically, one of the few projects in which there was a true intermingling of ideas was our examination of the Catasto. Yet the topic was not French; the society was not the *Ancien Régime;* the researchers did not come from the country under study; they did not know each other before beginning their collaboration; and they could easily have had strong differences in cultural traditions and professional, religious, or ideological positions.

So why did our project work? Except for the friendship that bonded us together as a team, and except for our common passion for Florence and Renaissance Italy, I cannot give a fitting answer. Without a doubt, I had deeply and lastingly internalized the ideals prevailing in my scientific French environment. In my first encounters with the American academic world, I was astonished, and perhaps slightly scandalized, by the pervasive atmosphere of individualism in its scholarly undertakings. It might be that precisely this combination of two different personal experiences of research—the tireless and pioneering personal energy of David on one side, and my own idealized conception of a somewhat mythical collective research on the other—made chemically active the explosive mixture of historians.

Would such an enterprise be possible today? David was hardly done with the Catasto when he started another huge project on the political archives of the Florentine commune. Again, it was a project involving the input into a computer of vast amounts of data. Since the Catasto, I have been working more on the margins of massive documentations and statistical evidence. But I feel deeply that all I am doing now results from our past collaboration and is possible only because David's daring and imagination led him to believe in the relevance of big numbers and big endeavors for historians and because he shared that adventure with me.

Part 1
Sex and the Family in the Middle Ages and the Renaissance

Genealogy and Marriage Alliance: Memories of Power in Late Medieval Florence

Anthony Molho, Roberto Barducci, Gabriella Battista, and Francesco Donnini

Giovanni di (son of) Pagolo Rucellai (1403–81) has attracted more than his share of historical attention. Jacob Burckhardt, Werner Sombart, and Robert Lopez, all three eminent contributors to their fields of scholarly inquiry, referred to him as exemplar of trends that each considered important in the history of late medieval Europe. More recently, monograph after monograph on fifteenth-century Florentine history has referred to his experience, generous selections from his writings were published in 1960, a little more than a decade ago an international symposium was held to discuss his career, and a magnificent volume— cosponsored by two of the most prestigious academic institutions in England and Italy—made available to the scholarly public the enormously learned and interesting papers presented in that symposium. No other personage of fifteenth-century Florence—with the possible exception of a handful of Medici—is better known, and none, perhaps, has been studied as thoroughly. Insights from his experience have been used to understand and measure broader social and cultural trends. For our purpose, his prominence rests on somewhat different grounds than those identified by other scholars. To be sure, he was rich and very well known to many of

An Italian version of this essay, part of a long-term research project on family and memory in late medieval Tuscany, appeared in *Quaderni Storici* 86, no. 2 (1994): 365–403. Some of the themes raised in this essay were also discussed in Molho 1994, where, however, the conclusions in chapter 7 are considerably different from those presented here. (Barbagli, Marzio. 1984. *Sotto lo stesso tetto. Mutamenti della famiglia in Italia dal XV al XX secolo.* Bologna.)

his important contemporaries—not in Florence alone, but also in Rome, Venice, Padova, and no doubt elsewhere. What counts for us, however, is not Giovanni's general distinction but his very particular prominence because of a set of marriage alliances which we shall examine below.[1] In fact, Giovanni was connected by marriage to the city's two premier lineages—the Strozzi, through his own marriage in 1428 to Palla Strozzi's daughter Iacopa, and the Medici, thanks to his son Bernardo's marriage in 1461 to Nannina, Cosimo de' Medici's granddaughter. These—and a small number of other—marriage alliances, and the connections they enabled Giovanni to make to a set of distinguished lineages in his city, endowed him with a complex sense of his own identity, which was itself based on his ability and his readiness to recollect these family connections. Our study addresses the particularities and singularities of Giovanni Rucellai's "memory" as it was conveyed in two brief documents he composed at different times in his life.[2]

Our study of this man's memory has led us to present, in this essay's conclusion, a brief series of hypotheses on the shifting images of his own past and of his familial identity, which Giovanni held in different periods of his long life. In the first place, our study shows how at least one Florentine—to be sure, someone of refined aesthetic sensibilities and a patron of prominent artists and thinkers, thoroughly imbued in contemporary humanistic culture, and endowed with high social rank—could represent his family past and in so doing fashion his own identity by relying on different types of genealogical representation according to the circumstances that confronted him. In a happy moment of his life, he prepared a classical genealogy, which represented the men of the Rucellai house—his *casato*—in a vertical, uninterrupted line, with its numerous ramifications, from his most remote ancestors to his grandsons. Later, after his economic circumstances had taken a decidedly unfavorable turn, Giovanni fashioned a document that highlighted a series of complex kin-

---

1. The most recent and complete study of Rucellai's life is Kent 1981; one should also consult Perosa 1981.

2. A selection of Giovanni Rucellai's writings is found in Rucellai 1960. The original version of Giovanni Rucellai's writings (hereafter cited as *Zibaldone*) is found in the private archive of the Rucellai family in Florence. We wish to thank Professor F. W. Kent for a microfilm copy of this document, which he most generously made available to us. The transcription of a part of the first of the two passages we analyze in this essay can be found in *Consorterie politiche* (1992, 58). We also offer our warm thanks to Count Cosimo Rucellai for his generosity in making it possible for us to consult the original codex of Rucellai's *Zibaldone* and for authorizing us to undertake an edition of the unedited portions of this valuable work.

ship ties brought to the Rucellai by the women who were married to them. Giovanni's sense of his own past and of his identity does not lend support to recent interpretations that have detected an almost linear change in the conception of their familial pasts among Tuscans of the late Middle Ages: from the dynastic, lineal ties of the thirteenth century to a family's horizontal extension (its cognatic ties) in the fourteenth through the mid-sixteenth centuries, and, in the early modern era, to the return to the vertical ties of consortial lineages. Rather, in the case of Giovanni, two systems of familial memory seemed to coexist in his consciousness, and he variously resorted to each according to contingencies at the time of composition. We believe that the study of Giovanni Rucellai's memory has led us to the rediscovery—and this would be a second hypothesis—of now lost meanings of two key terms, *consorteria* and *parentado*. To him, these terms were fundamental in his reconstructions of his familial past, as they are to us in our attempts to rediscover Giovanni's mental processes and the images evoked in his two documents. A third hypothesis regards the particular place that women occupied in Giovanni's complex and seemingly malleable memory of his past. Women do not emerge from our study as figures relegated to the margins of Giovanni's consciousness, as a recent historian rather dramatically suggested, at the same time exiles from their familial environments and temporary, fleeting presences in their married homes. Rather, what emerges from our study is Giovanni's difficulty in conceptualizing his past without assigning a privileged role to women of other families who, married to men of his own family, gave life to the successive generations of the Rucellai. Finally, there emerges from our investigation an image of the city of Florence, perceived by its leading citizens as an aggregate of the great families that, intermarrying among themselves generation upon generation—in marriages that, judged by the standards of Canon Law, often bordered on ecclesiastical illicitness—created a community of interests and a thick web of solidarities sustained over the course of generations by the memory of their cognatic bonds.

In 1457, Giovanni Rucellai, who, along with his entire family, had moved to the castle of San Gimignano to escape the plague, began a "Lenten notebook" *(zibaldone quaresimale)*. It was a book of annotations, "a salad of many greens," *(una insalata di più erbe)*,[3] as he called

---

3. *Zibaldone*, c.1 r.

it, in which he gathered all sorts of miscellaneous information about travels, readings, philosophical issues that agitated him, moral and business advice for his sons, and other diverse matters. A generous portion of this important manuscript has been published,[4] but a considerable portion of it remains unpublished. Among the unedited sections, two[5] concern directly the study of marriage and its links to economic life, the exercise of political power, and the function of memory.[6]

Rucellai opens his *zibaldone* with a passage in which he presents to his sons "notice of our family's descent and of other matters regarding the house's honor." "I find," he writes, "that the first who began and gave reputation to our family—of riches, state, and marriage alliances—was Nardo di [son of] Giunta d'Alamanno di Monte di messer Ferro around the year 1250."[7] Giovanni's evocation of this ancestor's genealogy, with its simple and clear lines of male descent, from Nardo, back to *giunta,* his father, then to his grandfather, and so on, gives a sense of his relentlessly agnatic focus in the reconstruction of his family.[8] Nardo had two wives, one from the Albizzi family and the other from the Tornaquinci, who bore him 13 male children. For each one Giovanni notes the name and alongside specifies either the descent or the extinction of the branch. This document spans 13 generations and includes a total of 197 names. What counted in this reconstruction were the biological links between one generation of men and the men of the preceding generations.[9] In this vision, men, and men alone, were responsible for the identity and the very existence of the family, the essence of which was its link to its male ancestors,

---

4. Rucellai 1960.

5. The first of these passages is composed of two folios (*Zibaldone*, ff. 1r–2v) commissioned by Rucellai to a copyist. In it, one finds a list of names to be given to Giovanni's sons Pandolfo and Bernardo for "their benefit" (*loro utile*). A few folios later (ff. 5r–v), there follows a series of annotations on the history of the Rucellai family, with references to Giovanni's grandfather's, his father's, his, and his sons' marriages. The notations in these folios, which refer to the years 1453–61, were made in Giovanni's own hand. In our analysis, we also use these passages, which in our estimation link the internal logic of the first document to that of the second (ff. 223r–224v), written about 20 years later. These two passages are published in the appendix of our article "Genealogia, parentado e memoria storica a Firenze nel XV secolo," to appear in the proceedings of the Congress "La memoria e la città."

6. This is an expression we use roughly in the accession of Fentress and Wickham 1992.

7. *Zibaldone*, f. 1r: "Truovo che 'l primo che diè principio et riputazione alla nostra famiglia di richeza, stato e parentadi ebbe nome Nardo di Giunta d' Alamanno di Monte di messer Ferro circa gli anni domini 1250."

8. Klapisch-Zuber 1991a.

9. Klapisch-Zuber 1991b identified 145 such men.

especially those responsible for bringing honor to the house. In the enumeration of Nardo's descendants, down to himself and his sons, Giovanni followed this principle with inflexible rigidity. Nardo had seven sons with his wife née Albizzi, of whom only two had any "descendants," by which term Giovanni obviously meant male descendants. And so the litany continued, from father to son and from Giovanni to his sons.

After the first reference to women who married into the Rucellai family, the wives of that illustrious ancestor Nardo, no names of women marrying into the family appear prior to the wives of Giovanni's grandfather, Messer Pagolo di Bingieri di Nardo.[10] In a sort of postscript to this genealogical compilation, Giovanni broke off for the first time from the logic of that first document and expressed in an emotion-filled sentence all the affection and esteem he had for his mother, who was his father's second wife: "She was a venerable woman, and it is worth remembering her because, although she was widowed at the age of nineteen, had three sons, and was expecting a fourth, she did not want to remarry so as not to abandon us; to her, we are greatly beholden" (È stata venerabile donna et degna di fare memoria di lei però che la rimase vedova d'età d'anni dicianove et avendo tre figliuoli et uno in corpo tutti maschi non si volle rimaritare per non ci abandonare alla quale siamo troppo obrigati). Giovanni's only wife was Iacopa, the daughter of Messer Palla di Nofri Strozzi,[11] considered the richest and most powerful citizen of Florence "at the time when I took her, which was in May of 1428." After extolling the merits of Palla Strozzi, Giovanni gave precise

---

10. From this entry, one learns that Messer Pagolo di Bingieri di Nardo had four wives, the first of the Bardi family, the second a Manetti, and the third a Buondelmonti. The fourth, Giovanni's grandmother, was Caterina Acciaiuoli (*Zibaldone*, ff. 5r–v).

11. On f. 5v of the *Zibaldone*, Giovanni quotes Leonardo Bruni, who had thus praised Palla Strozzi and Giovanni's decision to marry Palla's daughter: "Tu ài fatto parentado col più felice huomo non tanto della nostra città ma quanto mai avessi il mondo perché gli à tutte e sette le parti della felicità che non fu mai degli altri felici huomini che sono stati al mondo a chi non ne manchassi qualcuna e contommele tutte e sette, le quali noterò qui di socto nel modo che lui le disse a me: prima essere nato di nobile et di degna patria quanto abbi tutto l'universo mondo; la seconda essere di nobile sangue, la casa degli Strozzi essere degnissima, la donna degli Strozzi medesimi, la madre de' Cavalcanti, le sirochie et le figluole maritate nelle più degne case di Firenze; la terza essere dotato di bella famiglia, così di femine come di maschi; la quarta essere bello et sano di corpo . . . ; la quinta essere richo et di richezza bene aquistata; la sesta essere virtuoso et scientiato in greco e in latino; la settima ch'egli era molto amato . . . ."

information about his sons' marriages: Pandolfo, married to Caterina di Bonaccorso di Luca Pitti in 1453; and Bernardo, married in 1461 to Nannina di Piero di Cosimo de' Medici. Giovanni concluded this section of the *Zibaldone* by once again underscoring the great honor accumulated in his family as a result of these illustrious marriages: "And, as can be understood from what is written on this page, it appears that for the past hundred years our house has been able to make the principal marriage alliances of the city, first Messer Paolo my grandfather with Messer Donato Aciaiuoli, Paolo my father with Messer Veri de' Medici, I with Messer Palla Strozzi, Bernardo my son with Piero di Chosimo de' Medici, all of whom were the principal citizens of their time[12] . . . Pandolfo, my son, with Bonacorso di Messer Lucha Pitti, as mentioned above."[13] With this affirmation Giovanni interrupted his genealogy and addressed himself to his sons, offering them counsel on a range of subjects, including the risks of commerce, the effects of fortune on human affairs, and sundry others.

In this description, which we would today define as intensely virifocal, it is clear that Rucellai omitted an important element of his lineage's history. He himself seems to have recognized this when he wrote that his descendants should honor Nardo because of his ability not only to accumulate riches and gain political distinction but to arrange marriage alliances. If riches could be easily counted, and political distinction measured by the honors garnered in the political arena, the third criterion with which to measure reputation—marriage alliances—required a particular and separate treatment clearly absent from the zibaldone's opening passage. Yet, to focus on marriage alliances—to count and weigh the importance of the numerous *parentadi* struck by the Rucellai over the generations—was to formulate a different image of the family's past and of its identity. A recounting of generational successions of men was inadequate as a lineage's definition and history, for marriage alliances underlined the bonds—of blood, property, and sentiment—that linked one

---

12. There follows a short, indecipherable passage. In Rucellai 1960, 143, one reads: *e primi de la città.*

13. *Zibaldone,* f. 5v: "Et come si può intendere per quello ch' è scritto in questa carta apare che la chasa nostra da ciento anni in qua abbi per re[n]dita avuto d' avere fatti e principali parentadi della città, prima messer Paolo mio avolo con messer Donato Aciaiuoli, Paolo mio padre con messer Veri de' Medici, io con messer Palla de li Strozzi, Bernardo mio figliuolo con Piero di Chosimo de' Medici che in quelli tempi tutti sono stati e' primi . . . Pandolfo mio figliuolo con Bonacorso di messer Lucha Pitti chome detto di sopra."

lineage to others. One had to acknowledge the role of all the family's members not simply its men in establishing such blood connections. This discrepancy—between his intention to recount the "descent" *(discendentia)* of the Rucellai and the genealogy he had offered his sons in the opening pages of the zibaldone—must have stuck in Rucellai's mind, for eighteen years later, in 1475, when he had reached the ripe age of 72 and was enduring a series of unpleasant circumstances that threatened to destroy his material well-being and erode his family's honor, Giovanni undertook to reconstruct a part of his family's identity that he had overlooked in the earlier genealogical reconstruction.[14]

In 1476, then, Giovanni Rucellai inserted in his manuscript a section consisting of two densely written sheets in which he again went over much of the ground covered in the document he had redacted in 1457. He began with his great ancestor Nardo's grandson, Messer Paolo di Bingeri di Nardo, "my grandfather, who had four wives. The first was the daughter of Sandro di Bartolo de' Bardi, the second the daughter of Vanni Manetti, the third the daughter of Messer Uguccione Buondelmonti [of whom] there are no descendants, the fourth the daughter of Iacopo Acciaiuoli and sister of Messer Donato and of the cardinal; she was named Madonna Caterina."[15] Having dealt with his grandfather's wives, Giovanni shifted to the next generation, that of his father Pagolo and his aunt Nanna Rucellai. For Nanna, his father's sister, he noted her husband's name and their offspring. Nanna married Filippo di Biagio Guasconi, who, together with his sons, his daughters, and his daughters' husbands, was identified by Giovanni as belonging to his parentado. But not a mention is made here of the wives of Guasconi's five sons nor of their descendants. What follows is a systematically meticulous description of some, and only some, of the numerous and complex links that in the course of recent generations had bound the Rucellai to so many other Florentine lineages. One example should convey an idea of the tentacular extension of these familial links, which bound, in deeply knotted strands, so many lineages to each other, and which, collectively, comprised "our entire parentado" *(tutto il parentado nostro):*

> Madonna Caterina, the sister of the cardinal and of Messer Donato Acciaiuoli, my grandmother, had three sisters, one married, through

---

14. *Zibaldone,* f. 223r.

15. In the margin, with reference to the first three wives, he wrote, non ce n' è discendenti."

the mediation of the Great Acciaiuoli Seneschal, who was alive at the time, in the kingdom of Naples to a lord who was named [——][16] named Madonna Gismonda, from whom was born a girl named Bartolomea, who was married in Florence to Messer Mano Donati, who gave birth to a daughter, married to Messer Guglielino Tanagli, and another one married to Niccolò di Francesco Giraldi.

The aforementioned Madonna Caterina, my grandmother, had another sister named Madonna Andrea, married to Messer Mainardo Cavalcanti, of whom was born Messer Carlo Cavalcanti, who was my father Paolo's cousin, and of the said Messer Carlo were born Mainardo and Donato, who are my second cousins.

And she had another sister, named Madonna Francesca. . .

And so, with the punctiliousness of a skilled craftsman and the obsession for detail of someone used to striking his account book's debits and credits, Giovanni Rucellai produced a rich and complex image of his lineage's parentadi and of the multifarious links that, over the preceding three generations, had molded his house, binding him and his children to many of his contemporaries. With the sole exception of Nanna Rucellai, who was married to a Guasconi, he recorded only those parentadi brought by the women married into his branch of the Rucellai: his grandmother, his mother, his wife, and his daughters-in-law. For his grandmother, Acciaiuoli, he listed all her brothers and the marriages of her sisters, including their respective offspring down to the children of the paternal cousins, and in two cases to their children, for a total of 39 names. He then listed his mother Caterina's five siblings, with their children and grandchildren, for a total of 73. Finally, he undertook the same operation for his wife, Iacopa Strozzi, for whom he listed a total of 99 relatives, including uncles, brothers and sisters, cousins, nieces, nephews, grandnieces, and grandnephews. One peculiarity of this series of names immediately leaps to one's attention: invariably Giovanni reported the marriages of the sisters of the five women (Acciaiuoli, Pandolfini, Strozzi, Pitti, and Medici) who married into his branch of the Rucellai, with their offspring, but for the majority of the five women's brothers their spouses' names do not appear, and references to offspring are limited. In all, the

---

16. Here there is a blank space in the manuscript, extending for the length of about 30 letters.

1476 list includes 462 persons,[17] 345 men[18] and 117 women,[19] each name a pebble in a rich mosaic of personal links between the Rucellai and the city's other lineages, and each forming a small, if essential, part of *tutto il parentado nostro* ("all our parentado"). Compared to the first description, where 197 names appear over 13 generations, the names have more than doubled while the generations have been reduced to five, from Giovanni's grandfather to his grandsons.

At this point it becomes necessary to explain on the one hand the seeming complementarity of the two documents and on the other the probable existence of two different, regulated systems of omission: in the first, the systematic omission of marriage alliances; in the second, the inclusion of marriage alliances of only a limited number of women—those who either married into a specific branch of the Rucellai lineage or were related by blood to these women—and the omission of most marriage alliances struck by the vast majority of Rucellai men. In short, if Giovanni's thinking in compiling the first document is fairly obvious, one wonders to what rules (or criteria of inclusion and exclusion) he resorted when he compiled the second. The aim of much of the exercise that follows is to seek out traces of Giovanni Rucellai's memory of his own individual identity, while also searching for what we might define as his "social memory," that is, the memory of the social group to which he thought he belonged. Finally, we shall try to point to the particular events of Giovanni's biography that coincided with the drafting of the two texts, which could have had a bearing on his perspective and determined some of the differences in the conception and organization of the two documents.

It is not always easy to address these issues. A rapid rereading of the opening sentences of the two documents offers an initial suggestion of Giovanni's possible intentions. The first begins with these words: "First, I think that I should give you notice of the descent (*discendentia*) of our family, the Rucellai." In 1457, Giovanni limited himself to a list of the male "descent" of his ancestor Ferro who had, in some way, brought

---

17. In counting the number of people to whom Giovanni refers in this document, we included the names of his ancestors listed by implication in their descendants' patronymics. Thus, in the case of Pagolo di Bingieri di Nardo, who was Giovanni's grandfather, we counted three names, Paolo's, his father's (Bingieri), and his grandfather's (Nardo).

18. Of these, 103 names were considered to be listed by implication.

19. Of these, 74 are listed without names.

honor to the family. By contrast, the document of 1476 begins thus: "Herein I will make note of all our parentado" (*tutto il parentado nostro*), a group that, despite a modern reader's initial expectation, encompassed only a limited number of Rucellai and their marriages. As already noted, in this second document Giovanni recorded only those parentadi brought by the women who married into his branch of the Rucellai: his grandmother, his mother, his wife, and his daughters-in-law. In addition, he included his aunt Nanna Rucellai's husband and children. With the sole exception, then, of his father's sister, the marriages of the Rucellai girls who married "out of" the family, into other great lineages of the city, were systematically overlooked, as if their parentadi were less significant and honorable than those established by women who were not born Rucellai but who had given birth to the successive generations of the Rucellai. Sisters[20] and female cousins were not recorded in this honor roll, and their marriages were passed over in silence. Some time after completing this document, in an effort to explain (if not to justify) this sentence, Giovanni squeezed a seemingly puzzling note into the bottom margin of the last page: "I do not mention the parentadi of the Rucellai *consorteria*—of the girls who left and those who entered it—who are a very great number, because they carry with them half the city."[21]

Thus, despite Giovanni's intention to record "all our parentado," he found it natural to exclude from the list those whom he now relegated to the "parentado of the consorteria." In fact, the majority of the women married to men of the Rucellai family are excluded from the 1476 list, but, as we have noted, five of them are not only cited but occupy key positions in the *ricordanza*. How, then, did Giovanni determine that a woman married to a Rucellai belonged to "our entire parentado" and was not to be relegated to that indistinct (and somewhat puzzling) category of the "parentado di consorteria"? One can also ask how it was possible to consider the kin groups of the Acciaiuoli, the Pandolfini, the Strozzi, the Pitti, and the Medici as members of Giovanni Rucellai's

---

20. According to Passerini, Giovanni had a sister named Camilla, who was married in 1416 to Bartolomeo di M. Ciacchi. This alleged sister is not mentioned in any of the contemporary documents we consulted: the Monte delle doti, the Catasti, and the *Zibaldone* itself. Passerini also mentions that Giovanni had at least four nieces, of whom two were married, one to a Cavalcanti, the other to a Guidotti (Passerini 1861, 114, table 16).

21. *Zibaldone*, f. 224v: "Non fo menzione de' parentadi della chonsorteria de' Rucellai, delle fanciulle uscite e de l'entrate, che son grandissimo numero, per modo si tirano drieto mezza la città."

parentado while many of his own blood relatives were excluded from it. Or, to be more precise, under what rules of kinship could Giovanni have considered his grandmother's sisters and their children as belonging to "our" parentado while excluding from it his own brothers, their wives, their wives' kin, and their children? We shall shortly return to this question, but first we must note another order of omissions and inclusions that delimits the group of persons listed by Giovanni in this document. There exists, in fact, a marked disparity, seemingly based on a criterion of sexual discrimination, in Giovanni's treatment of the information at his disposal. The women belonging to the parentado, in their roles as mothers, sisters, daughters, or granddaughters of one of the five key women who entered into Giovanni's branch (but also the daughters of his aunt Nanna Rucellai), are often anonymous in the ricordanza, but as a rule their husbands' lineages are indicated, and often those of their offspring are as well. The lineage of these women's husbands is frequently followed in successive generations, even though it is very probable that the descendants noted represent only a fraction of the actual number. The brothers of these women are cited by name, but very little attention is given to their wives' lineages.

To illustrate the rules of composition of a similar aggregate, it would be useful to return briefly to the particular parentado that derives from Giovanni's Aunt Nanna, married to a Guasconi. Guasconi, together with his sons, his daughters, and his daughters' husbands, were inserted by Giovanni into his own parentado. But we have already observed that Giovanni passed over in silence Guasconi's five sons' wives. Giovanni did not consider them part of his parentado. Guasconi was drawn into the Rucellai parentado because he was the husband of a Rucellai woman. In the event that this rule was shared by Giovanni's contemporaries, Guasconi, as the father of five husbands, would consequently be part of the five different parentadi of his daughters-in-law, without, however, transmitting this quality to his closest acquired parentado, the Rucellai. In short, as the father of males, Guasconi represents an end point in the chain of every daughter-in-law's parentado, whereas, as the father of females, he represents a link that joins in one parentado the family of his father-in-law and that of his son-in-law. As a husband he is absorbed into the original parentado of his wife, and, correspondingly, as father of four daughters, he attracts four husbands into his parentado and into the closest of his acquired parentadi, that of the Rucellai. In this model, the connection between two families not linked by marriage is accomplished by an intermediary element that is simultaneously son-in-law and father-in-law of sons-in-law but not via an intermediary element that is simultaneously son-in-law and father-in-law of daughters-in-law.[22]

The reflection begun by Giovanni in 1457 was certainly simpler, and the destination of his compilation was much more evident than it was in 1476. The virifocal genealogical tree of 1457 could have been addressed to all the Rucellai, every one of whom should have found his particular branch in this tree and been able to trace his branch back to the trunk, thus discovering the blood links that connected him, over the preceding generations, to the common, illustrious ancestors responsible for the family's greatness.

On the contrary, the document of 1476 does not reveal immediately the parties for whom it was written: neither its opening phrase, nor the elliptical expression with which Giovanni closed it lends itself to a clear interpretation. So, if the terms he used to describe this document do not offer a sufficient explanation of its contents, we must search in the contents themselves and in their organization for clues to Giovanni's intentions and his audience. In turn, these clues may also help us understand the meaning of the terms used by Giovanni Rucellai. In his compilation, he applied a rigorous criterion not only of inclusion (the relatives acquired through the five women who married into the Rucellai family) but above all of exclusion. In fact, the most striking—initially, to us, almost mysterious—absence from this document is the list of his brothers' descendants, who, quite naturally, had been included in 1457. Other genealogical data reveal that Giovanni also excluded the branches generated by the brothers of his paternal grandfather (that is, his paternal great-uncles) and paternal cousins of various degrees. Instead, the document contains name after name of uncles, great-uncles, and cousins acquired through his grandfather's and father's marriages and of cognates and nephews acquired through his own marriage. What principle of compilation could justify the exclusion of his brothers and the insertion, instead, of uncles acquired on the female side? This complex of inclusions and exclusions—which, evidently, were not applied casually

22. There are some exceptions to this rule. They refer to Piero and to Donato di Neri di Donato di Iacopo Acciaiuoli, great-grandsons of Caterina Acciaiuoli, Giovanni Rucellai's grandmother. Piero was married to a daughter of Dietisalvi Neroni, while his brother Donato was married to a daughter of Piero Pazzi. Similarly, with regard to Francesca, Caterina Acciaiuoli's sister, who was married to Amerigo Cavalcanti, he mentions Francesco Castellani, father of his grandson Giovanni's wife.

but were result of carefully considered choices that, as we will suggest below, imparted upon his writing a pointedly practical character—furnishes important clues for identifying the audience to whom Giovanni addresses his message.

Our hypothesis can be somewhat clarified if we turn to the descendants of Bingieri Rucellai (Giovanni's great-grandfather) whom Giovanni excluded from his compilation: the brothers and sisters of Paolo di Bingieri (Giovanni's grandfather), the sons of the sons of Nanna di Paolo di Bingieri (but, notably, not Nanna herself, or her nine children), the sons of Giovanni's three brothers (Donato, Filippo, and Paolo), and then the descendants of Giovanni's daughters and of his son Pandolfo's daughters. This process of continuous exclusion—from his grandfather's generation to his own—had the effect of producing an increasingly narrow perspective, so that, in the end, the focus of Giovanni's compilation was cast sharply on the bloodline joining him to his father, his grandfather, and his two sons. In this representation, it could be said that each generation, from Paolo di Bingieri to Giovanni, transmitted to its descendants its blood and a portion of its honor, which, in successive generations, were enhanced (or modified) by the addition of blood and honor contributed by other, equally specific branches of other lineages, the Acciaiuoli, the Pandolfini, the Strozzi, the Pitti, and the Medici. Thus, it is hard to escape the conclusion that the only conceivable recipients of the message conveyed by the 1476 ricordanza were Giovanni's grandsons, the only persons among all those whom he cited in this document who, in addition to their Rucellai blood, shared the blood of the Acciaiuoli, Pandolfini, Strozzi, and either that of the Pitti or the Medici. It would seem that through this ricordanza of his old age, Giovanni wanted to identify the continuity of bloodlines and the portions of the family honor that he had amassed by virtue of being who he was: in the first place, the "undivided" blood heritage and honor shared by all the branches of the Rucellai, then the blood and honor that were specific to Giovanni, and finally those that he transmitted to his sons and grandsons. If this hypothesis is correct, it is fairly clear that, from the vantage point of Giovanni himself and then of his immediate descendants, the inclusions and exclusions of ancestors and relatives were made on the basis of a rigorous and consistent criterion of selection.

Before asking ourselves the meaning and the function of Giovanni's exploration of his familial past, we can already observe that the 1476 ricordanza defined Giovanni's individuality and that of his sons with much greater precision than could a virifocal genealogy. Indeed, the 1457 document, by highlighting the Rucellai bloodlines, offered necessarily only that fraction of each person's identity that was derived from his Rucellai name. The 1476 compilation suggests that Giovanni himself was acutely aware of the previous document's limitations and that he set out to define his own identity by casting it out of a portion of the Rucellai genealogy to which he grafted the partial genealogies of the great lineages allied by marriage with his immediate ancestors. Instead of placing the principal subjects of the second document's audience—Giovanni, his sons, and their sons—on branches of his lineage's genealogical tree, Giovanni now seems to have imagined them as standing in the center of a metaphorical "geometrical figure," which included only the cognatic relationships to which he referred in his second document, and which, systematically and self-consciously, excluded all other marriage alliances of the Rucellai.

Imagine, then, every head of family such as Giovanni Rucellai intent on mapping out the contours of the territory that encompassed the honor and blood transmitted to him by his ancestors. The perimeters of his territory—which defines the honor and blood that belong to his own, personal genealogical line—are determined by the boundaries of other, identical geometric figures, each of which has at its center a different Ego, who, nonetheless, shares the ancient portion of Giovanni's honor: in other words, a brother, or a cousin. A clear example of this is offered by Giovanni's decision to exclude from his second document his brothers' extremely prestigious marriage alliances, for, by the standards he applied while compiling "our entire parentado," they belonged to comparable geometric figures adjacent to Giovanni's own. Only for this reason was Donato's wife, a Panciatichi, overlooked, and similarly Donato's son Agnolo's bride, an Adimari, or Francesca da Diacceto, who married Giovanni's other brother Filippo, not to mention the very important marriages that distinguished the branch of Piero di Bingieri, the brother of Giovanni's grandfather.

Thus, it turns out that the reference to "half the city" was not, as one might have thought, a generic rhetorical expression with which Giovanni got out of offering a detailed enumeration of that chaotic tangle of ancient, indiscernible links of relationships, which, over the generations, had been forged by the Rucellai.[23] Giovanni stated that the women of the

---

23. This analysis and much of what follows should be read as a corrective to the concluding section of Molho 1994.

"parentado di consorteria . . . carry with them half the city" not to draw an arbitrary line around such an immense and indiscriminate agglomeration of familial connections but to define precisely the exterior limit of his part of this agglomeration, which, within this "half city," occupied a complexly shaped portion. Contiguous to Giovanni's "geometrical figure" within this "half city" would be a series of other such "figures," each constructed according to the same criteria and revolving around an Ego with the responsibility of transmitting to his immediate descendants his honor, bloodlines, and the knowledge (i.e., the memory) necessary for the construction of that particular "figure."

In late medieval Europe, for the vast majority of laymen, the essential function of memory was the regulation of endogamy. Over the centuries, and according to prevalent cultural norms, varying prohibitions had been imposed against marital unions between individuals related to each other by blood or other ties. The Fourth Lateran Council of 1215 established the definition of consanguinity, and consequently the nature of marriage impediments due to such blood relationships followed during the late Middle Ages. Its decisions made less stringent some of the church's previous prohibitions, while also offering a reasonably clear guide for calculating the degree of relationship between two individuals with a common ancestor.[24]

It is conceivable, then, that Giovanni's decision to include such a vast number of individuals in his parentado could have had an exquisitely cartographic character. That is, as his family's head, and the one responsible for the maintenance of its honor, he may have thought it necessary to present a map, as it were, of possible and prohibited marriages to the sons of his sons. And yet, after making the necessary canonical computations, we had to exclude the possibility that Giovanni's objective was that of drawing a map of prohibited relationships for his grandsons, who, on the basis of what we said earlier, were identified as the recipients of the ricordanza. Missing from this map are a large number of possible partners of the fifth and sixth degrees who surely existed in the agnatic and cognatic branches of brothers and paternal uncles.

If, then, Giovanni did not put on paper his "entire parentado" in order to facilitate the matrimonial choices of his grandsons—by pointing out a

---

24. Esmein (1891, esp. 1:87–90, 2:258–66, and 2:335–402) remains the best, clearest, and most authoritative discussion of these complex issues. See also Cimetier 1932. A useful and brief summary of the canonical definition of and ecclesiastical impediments to marriage (with an illuminating illustrative table) is found in Pettener and Niccolini 1980; and in Goody 1983, 56–59. See also Molho 1994, 256–60.

pool of acceptable marriage partners and warning them off those whom it would be inappropriate to marry—his aims must have been different. Of the various hypotheses that we pursued, we think the one that best explains his intentions has to do with the circulation of dowries among members of the Florentine ruling class. Studies in recent years have shown how, at least in the great Florentine families, a sort of accounting of dowries was kept—the dowries that entered the family with the marriages of sons and those that left it at the time of daughters' marriages.[25]

Dowries did not represent a portion of wealth that, having left the wife's family, entered the husband's to become his undisputed property. Husbands were no more free to dispose of the dowries they received than fathers were free from the responsibility of endowing their daughters. Every husband and his family had to provide elaborate guarantees to ensure that at the time of the marriage's termination a sufficient portion of his estate, equivalent to the dowry received, would be available to return to his widow or to her heirs if she predeceased him.[26] One can think of dowries as a sort of frozen wealth attached to a woman when she left her paternal home to enter married life. Families giving women away in marriage might consider the dowries carried by their womenfolk as deposits of such frozen wealth to which corresponded more or less exactly those other frozen deposits entered in their houses with the arrival of brides for their sons, who generally originated from the same circle of families.

Contemporaries, of course, were keenly aware of all this, and some even pointedly commented upon problems raised by the circulation of dowries. One of the most direct references among Giovanni's contemporaries was made by Bonaccorso di Neri Pitti, grandfather-in-law of one of Giovanni's sons, who justified his granddaughter's second marriage thus: "And the said Lisa [daughter of Luigi di Bonaccorso Pitti] having been widowed . . . and [because she was the] heir of the said Luigi . . . Bartolomeo [di Neri Pitti] took her for his wife so that the inheritance would not leave our house."[27] In short, dowries that left the house were marked

---

25. For an analysis of several of these themes, see L. Fabbri 1991; and Molho 1994.

26. On the circulation of women and dowries within the city's ruling class, see Molho 1994; Kirshner 1985; Kirshner 1991a; Kirshner 1991b; and, more generally, Kirshner and Molho 1978. On widows, see Chabot 1986; Chabot 1988; and Kuehn 1991.

27. Pitti 1986, 357–58: "E sendo rimasa la detta Lisa vedova e reda del detto Luigi di Bonaccorso Pitti, la tolse per moglie Bartolommeo, a fine che quella eredità non uscisse di casa nostra."

in a scarcely metaphorical account book under the entry "credits that could reenter," while dowries that came in had to be considered as debits, because, when the males of the lineage died, the widows, especially if they were childless, were likely to carry them back to their paternal homes.

Normally this type of transaction, which we can easily imagine as being registered in an account book kept in double entry, required the registration of two columns: "debits" for dowries that came into the family, "credits" for those that left it. The parentadi brought to Giovanni Rucellai by the Guasconi and the Acciaiuoli make clear a peculiar characteristic of the 1476 document. In it, Giovanni listed systematically the parentadi brought to his family by sisters and the female descendants of those who married him and his immediate ancestors and descendants. Men were generally recorded without their wives' names, and it is remarkable how little attention was paid to their descendants, particularly the male ones. In other words, in his work Giovanni showed a constant attention to the dowry movement generated by the marriage of women related to him in a continuous registration of what, metaphorically, we have called the debit dowry column. It should be noted, however, that Giovanni simultaneously took note of the dowries paid by the other lineages by marrying into the branches of the five wives of Paolo di Bingieri (Giovanni's grandfather), of Paolo di Paolo (his father), of Giovanni di Paolo himself, and of his sons Pandolfo and Bernardo.

Thus, the 1476 document reveals some unusual characteristics. First, and perhaps least striking, are the debts incurred by Paolo di Bingieri's branch of the Rucellai with the families of the five brides, the Acciaiuoli, the Pandolfini, the Strozzi, the Pitti, and the Medici. Yet Giovanni went beyond the registration of these debts. Additionally, and this is the document's most notable characteristic, he carefully traced the marriages of the sisters of all these Rucellai wives. That is, he made a list of the marriages (and, therefore, of dowries paid) by the sisters of his grandmother, Caterina Acciaiuoli, who had established ties between their natal family and the families into which they had married. He followed the same procedure for the parentadi brought to him by the Pandolfini and the Strozzi.

Why might Giovanni wish to list with such systematic rigor the marriages of females already related to him? Why would he want his grandsons to remember the names of the families who had received dowries from women who were already related by blood to the Rucellai? And why would he not be concerned with identifying the families that had paid dowries to men of the Rucellai family (other than to those who belonged to his immediate bloodline)? There appears to be only one answer to these questions: the families that had received in marriage one of the female relatives of the Rucellai, and also received her dowry, furnished to the sons of Giovanni's sons a list of families indebted, in a certain sense, to his immediate family members. In a moment of difficulty the knowledge of these past exchanges could offer to his grandsons useful references about families that, as debtors of the Acciaiuoli, Pandolfini, and Strozzi, could also be seen as indebted to the grandsons, inasmuch as they were the families' descendants through the female line.

To be sure, this is a complex explanation. Yet it is the only one that offers a key to interpreting this dense and unusual document. And there appears to be some additional evidence, external to the document here analyzed, which seems to lend support to our explanation.

At the time Giovanni wrote his genealogical "descent" of 1457, although he had not entirely overcome the difficult political position to which the Medici had relegated him since 1434, he was enjoying a period of considerable well-being. He had just concluded (in 1453) a good marriage contract for his son Pandolfo with Caterina Pitti, daughter of one of the city's premier politicians, and he was about to definitively overcome his political proscription by arranging the marriage of his son, Bernardo, to Nannina de' Medici, Cosimo de' Medici's granddaughter. In the Catasto (tax census) of 1457–58, Giovanni ranked as the third-wealthiest man in the city.[28] In the pages immediately following the genealogy of 1457, Giovanni exalted his family's status, listing its great political honors and mercantile successes, concentrating on the male, agnatic component of honor. The "great parentadi," arranged by the males, had brought about an increase in the family's "honor," even if by our reasoning they had contributed to the "dowry indebtedness" of the entire Rucellai lineage. But in that happy moment Giovanni did not pay attention to this aspect.

Instead he concentrated on showing off a great part of the honor accumulated by the house of the Rucellai and available to all its living members: the lineage's antiquity, which extended all the way back to a legendary relative, Messer Ferro, who, arriving in Italy from Brittany, stopped at the castle of Campi;[29] the Rucellai's participation in the city's public life, dating back to 1302, when Nardo di Giunta became prior, as

---

28. Archivio di Stato di Firenze, Catasto 817 (for the year 1458), c.74 r.
29. *Zibaldone*, f. 3v.

Giovanni informs us by inserting in the addendum to the genealogy a list of Rucellai priors and Standardbearers of Justice;[30] the considerable Rucellai wealth derived from the craft of dyeing cloth;[31] and the social status that the family had attained as early as the time of Cenni di Nardo, who had even given his name to the street in which he lived.[32] In this celebratory "genealogy" (*discendentia*) of 1457 the female component of this honor was excluded, even if "good parentadi" are declared to be manifest signs of honor, as Giovanni subsequently and repeatedly underlined.

The commemoration of Giovanni written later by his sons clarifies the components of this honor. In a passage they added to the zibaldone, they proudly wrote that "our house never had anyone who merited so much praise and so many commendations and who, following its beginning, brought greater honor to our family than the said Giovanni, our father, especially when one considers the worthy parentadi, the wealth (since he had been a great merchant who commanded great credit), the temporal and spiritual buildings that he caused to be constructed, and equally the gold brocade and other vestments [he donated to churches] and other worthy things: so much so, that it seemed to us that we should record all this in this book, may God concede him his holy grace."[33] We see here that the list of "worthy things" opens with the "worthy parentadi" arranged by Giovanni.

By the mid-1470s, Giovanni's situation had taken a dramatically different turn. One of his principal business ventures, in Pisa, had suffered huge losses because of the "betrayal" of his agent there. As a result of this crisis, Giovanni's bank practically disappeared, and he was obliged to sell

---

30. Such a list, which enhanced the family's honor, was placed in the *Zibaldone* immediately following the history of the family's accomplishments, on f. 6.

31. *Zibaldone*, f. 3v: "E nostri antichi furono tintori d'oricello et in quel tempo non era in Firenze né in tutta Italia che sapessi tignere di decto oricello . . . e da questo aviamento principiò la richeza et il buono stato della nostra famiglia perché era mestiero d'un grande utile. . . ."

32. *Zibaldone*, f. 3v: "Le case nostre in quel tempo erano inverso la piazza vecchia di Sancta Maria Novella, che volgarmente è chiamata la via di Cienni. . . ."

33. Kent 1981, 95: "la chasa nostra non n' ebbe mai niuno che meritasse tante dengne lode e chommendazioni, e che magg(i)ore onore abbi fatto alla famigla nostra poi che ll' ebbe principio che' l detto Giovanni nostro padre, chonsiderato massimamente e' dengni parentadi, la richezza, l' essere stato grande merchatante e di gran fede e chredito, e mediante le muraglie fatte per lui tenporali e spirituali, e paramenti di brochato d' oro e altre dengne chose : per modo che ci e' paruto meritamente farne memoria in questo libro che Dio gli choncieda della sua santa ghrazia."

the estates of Calenzano and Poggio a Caiano as well as staining himself with illegal actions and even risking excommunication for his debts. Although many old vexing questions regarding his political status had by now been resolved, in 1476 the composition of the "parentado" coincided with this serious financial crisis and the unsettled climate that prevailed in Florence immediately preceding the Pazzi conspiracy. Giovanni, in the face of an imminent catastrophe, struck an attitude that was altogether different from his optimistic stance of nearly 20 years before. Gone were the noble and honorable values that he had flaunted in the mid-1450s. Instead, he now assumed the attitude of a merchant who, in the face of a threatened catastrophe, seeks to shore up his financial position in order to avoid the humiliation of bankruptcy and the loss of his standing as an entrepreneur and a man of credit. His counsel to his sons was harsh, urging them as he did to withdraw from the international economic scene and high politics and to behave like shopkeepers. His sons, as far as Giovanni was concerned, were so visibly unsuited for the world of commerce and finance that they had to be counseled in a language devoid of euphemism: "The fact is that you are shopkeepers; which is to say that you must govern yourselves as wool manufacturers and silk manufacturers and as that sort are accustomed to doing, and to have the greater part of your business in Florence rather than keeping it abroad [invested] in merchandise, money, and debtors."[34] Giovanni not only showed a tendency to no longer conduct his affairs far from Florence, but elsewhere he added that it was preferable to conclude business within the narrow circle of the parentado. Based on this conviction, he left the details of the sale of his great estate at Poggio a Caiano to the buyer, Lorenzo de' Medici, "because we are dealing with cognates and relatives, not with strangers" (*ché con cognati e parenti abbiamo a ffare, non con istrani*).[35]

In this general situation, and in this state of mind, Rucellai produced a very private, almost hermetic, document that at first sight seemed only to refresh the memory of the heavy debts contracted by his branch of the Rucellai with the families of the five wives, the veritable protagonists of his 1476 account. In reality we are convinced that this account conveys an image of blood ties in which not so much the Rucellai as the families of the women who transmitted their blood to Giovanni's sons and grand-

---

34. Kent 1981, 95: "in facto che voi siate botteghai cioè che 'l fondamento del ghoverno sia chome chostumano fare e' lanaiuoli, e' setaiuoli et simili, d' avere le sustantie del traffico più tosto in Firenze che di fuori in mercatantie, danari et debitori."

35. We follow here Kent (1981, p. 90).

sons are brought into focus. In contrast to the logic of the virilinear genealogy, Giovanni's document now mapped out a system of horizontal alliances at the center of which were all the husbands who had received dowries from Giovanni's female relatives on his wife's, mother's, and paternal grandmother's sides (and who, therefore, shared on their mothers' sides their blood with him and his sons). Abandoning the logic of the genealogy, Giovanni now embraced the logic of the *sippe,* a horizontal system of kin networks that muted the family's antiquity and downplayed its exalted, noblelike status.

At the moment, this is the only explanation that we can offer for the stubborn and systematic absence from Giovanni's account of any reference to those women who, by marrying his male relatives-by-marriage, had "imported" their dotal capital into the five families with which the Rucellai were related by marriage. It would seem, therefore, that in 1476 Giovanni's memory served him for one precise and eminently practical purpose: to map out the sources of possible cognatic support among the families that, at some point in the course of the current and the preceding two generations, had entered into a marriage alliance with the women of the five families that had offered their women in marriage to the Rucellai. It was as if Giovanni conceived of his parentado's women as corresponding, in some way, to insurance policies, a portion of capital temporarily lost that could eventually return to its family of origin, but that, in the meantime, could have been a source of support and protection for his grandsons. In 1457, Giovanni Rucellai had struck too aristocratic a posture to dwell on details that would preoccupy him later. But in 1476, obsessed with the disaster that was about to engulf him, he cast aside his aristocratic pride and, rediscovering his mercantile vocation, returned to the calculating and meticulous mentality of the merchant. Now it was good to attend to the acquired parentadi, which, because of his new circumstances, could bring as much honor and utility to the family as had, by his preceding mental calculus, the glorious deeds of the ancient Rucellai.

Having until now focussed our attention on Giovanni Rucellai's intentions by analyzing the contents of his two genealogical reconstructions, we shift our focus to two terms, *parentado* and *consorteria,* which, it is now clear, were fundamental for the preceding analysis. We believe that our understanding of Rucellai's documents allows us to propose the semantic enlargement of these two terms. Furthermore, the meaning of the word *us* (*ours*), within the two ricordi, offers the possibility of extending our reflection on the meaning of these terms.

In fact, if we are to take at its face value the meaning of the adjective *all,* then *parentado* means "all the individuals mentioned in this ricordanza" and excludes those who are not cited (the very ones whose presence, initially, we had expected Giovanni to include in it). *Parentado* is, furthermore, delimited by the adjective *our,* for which we assume that the group of individuals present in the ricordo constitutes the parentado in its full extension (= all), relative to a group of persons (= us). At this point it is necessary to ask what extension we should ascribe to the pronoun *we* implied in *our.* If we look in Giovanni's texts for the occurrences of the term *parentado,* we can see how the meaning of the term was limited by, and in turn how it limited the meaning of, a series of other words such as *house, family, descent,* and *consorteria.* In a document contained in the zibaldone, which was defined by Giovanni's sons as "memory of the testament" (*memoria del testamento*), we discover that Giovanni attached quite precise meanings to a series of important terms: *sons, descendants,* and *consorteria.* Thus, the document states that "our Giovanni Rucellai made his will this day, December 13, 1465, drawn up by Ser Lionardo di Ser Giovanni da Cholle, and among other things he set a certain condition on our house that, in effect, his sons and descendants can neither sell it, nor mortgage it, nor bequeath it, nor rent, nor alienate it except and only among themselves to the end that it be inhabited only by his descendants." Proceeding, in the event that there was no extant descendant, he left it "to the oldest of the Rucellai family on the same condition" that he could not make "any contract nor bequeath it if not to those of the Rucellai consorteria." As the degree of family relationship became more distant Giovanni relied upon suitable terminology: from "sons" and "descendants," to "the oldest of the family of the Rucellai," to "consorteria."[36]

---

36. *Zibaldone,* f. 3r: "Giovanni Rucellai nostro fece testamento questo dì xiii di decembre MCCCCLXV rogato per ser Lionardo di ser Giovanni da Cholle e infra ll' altre chose fece certo legame della chasa nostra che contiene in effecto che suoi figliuoli e discendenti non possino né venderla, né impegnarla, né testarla, né appigionarla, né alienarla se non solamente fra loro medesimi per modo che l' effecto sia che lla non si possa abitare se non pe' suoi discendenti." If there were no direct descendant, he left it "al più anticho della famiglia de' Rucellai cholla medesima chonditione" that he cannot make "alchuno contracto né testarla se non a quelli della chonsorteria de' Rucellai."

Now it becomes clear that some of our initial difficulties in interpreting this document (and our initial puzzlement about the absence of certain names and Rucellai branches) were most likely the result of our ignorance of the fact that, during the last several centuries, a shift had taken place in the semantic field covered by the terms that interest us. In particular, the key term turned out to be *parentado,* repeatedly used by Rucellai. Among its various meanings, this word seems, over time, to have lost the one that was clearly impressed in Giovanni's mind, the one that allowed him to refer with great precision only to relationships of cognatic and never agnatic kin.[37] It is necessary to imagine a similar semantic "drifting" of the term *consorteria.* With such a word Giovanni seems at first glance to indicate all those members of his family who bore the name Rucellai and who, therefore, had a common ancestor. (This meaning echoes the use of the term in the commune's statutes of the year

---

37. We consulted Tommaseo's *Dizionario della lingua italiana*, tomo XIII (Milan, pp. 558–59), in which one reads: "Congiunzione per consanguineità o per affinità da Parentalis basso latino. Tra i significati compare anche <Far parentado>: divenir parente, contraendo matrimonio (Dino Compagni, 1,18; Boccaccio, *Decamerone*, g. 2, nov. VI, g. 5, nov. IV)"; Devoto-Oli's *Dizionario della lingua italiana* (1971, 1,623): "Parentado. Legame di parentela, particolarmente quello che si costituisce in seguito ad un matrimonio. Estens. Matrimonio. Concret. L' insieme dei parenti di una persona o di una famiglia (per lo più in espressioni ironiche o scherzose, dal lat. volg. parentadus, us)"; and Rigutini-Fanfani's *Vocabolario italiano della lingua parlata* (1893, 861): "Congiunzione per consanguineità. Stirpe, lignaggio. Matrimonio, unione matrimoniale. Nome collettivo di tutti i parenti." Other merchant-authors of books of *ricordi* use the term in the same accession used by Giovanni Rucellai. Such specialized use of the term is found in at least one other *libro di ricordi*, that by Donato Velluti, who clearly distinguishes between "e miei discendenti" and the "parentadi acquistati per mie donne e figliuoli." In another passage of the book, referring to his wife, Bice di Covone Covoni, he writes: "Cara, savia e bonissima donna, quanto non bella; e di lei molto mi contentai, e succedettemene ogni bene, di *parentado* e d'essere aventurato assai in questo mondo, mentre ch' ella vivette" (Velluti 1986, 543). Giovanni di Pagolo Morelli (1986, 169), in the section of his book in which he advises his sons, writes as follows: "Appresso, abbi riguardo ch' ella [a future wife] sia bene nata, di madre di gente da bene e di *parentado* onorevole." Remembering his own wife, he writes: "Tolsi moglie . . . la Caterina figliuola d'Alberto di Luigi degli Alberti . . . Credo che 'l detto *parentado* m' abbia tolto assai onore per avventura arei avuto del mio Comune, se avessi imparentato con altre famiglie, come arei potuto" (234). Bonaccorso Pitti writes in his ricordi (1986, 392): "Giunsi a Firenze e deliberai di torre moglie. E sendo Guido di messer Tomaso di Neri dal Palagio il maggiore e il più creduto uomo di Firenze, diliberai di torla per le sue mani e qualunche a lui piacesse, pure ch' ella fosse sua parente. Mandai a lui Bartolo della Contessa sensale che gli dicesse della mia intenzione, e ciò feci per acquistare la sua benivolenzia e *parentado*, a ciò ch' egli fosse obrigato d' adoperarsi a farmi avere la pace da' Corbizi."

1415, where the term *consorto* was defined.)[38] But a more careful analysis of his use of the expression reveals that in his use of it Giovanni rigorously excluded from it the group made up of himself and his direct descendants. For Giovanni it would seem that one of the meanings of the term, and the one he used in the document in question, has been entirely lost today: a "group of agnatic households (*ceppi*), each of which is headed by a brother (or possibly a cousin.)" This definition allows us to assign a precise meaning to the puzzling expression with which Giovanni closed the document of 1476: "parentado di consorteria," in reality the sum of fraternal parentadi created over many generations, which, in Giovanni's sense, were capable "of carrying with them half the city."

It is difficult to explain the reasons for the semantic impoverishment of the terms *parentado* and *consorteria*. Probably the difficulty resides in a common characteristic of the two words: they are collective terms that tend to delimit a group of persons bound among themselves by similar relationships. Such terms can be used by those who are excluded from the group just as they can be used by those who are included in it. Nevertheless, while from the outside the meaning of the terms coincides with the totality of all those who belong to the group, from the inside each Ego seems to carve out a subgroup in which he himself is included and which is subtracted from the general definition. Thus, the "consorteria of Paolo di Paolo Rucellai" (i.e., Giovanni's father) is a more comprehensive group than "the consorteria of Giovanni di Paolo di Paolo," in that the group of Giovanni was included in the first but excluded from the second. Each consorteria and parentado would have changed composition every time the terms were invoked on behalf of a different individual: thus, the parentado of Pandolfo would have been different from that of his brother Bernardo, just as that of Giovanni was different from that of Filippo.

It is clear from what has been said that the two documents were meant to trace the boundaries of the "territory" belonging to Giovanni's kin group. At the same time they suggest how other such affinal kin groups

---

38. Statuti del Comune di Firenze, anno 1415, c. 61v, Liber II, Rub. LXVI "De compromissis fiendis inter consortes": "Si aliqua quaestio, differentia vel controversia oriretur vel esset inter patrem vel matrem et filium vel filiam fratres vel sorores carnales vel uterinos vel uterinas patruum nepotem vel neptem vel alios consanguineos coniunctos seu consortes qui consortes sint de eadem stirpe per lineam masculinam etiam spurios usque in infinitum. . . ."

were configured. Taken together, these groups would represent the complex of those kin groups whose members, collectively, controlled their city's political and economic lives: they comprised Florence's ruling class. But, as we have observed, in this grid of kinships every relationship changes meaning according to its "focus," that is, according to the Ego from whose perspective it is examined. Every individual's identity could be defined only by a constant readjustment of his perspective as he sought to recognize the portion of his honor and blood that he shared with other (even close, blood) relations and the portion that was his alone, the part he could bequeath to his children. Thus, every individual would have had to reconstruct his kin group, defining in each instance his position in it. Giovanni's identity as his father's son would be slightly different (but different, nonetheless) from his identity as his sons' father. The difference would certainly be more evident and striking when Giovanni's identity as his sons' father was compared to his identity as his father's brother's nephew. In each instance, the key element in defining that identity would be provided by the links (of blood, money, and power) that connected him to other well-defined groups within the city's ruling class.

We can imagine that, in this system, blood was the vector of economic and political power, and its transmission from one kin structure to another was carried out by a woman. Every married woman was a link between attachable, modulelike, kin structures, each of which was made up of a lineage's fragments and organized around a "head of household." Together these kin structures formed the city's ruling class. If seen from outside the system, the function of the men was to conserve the sum of blood-money-power accumulated in each of the lineage's single modules, while the women, by moving from one family to another, exercised the function of transforming the balance by redistributing that sum within the ruling class. It was a system that maintained itself not in spite of but thanks to two largely arbitrary components: nature and economic-political fortune, which constantly reconfigured the power-money-blood balance. If it was the economic and political fortunes of the adult men in the recent past that determined the sums of money and power contained in each module, the proportion between male and female children, determined by nature, had a bearing on whether the available sums of money and power would be dispersed or concentrated in a centrifugal or centripetal motion. If there were more nubile daughters to marry than there were sons, the family's capital would be (at least temporarily) reduced, and its head would face the choice of either seeking husbands of inferior status (hypogamic practice), and by so doing save capital but diminish honor, or sacrificing wealth to arrange marriages with equal or greater status. Hypergamic practice for females would have an inverse effect on capital and honor.

While the organization of family memory does not ordinarily seem well equipped to maintain clear traces of the exchanges and the phases of redistribution that have already occurred, the 1476 ricordanza tends to underscore precisely these because, notwithstanding its small, built-in, virifocal genealogy (grandfather-father-Ego-sons-grandsons), the focus is placed above all on the horizontal, cognatic relations of each generation. The most important among the blood modules identified in 1457 (Giovanni's bloodline) was the natural recipient of the information about past marital and dotal exchanges contained in the text of 1476. This second text seems to indicate, however, the crisis that the branch of Giovanni Rucellai must have been experiencing if he truly had to resort to the drastic measure of preparing a written record to revive the vanishing links from which he and his descendants could draw strength. The memory of the elder Rucellai works like a shuttle along time's two vectors: it is bidirectional, and its remembrance of the past is conditioned by his perception of his immediate and future needs.[39] The two writings were conceived to serve a double function: they simultaneously constitute the "memory of something" and the "memory for something"; they are both record and project. The ricordo of 1476 shows itself to be a text intended for the use of a few, privileged readers—Giovanni's direct descendants—for it furnishes them with a map of alliances that do not concern even Giovanni's brothers. It is a map that outlines at once their social and unique individuality, shaped by the voluntary act of *far parentado* (making a marriage alliance) and of enlarging the parentadi inherited from past generations with a new one brought by a wife. Indeed, it could be said that an essential component of a wife's dowry (and a component that required no repayment of the cash and goods brought by the wife with her dowry but offered a persistent and resilient bond between the two families) was the very parentado brought by her to her husband.

Giovanni Rucellai's 1476 ricordanza is a magnificent instrument for

---

39. D. Fabbri (1990) presents a study on the "queen's memory." In Lewis Carroll's *Through the Looking Glass* the queen juxtaposes Alice's memory-only-of-the-past with a bidirectional memory (toward-the-past-and-toward-the-future). Fabbri borrows this expression as the title of her stimulating study, *La memoria della Regina*.

observing the evolution of memory in the crucial era that prepared the modern period: it still reflects a vision of kinship amply documented in the preceding centuries, but if we were to try to move it ahead a century we would find it an anachronistic and impossible operation. The transformation of the state into the principate and of the mercantile elite into a court nobility marks, in fact, an irreversible crisis of the memory of the cognatic kin, which expresses itself in the affirmation of the modern genealogy. This is not the place to discuss this complex problem, but the discrepancy between the old and new strategies seems clear. The latter depends on primogeniture, confinement to the nunnery of a high number of nubile women, and the simultaneous reduction of fertile lineal branches and cognatic links. The previous strategy, to the contrary, aimed to bring about the redistribution of economic fortunes and power alliances within the ruling class by relying on numerous and constantly renewed marriage alliances in an artfully combinatory game that often tested to its limit the ecclesiastical prohibition of endogamy.[40]

It has recently been said that women in premodern times, especially in patriarchal societies such as that of late medieval Florence, suffered the bitter destiny of being "expelled from memory."[41] In reality, until the great changes of the sixteenth century, they acted as infallible instruments for the cyclical renewal of the cognatic memory, which was entirely centered on the females. It was instead the adoption of primogeniture that hindered the mechanism that had functioned in the preceding era. This mechanism, regulated by the arbitrariness of nature in fixing the proportion of male to female children, had at once provided for the accumulation of capital, which consisted of blood-money-power, and for its constant redistribution. Men were responsible for its accumulation; women, by virtue of their movement from their natal to their married families, were responsible for its redistribution. By reducing to a single male and a sole female the children destined to reproduce themselves, families of the sixteenth century and beyond showed a desire to challenge nature's capriciousness, to fix for eternity the honor of the family (casato), and to place limits on the portion of wealth destined for the dowries of the daughters, with the aim of freezing the number of lineages

---

40. On endogamy in Florence's fifteenth-century ruling class, see Molho 1994.
41. One of the most suggestive presentations of this thesis is in Klapisch-Zuber 1990, especially the chapter entitled "Le complexe de Griselda. Dot et dons de mariage."

and the value of their properties in an unattainable and illusory dream of a perpetual balance of blood-money-power among a limited number of lineal kin modules.

One cannot pretend that the study of a single personage can make a decisive contribution to a theme as debated and complex as that of the history of the family and lineage in the late Middle Ages. Yet, the two documents of Giovanni Rucellai add some specific singularities to the vast materials accumulated on the subjects of the family and of late medieval Florentine memoirs (*libri di ricordi*).

The first of these singularities consists of the use on the part of a single person of multiple genealogical representations in different moments of his life. Giovanni Rucellai appears like a two-faced Janus, proud chronicler of the glory of his agnatic line, when he thinks it appropriate, and cryptic elaborator of a precise cognatic grid when he needs help. He does not express a preference for one or the other form of genealogical structure. In different ways and at different times, there coexist a vertical line, rooted in the Roman tradition, extended toward his ancient and even mythical ancestors, and a horizontal web of acquired kin groups, the sippe, of Germanic origin. These two systems of recalling the familial past were not abstract conceptions; rather, they had precise and concrete functions: glorify the lineage on the eve of an important marriage and identify a precise cohort of relatives who could render favors in time of need.

How did a Florentine family acquire its relatives by marriage, and in what ways and when did it bind itself to other families? Initially it did so by staying close to the boundaries of its neighborhood. At least this was the strategy of the Niccolini, who, only after they had solidified their position in their local ward (*gonfalone*), set out to extend their influence throughout the city by marrying into prestigious families and paying conspicuous dowries while also seeking out influential friendships and contracting spiritual alliances (through the institution of the godparenthood). From the ricordanza of Donato Velluti we can trace both the crisis of his lineage over the course of the fourteenth century and his systematic efforts to strengthen his horizontal alliances. Both of these cases have been studied recently, Niccolini's by Klapisch-Zuber and Velluti's by de la Roncière.[42] The analyses of these scholars have been indispensable

---

42. Klapisch-Zuber 1976; and de la Roncière 1977.

guides to the literature on memory and identity in late medieval Florence. But to read their accounts one would think that traces of alternative forms of memory had disappeared, as both Velluti and Niccolini set out to strengthen their relative positions in society by forging bonds—of marriage and friendship—without much regard for the old, vertical memories and sentiments of their ancestral traditions. This apparent linearity—from the genealogy to the sippe—is absent from the thought of Rucellai. In Rucellai's case, the second act of remembrance arrives unexpectedly, seemingly juxtaposed with the first. Following our interpretation, the document of 1476 might permit a better definition of the term *parentado,* distinguishing it from *consorteria.* Knowledge of one's own parentado—knowing, especially, its boundaries as well as its content—helps one to better resist economic reversals and the caprices of fortune.

The historiographical theme of the resilience of Florentine lineages has been amply debated. In the course of sometimes sharp controversies in the past two or so decades, there have emerged two strenuously opposed views. On one side are those, like Richard Goldthwaite, who insist upon the fragmentation and dissolution of the Florentine lineages; on the other are scholars such as F. W. Kent and P. J. Jones, who support the notion that lineages survived as viable and important institutions.[43] Other historians of the family have gradually grouped themselves around these interpretations. Giovanni Rucellai's experience does not offer support for either of these interpretations—it does not tip the interpretive balance to one or the other side. More simply, Giovanni seems to specify how to resist, by teaching, genealogically as it were, his sons' sons where they can ask for help and favors.

The 1476 ricordo reveals a particular selection of cognatic bonds of the horizontal alliance, often defined as sippe, that seems to have flourished in Giovanni Rucellai's strategy. This selection of bonds passes—and this might be the third small novelty of his reflection—through the feminine element implicated in the circulation of dowries. Attentive to cognatic bonds to the point of uncovering some that would otherwise be difficult to detect, Rucellai remains concurrently sensitive to the importance of agnatic descent. He is still far from the great sixteenth-century changes in familial ideology. His great preoccupation in 1476 seems to find a way of defining past marriage alliances so as to help his descendants draw some benefit from their remembrance.

---

43. Goldthwaite 1968; Kent 1977; Jones 1978.

In conclusion, we can return to the words of Giovanni Rucellai, who, when in old age he sold the Villa of Poggio a Caiano to Lorenzo de' Medici, commented that there was no need to worry about the details "because we have to do with cognates and relatives, not with strangers." But how could he distinguish between "relatives" (parenti) and "strangers," when he himself had affirmed that the Rucellai women, through the parentado of their "consorteria," carried along with them "half the city"? This was exactly the point, and Giovanni understood it as well as any of his contemporaries. Like any lineage of great antiquity and standing, the Rucellai were inseparable from "half the city," from dozens of other lineages of comparable distinction, with whose members, generation upon generation, parentadi were woven and rewoven into rich configurations of personal and material connections. Whatever other meaning the term *city* may have had for Giovanni Rucellai—the city as a physical space adorned by some of the structures that in other parts of his zibaldone he lovingly describes, or as political entity to whose governance he alternatively urges his sons to commit or desist from committing themselves—there is little question that for him one of the privileged meanings of the term *city* referred to it as the collectivity of those lineages with which over time the Rucellai had struck their parentadi. It was not a meaning that was his alone, for other men of his social standing—and women such as Alessandra Strozzi, Lucrezia Tornabuoni, and many others—would have unhesitatingly subscribed to it as well.

Bibliography

Barbagli, Marzio. 1984. *Sotto lo stesso tetto. Mutamenti della famiglia in Italia dal XV al XX secolo*. Bologna.

Bizzocchi, Roberto. 1991a. "Familiae Romanae. Antiche e moderne." *Rivista storica italiana* 102:355–97.

Bizzocchi, Roberto. 1991b. "Culture généalogique dans l'Italie du seizième siècle." *Annales* 46:789–805.

Bizzocchi, Roberto. 1991c. "La nobiltà in Dante, la nobiltà di Dante—Cultura nobiliare a, memoria storica e genealogia fra Medio Evo e Rinascimento." *I Tatti Studies. Essays in the Renaissance* 4:201–15.

Brucker, Gene. 1986. *Giovanni and Lusanna. Love and Marriage in Renaissance Florence*. Berkeley, Calif.

Calvi, Giulia. 1992. "Maddalena Nerli and Cosimo Tornabuoni: A Couple's Narrative of Family History in Early Modern Florence." *Renaissance Quarterly* 45:312–39.

Chabot, Isabelle. 1986. " 'Sola, donna, non gir mai.' Le solitudini femminili nel Trecento." *Memoria. Rivista di storia delle donne* 3:7–24.

Chabot, Isabelle. 1988. "Widowhood and Poverty in Late Medieval Florence." *Continuity and Change* 3:291–311.

Cimetier, F. 1932. "Parenté (Empêchements de)." In *Dictionaire de théologie catholique*, vols. 11–12, cols. 1,995–2,003. Paris.

Clark, Paula. 1991. *The Soderini and the Medici: Power and Patronage in Fifteenth-Century Florence.* Oxford.

Consorterie politiche e mutamenti istituzionali in età laurenziana. 1992. ed. Maria Augusta Morelli Timpanaro, Rosalia Manno Tolu, and Paolo Viti.

Duby, Georges, and Jacques Le Goff, eds. 1977. *Famille et parenté dans l'occident médiéval.* Rome.

Esmein, A. 1891. *Le mariage en droit canonique.* 2 vols. Paris.

Fentress, James, and Chris Wickham. 1992. *Social Memory.* Oxford.

Fabbri, Lorenzo. 1991. *Alleanza matrimoniale e patriziato nella Firenze del '400. Studio sulla famiglia Strozzi.* Florence.

Fox, Robin. 1983 [1967]. *Kinship and Marriage—An Anthropological Perspective.* Cambridge.

Goldthwaite, Richard. 1968. *Private Wealth in Renaissance Florence: A Study of Four Families.* Princeton.

Goody, Jack. 1983. *The Development of the Family and Marriage in Europe.* Cambridge.

Heers, Jacques. 1974. *Le clan familial au Moyen Age.* Paris.

Heritier, L. 1978. "Endogamia." In *Enciclopedia,* 5:397–411. Turin.

Heritier, L. 1980. "Parentela." In *Enciclopedia,* 10:363–417. Turin.

Jones, Philip. 1978. "Economia e società nell' Italia medioevale: La leggenda della borghesia." In *Storia d' Italia. Annali I, Dal feudalesimo al capitalismo,* 187–372. Turin.

Kent, Francis William. 1977. *Household and Lineage in Renaissance Florence: The Family Life of the Capponi, Ginori, and Rucellai.* Princeton.

Kent, Francis William. 1981. "The Making of a Renaissance Patron of the Arts." In *Giovanni Rucellai ed il suo Zibaldone.* Vol. 2: *A Florentine Patrician and His Palace,* 9–95. London.

Kirshner, Julius. 1985. "Wives' Claims against Insolvent Husbands in Late Medieval Italy." In J. Kirshner and S. Wemple eds. *Women of the Medieval World,* 256–303. Oxford.

Kirshner, Julius. 1991a. "Maritus Lucretur Dotem Uxoris Sue Premortue in Late Medieval Florence." *Zeiutschrift der Savigny-Stiftung für Rechtsgeschichte,* 108 bd., Kanonistische Abteilung, 77:111–55.

Kirshner, Julius. 1991b. "Materials for a Gilded Cage: Non-Dotal Assets in Florence (1300–1500)." In *The Family in Italy from Antiquity to the Present,* eds. Richard Saller and David Kertzer, 184–207. New Haven.

Kirshner, Julius, and Anthony Molho. 1978. "The Dowry Fund and the Marriage Market in Early *Quattrocento* Florence." *Journal of Modern History* 50:403–38.

Klapisch-Zuber, Christiane. 1976. "'Parenti, amici e vicini'. Il territorio urbano d' una famiglia mercantile nel XV secolo." *Quaderni storici* 33:953–82.

Klapisch-Zuber, Christiane. 1988. "Ruptures de parenté et changements d' identité chez les magnats florentins du XIVe siècle." *Annales* 43:1205–40.

Klapisch-Zuber, Christiane. 1990. *La maison et le nom. Stratégie et rituels dans l' Italie de la Renaissance.* Paris.

Klapisch-Zuber, Christiane. 1991a. "Kinship and Politics in Fourteenth-Century Florence." In *The Family in Italy from Antiquity to the Present,* David Kertzer and Richard Saller, eds., 208–28. New Haven.

Kuehn, Thomas. 1991. *Law, Family, and Women: Toward a Legal Anthropology of Renaissance Italy.* Chicago.

Lamaison, P. 1979. "Stratégies matrimoniales dans un système complexe de parenté: Ribennes en Gévaudan (1650–1830)." *Annales* 34:721–43.

Litchfield, Burr R. 1969. "Demographic Characteristics of Florentine Patrician Families: Sixteenth to Eighteenth Centuries." *Journal of Economic History* 29:191–205.

Molho, Anthony. 1989. *"Tamquam vere mortua.* Le professioni religiose femminili nella Firenze del tardo medioevo." *Società e storia* 43:1–43.

Molho, Anthony. 1994. *Marriage Alliance in Late Medieval Florence.* Cambridge, Mass.

Morelli, Giovanni di Pagolo. 1986. "Ricordi." In *Mercanti scrittori—Ricordi nella Firenze tra medioevo e rinascimento,* ed. V. Branca. Milan.

Palmieri, Matteo. 1982. *Vita civile,* ed. Gino Belloni. Florence.

Passerini, Luigi. 1861. *Genealogia e storia della famiglia Rucellai.* Florence.

Pettener, Davide, and Luciano Niccolini. 1980. "Ricerche sulla consanguineità nell'alta valle del Reno (sec. xvii–xx)—Impiego ed attendibilità delle fonti archivistiche." *Il Carrobio,* 291–99.

Pitti, Bonaccorso. 1986. "Ricordi." In *Mercanti scrittori—Ricordi nella Firenze tra medioevo e rinascimento,* ed. V. Branca. Milan.

de la Roncière, Charles M. 1977. "Une famille florentine au XIVe siècle: Les Velluti." In Duby and Le Goff 1977, 227–48.

Rucellai, Giovanni. 1960. *Giovanni Rucellai ed il suo zibaldone. I. "Il zibaldone quaresimale."* ed. Alessandro Perosa. London.

Starn, Randolph. 1971. "Francesco Guicciardini and His Brothers." In *Renaissance Essays in Honor of Hans Baron,* ed. Anthony Molho and John Tedeschi, 409–44. Florence.

Velluti, Donato. 1986. *"Ricordi."* In *Mercanti Scrittori—Ricordi nella Firenze tra medioevo e rinascimento,* ed. V. Branca. Milan.

Weissman, Ronald. 1982. *Ritual Brotherhood in Renaissance Florence.* New York.

Reproduction and Production
in Early Ireland

Lisa M. Bitel

The men and women of early Ireland married for many reasons: love and lust drove some, while kinfolk guided others into formal unions called *lánamnasa* (sg. *lánamnas*). Written sources produced by the literate elite (a homogeneous class of men educated in monasteries, most of whom were probably religious professionals) mirror this diversity of motives.[1] Sagas and other narratives from the eighth through the eleventh centuries romanticize and eroticize the relationship of marriage, while gnomic texts of the same period revile it and chastise the men so foolish as to wed. Legal tracts, also compiled by professional jurists between 700 and 1100, refer to legitimate marriage as *lánamnasa cumtusa comperta,* "contracts of union for the purpose of reproduction."[2]

Marriage could certainly be romantic or unhappy, as narratives and gnomic texts suggest. However, the laws come closest to describing the dominant purpose and experience of marriage in early Ireland, particu-

---

1. On the sources and the literati who composed and recorded them, see Kathleen Hughes, *Early Christian Ireland: An Introduction to the Sources* (London, 1972). See also Kim McCone, *Pagan Past and Christian Present in Early Irish Literature* (Maynooth, 1990); and, on the procreative ideologies of the literati, Lisa Bitel, "'Conceived in Sins, Born in Delights': Stories of Procreation from Early Ireland," *Journal of the History of Sexuality* 3 (1992): 131–202.

2. The early Irish legal tract *Cáin Lánamnae* (Law of Couples) deals with marriage, secondary marriage, and other formal legal unions as well as the property involved in such unions. See D. A. Binchy, ed., *Corpus Iuris Hibernici*, 6 vols. (Dublin, 1978) [hereafter *CIH*], 502–19; and W. N. Hancock et al., eds., *The Ancient Laws of Ireland*, 6 vols. (Dublin and London, 1865–1901) [hereafter *ALI*], 2:343–409. See also Rudolf Thurneysen et al., *Studies in Early Irish Law* (Dublin, 1936) [hereafter Thurneysen, *SEIL*], 1–74; Fergus Kelly, *Guide to Early Irish Law* (Dublin, 1987), 70–73; and Nerys Patterson, *Cattle-lords and Clansmen: Kinship and Rank in Early Ireland* (New York and London, 1991), 279–81.

larly for women. Whatever else it might be, marriage was, for most women, an economic arrangement aimed at the creation of a discrete domestic unit within which they practiced both reproduction and production.[3]

Marriage could provide a relatively equitable economic experience for women despite the gendered division of labor and legal restrictions on women as economic actors. At work within the walls of their houses and the hedges of their fields, men and women most closely approached similar status. When Cormac delved and Deirdriu span—or when both were hauling the harvest to the barn, slopping the pigs in a pelting rain, or anxiously tending a sick child—their labor became equally valuable to their mutual household. One economic partner could not maintain a house and farm without the other, and one alone could certainly not produce the children so necessary and precious to their little economic island, as well as to their families and society. Neither production nor reproduction could occur within the domestic economy without the capital and labor of both husband and wife.

Women's importance within the conjugal economy won them choices, just as they had choices to make about courtship, marriage, and procreation. Lawyers, literati, and the political elite believed that women's first duty was to bear legitimate children and that women's other economic tasks were to be adapted to this, their métier. Yet reproduction was not by any means women's only economic function, although the literati taught them, in a variety of formal textual genres, that it was their most important task. While they grew fat with child, while they nursed their babies and chased after their toddlers, women continued to do other jobs. When finally their babies had gone to fosterers or grown up enough to take care of themselves, women were free to devote themselves to other kinds of production.

What women did mostly was hard farmyard and household work or, if they were among the elite, farm and household-related managerial work. But what they were most valued for, after reproduction, was dairying and cloth production, especially the thoroughly feminine needlework that the lucky noble few had the opportunity to practice. Only occasion-

---

3. Although some elite women were able to become religious professionals and live in small communities of women, these were usually kin-based settlements situated on family land managed by a kinsman who was also a religious professional. The relationship of nuns to the male overseer was modeled on more traditional *lánamnasa*. See Bitel, *Land of Women: Tales of Sex and Gender from Early Ireland*, forthcoming from Cornell University Press.

ally did women participate in men's work away from the farmyard, and only the odd woman seems to have pursued prestigious, traditionally male callings such as poetry or healing. But, whatever their chores, women contributed their fair share to the conjugal economy, as even the most misogynous literati freely admitted. And women gained rewards for it: the ability to manipulate their own labor and its products, subject to some limits, and to accumulate profits by participating in the economy beyond the farmyard.[4]

Reproduction

The author of the ninth-century religious legislation *Cáin Adamnáin* (The Law of Adomnán) claimed that women were the producers of saints and bishops and righteous men; they were creators, *tustigud talman,* even as was Jehovah himself.[5] Inevitably, given the elite's desire for legitimate heirs and the whole focus of patrilineal ideology upon orderly procreation, women's most important domestic labor, in the eyes of the literati, was the labor of childbirth. A man could not discard his bride for shoddy housekeeping or lousy needlework, but a marriage contract could be broken if a woman failed to produce babies (or if her spouse proved unable to impregnate her).[6]

Ireland was no exception to the rule that, in traditional agrarian societies, particularly those practicing intensive plough agriculture, women get left at home.[7] Irish jurists recorded ideal evidence for Ester Boserup's classic association of a growing population with limited polygyny at elite levels, a dowry system, plough cultivation, and the devaluation and restriction of women's labor.[8] But the women and men of barbarian

4. Compare the situation in the medieval English village of Brigstock, where both spouses labored in the conjugal economy, but only husbands won the opportunity to move out to external markets (Judith Bennett, *Women in the Medieval English Countryside: Gender and Household in Brigstock before the Plague* [Oxford, 1987], 110–29).

5. Kuno Meyer, ed. and trans., *Cáin Adamnáin: An Old-Irish Treatise on the Law of Adamnán* (Oxford, 1905), 4.

6. H. Wasserschleben, ed., *Die irische Kanonensammlung* (Leipzig, 1885) [hereafter *Can. Hib.*], 186–87; *CIH*, 47–48, 1848.

7. Friedrich Engels, *The Origins of the Family, Private Property, and the State* (New York, 1972). See also Claude Lévi-Strauss, "The Family," in *Man, Culture, and Society,* ed. Harry L. Shapiro, 333–57 (New York, 1956); and Gerda Lerner, *The Creation of Patriarchy* (Oxford, 1986).

8. Ester Boserup, *Women's Role in Economic Development* (Aldershot and Brookfield, Vt., 1986). See also Jack Goody and Joan Buckley, "Implications of the

Europe would have found the depreciation of reproductive functions implicit in this paradigm truly appalling.[9] For, while this and other theories regarding the sexual division of labor and the economic oppression of women focus on motherhood, holding it accountable for women's low status and restricted economic roles, they also assume that reproduction limited the value of women and that babymaking was forced on women who would have preferred other economic tasks.[10]

Although it is true that Irish men and women put pressures both crude and subtle on potential childbearers to reproduce, women did not necessarily resist. *Cáin Adamnáin*'s effusive hymn to motherhood is just one of the subtler examples of pressure; calling contractual relations between women and men *lánamnasa cumtusa comperta* and constructing an entire political ideology based on patrilineages are other, less subtle instances. Yet, whether or not their alternatives were limited, women retained economically meaningful reproductive choices.[11] The importance of women as childbearers did not lend them social status or political power, nor were women always able to control the entire process of reproduction or its profits—their children—but motherhood did bring women economic value and status as legitimate economic actors. And women surely knew enough to exploit this status, manipulate their choices about childbearing, and use motherhood as a resource. Some men believed so. This is clear, for example, in the tale of Mugain, wife of King Diarmait mac Cerbaill, who was cursed with barrenness by another of her husband's women. Mugain was so desperate to reproduce and thus maintain her position as queen with all its resources that she sought the aid of holy men in conceiving. Her aim was to bear a son, keep her

Sexual Division of Labor in Agriculture," in *Numerical Techniques in Social Anthropology*, ed. J. Clyde Mitchell, 33–47 (Philadelphia, 1980); Judith K. Brown, "A Note on the Division of Labor by Sex," in *Women and Society: An Anthropological Reader*, ed. Sharon W. Tiffany, 36–47 (Montreal and St. Albans, Vt., 1979); Rae Lesser Blumberg, "Rural Women in Development: Veil of Invisibility, World of Work," *International Journal of Intercultural Relations* 3 (1979): 447–72.

9. Mina Davis Caulfield, "Equality, Sex, and Mode of Production," in *Social Inequality: Comparative and Developmental Approaches*, ed. Gerald D. Berreman, with Kathleen M. Zaretsky, 201–19 (New York, 1981).

10. Ellen Lewin, "By Design: Reproductive Strategies and the Meaning of Motherhood," in *The Sexual Politics of Reproduction*, ed. H. Homans, 123–38 (Aldershot and Brookfield, Vt., 1988).

11. Paola Tabet, "Fertilité naturelle, reproduction forcée," in *L'Arraisonnement des femmes: essais en anthropologie des sexes*, ed. Nicole-Claude Mathieu (Paris, 1985), also published in *Cahiers de l'Homme: Ethno.-Géog.-Ling.*, n.s., 24:61–146.

husband, and remain the rich and powerful woman she had become at marriage. Mugain's storyteller made clear that women's reproductive choices, like their other productive choices, allowed them to increase their economic participation generally and thus enhance their social status. Armed with such a strategy, women could endure and even counter the formal misogyny of their society.[12]

Besides a woman's choice to reproduce, her childbearing career depended upon her fecundity and her manipulation of it. In general, the fecundity of childbearers in early Ireland remains a demographic mystery, and family size is impossible to determine. If women turned themselves into economic actors by producing babies, then it seems logical that they would have sought maximum fertility because the more babies they had, the more valuable they became to their husbands and kin, and thus the more economic opportunities they won. In fact, as Josiah Cox Russell has shown, European women in the early Middle Ages averaged about twenty years of childbearing potential.[13] But all sorts of physiological and cultural factors could alter this span. Age at menarche, for example, could be considerably delayed if a girl did not get enough to eat. In hungry years and other bad times, social pressures as much as age at puberty set the age of marriage and legitimate childbearing; a girl might choose to wait, garnering her resources and wasting her reproductive years, before beginning a family of her own. Women, sometimes together with their men, also chose purposely to limit their fecundity for economic or religious reasons: some couples may have strictly observed Christian sexual prohibitions, and thus limited their moments of possible conception, or else they decided to limit the number of mouths they had to feed.

But, given all these conditions, if a woman chose to form a legitimate union with a man and begin bearing children when she was in her early to mid-twenties, as seems normally to have been the case, she could expect to continue reproducing regularly until well into her forties. Given the effects of nursing on conception, a woman might ordinarily conceive about every 32 months. Add the effects of diet and culture—whether a woman was healthy enough to carry successive fetuses to term, for instance, or notions about the proper seasons for conception and birth— and it would appear that the usual cycle of births during the Middle Ages

12. Standish O'Grady, ed., *Silva Gadelica* (London, 1892), 1:82–84, 2:88–91; Lewin, "By Design: Reproductive Strategies," 125.

13. Josiah Cox Russell, *Late Ancient and Medieval Population Control* (Philadelphia, 1985), 144–46.

was about three years. As sex ratios suggest, not every woman was such an efficient reproducer. Some died before their twenty years were up, while others survived the hazards of childbearing to marry more than once and continue reproducing. Hence, women in the early Middle Ages averaged between five and six children, the highest of the entire premodern period in Europe.[14]

The Irish kept no statistics, but the sources do confirm that women who were trained to reproduce did so with varying efficiency. The hagiographers told sad tales of desperate parents who begged the saints for babies when all other methods had failed. The jurists described in their divorce laws the possible fate of a woman who did not live up to her reproductive potential: her value as an economic partner in a sexual union fell to nothing. Yet, as the literati also made clear, a woman who produced a whole flock of babies was not necessarily the most valuable reproducer. If she produced quantity rather than quality, she was a bad wife and an expensive partner in *lánamnas*; a family needed only enough children so that one or two males would survive to adulthood and inherit property. As the author of a gnomic text, the eighth- or ninth-century *Senbríathra Fíthail* (The Advice of Fíthal), declared, "being heirless is better than great fertility."[15] Overproduction decreased value of both reproducer and products by reducing inheritance portions and fragmenting the family property, as women fully realized. St. Berach's hagiographer wrote how, during a famine, a well-to-do farmer went hunting, leaving his pregnant wife at home to deliver. His instructions to her were to kill the child as soon as it was born. After delivery, when her attendant asked the new mother what to do with the infant, she replied simply "a mharbadh": "kill it." Both parents made an economically informed decision for the good of their household, although the hagiographer believed it a bad decision, as is clear from the story's resolution and the baby's rescue.[16] The child's mother was not the only woman who chose to limit her production, one way or another, in order to maintain a viable conjugal economy and her own place within it; the penitentialists lamented that others practiced contraception, abortion, and infanticide.[17]

---

14. Russell, *Late Ancient and Medieval Population Control*, 147–48.

15. Roland M. Smith, "The *Senbriathra Fithail* and Related Texts," *Revue Celtique* 45 (1938): 19.

16. Charles Plummer, ed. and trans., *Bethada Náem nÉrenn* (Oxford, 1922), 1:40, 2:39.

17. Ludwig Bieler, ed. and trans., *The Irish Penitentials* (Dublin, 1975), 56, 76, 78–80, 100, 272.

The Irish considered a mother's product to be of better quality when it was both legitimate and male. Jurists rewarded the secondary wife (*adaltrach*) or concubine who gave birth to sons with more extensive legal rights of contract and more control over conjugal property than her childless counterpart.[18] Mugain's story would not have had a moral if she had produced a daughter instead of the great king Aed Sláine. And it may be no coincidence that the mother in Berach's *vita* ultimately chose not to kill her child because it was *mac,* a boy. No evidence exists for gender-specific infanticide in early Ireland, as elsewhere in Europe, but the legal system makes clear that the Irish literati and the elite they represented valued men more than women, legally, politically, and socially. As Berach's hagiographer suggested, women, too, were persuaded to apply this scale of values to the products of their childbearing labors.

Women's reproductive labors began with conception and often ended during their babies' early childhood when sons and daughters went to fosterers. Just as men seized the role of managers of reproduction, they also participated in parenting; for, although women produced the raw stuff that became farmers, warriors, and monks, male fosterers helped finish the product. In a sense, then, men helped with the reproduction of the workforce by taking the most precious products of women's labor—their male babies—and placing them in training with other men.[19] But women participated in the decision to foster out their children, and some took in fosterlings of their own. And, if men reproduced male laborers, then women reproduced the reproducers, training girls to become full partners in conjugal economies of their own.

A legitimately married woman who produced the desirable quantity and quality of babies gained economic opportunities that childless women—with the possible exception of some nuns—always lacked. A secondary wife or formal concubine could enhance her status and expand her economic experience by having legitimate sons. But a wife or concubine who produced inadequately or who failed to produce could lose not only economic opportunities but everything: man, household, and status.

Production: Dairying

A couple joined contractually usually set up house together, pooling their capital and deciding between them—guided by their vocational training,

---

18. *CIH*, 511–12, 513; *ALI*, 2:378, 384.
19. Janet Siskind, "Kinship and Mode of Production," *American Anthropologist* 80, no. 4 (1978): 864.

community opinion, and traditional expectations of gender roles—
exactly how to assign nonreproductive labor and its profits within the
union.[20] Around the farm, husband and wife ordinarily divided their
labors by sex. She minded the children and house, tended the farmyard
animals, particularly dairy cows, and cultivated the garden, while he
herded, ploughed, and planted. If they were wealthy, he managed the
male clients and slaves, while she oversaw the female laborers. He traded
gifts with his lord or landlord and took the surplus livestock to trade; she
carded, spun, wove, and sewed. Sometimes they may have helped each
other, but generally they kept to their own gender-specific tasks.[21]
According to most laws and narrative sources, women's labors took
place at home, in between or after their childbearing and childrearing.
Ideally, at least, housewives ranged only as far as the farmyard gate,
which contained and protected them and their work.

Within their yards, some of women's most important jobs were dairying and minding the farmyard animals. Every wife in the cattle-based
economy of early Ireland was a milker, churner, and cheese maker or a
manager of her dairymaids. Divorce laws, first recorded in the eighth century, make clear the meaning of women's labors in the dairy. One legal
commentator demanded nothing more of a good wife than that she be
home in time to milk the cows.[22] Other jurists, sorting out the division of
property at divorce, routinely assigned a portion of the dairy profits to
the wife on the simple principle that "every woman is a great worker in
regard of milk."[23] Hagiographers agreed that dairy production was
important both to the domestic economy and to a wife's working iden-

---

20. Irish laws allowed for other kinds of contractual arrangements, too; for
instance, one or the other partner might bring all the capital, or the two might not
actually form a permanent household. See Patterson, *Cattle-lords and Clansmen,*
277–81.

21. Similarly, when each brought his or her own property (*tinchor*) to the union,
both had some control over the common capital, but the property and its use normally
belonged to the original owner. If they should decide to divorce—the laws show that
there were plenty of reasonable grounds, everything from infertility to blabbing the
secrets of the marriage bed—lawyers ordered the redistribution of capital and profits
between the two, based on the investment of capital and labor by each partner. Given
the patriarchal bias that normally informed the early Irish laws, jurists came up with
a remarkably fair formula for settlement (Kelly, *Guide,* 73–75).

22. *CIH,* 43; *ALI,* 5:277. See also *CIH,* 1886.38; *ALI,* 5:152–53; and *CIH,* 1276,
where a dairymaid or milker (*bligre*) is paired with a male cowherd (*buachall*) as legal
types.

23. *CIH,* 508; *ALI,* 2:364–67.

tity. Even the foremost female saint of Ireland, St. Brigit herself, churned "as other women do," according to her seventh-century hagiographer.[24]

Dairying was so important because milk, butter, curds, and cheese formed a large part of any family's diet.[25] Thus, an efficient wife and mother produced, or oversaw the production of, what her family needed to live and to pay its rent. The eighth-century legal tract *Críth Gablach,* which details the rents owed by farmers to their landlords, routinely lists the "summer food" of dairy products as half a tenant's food rents, the other half consisting of grain and meat, the products of men's labor.[26]

What is more, a wife's dairying coincided perfectly with child care, for after nursing her own babies she could tote them with her when she went out at dawn to milk the cows, whereas she could not carry them off to the pastures at any distance from the house. Thus, women's dominion over cattle did not extend to herding oxen or driving them before a plough, although they sometimes helped; nor was it women's responsibility to slaughter cattle or dress their flesh.[27]

However, women's limited skills with the milk cows extended to the other animals kept in farmyard pens. In addition to milking, churning, and cheese making, women practiced what lawyers called "crud 7 biathad 7 méthad": penning the young calves and pigs, feeding them and

---

24. Cogitosus, *Vitae Sanctae Brigidae,* in Migne, *Patrologia Latina,* 72:777B. Another hagiographer associated soft, rich cheeses with the women who made them and women with the temptation that would lure a monk from his ascetic regimen (Plummer, *Bethada*), 1:166–67, 2:161.

25. A. T. Lucas, "Cattle in Ancient and Medieval Irish Society," *O'Connell School Union Record* (Dublin, 1958); Micheál O Sé, "Old Irish Cheese and Other Milk Products," *Journal of the Cork Historical and Archaeological Society* [hereafter *JCHAS*] 53 (1948): 82–87; Micheál O Sé, "Old Irish Buttermaking," *JCHAS* 54 (1949): 61–67. Women did not normally produce milk or butter for external markets, at least not until the nineteenth century (Nuala Cullen, "Women and Preparation of Food in Eighteenth-century Ireland," in *Women in Early Modern Ireland,* ed. Margaret Mac-Curtain and Mary O'Dowd, 267–68 (Edinburgh, 1991).

26. D. A. Binchy, ed., *Críth Gablach* (Dublin, 1941), 6 (l. 160), 8 (l. 203) (see 75–76 [*bés*] for discussion). See also J. O'Loan, "Livestock in the Brehon Laws," *Agricultural History Review* 7 (1959): 65–74.

27. When hagiographers depicted monks milking, it was probably a sign of their humble, nonwarrior status, in the same sense that *Cáin Adamnáin* included clerics with women and children among noncombatants. See the lesson about the sexual division of labor taught to St. Ailbe by an angel in W. W. Heist, ed., *Vitae Sanctorum Hiberniae,* Subsidia Hagiographica, no. 28 (Brussels, 1965), 129 (sec. 47). See also Plummer, *Bethada,* 1:46, 164, 2:46, 159. Patterson suggests that women drove the herds to summer pastures, but her evidence is slight and late (*Cattle-lords and Clansmen,* 73–75).

their herders, and fattening up the beasts.[28] Even when tending the pigs, women cared only for the special swine kept close by the farm, not the wild flocks let loose to eat mast in the woods. Male swineherds, who achieved the dubious reputation of shape-shifters and seers, took care of the herds beyond the civilized bounds of the farm.[29] But ordinary farmwives slopped the *mucca crai,* sty pigs, and fed them on grains or on the milk products, such as whey, that women themselves produced.[30] Pigs rooted around every farmyard, providing the bacon that helped feed the family and pay the rent but also worrying the mother, who could never quite keep track of all her small children: at least one saint was summoned to reconstruct a little one attacked and chewed by hungry swine, and jurists also worried about culpability in cases in which pigs devoured children.[31]

But the animal that figured most importantly in women's half of the conjugal economy was the sheep, despite the fact that sheep were not animals of the yard and barn but small-brained roamers of scrubby fields and stony hills. It may have been the case, as has been argued, that sheep were the dirty, low-status, feminine animal extraordinaire in the minds of the early Irish. Whereas men raided and traded cattle, women of pre-Christian Ireland supposedly celebrated their own fertility with a cult of sheep on February 1, Imbolc (later St. Brigit's Day).[32] Certainly male saints were known to flee at the bleat of a sheep, fearing that seductive women were not far behind.[33] However, women were not so closely identified with sheep that they always took responsibility for herding them. The *vitae* show as many boys as women herding sheep, perhaps because mothers could not traipse after the animals as they wandered the

---

28. *CIH,* 509; *ALI,* 2:366–77. *Crud,* which the legal commentators took for *crod,* "stock," should be read, with Thurneysen, as *cróud,* "penning" (see Thurneysen, *SEIL,* 34). Possibly the word could also mean *crúd,* "milking" (see E. G. Quin, gen. ed., *Dictionary of the Irish Language,* compact ed. [Dublin, 1983] [hereafter *DIL*], 161).

29. Proinséas Ní Chatháin, "Swineherds, Seers, and Druids," *Studia Celtica* 14–15 (1979–80): 200–211; Patterson, *Cattle-lords and Kinsmen,* 81–82.

30. *CIH,* 509; *ALI,* 2:367–69.

31. Whitley Stokes, ed. and trans., *The Tripartite Life of Patrick and Other Documents Relating to the Saint* (London, 1887), 198; Myles Dillon, ed. and trans., "Stories from the Law-tracts," *Ériu* 11 (1932): 44–45, 53.

32. Patterson, *Cattle-lords and Clansmen,* 82–86.

33. Molua was one who fled the bleating of sheep, fearing that seductive women would not be far behind (Heist, *Vitae,* 137).

hills, and it may not have been safe to send a young girl after them.[34] It was not so much the sheep themselves that belonged to women as what they produced, for, if babies bought a woman's place in the domestic economy, cloth was her most likely source of profit.[35]

Production: Cloth

Wool, like milk, was women's to work and finish. Women greased the wool, combed and spun it, and dyed the yarn; they also hung flax to dry before scutching it to extract the fiber from its casing and eventually dyeing it before turning it into thread. Then they made the thread into cloth and the cloth into clothing.[36] The writer of *Ca'in Adamna'in* claimed that women carried the spindle and clothed the world; if he meant that women were the managers as well as laborers at all stages of cloth production, this seems to have been true.[37] At divorce, their labor with wool and flax earned them half the finished product no matter who minded the

34. Heist, *Vitae*, 234–35 (where the sheep belong to the saint's aunt), 361, 383. See also episodes in which boys minded calves in Heist, *Vitae*, 357; and Plummer, *Vitae* 1, 6, 201–3. For boys minding pigs, see Plummer, *Vitae*, 172–73. Adomnán mentioned women herding sheep (A. O. Anderson and M. O. Anderson, eds. and trans., *Adomnan's Life of Columba* [London, 1961], 248–51). Plummer (*Vitae* 2, 42) refers to a noblewoman keeping sheep on an island pasture, but she certainly did not mind them herself. See also Kuno Meyer, ed. and trans., *Ca'in Adamna'in An Old Irish Treatise on the Law of Adamna'in* [hereafter *CA*] (Oxford, 1905), 14, which refers to women's flocks. One of the few exceptional shepherdesses was St. Brigit, who claimed to love herding sheep in the rain (Donncha Ó hAodha, ed. and trans., *Bethu Brigte* [Dublin, 1978], 16), but her mythic associations with sheep make her case problematic as evidence.

35. One of the few legal references to women herding sheep appears in the special context of cases of legal entry, a process by which the putative owner of a piece of property formally entered the land to claim it. The female claimant described in the laws drove sheep onto the land to signal her occupation and use of it, whereas men making formal entry normally drove cattle. But nothing in the episode suggests that the woman herself ordinarily chased the sheep around the countryside. The other equipment she brought along at legal entry, a kneading trough and sieve, were clearly symbolic of her economic functions upon the disputed land, just as were the sheep, and not implements she ordinarily carried with her: the trough and sieve were her means of making bread, just as the sheep were her source of cloth (*CIH*, 207–9, 378.26; Kelly, *Guide*, 187–88).

36. *CIH*, 510; *ALI*, 2:371–75. W. H. Crawford points out that linen production is labor-intensive work well suited to families, since some of the labor was difficult for women ("Women in the Domestic Linen Industry," in MacCurtain and O'Dowd, *Women in Early Ireland*, 256–67).

37. *CA*, 24. See also the long antiquarian discussion of cloth and the making of clothing in Eugene O'Curry, *On the Manners and Customs of the Ancient Irish* (Dublin, 1873), 3:112–23.

sheep, whose sheep produced the wool, or whose land fed the sheep; however, the less labor women put into the product, the fewer profits they gained when dividing the communal property. Similarly, women deserved more of the dyestuff derived from the plants called *róid* and *glaisen* (woad) and beans, called *seib*. They also took more of the linen and flax when they had worked to prepare the dye and finish the linen.[38]

Clearly, a good housewife was expected to take raw wool and flax and transform them into the fabric from which she made clothes; just as clearly, the value of her labors was acknowledged by the men who made the laws. The eighth-century legal tract *Di Cetharślicht Athgabála* describes the equipment of cloth production in such detail that it overwhelms the reader untrained in the weaver's craft. The tract concerns distraint, the process by which a plaintiff legally seized the property of a defendant who allegedly owed a debt to him or her; the Irish word for the procedure is *athgabál,* "taking back."[39] The tract's author assumed that women distrained the property of other women for cloth-making equipment borrowed and never returned or bought and not paid for. The lender could seize the sheep of someone who borrowed her wool bag, her weaving rod, a pattern for cloth that she had set out on a bit of leather, or a variety of other essential tools or raw materials. A woman could also sue over the price or wages she expected for finished cloth, or even for the blessing (*apartain*) she needed upon her work from another woman.[40]

Every bit of wool or flax, every tool, every step in the process, was valuable enough to sue over, according to the laws constructed and enforced by the men of Ireland. What is more, the legal tract implies a community of weaving, spinning, sewing women, some of whom were better equipped than others, who lent their tools back and forth, who sold some of their labor and its products, and who generally treated cloth making, if not as a business, then at least as an important sector of both

---

38. For *glaisin,* see *CIH,* 510; and *ALI,* 2:373–74. For *róid,* see *CIH,* 277; and *ALI,* 2:420–21; and *CA,* 32. See also Charles Plummer, ed., *Vitae Sanctorum Hiberniae* (Oxford, 1910), 1:95.

39. Kelly, *Guide,* 177–79; *CIH,* 378–39, 422; *ALI,* 1:146–51, 268–69. For a thorough discussion of the entire process of distraint, see D. A. Binchy, "Distress in Irish Law," *Celtica* 10 (1973): 22–71. Normally, a plaintiff gave formal notice of intention to impound the defendant's property in one to five days (always two days if the plaintiff was a woman). If the defendant did not begin to pay or negotiate, the plaintiff legally entered the other's property and took cattle or other livestock in the amount due. The plaintiff kept the animals separate from his or her own herd until the debtor settled or, after a proper amount of time, the plaintiff kept the impounded herd.

40. *CIH,* 379–81; *ALI,* 1:151–57.

the domestic economy and the external market. Although women may not have actually sat and worked together, cloth makers seem at least to have formed laboring networks in which they exchanged tools, similar to groups of men who shared ploughing equipment.[41]

Cloth making took place in the house, the seat of a woman's many social and economic functions and the site of her mothering. Nothing remains of looms or cloth, as at Scandinavian sites, to place cloth making in early Irish homes except specialized outbuildings, although the laws do not list dye houses, spinning rooms, or weaving sheds among other out-buildings and barns.[42] But the looms that Irish women used were proba-bly small and portable enough to fit into the tiny one- or two-room houses they inhabited, and no doubt they boiled the smelly cauldrons of dyestuff in the house or just outside, like the large-scale cooking that occasionally took place safely out-of-doors.[43] One of St. Ciarán's later hagiographers suggested that at least one stage of linen production took place at home when he mentioned the unfortunate mother of the saint who dried flax on the walls of her house; the stuff was a fire hazard, as she soon learned.[44]

Despite its acknowledged importance to the household economy, as well as to the larger economy of the community, cloth making and sewing remained the *lámthorad,* handwork or craft, of women.[45] Men did not seize or manage it as part of their own labor, heavy or skilled, until the Norman period.[46] The Irish words for women's and men's

41. David Herlihy, *Opera Muliebria: Women and Work in Medieval Europe* (New York, 1990), 28–29, argues against an Irish *gynaeceum* in the continental style.

42. Nancy Edwards, *The Archaeology of Early Medieval Ireland* (Philadelphia, 1992), 83, also 65–66; Nanna Damsholt, "The Role of Icelandic Women in the Sagas and in the Production of Homespun Cloth," *Scandinavian Journal of History* 9, no. 2 (1984): 83.

43. Herlihy, *Opera Muliebria,* 28; Damsholt, "Role of Icelandic Women," 82; Whitley Stokes, ed., *Lives of the Saints from the Book of Lismore* (Oxford, 1890), 121, 266–67.

44. Plummer, *Bethada,* 1:120, 2:116.

45. E. G. Quin, ed., *Dictionary of the Irish Language* (Dublin, 1983), 344, 420. See also R. Thurneysen, ed., "Aus dem irischen Recht III," *Zeitschrift für Celtishe Philologie* 15 (1925): 340–41. But see Kuno Meyer, ed., *Sanas Cormaic, Anecdota from Irish Manuscripts* 4 (1912): 15, where the goddess Brig/Brigit's craft work is referred to as *frithgnam.*

46. Later in the Middle Ages the Irish exported large quantities of woolen cloth; if the Scandinavian and continental evidence provides useful analogues, women may have been excluded from cloth making once wool became a profitable object of long-distance trade. See T. B. Barry, *The Archaeology of Medieval Ireland* (London and New York, 1987), 103–5; Herlihy, *Opera Muliebria,* 185–91; and Damsholt, "Role of Icelandic Women," 84–86.

work—"craft work" and "labor"—are themselves neutral, but their connotations were made profoundly gender specific. For instance, in the
tenth- or eleventh-century tale *Airec Menman Uraird Maic Coisse* (The
Plan of Urard mac Coisse), a humorous list of women includes Lenn
ingen Lámthora, "Cloak daughter of Handiwork," along with Lene
ingen Línghuirt, "Shift daughter of Linen–flax field," and Certle ingen
tSnímaire, "Kirtle daughter of Spindle," among others.[47] Nothing more
securely identified these figures as laboring women than cloth work, the
light work of the hands that women could take up during a break from
their other tasks. The wool would never spoil while a woman milked the
cows or cooked dinner, and the thread could wait while a mother busied
herself elsewhere. Having babies and clothing babies were all part of the
nurturer's duty, as *Cáin Adamnáin*'s author acknowledged. Similarly,
when St. Adomnán himself wrote his life of Columcille and searched for
the perfect metaphor for an exceptional pregnancy, he chose cloth making. St. Columcille's mother, about to give birth, had a vision of herself
weaving a marvelous cloak colored like the rainbow: the dazzling cloak
was her baby saint to be, Columcille.[48]

If cloth making was women's work, then its ultimate product was the
fine embroidery of a few highly skilled workers. The embroideress, *druinech,* did not find a place in any of the conventional status hierarchies
articulated in the laws; like every other woman, her honor price
depended on that of her male guardian. But lawyers listed the *druinech*
among seven people "difficult to maintain," by which they meant pro-
hibitively expensive for a guilty party to support when she became sick or
injured.[49] For, lawyers declared, when a *druinech* was temporarily lost to
the workforce, "there is needed someone who should perform [her]
work"; yet, like a king, hospitaller, smith, carpenter, or wise man, a well-
trained embroideress was so skilled, her talents so rare, and her product
so richly valuable that she was irreplaceable. The ability to create the dec-
orative cloth that adorned the shoulders of warriors and the shrines of

---

47. Mary E. Byrne, ed., "Airec Menman Uraird Maic Coisse," *Anecdota from Irish
Manuscripts* 2 (1908): 56. Cormac's eighth-century glossary identifies *lámthorad* with
abras, spinning or cloth production, but with class connotations: *abras* was the
lámthorad of an *inailt,* a serving girl (Kuno Meyer, ed., *Sanas Cormaic* [Dublin,
1912], 10 sec. 90).
48. Heist, *Vitae,* 366.
49. *CIH,* 53; *ALI,* 5:312–15; D. A. Binchy, ed., "Bretha Crólige," *Ériu* 12 (1934):
26–27 (for *ben lámtoruid,* glossed as "an embroideress and women who perform the
steeping and dressing [of flax]").

the saints could even raise a woman to sainthood. Such skills earned a few women the companionship of Pátraic himself, and St. Ercnat's chief claim to sanctity seems to have consisted of her duties as embroideress, cloth cutter, and seamstress for St. Columcille.[50] Measured by the value of her labor rather than her relation to men, a *druinech* ranked near the top of the social hierarchy.

Still, embroidery was never as necessary for the survival of the Irish as was the production of workaday cloth. A needleworker stitched her fine designs in precious metals and colored threads primarily for the secular and clerical elite, with their uniforms of gorgeously patterned cloaks and bordered tunics.[51] As a result, the work carried such connotations of prestige that it is never quite clear in the sources whether skill with a needle added to, or derived from, a woman's social cachet. According to fosterage laws, every daughter of a chieftain was to learn embroidery—which meant that her foster mother had to know the craft, too—along with sewing and cutting cloth.[52] Certainly, only women with a certain amount of wealth and leisure could be spared for such artistic training in the production of luxury goods.

Yet, according to the narratives, embroidery was as much a natural attribute as a learned skill of the noblewomen of early Ireland—and for the princesses of the otherworld, the *síd*. Fíthal's *senbríathra* advised that the very best kind of wife was a virgin with "good needlework."[53] In the secular narratives, too, embroidery marked a woman of good blood as surely as did her golden hair or slim ankle. When the hero Cú Chulainn tried to convince his wife, Emer, to allow him to continue his wild affair with an otherworldly temptress named Fand, he cited Fand's "shape and appearance and ability, needlework (*druine*) and handicraft and products of handicraft, good sense and prudence and fortitude" as justification for his infidelity.[54] But not every well-bred girl could have mastered the needle well enough to make her embroidery priceless in legal and market terms. Like the Victorian ladies who dabbled in piano and watercolors, some of the noble daughters of Ériu were mere dilettantes. By and large,

50. Stokes, *Tripartite Life*, 266, also 252; Whitley Stokes, ed., *Félire Oengusso Céli Dé* (London, 1905), 42.

51. *CIH*, 464; *ALI*, 5:382–83.

52. *CIH*, 1721.65; *ALI*, 2:156–57.

53. Smith, "Senbriathra Fithail," 56.

54. Myles Dillon, ed., *Serglige Con Culainn* (Dublin, 1953), 25. See also Eleanor Knott, ed., *Togail Bruidne Da Derga* (Dublin, 1936), 3: Étaín was raised "co mbo druinech maith, 7 ní buí i nHérind ingen ríg bad chaímiu oldás" ("so that she was a

they were expected to mark their status with just two kinds of labor: the reproduction of their husbands' lineages and the stitching of pretty patterns.

Clearly, needlework, like reproduction, became the focus of formal ideology. Enmeshed in myths and in laws of status, the capacity for wielding an embroidery needle—the actual ability to take the time to learn and practice the luxury craft—was a symbol of status as much as, or more than, production for material rewards. Further, like reproduction, embroidery came to represent more than the labor involved, more even than the identity of the class that practiced it or consumed its products. As the greater process of cloth making signified women and their work generally, so embroidery represented the crème de la crème of womanhood and all its ambivalent attributes.

In some mysterious way, embroidery—putting needle and thread to cloth—could steer the fortunes of the entire society. The author of *Imacallam in Dá Thúarad* (Colloquy of the Two Sages) best expressed the deep meaning of embroidery. He described two views of the world, one voiced by a chipper young poet and another by a dour old cynic. Néde, the upstart, considered the embroidery of women to be a fundamental sign of things going well; Ferchertne, the elder, knew that things were going to hell and predicted that "great skill in embroidery will pass to fools and harlots so that garments will be expected without colors."[55] War, bad weather, failed crops, moral degeneracy, and clothes without color were knotted together and dependent, somehow, upon women's needles.

The Ideology of Women's Production

In the formal ideology of early Irish culture, recorded by men, women's production, particularly of babies and clothing, had mythic connotations. Reproduction and cloth making carried meanings far beyond their basic economic value. The fertility of highly sexual goddess-figures

---

good embroideress, and there was no king's daughter in Ireland who was fairer than she"). See also R. I. Best, ed., "The Adventures of Art Son of Conn," *Ériu* 3 (1907): 168 sec. 25.

55. Whitely Stokes, ed., "The Colloquy of the Two Sages," *Revue Celtique* 26 (1905): 34, 42. For another prophetic text that mentions embroidery, see Kuno Meyer, ed., "Mitteilungen aus Irischen Handschriften," *Zeitschrift für Celtische Philologie* 9 (1913): 170 ("druinech cechla bean").

informed the most sacred sovereignty myths of early Ireland. Even milking suggested prosperity, fertility, and reproductive ideals for those
attuned to such notions.[56]

However, noble ladies, ordinary farmwives, and unfree female laborers also produced a great many other goods and services less subject to
mythmaking. Slopping the pigs or wiping a toddler's nose held little
romance for the scribes of early Ireland; tale-tellers and lawyers recorded
little, besides, of housekeeping, laundry, or the grinding of grain and
making of bread.[57] The source makers never wrote about men's labor,
either, except the glamorous work of warriors and the pious work of
monks.[58] We know that women must have filled their days with hard,
dull labors and distinctly unglamorous kinds of production; they must
have helped men trudge through the fields, planting, weeding, and reap-
ing when the season demanded. Some laws list sowing and harvesting
among women's duties, despite the gendered division of labor that otherwise prevails in the texts.[59]

The texts hint further that a few women imitated the most elite of male
labors; the eighth-century *Bretha Crólige* refers to female professionals,
including a wright and a physician, and a single entry in the monastic
annals mentions a *banfile* (woman poet).[60] There are even the odd references to illicit vocations such as witchcraft, which carried their own
mythic meanings.[61] But none of these labors and none of this production
merited the cultural meditation upon women's work called forth by baby
making and cloth production.

Perhaps women had their own ideologies of production, separate from
those of men. What could baby making and cloth making have meant to

56. One attribute of holy women and goddesses seems to have been the ability to
milk wild animals. See Heist, *Vitae*, 129; Stokes, *Tripartite Life*, 72; and the supernatural figure of Flidais in Whitley Stokes, ed., *Cóir Anmann*, in *Irische Texte mit
Ubersetzungen und Wörterbuch*, ed. Stokes and E. Windisch, Dritte Ser., 2 Heft,
294–95, secs. 25–26 (Leipzig, 1897).

57. For women grinding, see Heist, *Vitae*, 391. For women washing clothes, see
Plummer, *Vitae*, 1:96; and Plummer, *Bethada*, 1:217, 2:211. For women baking, see
CIH, 1766.14; and *ALI*, 2:176.

58. Lisa M. Bitel, *Isle of the Saints: Monastic Settlement and Christian Community
in Early Ireland* (Ithaca, N.Y., 1990), 128–44.

59. *CIH*, 509; *ALI*, 2:366–67.

60. Binchy, "Bretha Crólige," 26; Kelly, *Guide*, 49, 77. See Plummer, *Vitae*, 2:53,
for a reference to women practicing medicine. See Kuno Meyer, ed. and trans., *Liadan
and Cuirithir: An Irish Love Story of the Ninth Century* (London, 1902), for the story
of Liadan, *banfile*.

61. Binchy, "Bretha Crólige," 28; *CIH*, 233; *ALI*, 5:456; Kelly, *Guide*, 50.

them? Were the two activities linked in women's minds as in formally articulated ideologies? Were other modes of production more important to women? We have no *chansons de toile* from early Ireland, nor an Irish Christine de Pisan to detail women's ideologies of labor. The only clues Irish women have left are their prayers and spells: the blessing upon weaving that one woman could expect from another or the curse over which she might sue another; the prayers women sent to the saints when in hard travail; and the churning charms that have come down to us orally, from one woman's mouth to another woman's ear, thence to men's texts.[62] One late *vita* of St. Ciarán suggests that cloth making did have its own subculture exclusively for women and hence its own ideology. When the saint's foster mother set about dyeing her wool, she shooed the boy out of the house: no males were allowed to observe the secret art of dyeing or to contaminate the house where it occurred. Ciarán, ever the man, responded angrily by cursing the vats of dye so that the cloth would not take the color until his *muimme* begged forgiveness.[63]

Women's own interpretation of their production may well have conflicted with the formal ideology of women's labor constructed by men and shared by women. Women may have considered reproduction and cloth making more important than their other labors; on the other hand, they may have valued gardening, milking, or harvesting more highly—we cannot know. But Ciarán's hagiographer, at least, believed that the social meaning of women's work was different for the sexes. Ciarán's fosterer tried to go about her business—and it was *her* business—of cloth making while other women sought to control their own production and services. And, just as the boy-saint was bound to interfere in the name of excluded and threatened manhood, so husbands, fathers, and other male managers tried to restrict women's access to the products of their own labors and the profits of their own services.

Women had to labor as wives and mothers in the subsistence economy of early Ireland if they wished to become full economic actors. The procreative ideology that informed politics and the hierarchical social structure permitted them few other roles. Formal ideology intruded upon women's lives further when men emphasized two of women's labors

---

62. Anderson and Anderson, *Life of Columcille*, 434; H. D'Arbois de Jubainville, "Documents Irlandais publiés par M. Windisch," *Revue Celtique* 12 (1891): 154–55.
63. Whitley Stokes, ed. and trans., *Lives of the Saints from the Book of Lismore* (Oxford, 1890), 121, 266–67.

above all others, urging women to make heirs and to produce cloth, to have babies and to clothe them, complementary activities that placed women securely inside their houses. But this ideology also proved beneficial to women who could use their status as reproducers to win control of conjugal capital and their profits from cloth making to enter other economic arenas. For women who successfully collaborated with their male partners, or who avoided or subverted male management, their procreative and cloth-making labors were just the hard-won routes to more diverse economic opportunities.

The ideology of reproduction and cloth production expressed in formal texts remained, after all, only one ideology of many negotiated by the men and women of early Ireland. This ideology influenced attitudes toward women's economic activities and enhanced the status of fertile married women, but it remained an elaborate and occasionally contradictory expression of the agenda of one subgroup within the society. Women no doubt had their own ideas about labor, production, exchange, and men; they may well have shared these occasionally with their husbands and other men they met around the farm or fair. And the men who sweated in the fields beside them, who together with women created and loved and played with their babies, who wore the tunics woven by women and accompanied them to market, sued and were sued by them, and engaged in countless other economic interactions with women—these men knew that the women of early Ireland were not just the childbearers, dairymaids, and weavers of rhetoric. They were respectable companions in the struggle for subsistence.

Friends and Family, Politics and Privilege in the Kingship of Berengar I

Barbara H. Rosenwein

David Herlihy was drawn to medieval Italy. Its abundant documentation allowed him to explore the economic and social issues that preoccupied his life's work: shifts of wealth, changes in the nature of the family, relations between the sexes and classes. While he was interested in counting heads and documents (he was the preeminent pioneer in medieval studies of both statistics and computers) he brought to his work a moral passion that transcended numbers and made its focus both human greed and human bonds. I offer this study of Berengar I, king of Italy from 888 to 924, in homage to Herlihy's field of expertise, scholarship, and compassion.

Focused or Diffuse Patronage?

The common verdict pronounces Berengar I a weak king who frittered away the material resources of royal power—land, jurisdictions, rights

Parts of this essay are argued in more extended form in my monograph, "The Family Politics of Berengar I," forthcoming. I want to thank Professors Chris Wickham, Maureen Miller, and Steven Epstein for their helpful comments.

The following abbreviations are used.

Cod. Brix. = Memorial book of S. Salvatore/S. Giulia, Biblioteca Queriniana, Brescia Ms. G. VI.7.

DBer = Luigi Schiaparelli, ed., *I diplomi di Berengario I*, Fonti per la Storia d'Italia (Rome, 1903), followed by the charter number, date (where possible or relevant), and page number.

DLod = Luigi Schiaparelli, ed., *I diplomi italiani di Lodovico III e di Rodolfo II*, Fonti per la Storia d'Italia (Rome, 1910), 3–92.

DRod = Luigi Schiaparelli, ed., *I diplomi italiani di Lodovico III e di Rodolfo II*, Fonti per la Storia d'Italia (Rome, 1910), 95–141.

MGH = Monumenta Germaniae Historica.

MIÖG = Mitteilungen des Instituts für Österreichische Geschichtsforschung.

An asterisk preceding a charter number indicates that it exists in the original.

over public defensive structures such as castles and walls—with impru-
dent abandon to a vast assortment of recipients, most importantly the
bishops of northern Italy. His rule thus resulted in the fragmentation of
Italian political life and paved the way for the development of the communes. The verdict is summed up well by Giovanni Tabacco.

> The royal chancery continued to function, not in order to enact gen-
> eral measures but only to draw up diplomas: privileges addressed to
> the most disparate individuals, particularly churches and friendly aris-
> tocrats, centres of force which the king sought to link to his own
> power. . . . Berengar strengthened individual ecclesiastical patrimonies
> by extending his protection over them, renewed and conceded immu-
> nities, gave away serfs and tenant holdings, fiscal *curtes* and wooded
> mountains, extended fishing and navigation rights, gave exemptions
> from tolls, and conceded public revenues in ports, on bridges and
> roads, in market-places and from coinage.[1]

The granting of privileges generally rates failing marks from historians; kings are supposed to want to retain their power, and privileges
seem to surrender power. Some kings who granted numerous privileges
pass muster with historians, however, because there are other sorts of
documents against which one may balance their alienations.[2] Unfortunately for Berengar, the sources for his reign are extremely limited. We
have no narrative histories,[3] no political tracts from his advisors, and no
capitularies to tell us about his governmental goals. Indeed, the very lack
of capitularies has been taken to indicate that Berengar had no political
program whatsoever.

The diplomas are all that exist. But historians have not fully explored
their potential for elucidating the nature of Berengar's reign and (as I propose to do here) for discovering a policy behind his seemingly profligate

---

1. Giovanni Tabacco, *The Struggle for Power in Medieval Italy: Structures of Political Rule*, trans. Rosalind Brown Jensen (Cambridge, 1989), esp. 155–57. For further
references and a review of the historiography, see Rosenwein, "Family Politics."

2. Janet L. Nelson, *Charles the Bald* (London, 1992), esp. 267, placing his 354
charters in context.

3. There is a poem with some limited use as an account of Berengar's reign, the
Gesta Berengarii imperatoris (see n. 18), which paints Berengar as a great military
hero—an irony, since, as Chris Wickham has pointed out, Berengar, "in forty years of
campaigning, is not recorded as ever having won a battle" (Chris Wickham, *Early
Medieval Italy: Central Power and Local Society, 400–1000* [Ann Arbor, 1981], 171).

distributions. We are lucky to have 140 extant authentic charters, of which 73, or 52 percent, are originals: that is, the actual parchments drawn up by Berengar's chancery.[4] Naturally, we are faced with the usual problems connected with evidence of this sort, including the documents' uneven survival and their formulaic character. We may tease out hypotheses, but let us keep in mind their tentative nature.

For, as Herlihy remarked early in his studies of private charters, "we can hope indirectly to highlight . . . tendencies. . . . Let us repeat that word, tendencies."[5] This is precisely what historians have already done with Berengar's concessions, with harsh judgment of his scatter-shot approach. The thesis of the present essay is that the judgment is misplaced; there was pattern and concentration. Berengar had a political strategy: to use family, spiritual, and affective ties to bind select adherents to him. Berengar did indeed give away many privileges. But they were not given to a heterogeneous mélange of organizations or disparate individuals; they were given to family and friends.

Motives

Until the recent work of Aldo Settia, the common view was that Berengar granted concessions, particularly rights to build or keep castles, because he was confronted by desperate circumstances created particularly by Hungarian marauders who first arrived in Italy in 899.[6] However, Aldo

---

4. They are published in DBer. Vito Fumagalli, *Terra e società nell'Italia Padana. I secoli IX e X* (Turin, 1976), 84, counts 69 as originals, I cannot explain the discrepancy.

5. David Herlihy, "Treasure Hoards in the Italian Economy, 960–1139," *Economic History Review*, 2d ser., 10 (1957): 1–14, here 2, (*The Social History of Italy and Western Europe, 700–1500, Collected Studies*, Variorum Reprints [London, 1978], paper no. 1).

6. For a political narrative of the period, see Eduard Hlawitschka, *Franken, Alemannen, Bayern und Burgunder in Oberitalien (774–962)* (Freiburg im Breisgau, 1960), 67–94; Jörg Jarnut, "Ludwig der Fromme, Lothar I, und das Regnum Italiae," in *Charlemagne's Heir: New Perspectives on the Reign of Louis the Pious*, ed. Peter Godman and Roger Collins, 349–62 (Oxford, 1990); and G. Arnaldi, "Berengario," in *Dizionario Biografico degli Italiani* (Rome, 1960–), 9:1–26.

Regarding the Hungarians, the argument is that Berengar could not organize an adequate defense alone, so he allowed, indeed encouraged, others to build castles. See Pio Paschini, "Le vicende politiche e religiose del Friuli nei secoli nono e decimo," *Nuovo archivio veneto*, n.s. 10, 20 (1910): 229–44, and 21 (1911): 37–88, 399–435, esp. 61–74; and Gian Piero Bognetti, "Terrore e sicurezza sotto re nostrani e sotto re stranieri," in *Storia di Milano*, vol. 2: *Dall'invasione dei barbari all'apogeo del Governo vescovile (493–1002)*, 805–41, esp. 812–13 (Milan, 1954).

Settia has recently shown that the Hungarians were seldom in Italy before Berengar's death, and when they were they served him as mercenary troops.[7] This was the case for their incursions of 901 and 904, while, after Berengar's rival King Louis III was blinded in 905 and for as long as Berengar's position remained unchallenged, the Hungarians were not on Italian soil at all. When they returned, in 919/920, they did so again on orders from Berengar. But plenty of castles were built when there were no incursions.

Berengar did face a different sort of challenge: rival kings opposed him at the beginning and end of his career (888–98, again in 901–5, and finally in 921–24). But these moments of crisis do not neatly correspond with the periods in which Berengar drew up privileges. True, during the period 901–5, when he was opposing Louis III, Berengar granted 31 concessions (23 percent of the total).[8] But in the period 891–95, when he was contending against rival kings Guido and Lambert, Berengar made only three concessions (2 percent), while the next lowest point of gift giving (4.5 percent) was during 921–24 when he was battling Rudolf of Burgundy for the crown.

If we turn the question on its head and suggest that Berengar granted privileges in calm moments, here, too, we founder. For example, 906–10 was a period of both peace and royal parsimony (only 10 concessions), while 911–15, equally calm, saw the king granting 30 privileges.

Neither overt political emergencies nor placid routines, then, explain Berengar's privileges. However, laconic as the charters are, their very internal structure suggests a new avenue of approach to understanding Berengar's motives. The diplomas announce their own importance as social events. Invariably they involve at least three people: the king, a petitioner, and a recipient. Significantly, the documents often place the greatest emphasis on the petitioner, who is depicted as the necessary

7. Aldo A. Settia, "Gli Ungari in Italia e i Mutamenti territoriali fra VIII e X secolo," in *Magistra Barbaritas. I Barbari in Italia*, ed. Maria Giovanna Arcamone et al., 185–218 (Milan, 1984); Aldo A. Settia, *Castelli e villaggi nell'Italia padana. Popolamento, potere e sicurezza fra IX e XIII secolo*, 77–85, 128–70 (Naples, 1984); Aldo A. Settia, "Chiese e fortezze nel popolamento del Friuli," in *Chiese, Strade e Fortezze nell'Italia Medievale*, Italia Sacra; Studi e documenti di storia ecclesiastica, no. 46 (Rome: Herder, 1991), 99–129, originally published as "Chiese e fortezze nel popolamento delle diocesi friulane," in *Il Friuli dagli Ottoni agli Hohenstaufen. Atti del convegno internazionale di studi* (Udine, 1984), 217–44.

8. Here and in the following percentages, the total number of charters is considered to be 133 (the others being either *placita* or of uncertain date).

spark to fire up the heavy engine of royal munificence.[9] A kind of cosmic equation is set up in the rhetoric of the charter: the king, *rex divina favente clementia,* king by favor of divine clemency, was approached by so-and-so, who petitioned the king's *clementia* for a favor, that is, for a gift or a concession.[10] Thus, the intercessor was to the king as Berengar was to God, a view that made the actual recipient of the gift a less important figure in the drama. But this is not to downgrade the recipient; for, in fact, the person who was intercessor in one document was very often the recipient in another. These repetitions alert us to other connections among the documents.

I want here to discuss three important groups to whom Berengar gave his diplomas. These do not exhaust the clusters of people, both male and female, involved in Berengar's concessions; they are meant simply to illustrate the ways in which Berengar's concessions were connected to policies that linked family and friends rather than to improvisations that scattered gifts among diverse recipients.[11] The first group centers on two women in Berengar's immediate family: his first wife, Bertilla, member of the powerful Supponid family, and his daughter Berta, abbess of San Salvatore di Brescia; another centers on Adalbert of Ivrea, Berengar and Bertilla's son-in-law by their other daughter, Gisla; the third focuses on Grimaldus, a member of "the palace," by which is meant not a physical place but the traveling retinue of the king—his chancellors, notaries, palatine counts, and so on.

Royal Women

In the early phase of Berengar's kingship, Queen Bertilla was a key figure in his concessions. The charters refer to her not only as the king's *coniunx* (wife) but also as *consors,* a term of exceptional significance in her case. For, not only did it imply that she shared the prerogatives of the ruler (as it had done since the days of Louis the Pious), but it also immediately revived memories of her aunt, Queen Angilberga, wife of

---

9. On petitioners and petitioning, see Geoffrey Koziol, *Begging Pardon and Favor: Ritual and Political Order in Early Medieval France* (Ithaca, N.Y., 1992).

10. In 38 (52 percent, not counting *placita*) of Berengar's original diplomas, the intercessor petitions the king's *clementia;* of these, 22 (58 percent) speak of his being *rex* (or *imperator*) *divina favente clementia.*

11. For a more exhaustive survey, see Rosenwein "Family Politics."

Emperor Louis II and daughter of the powerful Suppo I.[12] Angilberga
was the first queen to be given the title *consors* in a royal privilege. When
the same term was used in the same sort of document to refer to Bertilla,
it recalled her family connections: not only to Angilberga but also to
Bertilla's brother Ardingus, who was bishop of Brescia, Berengar's
archchancellor, and a frequent petitioner in his charters; and to another
brother, Wifred, who was count of Piacenza and who also served as a
petitioner in royal charters.[13]

Bertilla was the most important petitioner in Berengar's early charters.
Indeed, she was the impresario of the great surge of concessions during
the period 901–5, petitioning nearly a third of the 31 privileges given out
during that period.[14] In a single year, for example, she intervened on
behalf of the church of Reggio; twice for Federico, the patriarch of
Aquileia; and once in favor of Adelbert, the bishop of Treviso.[15] Why

---

12. On the significance of *consors*, see Carlo Guido Mor, "'Consors regni': La
Regina nel diritto pubblico italiano dei secoli IX–X," *Archivio giuridico* 135 (1948):
7–32; Thilo Vogelsang, *Die Frau als Herrscherin im hohen Mittelalter. Studien zur
'consors regni' Formel* (Göttingen, 1954), esp. 18–21; and Paolo Delogu, "'Consors
regni': un problema carolingio," *Bullettino dell'Istituto storico italiano per il Medio
Evo e archivio muratoriano* 76 (1964): 47–98. For the title as a "female tradition"
among Supponid women, see Silvia Konecny, *Die Frauen des karolingischen
Königshauses: Die politische Bedeutung der Ehe und die Stellung der Frau in der
fränkischen Herrscherfamilie vom 7. bis zum 10. Jahrhundert*, Dissertationen der Uni-
versität Wien, no. 132 (Vienna, 1976), 118–28. On Suppo I, see Hlawitschka,
Franken, Alemannen, 269.

13. On Wifred and Ardingus, see Hlawitschka, *Franken, Alemannen*, 299–307.
The charters sometimes make the Supponid association explicit. For example, see
DBer *55 (17 June 905), 156–58: at the intervention of Bertilla, "dilectissimae coniugis et consortis," Berengar gives a concession to the abbess of S. Resurrezione, "quod
olim Angilberga gloriosa imperatrix a solo construxit." Further, the charter notes that
the monastery had been given "pro remedio quoque animae domni Hludovuici
gloriosissimi imperatoris" and goes on to connect the monastery to Angilberga's
daughter Ermengarda as well. The document was drawn up by "Ambrosius cancel-
larius ad vicem Adingi [i.e., Ardingus, Bertilla's brother] episcopi et archicancellarii."

14. She petitions (as *coniunx et consors* except where noted) in the following: DBer
*10 (3 Nov. 890), p. 38; *14 (30 Apr. 896), p. 48; *20 (6 Nov. 898), p. 61; 32 (7 June
900), p. 96; *38 (19 Jan. 903), p. 510; 40 (11 Sept. 903), p. 116; *42 (4 Jan. 904), p.
123; 49 (904?), p. 142; 50 (June 904?), p. 144; *52 (9 Jan. 905), p. 150; *55 (17 June
905), p. 156; *56 (31 July 905), p. 159; *60 (1 Aug. 905), p. 166; 62 (2 Aug. 905), p.
171 (*coniunx* only); 67 (5 Aug. 908), p. 182; 72 (27 July 910), pp. 194–95; 104 (ca.
911–15), p. 270; 113 (916?), p. 292 but "molta dubbia" (*coniunx* only). Total: 18. In
DBer *34 (23 Aug. 901), p. 102, a gift is given "pro longevitate . . . regni nostri sempi-
ternoque nostrae animae remedio seu coniugis nostrae."

15. For the church at Reggio, see DBer 42 (4 Jan. 904), p. 123; for Federico in 904
(probably), DBer 49, pp. 142–43 and DBer 50, pp. 144–46; for Adelbert, see DBer
*52 (9 Jan. 905), pp. 150–51.

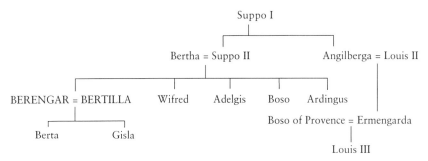

Fig. 1. Genealogical table

was she so influential at this time? The answer lies, I suggest, in the domain of family connections. During 901–5, Berengar's kingship was challenged by Louis III, the grandson of Angilberga and Louis II. Bertilla's Supponid connections counterbalanced the prestige of the Provençal king. Her place in Berengar's privileges helped to ensure her husband's claim to follow in the footsteps of Louis II, a claim that he tried to stake not only through her forebears but through his actions and the very vocabulary that was used to describe his kingship.[16]

Yet ancestors alone were weak trumps for a queen. Bertilla lacked the son that might have ensured her continued influence and, ultimately, her survival.[17] Vilified at Berengar's court, she died by poison sometime before his coronation as emperor at the end of 915.[18]

In some ways her place was taken by one of her daughters, Berta. But Berta's position was more secure; clearly the importance of progeny was

---

16. On this imitative aspect of Berengar's reign, see Settia, *Castelli,* 45–47. For his "access" through Bertilla to the glorious reign of Louis II and his wife, see DBer *55, discussed in note 13 above.

17. We know that the family and personal ties of early medieval queens were crucial to both their survival and their success. See Janet L. Nelson, "Queens as Jezebels: Brunhild and Balthild in Merovingian History," in her *Politics and Ritual in Early Medieval Europe,* 1–48 (London, 1986); Suzanne Fonay Wemple, *Women in Frankish Society: Marriage and the Cloister, 500 to 900* (Philadelphia, 1981), 63–70; Elizabeth Ward, "Caesar's Wife: The Career of the Empress Judith, 819–829," in Godman and Collins, *Charlemagne's Heir,* 205–27; and Pauline Stafford, "Charles the Bald, Judith and England," and Jane Hyam, "Ermentrude and Richildis," both in *Charles the Bald, Court and Kingdom,* ed. Margaret T. Gibson and Janet L. Nelson, 139–53 and 154–68, respectively (Aldershot, 1990).

18. On her vilification and death, see *Gesta Berengarii imperatoris* 2, lines 77–80, ed. Ernst Dümmler, 101 (Halle, 1871).

more enduring than that of queen mother in this instance. By 915, Berta was abbess of San Salvatore di Brescia. At that juncture, around the time of Bertilla's death, Berengar gave Berta and her monastery the right "to dig moats and build fortifications" at a nearby castle.[19] In the following year she and her monastery received another privilege, this time to construct a castle on the Ticino River.[20] In 917, Berengar gave her the monastery of S. Sisto at Piacenza, which had been founded by Empress Angilberga; Berta was made its *domina et ordinatrix atque rectrix,* in other words, its head in matters both spiritual and temporal.[21]

Thus, Berta's importance in the diplomas comes precisely at the time when Bertilla's influence ends, coinciding with Berengar's greatest (and terminal) gift-giving period (915–20). Although she was a recipient of his privileges rather than a petitioner, she also functioned, by a different means than Bertilla did, as an intermediary between Berengar and his adherents. The convent of San Salvatore included two nuns who were daughters of Berengar's chief palatine *fidelis,* count Grimaldus. In the confraternity book of San Salvatore, begun ca. 824 and steadily augmented during the ninth and tenth centuries, Grimaldus appears on one page handing over his daughters while on another folio his name is surrounded by those of his family members. Of these, we know that Sibico and Ingelfredus were also part of the "palatine group" of Berengarian adherents.[22] We shall return to them in due course. This is the place, however, to note the web of familial and amicitial relationships that made Berta's monastery more than merely the recipient of a few royal concessions. Grimaldus and his family had a "real presence" at Berta's convent: not only were his daughters nuns there but their names and his, inscribed in the confraternity book kept upon the convent altar, were read aloud during the liturgy.[23] San Salvatore and Berta in this way

---

19. DBer *96 (4 Mar. 915), pp. 253–54.

20. DBer *110 (25 May 916), pp. 281–83.

21. DBer 115 (25 Aug. 917), pp. 296–99.

22. For Sibico and Ingelfredus, see Cod. Brix., fol. 37r (33r). The old folio numbering is in part effaced; the new, given in this instance in parentheses, is always four folios behind the old. Henceforth, the old will be cited because it is the one used in the published edition of Andrea Valentini, ed. *Codice necrologico-liturgico del monastero di S. Salvatore o S. Giulia in Brescia* (Brescia, 1887). For the daughters of Grimaldus, see fol. 44r: "Grimohald[us] comes tradidit filias suas (Rotpern) et Reginberga." For further discussion, see below, n. 46.

23. On the sense of community between living and dead, between those named and those naming, see Otto Gerhard Oexle, "Memoria und Memorialüberlieferung im früheren Mittelalter," *Frühmittelalterliche Studien* 10 (1976): 70–95.

played an intermediary role, continually associating, through the liturgy, the families of the king and his adherents.

Dilectissimus gener

Berengar's other daughter was Gisla, married to Adalbert, marquis of Ivrea. None of the king's diplomas mentions her by name, but she nevertheless lurked behind many of his concessions, for she was the link that bound the powerful family of Anscar, Adalbert's father, to Berengar. When Berengar's rival King Lambert died in 898, Anscar, who had supported Lambert, turned to Berengar. We find him that very year petitioning the king alongside the royal archchancellor, Bishop Peter of Padua, and his notary, Restaldus; all three were termed *summos consciliarios nostros* (our most important councillors).[24] Perhaps at this time Adalbert married Gisla.[25] Nevertheless, our earliest sources place Adalbert by the side of Louis III, called in from Provence by a faction of the Italian magnates (doubtless including Adalbert) to oppose Berengar. By 902, Adalbert dominated much of northern Italy as one of Louis's *dilectissimi fideles*.[26] Yet soon enough, once Louis had been blinded and packed off to Provence, Adalbert was at Berengar's side, petitioning him on behalf of Viscount Gariardus.[27] The next we hear of him, he is in possession of an unusually grand title: *Adalbertus gloriosus marchio dilectus gener et fidelis noster* (Adalbert, glorious marquis, beloved son-in-law, and our *fidelis*).[28] The endearments continued until 913.[29] Perhaps this is when Adalbert remarried, this time to the daughter of Adalbert, marquis of

---

24. DBer 23 (1 Dec. 898), pp. 69–71. For Anscar, see Hlawitschka, *Franken, Alemannen,* 128–30, and for Adalbert, 100–104.

25. Hlawitschka argues (*Franken, Alemannen,* 100 n. 1, and 129 n. 6) that the marriage with Gisla must have taken place ca. 900 because Berengar II, the son of their union, was already sitting as *nepus et missus domni et gloriosissimi Berengarii . . . imperatoris avio et senior eius* in Milan in April 918. See Cesare Manaresi, ed., *I placiti del "Regnum Italiae,"* 3 vols., Fonti per la Storia d'Italia, vols. 92, 96, pts. 1 and 2, 97, pts. 1 and 2 (Rome, 1955–60), 1:485, no.*129. The first certain evidence of the union comes from 910, when Berengar refers to Adalbert as *gener* (DBer 71, p. 193); but it seems unlikely that the son of a union of this late date would have held the office of *comes et missus discurrens* in 918.

26. DLod *18, pp. 51–53.

27. DBer 68 (14 Aug. 908), pp. 183–85.

28. DBer 71 (910), pp. 192–93.

29. DBer 87 (26 Jan. 913), p. 233.

Tuscany;[30] thereafter he took an increasingly independent line, joining various conspiracies against Berengar.

Adalbert was a petitioner only three times in Berengar's concessions and never once a recipient.[31] But his importance in orchestrating Berengar's gifts, though hidden, may at times be glimpsed. This is easiest in the case involving Berengar's confirmation of the monastery of Fontaneto to Viscount Gariardus; the petitioner was Dagibert, bishop of Novara, but we know (the charter says so) that Gariardus was Adalbert's *fidelis*.[32]

Less obvious, but equally telling, is the case of Audax, bishop of Asti. In 904, Berengar conceded a diploma to the church of Asti, where Audax was bishop, confirming its possessions, including its castles and markets.[33] It seems an isolated event: neither before nor afterward did Berengar trouble himself about Asti. Who was this Audax who momentarily gained the king's attention? We know very little about him, but what we do know shows that he had an unusually cozy relationship with the local viscount, Otbert. In March 905, when he gave a donation to the canons of his church, he reported that he acted "with the advice (*consilio*) of viscount Otbert."[34] This deference to secular authority suggested to Cipolla that the incident showed the "valore dell'autorità della *pars regia*."[35]

A closer look reveals that Otbert did not represent the king but rather the king's son-in-law. It was Adalbert who intervened on Otbert's behalf when Berengar gave the viscount a *curtis* at Cairo; and much later, after Berengar's death, Adalbert's sons and widow would petition King Rudolf

30. We do not know the date of this remarriage. However, Anscar, son of this second alliance, was shown petitioning alongside his half-brother Berengar in 924, with both referred to as "illustres marchiones," which seems to indicate that he was not considered a child (DRod 4, p. 104 [18 Aug. 924]). The earliest possible birth date for Anscar is late 913, with the remarriage having taken place early that year.

31. He participated in the following: DBer 71 (13 June 910), pp. 192–93; DBer 87 (26 Jan. 913), pp. 232–34; and DBer 93 (ca. 913), pp. 247–48.

32. DBer 68 (14 Aug. 908), pp. 183–85. On Gariardus (or Gaddo), see Hlawitschka, *Franken, Alemannen,* 183–84; Giancarlo Andenna, "Grandi patrimoni, funzioni pubbliche e famiglie su di un territorio: Il 'comitatus plumbiensis' e i suoi conti dal IX all'XI secolo," in *Formazione e strutture dei ceti dominanti nel medioevo: marchesi, conti e visconti nel regno italico (secc. IX–XII),* Atti de primo convegno di Pisa, 10–11 May 1983 (Rome, 1988), 205–7 and Tav. 1.

33. DBer 51 (15 July 904), pp. 146–49.

34. Ferdinando Gabotto, ed., *Le più antiche carte dell'archivio capitolare di Asti,* Biblioteca della Società storica subalpina, no. 28 (Pinerolo-Turin, 1904), 59, no. 37.

35. Carlo Cipolla, "Di Audace vescovo di Asti e di due documenti inediti che lo riguardano," *Miscellanea di Storia Italiana* 27 (1889): 189 n. 1.

to bestow on Otbert the Castel Vecchio at Asti and the church of St. Ambrose and its dependencies.[36] Meanwhile, Otbert named one of his own sons Adalbert,[37] and at the end of his life he entered Novalesa, a monastery particularly favored by Adalbert.[38]

Thus Bishop Audax deferred to Otbert, and Otbert to Adalbert.[39] Adalbert *gener* stands behind the seemingly unrelated concessions of Berengar to Otbert and Audax.

Grimaldus

Grimaldus was a member of Berengar's entourage beginning perhaps as early as 900; he was certainly Berengar's *illustris vir ac devotus fidelis noster* in 905. He remained the most active of Berengar's petitioners.[40] The documents celebrate him with encomia and promotions: in 911, he

---

36. On the gift from Berengar, see DBer 93 (ca. 913), pp. 247–48. On the gift of Rodolfo, see DRod 10 (Dec. 5, 924), pp. 122–25. On Otbert and the general political context, see Renato Bordone, "Società e potere in Asti e nel suo comitato fino al declino dell'autorità regia," *Bollettino storico-bibliografico subalpino* 73 (1975): 379–84. Elsewhere in the article, on page 419, he speaks of Berengar as a "re ostile agli Anscarici" and sees Audax in Berengar's camp. See also Giuseppi Sergi, "Una grande circoscrizione del regno italico: La marca arduinica di Torino," *Studi Medievali*, 3d ser., 12, no. 2 (1971): 687.

37. Gabotto, *Asti*, *55 (14 Mar. 940), pp. 96–101.

38. Carlo Cipolla, ed., *Monumenta Novaliciensia vetustiora*, vol. 2: *Chronicon Novaliciense*, Fonti per la Storia d'Italia, no. 32 (Rome, 1901), 5.xxiv, 266. For Adalbert's special place at Novalesa, see *Chronicon Novaliciense*, 5.v, 247.

39. In addition, we know that Adalbert was an important landowner in the vicinity and well known to Audax: the bishop made a number of exchanges of lands that were described as bordering on the land of Marquis Adalbert (Gabotto, *Asti*, no. *42, p. 68; no. *44, pp. 73–77).

40. He appears in the following: DBer *54 (26 May 905), pp. 154–55; *66 (24 Apr. 908), pp. 178–80; 77 (15 Aug. 911), pp. 210–12; 78 (19 Aug. 911), pp. 212–14; *85 (9 Aug. 912), pp. 226–30; 87 (26 Jan. 913), pp. 232–34; *89 (25 May 913), pp. 240–42; *91 (19 Sept. 913), pp. 244–45; 93 (ca. 913), pp. 247–48; 104 (ca. 911–15), pp. 269–70; 105 (ca. 911–15), pp. 271–73; 112 (1 Sept. 916), pp. 285–89; *114 (916), pp. 294–96; *117 (Jan. 918), pp. 302–8; 120 (18 Dec. 917 or 918), pp. 313–15; 121 (26 Dec. 918), pp. 315–17; *123 (17 Nov. 919), pp. 319–22; *131 (Oct. 920), pp. 338–40; *132 (20 Dec. 920), pp. 340–42; 136 (3 Oct. 921), pp. 348–51; 138 (28 July 922), pp. 354–56; and 140 (24 Dec. 915), pp. 361–62. In all but three of these, *85, *117 (*placita*), and 104 (where he is the recipient), Grimaldus appears as a petitioner. If Gabotto's argument for the authenticity of DBer † (forgery) 5 (8 July 900), pp. 376–77, is accepted, Grimaldus was in Berengar's entourage as *dilectus vassus fidelis noster* as early as the turn of the century. See Ferdinando Gabotto, "Un contrasto dei vescovi di Novara e di Vercelli," *Bollettino storico per la provincia di Novara* 7 (1913): 1–9.

was *gloriosus comes;* by 913, when he had probably become the king's treasurer, he was "fidelissimus" and "dilectissimus."[41] By 919, he was *marchio,* a marquis.[42] Grimaldus's social circle intersected with most of the other important associates of Berengar. Furthermore, he was intimately involved in the royal "family" monastery of San Salvatore.

The interconnections between Grimaldus and other recipients of Berengar's largesse may be illustrated by the complex but telling case of Sibico, bishop of Padua. In 912, Berengar confirmed all the former rights of the Paduan church and then gave Sibico the right to "build castles [*castella*] . . . under such terms that no public personage, small or great, may dare to enter by his own power [*sua virtute*], nor distrain, nor take anything from the inhabitants there unjustly and contrary to law."[43] We have only half the story here because we do not know who petitioned on Sibico's behalf.

We, can, however, guess who the "gloriosi marchiones dilecti fideles [nostri]" were who petitioned Berengar to grant to Sibico's church the public roads along the river valleys of the Brenta and Solagna together with the regnal lands alongside the roads, judicial jurisdiction, and all fines, taxes, and dues.[44] Berengar did not have very many *gloriosi marchiones* around him: the possibilities are Adalbert, Anscar, Waltfredus, Odelricus, and Grimaldus. The latter two are the only ones who appear together in Berengar's charters.[45] They are very likely the petitioners for Sibico.

The association of Sibico with Grimaldus is confirmed by the confraternity book of San Salvatore, Berta's monastery. Grimaldus headed up a list on fol. 37r, all of it written by the same scribal hand:

---

41. As *comes,* see DBer 77. As treasurer, see DBer 105. Hlawitschka (*Franken, Alemannen,* 190 n. 5) connects the use of superlatives with Grimaldus's role in a case of infidelity on the part of one Adelardus and his men and of Boso, brother of Bertilla.

42. DBer *123 (17 Nov. 919), p. 321.

43. DBer 82 (25 March 912), pp. 220–22.

44. DBer 101 (before 915), pp. 264–66: "terram juris regni nostri . . . et omnem iudiciariam potestatem . . . cum bannis, censibus et redditibus."

45. They appear together in DBer *114, 119, 121, and *123 (pp. 295, 314, 316, and 321). On the association of Odelricus and Grimaldus, see Adolf Hofmeister, "Markgrafen und Markgrafschaften im Italischen Königreich in der Zeit von Karl dem Grossen bis auf Otto den Grossen (774–962)," *MIÖG Ergänzungsband* 7 (1907): 215–435, esp. 379–81. For a more extended argument in favor of Odelricus and Grimaldus as the petitioners of DBer 101, see Rosenwein, "Family Politics."

Grimaldus commes
Ingelfredus commes
Egitingus commes
Cadolo
Sibichus episcopus

followed by others, including two more people named Grimaldus and three others named Cadolo. In short, the list seems to describe a family group. Sibico certainly was closely aligned with this kindred, perhaps even part of it: just after his name (Sibichus episcopus) came Teopertus, followed by the names Rotpern and Regimberga—the names of Grimaldus's daughters—and then yet another Rotpern.[46] Ingelfredus commes was count of Verona 913?–21; we know from a donation charter that he was Grimaldus's son and that his own son was Aitingo (the Egitingus commes of the San Salvatore confraternity book).[47]

With Sibico, therefore, we find links to Grimaldus, and with Grimaldus we return to Berta. Sibico's case, on its face isolated from Berengar's other privileges, upon closer examination nicely illustrates Berengar's policy of issuing privileges to and on behalf of an extremely close network held together by family and spiritual ties. Furthermore, as we shall see, these bonds had an affective component as well.

A Family Politics

In his book *Medieval Households,* David Herlihy argued that from about the eleventh century "a distinctive set of emotional ties links the members of the medieval family. It is not true, as has often been assumed, that medieval people were emotionally indifferent to their closest relatives, with whom in intimacy they passed their lives."[48] This "distinctive set of emotional ties" consisted of the love between husband and wife, parent

---

46. The name Immeltruda is thirteenth on the list; she, too, was one of Grimaldus's daughters. See P. S. Leicht, *Scritti vari di storia del diritto italiano,* vol. 2, pt. 2 (Milan, 1948), no. 1 (21 Nov. 927), 40–41: "Ego . . . Imeltruda honesta femina . . . per salutem et remedium anime . . . Grimoaldo genitori meo" gives property to S. Maria di Sesto in Cividale (Friuli). The document is signed by "Aitingo con . . . eiusdem femine," i.e, her nephew (see Hlawitschka, *Franken, Alemannen,* 174).

47. Andrea Gloria, ed., *Codice diplomatico Padovano dal secolo sesto a tutto l'undecimo,* Monumenti storici dalla deputazione Veneta di storia patria, vol. 2, ser. 1, Documenti (Venice 1877), 45–47, no. *29.

48. David Herlihy, *Medieval Households* (Cambridge, Mass., 1985), vi.

and child. It was presumably the result of the new insistence on mutual consent between bride and groom before marriage, of the "triumph of monogamy"[49] (which, along with the decline of household slaves, brought new intimacy to the conjugal household), and of the new emphasis on children in the patrilineal family (male children to inherit, female children to procreate).[50] But I would like to suggest that affective ties did not necessarily await these developments: we can, for example, dimly glimpse them in the documents connected with Berengar.

At first glance, it is hard to see what relevance family feeling might have had for a king whose first wife was accused of witchcraft and whose son-in-law spearheaded the groups that called rival kings into Italy. Yet even the archetypal affective family, that of the modern West, alerts us to the hatreds and vituperations that all too easily rend them.

In the face of a near absence of direct evidence of tender feelings within even the late medieval family, Herlihy ingeniously called upon the evidence of metaphors in saints' lives and mystical writings.

> [T]he evocations of motherhood, childhood, and fatherhood contained in the [mystical experiences described in the] lives must bear some correspondence with the ways in which mothers, children, and fathers were viewed in the real world. These images were designed to evoke an emotional response on the part of readers or listeners; the sentiments expressed in a devotional context must have had parallels in feelings that prevailed in the natural family, for which we have no records.[51]

The diplomas of Berengar are a far cry from mystical literature, but they, too, betray a perhaps surprising belief that bonds between family members were of supreme importance. We have no reason to imagine that Bertilla "consented" to her marriage to Berengar, but her role and title in his early concessions suggest a form of conjugal equality between the two. Berengar's gifts to his daughter and her monastery are even more telling. It is true that San Salvatore had enjoyed a long tradition of royal favor; even before Berta became its abbess Berengar had given it a gift: a little house (*mansiuncula*) at Brescia.[52] But political expediency or mili-

---

49. Ibid., 86.
50. Ibid., chaps. 4, 5.
51. Ibid., 115.
52. DBer *5 (889), pp. 28–29. On the history of the monastery and its royal privileges, see Cinzio Violante, "La chiesa bresciana nei secoli IX e X," in *Storia di Brescia*, ed. Giovanni Treccani degli Alfieri, vol. 1: *Dalle origini alla caduta della signoria*

tary emergency, which some historians have invoked to explain Berengar's grants of castles to bishops and *fideles,* cannot explain his concessions of fortifications to San Salvatore: the abbess of a convent could not be responsible for the defense of a city. How do the charters themselves justify their contents? As gifts to "Berta, most devout [*religiosissimam*] abbess of the monastery of S. Giulia [used here for the first time as the alternative name for San Salvatore] and our dear [*dilectamque*] daughter" (52 bis). As Herlihy took metaphors seriously, so we need to take seriously the seemingly formulaic vocabulary of the charters. Indeed, along the very lines of Herlihy's argument, these *formulae* were such precisely because they expressed a commonly accepted—a culturally "meaningful"—ideal. Why invoke Adalbert's status as *gener* if this made no difference? On the contrary, the charters meant to be clear: Adalbert was Berengar's "dilectissimus gener," most beloved.

As far as we know, Grimaldus was not related by blood to Berengar. But the families were closely associated. On fol. 8r of the San Salvatore book were listed, in order,

Domnus Loduicus imperator [i.e., Louis II]
Domna Ingelberga imperatrix [i.e., Queen Angilberga]
Domna. Berta abbatissa. Domna Adeleida abbatissa.

Berta was Berengar's daughter; beneath her name came the names of her ancestors, including Berengar, his brother Unruoc, and his mother and father, Everard and Gisella. Unruoc had been married to Ava, daughter of Liutfrid; her name, too, was listed, as was her father's.[53] The scribes who entered the names were not working at the same time; the page is a

Viscontea (Brescia, 1963), 1,001–27; and Suzanne F. Wemple, "S. Salvatore/S. Giulia: A Case Study in the Endowment and Patronage of a Major Female Monastery in Northern Italy," in *Women of the Medieval World: Essays in Honor of John H. Mundy,* ed. Julius Kirshner and Suzanne F. Wemple (Oxford, 1985), 85–102. See also Katherine Fischer Drew, "The Italian Monasteries of Nonantola, San Salvatore and Santa Maria Teodota in the Eighth and Ninth Centuries," *Manuscripta* 9 (1965): 131–54, esp. 134–38.

53. Hlawitschka, *Franken, Alemannen,* 221–23, esp. 223 n. 19; and Hagen Keller, "Zur Struktur der Königsherrschaft im Karolingischen und Nachkarolingischen Italien. Der 'consiliarius regis' in den italienischen königsdiplomen des 9 und 10 Jahrhunderts," *Quellen und Forschungen aus italienischen Archiven und Bibliotheken* 47 (1967): 211–12.

compilation.[54] But the scribes wanted to associate the names on the same page; we know from burials *ad sanctos* that physical placement was a powerful form of association.[55]

Nearly 30 pages separate the Louis II page from the Grimaldus page (37r). Nevertheless, there are connections that tie Grimaldus to Berengar's family by more than the important association of confraternity. In the second column of the Grimaldus page are Liutfrid and other members of his family (though not Ava); they were treated as members of the same group of relations.

There is one other connection. On fol. 42r begins a long list of oblations, headed, on fol. 42v, by Lothar, who *tradidit filiam suam domnam Gislam*. Everard appears at the top of fol. 43v handing over *his* daughter (Berengar's sister), Gisla. On the facing folio, 44r, at the top of the second column, is Grimaldus, giving away two of his own daughters. The physical parallel of the names suggests deeper associations.

Thus, we should take seriously the fact that Berengar called Grimaldus "dilectus . . . fidelis noster."[56] The affective bonds of feudal and familial relationships are chronologically parallel and may perhaps be interrelated. Taken together with the dossiers of Bertilla and Adalbert, Grimaldus's case suggests at least the powerful hold of familial metaphors and perceptions upon the political (and, inescapably, religious) activities of the tenth century. If we understand Berengar's kingship in the light of these examples, we see not "privileges addressed to the most disparate individuals," depleting and transforming the state, but a strategy in which Berengar strengthened and supported the groups that were close to him through ties of blood, both real and metaphorical.

---

54. Karl Schmid, *Kloster Hirsau und seiner Stifter*, Forschungen zur oberrheinischen Landesgeschichte, no. 9 (Freiburg im Breisgau, 1959), 83–84, 133.

55. The importance of the placement of names is, indeed, the idea behind the massive *Gruppensuchprogramm* at the University of Münster, presided over by Joachim Wollasch, Maria Hillebrandt, and Franz Neiske. On burial *ad sanctos*, see Dietrich Poeck, "Laienbegräbnisse in Cluny," *Frühmittelalterliche Studien* 15 (1981): 68–179; and Meghan McLaughlin, *Consorting with Saints: Prayer for the Dead in Early Medieval France* (Ithaca, N.Y., 1994). On the importance of order and physical proximity in general, see Heinrich Fichtenau, *Living in the Tenth Century: Mentalities and Social Orders,* trans., Patrick J. Geary (Chicago, 1991).

56. As in DBer *132 (20 Dec. 920), p. 341.

Clotild's Revenge: Politics, Kinship, and Ideology in the Merovingian Blood Feud

Stephen D. White

Introduction

Sometime after the death of the Frankish king Clovis in 511, according to Gregory of Tours, his widow Clotild, daughter of the deceased Burgundian king Chilperic, met with her three sons to instigate an attack on two of her cousins, Sigismund and his brother Godomar (III.6),[1] whose father Gundobad, Clotild's patrilateral uncle, had killed his brother Chilperic and Chilperic's wife (II.28). Addressing Chlodomer and her two other sons, Childebert I and Lothar I, Clotild declared:

> "My dear children, . . . do not give me cause to regret the fact that I have brought you up with such care. You must surely resent the wrong[2] which has been done to me. You must do all in your power to avenge the death of my mother and father." When they had listened to her appeal they set out for Burgundy. They marched their troops against Sigismund and his brother Godomar. (III.5)

The Franks defeated the Burgundians. Godomar fled and Sigismund was captured, along with his wife and children, by Chlodomer, who brought

---

1. Parenthetical references in the text and notes are to book and chapter numbers in Gregory of Tours, *Decem Libri Historiarum*, ed. B. Krusch and W. Levison, *Monumenta Germaniae Historica, Scriptores Rerum Merowingicarum*, vol. 1, pt. 1 (revised edition; Hanover/Leipzig, 1951). Translations are taken or adapted from Gregory of Tours, *The History of the Franks*, trans. Lewis Thorpe (Harmondsworth, Middlesex, 1974).

2. Throughout this essay, I use *wrong* in preference to Gregory's term *injuria* (see, e.g., III.6 [bis] and III.7).

them back as prisoners to the Orléanais. When the Frankish kings had departed, Godomar won back his kingdom. After killing Sigismund, his wife, and their children, Chlodomer attacked Godomar with support from his half brother Theuderic, who had previously married a daughter of Sigismund (III.5).[3] In the ensuing battle, Godomar's army cut off Chlodomer's head, "stuck it on a stake and raised it in the air." But the Franks recovered and drove out Godomar: "They conquered the Burgundians and took over their country." Later, Godomar won back his kingdom (III.6).[4]

Even though this conflict between the Franks and the Burgundians involved relatively large groups, was waged partly for control of territory, and presumably led to the deaths of many people who were not kin of the principals,[5] it can still be understood as a feud since it displays so many other features characteristic of this kind of process.[6] Instead of representing the deaths of Sigismund and Chlodomer and the defeat of Godomar as isolated events, Gregory of Tours's *History*[7] locates them in

3. The daughter, I assume, was born of Sigismund's first wife and was thus a full sister of Sigeric (see below).

4. On this episode see, in particular, J. M. Wallace-Hadrill, "The Bloodfeud of the Franks," *Bulletin of the John Rylands Library* 41 (1959); reprinted in J. M. Wallace-Hadrill, *The Long-Haired Kings* (Toronto, 1982), 121–47; I. N. Wood, "Clermont and Burgundy: 511–534," *Nottingham Medieval Studies* 32 (1988): 119–25; and Ian Wood, *The Merovingian Kingdoms, 450–751* (London, 1994), 43, 52–54, which appeared after the present study was substantially complete. See also Roger Collins, *Early Medieval Europe, 300–1000* (New York, 1991), 155–56; and Edward James, *The Franks* (Oxford, 1988), 85–86, 93–94.

5. In these respects the conflict differs from medieval Icelandic feuds, as analyzed and outlined in William Ian Miller, *Bloodtaking and Peacemaking: Feud, Law, and Society in Saga Iceland* (Chicago, 1990), 180–81.

6. Wallace-Hadrill treated it as a "royal feud" between "two royal kins, related by marriage but distinct and separated by a considerable distance" ("Bloodfeud," 131). The conflict exhibits most features of feuds identified by Miller (*Bloodtaking and Peacemaking*, 180–81).

7. On the *History*, see Louis Halphen, "Grégoire de Tours, historien de Clovis," in *Mélanges d'histoire du moyen âge offerts à M. Ferdinand Lot par ses amis et ses élèves* 235–44 (Paris, 1925); Wallace-Hadrill, *The Long-Haired Kings*, 49–70 and passim; Walter Goffart, "From Historiae to *Historia Francorum* and Back Again: Aspects of the Textual History of Gregory of Tours," in *Religion, Culture, and Society in the Early Middle Ages*, ed. T. F. X. Noble and J. J. Contreni (Kalamazoo, 1987), reprinted in Walter Goffart, *Rome's Fall and After* (London, 1989), 255–74; I. N. Wood, "Gregory of Tours and Clovis," *Revue Belge de philologie et d'histoire* 63 (1985): 249–72; I. N. Wood, "The Secret Histories of Gregory of Tours," *Revue Belge de philologie et d'histoire* 71 (1993): 253–70; Wood, *The Merovingian Kingdoms*, esp. 28–32; and Yitzhak Hen, "Clovis, Gregory of Tours, and Pro-Merovingian Propaganda," *Revue Belge de philologie et d'histoire* 71 (1993): 271–76.

a single narrative and suggests, as well, that participants understood them as phases in an ongoing conflict between two groups.[8] The leaders of each group were clearly recruited or identified on the basis of kinship: the Franks' attack on the Burgundians was instigated by the daughter of Gundobad's two homicide victims and led by their grandsons; and the Burgundians were led by Gundobad's sons. Notions of collective liability animated the entire conflict:[9] vengeance for the deaths of Clotild's parents was taken by their grandson on their slayer's son, Sigismund, and on Sigismund's wife and children; vengeance for Sigismund's death was taken on Chlodomer by Burgundian followers of Sigismund's brother Godomar.

The entire conflict was governed by "a notion of exchange . . . a kind of my-turn/your-turn rhythm, with offensive and defensive positions alternating after each encounter."[10] Each attack sooner or later elicited a counterattack that could be represented as an act of retaliation for a previous wrong. Chlodomer's homicides were clearly represented as vengeance killings, committed after he was charged with the task of avenging his matrilateral grandparents' deaths. Furthermore, he chose a well-known method of killing that was deemed especially heinous under Frankish law;[11] that clearly recalled the drowning of his mother's mother; and that compensated Clotild for the wrong Gundobad had previously done to her, since the deaths of Sigismund, his wife, and their children balanced the deaths of Chilperic and his wife and the exile of their children.[12] In response to Chlodomer's killings, the Burgundians marked Chlodomer's death as a vengeance killing by displaying his sev-

---

8. According to Wallace-Hadrill's "working definition," feud is: "first, the threat of hostility between kins; then the state of hostility between them; and finally, the satisfaction of their differences and a settlement on terms acceptable to both" ("Bloodfeud," 122).

9. "Feud involves collective liability. The target need not be the actual wrongdoer, nor, for that matter, need the vengeance-taker be the person most wronged" (Miller, *Bloodtaking*, 180).

10. Miller, *Bloodtaking*, 181.

11. On the unusually high compensation to be paid for *mathleodi* (killing by throwing down a well or holding under water), see *The Laws of the Salian Franks*, trans. with an introduction by Katherine Fisher Drew (Philadelphia, 1981), 104–5, 180–81. For archaeological evidence bearing on this method of killing or disposing of dead bodies, see, e.g., P. Schröter, "Skelettreste aus zei römischen Menschenopfer bei den Germanen der Kaiserzeit," *Das Archäoloqische Jahr in Bayern* (1984): 118–20. I thank Thomas S. Burns for this reference.

12. On keeping score in feuds, see Miller, *Bloodtaking*, 181.

ered head on a stake to the Franks.[13] Indeed, balanced exchange was explicitly invoked and endorsed as the principle underlying divine vengeance by St. Avitus. After telling Chlodomer that if he showed respect to God by sparing his prisoners the Lord would support him, the saint then warned him that if he killed his prisoners, "you will fall into the hands of your enemies and you will suffer a fate similar to theirs. Whatever you do to Sigismund and his wife and children, the same will be done to you, your wife, and your sons" (III.6). Since Gregory's narrative later shows that the saint's prophecy about how God would respond to Chlodomer's killings was partially fulfilled by the subsequent killings of Chlodomer (III.6) and two of his sons,[14] it appears that for Gregory "God's vengeance is of the same nature as that of any head of a family or warband."[15]

Although many features of the Frankish-Burgundian conflict, as Gregory narrates it, become readily comprehensible if we treat it as a feud, others remain puzzling, partly because Gregory of Tours never explicates them fully and may have misrepresented the episode[16] and partly because they raise questions that general models of feuding are not designed to answer. In spite of its errors and inaccuracies, Gregory's account of the feud is worth analyzing closely not only because it provides evidence about how he thought feuds were carried on but also because it poses problems of interpretation that frequently arise in accounts of feuds but that historians rarely confront. First, because the feud started so long after the killings it was meant to avenge[17] that it cannot have been initi-

---

13. See Wallace-Hadrill, "Bloodfeud," 131–32.

14. Two of Chlodomer's children were killed by Lothar; the third escaped and became a priest. After his death his widow Guntheoc married Lothar (see below).

15. Wallace-Hadrill, "Bloodfeud," 127. Gregory, he asserts, sees divine vengeance as "nothing less than God's own feud in support of his servants, who have no other kin. God will avenge crimes specially heinous in the Church's eyes—parricide, for example, crimes within the family generally and crimes involving all who lack natural protectors. The agent may be God himself directly intervening to strike down the culprit (for instance with sickness) or it may be a human agent, [such] as the king. . . . He strikes to kill, to avenge insult—to himself, to his children or to his property. The Frankish churchmen cannot in any other way see *ultio divina* in a society dominated by the bloodfeud."

16. See Wood, "Clermont and Burgundy," esp. 122–25; and Wood, "Gregory of Tours," 253–56.

17. It commenced about thirty years later according to Wood ("Gregory of Tours," 253).

ated in "hot blood,"[18] and because it eventually led to Frankish territorial conquests as well as vengeance killings, it is worth asking what
motives or strategic considerations were actually involved in initiating it
at this particular moment.[19] Why did the feud break out when it did?
Since Clotild could have invoked her stated rationale for the attack *any*
time after her parents died, did she do so at this time because she finally
had the practical means to avenge her parents' deaths, because she and
her sons needed a pretext for launching an attack on the Burgundians
that they had other grounds for initiating, or because she had other reasons for considering this an opportune time for waging a feud? If revenge
was the real motive for the attack, why wasn't it invoked more consistently by Frankish participants such as Chlodomer, who justified his
killings by explaining that they made good military sense? If Clotild's
desire to avenge her parents was simply a pretext for attacking people
whom she and her sons had other reasons to attack, was the conflict she
initiated with the Burgundians really a feud rather than a war?[20]

Second, Theuderic's belated decision to support the Franks in a feud
between his half brothers and his Burgundian affine Sigismund also raises
many interrelated questions about timing, motives, and strategy.[21] Why,
for example, did Chlodomer summon Theuderic after Sigismund was
dead and not before? Why did he summon him at all? Why didn't Theuderic support the Franks from the very beginning of the feud? Absent from
his stepmother's meeting with his half brothers, which postdated his marriage to Sigismund's daughter (III.5), Theuderic played no part in the
early phases of the feud. Why did he join it at all, instead of remaining
outside it or supporting Godomar in avenging "the wrong done to his

---

18. On revenge killings committed in "hot blood," see Wallace-Hadrill, "Bloodfeud," 124 25.

19. Wood's solution to the problem is to assume that the "vengeance motif" is
Gregory's interpolation ("Gregory of Tours," 253, 255; "Clermont and Burgundy,"
122).

20. To show that historians have exaggerated the importance of feuding in early
medieval Europe, Peter Sawyer argues, inter alia, that the Franks' conflicts with the
Burgundians, Thuringians, and Visigoths were wars not feuds ("The Bloodfeud in
Fact and Fiction," *Tradition og Historie-Skrivning, Acta Jutlandica,* 63, Humanistisk
serie, no. 61 [1987]: 29).

21. If Wood is right to contest "Gregory's belief that Theuderic supported
Chlodomer" ("Clermont and Burgundy," 122), then explaining this alliance disap-
pears as a problem in Frankish history but not as a problem in the history of representations of feuding.

father-in-law" Sigismund (III.6)?[22] If Theuderic joined Chlodomer against Godomar because his obligation to support his Frankish half brothers outweighed his duty to avenge his father-in-law and his duty to support his Burgundian wife and affines, why didn't he support the Franks earlier, joining their feud immediately? Did he have other reasons for finally allying himself with the Franks against the Burgundians?

Finally, why, in Gregory's estimation, did God participate in the Frankish-Burgundian feud only intermittently and ambiguously, implicating himself only obliquely in certain acts of Frankish revenge against the Burgundians and even taking vengeance on the Franks for one of their acts of vengeance, namely, Chlodomer's killings? In separate passages, Gregory represents Sigismund and his brother Godomar, respectively, as targets of divine vengeance. But, by condemning Chlodomer's killings through the mouth of St. Avitus and thereby treating them as wrongs that God would avenge, Gregory also implicated God not only in the vengeance killing of Chlodomer by the Burgundians but in the subsequent killings of Chlodomer's sons by their patrilateral uncles, Lothar and Childebert. How, then, did Gregory understand the relationship between God's vengeance and the vengeance taken by the Franks in their feud with the Burgundians? Why, in this particular feud, did God support the Franks only intermittently, withholding from them the full support he had previously given them in wars waged by Clovis?[23]

These questions about feuding practices and strategy, including God's, cannot be answered by consulting general models, which of necessity privilege selected features and functions of feuding. By representing the feud as being relatively rare among the Franks,[24] by treating it primarily as a sanction behind "every feud settlement,"[25] and by explaining why feuds were likely to be settled,[26] structuralist-functionalist models of

---

22. By using *vindicare* and *injuria* soon after using the same words in recounting Clotild's speech to her sons, Gregory pointedly contrasts Theuderic's behavior with that of Clotild's sons, who did avenge a wrong to a relative.

23. See, e.g., II.40.

24. "It must be wide of the mark to conceive of the Franks being at all often engaged in major kin-warfare" (Wallace-Hadrill, "Bloodfeud," 126).

25. Wallace-Hadrill, "Bloodfeud," 126.

26. "[T]he mere elaboration and interdependence of kin-groups may ensure a kind of immobility. Common blood and propinquity will always make for settlement" (Wallace-Hadrill, "Bloodfeud," 125–26). See also Alexander Callendar Murray, *Ger-*

feuding[27] illuminate the Frankish-Burgundian feud mainly by identifying pressures against feuding that were evidently overcome in this particular case. Models of the feud that represent it as an exchange of retaliatory attacks between hostile groups[28] do not explain, among other things, the timing of individual moves in a feud, such as Clotild's meeting with her sons or Chlodomer's summons of Theuderic. Nor do they show how participants in feuds could not only achieve vengeance but also serve other strategic purposes such as territorial conquest or the reinvention of kinship groups. Models representing the feud as a method of competing for scarce resources[29] do not leave much room for the multiple strategic purposes that the Frankish-Burgundian feud may have served.

Juridical models are no more useful for the purpose of answering our specific questions about the Frankish-Burgundian feud. If we treat the feud as a legal institution,[30] which was based on a generally recognized "obligation to participate in interkindred feuds on behalf of one's kin"[31] and was also limited by "a special 'peace' that made violent conflict within the clan a crime for which no compensation or atonement could be made,"[32] we can both see how the Franks' feud with the Burgundians could have been justified and identify a desire to avenge wrongs to Clotild as a possible motive for it. But the model does not tell us why the wrong Clotild suffered was avenged through feud, while other wrongs were not; why the feud started when it did; or what strategic considerations other than vengeance were incorporated into it. Moreover, although the model indicates that the "kin" of those wronged by Chilperic were obliged to avenge this wrong, and could justifiably do so

manic Kinship Structure: Studies in Law and Society in Antiquity and the Early Middle Ages, Pontifical Institute of Medieval Studies: Studies and Texts, vol. 65 (Toronto, 1983), 137.

27. A model of this kind underlies the discussion of feuding in Edward James, *The Origins of France: From Clovis to the Capetians, 500–1000* (London, 1982), 87–88, 92.

28. A model of this kind could be constructed out of Miller's deliberately open-ended discussion of feuding (see *Bloodtaking*, 180–81).

29. See, for example, E. L. Peters's foreword to Jacob Black-Michaud, *Feuding Societies* [also published under the title *Cohesive Force*] (Oxford, 1975), xxii, xxvi, xxvii.

30. "The tribal law did not so much forbid or discourage interclan violence as it set the rules according to which these feuds were to be carried on" (Patrick J. Geary, *Before France and Germany: The Creation and Transformation of the Merovingian World* [New York, 1988], 54).

31. Geary, *Before France and Germany*, 52. See also James, *Origins of France*, 87, 88; and James, *The Franks*, 172.

32. Geary, *Before France and Germany*, 52.

against Chilperic's kin, it does not specify these kin precisely or explain why some of them joined the feud while others did not. Nor does it explain how the main participants on the Frankish side, including Theuderic as well as Clotild and her sons, negotiated the problem of feuding with a group to whom they were linked by kinship and/or marriage. Treating feuding practices as the product of obedience to determinate rules,[33] juridical models do not fully explain the role played in feuds by people such as Theuderic, who, depending on how the "rules" were interpreted, could have justifiably joined either side in the feud or avoided participation in it altogether. Treating the conduct of the feud as equally rule-bound,[34] juridical models cannot explain how killings such as the ones committed by Chlodomer could be interpreted *either* as fitting acts of revenge or as blatant violations of feuding norms. Finally, because conventional models represent the feud primarily as a political process, rather than as an ideological schema for interpreting politics, they provide no way of analyzing either the retrospective narratives of feuds that observers such as Gregory constructed or the stories about feuds that participants such as Clotild told and that were indispensable to the feuding process.

To answer our questions about why the Frankish-Burgundian feud proceeded as it did when it did and what roles in it Gregory assigned to God, we need to see how it intersected with other kinds of political processes that are necessarily excluded from general models of feuding. We also need to view the Merovingian feud not just as a political process but also as a coherent yet flexible cultural schema for organizing political practices and imagining politics. Without the schema, no feud could have taken place. This approach is both facilitated and justified by Gregory's story of the feud,[35] which he carefully linked to other story lines: one about Frankish-Burgundian relations down to the time of the Frankish conquest of Burgundy in 534; another about power struggles within the Frankish royal family after Clovis's death in 511; and a third about

---

33. On "the fallacies of the rule" as a method of explaining practices, see Pierre Bourdieu, *Outline of a Theory of Practice*, trans. Richard Nice (Cambridge, 1977), 22–30.

34. See, e.g., the passage quoted above in note 30.

35. In the preface to book III of his *History*, Gregory cites Godomar's loss of his homeland, inter alia, as proof that heretics would suffer divine punishment. Just before narrating the Frankish-Burgundian feud, he concludes the story about Sigismund's murder of his own son with the cryptic remark that Theuderic's marriage to Sigismund's daughter constituted an act of divine vengeance against Sigismund (III.5).

God's feuds with Arians and others meriting divine vengeance. An examination of these different story lines and their interrelationships provides a framework of addressing our questions about the Frankish-Burgundian feud. It also shows that feuding ideology was so capacious and manipulable and that feuding practices could incorporate so many different strategic considerations and goals other than revenge that the Merovingian feud could have constituted "one of the key structures in which the competition for power, the struggle for dominance, [was] played out."[36] Although this view of the Merovingian feud will be developed mainly through a study of the Frankish-Burgundian conflict, its applicability to several other Frankish feuds will be discussed in passing.

Other Story Lines

Having considered Gregory's account of the Frankish-Burgundian feud, we now need to examine the other stories with which he associated it.

Franks and Burgundians

In Gregory's *History,* the feud fits into a longer story about Frankish-Burgundian relations from Clovis's reign down through the definitive Frankish conquest of the 530s. The main events in the story are as follows.

1. After killing his brother Chilperic and Chilperic's wife and exiling their daughters, Clotild and Chroma, Gundobad acquiesced in Clovis's marriage to Clotild (II.28).
2. In return for several promises that were never honored, Clovis helped Godigisel to defeat Gundobad (II.32).
3. After agreeing to pay an annual tribute to Clovis, who had withdrawn from Burgundy, and then paying for only one year, Gundobad killed Godigisel, became sole ruler of the Burgundians (II.33), and converted from Arianism to orthodoxy without, however, espousing the Trinity publicly (II.34).
4. Upon the death of Gundobad, his son Sigismund inherited the kingdom and, at the urging of his second wife, killed Sigeric, his

---

36. Miller, *Bloodtaking,* 181; see also 179.

son by his first wife. Sigismund's daughter by his first wife then married Clovis's son Theuderic (III.5).

5. The feud with the Burgundians instigated by Clotild left Godomar in control of his kingdom (III.6).

6. Much later, Lothar and Childebert put Godomar to flight and conquered "the whole of Burgundy," doing so without support from Theuderic, who had refused to join them (III.11).

This factitious chronicle reveals that the Frankish-Burgundian feud immediately followed Theuderic's marriage to Sigismund's daughter and permanently transformed Frankish-Burgundian relations, as the Franks now expanded their power into Burgundy by trying to conquer it militarily, and not, as heretofore, by supporting one Burgundian faction against another in return for tribute and/or limited territorial control. Although the question of how the marriage, the feud, and the political transformation were connected can be fully explored only by considering internal Frankish politics, as well as the Franks' relations with the Burgundians and other peoples, several points are clear. First, Gregory posited a connection between the marriage and the feud not only by treating them as successive events in his story but also by linking them in another way that has to be decoded. Having represented Theuderic's marriage to Sigismund's daughter as an act of divine vengeance on Sigismund for killing his own son Sigeric,[37] Gregory then shows that in the feud waged to avenge killings committed by Sigismund's father, Sigismund was killed, along with his second wife and their children, and was not avenged by his son-in-law Theuderic. Gregory's narrative remains unintelligible unless we assume that the marriage had dire—and divinely sanctioned—consequences for Sigismund. The marriage, we can assume, somehow led to Sigismund's death. Since the only way of linking the marriage and the death is to treat the cause of the death—that is, the feud—as a consequence of the marriage, we must assume that, in Gregory's estimation, the marriage triggered the feud, even though the Franks and God did not posit the same kind of relationship between the two events.

Whereas Clotild represented the attack on the Burgundians simply as

---

37. After describing Sigismund's killing of Sigeric and the penance he did for it, Gregory concludes chapter 5 of book III by noting that "[Sigismund] returned to Lyons with divine vengeance (*ultione divina*) following in his tracks. King Theuderic married his daughter" (III.5).

a means of avenging the killings of her parents committed long ago by Sigismund's father,[38] the participants could have understood it, as Gregory did, as a response to Theuderic's recent marriage to Sigismund's daughter. The marriage posed an immediate threat to Clotild and her sons because, sooner or later, it could have facilitated interventions in their own territories by the Burgundians and because it immediately enhanced the power of Theuderic, whose power already threatened that of his half brothers and stepmother.[39] Of the four sons of Clovis who divided his kingdom (III.1), Theuderic was in the best position to dominate the others, since he was the eldest, the only one with an adult heir by a previous marriage (see III.3), and the only one not born of Clotild. As Gregory shows, Theuderic was, in fact, the first of Clovis's sons to assert his power after 511.[40]

Clotild's feud met the threats posed by Theuderic's alliance with Sigismund with counterthreats against both of them, doing so by dramatically transforming Frankish-Burgundian relations into a state of feud. Putting direct military pressure on Sigismund by targeting him for revenge and his kingdom for conquest, the feud also threatened to split Sigismund's alliance with Theuderic, who was forced to choose among several potentially dangerous strategies. Whether Theuderic supported Sigismund or his half brothers, he would incur the wrath and enmity of a former ally. In theory, at least, he was well positioned to mediate between the Franks

---

38. Gregory's account of Clotild's meeting with her sons can be read in the light of anthropological studies showing how "what may have initially been accepted as an accidental death can quite well blossom after a generation or two in the minds of the victim's kin into a deliberately gory atrocity seen as the first step in an eternal feud" (Black-Michaud, *Feuding Societies*, 19, summarizing E. L. Peters's findings).

39. Viewed in the context of previous relations between Franks and Burgundians, the marriage replicated both the short-term practices and a long-term political strategy of infiltration (as opposed to confrontation) that Theuderic's father Clovis had used when trying to expand his power into Burgundy. In the short run, Clovis gained support within Burgundy through his alliances, first with Godigisel, later with Gundobad, and, perhaps, through his marriage to Clotild. These alliances also constituted elements in a longer-term strategy of infiltration because they sooner or later gave Clovis grounds for feuding not only with the Burgundian enemies of his Burgundian allies but with those Burgundian allies whom he could represent as having betrayed him. Theuderic's marriage to Sigismund's daughter could have had the same outcome.

40. Previously, "Clovis sent . . . Theuderic through Albi and the town of Rodez to Clermont-Ferrand. As he moved forward Theuderic subjected to his father's rule all the towns which lay between the two frontiers of the Goths and the Burgundians" (II.37). Before marrying Sigismund's daughter, Theuderic had acted as a political patron in Tours (III.2), fought against Danish invaders (III.3), and intervened in

and the Burgundians.⁴¹ But this strategy would have involved a vast expenditure of political capital and had little chance of success. Any effort to attain even a short-term truce could have been construed as a duplicitous and/or cowardly refusal to provide support in a feud. By withholding such support from either party, he ran the twin risks of incurring the anger of both and of losing the support of his own followers, whom Gregory later represents as goading him into military action.⁴² In any case, Theuderic showed no interest in making peace. After a period of nonparticipation, and perhaps indecision, Theuderic was drawn into Clotild's faction by Chlodomer's summons. Leaving it to the troops following his wife's father's brother Godomar to avenge his father-in-law, Theuderic participated in the conquest of their territory by his half brothers. In this way, Clotild's vengeance raid reconfigured Frankish-Burgundian relations in a way that grew out of earlier political strategies (since it depended on a kinship connection between the Franks and the Burgundians) but that served two new political purposes. In the short run, it met the threats posed by Theuderic's marriage to Sigismund's daughter, which continued an earlier style of Frankish-Burgundian relations. In the long run, it laid the basis for the conquest of Burgundy.

Viewed as a means of avenging a wrong, transforming the Franks' relations with a neighboring kingdom, and countering a seemingly unrelated political threat, the Frankish-Burgundian feud resembles the feud that Theuderic later initiated with the Thuringians. After Hermanfrid had killed his brother Berthar, he was shamed by his wife Amalaberg into attacking his other brother Baderic so that he could become sole ruler of Thuringia. To secure support for this undertaking, Hermanfrid first promised half the kingdom to Theuderic, who helped him defeat Baderic. Later, however, Hermanfrid broke his promise to Theuderic, creating "great enmity between the two kings" (III.4). Unable to "forget the wrongs done to him by Hermanfrid," Theuderic decided to attack him, doing so just after Clotild had adopted the sons of the deceased Chlodomer and after Lothar had married Chlodomer's widow (III.6). To

---

Thuringian politics by allying himself with King Hermanfrid (III.4). Hermanfrid had previously killed his brother Berthar in battle and later killed his other brother, Baderic, at the instigation of his wife and with help from Theuderic, whom he later betrayed (III.4).

41. On mediation by someone linked to both sides in a feud, see, e.g., Miller, *Bloodtaking and Peacemaking*, 261–67.

42. See below.

secure support for this attack, Theuderic promised "his brother" Lothar "a share in the booty" and told his own men that they should feel resentment against the Thuringians "both because of the wrong done to me [by Hermanfrid] and for the slaughter of your own kin" in a previous episode, which Theuderic then described in lurid detail.[43] Theuderic's force then massacred many Thuringians, "took over the country and subjected it to their own rule" (III.7). Later, Theuderic killed Hermanfrid (III.8). Like Clotild's feud with her Burgundian kin, Theuderic's feud with the Thuringians achieved more than revenge for old wrongs. It transformed Frankish relations with another kingdom, into which the Franks now expanded their power militarily rather than through the policy of subversion that Theuderic, like Clovis, had followed by allying himself with one faction in a neighboring kingdom against another. At the same time, by securing Lothar's support for his feud with the Thuringians, Theuderic reactivated a kinship connection with the Frankish royal house from which he had, in a sense, been excluded by Clotild's adoption of Chlodomer's sons and Lothar's marriage to Chlodomer's widow.

Like Theuderic's feud with the Thuringians and Clotild's feud with the Burgundians, Childebert I's feud with the Visigothic king Amalric served multiple political purposes. It, too, transformed the Franks' relations with another kingdom and constituted a response to an event that was not openly represented as its cause. After receiving the younger Clotild in marriage from her brothers, Clovis's four sons (III.1), Amalric mistreated her because she was a Catholic not an Arian. "Finally he struck her with such violence that she sent to her brother [Childebert] a towel stained with her own blood." Greatly moved, Childebert "left immediately for Spain," where a soldier of his killed Amalric. He "planned to take his sister home with him and . . . carry off a large mass of treasure" (III.10). Although this feud, like the ones waged by Clotild and Theuderic, was meant to avenge a wrong to a relative, it, too, served other political purposes, as we can see by considering once more the crucial issue of timing. In introducing the feud, Gregory went out of his way to note that Childebert left Clermont-Ferrand for Spain to support his sister Clotild only after he was certain that Theuderic had returned safely from Thuringia (III.10). The news about Theuderic was important since a false rumor

---

43. Just as Clotild tells her sons that they should resent (*indignate*) a wrong (*injuriam*) that she had suffered (III.6), so Theuderic tells his men to resent (*indignamini*) a wrong (*injuriam*) that he had suffered (III.7).

about Theuderic's death in Thuringia had led a senator of Clermont to help Childebert enter this city of Theuderic's. Childebert's subsequent expedition to Spain can thus be interpreted not just as a vengeance raid but as a means of escaping from, and securing compensation for, a failed political undertaking.

Although the three feuds just considered were all meant to avenge wrongs, each of them served at least one other tactical or strategic purpose, which was never openly acknowledged and could not necessarily have been achieved if the feud had been waged at another time. By feuding with the Burgundians, the Franks not only avenged the deaths of Clotild's parents but also put political pressure on Theuderic and made the Burgundians into enemies to be conquered. By attacking Amalric, Childebert did more than avenge the dishonor suffered by his sister. By transforming an ally of the Franks into a target for revenge, the feud provided Childebert and his men with an enemy to plunder just when he needed to extricate himself from a humiliating position in Clermont-Ferrand. After initially trying to undermine the Thuringian kingdom by allying himself with Hermanfrid against Baderic, Theuderic construed Hermanfrid's treachery as a wrong that he could avenge, with support from Lothar, by conquering Thuringia at a time when he needed to reactivate his links to the Frankish royal family. Waging a feud was thus a way of making enemies at a moment when having them was politically useful.

The Frankish Royal Family

We now need to consider how the same process of feuding also served as a means of reinventing friendship with kin and followers. As the preceding discussion implies, Gregory locates Clotild's feud not only in the history of Frankish-Burgundian relations, but also in another narrative concerned with internal Frankish politics. Although the second story line features civil war and intrafamilial conflict among Frankish leaders such as Theuderic and Lothar, it also describes successive alliances that these same leaders forged as they competed for power both inside and outside the kingdom. The early phases of the story run as follows.

1. After Clovis's death, his four sons Theuderic, Chlodomer, Childebert, and Lothar divided his kingdom equally (III.1), while his widow Clotild's political position remained uncertain.

2. Clovis's four sons gave their sister, the younger Clotild, in marriage to the Visigothic king Amalric, son of Alaric (III.1).

3. Acting independently of Clotild and her three sons but supported by his own son Theudebert (see III.1), Theuderic intervened in Tours (III.2), in coastal regions of his kingdom (III.3), and in Thuringia (III.4).

4. Theuderic married a daughter of Sigismund's by his first wife (III.5).

5. Clotild persuaded Chlodomer and her other two sons to avenge the deaths of her parents by attacking the Burgundians, who were led by Sigismund and his brother Godomar (III.6).

6. Sigismund, his second wife, and their children were killed by Chlodomer (III.6).

7. Chlodomer summoned Theuderic, who joined him in attacking Godomar (III.6).

8. Godomar's men killed Chlodomer (III.6).

9. Lothar married Chlodomer's widow, while Clotild took Chlodomer's sons—Theudovald, Gunthar, and Chlodovald (whom St. Avitus had marked as targets for vengeance)—into her household and brought them up (III.6), just as she had brought up their father and his brothers (III.6).

10. Lothar and Childebert killed Theudovald and Gunther and tried to kill Chlodovald, who became a priest (III.18).

Instead of rejecting all claims of kinship and engaging as isolated individuals in wars of all against all, Clotild and Clovis's descendants selectively used the idioms of kinship to organize themselves successively into different alliances, which included some of their kin and excluded others. The claims to kinship on which such alliances were based could not be deduced and enforced simply by reference to genealogical position,[44] as we can see by considering the attack by Clotild's sons on their mother's father's brother's sons, Theuderic's failure to avenge his father-in-law, and many other episodes in Gregory's *History* in which kin either failed to support kin or even attacked each other. Kinship claims had to be activated, as they were, for example, by Clotild's speech to her sons, by Chlodomer's summons of his half brother Theuderic, and by the bloody

---

44. According to Murray, "the vengeance group . . . is best seen not as a strict kin group at all but as a kindred-based group of interested relatives, friends, and dependents" (*Germanic Kinship*, 136).

token the younger Clotild sent to Childebert.[45] Although the activation of a kinship claim could take many different forms, it sometimes involved an effort by the claimant to engage the other's sense of honor while constructing "honor" in such a way as to suggest that the pursuit of it might yield practical advantages to the pursuer.[46] The successful activation of a kinship claim for one purpose did not insure that the claim could later be reactivated for another. But it still kept the claim "in working order."[47]

Since the Franks' feud with the Burgundians was waged by two overlapping kin groups—one composed of Clotild and her three sons and the other composed of Chlodomer and Theuderic—it provided each of them with occasions for redefining his or her kinship identity in such a way as to renegotiate political relations with the others. Consider, first, the different kinship identities assumed, successively, by Clotild's sons and the political claims associated with those identities. When Chlodomer, Childebert, Lothar, and Theuderic inherited their respective kingdoms and later gave their sister Clotild in marriage to Alaric, each assumed the identity of a son of Clovis without regard to the fact that they were not all born of the same mother. However, the difference between Theuderic's genealogical position and that of Clovis's other three sons was soon manifested when Theuderic, sometimes supported by his son Theudebert, exercised political power independently of his brothers and when he independently allied himself by marriage with Sigismund. The absence of full brotherhood between Theuderic and Clovis's three other sons took on heightened political significance when the latter, now identified as sons of Clotild, not Clovis, sought to avenge the deaths of Chilperic and Chilperic's wife by feuding with a group led by the father of Sigismund's wife. In this feud Chlodomer, Childebert, and Lothar enacted their common brotherhood, their common tie to Clotild and her parents, and their common claim to avenge their matrilateral grandparents by fighting the Burgundians. They also distanced themselves, for the time

---

45. Before Theuderic could feud with the Thuringians, his followers had to give him their support, which he claimed partly by invoking their dead kin's claim on them (III.7). On methods of imposing or activating an obligation to take vengeance, see William Ian Miller, "Choosing the Avenger: Some Aspects of Bloodfeud in Medieval Iceland and England," *Law and History Review* 1 (1983): 159–204.

46. Miller's recent discussion of honor in medieval Iceland is instructive for other medieval European societies. See William Ian Miller, *Humiliation* (Ithaca, N.Y., 1993), esp. 93–130.

47. See Bourdieu, *Outline*, 35, where "kinship relationships" are represented as "something people make, and with which they *do* something" (author's italics).

being, from Theuderic, who was now the son-in-law of the son of their maternal grandfather's slayer, and they completely disavowed all kinship with their mother's father's brother's sons,[48] Sigismund and Godomar, so that when Chlodomer killed Sigismund he was not committing an intrafamilial killing.

Viewed from the perspective of both kinship identity and associated claims to support from kin, the Frankish-Burgundian feud held different meanings for Theuderic than it did for Clovis's other sons, and these meanings changed as the feud progressed through several different phases. Initially, Clotild's decision to seek vengeance for the deaths of her parents by initiating an attack on Sigismund and Godomar placed Theuderic in a tricky position because it provided an occasion for activating at least three different kinship claims on him, each of which involved a different way of construing his kinship identity. Even though Theuderic was not descended from Chilperic, the Franks could still have claimed his support in their feud, as Chlodomer eventually did, because he was the brother of Clotild's sons. Because Theuderic was the husband of a daughter of Sigismund, the Burgundians, too, had a claim on his support, as Gregory implied by noting that Theuderic later failed to avenge his father-in-law. Finally, because Theuderic was the husband of the sister of Sigismund's victim, Sigeric, he could have been charged with the duty of taking vengeance against his own father-in-law. Like his brothers, he was thus a potential enemy of Sigismund, though for different reasons. None of these conflicting kinship claims on Theuderic, however, was activated during the early stages of the feud. Perhaps they were understood to cancel each other out. Perhaps Theuderic himself had no political interest in privileging any one of them over the others. In any case he simply remained outside the feud until Sigismund was dead, at which point he accepted Chlodomer's summons to fight Godomar instead of trying to avenge Sigismund by fighting on the other side.

Theuderic's position in the feud changed after Chlodomer first killed Sigismund, Sigismund's second wife, and their children and then secured Theuderic's support against Godomar.[49] But the transformation was open to different interpretations, depending on how Theuderic's kinship

---

48. The physical distance separating the Franks from the Burgundians must have facilitated this process, though it did not necessitate it.

49. Because the killing of Sigeric would not have served the purposes of Sigismund's second wife if Sigismund had had other surviving sons by his first wife, I assume that the children killed in the Orléanais were born of the second wife.

identity was construed. We can imagine him as leaving his father-in-law unavenged and following his father-in-law's slayer against his father-in-law's brother. We can think of him as supporting his brother and fellow-Frank against a Burgundian leader with whom he had had an indirect, affinal, genealogical connection that had never been activated and was totally severed when Sigismund died. Finally, if we think of Theuderic as Sigeric's brother-in-law and as the brother of Chlodomer, we can imagine him as participating vicariously and retrospectively in the vengeance taken for Sigeric's death on Sigeric's slayer, on the instigator of the slaying, and on their children. By joining in Chlodomer's attack on Godomar, Theuderic chose to incorporate himself into the second script and possibly into the third as well. Once again, he was a brother of at least one of Clotild's sons.

Clotild's participation in the feud is also worth analyzing in terms of both kinship identity and the formation of kinship groups because it involved efforts not just to avenge an old wrong but also to exercise political power by manipulating the idioms of kinship. Her meeting with Chlodomer and his brothers activated and validated her kinship claims on each of them while separating them from their half brother Theuderic, who was not her son. Having lost, through Clovis's death, her status as the wife of a Frankish ruler, she could use the feud to reinvent herself, so to speak, as the mother of three Frankish rulers and as the daughter of the Burgundian Chilperic. Later, after her son Chlodomer had been killed to avenge a killing that he had committed to avenge a wrong against her, she assumed the identity of foster mother, or even mother, to his three children.

The activation of these kinship claims and kinship identities through the mediation of the Frankish-Burgundian feud did not, of course, unite Clotild and Clovis's descendants into an enduring political alliance. But it still had implications for subsequent Frankish history, as Gregory narrates it. After Chlodomer's death, the kinship tie with Clotild that he had previously acknowledged most dramatically by killing Sigismund was, in a sense, perpetuated when they entered their father's mother's household, where they were treated so affectionately that their father's brother Childebert thought they were entering the line of succession (III.18). Childebert's fears are understandable if we assume that Clotild's adoption of Chlodomer's children and the favor she subsequently showed them were methods of reasserting an identity as the mother of Frankish kings that she had previously enacted by instigating the Frankish-Burgundian feud. Although the alliance among Clovis's descendants forged in that feud was not reproduced subsequently, several of the kinship claims that were activated in it did not entirely lapse. Lothar supported Theuderic in the latter's feud with the Thuringians (III.7), and, in association with Childebert, he conquered the Burgundians (III.11) and killed Chlodomer's children (III.18). Theuderic and Childebert made a treaty together (III.15) and later marched against Lothar (III.28).

Although Gregory says nothing about how the Frankish leaders recruited followers for their raids into Burgundy, his references to the plunder taken in feuds suggest that they used feuding as a means of maintaining ties with followers as well as with kin. This point is directly confirmed by Gregory's account of Theuderic's feud with the men of his own city of Clermont—a story that also shows how a feud could be triggered by events unrelated to the feud's ostensible cause. By initiating a feud in which he licensed his men to take plunder, Theuderic did more than take vengeance on a community whose leaders, he feared, would betray him. He retained control over followers who had threatened to desert him when he refused to support Lothar and Childebert's attack on Burgundy. By feuding with the men of Clermont, Theuderic could achieve the second goal, as well as the first, because, as he explained to his men, the feud would provide them with an opportunity to take as much plunder as they might have taken in Burgundy (III.11). By ravaging the region around Clermont (III.12), Theuderic gained political independence from his brothers, avoided involvement in a war against the Burgundians, retained control over his men, acquired a large stock of plunder for himself, reasserted his power in an important region, and avenged the treachery of some troublesome enemies. In their feud with the Burgundians, the Franks achieved something similar.

The conclusion to be drawn from these examples of intrafamilial alliance—which can be matched by numerous examples of intrafamilial treachery—is not, of course, that kinship claims were regularly respected by Frankish leaders but rather that, under certain circumstances, such claims could be effectively activated in ways that were thinkable only if the claims and the identities associated with them had been kept in working order. Feuding was one way of keeping them so.[50]

---

50. In considering how Clotild, her sons, and Theuderic manipulated their own kinship identities for political purposes, it is important to keep in mind that, instead of simply promoting so-called family solidarity, claims to kinship identity could also engender conflict because claiming kinship with a person, living or dead, was a means of claiming that person's enemies as one's own. It was a way of opting into a feud.

God's Vengeance

Although God participated in the Frankish-Burgundian feud, his role in it was even more ambiguous than that of Theuderic, because, instead of fully allying himself with either party to the feud, he used both parties as instruments of different kinds of vengeance. First, since the feud enabled God to take vengeance on those who had betrayed him and his kin (i.e., the Trinity) by espousing Arianism, he sometimes appears in the feud as the enemy of the Burgundians, using the Franks as an instrument of his vengeance. Before treating Godomar's loss of his kingdom as part of the Frankish-Burgundian feud (III.6), Gregory had cited the same event as an example of how God took vengeance on his enemies and supported his friends. He first noted that, whereas Clovis, "who believed in the Trinity, crushed heretics with divine help and enlarged his dominions to include all Gaul," the Visigothic king Alaric, "who refused to accept the Trinity, was therefore deprived of his kingship, his subjects and, what is more important, the life hereafter" (III.pref.). As further proof that God gave little to heretics and took what they had from them, Gregory then cited the fates of Godigisel, Gundobad, and Godomar, who "lost their home-land and their souls at one and the same moment" (III.pref.).[51] More-over, if Theuderic's marriage to Sigismund's daughter could be repre-sented as an act of divine vengeance against Sigismund because it triggered a feud in which Sigismund, his second wife, and their children were killed, then God must have used Chlodomer as an instrument of divine vengeance against those responsible for killing Sigeric.[52] Never-theless, because God, as represented by St. Avitus, clearly condemned Chlodomer's killings and treated them as wrongs demanding divine vengeance on Chlodomer and his kin, God used the Burgundians as instruments of his own vengeance when they avenged Sigismund by killing Chlodomer and later used Chlodomer's brothers, Lothar and Childebert, for the same purpose when, for their own reasons, they killed Chlodomer's sons.

Although Gregory twice implicated God in the Frankish-Burgundian

---

51. Gregory had previously shown that the Burgundians were appropriate targets for divine vengeance by first noting their belief in the Arian heresy (II.9) and then iden-tifying King Gundioc—the father of Gundobad, Godigisel, Childeric, and Gundo-mar—as a kinsman of the Gothic king Athanaric, who persecuted Christians (II.28).

52. The vengeance was appropriate, moreover, because Chlodomer's victims included not only Sigismund but also his second wife and her children.

feud, first by representing Godomar's loss of his kingdom as an act of divine vengeance and then by indicating that Sigismund became a target for divine vengeance by killing Sigeric, the *History* does not treat the entire feud, which ultimately led to the conquest of Burgundy, as being directly analogous to Clovis's conflicts with Alaric and other enemies. Why, then, did Gregory refrain from representing the Franks unambiguously as instruments of divine justice in their feud with the Burgundians? The obvious, though speculative, answer is that Chlodomer's killings were not fully acceptable as instances of divine vengeance because, as prisoners, Chlodomer's victims were entitled to mercy; because, as orthodox Christians, they were inappropriate targets of God's anger against their Arian kin; and because, as someone who had done penance for his killing, the main victim, Sigismund, was an inappropriate target in a feud.[53] Gundobad's private conversion to orthodoxy and Sigismund's public one had complicated the story of Frankish-Burgundian relations, preventing Gregory from treating all subsequent wars between the two peoples as phases in the long, divinely sanctioned feud between loyal followers of the Trinity and treacherous followers of Arius.

The relationship between God's feuds with humans, on the one hand, and human feuds, on the other, was thus subtle and complex. Moreover, God, like humans, waged feuds in ways that were mysteriously selective and opportunistic, though not totally unpredictable. After Clovis openly espoused the Trinity, his feuds with neighboring peoples were fused in Gregory's imagination with God's feuds against Arians and pagans. God not only fought on Clovis's side against the Alemanni and the Visigoths (II.30, 35, 37), but he refrained from taking vengeance on Clovis after he killed his own kin (II.42). After Clovis's death in 511, however, the relationship between the Franks' feuds and God's was transformed both by the conversions to orthodoxy of neighboring rulers such as Gundobad and by the accession of new Frankish kings whose external wars could not necessarily be configured as holy wars, whose military adventures could not necessarily be configured as holy wars, and whose intrafamilial killings and treacheries, unlike Clovis's, served no clear religious purpose. In this phase of Frankish history, God did not withdraw his support from the Franks or turn against them completely. But his participation in their feuds took on a new character. For one thing, although God, like

---

53. Because Chlodomer's victims were, under one interpretation, his kin, he was not necessarily justified in killing them.

Clotild and her sons, sought vengeance against Sigismund, his reasons for doing so differed from theirs. They held Sigismund vicariously liable for his father's killings of Clotild's parents; God took vengeance against him for killing his son. In later stages of the Frankish-Burgundian conflict, the relationship between the divine feud and the human one assumed a slightly different aspect, as God took vengeance against Godomar for betraying the Trinity while the Franks attacked him initially to avenge his father's killings of Clotild's parents and subsequently to avenge the killing of Chlodomer by Godomar's followers. Furthermore, although God indirectly implicated himself in the killings of Sigismund, his second wife, and their children—by means of which Sigismund's killing of his son Sigeric was avenged—God also treated these homicides of Chlodomer's as wrongs demanding vengeance, which was eventually taken first on Chlodomer and later on Chlodomer's children. Paradoxically, Chlodomer became liable to God's vengeance when he acted, in effect, as an instrument of God's vengeance by killing Sigismund. Similarly, although Godomar, along with his men, acted as instruments of God's vengeance when he avenged Sigismund by killing Chlodomer, he later suffered God's vengeance for his own treachery against the Trinity.

Conclusion

Whether we treat Gregory's *History* as usable, if flawed, evidence about early Frankish feuding practices, as well as one author's view of feuding,[54] or whether we largely dismiss his accounts of Frankish feuds as inaccurate,[55] Gregory's account of the Frankish-Burgundian conflict is still an important source for the study of a culture in which the feud is an important schema for imagining and experiencing politics in both the human and the supernatural spheres. If we understand the feud as both a cultural schema and a political process organized in accordance with that schema, then even inaccurate stories about feuds will provide evidence about feuding practices because no one could fully participate in a feud without locating himself or herself in a story about the feud in which he

---

54. Commenting, for example, on the historical value of Gregory's account of the Frankish-Burgundian conflict, Wallace-Hadrill observed: "Some historians look upon the story as essentially a myth. I do not know why" ("Bloodfeud," 131 n. 3).

55. See Wood, "Gregory of Tours," 253–57; Wood, "Clermont and Burgundy," 122–25; and Sawyer, "Bloodfeud," 29.

or she participated. Feuds were much more than stories about feuds, but without such stories feuding is unthinkable.

Surveying the role that Gregory assigned to God in Frankish politics, both before and after Clovis's death, we can see that, although the bishop did not always view God's feuds and the feuds of Frankish kings as being fused, he believed that the Franks and the God of the Franks feuded in similar ways. When it came to feuding, God did not consistently conform to juridical models any more than the Franks did; instead, he made strategic choices, just as they did. He was selective in construing certain political acts as wrongs that needed to be avenged, in recruiting supporters for his feuds, in identifying targets for vengeance, and in deciding what forms of vengeance were acceptable. At the level of ideology and overall political strategy, however, both God and his Frankish subjects consistently used the feud both as a way of competing for power and territory and as a schema for interpreting, representing, and evaluating the competition.

It is relatively easy to think of the feuding *either* as a juridical and political institution *or* as an ideological schema justifying efforts to compete for scarce resources. But in the preceding analysis of the Frankish-Burgundian feud I have followed William Miller in merging the two approaches, treating the feud simultaneously as both an ideological structure and a political process. Out of a tangled web of past treacheries, any one of which could have been construed as calling for vengeance, certain acts had to be identified as wrongs or injuries.[56] Out of a large set of people who could have been held liable for these wrongs and targeted for revenge, a definable group of "enemies" had to be constructed. To avenge the wrong against the enemy, a vengeance group was recruited out of a large, ill-defined class of potential avengers. Then, certain hostile acts had to be construed as vengeance by the avengers and seen as such by targets and third parties. As the feud proceeded, its dimensions had to

---

56. The history of Frankish-Burgundian relations down to the time of Clotild's feud was replete with what could have been interpreted as acts of treachery, including the following. *Treachery to kin:* Gundobad killed Chilperic and Chilperic's wife (II.28); Godigisel conspired with Clovis against Gundobad (II.32); Sigismund killed Sigeric (III.5). *Wrongs to followers:* Godigisel ejected his engineer from Vienne (II.33). *Treachery to lords:* Aridius betrayed his own lord Gundobad by helping Clovis (II.32); Godigisel's engineer facilitated an attack on Godigisel by Gundobad (II.33). *Treachery to God:* the Burgundians espoused Arianism (II.9); Gundobad refused to acknowledge the Trinity publicly (II.34). *Treachery to allies:* both Godigisel and Gundobad broke promises to Clovis (II.32, 33).

be continually tailored and retailored to fit changing circumstances. Through this complex process, both participants and observers could attain many different political and ideological goals as they refashioned the political world. Mediated by a specific, yet highly flexible, schema for configuring politics and experiencing several different kinds of conflict, the feud was a process into which multiple strategies could be enfolded. The feud was a deterrent to wrongdoing and to breaking settlements as well as a method of actually punishing wrongdoing. It was also a vehicle for achieving honor by avenging shame, for openly expressing anger and fury, for constructing enemies to be plundered, killed, and conquered, for reinventing kinship identities and kinship groups, for consolidating other kinds of political groups, and for meeting political threats that were seemingly unrelated to the feud itself. The feud could never have served these many different strategic purposes if it had not also been a complex cultural schema, deeply encoded with ideas of honor, wrong, liability, divine justice, exchange, kinship and friendship, lordship, anger, and revenge. That was a feud.

The Twilight of *Morgengabe*

Barbara M. Kreutz

Some fifteen years ago, Diane Owen Hughes tracked the history of medieval marriage settlements and concluded that their changing form in Italy had mirrored changes in family structure and familial imperatives.[1] Her demonstration was convincing, particularly for the twelfth century onward. But one notable development warrants further consideration: the abandoning of *morgengabe* and the adoption in its stead of a dowry system.

For 600 years, from the arrival of the Lombards in Italy, it had been customary for husbands to provide for the economic security of their wives by means of this "morning gift." (Whatever the original connotation of *morgengabe,* this in fact came to be its function.)[2] Round about the twelfth century, however, and quite abruptly, we find this responsibility assumed instead by the family of the wife. This was a dramatic cultural shift. Hughes and others have argued that it cannot be attributed to demographic trends, an oversupply of potential brides; she linked it instead to the role played by large family units in the central Middle Ages

---

1. Diane Owen Hughes, "From Brideprice to Dowry in Mediterranean Europe," *Journal of Family History* 3 (1978): 262–96.
2. Originally the bestowal came the morning after the marriage ceremony, apparently as acknowledgment of the bride's virginity. But by the ninth century the grant was as likely to be made on the wedding day itself. See Antonio Marongiu, *Matrimonio e famiglia nell'Italia meridionale: sec. viii–xiii* (Bari, 1976), 80; and Manlio Bellomo, *Ricerche sui rapporti patrimoniali tra coniugi* (Rome, 1961), 3. Many of the charters surveyed for this article are ambiguous as to timing, but some do firmly state "in die coniunctionis adque copulationis nostre" (for example, *Codex Diplomaticus Cavensis,* ed. M. Moraldi, M. Schiani, and S. De Stefano, 8 vols. [Naples, Milan, and Pisa, 1873–93], [hereafter as *CDC*], *CDC* I, no. 86, 882). It should perhaps be noted that these charters never refer to any other gifts the Lombard laws associated with marriage, although something from the bride's father mentioned in *CDC* II, no. 257 (968), may indicate some survival of *faderfio.*

131

("newly strengthened kin groups") and a diminution of emphasis on the "conjugal bond" in and of itself.[3] The change does indeed correlate with this development. It also roughly correlates with the rediscovery of Justinian's legal *corpus,* which provided a system of law far more compatible with dowry than with "morning gifts" from husbands.[4]

Yet does major social change ever happen quite so neatly? Should we not also look further back in time, for factors that built a predisposition for change? Kin groups, after all, had mattered earlier as well, even if not then cohering physically within cities. And yet *morgengabe* had survived. It had also survived despite the fact that here and there in Italy many individuals and population clusters had remained sufficiently familiar with Roman law to think of themselves as practicing it. They—and their Lombard neighbors—seem clearly to have recognized a difference between Roman and Lombard law, especially in relation to women. But in earlier centuries, as we shall see, any drift from one to the other system was likely to be toward, not away from, the Lombard approach.

All in all, it seems advisable to explore more thoroughly the situation before the twelfth century. Manlio Bellomo has noted that in northern Italy, in the latter part of the eleventh century, certain properties began to be exempted from the *morgengabe* fourth to which a wife could lay claim.[5] This suggests one issue that deserves more attention. But we must also examine the full reality of women under Lombard law in what might be called the final heyday of *morgengabe.* And for that same period we must investigate the attraction of Lombard practice for those who thought of themselves as "Roman." In other words, we need to know not only what ultimately caused change but also what kept the Lombard approach in place for so long.

Contractual documentation for these early centuries is generally sparse, mostly useful only for tracing land acquisition by ecclesiastical institutions. Yet early medieval charters (when they survive in their original form) have one notable virtue: the formulas that render opaque so many later contracts had not yet been invented. Sometimes a key detail is omitted, but what is recorded tends to be engagingly revealing; genuine

3. Hughes, "Brideprice," 285–88.

4. It also correlates roughly with Gratian's canon law commentaries, which included unequivocal statements on women and marriage. See Susan Mosher Stuard, "From Women to Woman: New Thinking about Gender c. 1140," *Thought* 64 (1989): 208–19. I am much indebted to Susan Stuard for stimulation and suggestions during the early stages of this article.

5. Bellomo, *Ricerche sui rapporti,* 5–8; see also Hughes, "Brideprice," 227.

human concerns emerge from these documents, much more clearly than would later be the case. Furthermore, there is one region of Italy for which we have a large number of strictly *lay* contracts for the period preceding the twelfth century: the region encompassing the Lombard principality of Salerno and the Romanic, or quasi-Byzantine, city-state of Amalfi.

Particularly in the tenth century, these two entities had a symbiotic relationship. Amalfitans increasingly acquired property within the principality of Salerno, and Salernitan Lombards became ever more entrepreneurial in their own approach to landholding, seemingly lured by the marketing opportunities Amalfi offered.[6] In the nineteenth century, several hundred contracts reflecting all of this activity were published in the *Codex Diplomaticus Cavensis;* especially if compared with charters in the *Codice Diplomatico Amalfitano,* these documents can shed considerable light on issues relating to women.[7] Moreover, they illustrate the interaction of two legal systems, since many Salernitan charters involved Amalfitans.

In size, the principality of Salerno was far more impressive than the city-state of Amalfi. The latter could claim little more than the southern flank of the Amalfitan peninsula, whereas Salernitan territory encompassed roughly half of modern Campania, stretching north almost to the city of Naples; it also stretched east and south to include portions of modern Basilicata and Calabria. Despite this difference in size, however, Amalfi and Salerno had one characteristic in common; both had achieved importance only in the early medieval period. According to local legend, Amalfi was founded by refugees fleeing Rome after the center of power moved to Constantinople. And Salerno, as an independent principality, dated only to the 840s, when it split off from the old Lombard duchy of Benevento.

One might expect such relatively new creations to be unencumbered by the past. But in fact both attached great importance to their roots. Amalfi thought of itself as thoroughly Roman in its traditions and maintained a strong (and highly useful) link with Byzantium. Salerno was

---

6. On Amalfi and Salerno, their histories, and their interactions, see my *Before the Normans: Southern Italy in the Ninth and Tenth Centuries* (Philadelphia, 1991), esp. chaps. 5 and 6.

7. *CDC; Codice Diplomatico Amalfitano,* vol. I, ed. Riccardo Filangieri di Candida (Naples, 1917), cited hereafter as *CDA*. For the period surveyed here (through the tenth century), the latter contains only 17 charters, but they are sufficiently varied to be highly useful.

aggressively Lombard, enormously proud of the Lombard past in Italy and of its own resistance to outside influence. While Benevento had been the original center of Lombard power in the south, by the latter part of the tenth century only Salerno could claim to have remained virtually free of interconnection with the Carolingian and Ottonian worlds. And Salernitans demonstrated their special sense of "Lombardness" through constant reference to Lombard practices and Lombard law. It is, of course, true that elsewhere in southern Italy, and in the north as well, Lombard law persisted. Yet nowhere else did it seem so interwoven with self-esteem as in the defiantly independent principality of Salerno.

What did this mean for the legal and economic position of Salernitan women? The generally held view is that the Lombards were the most "conservative" of all Germanic peoples as far as women were concerned, with *mundium*—every woman firmly controlled by a male guardian—the prime evidence.[8] Katherine Fischer Drew, translator of the Lombard laws, described *mundium,* or guardianship, as usually passing from a woman's father to her husband at the time of marriage.[9] Since *mundium* presumptively included control of a woman's property, and the laws stated that women were not legally competent,[10] the picture conveyed is that of a tightly meshed cage.

Yet this picture is a still photograph of something that in fact was continuously in motion. The first—and best known—encoding of the Lombard laws had taken place in 643: the Edict of Rothari [or Rothair, as Drew prefers], containing 388 individual laws or chapters. But major additions were promulgated during the long reign of Liutprand (712–44). Ratchis, in 746, and Aistulf, in 750 and 755, issued still more chapters. Drew did note that some of these eighth-century laws repre-

---

8. David Herlihy, "Land, Family, and Women in Continental Europe, 701–1200," in *Women in Medieval Society,* ed. Susan Mosher Stuard (Philadelphia, 1976), 14, first published in *Traditio* 18 (1962). Others have used harsher terms than *conservative.* But Edward Peters once wisely urged historians to explore "to what extent the [Lombard] law codes reflect actual conditions and what means existed for circumventing them" (foreword to Katherine Fischer Drew, *The Lombard Laws* [Philadelphia, 1973], xxi).

9. Drew, *The Lombard Laws,* 32; see also "Notes on Lombard Institutions," in her *Law and Society in Early Medieval Europe* (London, 1988), IV:61.

10. Drew, "Lombard Institutions," IV:17. The relevant laws are Rothair [Rothari] 204 and Liutprand 93. All laws are cited here as in Drew's 1973 translation (see note 9, above). The traditional Latin edition (with the same numbering) is that of F. Bluhme (*Leges Langobardorum*) in *MGH Leges,* vol. 4 (Hanover, 1869).

sented an improvement in the position of women, particularly in relation to inheritance rights.[11] But she perhaps did not make enough of this, for increasing attention to the rights and concerns of women, as well as evidence that they were beginning to constitute a significant economic factor, is in fact, a prime characteristic of the eighth-century additions.

Of Liutprand's first six laws, for example, five related to women, including new or broadened authority for sisters and daughters to inherit.[12] Then, in 717, he decreed that the morning gift should not exceed a quarter of a man's estate, and in 728 that no husband should ever give his wife more than had been provided as a marriage portion.[13] Plainly, the intent here was restrictive, but the 717 maximum came to be the standard award and *quarta* became a synonym for the *morgengabe*. Furthermore, in 721, Liutprand issued a law safeguarding women's property. It stated that if a woman wished to sell her land ("with the consent of her husband or in community with him") two or three of her male relatives should be summoned so that she could be questioned, in their presence, as to whether she was acting under compulsion; if so, the sale could not take place.[14] Perhaps this reflected increasing Christian influence. One of Aistulf's laws urged nephews to provide for unmarried aunts "so that they will not suffer need."[15] Whatever the motivation, however, the net result undeniably was an improvement in women's situation. This was further demonstrated by another of Aistulf's laws, in which he decreed that, since a widow would in any case have her *quarta,* a man should not bequeath to his wife more than half the usufruct of [the rest of] his property if he also left children by her, or a third if he left children by an earlier wife.[16] What this *permits* him to leave to his wife is remarkable. Heretofore, according to Lombard law, all but the *morgengabe* share of a man's estate passed to sons (or sometimes daughters). Now widows could have not only their *quarta* but also at least the income from considerable additional property.[17]

11. Drew, "Lombard Institutions," IV:68–70.

12. Liutprand 1–4. Heretofore, inheritance by women had been permitted only if a man left no legitimate sons.

13. Liutprand 7 (717), and 103 (728).

14. Liutprand 22 (721). All quotations from the laws are from the Drew translation.

15. Aistulf 10.

16. Aistulf 14.

17. Hughes indicated that Lombard widows did not retain their *morgengabe* portion ("Brideprice," 271), but if ever this had been true, it was no longer the case, as Aistulf's law and the Salernitan charters make clear.

Of course, under Lombard law women were still circumscribed in their actions. And, overall, the society we glimpse through the prism of the laws is still a harsh one. Yet, as Bellomo has observed, the new decrees made the law more "gentile."[18] We therefore need now to move on to the real world, examining charter evidence to see which strictures of Lombard law were actually observed—and with what consequence.

Practices in relation to *mundium* and *morgengabe* require particular attention, but first some evidence touching the legal capacity of women needs to be noted. In the principality of Salerno, in the ninth century, charters sometimes had as many as 14 witnesses (exclusive of principals). Notaries had not yet achieved official status; in ninth-century Salerno it was witnesses who lent legitimacy to the contract. Assumed to be disinterested, they were somewhat analogous to the *boni homines* convened locally to resolve controversies.[19] And among the witnesses to six sale contracts executed between 824 and 848, and involving small plots of land, we find two women.[20] Only their gender marks these two witnesses as exceptional. All of the witnesses were Lombard, but none represented the ruling elite; they were not "*maiores,*" to use the terminology of local chronicles. Indeed, according to several of the indictions, the documents were drawn up "by the baking ovens in the marketplace" in two market towns within the principality.[21] We can picture the scene; notaries obviously set themselves up in the market to serve local landowners, and, since the same two women keep appearing, we must assume that they, too, did business in the market. (One of the women, Walfreda, turns up in both towns, as does one of the notaries.) Altogether, four different notaries were involved in these transactions, and five of the charters had one woman witness while one charter had two.

---

18. Manlio Bellomo, *La condizione giuridica della donna in Italia* (Turin, 1970), 29.

19. On the role of witnesses in this region, see Maria Galante, "Il notaio e il documento notarile Salerno in epoca longobarda," in *Per una storia del notariato meridionale* (Rome, 1982), esp. 76–77. As many have observed, a concept of public order never really disappeared in Italy; the Salernitan approach to witnessing reflected this fact.

20. *CDC* I, nos. 14, 16, 20, 24, 27, 30. The women are Walfreda and Gaidelfreda, and they are unquestionably female; not only do their names suggest it but each signature is followed by a clearly scripted "*filia*" of so-and-so. (I have examined the original charters at Ssa. Trinità di Cava.) Later, between 875 and 903, in five charters, another Walfreda and an Odelfreda served as witnesses in one of the same market towns, but there is no *filia* following their names and thus no absolute proof that they were women.

21. "Actu tostatiu in ipso mercatu [*sic*]": *CDC* I, nos. 14 (824), 16 (836).

Despite the strict Lombard laws pertaining to women's legal capacity, Walfreda and Gaidelfreda presumably would have been among those testifying if the contracts had later been contested. And this anomaly cannot be dismissed as representative only of unsophisticated rural areas. An 894 document reports a hearing at the royal palace in the city of Salerno, "in the presence of gastalds and judges," in which a woman was the chief participant, personally testifying to a grant made by her late father.[22] The grant had been made to St. Maximus, the abbey-church of Salerno's ruling family, and the abbot himself was present. With such high-level interests at stake it was apparently thought quite all right to turn a blind eye to the law.

After the start of the tenth century, the surviving charters show no women witnessing contracts in Salerno. Yet one ninth-century element did persist. Whenever a woman disposed of her property (whether inherited or derived through *morgengabe*), notaries typically recorded her action in the first person, just as was done in the case of a man. In other words, the woman speaks, as it were, in her own voice ("Ego Wiseltruda . . .").

It would be a mistake to make too much of this. With married women, husbands always confirmed or consented. And in all cases, as we shall see, the woman's male relatives participated as well. Yet all of these scraps of evidence indicate that attitudes had changed in relation to women. The Lombards had come a long way from bride-price and all that it connoted, and a long way, too, from the era of Rothari. The old laws still stood, and the local Lombards took pride in observing them. But, as Alan Watson has noted, the rules of private law can have a different effect at different times within the same society.[23]

This seems particularly true in the case of *mundium*. Originally, a woman's *munduald* (normally first her father, then her husband, or, if neither survived, a brother or a son) exercised a virtual property right over the woman herself, not merely over her property. Bellomo has observed, however, that as early as the start of the ninth century the role of *munduald* came more to resemble that of an *advocatus* or defender.[24] And certainly our Salerno charters indicate some change. In 5 out of 44 ninth-century charters involving women, we do encounter the terms

22. CDC I, no. 105.
23. Alan Watson, *Legal Transplants: An Approach to Comparative Law* (Edinburgh, 1974), 19–20.
24. Bellomo, *Condizione giuridica*, 29.

mundualdus or *mundium*. But in 4 of these instances the terms seem merely one among many rhetorical flourishes in elaborately drawn documents recording land acquisition by a member or close associate of Salerno's ruling family or by the royal abbey-church.[25] In the rest of these 44 charters, mostly involving lesser folk, the terms do not appear at all. In the tenth century, one or the other term does appear in roughly one-third of women-related charters, but usually the *munduald* does then seem more spokesman than all-powerful "controller."[26] Only toward the end of the century do we once again find women—especially if high-born—consistently proclaiming themselves subject to the *mundium* of their husbands.[27]

Use of the term certainly added a fine legalistic flavor to charters. Moreover, *mundium* connoted "Lombardness"; renewed reference to *mundium* at the end of the tenth century may have signified a reassertion of ethnic identity as the German emperors increased their pressure on southern Italy. As a practical matter, however, by now *mundium* appears to have had considerably less significance than one of Liutprand's eighth-century stipulations: the requirement that a woman's male relatives participate in any transaction affecting her interests. This law, noted earlier, was designed to protect women from being forced to sell through violence or the threat of violence on the part of their husbands. It begins:

> [I]f a woman wishes to sell her property with the consent of her husband or in community with him, the man who wishes to buy . . . shall notify two or three relatives of the woman. . . . If in the presence of these relatives the woman says that she acted under compulsion, [the sale] shall not be valid.

---

25. CDC I, nos. 65, 66, 86, 98: sales to Salerno's current ruler, to his son, to the abbot of St. Maximus, and to "Josep medicus," who seems to have been the palace physician. The fifth charter (no. 37) was drafted in a rural area, and the notary proudly proclaimed it to be "secundum legem in edicti."

26. Forty years ago, in a lengthy and provocative article, Ennio Cortese traced the history of *mundium* and its evolution over time ("Per la storia del mundio in Italia," *Rivista italiana per le scienze giuridiche* 91 [1955–56]: 323–474). He denied that the *munduald* became merely an *advocatus* (445–49) but he also insisted that, despite the usual view, *mundium* was never the primary "forza unificatrice della famiglia e l'anima del diritto domestico" (328). In conclusion, he noted the elasticity of the term, and suggested that in southern Italy the approach to *mundium* was affected by the survival there of ancient Roman practices (470–74).

27. In one, for example, it is a titled Salernitan woman giving extensive lands to a monastery (CDC III, no. 534).

The law then goes on to mandate that such hearings take place before a judge and ends by stating that if the woman denies compulsion, and either those male relatives or the judge sign the charter, the sale is valid.[28]

If the evidence of our charters can be trusted, no Lombard law was observed more scrupulously. Transactions involving women—whether widowed or with living husbands—always take place in the presence of a *judex,* or *sculdais* (an official whose duties included judgments), or sometimes even a *gastald*. And two or three *propinqui parentes* (the woman's nearest male relatives) are always present, and vocal.[29]

Liutprand surely did not anticipate how this law would affect *mundium* in centuries with an active market in land. With widows, there was no problem, since a widow's *mundium* reverted to some male member of her family—in other words, to one of her *propinqui parentes*. With a married woman, however, this law in effect sideslipped the husband by granting her own family considerable control not only over anything she might have inherited but also over her *quarta*. Should she propose to sell the latter, a woman might describe herself as subject to the *mundium* of her husband, but obviously that was not what mattered most. The woman's relatives had only to declare themselves unsatisfied, or refuse to sign, for the sale to be invalid.

For the ninth century, there are 10 Salernitan contracts recording either the sale of land by a married woman or a joint (husband and wife) sale that included the wife's quarter share.[30] In all but one, the *propinqui parentes* consent to the transaction (and the exception is a damaged document with sentences missing). We of course have no way of knowing how many sales fell through for lack of such consent; such instances would leave no trace. But one judgment-charter is tantalizing in its implications. Though somewhat hard to decipher, it appears to record the reclaiming of land a husband and wife had sold—land that was the wife's *morgengabe* share from her first marriage.[31] The wording suggests that the sale had not been properly conducted. Does this mean that the woman's relatives had not been involved? Very likely—for the reclaimed land was awarded to the wife's father.

The *Codex Diplomaticus Cavensis* supplies 422 charters for the tenth

28. Liutprand 22.
29. If a woman had no male relatives available, some official deputizing for the ruler questioned her closely as to free will.
30. CDC I, nos. 24, 28, 29, 32, 37, 39, 48, 66, 68, 94.
31. CDC I, no. 27 (847).

century.[32] And they show much undeveloped land put to use; leases abound. Sales, on the other hand, become relatively rare. The decline begins early in the tenth century, and in the last decade there are only nine sales, as opposed to 32 leases, 25 confirmations or judgments relating to property, and 21 trades or gifts of land (not including intrafamily arrangements). Admittedly, the *Codex* does not represent a systematic collection; its charter rolls were perhaps haphazardly preserved and may not provide a totally valid overview. Yet a decrease in sales is plausible. Ninth-century charters had shown the *maiores* acquiring more and more land from small landowners. Perhaps there really did come to be diminished opportunity for purchase. Plainly, too, leases were now proving profitable. In addition, however, the difficulties inherent in buying and selling land, as a result of Liutprand's dictum, may well have had a chilling effect.

For there was no end to the ramifications of the *propinqui parentes* requirement. *Morgengabe,* deeply embedded in custom and the Lombard laws,[33] traditionally gave to the wife an *undifferentiated* fourth of her husband's holdings. In the case of a small landowner, a fourth of the husband's property might be relatively easy to determine.[34] But with the *maiores,* a typical *morgengabe* charter read:

> I grant and hand over to you [the wife] a fourth part of everything I possess, including buildings and the contents of buildings; vineyards and arable land; pastures and woodlands; gardens, chestnut and oak trees, olive trees and cane plantings, trees trimmed as vine-supports and also [untrimmed] hazelnut trees, fruit trees whether bearing or not; in the mountains or on the plains, whether [the land is] cultivated or not; possessions moveable or fixed, slaves and serving women, any and all money-wealth; in other words all of my resources, however gained, whether from my father or my mother, and whatever I may in

---

32. For the ninth century, the *CDC* provides 111 charters; the total for the two centuries is thus 533 (of which some few have recently been redated). Not all *CDC* charters were redacted within Salernitan territory, but most were. In the tenth century, some of these, though drafted by Salernitan notaries, recorded Amalfitan actions.

33. As an indication of the importance attached to *morgengabe,* Adelchis, ruler of Benevento and the last Lombard "legislator," devoted the third of his eight laws to it, decreeing that loss of her *morgengabe* charter should not prejudice a woman's right to a quarter share (*Capitula Domni Adelchis Principis* [866], *MGH Leges* 4:211).

34. For example, in 853 a married woman in a rural area sold her *quarta,* and it seemed to be only one small vineyard (*CDC* I, no. 37); in 868, another woman's *quarta* was a fourth of each of two houses in the city of Salerno (*CDC* I, no. 65).

future obtain or collect by whatever means, in accordance with Lombard law.[35]

If this wife wished to sell her *morgengabe* share—or her husband persuaded her to raise money in that way—not only did the *propinqui parentes* have to approve, but the actual parameters of the *quarta* had to be agreed upon, surely not an easy task. And the wife's relatives were undoubtedly involved in that, too.

As has been noted, their participation was also required in the case of a joint sale in which the wife's *quarta* constituted part of the land sold. (In one joint sale, even this failed to satisfy the cautious buyer; he asked that the wife herself indicate consent by giving a *signam manus* in the presence of the judge.)[36] And finally—doubtless the most irritating complication—if ever the husband wished to sell any part of his holdings, he was well advised to secure the approval of his wife and her relatives. Otherwise they might later claim that the property sold had included part of the wife's share.

If all of this made matters awkward for the husband as seller, the potential complications clearly could terrify a prospective purchaser. Thus, almost all Salernitan sale charters—if not including proof of the wife's consent—contained some variation on the following wording.

> And if my wife should enter upon [*introierit*] this land I have sold, and take it from you, then you [the buyer] may take, from my other holdings, land equivalent in worth.[37]

Often the seller notes that he is selling only half of his land in a given area, so that if compensatory land should be required it can be taken from the other half. When this was not a viable option, compensation in *solidi* was guaranteed, the value of the land wrested back by the wife to be determined by *boni homines*.[38]

---

35. *CDC* I, no. 166 (940). Virtually identical wording appears in most tenth-century *morgengabe* charters involving the *maiores*.

36. *CDC* I, no. 29 (848). The purchaser here was again "Josep medicus" (see note 25). A "signum manus" is reported several times in the first half of the ninth century; in nos. 24, 32, and 40, both husband and wife make the sign when the wife sells land.

37. *CDC* I, nos. 23 (843), 47 (856), 59 (860), 81 (877), 84 (880), 88 (882), 138 (920). In *CDC* II, no. 191 (956), and III, no. 493 (996), the phrase is "and if my *mother* [italics mine]."

38. *CDC* I, nos. 42 (855), 167 (940).

Surely even this was not enough to fill prospective purchasers with confidence; actually acquiring the compensatory land or *solidi* could prove difficult. And the problems associated with *morgengabe* rights affected even secondary sales. If any portion of land being sold had been purchased from a woman whose *quarta* it represented, it was incumbent on the seller to provide documentation showing that the formalities had been properly observed when he made the purchase.[39] Altogether, it is no wonder that sales declined while leases proliferated. The "and if my wife" clause appears once in relation to land pledged for a loan, but never in connection with a lease; husbands could apparently lease out land with total freedom.[40]

In the tenth century, Salernitan *morgengabe* charters became increasingly generous in their provisions. As in the example quoted earlier, most emphasize that the wife's fourth applies not only to what the husband currently possesses but also to what he may inherit from his father or mother.[41] One charter even stated that if the husband predeceased his parents the widow would receive a quarter share of what they would have left him.[42] In another, the bride's father stipulates that the husband is to treat his wife well—and if by ill chance she is captured in an Arab raid the husband is to pay two-thirds of her ransom.[43] And always, as had been true in the ninth century, it is firmly declared that the *quarta* is the wife's in perpetuity, to dispose of as she wishes, with no interference ever from anyone on the husband's side.[44]

All in all, one would expect husbands to feel beleaguered. And, of course, it was not merely husbands; a man's family was inevitably affected by, indeed usually involved in, his *morgengabe* grant. In the very first Salernitan charter, from 792, the husband makes his commitment with the permission of his father, and this is stated again in two tenth-

---

39. For example, see *CDC* I, nos. 54 (858), and 84 (880).

40. For the loan, see *CDC* I, no. 70 (871). *Propinqui parentes* are never mentioned in leasing contracts, nor is there mention of a wife's consent, even when the land is described as hers or when (*CDC* II, no. 271) it is a partition lease, a portion of which would be permanently alienated.

41. *CDC* I, nos. 166 (940), 210 (960); *CDC* II, nos. 294 (976), 411 (989).

42. *CDC* I, no. 166. A *morgengabe* charter from Avellino, in Beneventan territory, also includes this promise (*CDC* II, no. 272 [972]).

43. *CDC* I, no. 163 (937).

44. [P]otestatem iuxta legem faciendum exinde omnia que vobis placuerit; et neque a me [the husband] neque a nostris heredibus, neque a nullusquenquam hominibus abeatis exinde aliquando aliqua requisitione, set perpetuis temporibus securo . . . abere et possidere [*sic*]" (*CDC* I, no. 210).

century charters.[45] In two sales, the "and if my wife" clause is expanded to include "or my daughter-in-law," indicating that the latter had a claim on the seller's estate.[46] One woman sells her *quarta* land with the consent of her father-in-law, and a later charter notes that the father-in-law had provided the morning gift for a woman's first marriage.[47] Surely even the exempting of certain properties from the *quarta* (noted by Bellomo in eleventh-century northern Italy) would not have sufficiently eased the pressures on husbands and their families.

Furthermore, the morning gift was not the only way in which women were in effect acquiring control of land. In Salernitan charters through the tenth century, only once does a Lombard woman actually buy property.[48] Given women's enhanced right to inherit, however, many women must have gained possession of entire estates. One obvious indication is that phrase in *morgengabe* contracts: "anything I have inherited or may inherit from my father *or my mother.*" This phrase provides evidence we cannot gain directly from wills, since wills appear to have been made only when there was deviation from the norm—and eighth-century Lombard laws had made daughters (and sometimes sisters) legitimate heirs. But the derivation of property was often recorded in connection with sales, and in that way we learn that daughters inherited from their fathers; they inherited or received gifts of land from their mothers; mothers sometimes inherited from sons who died young; a man might leave his property to his sister-in-law; and some husbands were exceptionally generous, one leaving his wife half his estate (and not merely the usufruct).[49] Mothers and sisters-in-law are nowhere mentioned in the laws as permissible legatees, and wives were not supposed to inherit half the estate outright. But it would seem that almost anything had become possible, if done by charter, and women were benefiting from this.

In due course, much of this property may have flowed back into male hands; three charters refer to sons inheriting from mothers.[50] Yet one could not always count on this. In one instance, a widow with living sons

45. *CDC* I, no. 1 (792); *CDC* II, nos. 294 (976), 411 (989): "per verbum et absolutionem ipsius genitori."

46. *CDC* I, nos. 34 (850), 47 (856).

47. *CDC* I, no. 37 (853); *CDC* II, no. 344 (982).

48. In the mid–ninth century, a rural widow in Salerno twice bought property together with her (apparently minor) sons (*CDC* I, nos. 33, 34).

49. Daughters from fathers: *CDC* I, nos. 68, 173; *CDC* II, nos. 241, 248. Daughters from mothers: *CDC* III, nos. 490, 505. Mothers from sons: *CDC* I, no. 109; *CDC* II, no. 235. Man to sister-in-law: *CDC* I, no. 118. Husband to wife: *CDC* II, no. 257.

50. *CDC* I, nos. 153 (933), 168 (940); *CDC* II, no. 213 (961).

left her estate to a monastic church, merely giving her sons an option to
buy the land (presumably from the abbot) if they could come up with the
money within seven days of her death.[51]

What, then, was the solution to the problems associated with women
and property? It is time to consider Amalfi, Salerno's nearest neighbor,
where Roman law was theoretically the rule. We cannot be sure what
contemporary Amalfitans meant by "*lex romanorum.*" Nonetheless, one
interesting fact has recently come to light. An old legend held that the
Codex Pisanus (an early copy of the *Digest*) had been taken from Amalfi
in the Pisan raid of 1135. Scholars were skeptical, but thirty years ago it
was discovered that the margins of the *Codex Pisanus* bore notations in
ninth-to-eleventh-century Beneventan script, proof that it had at least
been in southern Italy in that period.[52] Since there is also a Beneventan
copy of the *Novellae,* conceivably the Amalfitans could indeed have had
some knowledge of Justinian's Roman law.[53] In any event, widows in
Amalfi bought and sold land with what appeared to be total freedom.[54]
Even married women sometimes undertook transactions on their own,
perhaps because their husbands were so often gone; in one instance, a
wife exchanged property with another Amalfitan while her husband was
on a voyage to Egypt.[55] But this was not the only contrast with Salerno.
Most tenth-century sales executed at Amalfi reveal husbands and wives
acting as joint principals in a manner suggesting community property.[56]
Other female family members were often prominently involved as well.
Acting together, a man, his wife, and their daughter-in-law sold land to a

51. *CDC* II, no. 218 (962).
52. I owe word of this to Prof. Francis Newton, who plans to publish a comment
on these notations. He also kindly informed me of an article by Juan Miquel, who first
identified the glosses as Beneventan and noted their significance for the Amalfitan legend. See Juan Miquel, "Mechanische Fehler in der Überlieferung der Digesten,"
Zeitschrift der Savigny-Stiftung fur Rechtsgeschichte, 80 (1963), II: Romanistische
Abteilung, 283.
53. The *Novellae* in Beneventan script is thought to be the copy made at Monte
Cassino in the eleventh century during the abbacy of Desiderius. See E. A. Loew, *The
Beneventan Script,* 2d ed., by Virginia Brown, 2 vols. (Rome, 1980), 1:12, 2:49. If this
manuscript was copied from another already in southern Italy (as seems likely), tenth-
century Amalfitans may have known the *Novellae* as well as the *Digest.*
54. Indeed, the largest transaction recorded in tenth-century Amalfitan charters
was the sale by a widow, for 70 *solidi,* of a waterfront lot and buildings in the port of
Atrani (*CDA* I, no. 8 [970]). Many Amalfitans cited in this article were actually from
Atrani, which adjoins the much larger city of Amalfi.
55. *CDC* II, no. 292 (976). Although it is included in the *CDC,* this charter was
redacted at Amalfi by an Amalfitan scribe.
56. *CDA* I, nos. 1 (907), 3 (931), 11 (984), 12 (985), 13 (987), 15 (993), 17 (998).

widowed aunt, and two men divided land with their uncle with the consent of their sister.[57]

As Richard Saller has observed, Roman law "offered a diverse and highly flexible tool kit."[58] Amalfitans could doubtless believe they were adhering to it, particularly if they not only knew something of Justinian's version but had also absorbed—perhaps by way of Naples—some smattering of classical Roman law. (We can only be certain that they were not heeding contemporary Byzantine codes, hardly sympathetic to women operating independently.)[59] At any rate, in one respect the Amalfitans clearly were "Roman." Amalfitan wives were dowered, apparently without even a countergift on the part of the husband.[60]

Yet this statement needs to be qualified. Dowry seemed certain only when Amalfitans married each other. And increasingly in the tenth century Salernitans and Amalfitans were intermarrying, with interesting results. In a 997 charter drawn at Amalfi, a powerful Amalfitan and his Lombard wife and mother sold some Amalfitan property to another Amalfitan "secundum legem et consuetudinem romanorum"—but noted that the women's *morgengabe* shares formed part of the sale.[61] The Lombard wife of a duke of Amalfi presented some Amalfitan land to Nicetas, imperial *protospatarius*—with the consent of her husband, in whose *mundium* she declared herself to be.[62] At a much lower level of society, in a rural area within Salerno, a settlement was recorded between a local Lombard family and the Amalfitan widow of their son; now married to her second Lombard husband, she had sued to gain the *quarta* from her first marriage.[63]

It is not surprising that the wife in the third example had received a morning gift, since she had married a Lombard. But it is striking that

---

57. *CDA* I, nos. 6 (947), 4 (939).

58. Richard P. Saller, "Roman Heirship Strategies in Principle and in Practice," in *The Family in Italy from Antiquity to the Present*, ed. David I. Kertzer and Richard P. Saller (New Haven and London, 1991), 47.

59. On Byzantine law in relation to women and the new codes of Basil I (867–86) and Leo VI (886–912), see Joëlle Beaucamp, "La situation juridique de la femme à Byzance," *Cahiers de Civilisation Médiévale* 20 (1977): 145–76. I am grateful to Prof. Charles Brand for pointing me toward this article.

60. On the dowry in medieval southern Italy, see Marongiu, *Matrimonio e famiglia*, esp. 131–36, 202. But note that Marongiu, covering a large area over many centuries, tends to disregard or blur local variations.

61. *CDA* I, no. 16.

62. *CDC* II, no. 386 (986).

63. *CDC* I, no. 185 (954). Adhering to Lombard practice, her second husband then rented out the property on her behalf (*CDC* I, no. 187).

morgengabe and *mundium* appear in the first two charters even though the husbands were Amalfitan—and despite Liutprand's decree (law 127) that a Lombard woman who married a "Roman" became Roman herself and subject to Roman law. In fact, however, this is typical of the extent to which Lombard legal practices were adopted by Amalfitans. The trend is apparent in many tenth-century sales and leases; Amalfitans enthusiastically embraced the Lombard use of *guadia* and *mediatores* (pledges and guarantors) even when dealing with fellow Amalfitans.[64]

The reasons for this become apparent when contracts drawn at Amalfi are compared with Salernitan contracts. A typical Amalfitan charter rambled on for pages, circling round and round the fine points. A Salernitan charter was far more succinct, the transaction firmly lodged within the framework of Lombard law. It is easy to make fun of the Lombard laws: the meticulous spelling out of penalties for cutting off a horse's tail or the like. Particularly in the later laws, however, there were strictures eminently useful in the ever more commercial world of the tenth century. Agreements that Salernitan notaries drafted, stitched together with legal tag-words familiar to any Lombard *judex,* gave real assurance of security in contract.

Here, surely, lies the explanation for the survival of *morgengabe.* Bestowal of the morning gift placed a heavy burden on a man's family, and after marriage the *propinqui parentes* could severely limit a man's freedom of action.[65] But *morgengabe* was an integral part of a great web of law—an exceptionally solid, overarching structure that attracted even the "Roman" Amalfitans, whose own approach to women and property

---

64. There are many examples of Amalfitans using *guadia* and *mediatores.* In one instance, two Amalfitan men and their young nephew (accompanied by his tutor) seem specifically to have come to Salerno to have their division of lands recorded, Lombard-style by a Salernitan notary (*CDC* III, no. 532). We also find Amalfitans sealing intrafamily land transfers with *launegild* (a return gift) "as prescribed by Lombard law." One example is *CDC* III, no. 486 (995), in which *guadia* and *mediatores* also appear.

65. Not only did the *propinqui parentes* requirement limit a husband's action; Huguette Taviani-Carozzi has observed that its effect was to bind together the families of the husband and wife within a *consanguinitas* newly defined. On this, and its ramifications in the political sphere, see Taviani-Carozzi, *La principauté lombarde de Salerno, IX–XI siècle,* 2 vols. (Rome, 1991), 1:384–409. Her case may rest too much on widely scattered evidence and some questionable generalizations by Marongiu (see note 60, above), but she makes some very important points. And, if one accepts her view, the twelfth-century changes must then be described as a move not from the conjugal family to a broader unit but, instead, from an overly broad congerie of relationships to something more manageable.

seemed shapeless in comparison. Reference was made earlier to an Amalfitan woman exchanging land with another Amalfitan while her husband was absent. That charter was executed at Amalfi, and the aftermath is revealing. When the husband returned from Egypt, he reconfirmed the exchange—in a charter drawn at Salerno by a Salernitan Lombard notary.[66]

The documentation available for Salerno and Amalfi makes it possible to take a close look at the real world, and what we find makes it less surprising that *mundualdi* would still serve a function in fifteenth-century Florence.[67] Lombard legal concepts offered both rigor and an appealing simplicity; it is no wonder that a few survived. As for *morgengabe,* it was obviously presenting serious problems well before the twelfth century. Nonetheless, it was deeply embedded in Lombard law, a secure and all-encompassing system that was unlikely to be abandoned absent some other equally strong framework for the sustaining of family and property interests. Only in the twelfth century—when *lex romanorum* ceased to mean merely a disparate collection of maxims and, thanks to the work of many jurists, acquired impressive new and authoritative forms—could *morgengabe* fade from view.

---

66. *CDC* II, no. 300 (978).

67. On this survival of a Lombard concept, see Thomas Kuehn, *Law, Family, and Women* (Chicago and London, 1991), chap. 9: "'Cum Consensu Mundualdi': Legal Guardianship of Women in Quattrocento Florence." The Florentine *munduald* was actually a *mundualdus ad negotiam,* court-appointed (or court-approved) for a specific transaction—one might say the early drift toward *advocatus* carried to its logical conclusion.

The Medieval Family: A Place of Refuge and Sorrow

Steven A. Epstein

In *Medieval Households,* David Herlihy quotes from the *Epistles* of Horace: "If you know something more accurate than the things written here, then openly share it; if not, use these with me."[1] Anyone attempting to distill the experience of millions of households that existed centuries ago into a book of some 200 pages inevitably becomes a target for criticism, but in more optimistic terms it provides a place for the rest of us to begin.

To summarize a brief book on a big subject is a mistake, so instead let us look at Herlihy's own conclusions. The important distinction between the household and the family is the central message of the book. As much as Herlihy may have wished to call this book *The Medieval Family,* he did not for good reasons. We know much more about the household than the family in the Middle Ages because, unlike the situation in classical antiquity, these households are commensurable, that is, they can be counted and compared. Why is it important that these households can be counted and compared? To the extent that these domestic units increasingly became recognizable families and not simply collections of free and unfree people living under the same roof, the medieval household became something more than a human stable. What particularly interested Herlihy about the medieval household was its tighter moral and emotional unity, especially when compared to the ancient household.[2] Although households were commensurable, they were not the same and were never

1. David Herlihy, *Medieval Households* (Cambridge, Mass., 1985), vii, his translation of "si quid novisti rectius istis, candidus imperti; si nil, his utere mecum"(*Epistles* I:6, 67–68).

2. For more on the ancient household, see Keith R. Bradley, *Discovering the Roman Family: Studies in Roman Social History* (Oxford, 1991), 140, for views on

static. People were always entering or leaving households, whether by being born, dying, or marrying, or by being adopted, abandoned, divorced, or murdered. The ability to count and compare these households, granted by precious surviving sources like the surveys of Carolingian monastic estates or the tax records of Renaissance Florence, freezes them for a moment, but the still frame lasted, we must remember, for only an instant.

This dynamic quality of household life is also apparent in the great changes Herlihy found over the course of the Middle Ages. The Christian church insisted on monogamy and exogamy (one marriage at a time to nonkin) and attempted, at least in theory, to impose the same rules on everyone. After the demise of resource polygyny, so memorably revealed in the family life of the early medieval Irish, women could look forward to more than being collected, or simply accumulated (a terrible word and fate for any people) in the households of the powerful. A late age for first marriage was the medieval norm throughout society, but during the later Middle Ages it dropped dramatically for women, at least for Florence and southern Europe. The age difference between wife and husband placed women in the difficult and perhaps dangerous role of intermediary across the generations between their older husbands and their children. Even these age differences did *not* sap the level of affection within the family and household. Philippe Ariès's contention that childhood was discovered in the early modern period or Lawrence Stone's idea that the eighteenth century witnessed the rise of affective ties within the family, always struck Herlihy as unproved, and, more importantly, implausible.[3] Herlihy concluded his book with two points he would pick up in a later work—paternal care as exemplified in the rise of the cult of St. Joseph, and the idea that society was after all a collection of households. The common values that helped to bring families into some larger unit constituted the cement of society.

Herlihy's last work, starkly titled "Family," his presidential address to the American Historical Association, was not simply the medieval family

---

emotional investment in children, and 7–8 for the emotional content of Roman marital ties. The latter are also analyzed and their emotional content stressed by Susan Treggiari in *Roman Marriage* (Oxford, 1991), 229–61.

3. Philippe Ariès, *Centuries of Childhood: A Social History of Family Life* (New York, n.d.); Lawrence Stone, *The Family, Sex, and Marriage in England, 1500–1800* (New York, 1977).

and households revisited.[4] In this piece Herlihy responded to his own challenge to know more and to know it more deeply. He wanted to explore the double vision of the family—itself as loving, the outer world as loveless—in other words, the family as a moral unit. Again, rather than give a précis of this impressive and brief synthesis, let us look at his conclusions. With sources ranging from biblical exegesis, to the law, to private and personal records, he illuminated love in the family and the necessary tension between authority in the family and the family itself as a place of refuge in a cold world. Again noticing important change, Herlihy saw a gradual weakening of paternal authority during the Middle Ages, balanced by a growth of love within the household.[5] The bubonic plague of 1348, one of the great killers in the history of humanity, swept away a third of Europe's people and reinforced fears of a capricious and hostile outer world, while at the same time testing the worth of the family as refuge. By the time Herlihy wrote these words he was in the grip of illness himself, and so he knew well how important a place of refuge was and how inadequate impersonal institutions like hospitals, and indeed universities, can be when one begins the process of saying farewell to the outer world.

In order to build upon these fundamental insights on the medieval household and family we shall have to approach the topics from different directions, to test some of the assumptions of Herlihy's work. His basic optimism about human kindness, as well as his own experience of family life, led him to write history that sustained the value of the family and the emotional ties that welded it together. Although an optimist, Herlihy was not naive about what passes for real life, so he certainly knew that some families fail and become more of a prison than a refuge, harboring domestic violence and abuse and providing a refuge from the law and punishment for just the sort of people we would rather not see protected. Murder, divorce, incest, cruelty, and abandonment happen, and those whose experience of family life conjures up these images will feel a chill rather than a warm glow when they see an essay entitled "Family." From its very beginnings, and especially in the Middle Ages, part of the Christian message seemed to want to abolish family life or at least offer to some a higher and safer calling. Medieval Christianity was sometimes hostile to family life as it responded to the need that many people felt for something more, and, in particular, for some people the call to abandon

4. David Herlihy, "Family," *American Historical Review* 96 (1991): 1–16.
5. Ibid., 5.

their families and follow Christ was the best possible news. So, at least for a few people, the outside world may have been the loving place, a refuge from the miseries of family.

But it is not news to us that some families destroy their members and nurture hatred, violence, and twisted lives. These families are never the majority, for if they were the calls to abandon family life would have been answered a long time ago. Herlihy understood this and chose to begin with the ideal of the positive, life-enhancing aspects of family life. I propose here to explore the downside, the sort of families that crawl out when you turn over the rock and look below. The question to be asked of the accumulated unhappy experiences of the family and household must be: what can society do about bad family members and the harm they cause without undermining the positive and strong role for autonomous family life? Since society is a collection of families held together by some common values, how could outsiders have saved people from the worst excesses of medieval family life? This question needs no defense, but the attempt to answer it is useful for several reasons. To the extent that the Middle Ages witnessed the emergence of a recognizably modern family, it should also reveal the first efforts to salvage the bad ones. Second, the question itself is an antidote to the tendency (not in Herlihy's work) to romanticize the family and gloss over its problems.

It is by now a commonplace that victims and their killers tend to know one another, and a distressingly high percentage are actually related and/or are part of the same household.[6] Here is a story of family life in thirteenth-century Genoa, a city whose surviving source materials offer an unparalleled volume of information on the realities of family life. On 15 November 1226, Giovanna Pevere, the wife of the late Nicola Embrone, made a series of remarkable statements intended to help her out of a predicament.[7] At this time Giovanna found herself a member, as a sort of lady companion, in the Hospital of San Giovanni in Genoa. This religious house, the local headquarters of the Hospitaller order, had sheltered Giovanna since sometime earlier in the year when she had sought refuge "because my husband had been lately and recently slain." Giovanna now claimed that she had been out of her mind with grief at the

---

6. This has been demonstrated by James B. Given in *Society and Homicide in Thirteenth-Century England* (Stanford, 1977). See, especially, 55–56, where he shows that the low absolute percentage of kin-kin murders masks a high rate; the high overall murder rate makes murder in the family look like a less serious problem than it was.

7. For what follows, see my *Wills and Wealth in Medieval Genoa, 1150–1250* (Cambridge, Mass., 1984), 91–96.

time she made a vow and became a member of the order and she no longer wanted or consented to be there. This declaration stood at the beginning of what must have been a long, expensive, and complex legal effort to extract Giovanna from the religious life. Loyally at Giovanna's side in this crisis were her brothers, Sorleone and Sozo Pevere, two of the men who had murdered their brother-in-law, Nicola Embrone. A long story of high politics and revenge is embedded here, for the Embrone and Pevere were among the most noble of families in the city. A marriage between a man with grown children and a much younger woman was supposed to close a breach or confirm an alliance. But instead the marriage failed and ended in murder. Years later, in 1232, an Embrone attempted to assassinate the Pevere brothers, revealing that this feud was difficult to end. Unfortunately, the sources do not reveal why Nicola Embrone had been killed in 1226, and we know little about the end of this phase of the story. In 1227, the *podestà* of Genoa arranged for the Pevere and Embrone families to exchange a kiss of peace in public, but this act failed to signal the participants in the feud to cease their brawling and assaults.

Failure in family life is not always so easily or fairly defined, but the marriage of Nicola and Giovanna failed when the wife's brothers killed their brother-in-law. The marriage ended up causing more problems than it solved.[8] When the family bond is asked to accomplish goals beyond its scope, like forging political alliances or relieving poverty, it sometimes fails. Expecting from the family more than it can deliver may in some cases doom particular families. The exterior world, in this instance the legal system of medieval Genoa, did not pursue Sozo and Sorleone Pevere as murderers, and in the end they were merely and literally asked to kiss and make up with the unforgiving kin of their victim. This curious double standard applied to violence within the family, that somehow a kin-kin murder does not threaten society in the same way that random violence among strangers does, emerges again and again in the sources, down to today's newspaper. In this case the Pevere were also rich and powerful, circumstances that always affect the wheels of justice. But the crime of passion within the family, which in some ways seems to strike at the cohesion of society, instead seems to strike people as something not likely to threaten them or as something unique and not apt to repeat

---

8. For more on family squabbles among the nobles, see Diane Owen Hughes, "Urban Growth and Family Structure in Medieval Genoa," *Past and Present* 66 (1975): 3–28, esp. 8–13.

itself. The Pevere brothers walked away from a murder because it was all in the family.

In another declaration, made before a notary, we see a second example of how death within the family fell into a legal and moral gray zone. On 18 August 1226, Castagna de Montanesi appeared before a notary to state for the record that he did not believe, and had never believed, that his wife Archesia had killed his daughter Giacoma or otherwise caused her death.[9] This bald declaration betrays no sign of why it was made. No trial or legal process appears to be at stake here. Perhaps Castagna wanted to silence gossip and slander about his family; certainly he, for one, regarded his wife as innocent. Giacoma's age is unknown, so we do not know if this may be a case of crib death (sudden infant death syndrome) or the more notorious "laying over." Archesia was viewed with suspicion by someone, which was often the fate of women, held responsible in moral if not legal terms for the deaths of their children. This time, again, no institution outside of the family intervened.

But by the thirteenth century there were some efforts by the commune to step in and rectify problems within a family. For example, in 1201, the consuls of the *pieve* of Bavari (a neighborhood of Genoa) decided that Baldo de Pomario should have compensation in the amount of three lire for raising his brothers Rollando and Fulcone for two years, the money to come from the property of the brothers.[10] Their father was dead and their mother, Alda, had married again. She had dismissed the young children and did not want to raise them. So the consuls decided to provide for their needs in a realistic manner that surprisingly let Alda off the hook. A widow's remarriage did not have to entail disregard of her children. Yet Genoese men had a common nightmare that they were not able to control their widows and hence their children might be at risk, as were the ones in question here. A mature brother was present in this case, and a court took an interest. These neighborhood officials began to assume a general concern for all minors left in custody, and the guardians were forced to come to court to account for their handling of their wards and their estates.

Beyond the specter of violence and neglect, one problem with the family was that, in an age before comprehensive censuses and vital statistics,

9. Arturo Ferretto, *Liber Magistri Salmonis Sacri Imperii Notarii, 1222–1226,* Atti della società ligure di storia patria, no. 36 (1906), N. 1230.

10. Margaret W. Hall-Cole, Hilmar C. Krueger, Ruth G. Renert, and Robert L. Reynolds, *Giovanni di Guiberto* (Turin, 1939), N. 134, 78.

it was sometimes difficult to say just what group of people constituted a family. In Genoa, as in other Italian city-states, this type of problem often fell within the purview of the church. Ottone, the archdeacon of Genoa, on 28 February 1192, heard a marriage dispute between Giacomo Rosso and Matilda, a widow.[11] Giacomo claimed that Matilda was his wife, and she denied it.[12] In this period, with no parish registers, proving the existence of a marriage depended on witnesses rather than paper. Matilda produced witnesses, described by the notary as suitable, who testified that Giacomo had had another wife, named Sibilia, and a son by her, before he married or became engaged to Matilda. (The word *desponsare* here is difficult and reflects the vagueness about what actually constituted a marriage.) But Sibilia was alive, so whatever rite joined Giacomo and Matilda together did not matter. Archdeacon Ottone absolved Matilda from Giacomo, giving her license to marry as she wished. Thus, a woman managed to escape a family by proving that her so-called husband already had one, although the abandoned Sibilia's fate remains a mystery that probably ended unhappily.

Three other cases of alleged bigamy, all from 1236, were treated as civil matters and heard before a judge and a public meeting (*parlamento*) of the people of Genoa.[13] In all the cases a woman, claiming to be the wife of an accused man, complained that her husband had married someone else. In this century the commune of Genoa, relying on the many precedents in Roman law, still defended its jurisdiction over marriage as a civil matter. The court found the men innocent in all three cases and absolved them from the accusations. Unfortunately, no evidence or reason for these decisions emerges from the terse notices of acquittal. The historian Laura Balletto believes that the three women may have been concubines whose status before the law was perilous at best.[14] Hence, the court and common opinion were not likely to intervene on their behalf

---

11. Margaret W. Hall, Hilmar C. Krueger, and Robert L. Reynolds, *Guglielmo Cassinese* (Turin, 1938), N. 1641, 2:212–13.

12. Gene Brucker has described in wonderful detail a similar kind of case in his *Giovanni and Lusanna: Love and Marriage in Renaissance Florence* (Berkeley, 1986). In this case, the woman was trying to prove that she was the lawful wife of a man who denied it.

13. All the cases are from Archivio di Stato di Genova (ASG), Cartolari Notarili (CN), Cartolare N. 18, parte II, Bartolomeo de Fornari notary, and have been edited and published by Laura Balletto in "Cause matrimoniali a Genova nel 1236," *Archivio storico sardo de Sassari* 4 (1978): 73–84.

14. Ibid., 75.

and upset a legal marriage. A legitimate union between man and woman, requiring the proper words ("I do") in the present tense (not "I will") could only be proved by witnesses, and in these cases no witnesses apparently came forward to testify. Most likely these women were concubines, a relationship recognized in Roman law and common practice but not one conferring any particular rights on the woman. And it was a relationship that might end suddenly. If there were more cases, it would be tempting to speculate that women found a more favorable hearing in the church courts and men might rely on the civil courts to give them the edge.[15]

In a remarkable contract made in Laiazzo in the kingdom of Armenia on 31 March 1279, concubinage emerges into the sharp light of a legal document. Cerasia Ciliciana, probably of Armenian and Genoese parentage, promised Jacopo Porco that she would stay and live with him in his house forever as a good woman and not lie with or allow herself to be known carnally by any other man.[16] Cerasia further promised to be content with the clothing, shoes, and food she received and to perform any and all legal services, inside and outside the house. If she fled or failed to do all this, she gave Jacopo the right to cut (*incidere*) her nose, hand, or foot, as it seemed best to him, or he could put her in irons. Jacopo had this right without any fear of punishment by the Genoese, the Pisans, or the king of Armenia. Finally, Cerasia specified an escape clause that would cancel the contract if she wished to enter the religious life. In turn Jacopo promised to provide her with food and clothing, not punish her for anything she may have done before, and pay her 400 new dirhems of Armenia. I think this contract could not have been made in Genoa proper, but in distant Armenia the facts of concubinage were more frank and brutal. If Jacopo Porco ever returned to Genoa and married, the "lessons" he had learned about women in the east would not have made his house a refuge for anyone.

---

15. In the Florentine case cited above, Brucker concluded that the archbishop of Florence, the saintly Antoninus, found for the woman because he believed her witnesses, he focused on the issue of consent, and he took seriously his role as the protector of the weak (op. cit., 63–75).

16. For what follows, see the contract reproduced in Laura Balletto, *Notai genovesi in Oltremare: Atti rogati a Laiazzo da Federigo di Piazzalunga (1274) e Pietro di Bargone (1277, 1279)* (Genoa, 1989), 344–45. It was canceled on 8 April, so the arrangement only lasted a week. Cerasia had two Genoese men serve as her *vicini* and *propinqui*, the latter term suggesting that they may have been kin. If so, she might have been part Genoese, though the surname Ciliciana suggests a local origin.

Marriage in thirteenth-century Genoa remained at times curiously unstable. On 8 October 1225, Ugone Fornario appeared before a notary to record that after he returned from Tunis he was not able to find his wife Alda. After looking for her inside and outside Genoa, Ugone stated that she was absent against his will and presumably had run away.[17] Church and state could do little for Ugone except lay the foundation for permitting him to marry again. In December of 1222, Giovanni, the archdeacon of Genoa, attempted to make peace between a couple, Pietro and Druda. In this case the wife had fled her husband's house. Archdeacon Giovanni ordered Pietro to take Druda back and treat her with marital affection, which he defined in these terms: Pietro should lie with her in the same bed, pay his marital debt, and share their meals.[18] Pietro was also not allowed to wound Druda, do anything that would detract from her mental or physical health, keep a concubine publicly where he lived, or bring one into his house. In turn Druda was directed to obey her husband and serve him in all things like a good wife. This recipe for a successful Genoese marriage suggests that Pietro was mainly at fault.

Genoese society tried to clarify the uncertainties of marriage by being more specific about just what made a couple married. In 1262, Percivale de Finario married Peroneta by placing a gold ring with a gem on her ring finger.[19] By 1304, a notarial marriage contract noted that both the husband Pietro and the wife Beatrice had answered "yes"—to the questions: did he want her as a wife and would he keep her as such? She had answered the same to the questions: did she want him as a husband and did she consent to the marriage?[20] Finally, in 1203, Gerardo Christiano promised the wealthy and prominent Genoese merchant Guglielmo Streiaporco that he would marry Fatima, Guglielmo's slave, when he made her a Christian and manumitted her.[21] Muslim slaves were no rarity in Genoa, but Gerardo's additional promise is odd: "tenebo eam pro uxore et quod non deriliquam pro meliori vel priori quam possem habere nisi quantum licentia tui guilielmi"—in other words, he "promised to

17. Luigi T. Belgrano, *Della vita privata dei genovesi* (Genoa, 1875), 415–16.

18. Ferretto, op. cit., 284–86: "tractet eam maritali affectu scilicet iacendo cum ea in eodem lecto et redendo sibi debitum coniugii et cum ea comedendo ad discum in una paraside." Since both parties had sworn to obey the archdeacon, he could order them to do these things.

19. ASG, CN, Cartolare N. 52, 172v, Baldoino de Predono notary: "imponendo manu sua anulum deauratum cum gemma in digito anulari dicte Peronete." I am indebted to Robert S. Lopez for this reference.

20. Belgrano, op. cit., 413.

21. Giovanni di Guiberto, N. 1020, 13 November 1203.

keep her as a wife and not abandon her for a better one, or a previous one that he might have had, without Guglielmo's permission." So often more was going on than the notary needed or cared to reveal. Gerardo Christiano may himself have been a convert with a family in some other part of the Mediterranean world. But in an age when church and society increasingly saw marriage as "till death us do part," the promise not to leave a spouse for a better one is itself intriguing, and a previous one is even more revealing of the occasionally fluid nature of the family, which people were able to leave in more ways than we might expect.

One last issue in the gray zone concerns birth and this special way of entering a family. Even here, some notorious ambiguity remained, for, as Genoa's famous archbishop and preacher Jacopo da Voragine never tired of reminding his flock, a woman always knew a child was hers and a man might only hope that a baby was his.[22] In the matter of determining paternity, the law and the notaries offered the illusion of certainty in an uncertain world. On 18 January 1256, Giovannetta Sarda acknowledged to Guglielmo Cerexia that she "had and born from you" a masculine child not yet a Christian (not baptized) and not of any other man.[23] This man and woman were clearly not married, and little may have tied them together except the existence of this unnamed infant. Genoa had its share of illegitimate children, and in some cases these natural heirs were all the family a person might possess and were cherished; other such children were raised as an act of charity by strangers.[24] But in the matter at hand Guglielmo had to accept the legal declaration of paternity, and presumably he wanted to be thus assured that the child was his. In an age before blood tests and DNA screening, the legal statement of his paternity and the promise that Giovannetta would give this child only to him gave to Guglielmo all that he wanted. This the law could do, but since they did not marry the child's refuge depended on Guglielmo's subsequent life. If, for example, Guglielmo eventually married and had legitimate heirs, his bastard could not count on much, especially if Guglielmo died before his wife, who would protect her own children's rights against the claims of an interloper.

---

22. See my *Wills and Wealth* (op. cit., 67–69) for more details on this theme in his preaching, certainly one not unique to him.

23. ASG, CN, Cartolare N. 31, parte I, 196r, Matteo de Predono notary: "Habui et substuli ex te."

24. There are many testaments that reveal these adoptions—a subject not considered by John Boswell in his *The Kindness of Strangers: The Abandonment of Children in Western Europe from Late Antiquity to the Renaissance* (New York, 1988).

All the different families discussed thus far reflect many situations, some tragic, some difficult, some simply part of normal life. I have discussed these people and their families because their circumstances complicate the vision of the family as refuge, at least for everyone. Sometimes society, through the law or some other institution, rescued people whose families were not able to care for them. Medieval society was prepared to take such steps because it knew how the family was supposed to work and hence could recognize trouble. The sources do not permit us to estimate which families were refuges and which were places of sorrow. What we can see is a growing desire to help families survive tragedies. This help could be very personal as well as institutional. Brother Jacopo, prior of the Dominicans in Genoa, was executor of the estate of the well-known Genoese notary Maestro Salmone. In 1248, Jacopo gave an apartment in the late notary's house to a certain Giovanni, "useless with his hands and a pauper," so that he, his wife, and family would have a place to stay for 10 years without rent.[25] This act of charity benefited Maestro Salmone's soul but was also evidence of an evolving ethic of social responsibility.

With all these examples in mind, the question to answer is: what were things normally like in the medieval family? And how can we possibly find out? Some historians believe that statistics reveal the range of life and help to identify average experience. But before the Florentine Catasto of 1427 few reliable sets of data for exploring the composition of medieval families survive. One way to find the normal, or representative, is to look in that most prosaic of sources, the dictionary.[26] Now it so happens that the great Latin dictionary of the Middle Ages, the *Catholicon* of Giovanni Balbi, was completed by this Genoese Dominican monk in 1286.[27] This huge work was more than the jumbled collection of his predecessor Isidore of Seville or the terse word list of his fellow lexicographer Papias (active ca. 1050). The *Magnae Derivationes* of the famous canonist Uguccio, bishop of Ferrara (d. 1210), served as a model for Balbi's more orderly and systematic dictionary, but Uguccio did not

25. ASG, CN, Cartolare N. 22, 110v, 24 April 1248, Bonovassallo de Maiori notary: "inutilatus manibus et pauper," and a nice use of the word *familia* for family.

26. The history of Latin dictionaries in the Middle Ages has not been reconsidered for some time. See George Goetz, *De Glossariorum latinorum origine et fatis* (Leipzig, 1923), text in Latin, for a study of the principal dictionaries, excerpts from their prefaces, and old lists of manuscripts.

27. For what few biographical details are available, see *Dizionario biografico degli italiani*, 5:369–70.

organize his entries in strict alphabetical order, so his text is difficult to consult. But Balbi certainly followed in the footsteps of these predecessors and often simply passed on very old observations that are easy to mistake for contemporary comment. He supplied illustrative quotations for some words and occasionally offered long discursive essays on certain key words, particularly in the two areas that most interested him, theology and science. The task here is to take dictionaries from the seventh, eleventh, and thirteenth centuries and look for changes in the definitions of words relating to the family. This is complicated, because Balbi could draw directly from Isidore and skip over Papias or Uguccio for some meanings, so we should not expect all changes to be cumulative and chronological.

Balbi was not the Samuel Johnson of medieval Latin, but we have something here that no other city in Europe can claim—a great dictionary that fixed the meaning of words, the same ones that appear in the notarial documents we have just considered. For example, Balbi defines *concubina* as a woman "held for illegitimate carnal use," a clear sign that contemporary standards were turning against this old relationship.[28] The dictionary was also a compendium of esoteric learning; where else would the casual reader learn that the elephant, a wonder of chastity, gave up sex after the death of his spouse, no easy feat when his life span sometimes reached three centuries. Papias recorded this information about elephants and even knew that Pyrrhus was the first to bring the animal to Italy.[29] Isidore knew about Pyrrhus but wrote nothing about the chastity or longevity of elephants.[30] Even here, elephants, like good Genoese women, shied away from second marriages. Genoese men certainly did not.

What does the humble dictionary reveal about the family? The Latin language preserved separate words for paternal (*amita*) and maternal (*matertera*) aunts, and the Genoese records confirm that through the thirteenth century these distinctions were still important. Balbi occasionally appears to venture into social and religious theorizing, as he did in his definition of *maritus* (husband). This discursive definition offers the view that in selecting a husband four things matter: *virtus* (manly virtue),

28. Giovanni Balbi, *Catholicon* (Mainz, 1460, anastatic reproduction, 1971). The work is unpaginated but in alphabetical order, so this and other citations are to this edition, by order.

29. Papias, *Vocabulista* (Venice, 1492), 103.

30. Isidore, bk. XII, chap. 2, 14–15, 2:71–72.

genus (family), *pulchritudo* (beauty), and *sapientia* (wisdom). Of these qualities wisdom was the most important, at least to a university-trained lexicographer. But Isidore of Seville, writing nearly seven centuries earlier, had provided the same four qualities in the same order, and he even had a verse from Vergil to illustrate the importance of wisdom.[31] In choosing a wife four qualities should receive the most attention: *pulchritudo* (beauty), *genus* (family), *divitie* (riches), and *mores* (morals). Balbi again copied Isidore and Papias in stating that morals were more important than beauty. Yet what confidence can we have in an analysis of marriage that was content to use in this case an old source with almost no change? What are we learning about thirteenth-century Genoa when Balbi re-presents Isidore? Surely marriage in Visigothic Spain did not mirror family life in Genoa, and perhaps Isidore may himself have copied these comments from a source that seemed old and venerable to him.

So we must be wary of this dictionary and on the lookout for a few modest signs of original thought. Balbi also noted the three reasons for marriage—having offspring, providing companionship (*adiutorium*), and avoiding vice. He justified the middle reason with the simple words used in Genesis to explain the creation of Eve—"for it is not good for a man to be alone."[32] All of this information appears in the definition of the word for "husband," but, again, it all appears in Isidore on "marriage" and in Papias on "wives."

For *matrimonium* Balbi repeatedly insists that consent makes a marriage, and, conversely, that without consent there is no marriage, a point Herlihy stresses in his book as one of the significant legacies of the Middle Ages, and, happily for our purposes, a thought that had not occurred to Isidore or Papias. Here, in a dictionary, the consensual nature of marriage is embedded in the very meaning of a word. For Balbi, marriage is also a sacrament, with all that entails, revealing again one of the great changes that had taken place in the theology of marriage since the time of Isidore.[33] This emphasis on consent improved the circumstances of women within marriage and may have helped some to avoid undesired ones. But, as Balbi also stresses, the husband and father is more worthy than the wife and mother, who is the one more burdened with the cares

---

31. Isidoro de Sevilla, *Etimologías*, ed. Jose Oroz Reta and Manuel-A. Marcos Casquero (Madrid, 1982), 800. Papias included the same information in his definition of *uxores* (Papias, op. cit., 379).

32. Balbi, op. cit.: "non est bonum hominem esse solum," exactly as in Gen. 2:18, and cited as well by Isidore (op. cit., 800).

33. Papias also stressed that marriage was a sacrament (op. cit., 379).

of raising the children. Balbi derives all this himself, for a change, from his fanciful etymology *matris munium* (the duties of motherhood), a revealing meaning for the word *marriage*.

Any woman turning to the word *mulier* (wife) would learn that "the virtue of the husband is greater and that of the wife less," that the wife is actually "weak with respect to the husband," and that the woman is under the authority of her husband because of "guilt and not by nature."[34] (The last reason must refer to Eve but suggests that there may have been equality in natural marriage before the Fall.) On this subject Balbi has gone beyond Isidore by expressing his own ideas about women. Now, if our dictionaries defined *wife* in this way we would surely object, but in this world women would have to wait for the daughter of a Venetian physician, Christine de Pizan, to raise her voice against this almost casual misogyny.

In broader terms Balbi hardly bothers to define *familia,* which came up in the meaning of *filius* (son), derived from *famulus* (slave or servant) and hence *familia*—the great collection of people living under one roof. Balbi's *familia* begins with the great-great-great-great-grandfather, everyone with a common ancestor beyond six generations. With his love of lists, Balbi notes in his definition of *brothers* that there were four types: the first two natural (like Jacob and Esau, Peter and Andrew—two different pairs here), and cognate (of the same family and common blood, like Abraham and Lot). Balbi then distinguishes brothers by common affection, almost friendship, and special fraternal ties among Christians. Thus far Balbi closely follows Isidore and Papias, but then he introduces something that had developed and changed since the early Middle Ages, spiritual kinship.[35] Balbi explores the issue of whether or not a man and woman having the same godparent can marry—his answer is no. Spiritual kinship is important because the medieval family sustained itself and its members by fostering an alternative network based on the voluntary tie of godparenthood to save some people from the problems described above.

Incest is another key word whose definitions provide insight into family troubles. Isidore defined *incest* as a particular way of violating chastity

---

34. Balbi, op. cit.: "virtus viri est maior et mulieris minor," "debilis respectu viri, mulier sub dominio est," "hoc accidit ex culpa non est natura."

35. Papias gave a vague definition of *compater*, a word related to godparenthood, but he wrote very little on the subject (op. cit., 72): "compater cum aliquo eiusdem filii pater"—not in Isidore. See, in general, Joseph H. Lynch, *Godparents and Kinship in Early Medieval Europe* (Princeton, 1986).

and more narrowly as a male crime involving illicit sex with a conse-crated virgin or a close blood relative.[36] Papias extended the class of vic-tims to consecrated virgins, widows, and close blood relatives. He also made the important point that anyone who violated the laws of legiti-mate matrimony in this matter committed incest.[37] Uguccio considered this matter in his definition of *castus* (chaste).[38] He tersely defined incest as *coitus illicitus,* drawing attention to the heart of the taboo. Uguccio also noted that incest stained those who slept with nuns, close blood rel-atives, or virgins. Here, too, Uguccio saw incest as violating the legiti-mate marriage bond, but his emphasis remained at least as much on the sexual nature of the act as on the marital question. Balbi's definition of incest actually cited Uguccio and closely followed his emphasis on illicit intercourse and the violation of protected groups of women. Balbi did not make any references to marriage.[39] The common thread here is that incest was a male sin or crime, in the first instance concerning sex but by extension marriage as well. Incest, as a category of prohibited sexual partners, extended beyond the kin group to other women close to God, and here it is a clue for understanding that consanguinity does not tell the entire story of medieval fears of incest.

From these dictionaries we learn to look closely at consent, the status of women, incest, and godparents as subjects for which the dead hand of the past would not point to old and irrelevant comments. Let us look at one of these topics, incest, in detail.[40] The Middle Ages witnessed impor-tant changes in an area of family life, in the evolving rules on marriage between relatives—consanguinity, more commonly referred to as rules

---

36. Isidore, op. cit., bk. V, chap. 26.24, p. 530, and bk. X, chap. 148, p. 826.

37. Papias, op. cit., 154.

38. Uguccio da Pisa, bishop of Ferrara, *Magnae Derivationes*, Bodleian Library, Manuscript Laud 626—various definitions of *castus* and *castitas* on 23v, then the fol-lowing on 24r: "ceston indeclinabile in cingulum veneris quo attinguntur et utuntur in legittimis nuptiis et de ceston quia caston. qua in feminis maritatis significationem castitatis sit. Unde primo quin pro legittima copula et maritali concordia vel castitate. Unde Statius in Thebaid. . . . incestus, a, um, qui cum moniali vel consanguinea vel vergine concumbit. Unde hoc incestum et incesta, ta, tui, talis coitus illicitus et incesto, as, verbum activum talem impudicare.

39. Balbi, op. cit., *incestus.*

40. I know of no historical study of incest, but for a classic look at contemporary problems, see Ruth S. Kempe and C. Henry Kempe, *The Common Secret: Sexual Abuse of Chidren and Adolescents* (New York, 1984), 47–79. Carl N. Degler, in *In Search of Human Nature* (Oxford, 1991), surveys different views on the incest taboo in the last hundred years (245–69).

about incest.[41] Herlihy saw the rules prohibiting relatives from marrying one another as primarily intended to foster exogamy and bring about a "wider circulation of women through society" and a "breaking of the monopoly of the powerful over women."[42] Herlihy also cited Peter Damian, who declared that the "right to inherit from a person and the right to marry that person were mutually exclusive."[43] Here Herlihy casts some doubt on the thesis put forward by Jack Goody that the church's rules on marriage resulted in part from its desire to make marriage harder to achieve and therefore increase the chances that the church would inherit the property of the faithful.[44] In Herlihy's view this "policy" was too devious to be credible and is not supported by any evidence.[45] More recently, James Brundage also criticized the Goody thesis and pointed out that the stricter rules on marriage between relatives may have been an attack on pagan customs.[46] But, as Brundage himself noted, the ancient Greeks and Romans, as well as the barbarian Germans, either disapproved of or had laws against marriage between close kin, and the latter two extended the bans to people related by marriage.[47] Christopher Brooke, while praising the insights Goody brought to the study of the medieval family, also doubted that the church's inheritance strategies adequately explained the extended incest prohibition.[48] Brooke, too, emphasizes the role Peter Damian played in the eleventh-century changes in the way the church determined degrees of kinship. The personal factor also counted for Brooke, who found Peter Damian's "quite exceptional horror of human sexuality" the motive for finding any means of discouraging marriage by limiting the range of potential partners.[49]

---

41. The most comprehensive treatment of the canon law on marriage remains Adhémar Esmein, *Le mariage en droit canonique* (Paris, 1929–35), 1:370–93, on the impediments to marriage raised by blood, adoption, and spiritual kinship.
42. Herlihy, *Medieval Households*, op. cit., 61–62.
43. Ibid., 136.
44. Jack Goody, *The Development of the Family and Marriage in Medieval Europe* (Cambridge, 1983). This is a central theme of the book, but see pages 95 and 214–15 for clear summaries of the thesis.
45. Herlihy, *Medieval Households*, op. cit., 11–13. See also his illuminating essay, "Making Sense of Incest: Women and Marriage Rules of the Early Middle Ages," in *Law, Custom, and the Social Fabric in Medieval Europe: Essays in Honor of Bryce Lyon*, ed. Bernard S. Bachrach and David Nicholas (Kalamazoo, 1990), 1–16.
46. James Brundage, *Law, Sex, and Christian Society in Medieval Europe* (Chicago, 1987), 88–89, 606–7.
47. Ibid. (Greeks, 14; Romans, 36; Germans, 130–31).
48. Christopher Brooke, *The Medieval Idea of Marriage* (Oxford, 1989), 135.
49. Ibid., 136.

Goody believed that this heightened emphasis on incest, again apparent in Peter Damian's success in changing the system of reckoning kinship, partly resulted from the desire to refute the secular claims of Roman law. In addition, the church was interested in diminishing the influence of the collateral kin and stressing the creative role of the marriage bond.[50] Once again Goody saw the desire for property as the culprit, in this case the tradition that the collateral kin had the right to consent to or to challenge gifts made to the church. People without close kin were more likely to name the church as their principal heir, but would preventing them from marrying relatives make them less likely to marry at all? It is not clear why prohibiting marriage among collateral kin would affect their desire, one way or the other, to give land to the church or their inclination to consent to such gifts by other relatives. Herlihy's point about deviousness is again relevant; Goody tends to see the medieval clergy as rather self-conscious social engineers or even applied anthropologists. At the Fourth Lateran Council of 1215, the church retreated from the broad ban and prohibited marriages only within the fourth degree of kinship. As Georges Duby suggested, the changes in 1215 were a compromise between lay and church conceptions of marriage, and they also closed a loophole that had enabled some couples to have their marriages annulled on the most tenuous claims of consanguinity.[51] The church was also increasingly free with dispensations for cousin marriages because consent prevailed over vague scruples about distant relationships. But, to follow Goody's analysis, we might conclude that the church was less interested in acquiring property in the thirteenth century. No evidence known to me would support that hypothesis unless the changes in 1215 resulted from secular pressures.

Goody relied on Thomas Aquinas, as most scholars do, to explain why the church prohibited incest.[52] First, incest violated the spirit of honor in the family, presumably here a respect for proper status and a desire to avoid polluting the family name. Second, if incest was not prohibited, proximity would make it too easy and hence universally practiced. Third, "incest would prevent people [from] widening their circle of friends"—

---

50. See Goody, op. cit., 136, for Damian, and 142 on the collateral kin.
51. Georges Duby, *Medieval Marriage: Two Models from Twelfth-Century France* (Baltimore, 1978), 80–81.
52. Goody, op. cit., 57–58; Thomas Aquinas, *Summa Theologica* (Rome, 1922), 3:1006–8, 2.2 question 154, art. 9. The third reason is Thomas Gilby's translation of "quia per hoc [incestus] impediretur multiplicatio amicorum, dum enim homo uxorem extraneam accipit, junguntur sibi quadam speciali amicitia omnes consanguinei uxoris . . ."

an overlooked consequence of inbreeding. Last, Aquinas cited Aristotle's view that lust, when combined with the natural affection for kin, produced an evil situation. Aquinas concluded that incest was indecent and repugnant to natural reason as well as divine law. As we will see, modern theories support his views on honor and confused affections in the family, discount the opinion on the role of proximity, and take the circle of friends observation seriously.

Historians and anthropologists continue to focus on the incest taboo and for complex reasons have less to say about the actual practice, prevalence, or meaning of incest in society.[53] There is certainly a difference, as W. Arens points out, "between rules about exogamy, which govern marriage, and rules about sex, which determine incest."[54] According to the teaching of the church, sex outside marriage was always wrong, so any rules about who was able to marry whom, i.e., exogamy, were the rules on sex as well. But can this distinction between exogamy and the incest taboo explain changes in the rules governing marriage? Here we must consider some theories on incest.[55] First, exogamy does not exclude or preclude incest—sadly the two can go hand in hand, as our own society and its appalling level of incest proves. We tend to see incest as a problem inside the family, as inappropriate sexual contact between close kin. Although it is illegal for siblings to marry, for example, and society can usually prevent it, the family sometimes shields a sexual relationship from the eyes of the law, particularly when incest is compounded with the crime of child abuse. A functionalist approach suggests that incest within the family is dysfunctional; it reveals that the family has broken down in some profound way. Yet this dysfunction is not likely to be the cause of the prohibition. Claude Lévi-Strauss concluded that the incest prohibition was the link between nature and culture—"where nature transcends itself."[56] This insight is of little use to historians. Most anthropologists conclude that human culture invented incest in order to describe what happens when someone overcomes the innate trait of avoiding sexual contact with close kin.[57] Various observations support

53. W. Arens, *The Original Sin: Incest and Its Meaning* (New York, 1986), 3—a principal theme of this book.

54. Ibid., 9.

55. For a general summary, see Claude Lévi-Strauss, *The Elementary Structures of Kinship* (Boston, 1969), 12–25. Sigmund Freud, in *Totem and Taboo* (New York, 1950), puts forward a theory of incest based on the Oedipus complex and the activities of the primal horde. No documents illuminate these activities or the theory.

56. Lévi-Strauss, op. cit., 25.

57. W. Arens, op. cit., 92–94.

this conclusion, ranging from studies of monkeys and apes, demonstrating that incest is much more common among humans than among our nearest kin, to studies of children raised on a kibbutz showing a lack of physical attraction between people raised together, kin or not.[58] So an inherited trait, an inclination to avoid sex with familiars, explains the incest taboo. There is, as usual, a gray zone, for example, marriage between cousins, where the familiarity is not intense and hence culture determines whether or not particular societies will permit such unions.

What insights does this theory offer for the Middle Ages? On the most basic level the incest taboo, at least as it concerns close kin, is a given in human societies, even though the taboo is not universal in any recognized sense, because of the problem of determining what group of people constitutes a family. For example, I know of no other culture except the one considered here that disallowed marriage to a sixth cousin. So the innate trait is universal but it manifests itself in different ways according to the cultural rules at hand. The Middle Ages witnessed changes in the scope of the taboo: the first greatly expanded on the pagan Roman concept of incest; the second, more easily dated to the Council of Rome in 1059, built on the previous rules to double the scope of the prohibition; and the third pruned back the bans in 1215. All these changes reflect deeper currents and not simply the whims of one person, like Peter Damian, no matter how influential he may have been.

The family should be a refuge from sexual abuse, so nothing is worse than when it becomes a haven for it, whether through marriage, parental abuse of children, or sibling abuse. In the same vein, the family should be a happy place in a world filled with sorrow, so nothing is worse than when sexual experiences confuse the normal bonds of affection within the family. So the rules on incest accomplish what Herlihy and Brundage have noted, but they also do more. The first change in the early church was an antidote to paganism and a way to distinguish Christian families. The second change, in the eleventh century, doubled the scope of the taboo. Why would anyone want to do that? Apart from Damian's weird

---

58. Jane Goodall describes incestuous matings between chimpanzees—sexually mature males and their mothers, and brother-sister pairs—as "extremely uncommon." See her *The Chimpanzees of Gombe* (Cambridge, Mass., 1986), 466–70, esp. 466. Goodall also found a "high level of familiarity that presumably underlies incest avoidance between mothers and sons and maternal siblings" (469), a familiarity that is absent in other relationships, like that of father-daughter, where incest is more common. For a survey of research on children raised on a kibbutz, see Joseph Shepher, *Incest: A Biosocial View* (New York, 1983), esp. 51–67.

mind, or perhaps his victimized past, people are protected when society extends the boundaries in which sex is not allowed. The third change (in 1215) was more realistic and enforceable; it did not diminish the power of the family but rather made its boundaries more plausible and clear.

These changes become clearer if we look outside Christian culture. In Islamic societies the category "Mahram" includes all people to whom marriage is forbidden, whether because of a relationship by blood, marriage, or sexual act, or because of a category special to Islam, that of milk relatives, in which the tie was established by wet-nursing.[59] Jane Khatib-Chahidi observed that those not allowed to marry one another "are permitted to be on familiar terms with each other and share the same physical space; those not related in this way, should avoid each other's company."[60] So in the Muslim world the incest taboo serves the additional function of defining which men and women can be on easy and familiar terms—only those who should not have sex. Those who could marry were denied the opportunity of social interaction and women especially remained private persons outside the public eye, except for their *mahram* males. Since the ordinary punishment for incest was decapitation, clearly Islam had strict rules on the matter.[61] Because some Muslim men have up to four wives and children sometimes a generation apart, family life is complex. In a case known to Emrys Peters concerning the Bedouin of Cyrenica, a male and his aunt (of the same age) had a child who was abandoned in the desert. The girl was sent away in disgrace while nothing happened to the male.[62] The penalties of incest tended to fall more heavily on women and children.

The private social world of men and women in the medieval Christian West remains a mystery; we know only a little about court life and even

---

59. Jane Khatib-Chahidi, "Sexual Prohibitions, Shared Space and Fictive Marriages in Shi'ite Iran," in *Women and Space: Ground Rules and Social Maps*, ed. Shirley Ardener, 112–35 (New York, 1981) (see esp. 114–17). Sour milk plays an important part in Zulu kinship, where only relatives may eat it together. See W. D. Hammond-Tooke, "Twins, Incest, and Mediators: The Structure of Four Zulu Folk Tales," *Africa* 62 (1992): 203–20, esp. 211.

60. Khatib-Chahidi, op. cit., 112.

61. Guido Ruggiero found a Venetian case of father-daughter incest in 1457 for which the father was sentenced to prison for 10 years and then perpetual banishment. In a case of father-stepdaughter incest in 1467, the punishment was 2 years in prison and perpetual banishment. See his *The Boundaries of Eros: Sex Crimes and Sexuality in Renaissance Venice* (Oxford, 1985), 42, 107.

62. Emrys L. Peters, *The Bedouin of Cyrenica: Studies in Personal and Corporate Power* (Cambridge, 1990), 192.

less about townspeople and peasants. In a society with stern rules on sexual behavior, increasing the scope of the incest taboo also widened the circle of more free and trusting, less sensually charged relationships among men and women. J. K. Campbell noted among the Sarakatsani people of northwestern Greece that "only in the family and kindred is it possible for unmarried persons of the opposite sex even to hold conversation."[63] So, in a paradox, a broader incest taboo increased trust, decreased suspicion and sexual tensions in the kinship group, and allowed men and women to share the same space casually and without shame. This wider circle in which sex was a crime also served to protect children, whether kin or not, from sexual abuse in a society in which strong beliefs on consent and consanguinity protected blood relatives not of an age to consent to anything. Even when this protection broke down, as it did in a case of father-daughter incest among the Sarakatsani, the shepherds could "only understand this enormity as a plot of the Devil," so horrible was it to them.[64]

Apart from relaxing tensions among adult kin, medieval views on incest may also have addressed the problem of child abuse. People hate child abuse, and are even more scandalized by incestuous exploitation of children, but what can society do? Make it illegal, surely, but the law does not easily enter family life and it is better at picking up the pieces than at preventing abuse. In the Middle Ages it was one thing to prevent third cousins from marrying and another to protect little children. Urbanization in the eleventh and twelfth centuries permitted an increased reliance in the middle and upper classes on wet nurses. This practice probably weakened the innate lack of sexual interest in people raised together, especially when the wet nurse did not live with the family. This weakening of the trait would lead to more sibling incest/child abuse within the family and undercut opposition, based on some fear of pollution, to cousin marriages.[65] Contemporaries were probably not conscious of this cause-and-effect relationship, but heightened concern to define incest could result from more personal experience and knowledge

63. J. K. Campbell, *Honour, Family and Patronage: A Study of Institutions and Moral Values in a Greek Mountain Community* (Oxford, 1964), 101.

64. Ibid., 336.

65. For more on the recently emphasized special problems of sibling sexual abuse, see Vernon R. Wiehe, *Sibling Abuse: Hidden Physical, Emotional, and Sexual Trauma* (Lexington, Mass., 1990), esp. 49–71. Wiehe raises the possibility that some older siblings, who are forced to act as parents but cannot handle the responsibility, may become abusers (151), but he has nothing to say about the taboo and innate traits.

of the problem. Jean Gerson saw the problem of familiarity the other way; in a sermon on lechery he praised the French for making their infants sleep alone in small beds, not like the Flemish, who allowed them to sleep with their sisters and others.[66] More likely, children no longer raised and sleeping together would miss the opportunity to develop a lack of physical attraction to siblings, and for them a stronger incest taboo might serve to counteract feelings of attraction that might have arisen when the children returned from the wet nurses. The growing interest in Jesus as infant and in his perfect childhood makes more sense in this atmosphere of concern about incest and the sexuality of children. By making the circle of the taboo so broad, the new definition of incest could succeed in diminishing sexual contact among close kin even as it fostered nonsexual relations between male and female relatives. By 1215, some realism set in, but the key to understanding the church's motives in my view remains the children—either the sexual abuse of them or the production of tainted children through incestuous unions.

If there is anything to the connection I have made between shifting def- initions of the incest taboo and the problem of child abuse within the family, then more research into dysfunctional families may reveal other ways in which church and society with the best of intentions pried into the intimacies of family life. For example, Gerson also warned against kissing and touching children in their secret or special spots, and he believed that the children should be encouraged to report such contact to confessors, who should in turn ask them about their own desires.[67] What effect did (or does) oral confession have on the practice of incest and child abuse? Herlihy was surely right to emphasize the family as a place of refuge, even as he recognized that to some it was a prison. Medieval governments began to intervene and save some families from poverty or worse. The rules governing incest may have seemed to some to be an unwarranted intrusion into private matters, but the motivation may have been a desire to help. Most of the time the family was a refuge from the troubles of the world and perhaps even the well-intended acts of reform- ers and do-gooders. Herlihy's speculations about medieval family life rested on a firm grasp of the evidence as well as optimism about human

---

66. Jean Gerson, *Oeuvres complètes,* vol. 7 (Paris, 1968), 831, in an advent ser- mon of 1402.

67. Gerson, op. cit., 838: "Je di oultre on ne doit pas moins abaisier ou tenir nus, en lieu secret par especial, enfans malle que femmes ou filles," alluded to by P. Ariès, op. cit., 107.

nature and the intentions of the medieval church. He would have been suspicious of any theory about the incest taboo that located its origins solely in inheritance strategies or the alleged genetic deficiencies of children born through incest. Alleviating the sorrows of family life became an aim of church and government in the thirteenth century for the twin goals of achieving salvation and creating a stable society.

Part 2
Power and Patronage in the Middle Ages and the Renaissance: Local History

Writing, Memory, and Landholding in Medieval Provence

Stephen Weinberger

From reading the medieval sources—chronicles, saints' lives, law codes, charters, and edicts of church councils—it seems that no subject was more important for those who sought wealth, power, and prestige than amassing and securing real property. It was largely to achieve these ends that armies were raised, fortifications constructed, and battles waged.

Yet, while armed combat was clearly the most spectacular way of acquiring, recovering, or maintaining control over property, it was certainly not the most common, nor was it necessarily the most effective, means of realizing these goals. Although violence was certainly common in the Middle Ages, the existence of tens of thousands of charters attests to the fact that property normally changed hands in an orderly and peaceful manner. Moreover, these documents make it clear that when disagreements occurred over the ownership of property they were most often resolved not through physical force but in court or in informal public hearings. Indeed, during the past three decades a very substantial body of literature has appeared that discusses and analyzes the ways in which property disputes were resolved.[1]

---

1. W. Davies, "Disputes, Their Conduct and Their Settlement in the Village Communities of Eastern Brittany in the Ninth Century," *History and Anthropology* 1 (1985): 289–312; W. Davies, "People and Places in Dispute in Ninth-Century Brittany," in *The Settlement of Disputes in Early Medieval Europe,* ed. Wendy Davies and Paul Fouracre (Cambridge, 1986), 45–65; J.-P. Delumeau, "L'exercice de la justice dans le comté d'Arezzo (IXe–debut XIIIe siècle)," *Melanges de l'École française de Rome. Moyen âge, Temps modernes* 90 (1978): 563–605; J. Nelson, "Dispute Settlement in Carolingian West Francia," in *The Settlement of Disputes,* ed. Wendy Davies and Paul Fouracre, 45–64; S. Weinberger, "Cours judiciaires, justice, et résponsabilité sociale dans la Provence médiévale: IXe–XIe siècles," *Revue Historique* 267 (1982): 273–88; S. White, "Pactum . . . legem vincit et amor judicium: The Settlement of Disputes

The purpose of this study is not to consider the outcome of various judicial hearings or the ways in which these bodies functioned but to evaluate the role of writing in securing the ownership and possession of property.[2] More specifically, we shall discuss what were the strengths and the weaknesses of written instruments as a means of controlling property. And we shall consider this issue both from the point of view of those who relied on such documents and from that of those who did not.

The scope of this investigation will concentrate on Provence between the ninth and eleventh centuries. Located in the southeastern corner of France, Provence had the distinction of being the most thoroughly Romanized province of the empire, as well as being the last one in Gaul to remain under Roman control. Thus the Roman tradition of requiring written documentation for the legitimate transfer of property was well established in this region. Indeed, numerous Provençal charters begin by recalling this tradition, stating that "Authority clearly shows and Roman law orders that any person who wishes to give, sell, exchange, or transfer his property to another person should list it in the page of a testament, so that it shall remain secure and undisturbed for a very long time."[3] Fur-

---

by Compromise in Eleventh-Century Western France," *American Journal of Legal History* 22 (1978): 281–308; S. White, "Feuding and Peace-Making in the Touraine Around the Year 1100," *Traditio* 42 (1986): 195–263; P. Geary, "Vivre en conflit dans une France sans état: Typologie des mécanismes de règlement des conflit (1050–1200)," *Annales E.S.C.* 5 (1986): 1107–33; F. Cheyette, "Suum cuique tribuere," *French Historical Studies* 6 (1970): 287–99; R. Fossier, *Enfance de l'Europe, Xe–XIIe Siècles: Aspects économiques et sociaux* 1 (Paris, 1982): 394–440; R. Collins, "The Role of Writing in the Resolution and Recording of Disputes," in *The Settlement of Disputes*, ed. Wendy Davies and Paul Fouracre, 207–14; E. Tabuteau, *Transfers of Property in Eleventh-Century Norman Law* (Chapel Hill, 1988); Barbara Rosenwein, Thomas Head, and Sharon Farmer, "Monks and Their Enemies: A Comparative Approach," *Speculum* 66 (1991): 764–96; Constance Bouchard, *Sword, Miter and Cloister in Burgundy, 980–1198* (Ithaca, N.Y., 1987); Barbara Rosenwein, *To Be the Neighbor of Saint Peter: The Social Meaning of Cluny's Property, 909–1049* (Ithaca, N.Y., 1989).

2. Among the works that deal with literacy in the Middle Ages, see especially M. Clanchy, *From Memory to Written Record: England, 1066–1307* (Cambridge, 1979); B. Stock, *The Implications of Literacy: Written Language and Models of Interpretation in the Eleventh and Twelfth Centuries* (Princeton, 1983); J. Nelson, "Literacy in Carolingian Government," *The Uses of Literacy in Early Medieval Europe* (Cambridge, 1990), 258–96; R. McKitterick, *The Carolingians and the Written Word* (Cambridge, 1989); M. Parkes, "The Literacy of the Laity," in *Literature and Western Civilization: The Medieval World*, ed. D. Daiches and A. K. Thorlby, 555–77 (London, 1973).

3. *Cartulaire de l'abbaye de Lérins*, ed. H. Moris and E. Blanc (Paris, 1883), #192 (1046–66).

thermore, the period under consideration witnessed a number of major political disruptions. Following the collapse of the Carolingian Empire, Provence experienced the effects of civil war and a prolonged series of raids by the Saracens, who succeeded in establishing a fortified base at Garde-Freinet. Although a degree of political order was established in 972 when Count William II (d. 993/94) drove the Saracens from their stronghold, this stability was short-lived, and by the second decade of the eleventh century civil strife had once again returned to the region. Under these conditions, the control of property was extremely insecure. The charters of this period are filled with references to lands being lost through usurpations and to numerous judicial hearings being held to resolve property disputes. This period in Provençal history is therefore rich for evaluating the role of writing as a means of making landholding secure.[4]

Before turning to the matter at hand, we need to address certain misleading impressions left by the charters regarding the differences between clergy and laity. First, one might reasonably conclude that only the clergy appreciated and relied upon writing to secure their landholdings. In the descriptions of property disputes, it was the clergy alone who presented written documents at public hearings to prove their ownership. In none of the Provençal disputes did laymen offer this form of proof. Instead, they relied exclusively on the testimony of witnesses and oral arguments to prove that the property in question was theirs by right of possession, inheritance, or enfiefment.[5]

However, though laymen did not present documents in these disputes, there is nonetheless good reason to believe that they regularly used documents when exchanging property. Provence, after all, was the land of the *droit écrit*. The fortuitous inclusion in ecclesiastical cartularies of a small number of charters detailing the sale, gift, or donation of land between laymen demonstrates that, at least for those members of the laity claiming to live in accordance with Roman law, written documents were regarded as a normal and necessary component of land transfers.[6]

---

4. For a detailed discussion of this period, see J.-P. Poly, *La Provence et la société féodale, 879–1166* (Paris, 1976), 3–29, 172–81.

5. *Cartulaire de l'abbaye de Saint-Victor de Marseille*, ed. B. Guérard (Marseilles, 1857), #26 (845), #27 (1010); #341 (1074).

6. *Cartulaire de l'église d' Apt (835–1130?)*, ed. N. Didier et al. (Paris, 1967), #4 (890), #36 (986–87), #40 (991), #52 (983–90), #53 (983–90), #66 (1010–32), #67 (1020–40); *Lérins*, #31 (1032), #120 (1047).

Second, the documents appear to indicate that the clergy were almost always successful in their struggles with laymen over the ownership of property. Virtually all disputes between laymen and clergy concluded with the latter recovering the ownership and usually the possession of the contested property. While in a few instances laymen might receive the land's usufruct, the documents clearly indicate that the clergy were the rightful and acknowledged owners who, in a spirit of generosity and compromise, permitted their lay adversaries to possess the property for a limited time.[7] Here, again, this impression of consistent clerical triumph over the greed of laymen is due more to the nature of the documents than to the actual outcome of disputes. The charters, after all, served primarily as a record of land acquisition. If a religious house failed in its attempt to acquire or recover certain lands, and instead the disputed property was awarded to its lay adversaries, then the clergy would not normally produce a charter. On those occasions when charters do refer to the loss of ecclesiastical lands to laymen, these discussions normally recount how the clergy eventually recovered the property in question. For example, a charter from 1055 begins by recounting how the monastery of Saint-Victor, "destroyed by pagans . . . reduced to solitude,"[8] had lost the village of Roquebrune. The charter then describes in considerable detail how the monks ultimately recovered the village.[9] Had the monks been unsuccessful and Roquebrune remained in the hands of laymen then the usurpation would undoubtedly have resulted in silence.

In terms of their content, the charters seem ideally suited to serve as convincing proof of one's ownership of a specific piece of property. Following a highly standardized format, these documents first listed the names of donors, vendors, and family members. This was normally followed by a statement regarding the origin of ownership, whether by inheritance or purchase, and a description of the land and its buildings. Further, its location and borders were listed, followed by a malediction against anyone who might contest the right of the new owners to the property in question. This warning contained the spiritual threat of incurring the wrath of God as well as monetary penalties fixed either in pounds of gold or double the value of the land. The charter would conclude with the signatures of the parties involved and the witnesses.

---

7. *Les chartes du pays d'Avignon, (438–1040)*, ed. G. de Manteyer (Mâcon, 1914), #109 (1006–14); *Saint-Victor*, #341 (1074).

8. *Saint-Victor*, #565 (ca. 1055).

9. Ibid.

Clearly, the charters constituted formidable evidence in support of one's property claims, and great care was taken in the preparation and preservation of these documents. Indeed, many charters begin with a general assertion that written documents were essential in making property ownership secure. Only possession of such documents could provide rightful landowners with the assurance that, as one charter affirms, "no one can claim it [the property] either by force, ignorance, envy, or any other form of malice."[10] This attitude is reflected even more strikingly in a charter issued at the request of the monks of Saint-Victor by Fulk and William, the viscounts of Marseilles. The viscounts explained that their deceased father had donated land to the monastery of Saint-Victor and that the monks now wished to build on the property but were reluctant to do so without the security of a charter. Accordingly, the two brothers agreed to issue the document "so that after our death no one will molest them [the monks], by giving money, which we see being done daily, since faith is rare and malice is far more common."[11]

In the great majority of property disputes in which plaintiffs presented charters as proof of ownership, the outcome was decided either in court before judges or in informal hearings before prominent local figures. Occasionally, however, the charter itself was of sufficient force to effect the return of property without the need for intermediaries. In one such case Counts Geoffrey I and Bertrand I announced before a gathering of prominent figures that they were returning the village of Chaudol to the monastery of Saint-Victor.[12] They explained that they had reached this decision after having seen the ancient charter of donation made to the monks by the *patricius* Nemfidius and his family and from fear of incurring the awesome wrath of God.[13]

Yet, while charters were much valued by property owners, they were certainly not without their limitations. First, they could be challenged in court. The widespread existence and awareness of forged documents meant that questions could always be raised about the authenticity of a particular charter. In one such instance, the monks of Saint-Victor became involved in a dispute with a certain Aldebert of Saint-George and his sons. According to the proceedings, although the monks possessed a

---

10. *Lérins*, #139 (1030–46).
11. *Saint-Victor*, #56 (1035).
12. Ibid., #737 (1048).
13. Ibid.: "visa eciam carta pervetusta . . . et ne iram Dei, quod est orrendum et valde metuendum . . ." See also #31 (780).

supporting document, their adversaries "attempted to falsify . . . that charter."[14] Admittedly, the preceding phrase is somewhat ambiguous. While it might mean that Aldebert disputed the authenticity or content of the charter, it might also mean that he tried to tamper with it. In either case, however, Aldebert was not prepared to allow the charter to be placed in evidence without challenging it. And, second, while a charter might be accepted as authentic, questions could be raised about the previous owner of the disputed land. If it could be demonstrated that he had acquired the property illegally, then the charter by which he alienated the land to the present owner would be invalid.[15]

Even during the relatively stable Carolingian period, when public officials and courts possessed the authority and power to enforce the law and render binding judgments, those relying on charters to prove their ownership could never be entirely secure. The descriptions of Carolingian courts makes it clear that while a written document was an important form of evidence it was not necessarily sufficient. For example, in 845, a court was held at Cadarosc to settle a dispute between the bishop of Marseilles and the vicar Rothbert over control of the customs tolls collected at the village of Ligagnau. Each of the disputants was represented in court by an *advocatus*. While both sides made oral arguments supporting their conflicting claims, the bishop's *advocatus* also presented documents issued by Pepin, Charlemagne, Louis the Pious, and Lothair to support his case. Following this, 20 *pagenses* (men of the district who were deemed to be knowledgeable about this case), each identified by name, gave testimony. On the basis of all of this evidence, the dispute was decided in favor of the bishop of Marseilles.[16]

This case and several others in which both written documents and the testimony from witnesses were introduced raise the question of the relative weight of each form of evidence. While both are regarded as normal and important to a case, it is not clear whether a charter possessed an inherently greater value as evidence than did the memory of a living witness. In the case just described, the two forms of evidence did not disagree. However, in the event that witnesses contradicted the charter, the judge would obviously have a more difficult time reaching a verdict.

---

14. Ibid., #605 (ca. 1090): "Quam cartam . . . idem Aldebertus et filii ejus falsare niterentur . . ."

15. For instances of this, see the discussion in C. Wickham, "Land Disputes and Their Social Framework in Lombard-Carolingian Italy, 700–900," in *The Settlement of Disputes*, ed. Wendy Davies and Paul Fouracre, 105–24.

16. *Saint-Victor*, #26 (845).

Aside from what might be considered formal limitations, under which charters could either be negated by challenges or neutralized by the conflicting testimony of witnesses, there were also certain inherent problems in relying upon written documents as proof of ownership. In particular, those who had designs on ecclesiastical property could conspire to destroy the clergy's proof of ownership. In one such case, dating from the late eighth century, the *patricius* Antenor attempted to wrest control of the village of Chaudol from the monks of Saint-Victor by having their charter destroyed.[17] Fortunately for the monks, Antenor failed, and the charter remained safe. Yet the incident does reveal that property ownership that relied upon written documents was not as secure as one might imagine and could be undermined by a determined and unscrupulous rival.

If there were risks, or at least uncertainties, in relying upon written documents during the Carolingian period, the Saracen raids and civil war that raged in Provence during most of the ninth and tenth centuries made it clear just how vulnerable this form of proof was. In the wake of these disruptions many religious houses were abandoned and their contents destroyed. Having lost their charters, clergy often found themselves unable to support their claims to their former vast estates. In a highly emotional appeal for comital aid, Riculfe, bishop of Fréjus, described a condition that was no doubt common to many churches and monasteries. "The city of Fréjus," he lamented, "in which this church was constructed, has been destroyed by the cruelty of the Saracens and reduced to solitude, its inhabitants having been exterminated or dispersed through fear. No one remains who can designate the properties and possessions of this church. We have lost our old charters, the edicts of our kings have disappeared, the titles containing our privileges and other documents have perished from age or have become the victim of the flames. Only the name of my bishopric remains."[18] In similar terms the monastery of Saint-Victor was described as "destroyed by the Vandals [i.e., the Saracens], its possessions dispersed, and its charters lost or burned . . ."[19]

Although Count William II (d. 993–94) managed to restore order to the region following his victory over the Saracens in 972, this respite was

---

17. Ibid., #31 (780).
18. *Gallia christiana*, vol. 1, inst. 82.
19. *Saint-Victor*, #15 (ca. 1030).

short-lived. By the first decades of the eleventh century, Provence, like many other regions in France, experienced a rapid deterioration in public authority and a dramatic increase in property disputes. One result of renewed instability was to diminish the value of written documents as proof of landownership. Perhaps the most striking example of this was the refusal of public officials to acknowledge the charters presented before them. For example, in 1020, the monks of Saint-Victor appeared in court before William II and his brother Fulk, the viscounts of Marseilles.[20] At issue was the ownership of the village of Caravaillon. Claiming that the property had been usurped during the chaos of the tenth century, the monks presented an ancient charter by which *vir nobilissimus* Sigfried and his wife had donated the village to the monastery. Although the viscounts praised Sigfried, they chose to postpone the case until just before the festival of Saint John the Baptist. When the appointed day finally arrived, the monks' adversaries requested and received yet a second delay.

When at last a trial was held, the viscounts decided not to settle it in the traditional way by means of the presentation of written documents and the testimony of witnesses. Instead, the ordeal by fire would determine the outcome. Although this ended in favor of the monks, their adversaries remained intransigent and insisted on a second ordeal—that by water. Again the viscounts acquiesced, the trial was arranged, and for a second time the outcome supported the claims of the monks. This time, however, the result proved to be conclusive, and the viscounts ordered the village to be returned to the monks.

What seems peculiar about this case is the viscounts' decision to ignore the charter of Sigfried and their apparent reluctance to render a prompt verdict. It is certainly possible that the monks' adversaries were prominent people whom the viscounts did not wish to offend. More likely, family interests appear to have influenced their decision. Following the description of the second ordeal and the recovery of the land, the document adds that the greater part of Caravaillon still remained in illegal hands—those of Pons II, who happened not only to be the bishop of Marseilles but was also the son of Viscount William II.

While their motivations must remain an object of speculation, what is clear is that the viscounts chose not to rely on the evidence of the original

20. Ibid., #27 (ca. 1020).

charter of donation in deciding the case. In this situation the monks could do little but tolerate the delays and trials by ordeal.

As public officials proved to be unreliable or ineffective in resolving disputes and rendering justice, those who had traditionally relied upon the courts and written documents faced a very distressing situation. In 1067, for instance, after mentioning their recent losses, the monks of Montmajour complained about the state of affairs in which "there is now neither a duke nor a marquis to render justice, but from the lowest up to the greatest of the lay order, they daily commit injustices."[21] At about the same time, a monk wrote to Bernard, the newly elected abbot of Saint-Victor, urging that he be allowed to study law at Pisa. He explained that he would then employ this legal knowledge on behalf of the monastery, which he described as "being harassed by clergy and laymen as they please."[22]

Within these conditions, we find that after 1020 disputes were no longer resolved in formal court hearings but informally through the influence of mediators or between the adversaries themselves. Unlike the earlier Carolingian courts, which rendered clear verdicts and awarded the disputed property to one of the claimants, compromise, with each side receiving some material satisfaction, now became the preferred means of dispute resolution.[23] Regardless of the strength of a case or whether one possessed a charter, one could always expect to benefit in some fashion.

To make this point more clearly, we might briefly mention certain cases that seem to be typical of the general pattern. In one, which dates from 1006/1014, the widow of a certain Salvator challenged an agreement over the possession of property that her former husband had made with the monks of Saint-André of Avignon. The dispute ended when two prominent laymen mediated a settlement allowing the widow to retain possession of the property for four years, after which time it would revert to the monastery.[24] In a second dispute from midcentury, Rostang, the bishop of Avignon, acknowledged that he and his brother had illegally

---

21. "Histoire de l'abbaye de Montmajour," ed. Dom Chantelou, *Revue d'histoire de Provence* 1 (1890–91): 179 (1067).

22. E. Martène, *Veterum scriptorum et monumentorum historicum, dogmaticorum, moralium; amplissima collectio* (Paris, 1724) 1, 469–71.

23. For discussions of compromise settlements, see Davies, "People and Places"; White, "Pactum"; Geary, "Vivre en conflit"; Cheyette, "Suum cuique tribuere"; Weinberger, "Cours judiciaires"; Bouchard, *Sword*; Rosenwein, *Saint Peter*.

24. *Avignon*, #109 (1006–14).

retained land that their uncle had sold to the monastery of Saint-Victor. With his brother having given up his claim to the land before his death, the seemingly repentant bishop now did the same. However, the settlement concluded with Rostang adding that "Since I am not able to abstain from the payment of temporal goods, I receive 40 *solidi* in Ottonian money."[25] Another case from the end of the century involved land that three brothers had sold to the monks of Saint-Victor. This sale was challenged by two men, Aicard and Guiran, who, as relatives of the vendors, insisted that they had never consented to the sale. To resolve the matter the monks gave Aicard and Guiran a pack animal, and they in turn dropped their challenge.[26] Another dispute, also from midcentury, involved the sale of land by a certain Amic of Calcia to the cathedral of Nice. After several years the son of Amic confronted the canons of the church and demanded the return of the land. To settle the matter a hearing was arranged, and in the presence of *boni homines* the son relinquished his claim and received 20 Ottonian *solidi*.[27] Last, in 1074, the monks of Saint-Victor became involved with Aicard and Laufred, the sons of Gerald Episcopalis, over property in Brignolles.[28] Although the brothers claimed that the property was part of their family estate, the monks presented a charter showing that Gerald had actually donated it to the monastery. This proof was apparently sufficient to convince everyone, including the two brothers, that the property belonged legally to Saint-Victor. However, the matter did not end there. Instead, the description of the hearing states that "The abbot and the monks, on the advice of the *boni homines,* returned it to them [the brothers] as a fief . . ."[29]

The point that these and most other eleventh-century property disputes raise involves the efficacy of written instruments as a safeguard of one's property. Since these documents could be challenged and ignored, and those without charters could still advance claims to the property and reasonably expect to receive some material settlement, we might then ask whether there was some other benefit to be derived from possessing a charter that placed all potential claimants without documents at a distinct disadvantage. The answer, it seems, rests in the fact that written

---

25. *Saint-Victor*, #664 (1040–80).

26. P.-A. Amargier, "Chartes inédites (XIe siècle) du fonds de Saint-Victor de Marseille," typescript, 1967, #128.

27. *Cartulaire de l'ancienne cathédrale de Nice*, ed. E. Cais de Pierlas (Turin, 1888), #20 (1081).

28. *Saint-Victor*, #341 (1074).

29. Ibid.

documents provided those who possessed them with testimony that could transcend the limits of human memory and indeed of time itself. Moreover, those who relied on documents were clearly aware of this. In one charter from the monastery of Lérins, the monks prefaced the details of a donation by explaining that such transactions should be committed to writing "so that memory which is subject to forgetfulness will not decide."[30]

Another charter is even more emphatic in making the point that the passage of time is of no consideration when it comes to recovering lost property. It asserts that "ecclesiastical property, acquired by a person of any order and by whatever means, however long he has possessed it, even if it were improved by buildings and possessions, will soon be demanded by Church officials to whom the properties legally belong, and they must be returned without any conflict."[31]

Documents were important not only for recording the details of sales, donations, and exchanges of property but for citing the injustices one had suffered. By possessing in writing the details of property lost through usurpation or deception, a family or religious house could keep the memory of that loss alive indefinitely and therefore could nurture the hope of a recovery at some future date. In one such instance, dating from the end of the tenth century, the abbot of Saint-Victor began his discussion of the injustices done to his monastery by telling the reader "I want to write this . . . so that present and future generations will know what to believe and what to deny."[32] He then proceeded to relate how his predecessor had been deceived by the viscount of Marseilles, who, despite his promises to the contrary, retained monastic lands for himself and his family.

If the above examples demonstrate how writing served to perpetuate the memory of property losses, this point is made even more strikingly for those who did not possess documents. When looking at the numerous property disputes appearing in the eleventh-century documents, certain patterns appear. Although several disputes are described in a most cursory fashion, many others offer important details regarding those who were the adversaries of the clergy and in particular about the nature of their claim to the disputed property. First, unlike the clergy, these individuals never supported their claims to the property with written documents. Instead, since the lands they disputed had usually belonged to or

30. *Lérins*, #1 (1094).
31. *Saint-Victor*, #155 (ca. 1030).
32. Ibid., #77 (993).

at least been possessed by their families, they tended to base their claims on hereditary rights or at least on familial attachment to the property.[33] For example, in the dispute involving the widow of Salvator, her husband had originally held the land in benefice from a certain Rostang and then from the monastery of Saint-André.[34] In the other four cases discussed above, the property in question had been donated or sold to the clergy by a member of the disputant's family. Rostang, bishop of Avignon, usurped land that his deceased uncle Miro had donated to Saint-Victor;[35] Aicard and Guiran challenged a sale of land made by their relatives,[36] as did the sons of Gerald Episcopalis.[37] The son of the recently deceased Amic of Calcia did the same for the land his father had sold.[38]

Second, insofar as it is possible to tell, these people tended to postpone their challenges until the family member who had alienated the property had died.[39] In those few instances in which the original donor/vendor was still alive, he tended to become involved in resolving the dispute between his relatives and the clergy. For example, in 1050, when Peter Saumada had usurped land that his uncle Fulk, the viscount of Marseilles, had donated to the monastery of Saint-Victor, the angry viscount personally restored the donation and then warned that "if any of my nephews or heirs will disrupt this gift in any way he shall have nothing that I have given him from my inheritance.[40] Similarly, following a sale made by a certain Amalric and his family to Saint-Victor, his two nephews disputed the transaction. To resolve the matter, Amalric offered other lands to the monks and gave the disputed property to his

---

33. S. Weinberger, "Les conflits entre clercs et laics dans la Provence du XIe siècle," *Annales du Midi* 92 (1980): 269–79. This situation was certainly not unique to Provence. Writing at the turn of the twelfth century, Abbot Guibert of Nogent offered a strikingly similar picture of the situation in northwestern France. He lamented that "alas, those gifts which their parents, moved with love of such things, made to the holy places, the sons now withdraw entirely or continually demand payment for their renewal, having utterly degenerated from the goodwill of their sires" (Guibert of Nogent, *Self and Society in Medieval France: The Memoirs of Abbot Guibert of Nogent*, ed. J. Benton [New York, 1970], 66). See also P. Johnson, *Prayer, Power, and Patronage: The Abbey of la Trinité Vendôme, 1032–1187* (New York, 1981), 97.

34. *Avignon*, #109 (1006–14).

35. *Saint-Victor*, #664 (1040–80).

36. "Chartes inédites," #128.

37. *Saint-Victor*, #341 (1074).

38. *Nice*, #20 (1081).

39. S. Weinberger, "Aristocratic Families and Social Stability in Eleventh Century Provence," *Journal of Medieval History* 8 (1982): 149–57.

40. *Saint-Victor*, #452 (1050).

nephews.[41] These, however, are exceptional cases. The great majority of property disputes did not involve the original donor/vendor because his relatives, out of either respect or fear, waited until he had died.

Third, and most striking, is the relationship between those who disputed the donation/sale and the relative who had made it. In virtually every instance for which information is supplied, those who challenged the clergy were of the same generation as, or at most only one generation removed from, that family member. That is to say, the disputants were the widows, sons, nephews, and cousins of those who had donated or sold the land. Virtually never do we find grandchildren, grandnephews, or more distant family members initiating property claims.

Taken together these three points suggest that those who did not possess documents but wished to reclaim property that had earlier belonged to their families were forced to act within limited confines. They had to delay their challenge until the original alienator had died but not so long that the task of recovery became the responsibility of the next generation. Generally, after only one generation outside the family, the memory of and attachment to that property seem to have succumbed to time. It was lost forever.[42]

In the final analysis, while the possession of a document was clearly no guarantee that one's property would remain secure, it did provide enduring and unchanging testimony of one's claim to that property. In an age in which violence was common and the physically powerful often achieved their ends through the exercise of force, written documents served in some ways as a counterbalance. While they certainly could not prevent usurpations or ensure a successful outcome to a property dispute, they allowed the memory of lost property to remain alive indefinitely.

---

41. Ibid., #51 (1051). See also #299 (1053).
42. Johnson, *Prayer*, 95.

Praesidentes Negotiis: Abbesses as Managers in Twelfth-Century France

Bruce L. Venarde

With the publication in 1962 of "Land, Family, and Women in Continental Europe, 701–1200," David Herlihy embarked on a 30-year investigation of medieval women. The findings from his search are numerous articles and the considerable portions of *Les toscans et leurs familles* and *Medieval Households* that focus on women. Herlihy's last book, *Opera Muliebria,* was an attempt to outline the experiences of women in various kinds of work, ranging from agricultural labor, to medicine, to sacred scholarship, in late antiquity and across the medieval millennium.

In *Opera Muliebria,* Herlihy at last appeared to be in accord with the conclusion of a "feminist historiography" (his term) he had previously approached with caution. Among American scholars, the paradigm has been most forcefully argued by Jo Ann McNamara and Suzanne Wemple, whose classic 1977 essay posited that "women of the high and late Middle Ages (1100–1500) found their rights and roles increasingly curtailed and their ambitions frustrated."[1] In 1970, Herlihy found that, despite the burdens and prejudices women accumulated across the course of the Middle Ages, "the balance of change was in their favor."[2] But 15

My thanks to Jack Eckert, Mary M. McLaughlin, Maureen Miller, and the editors of this volume for their help.

1. Jo Ann McNamara and Suzanne Wemple, "Sanctity and Power: The Dual Pursuit of Medieval Women," in *Becoming Visible: Women in European History,* ed. Renate Bridenthal and Claudia Koonz (Boston, 1977), 116. See also Joan Kelly-Gadol's essay "Did Women Have a Renaissance?" in the same volume. For an argument focusing specifically on the twelfth century as a period of decline, see Jo Ann McNamara, "Victims of Progress: Women and the Twelfth Century," in *Female Power in the Middle Ages,* ed. Karen Glente and Lise Winther-Jensen (Copenhagen, 1989), 26–37.

2. David Herlihy, *Women in Medieval Society* (Houston, 1971), 14.

years later, he acknowledged that the opposite view "carries much conviction."[3] In *Opera Muliebria,* the answer, at least concerning women and work, was quite clear. From antiquity until the twelfth or thirteenth century, women were "prominent participants in many forms of productive activity," but by the fifteenth century their role in economic life "had become circumscribed."[4] In his last years, then, David Herlihy joined the chorus of scholars—many of whom had made use of his quantitative evidence—who believed that the position of women did indeed deteriorate across the Middle Ages.

That conclusion, in combination with the exponential increase in sources for social history in the later Middle Ages, has produced an odd effect. Apparently finding the greatest inspiration in either the broad scope of women's activities in the early Middle Ages or the multiplication of sources from the thirteenth century onward, students of medieval women have written far more about these periods than about the years 1000–1250. The English translation of Edith Ennen's *Frauen im Mittelalter,* which surveys the era from 500 to 1500, devotes 73 pages to the early Middle Ages, and 119 pages to the late Middle Ages, but a scant 51 pages to the period from 1050 to 1250.[5] In a recent collection by American scholars entitled *Women and Power in the Middle Ages,* only 3 of 11 essays devote more than a few words to women in the eleventh and twelfth centuries.[6] We are still far better informed about early or late medieval women than about their counterparts in the central Middle Ages. If women's status began to decline after A.D. 1000, it is all the more important to investigate their activities in an era of transition.

This essay follows the traces of a few twelfth-century nuns as they manage monastic property. I do not pretend to consider typical figures; it is difficult to make a claim of "representativeness" for any medieval woman whose achievements were significant enough to be recorded. However, the field for a great deal of this kind of women's work existed: several hundred nunneries were founded in France between the turn of

3. David Herlihy, "Did Women Have a Renaissance?: A Reconsideration," *Medievalia et Humanistica,* n.s., 13 (1985): 16.
4. David Herlihy, *Opera Muliebria: Women and Work in Medieval Europe* (New York, 1990), xi.
5. Edith Ennen, *The Medieval Woman,* trans. Edmund Jephcott (Oxford, 1989).
6. *Women and Power in the Middle Ages,* ed. Mary Erler and Maryanne Kowaleski (Athens, Ga., 1988).

the millennium and the mid–thirteenth century.[7] What follows may serve both as a gloss on *Opera Muliebria* and a suggestion that we should acknowledge, and seek to uncover, twelfth-century women's opportunities and accomplishments.

At the turn of the twelfth century, the errant evangelist Robert of Arbrissel settled a band of his followers in a forest just south of the Loire, where Anjou, Touraine, and Poitou meet.[8] Robert gathered together men and women of all sorts and conditions whom he regarded simply as the poor of Christ. The huts in which these seekers gathered were soon overcrowded, and the erection of more substantial buildings began.[9] Such were the modest beginnings of Fontevraud, which grew at a remarkable pace in the first half of the twelfth century. Although it was in large part his charismatic preaching that drew people to Fontevraud, Robert did not wish to supervise the monastery and never became a monk or superior there. Only a few years after founding the community, with the work of building still going on, he returned to the apostolate. He continued his ministry across western France, with frequent stops at Fontevraud, until his death in 1116.

Before he left the newly established community, Robert needed to establish some form of organization for the supervision of construction and other business. He chose from the ranks of the sisters a leader, Hersende, a woman of "great devotion and equally great wisdom," and an assistant, Petronilla, an "experienced estate manager." As events proved, this was indeed a "wise, hard-working and very cautious" team.[10] Hersende, a native of Burgundy, was the widowed mother-in-law

---

7. On this phenomenon, see my "Women, Monasticism, and Social Change: The Foundation of Nunneries in Western Europe, c.890–c.1215," Ph.D. diss., Harvard University, 1992, esp. 23–57. For a thorough description of several contexts of female monastic life in the central Middle Ages, see Penelope D. Johnson, *Equal in Monastic Profession: Religious Women in Medieval France* (Chicago, 1991).

8. Two *vitae* of Robert written shortly after his death are printed in the *Patrologiae cursus completus, Series latina*, ed. J.-P. Migne, 221 vols. (Paris, 1844–64) (hereafter *PL*), 162:1043–78. The most important recent work on Robert and the early history of Fontevraud is by Jean-Marc Bienvenu, some of whose writings are cited below.

9. *PL* 162:1053: "quos alio nolebat censeri vocabulo, nisi pauperes Christi. Multi confluebant homines cujuslibet conditionis; conveniebant mulieries, pauperes et nobiles, viduae et virgines, senes et adolescentes, meretrices et masculorum aspernatrices. Nec iam innumeram copiositatem praeparata capiebant tuguriola, imo capacioribus tirunculi Christi indigebant mansionibus."

10. *PL* 162:1054: "Constituit igitur ex sororibus unam responsis et operibus assistricem, et magistram, Hersendis nomine . . . Vivebat autem Hersendis et magnae

of Gautier of Montsoreau, one of Fontevraud's earliest patrons. Petronilla came from northern Anjou—she was a cousin of Abbot Geoffrey of Vendôme—and had married into the family of the lords of Chemillé.[11] Robert's message seems to have been particularly attractive to women; he centered his community around these two from the outset.[12] Hersende died sometime before 1113 and was succeeded by Petronilla. When Robert died in 1116, his ascetic community had already been transformed into a prosperous abbey, the head of a congregation of 15 monasteries.

The choice of women for leadership in a mixed community of men and women was something of a risk, as Robert doubtless realized. Submission of male religious to female superiors was practically unknown in Western Christendom by 1100. Furthermore, the early charters of Fontevraud are filled with names suggesting the tenor of life in the area; it was probably no easy task to keep peace with locals known as Jerorius Fat Lips, Ogerius Sword-Rattler, Peter Booty-Seizer, Geoffrey Bad Monk, and Raginald Who Folds Up Peasants,[13] to say nothing of monastic and episcopal neighbors. Jerorius, Geoffrey, and many others (including Arraudus Livid and his brother Andrew Livid, as well as Honey-Sated John)[14] were early donors to Fontevraud. More than 200 charters from the first two decades of the history of Fontevraud have survived in a fragment of what was once a much fuller cartulary.[15] In these and later doc-

---

religionis et magni pariter consilii. Huic autem Hersendi conjunxit et Petronillam procurationis mansionariae gnaram . . . Has itaque duas feminas quoniam congnoverat prudentes et industrias et magnae cautelae personas, aliis, ut dictum est, praefecerat sororibus."

11. Jean-Marc Bienvenu, "Aux origines d'un ordre religieux: Robert d'Arbrissel et la fondation de Fontevraud," *Cahiers d'histoire* 20 (1975): 241.

12. A charter of 1106 from Bishop Peter of Poitiers (*PL* 162:1090) notes that "ipse [Robertus] vero in predicta ecclesia plures congregavit mulieres, quas sanctimoniales constituit, ut ibi regulariter viverent . . ." without any mention of the men who prayed and worked together with them at Fontevraud.

13. Paris, Bibliothèque Nationale (hereafter BN), ms. nouv. acq. lat. 2414, folios 31v. (#663, "Jerorius crassa labra"), 82v. (#803, "Ogerius verberans ferrum"), 12r.–v. (#598, "Petro trahente predam"), 8v. (#587, "Gaufridus malus monachus"), 135r.–v. (#913, "Raginaldus plicat vilanum").

14. Ibid., folios 31v.–32r. (#664, "Arraudus Lividus"), 83r. (#804, "Johannes Saturatus Melle").

15. These charters are in the so-called Great Cartulary, of which only a fragment still exists (BN, ms. nouv. acq. lat. 2414). See R. I. Moore, "The Reconstruction of the Cartulary of Fontevrault," *Bulletin of the Institute of Historical Research* 41 (1968): 87–95. To the portion of this volume that Moore argues must have been redacted in the period shortly after Robert of Arbrissel's death, I would add an additional 6 folios

uments we may see Hersende and Petronilla at work, presiding over the
growth of Fontevraud's patrimony and assisting Robert and others in the
foundation of daughterhouses first peopled with nuns and monks from
the motherhouse. Both women were more than equal to the guidance of
external and practical matters as well as internal and spiritual ones.[16]

Fontevraud amassed a considerable landed patrimony from its earliest
years. The speed with which the nuns accumulated wealth is clear from
the amount of cash involved in their transactions only a few years after
the monastery was founded. Two documents which date to 1106–8 show
payments totaling 18 pounds, in one case a sale price of 8 pounds, in the
other 10 pounds, the cost of an overlord's concession when land of his
fief was given to Fontevraud.[17] Other transactions in or before 1108 have
Hersende returning four horses, two sets of saddle and reins, a cow, a
chicken, a tunic, and a total of over 70 *solidi* to lay people.[18]

A religious institution that could draw on such resources only a few
years after its founding was fortunate, and Hersende pressed the advantage as a ready participant in the complexities of the local and regional
economy. Not content to own lands for cultivation and pasturage, the
nuns were especially careful to gather up mill rights. In one case,
Hersende was forced to act vigorously to enforce ownership. A man and
his wife donated a mill upon the "reception of our daughter into the
church of the new congregation of nuns at Fontevraud." The donation
was recognized by the overlords of the property but was subject to two
challenges within a few years. Some relatives of the donors seized grain
from the mill and were compelled to return it only when Hersende took
them to a feudal court in Loudun. Another man, admitting (as the char-

---

(quire xix, folios 9–14). This makes a total of 223 charters from the first two decades
of the history of Fontevraud that still exist in nearly contemporary copies.

16. On the institutionalizing of the relationship between the sexes and Robert's
insistence on "woman-centeredness," see Penny Schine Gold, *The Lady and the Virgin: Image, Attitude, and Experience in Twelfth-Century France* (Chicago, 1985),
93–113. Gold touches on the matter of business and management, primarily to make
the point that it was useful for Fontevraud to have monks available for matters outside the cloister. I agree, but here put more emphasis on the role of the female superiors. For an extension of Gold's thesis, see Carl Kelso Jr., "Women in Power:
Fontevrault and the Paraclete Compared," *Comitatus* 22 (1991): 55–69.

17. BN, ms. nouv. acq. lat. 2414, folios 80r. (#795), 100 r.–v. (#846).

18. Ibid., folios 10v.–11r. (#591), 12v. (#600), 37v.–38r. (#681), 43v. (#697),
80r.–v. (#796), 115v. (#867), 131r.–v. (#906).

ter puts it) that he had "long suffered poor judgment," came to Fontevraud to give up his own claim to the same mill.[19]

Still more complicated was the acquisition and oversight of property around what is now the hamlet of Raslay, not far from Fontevraud on the Petite Maine, a Loire tributary. Here, too, Fontevraud began to gather property at a very early date. Starting about 1108, the nuns collected arable, meadow, and forest lands, fishing areas, and the watercourse and mill at Raslay. This involved at least six different transactions of donation and sale. Once again, Hersende had to act personally to enforce Fontevraud's rights to new property. A neighbor of the lord who had donated the waterway made a claim against the nuns, which he withdrew when Hersende offered him 40 *solidi*. Another claim, on the mill itself, was settled without cost to the nuns. Finally, Hersende manipulated a second claim to the waterway to her advantage: the claimant gave up the suit and proceeded to donate two pieces of land to Fontevraud, receiving in return small countergifts (*de karitate*) for herself, her son, and her daughter.[20]

Hersende also oversaw the founding of Fontevraud's earliest dependent houses. The first of these was Les Loges, located north of the Loire in eastern Anjou. The property was donated by Gautier of Montsoreau, Hersende's son-in-law.[21] A few years later, Hersende traveled to eastern Poitou in order to ensure the transfer of another settlement to the care of Fontevraud. Some hermits had settled in a place called Villesalem late in the eleventh century. Around 1108, the hermits gave their property to Fontevraud. But the abbot of nearby Fontgombaud claimed ownership, so Hersende traveled to the site to settle the matter. She granted a few concessions to the monks, and the property was once and for all ceded to Fontevraud. It was soon after settled, like other dependent houses, with colonists from the motherhouse.[22]

Hersende died sometime before 1113. On his deathbed, in 1116,

---

19. Ibid., folio 125v. (#892, "pro Dei amore et filiae nostrae in ecclesia novae congregationis monacharum Fontis Evraudi susceptione"), 128v. (#899), 121v.–122r. (#885), 126r. (#893, "Ego Radulphus . . . diu malo consilio abusus"). For the process of obtaining another mill, see ibid., folios 126r.–127v. (#894–95).

20. Ibid., folios 111r.–v. (#859), 12r. (#600), 124v. (#890), 133v.–134r. (#911), 81r. (#798), 30r. (#659), 129v. (#902), 30v. (#660).

21. Jean-Marc Bienvenu, *L'étonnant fondateur de Fontevraud, Robert d'Arbrissel* (Paris, 1981), 108–10.

22. Jacques de Bascher, "Villesalem: L'ermitage fontgombaldien et les origines du prieuré fontevriste," *Revue Mabillon* 61 (1987): 106–8, 116–19.

Robert of Arbrissel asked to be buried at Fontevraud with "my good assistant, who gave counsel and labor in the construction of Fontevraud."[23] A short time before, Robert had decided to appoint an abbess to lead the monks and nuns, insisting on the importance of practical abilities. "But how," Robert asked, "can any claustral virgin, who knows only how to sing psalms, suitably manage our external affairs? Tell me: did one always accustomed to being occupied with spiritual things ever direct mundane matters rationally?"[24]

Not surprisingly, Robert's choice was Petronilla. "Indeed, it seems to me fitting that one who bore along with me the labor of traveling and poverty should also bear any burden of support and good fortune. Although she is once-married, it seems to me that by virtue of necessity, no one is more suitable for this prelacy."[25] So, in 1115, Petronilla became the first abbess of Fontevraud. For more than 30 years she fostered and supervised the growth of the abbey and its congregation. The vigor with which Petronilla pursued Robert's charge, even long after his death, is evident in the numerous charters of her abbacy. The patrimony of Fontevraud continued to grow. Like Hersende before her, Petronilla was a careful steward of the properties of Fontevraud and brooked no interference with them.

> I, Petronilla, who then by the grace of God held the primacy of Fontevraud, have taken care to commend to the memory of the living and of posterity that one day, while I was refreshing myself briefly at La Pignonnières, Helignandus of Longchamp and Elisabeth, wife of the oft-mentioned Achardus, came up together for the sake of visiting me. And when we had said quite a lot, among other things I reminded Elisabeth that her son Buccardus should concede to lord Robert and the nuns subject to him the land which his father Achardus and she herself had conceded to them in perpetual ownership. She replied to me in words to this effect: the land had been bought and acquired by

23. *PL* 162:1074: "Ibi jacet Hersendis monacha, bona coadjutrix mea, cujus consilio et opere construxi Fontis Evraldi aedificia."

24. *PL* 162:1060: "Sed quomodo poterit quaelibet claustrensis virgo exteriora nostra convenienter dispensare, quae non novit nisi psalmos cantare? Quid enim rationabiliter cantavit terrestria, semper consuevit operari spiritualia?"

25. Ibid., 1061: "Dignum quippe mihi videtur, ut quae portavit mecum laborem peregrinationis et paupertatis, portet enim pondus qualecunque consolationis nostrae et prosperitatis. Licet enim monogama fuerit, cogente tamen necessitate, nulla mihi convenientior videtur huic praelationi."

her [or "them"] so that they could leave it and give it to whomever they pleased, freely and peacefully. Then I, Petronilla, not wishing to acquiesce to her statement, with the advice of our friends and with her assent, on this account went to the place called Escharbot with some brothers and laymen . . .

At these proceedings, the right of the nuns was confirmed and another lay patron gave Buccardus a small money tribute to recognize that he *had* given the land to Fontevraud.[26] Petronilla's insistence was both understandable and necessary, for the nuns had paid 10,000 *solidi* for the estate, which had subsequently been subject to two claims, the first by the grandson of the vendor, who was declared to be underage and his suit dismissed. The second claim was by Archardus Escharbot and Elisabeth, who had in fact been given 300 *solidi* and a horse to concede La Pignonnières to Fontevraud shortly before the proceedings described in the document quoted.[27]

Such determined action was not unusual for Petronilla, who saw no conflict between spiritual aims and temporal necessities. "Often putting aside the glory of reading and prayers, we turn to management of temporal goods for the advantage of our successors, which indeed we do for this reason: that when we are sleeping in our tombs, we may be helped by their prayers before God."[28] Shortly after becoming abbess, Petronilla appealed to Count Fulk of Anjou for the restoration of properties

---

26. BN, ms. nouv. acq. lat. 2414, folio 103r.–v. (#849): "Memoriae tam presentium quam posterorum commendare curavi quod ego Petronilla quae tunc Dei gratia Fontis Ebraudi prioratum tenebam, dum uno die apud Pignorariam paululum me recreassem, Helignandus de Longo Campo et Elisabet uxor sepedicti Achardi, me visitandi gratia, pariter ad me venerunt. Cumque satis plura dixissemus, haec inter cetera ipsi [*sic*] Elisabet reduxi memorie ut filius suus Buccardus domno R[oberto] et feminis sibi subpositis concederet terram quam pater eius Achardus et ipsa perpetuo eis tenendam concesserat. Quae meis itaque verbis huiusce modi verba respondit: quia predicta terra de emptione sua et adquisitione fuerat et cui ipsi voluissent eam libere vel quiete dare ut dimittere potuissent. Tunc ego Petronilla nolens suis adquiescere dictis, consilio amicorum nostrorum et suo assensu, ad locum qui vulgo Escarbot appellatur de fratribus et saecularibus hominibus huius rei gratia transmisi . . ." These events date to the earliest period of Petronilla's abbacy, or possibly even before it, since Robert of Arbrissel was apparently still alive.

27. Ibid., folios 97v.–100r. (#845 and 845 bis), 101r.–102v. (#848).

28. Ibid., folio 71v. (#768, dated 1119): "Sepe postpositis lectionis oracionumque floribus, ad disponenda temporalia propter successorum utilitatem nos inclinamus, quod nimirum idcirco facimus ut cum in sepulchris dormierimus, earum precibus apud Deum adiuvari valeamus."

claimed by a foreigner acting, as the document has it, on the devil's inspiration.[29] Some years later, two brothers seized mills belonging to
Fontevraud. The abbess, called "a very wise woman," arranged that the
claimants "not only humbly made amends for the wickedness they had
committed, begging for mercy, but also confirmed the gift of their
brother [who gave the mills], confessing to have done evil against the
family of God."[30] Such remarks suggest a powerfully persuasive aspect of
Petronilla's character.

Petronilla also knew the importance of a written record, as the proems
to several charters show. "The goods of the church of the holy mother of
God at Fontevraud are committed to writing, lest on account of the swift-
ness of fleeting life they be given over to oblivion by our successors.
Therefore, Lady Petronilla, first religious abbess, ordered that gifts to the
above-mentioned place made in her time be written down . . ."[31] It was
probably at Petronilla's behest that the first cartulary of Fontevraud was
redacted, shortly after the death of Robert of Arbrissel.[32]

The size of the Order of Fontevraud, as it came to be known, grew
steadily through the first half of the twelfth century. Starting with Pascal
II, in 1106, every pope except the short-lived Celestine II confirmed to
Fontevraud and its dependent houses privileges and properties, strengthening ties between the abbey and Rome. In 1119, Calixtus II dedicated
the Romanesque abbey church at Fontevraud.[33] Abbess Petronilla's energies remained undiminished into the 1140s, when she took advantage of

---

29. Ibid., folio 105v. (#852): "denuntiamus quamdam iniuriose calumpnationis iniuriam quam quidam vir advena, Gireus nomine . . . diabolico instinctu nobis fecit . . ."
The document is undated but must be early because one of the witnesses is Fulk's
mother, the one-time queen of France, Bertrade (d. 1116).

30. Ibid., folio 64r. (#746): "Abbatissa itaque tunc temporis de Chimilliaco
Petronilla, mulier sapientissima, adeo ut eos contigit non tantum quod male fecerant
misericordiam eius implorantes suppliciter emendarent, verum eciam donum fratris
sui se contra Dei familiam male fecisse confitentes, confirmaverunt."

31. Ibid., folios 58r.–v. (#734): "Bona ecclesie sancte Dei genetrici Marie Fontis
Evraudi in scriptis mittuntur, ne a posteriis nostris, propter velocitatem transeuntis
vitae, oblivioni tradantur. Ideoque domna Petronilla prima religiosa abbatissa illius
loci dona supradicti suo tempore facta scribere [sic] iussit . . ."

32. Moore, "The Reconstruction of the Cartulary of Fontevrault," 94–95.
Although I think Moore underestimates Robert of Arbrissel's practicality—he did
choose Hersende and Petronilla, after all, to attend to business matters—I agree that
Petronilla frequently showed herself "determined to secure the rights of her abbey
against all comers and exercised a high degree of competence in doing so."

33. *PL* 163:1121. The church and several other twelfth-century structures, including a fascinating octagonal kitchen, have survived.

papal connections during a protracted wrangle with Ulger, the bishop of Angers. The immediate cause of the quarrel was the maltreatment of one of Petronilla's secular allies, a man known to us only as Basset, whose houses were wrecked and possessions stolen by agents of Bishop Ulger. The matter became a cause célèbre. Bernard of Clairvaux sent an outraged letter to the bishop, lamenting the *scandalum,* as he called it. "Tears," began the abbot, "are more suitable than letters."[34] Basset went to Rome to appeal in person to Pope Innocent II.[35] However, as Jean-Marc Bienvenu has demonstrated, the difficulty was not simply maltreatment of Petronilla's ally. Basset held lands adjacent to those of the bishop along the Loire. The violence against him was thus connected to a larger and more important issue: Fontevraud's rights on the Ponts-de-Cé near Angers, at that time the only passage over the Loire in Anjou and hence an extremely lucrative property. In 1144, Pope Lucius, writing to Petronilla about the ongoing troubles between her and Ulger, appointed a commission of five bishops to settle the case. Arbitration over rights on the Ponts-de-Cé was completed by the following year, and Fontevraud's rights were confirmed, but not until the early spring of 1149 was restitution to Basset settled at 1,000 Angevin *solidi.*[36]

A few weeks later, Abbess Petronilla died after 50 years of service at Fontevraud. The necrology of Fontevraud refers to her as "our incomparable and irrecoverable mother."[37] Owing in large part to Petronilla, and to Hersende before her, there were by 1149 more than 50 monasteries in the order. All of them were, like Fontevraud, mixed communities headed by a female superior, distributed across the region bounded by northern Champagne, Lyonnais, and Aragon. The number of daughterhouses grew some in the decades that followed, but until the French Revolution the Order of Fontevraud remained very much what it had become under the guidance of Hersende and Petronilla: the largest and wealthiest federation of monasteries for women in Western Europe.

34. [Bernard of Clairvaux], *Sancti Bernardi Opera,* ed. J. Leclercq, C. H. Talbot, and H. Rochais (Rome, 1957–), 8:57 [letter 200]: "Lacrimas magis dare quam litteras libet."

35. *PL* 179:635–36.

36. Jean-Marc Bienvenu, "Le conflit entre Ulger, évêque d'Angers, et Pétronille de Chemillé, abbesse de Fontevrault (vers 1140–1149)," *Revue Mabillon* 58, no. 248 (1972): 113–32. The document concerning the final settlement, which is known only through a seventeenth-century edition, is printed at the bottom of the columns in *PL* 179:923–26.

37. Angers, Archives départementales de Maine-et-Loire, 101 H, 225 bis, p. 242: "incomparabilis et irrecuperabilis mater nostra."

There is similar evidence of managerial skill on the part of another quondam wife turned nun, who is arguably the most famous woman of the twelfth century. Heloise, whose parentage is unknown, was probably of a lineage similar to Petronilla's. She was raised in the nunnery of Argenteuil in Paris.[38] As a teenager, in the care of her uncle Fulbert, a canon of the cathedral of Notre-Dame, she became the student of the fiery Peter Abelard. The story is well known. The two became lovers; Heloise had a child; she and Abelard married but soon after parted. At her husband's insistence, Heloise returned to Argenteuil. Fulbert proceeded to take violent revenge on the man he suspected of spurning his niece: Abelard was castrated. Abelard became a monk and retired to Champagne, living in a hermitage called the Paraclete located a few miles from the Seine, northwest of Troyes. Called to be abbot of a monastery in his native Brittany in 1126, he remembered that his isolated oratory was deserted when he heard that the nuns of Argenteuil, now led by Heloise, had been expelled by Abbot Suger of Saint-Denis, who laid claim to the property. In 1129, some of the community went to the Paraclete, where Abelard came to install the nuns and pay a rare visit to Heloise.

Heloise is best known through her correspondence with Abelard. Most of the letters concern personal and theological matters, but Heloise also asked Abelard to write a rule for the Paraclete, pointing out that the Rule of Saint Benedict was inadequate for women.[39] Most of the lengthy reply addressed matters of internal organization and practice, but Abelard did make some telling remarks about the choice of a superior. He scorned the "pernicious practice" of electing virgins instead of those who have known men, and younger women over older ones, echoing the sentiments of Robert of Arbrissel (whom he did not mention). Abelard also cautioned against the choice of powerful noblewomen as abbesses, for they might become proud to the disadvantage of the convent, especially if they were local people whose families might interfere with

---

38. See Enid McLeod, *Heloise: A Biography* (London, 1971), 8–12, Charlotte Charrier, *Héloïse dans l'histoire et dans la légende* (Paris, 1933), 50–52; and Robert-Henri Bautier, "Paris au temps d'Abélard," in *Abélard en son temps* (Paris, 1981), 75–77, for speculations on Heloise's parentage.

39. [Abelard and Heloise], "The Letter of Heloise on Religious Life and Abelard's First Reply," ed. J. T. Muckle, *Mediaeval Studies* 17 (1955): 241–53, esp. 242–44. The translation is published in *The Letters of Abelard and Heloise*, trans. Betty Radice (Harmondsworth, 1974), 159–79.

monastic life.[40] Heloise, neither a virgin nor of local origin, proved to be a remarkable leader. Peter the Venerable, abbot of Cluny, admired Heloise's community, wished that she were a nun at the Cluniac nunnery of Marcigny, and praised her as a philosopher for having exchanged logic for the Gospel, Plato for Christ, and school for the cloister.[41]

Less well known are Heloise's skills in management of temporal matters, but these were quite exceptional. The Paraclete was a poor foundation at the beginning; Abelard notes that the nuns' life there "was full of hardship at first and for a while they suffered the greatest deprivation . . ."[42] But this period of want was over by 1147, when Pope Eugenius III issued a bull confirming the possessions of Heloise and her nuns.[43] Eugenius named more than 50 donors, including Count Theobald of Champagne (twice) and his countess, a viscountess, the bishop of Troyes, and the archbishop of Sens. The rest of the Paraclete's patrons were of lesser rank, a few identified as *miles,* most of them obscure landed men and women. Less than 20 years after the refugees arrived, the Paraclete controlled property in more than 80 places, mostly land but also mills and annual tributes. Unlike Fontevraud, which a few years after its founding had possessions spread across a large portion of western France, the Paraclete's holdings were far more compact. With one exception, all of the Paraclete's properties in 1147 were within 20 miles of the motherhouse. A vast majority were within 10 miles, in a region reaching north from the nunnery across the Seine and south and east toward Troyes. There were also properties further south, along a smaller river, and several near Provins, a town 15 miles northwest of the Paraclete. Because most of the original charters of the Paraclete have not survived, it is difficult to know much about the process by which its patrimony was assembled. But the surviving evidence hints that the model of Fontevraud holds in this case:

---

40. [Abelard], "Abelard's Rule for Religious Women," ed. T. P. McLaughlin, *Mediaeval Studies* 18 (1956): 252–54; translated in *Letters of Abelard and Heloise,* 200, 202.

41. Peter the Venerable, *The Letters of Peter the Venerable,* ed. Giles Constable, 2 vols. (Cambridge, Mass., 1967), 1:303–8; translated in *Letters of Abelard and Heloise,* 277–84. The abbot wrote to Heloise in 1144.

42. Abelard, *Historia calamitatum,* ed. Jacques Monfrin (Paris, 1959), 100; *Letters of Abelard and Heloise,* 97.

43. *Cartulaire de l'abbaye du Paraclet,* ed. Charles Lalore, vol. 2 of *Collection des principaux cartulaires du diocèse de Troyes* (Paris, 1878), 6–14. On the early properties of the Paraclete, see the remarks in Charrier, *Héloïse dans l'histoire,* 261–73. The observations that follow will be superseded shortly by Mary Martin McLaughlin's forthcoming study of Heloise and the Paraclete.

a skilled manager's careful handling of goods acquired primarily through donation by pious local people.

A charter of 1133 outlines the donation of some properties in and around Provins, including 40 *solidi* in tithes at Provins and nearby Lesines, with the proviso that if some or all of the sum cannot be obtained there, the donor is obliged to make up the difference from another holding. It is then repeated that the tithes at Lesines are granted by the donors, one of whom entered the Paraclete; this woman noted that her brother Robert, too, had granted them.[44] Heloise apparently realized two things about such a donation. First, a gift of tithes would constitute a reliable source of income only if carefully acquired. Second, often more than one or two people considered themselves to have title to a property or right in the early twelfth century, and it was necessary to specify who they were. This is clear from a document written three years later in which the archbishop of Sens, acting at Heloise's request, gave to the Paraclete the tithe of Lesines, which he noted that the same Robert and another man had previously conveyed to him personally.[45] Such complexities aside, Heloise had presided over the multiplication of the Paraclete's properties to the extent that by 1146 the nuns could afford to pay 120 pounds for lands and tithes near the monastery.[46]

Abelard observed that once he left Heloise and the nuns "their worldly goods were multiplied more in a single year than mine would have been in a hundred, had I remained there, for as much as women are weaker, so much the more pitiable is their poverty, which easily rouses human sympathy, and the more pleasing is their virtue to God and to men."[47] Despite Abelard's insistence on female frailty, it is unlikely that Heloise

---

44. *Cartulaire du Paraclet*, 62–63: "Galo et Adelaudis, uxor ejus, soror Ermeline, que se Deo et ecclesie Paracliti in sanctimonialem dedit, laudaverunt et concesserunt . . . et XL solidos census. Et in hoc censu habebunt sanctimoniales Paracliti censum Pruvini, et hoc quod restabit ad percipiendum de XL solidis capient apud Lesinas, si ibi inveniri poterit; si vero ibidem inveniri non poterit, prefatus Galo in propinquiori loco quem habuerit, predictos XL solidos census perficiet . . . prenominatus Galo et Adelaudis . . . et ipsa Ermelina laudaverunt et concesserunt Deo et dicte ecclesie Paracliti decimam de Lesignis, quam Robertus Goisias dederat eidem ecclesie . . ."

45. Ibid., 64: "Henricus, Dei gratia Senonensis archiepiscopus, notum fieri volo tam presentibus quam futuris, quod Heloysa venerabilis abbatissa totusque ejusdem loci sanctissimus conventus, humiliter a nobis petierunt decimam de Lesignis, quam Robertus Goes de Turre et Girardus Ispanellus diu possiderant et in manu nostra dimiserant, eis daremus. Quarum pie petitioni assentientes . . ."

46. Ibid., 70–71.

47. Abelard, *Historia calamitatum*, 100–101.

and her community were simply passive recipients of pious donations. The relative compactness of the Paraclete's possessions suggests that Heloise gathered wealth quite deliberately, perhaps often exchanging or buying lands nearby, as she did in 1146. Furthermore, the same pattern is visible in the patrimony of a daughterhouse of the Paraclete. La Pommeraie was founded in the early 1150s on lands of Mathilda, dowager countess of Champagne, not far from the Yonne River north of Sens.[48] A papal bull of 1157 lists the properties of the new house, which were mostly along the banks of the lower Yonne and near the confluence of the Yonne and the Seine.[49] One of Heloise's modern biographers refers to her "strong practical sense which might almost be called business ability."[50] No such qualification is necessary, for Heloise was obviously a successful businesswoman whose legacy as abbess included both her reputation for learning and piety and the landed wealth that assured that by the late twelfth century 60 nuns could worship in the Paraclete.[51]

For abbesses and their deputies to be in charge of property and other business was, at least at Fontevraud and the Paraclete, a matter of course. When he appointed Petronilla as abbess, Robert of Arbrissel also drew up a set of rules for Fontevraud. Stipulations about the conditions under which the abbess, prioress, and other nuns might be allowed to leave the cloister show that travel for the purposes of doing business was normal. The *maior priorissa,* Robert decreed, was to be received in all of Fontevraud's churches and cells and was to be second only to the abbess in executing the business of the community ("habeatque potestatem post abbatissam de negotiis ecclesiae agendis").[52] The Paraclete statutes known as *Institutiones nostrae,* which date to Heloise's time, contain regulations anticipating this same need for mobility in order to conduct business. As a modern commentary on the *Institutiones* puts it, the rules are "quite liberal: nuns and lay-sisters are authorized to handle business

---

48. For the foundation charter, see *Cartulair générale de l'Yonne,* ed. Maximilien Quantin, 2 vols. (Auxerre, 1854–60), 1:493–94.

49. *Cartulaire du Paraclet,* 18–20.

50. McLeod, *Héloïse,* 211.

51. *Cartulaire du Paraclet,* 33–34, is a papal letter of 1196, enjoining that the number of nuns not exceed 60. Such a request suggests, of course, that the community was or had been larger.

52. Johannes von Walter, *Die ersten Wanderprediger Frankreichs: Studien zur Geschichte des Mönchtums,* 2 vols. (Leipzig, 1903–6), 1:191 (on leaving the monastery), 1:193 (on the duties of the *maior priorissa*). Pages 189–95 contain the most complete text of the rule, which is edited in briefer form in *PL* 162:1079–86.

which might otherwise have been delegated to bailiffs and other officials charged with monastery affairs."[53] So the superior's job included the distribution of tasks to other nuns. In the twelfth century, management of *temporalia* by women like Hersende, Petronilla, and Heloise was, in theory and in fact, a central and legitimate responsibility of abbesses.[54]

Unfortunately, we can discover far less about most superiors of new nunneries in the central Middle Ages than about their status in local economic and social structures. But surely these women were significant figures whose practical acumen could be a useful attribute in monastic leadership, albeit on a smaller scale than at Fontevraud or the Paraclete. A telling hint is provided by the earliest surviving charter from a nunnery near Carcassonne. An 1162 donation is addressed to "God and the church of the Blessed Mary of Rieunette and to you, humble Raina, business manager [*praesidenti negotiis*] of the monastery of this church."[55] Since the document was drawn up at the convent, its language emphasizes that the nuns and their patrons regarded highly the mundane aspect of the superior's duties. Sadly, lists of twelfth-century abbesses and prioresses are incomplete, and often nothing more than names survive. Their very obscurity suggests that they were, like the men and women who founded and endowed their houses, of less than exalted lineage. But, like the women discussed here, they were charged with the direction of possessions as well as prayer.[56]

---

53. *The Paraclete Statutes: Institutiones Nostrae*, ed. Chrysogonus Waddell (Trappist, Ky., 1987), 116.

54. Johnson, *Equal in Monastic Profession*, 207–26, addresses female monastic participation in the economy, usually citing thirteenth-century documents.

55. *Cartulaire et archives des communes de l'ancien diocèse et de l'arrondissement administratif de Carcassonne*, ed. Alphonse Mahul, 6 vols. (Paris, 1857–82), 5:22: "damus Deo et Ecclesie B. Mariae de Rivo nitido, et tibi humili Rainae praesidenti negotiis domus istius ecclesiae . . ."

56. It is noteworthy that these women sometimes appear to be confronting an older understanding of property explained in Barbara Rosenwein's brilliant study of the tenth- and eleventh-century charters of Cluny. According to Rosenwein, until 1050 or so, title to the transfer of property as we understand it was the less important of two meanings of property, the other being the establishment of an ongoing relationship between the parties involved in any transfer. In such cases, property had symbolic meaning and existed to be given, sold, or exchanged repeatedly. Possessions could in some sense "belong" to a number of individuals and groups, who used transactions concerning it as a means of creating or maintaining bonds, so that property acted as a kind of "social glue." See Barbara H. Rosenwein, *To Be The Neighbor of Saint Peter: The Social Meaning of Cluny's Property, 909–1049* (Ithaca, N.Y., 1989), esp. 109–43. Such a conception of property would account for the difficulties Petronilla had in establishing title to Pignonnières and make sense of Elisabeth's claim that

Hersende, Petronilla, and Heloise may well be, as I have suggested, Raina writ large. A careful sifting through the surviving records, especially charters and other documents of practice, may yield important results and uncover, if not many Petronillas, more than a few Rainas. These very successful managers might represent only the tip of the iceberg, the easily visible portion of a much larger story of work done by monastic women in the twelfth century. Whatever lies below the surface tends to appear dim and uninviting, not wholly unlike a sheaf of charters at first approach. However, as I hope I have suggested, there is a great deal to be discovered in these apparently dry documents, especially those from the eleventh and early twelfth centuries.

If we assume that the women who came after a golden age in the early Middle Ages were hapless casualties of social and ideological change, we are more likely to pity them than understand them. They will almost certainly seem dull. All the more reason, then, to seek out women of all descriptions in medieval charters, in which, as a great nineteenth-century scholar-archivist put it, we can find "the true countenance, interests, passions, laws, and beliefs of the epoch."[57] Charters of the central Middle Ages also shed light on the activities of people who might well go entirely unnoticed otherwise: women of the lower aristocracy like Hersende, Petronilla, Raina, and their deputies, far less visible in narrative sources than are the saints and queens of an earlier era. I strongly suspect that we will discover in documents of practice something other than steady and uniform erosion of women's opportunities in the medieval West.

We must at all costs refrain from taking at face value the opinions and observations of powerful and articulate men about their female contem-

---

the land was hers to do with it as she pleased, even though she had recognized Fontevraud's ownership only a short time before. The same may well apply to the tithes of Lesines, which a number of people claimed the right to alienate before they came firmly under the control of Heloise and the Paraclete. Constance Bouchard finds a similar "semi-ambiguity in property ownership" among Burgundian Cistercians and their knightly neighbors even in the later twelfth century, arguing that this understanding of the meaning of property had moved down the social scale since the tenth and eleventh century (Constance B. Bouchard, *Holy Entrepreneurs: Cistercians, Knights, and Economic Exchange in Twelfth-Century Burgundy* [Ithaca, N.Y., 1991], 178–81). Although neither of these excellent studies is explicitly based on David Herlihy's work, the use of charters to explore otherwise hidden aspects of medieval culture follows very much along the same lines.

57. Paul Marchegay, "Recherches sur les cartulaires d'Anjou," *Archives d'Anjou* 1 (1843): 186.

poraries. In 1144, Pope Lucius II, confirming the privileges of a monastic house, noted that "as much as the feminine sex is the more fragile, so much do we want to show paternal care and solicitude toward you and defend the rights of your monastery from the incursions of wicked people."[58] Such boilerplate can conceal more than it reveals, in this case making the rather ludicrous suggestion that the addressee, Abbess Petronilla of Fontevraud, was a weak and defenseless creature. The truth of the matter was quite different, as a careful reading of the charters of Fontevraud amply demonstrates. David Herlihy's counsel for historians of late medieval Italian urban women applies to all who study European women in the Middle Ages: "They must learn to be alert, patient, sensitive listeners."[59]

58. PL 179:864: "Quanto ergo femineus sexus exstat fragilior, tanto magis erga vos paternam curam atque sollicitudinem volumus exhibere, et jura vestri monasterii a pravorum incursibus defensare."

59. David Herlihy, "Women and the Sources of Medieval History: The Towns of Northern Italy," in *Medieval Women and the Sources of Medieval History,* ed. Joel T. Rosenthal, 147 (Athens, Ga., 1990).

A Medieval Inquisitor at Work: Bernard Gui, 3 March 1308 to 19 June 1323

James Given

The thirteenth and early fourteenth centuries were a turning point in the political history of medieval Europe. The small-scale organizations of the earlier Middle Ages, limited both in geographical scope and in their ability to mobilize the resources of their subjects, were replaced by larger organizations. These organizations—whether kingdoms, principalities, or city-states—not only exercised authority over larger territories, but they increasingly developed improved means for coordinating the activities and mobilizing the resources of their subjects. By the end of the fourteenth century it was clear that, despite their propensity to entangle themselves in war and domestic strife, the political future would belong to these new, larger, political organizations.

As these organizations grew they developed a number of organs of governance and techniques of rule: mechanisms for accounting, record keeping, dispute settlement, ideological persuasion, and so on. Of these improved instrumentalities, pride of place must be given to legal mechanisms. For a long time courts were the primary, and most effective, means that the rulers of the new, enlarged, political organizations had at their command for intervening in the affairs of their subjects.

Historians have examined the learned aspects of medieval law for generations. But it is only in the last few decades that the serious study of the social and political aspects of medieval legal systems has begun. This essay is a contribution to this growing body of literature. It takes as its subject one of the most interesting legal organizations of the thirteenth and fourteenth centuries, the inquisition of heretical depravity. The development of inquisitorial procedure, in which judges could undertake the investigation of criminal actions *proprio motu,* without first receiving a formal accusation or denunciation, was one of the most important innovations in European legal history.[1] Although inquisitors of heretical depravity were free of some of the common restraints imposed on investigating magistrates, the use of inquisitorial procedures to pursue heretics was part of this larger generalization of inquisitorial procedures.[2]

The inquisitors, however, were among the most determined and resourceful users of this new-fangled mode of legal proceeding. In Languedoc, the area of concern in this essay, the Dominican inquisitors established heresy-hunting tribunals at Toulouse and Carcassonne. In cooperation with those prelates, such as the bishops of Albi and Pamiers, who established their own inquisitorial tribunals, they conducted a largely successful campaign against the heretics, principally Cathars, who had found Languedoc a fertile ground for their heterodox messages.[3]

Bernard Gui's *Liber sententiarum*

In this essay I shall examine the data contained in one of the best-known documents of the Languedocian inquisition, the *Liber sententiarum* of

---

1. For recent discussions, see Edward Peters, *Inquisition* (New York, 1988); and Richard M. Fraher, "Conviction According to Conscience: The Medieval Jurists' Debate Concerning Judicial Discretion and the Law of Proof," *Law and History Review* 7 (1989): 23–88.

2. For an argument that "there was not a single provision of the original *ordo juris* or rules of procedure for inquisition that privileged heresy cases over all other kinds of cases or limited due process for persons charged with heresy in ways that were not permitted for persons charged with other crimes," see Henry Ansgar Kelly, "Inquisition and Prosecution of Heresy: Misconceptions and Abuses," *Church History* 58 (1989): 439–51 (the quotation is from p. 443). The views expressed in this essay should, however, be compared with the careful survey of papal decrees relating to the powers of inquisitors in Albert Clement Shannon, *The Popes and Heresy in the Thirteenth Century* (rpt.; New York, 1980), 48–89.

3. The reader should note that in the bulk of this essay I will be using the term *heretic* in a broader fashion than did the medieval inquisitors. In Languedoc the inquisitors generally used the term *heretic* to describe the elite of the Cathar sect, the Bons Hommes, or *perfecti*, the men or women who had received the *consolamentum*, the baptism of the Holy Spirit that washed away the effects of sin and guaranteed escape from the prison of this world, and who lived a life of strict asceticism devoted to the spreading of the sect's message. Most of the people prosecuted and condemned by the inquisitors were not heretics in this narrow sense. To describe this group the inquisitors employed a large vocabulary distinguishing different forms of aiding and abetting of the heretics proper. To avoid excessive circumlocution, I shall refer to all those who supported heresy of all types, Cathar *perfecti* or not, as heretics.

Bernard Gui.[4] This register was subjected to a form of quantitative analysis by Célestin Douais in 1900.[5] His findings have done much to shape subsequent historians' understanding of the operation of inquisitorial tribunals. Working in a period before electronic data processing, Douais could discover only the simplest and most obvious patterns in the data. The way in which he presented the data, however, was occasionally not only misleading but erroneous. Since Douais, only Jacques Paul and Annette Pales-Gobilliard have attempted quantitative examinations of Gui's register. Paul's 1981 essay on the "mentality" of the inquisitor makes a number of interesting observations, but it examines only a fraction of the data, that is, the sentences imposed on 5 April 1310.[6] Similarly, Pales-Gobilliard's 1991 essay discusses in detail only part of the information in the register.[7]

Gui's register contains the largest set of surviving sentences recorded by a medieval inquisitor. As part of a project dealing with the Languedocian inquisitors, I have subjected the *Liber sententiarum* to a new quantitative examination. In this essay I shall set out some results of this investigation, correcting Douais's errors and exploring facets of the data that he was unable to investigate.[8]

---

4. This text was published by Philipp van Limborch as an appendix to his *Historia inquisitionis, cui subjungitur Liber sententiarum inquisitionis Tholosanae ab anno Christi MCCCVII ad annum MCCCXXIII* (Amsterdam, 1692) (cited hereafter as *LS.*). For many years students of the Languedocian inquisition thought that the original manuscript of this register had been lost. However, as M. A. E. Nickson pointed out in the early 1970s, Gui's register had been residing for some time in the British Library ("Locke and the Inquisition of Toulouse," *British Museum Quarterly* 36 [1971–72]: 83–92) as Add. MS. 4697. As Jean Duvernoy has noted, Limborch's transcription of the original text was a very good one ("L'Edition par Philippe de Limborch des sentences de l'Inquisition de Toulouse," *Heresis* 12 [1989]: 5–12). In constructing my data set, I have relied primarily on Limborch's edition, but all the data have been checked against a microfilm of Add. MS. 4697.

5. C. Douais, ed., *Documents pour servir à l'histoire de l'Inquisition dans lo Languedoc*, 2 vols. (Paris, 1900), 1:ccv. Henry Charles Lea also tabulated the data in the *LS.* Unlike Douais, who counted individual sentences and commutations of previously imposed sentences, Lea evidently used as his unit of analysis the individuals who appeared before Gui. See his *A History of the Inquisition of the Middle Ages*, 3 vols. (New York, 1955), 1:495.

6. Jacques Paul, "La Mentalité de l'Inquisiteur chez Bernard Gui," in *Bernard Gui et son monde, Cahiers de Fanjeaux* 16 (1981): 279–313.

7. Annette Pales-Gobilliard, "Pénalités inquisitoriales au XIVe siècle," in *Crises et réformes dans l'église de la réforme grégorienne à la préréforme*, Actes du 115e Congrès National des Sociétés Savantes (Avignon, 1990), Section d'Histoire Médiévale et de Philologie (Paris, 1991), 143–54.

8. Not all of the material in the register, however, has been used for this essay. Although almost all of the sentences or commutations of sentences in the register

Gui's register is a complex document, and we need to clarify the terminology that will be used in discussing it. Gui's register contains 907 different "acts," recorded between 3 March 1308 and 19 June 1323, relating to individuals convicted of heresy. In 633 of these acts Gui imposed some form of penance or punishment on an individual. Of these, 544 (85.9 percent) were imposed on individuals who were alive at the time, while 89 (14.1 percent) were imposed on individuals who were deceased. These 633 acts will be referred to as sentences or punishments throughout this essay. The other 274 acts consisted of the commutation of a previously imposed penance into a lesser penalty. These will be referred to as commutations. The 907 acts in the register relate to only 637 individuals. Of these 413 appear only once in Gui's register, 178 two times, and 46 three times. In this essay, individuals will be referred to as either individuals or cases.[9]

Most of the individuals recorded in the register had been tried and condemned by Gui. Some, however, had not. Some were individuals who had been given penances by other inquisitors, which Gui, acting as their successor in office, commuted at a later date. Some were individuals who had been tried primarily by other inquisitors. According to the reforms instituted by Pope Clement V at the Council of Vienne (1311–12), inquisitors and local bishops were for certain matters required to act together. Therefore, some of the sentences in the *Liber* relate to people who were tried primarily by Jacques Fournier, bishop of Pamiers. One person, the notorious Franciscan Bernard Délicieux, was tried by a specially appointed papal commission. But, since Bernard had been extremely active in leading opposition to the inquisitors, Gui was careful to record his sentence.

The Types of Heresy

In 91 percent of the cases, the *Liber sententiarum* notes the offense for which an individual was condemned. Material in Jacques Fournier's reg-

---

relate to single individuals, the *LS* contains two "collective" sentences, a "reconciliation" with the community of the *castrum* of Cordes, and an order for the destruction of copies of the Talmud confiscated from Languedocian Jews. Both of these anomalous sentences have been excluded from the present analysis.

9. Douais's failure to make clear the fact that "acts" do not equal individuals has led into error some of those making use of the table he printed in his *Documents*. For an example, see James Given, "The Inquisitors of Languedoc and the Medieval Technology of Power," *American Historical Review* 94 (1989): 353.

ister specifies the offenses of another 5 percent.[10] Not surprisingly, by far the most common type of heresy was Catharism (see fig. 1). Since the twelfth century this dualist sect had been well established in Languedoc. Indeed, its presence had been responsible for the Albigensian Crusades, which brought the region under the French monarchy's control. Fully 475 (74.6 percent) of the individuals recorded in Gui's register were accused of this heresy. Only 3 were members of the Cathar elite, the Bons Hommes, or *perfecti,* who had received the baptism of the Holy Spirit and led lives of strict asceticism devoted to preaching and ministering to the sect's followers. The overwhelming majority were simple *credentes,* who had sympathized with and protected the Bons Hommes.

Catharism was by far the most popular heresy in early-fourteenth-century Languedoc. The second most common heresy was Waldensian-ism, represented by 90 individuals (14.3 percent of the total). Nineteen individuals (3 percent of the total) were guilty of what I shall call Beguin-ism. These individuals, usually members of the Franciscan Third Order, were followers of the Spiritual Franciscans.[11] They adhered to a rigid interpretation of the meaning and role of poverty in St. Francis's rule, regarded the Franciscans who had been burned at Marseilles in 1318 as martyrs, revered the Languedocian friar Pierre Jean Olivi as a great teacher and saint, and looked on Pope John XXII as the mystical Antichrist.

Another 26 (4.1 percent) comprised an eclectic grab bag of religious dissent and moral peculation. Four had fled the inquisition's jurisdiction and were condemned in absentia. Although their offenses are not men-tioned, it is reasonable to assume that they were probably involved with Catharism in one fashion or another. Two were Jews who had converted to Christianity, only to revert to Judaism.[12] One man, from Lugo, in Galicia, was a Pseudo-Apostle, a follower of the Italian heretic Gerard Segarelli.[13] Another man was condemned for saying mass even though he was not a priest.[14] Against one man the chief charge seems to have been

---

10. Fournier's register has been published in Jean Duvernoy, ed., *Le Registre d'in-quisition de Jacques Fournier, évêque de Pamiers (1318–25),* 3 vols. (Toulouse, 1965).

11. On these heretics, see Raoul Manselli, *Spirituali e Beghini in Provenza,* Istituto Storico Italiano per il Medio Evo, Studi Storici, fasc. 31–34 (1959). This work was translated into French by Jean Duvernoy in *Spirituels et Béguins du Midi* (Toulouse, 1989).

12. *LS,* 167, 230.

13. *LS,* 360.

14. *LS,* 251.

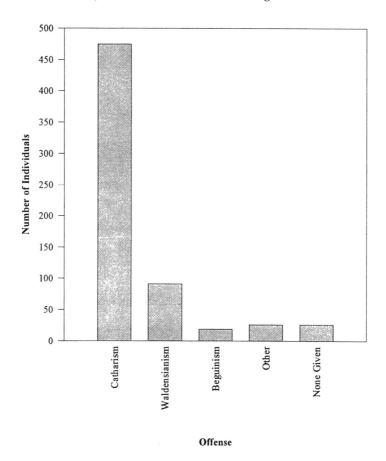

Fig. 1. Offenses of individuals who appeared before Bernard Gui (*N* = 637)

a failure to pay tithes.[15] Another was a priest who openly maintained a concubine and aided her when she tried to escape from Jacques Fournier's investigations.[16] One poor devil was the commander of a *leprosarium* in the diocese of Pamiers; he was condemned for participating in a fantastic and wholly imaginary plot in which the lepers of southern France supposedly tried to poison all nonlepers.[17] Six people were condemned for a variety of unorthodox ideas. Among these were the beliefs

15. *LS*, 295; Duvernoy, *Registre*, 2:160–69; J.-M. Vidal, "Le Tribunal d'inquisition de Pamiers," *Annales de Saint-Louis-des-Français* 8 (1903–4), 411–12.
16. *LS*, 294; Duvernoy, *Registre*, 1:251–59; Vidal, "Tribunal," 396–97.
17. *LS*, 295; Duvernoy, *Registre*, 2:135–47; Vidal, "Tribunal," 410.

that the world had neither beginning nor end;[18] that the soul was merely air and blood;[19] that fornication with a prostitute was not a mortal sin;[20] that God and the Virgin were nothing other than this visible world; that Christ's birth was natural and the soul was only blood;[21] that there would be no bodily resurrection at the Last Judgment;[22] and that God did not create the devil or creatures injurious to man.[23]

The inquisition's old enemy, Bernard Délicieux, was condemned for impeding the inquisition and for necromancy.[24] Eight individuals (1.3 percent) were condemned for falsely accusing innocent people of heresy.[25] (Another two individuals, primarily guilty of involvement with Catharism, were also condemned for bearing false witness.)

A Flexible System of Punishment

With this sketch of Gui's "clientele" out of the way, we can turn to the sentences he imposed, either alone or in cooperation with other inquisitors. Much could be said about these sentences. In this essay, however, I will point out only some of the most striking and obvious patterns in the data.

As I have argued elsewhere, one of the distinctive features of the inquisitors' work was the great flexibility they displayed in imposing punishment on those they found guilty.[26] This made their tribunal very different from most contemporary courts. In general, when medieval judges sentenced malefactors, they did not have available a wide array of

---

18. *LS*, 294; Duvernoy, *Registre*, 1:160–68; Vidal, "Tribunal," 393–94.

19. *LS*, 294; Duvernoy, *Registre*, 1:260–67; Vidal, "Tribunal," 397.

20. *LS*, 393; Duvernoy, *Registre*, 3:296–304; Vidal, "Tribunal," 428.

21. *LS*, 295; Duvernoy, *Registre*, 2:118–34; Vidal, "Tribunal," 409–10.

22. *LS*, 393; Duvernoy, *Registre*, 3:7–13; Vidal, "Tribunal," 423.

23. *LS*, 294; Duvernoy, *Registre*, 2:378–81; Vidal, "Tribunal," 402. Some of these offenses savor of Catharist belief, but it is difficult to tell whether the people who held them were really sympathizers with that sect.

24. *LS*, 268. For the career of this opponent of the Languedocian inquisitors, see Michel de Dmitrewski, "Fr. Bernard Délicieux, O.F.M., sa lutte contre l'Inquisition de Carcassonne et d'Albi, son procès, 1297–1319," *Archivum Franciscanum Historicum* 17 (1924): 183–218, 313–37, 457–88; 18 (1925): 3–32; and B. Hauréau, *Bernard Délicieux et l'Inquisition albigeoise (1300–1320)* (Paris, 1877).

25. False denunciations seem to have been a significant problem. For a detailed study of one incident, see James Given, "Factional Politics in a Medieval Society: A Case Study from Fourteenth-Century Foix," *Journal of Medieval History* 14 (1988): 233–50.

26. Given, "Inquisitors of Languedoc," 352–56.

options. For the most part custom prescribed what type of punishment could be imposed for a particular offense: execution, mutilation, exile, a fine, and so on. Beginning in the thirteenth century this inflexibility came to be seen as a hindrance to the effective administration of justice. Increasingly legal professionals began working toward giving judges greater discretion in sentencing the guilty.[27]

Of all medieval judges, probably few were as resourceful as the inquisitors in devising a varied and flexible set of punishments. Not only could they make fine distinctions among various degrees of culpability, but their ability to alter the punishments they imposed, if those they sentenced proved cooperative, enabled them to operate something akin to a parole system. The penalties employed by the inquisitors were thus not simply punishments, but, taken as a whole, constituted a system for the long-term manipulation of those who had fallen into their clutches.

Gui's register contains a total of 633 penalties (see table 1 and fig. 2). The least severe punishment in the inquisitor's tool bag was the requirement to perform penitential pilgrimages. This penalty was generally reserved for those whose involvement with heresy had been relatively minor and who readily made complete confessions. Gui recorded a small number of such penalties, only 17, or 2.7 percent, of the total.

For individuals whose involvement with heresy was more serious, there were more severe penalties. When the inquisitors did not think that pilgrimages alone were sufficient, they required the wearing of crosses. These were made of yellow cloth and were to be worn at all times on the front and back of one's clothing. In a society such as that of Languedoc, where people were much concerned with honor and reputation, such a penalty was peculiarly humiliating. Of the sentences recorded by Gui, 136 (21.5 percent) were for this form of punishment. Within this category, there were gradations. Those who had cooperated and confessed quickly were required to wear only a single set of crosses. Seventy-nine sentences (12.5 percent) fell into this category. Those who had not been as cooperative, or who were felt to be more deeply compromised, had to wear a double set. Gui recorded 57 such sentences (9 percent of the total).

If those sentenced to wear crosses behaved properly, they could look forward to a day when they would be allowed to lay them aside. For 121 people sentenced to wear crosses, we can calculate how long they did so

27. On this, see Bernard Schnapper, "Les Peines arbitraires du XIIIe ax XVIIIe siècle (doctrines savantes et usages français)," *Tijdschrift voor Rechtsgeschiedenis* 41 (1973): 237–77; 42 (1974): 81–112.

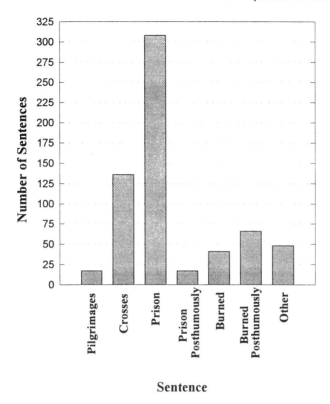

Sentence

Fig. 2. Types of sentences imposed by Bernard Gui (*N* = 633)

(see fig. 3).[28] For this group, the mean time spent wearing crosses was 4.4 years (1,601 days), with the median and the mode both being 2.95 years (1,078 days). The shortest period of cross-wearing was a little less than a year, 315 days, the longest 13.3 years (4,858 days).

The next penalty in the hierarchy of punishments imposed by the inquisitors, imprisonment, represented a significant increase in severity. This was almost invariably for life and also entailed the confiscation of one's property. Of the sentences recorded in Gui's register, almost half, 308 (48.7 percent) were of this type. The inquisitors recognized different forms of imprisonment. The normal regime, known by the shorthand term of *murum largum,* was evidently not very harsh. Direct evidence on

28. Information on two of these individuals (1.7 percent) is derived from Vidal, "Tribunal."

TABLE 1.   Acts Recorded in Bernard Gui's Register

Sentences Imposed	Number	Percentage
Pilgrimages	17	2.7%
Simple crosses	79	12.5%
Double crosses	57	9.0%
One-year prison term	1	0.2%
Perpetual imprisonment, normal regime	268	42.3%
Perpetual imprisonment, normal regime, and house destroyed	8	1.3%
Perpetual imprisonment, strict regime	31	4.9%
Burned alive	41	6.5%
Deceased but would have been imprisoned if alive	17	2.7%
Deceased but would have been burned if alive	3	0.5%
Burned posthumously	52	8.2%
Burned posthumously, house destroyed	14	2.2%
Remains to be exhumed	3	0.5%
Condemned in absentia	40	6.3%
Ordered on crusade	1	0.2%
Reserved for other judgment	1	0.2%
Total	633	
Commutations of previously imposed sentences		
Released from prison, to wear crosses	139	50.7%
Allowed to lay aside crosses	135	49.3%
Total	274	
Grand total	907	

conditions in the inquisitorial *mur* in Toulouse is, unfortunately, rather scarce. We are better informed about conditions in Jacques Fournier's prisons. The regime employed in the Tour des Allemans seems to have been fairly lax. Some prisoners were allowed to wander about relatively unsupervised. Indeed, the infamous Bernard Clergue of Montaillou, admittedly only under investigation at the time and not yet condemned, was able to secure a set of keys to the castle's internal doors.[29] Gui recorded 268 sentences to the *murum largum* (42.3 percent).

29. Duvernoy, *Registre*, 2:289–90.

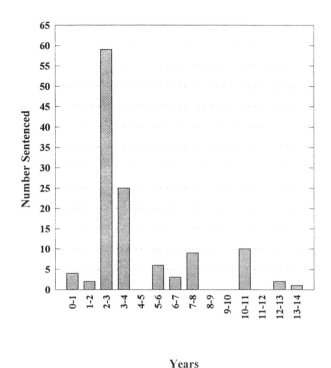

Years

Fig. 3. Length of time spent wearing crosses (N = 121)

Imprisonment, however, could be either supplemented with other penalties or intensified. Some individuals, in addition to being imprisoned, had their houses destroyed. These people had sheltered the Cathar Bons Hommes or allowed them to perform the Cathar baptism, the *consolamentum,* in their homes. These houses were torn down and turned into rubbish dumps as a sign of disgrace and a perpetual reminder of the fate of Cathar sympathizers. Eight sentences to the *murum largum* (1.3 percent) involved this additional indignity. Individuals who tried to bend the inquisition to their own ends by concocting false accusations of heresy could expect not only a term in prison but a period of exposure to public obloquy as well. Two individuals sentenced to the *mur* for making false accusations were also exposed to public view for several days on specially erected ladders, with red tongues sewn on their clothing. One individual, who had forged a letter in the name of the inquisitors, was exposed to public view with a red letter attached to his clothing.

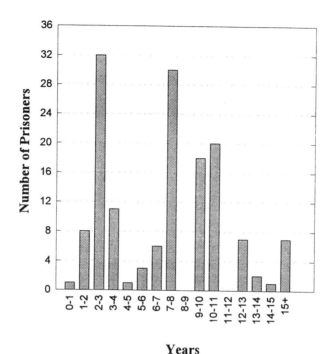

Years

Fig. 4. Length of time spent in prison (*N* = 147)

For those whom they wished to punish severely, the inquisitors had available a particularly harsh form of imprisonment. Those who had been deeply involved with heresy, or who had tried to deceive the inquisitors, were sentenced to what was known as the *murum strictum*. Individuals thus condemned were locked up in cells, shackled to the walls, and fed on bread and water. Thirty-one such sentences (4.9 percent) were recorded in Gui's register. In one anomalous case, a single individual was sentenced to a term of one year in prison.

Although virtually all those immured were supposedly sentenced to life in prison, many could look forward to eventual release. We can calculate the amount of time 147 people spent in prison (see fig. 4).[30] The average period of incarceration was 7.49 years (2,734 days).[31]

---

30. Information on the length of time spent in prison by 15 (10.6 percent) of these people is derived from Vidal, "Tribunal."

31. The median and the mode were both 7.44 years (2,716 days). The shortest period spent in prison was a little under a year, 315 days, while the longest was 33.83 years (12,348 days). Of this group, one-quarter spent 2.95 years (1,078 days) or less in prison; one-half spent 7.44 years or less (2,716 days); and three-quarters spent 10.36 years or less (3,780 days) in prison.

The inquisitors' most severe penalty was death by fire. Technically, of course, the inquisitors, being priests forbidden to shed blood, did not actually condemn anyone to death. They merely relaxed culprits to the secular authorities, who were expected to carry out the executions. Forty-one such relaxations to the secular arm were recorded in Gui's register, 6.5 percent of the total.[32]

Most modern historians have been struck by the small number of executions decreed by the medieval inquisitors.[33] At first glance Gui's register might seem to bear out this picture of inquisitorial clemency. But before we accept this picture we need to examine the data in more detail. Certainly, from the evidence in Gui's register one cannot argue that he and his fellow early-fourteenth-century inquisitors went in for wholesale slaughter. The 41 people sent to the stake constituted 7.9 percent of the 519 who both received a sentence and were alive at the time.

From the perspective of the end of the twentieth century, with its record of death camps, administrative massacres, and massive killing of civilians during wartime, this may seem a modest toll. Yet no modern European or North American court imposes death sentences with anything approaching this frequency.[34] One may object that the early fourteenth century employed a different standard in handing out punishment. Unfortunately, this is a very difficult proposition to evaluate. Some courts were indeed much harsher than those of Gui and his colleagues. This seems to have been especially true of the royal courts of northwestern Europe. Between 1389 and 1392, for example, the court of the royal *prévôt* of Paris, held in the Châtelet, sent more than 30 people a year to their deaths.[35] Gui, by contrast, recorded the executions of only about 2.7 people a year.

---

32. We should note two anomalous penalties recorded in Gui's register. In one case an individual was sentenced to take part in the next crusade to the Holy Land, pending which he was to remove himself into exile. And in another case no punishment was imposed until further deliberation could be conducted concerning his case.

33. Lea, *History,* 1:549–51; Yves Dossat, *Les Crises de l'inquisition toulousaine au XIIIe siècle (1233–73)* (Bordeaux, 1959), 265, 268; Walter Wakefield, *Heresy, Crusade and Inquisition in Southern France, 1100–1250* (Berkeley, 1974), 184–85.

34. The classic study of criminal homicide in Philadelphia during the years 1948–52 found that, of the 387 individuals who were found guilty of a criminal homicide and sentenced, only 7 (1.8 percent) were given the death penalty. See Marvin E. Wolfgang, *Patterns in Criminal Homicide* (New York, 1966), 302–5.

35. See Bronislaw Geremek, *The Margins of Society in Late Medieval Paris,* trans. Jean Birrell (Cambridge, 1987), 47–53.

The surviving register of the Châtelet seems to record only the trials of people who were found guilty.[36] It is therefore impossible to determine what proportion of all people who appeared before the court was likely to be condemned and executed. For information on the likelihood that any particular defendant would be executed, we must cross the Channel to England. English criminal law was peculiarly drastic in its system of punishments; virtually the only penalty for all types of felony was death by hanging. This punishment seems to have been imposed more frequently by English judges than by Languedocian inquisitors but not all that much more frequently. In a study I did of patterns of homicide in a number of English counties, 3,492 people were formally denounced as suspected murderers. Of these, 1,251 appeared in court, and 247 were executed. These 247 constituted 19.7 percent of those who were actually tried, and 7.1 percent of those suspected.[37] Barbara Hanawalt found that 22.9 percent of her sample of 15,865 individuals who were tried at gaol deliveries in the first half of the fourteenth century were convicted and presumably executed.[38] Philippa Maddern has found that, of the 2,476 people tried in gaol deliveries in East Anglia between 1422 and 1442, 10 percent (248) were executed.[39]

For fifteenth-century Florence we not only know how many people were executed in a particular year, but we can also calculate an execution rate that reveals with what frequency Florentines perished at the gallows. In Florence a lay confraternity, the Compagnia di Santa Maria della Croce al Tempio, took on the somber task of accompanying to the gallows and offering spiritual comfort to those who were to be executed. The confraternity kept a register, the *Libro dei giustiziati,* of all the executions serviced by its members. This material has been tabulated by Samuel Y. Edgerton Jr.[40] In the case of Florence, we are in the happy

36. See Henri Duplès-Agier, ed., *Registre criminel du Châtelet de Paris du 6 septembre 1389 au 18 mai 1392,* 2 vols., Société des Bibliophiles Français (Paris, 1861–64).

37. James Given, *Society and Homicide in Thirteenth-Century England* (Stanford, 1977), 137.

38. Barbara A. Hanawalt, *Crime and Conflict in English Communities, 1300–1348* (Cambridge, Mass., 1979), 59. Hanawalt's data are very unreliable, gathered in an inconsistent fashion and riddled with arithmetical errors, but the order of magnitude is consistent with what I found in my study of homicide.

39. Philippa C. Maddern, *Violence and Social Order: East Anglia, 1422–1442* (Oxford, 1992), 50.

40. Samuel Y. Edgerton Jr., *Pictures and Punishment: Art and Criminal Prosecution during the Florentine Renaissance* (Ithaca, N.Y., 1985), 234–38.

position of knowing the size of the population that was at risk for execution. According to the Catasto of 1427, the city's population was about 37,000.[41] From 1400 to 1439, the *Libro dei giustiziati* recorded 196 executions, for an average of 9.8 a year. This works out to an annual execution rate of 26 per 100,000, which seems impressive.

This figure probably *overestimates* the true execution rate. Undoubtedly some of those executed at Florence were not inhabitants of the city of Florence but of its *contado*. In 1427, the *contado*'s population was 126,831.[42] The total population of the Florentine state was thus 164,077 (which will be rounded to 164,000 in the following calculations). If we assume (undoubtedly incorrectly) that all executions in the Florentine state took place in the city of Florence, we then come up with an annual execution rate of 6 per 100,000. The true annual execution rate therefore lies somewhere between 6 per 100,000 and 26 per 100,000.

None of these figures are exactly comparable to the data in Gui's register. In dealing with Gui's register, we lack information about the number of people against whom investigations were begun but who were cleared of any taint of heresy, and we certainly do not know, except in the most crude fashion, the size of the population that was at risk of falling into the Languedocian inquisitors' hands. It does appear, however, that inquisitorial judges were less likely to impose capital sentences than were their secular French, English, and Florentine counterparts.

But can we say that Gui and his colleagues displayed greater mansuetude than all medieval judges? The answer to this question must be unclear, since with only a few exceptions the abundant judicial records of most other areas of medieval Europe have not been subjected to rigorous quantitative analysis. Some of the available evidence suggests, however, that many medieval courts were reluctant to impose harsh punishments. For example, Martin Schüssler found in his study of crime in the German city of Nuremberg between 1285 and 1403 that only 87 people were executed.[43] In addition to analyzing the data from Nuremberg, Schüssler

41. The Catasto gives a figure of 37,246, which I have rounded to 37,000. The figure comes from David Herlihy and Christiane Klapisch-Zuber, *Tuscans and Their Families: A Study of the Florentine Catasto of 1427* (New Haven, 1985), 56.

42. Herlihy and Klapisch-Zuber, *Tuscans*, 56.

43. Martin Schüssler, "Statistische Untersuchung des Verbrechens in Nürnberg im Zeitraum von 1285 bis 1400," *Zeitschrift der Savigny-Stiftung für Rechtsgeschichte, Germanistische Abteilung* 108 (1991): 163, 172–74.

carried out a thorough survey of the existing secondary literature on medieval crime. He found that in many places in Germany, Flanders, and Italy courts were very reluctant to impose capital sentences on those they condemned.[44]

It thus appears that the Languedocian inquisitors were, as historians have long noted, not the blood stained butchers of popular myth. The comparative material suggests that they were not the most severe judges to be found in thirteenth- and fourteenth-century Europe. They did, however, preside over a court that may have been, in comparison with many others in medieval Europe, highly prone to hand down capital verdicts.

Gui and his collaborators were more likely to send men than women to the stake. Of the 41 people listed in Gui's register who were burned, 32 (78 percent) were men, and 9 (22 percent) were women (see table 2). The 32 men burned constituted 10.2 percent of the 315 living males listed in Gui's register who received some sort of punishment; the 9 women equaled only 4.4 percent of the 204 living women punished.[45]

A less striking difference appears if we break down the offenses for which people were executed (see table 3). Thirty Cathars were burned, as were 7 Waldensians and 4 Beguins. However, these raw figures are slightly misleading. Although Cathars made up the largest number of people burned, individuals convicted of Catharism actually ran the smallest risk of being burned (see fig. 5). The 30 people burned for Catharism made up 7.6 percent of the 393 living individuals sentenced for this type of heresy. The inquisitors took a slightly tougher line with Waldensians, burning 8.4 percent of the 83 living people convicted under this heading.[46] The heretics most often burned were the Beguins. Four of the 19

---

44. Schüssler, "Statistische Untersuchung," 162–68. On the whole, high rates of execution seem to be more characteristic of early modern than of medieval society. On this, see Robert Muchembled, *Le Temps des supplices: De L'Obéissances sous les rois absolus, XVe–XVIIIe siècle* (Paris, 1992), 48–51, 105–15.

45. This is a statistically significant relationship. For this distribution, chi-square = 5.62 with one degree of freedom; $p = 0.018$. This allows us to reject the null hypothesis that there is no relationship between sex and the likelihood of being burned at the stake. The reader should note that the figures given in this paragraph for the percentages of men and women burned differ slightly from those in table 2. This difference arises from the fact that in table 2 I have included all those who were punished by Gui, whether living or dead at the time of their sentencing. In this paragraph, however, I discuss only individuals who were alive at the time of their sentencing.

46. Note that the percentages given in this paragraph for those burned alive differ slightly from those given in table 3. This difference arises from the fact that in table 3 I have included all those who were sentenced by Bernard Gui, whether they were alive at the time of their sentencing or not. In this paragraph, however, I discuss only those individuals who were alive at the time of their sentencing.

(21.1 percent) Beguins, all alive at the time they were sentenced, were sent to the stake.[47]

To round out this discussion, we should note that 40 sentences con-

TABLE 2.   Individuals and Their Penalties Broken Down by Gender

Penalty	Men	Women	Total
Pilgrimages	8	9	17
	2.3%	3.6%	2.8%
Crosses	72	64	136
	20.4%	25.3%	22.4%
Prison	190	118	308
	53.8%	46.6%	50.8%
Deceased but would have been imprisoned	9	8	17
	2.6%	3.2%	2.8%
Burned alive	32	9	41
	9.1%	3.6%	6.8%
Deceased but would have been burned	3	0	3
	0.9%	0.0%	0.5%
Burned posthumously	25	41	66
	7.1%	16.2%	10.9%
Remains exhumed	2	1	3
	0.6%	0.4%	0.5%
Other	35	7	42
	9.9%	2.8%	6.9%
Total	353	253	606

Note: The unit of analysis in this table is the individual not the sentence. Since some individuals received more than one sentence, they are counted more than once in this table. Therefore, column totals sum to figures greater than those shown, and percentages sum to more than 100 percent.

47. This is not a statistically significant distribution. If we perform a chi-square test on only those individuals convicted of Catharism, Waldensianism, and Beguinism, we find that chi-square = 4.3 with two degrees of freedom; $p = .12$. Therefore, we cannot reject the null hypothesis that there is no relationship between type of heresy and likelihood of going to the stake.

TABLE 3. Individuals and Their Penalties Broken Down by Offense

Penalty	Cathars	Waldensians	Beguins	Other	Unknown	Total
Pilgrimages	10 2.1%	7 7.8%	0 0.0%	0 0.0%	0 0.0%	17 2.8%
Crosses	107 22.7%	19 21.1%	1 5.3%	7 31.8%	2 50.0%	136 22.4%
Prison	249 52.9%	36 40.0%	13 68.4%	9 40.9%	1 25.0%	308 50.8%
Deceased but would have been imprisoned	16 3.4%	1 1.1%	0 0.0%	0 0.0%	0 0.0%	17 2.8%
Burned alive	30 6.4%	7 7.8%	4 21.1%	0 0.0%	0 0.0%	41 6.8%
Deceased but would have been burned	3 0.6%	0 0.0%	0 0.0%	0 0.0%	0 0.0%	3 0.5%
Burned posthumously	58 12.3%	6 6.7%	0 0.0%	2 9.1%	0 0.0%	66 10.9%
Remains exhumed	3 0.6%	0 0.0%	0 0.0%	0 0.0%	0 0.0%	3 0.5%
Other	19 4.0%	15 16.7%	3 15.8%	4 18.2%	1 25.0%	42 6.9%
Total	471	90	19	22	4	606

Note: The unit of analysis in this table is the individual not the sentence. Since some individuals received more than one sentence, they are counted more than once in this table. Therefore, column totals sum to figures greater than those shown, and percentages sum to more than 100 percent.

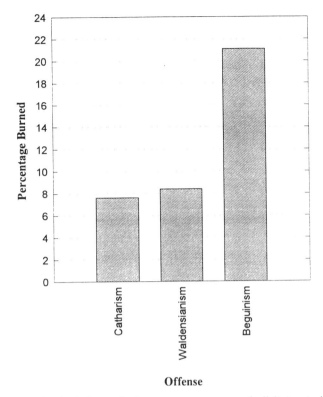

Offense

Fig. 5. Individuals burned alive as a percentage of all living individuals punished ($N = 519$)

sisted of the condemnation of individuals in absentia (6.3 percent of the total). These were people who had either failed to heed citations to appear before the inquisitors to have their beliefs examined or who, having confessed to heretical dealings, failed either to appear to hear their sentences or fled without completing their penances.

The inquisitors also pursued the dead. Gui and his fellow inquisitors imposed 89 sentences (14.1 percent of the total) on individuals who were deceased. The majority of these sentences, 66 in all (11 percent of the total), consisted of orders to exhume and burn the corpses of the deceased. On 14 occasions an order for the destruction of the house of the person concerned was also issued. In 3 instances Gui declared that the individuals in question, had they lived long enough to be sentenced, would have been burned. Another 3 sentences consisted of orders to exhume, but not burn, the corpses of the deceased.[48] And on 17 occasions, usually involving people who had confessed to heretical dealings but had died before penances could be imposed on them, it was proclaimed that they would have been immured had they lived.

The Varying Treatment of Men and Women

We have already noted that the inquisitors were more likely to burn men than women. It is worth examining our data further to see what else is revealed about the impact of gender on the prosecution and punishment of heresy. A little over two-fifths, 266, or 41.8 percent, of those individuals listed in Gui's register were women. This is a remarkably large percentage. The "clientele" of most medieval courts was overwhelmingly male. This was especially true of courts that handed down afflictive punishments for various types of wrongdoing. At least in English criminal courts, women made relatively infrequent appearances. In my sample of 1,251 individuals who appeared in court to stand trial for homicide in thirteenth-century England, only 123 (9.8 percent) were female.[49] Similarly, the early-fourteenth-century English gaol deliveries analyzed by Hanawalt show that only about 10 percent of those tried were women.[50] The fact that women made up a large proportion of those who passed through the hands of Bernard Gui and his associates is one of the most striking aspects of the work of the Languedocian inquisitors. The inquisitorial tribunals were involved much more thoroughly than almost any other medieval courts in trying to regulate the behavior and attitudes of the female part of the population.

Women were not equally represented among the ranks of the different heresies (see table 4). They made up a larger proportion of those punished for Catharism than for any other heresy, 46.3 percent. They were less well represented among the ranks of other heresies. They made up only a little more than a third of the Waldensians, 36.3 percent. And Beguinism appears to have been, at least in Gui's register, an almost exclusively male phenomenon, women constituting only 10.5 percent of these heretics.

---

48. These were individuals who were sympathizers with the Cathar heretics but who had not received the *consolamentum* (Bernard Gui, *Practica inquisitionis heretice pravitatis*, ed. C. Douais [Paris, 1886], 85).
    49. Given, *Society and Homicide*, 137.
    50. Hanawalt, *Crime and Conflict*, 118.

The women whose sentences were recorded in Gui's register seem to have received less rigorous treatment than men (see table 2). They were slightly more likely than men to receive one of the lighter penances. Among women 3.6 percent, as opposed to 2.3 percent of men, received penances consisting only of pilgrimages, and 25.3 percent of women, as opposed to 20.4 percent of men, were only required to wear crosses. Although women were slightly more likely than men to be required to wear crosses, there was virtually no difference in the length of time that men and women wore these badges of infamy. We can calculate the length of time that crosses were worn for 66 men and 55 women. The average time for the two sexes was very nearly the same, men wearing crosses for an average of 4.36 years (1,592 days) and women for 4.41 years (1,611 days) (see fig. 6).[51]

Men were more likely than women to be sentenced to prison, 53.8 percent as opposed to 46.8 percent. Interestingly, however, those women

TABLE 4. Nature of Offense Broken Down by Gender

Offense	Male	Female	Total
Catharism	255 53.7%	220 46.3%	475
Waldensianism	58 63.7%	33 36.3%	91
Beguinism	17 89.5%	2 10.5	19
Other	25 96.2%	1 3.8%	26
None Given	16 61.5%	10 38.5%	26
Total	371 58.2%	266 41.8%	637

51. The variability around the mean was somewhat greater for men, who had a standard deviation of 1,048 days as opposed to a standard deviation of 961 days for women. But there is no statistically significant difference in the mean time spent by men and women wearing crosses.

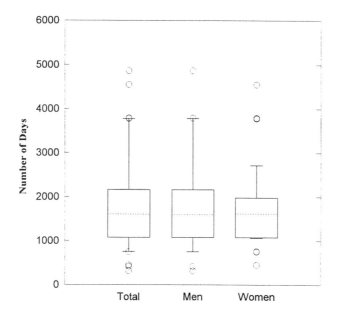

Fig. 6. Time spent wearing crosses broken down by gender (*N* = 121). Each box indicates the range between the 25th and 75th percentiles of the data. The dashed horizontal lines indicate the means of the respective boxes. Capped bars indicate the 10th and 90th percentile points. The circles indicate extreme cases lying beyond the 10th and 90th percentiles (From Liber Sententiarum and Vidal, "Tribunal")

who were immured may have had to spend more time incarcerated than did their male counterparts. We can calculate how much time 97 men and 50 women spent lodged in the inquisitorial prisons. On average, women spent almost three-quarters of a year longer in prison than men did. The mean prison stay for men was 7.25 years (2,645 days) versus 7.97 years (2,909 days) for women (see fig. 7).[52]

Men were more than twice as likely as women to go the stake; 9.1 percent of all men, whether living or dead, were burned, as opposed to 3.6 percent of the women.[53] However, women were more than twice as likely

---

52. The variability around the mean was somewhat greater for men than for women. The standard deviation was 1,910 days for men and 1,778 days for women. The difference in means between men and women is not statistically significant.

53. Readers will note that the percentages given in this and the following paragraph concerning the number of people burned by Bernard Gui differ slightly from those given above. This is due to the fact that in the earlier discussion of individuals burned by Gui, I considered only individuals who were alive when they were sentenced. In this section I am including all individuals, whether dead or alive at the time of their sentence. The relationship between sex and the chances of being burned seems

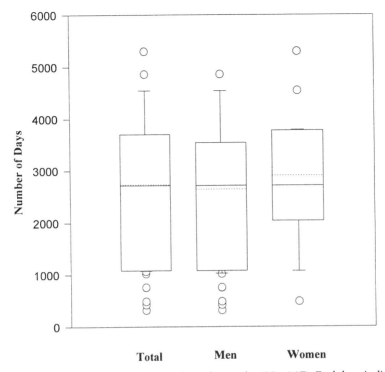

Fig. 7. Time spent in prison broken down by gender (N = 147). Each box indicates the range between the 25th and 75th percentiles of the data. The solid horizontal lines indicate the 50th percentile; the dashed lines the mean. Capped bars indicate the 10th and 90th percentile points. The circles indicate extreme cases lying beyond the 10th and 90th percentiles (From Liber Sententiarum and Vidal, "Tribunal")

to be burned *posthumously* than were men. Whereas only 7.1 percent of the men whose sentences are recorded in the *Liber sententiarum* were dug up and burned, this happened to 16.3 percent of the women.

The Varying Treatment of Different Types of Heresy

Just as we can see differences in the way the inquisitors treated men and women, so we can detect differences in the way they dealt with different types of heresy (see table 3). Beguins seem to have received the harshest

to be statistically significant. If we look at only those individuals who were alive at the time Gui recorded their sentences, we find that 10.2 percent of the men (32 of 315) were burned alive, as opposed to 4.4 percent of the women (9 of 204). Chi-square for this distribution is 5.62 with one degree of freedom; $p = .018$. This allows us to reject the null hypothesis that there is no connection between sex and the chances of being burned.

treatment. As I have already remarked, Beguins had the greatest chance of being burned, with 21.1 percent of this group going to the stake. Smaller proportions of Waldensians and Cathars were burned, 7.8 percent and 6.4 percent, respectively.[54]

Beguins were also more likely to be sentenced to periods of imprisonment. More than two-thirds, 13 in all (68.4 percent), were immured. Cathars and Waldensians were subjected to less rigorous treatment. Of the 469 Cathars in Gui's register, a little over half, 249 (53.1 percent), were imprisoned, while only 36 of the 89 Waldensians (40.4 percent) received a similar punishment. In the case of 122 Cathars[55] and 13 Waldensians,[56] we can tell exactly how long they remained in prison. Waldensians on average spent 2.83 years (1,032 days) in the *mur*. For this group the median and the mode were both 2.95 years (1,078 days). Cathars spent much more time in prison. Their average stay was 7.26 years (2,650 days), with a median and a mode that were both 7.44 years (2,716 days).[57] One would like to know how long Beguins spent in the inquisitorial prisons, but the data in Gui's register unfortunately cast no light on this problem.

The lighter penalties inflicted by the inquisitors also show variation with respect to the different types of heresy. As might be expected, only one Beguin (5.3 percent of the total) was sentenced to wear crosses. Waldensians and Cathars received this type of penalty more frequently, in about equal proportions, with 21.3 percent of Waldensians and 22.8 percent of Cathars being sentenced to wear these badges of infamy. Of those sentenced to wear crosses, we know exactly how long 105 Cathars and 13 Waldensians had to do so.[58] Those condemned for Catharism seem to have been treated more rigorously. On average, convicted

---

54. This does not seem to be a statistically significant distribution. If we consider only those people who were alive at the time they were sentenced for either Catharism, Waldensianism, or Beguinism, we find that 7.6 percent of the Cathars (30 of 393), 8.4 percent of the Waldensians (7 of 83), and 21.1 percent of the Béguins (4 of 19) were burned alive. Chi-square for this distribution is 4.3 with two degrees of freedom; p = .117. We therefore cannot reject the null hypothesis that there is no connection between heresy and the likelihood of being burned.

55. Information on the length of stay in prison for nine of these people is derived from Vidal, "Tribunal."

56. Information on the length of stay in prison for one of these people is derived from Vidal, "Tribunal."

57. This is a statistically significant difference. However, the fact that 12 of the 13 Waldensians served exactly the same amount of time, all being imprisoned on 30 September 1319 and released on 12 September 1322, makes this a not very meaningful statement.

58. Information on one of the Waldensians is derived from Vidal, "Tribunal."

Cathars wore their crosses for 4.6 years (1,696 days) while convicted Waldensians wore theirs for only 2.89 years (1,054 days). For the Waldensians the median and the mode were both 2.95 years. For the convicted Cathars, the median time spent wearing crosses was 3.57 years (1,302 days) and the mode 2.95 years (1,078 days).[59] No Beguin received the lightest possible penalty, the requirement to perform only a number of penitential pilgrimages. Of the condemned Waldensians, 7.8 percent received this penalty, whereas only 2.1 percent of the condemned Cathars did.

Conclusion

Some of the conclusions that emerge from this reexamination of Bernard Gui's register will not come as a surprise to students of heresy and the inquisition. That the most popular heresy in Languedoc was Catharism, followed by Waldensianism as a distant second, is well known. The importance given by the inquisitors to the persecution of Beguins, a heretical movement that deserves more general attention than it has received, is also something of which specialists on Languedocian history have long been aware.[60] The great variety of penalties imposed by the inquisitors has been noticed by virtually every commentator on the medieval inquisition. I have argued elsewhere that this flexible system of punishments enabled the inquisitors to create a readily identifiable and stigmatized social outgroup that they could easily manipulate and turn into a tool to help them in the further repression of heresy.[61]

Our fresh examination of Gui's register also reveals some patterns that no other commentator on the inquisition has noticed. One of the most interesting observations is the great frequency with which women appeared before Gui and his fellow inquisitors. At a time when women seldom appeared in European courts, more than 40 percent of those recorded by Gui were female. Although the inquisitors do not appear to

---

59. This is a statistically significant difference. However, 12 of the 13 Waldensians wore their crosses for exactly the same period, all sentenced on 30 September 1319 and allowed to lay aside their crosses on 12 September 1322. To say that this is a statistically significant difference is, once again, to make a not very meaningful statement.

60. See Raoul Manselli, "Bernard Gui face aux Spirituels et aux Apostoliques," in *Bernard Gui et son monde*, 265–78.

61. Given, "Inquisitors of Languedoc," 353–56. This is a subject I propose to treat in greater length in a book dealing with the Languedocian inquisitors.

have been as rigorous with them as with men, it is clear that this particular tribunal was unusually interested in policing the behavior of medieval women.

Our examination of the data also reveals interesting differences in the ways in which the inquisitors dealt with different types of heresy. The heresy that evoked the harshest set of penalties was also the newest, Beguinism. Its novelty, and the fact that its ideas about the poverty of Christ and the corruption of authority within the church, which seemed to pose a real threat of major social and religious upheaval, provoked the inquisitors to unusual displays of wrath. More than a fifth of those convicted of this heresy were burned, and almost 70 percent were immured. The older, one might almost say traditional, heresies of Languedoc evoked less severe treatment. Catharism, which was clearly on its last legs in the region, provided the bulk of the inquisitors' business, but was not punished with the same draconian fury as was Beguinism. Less than 7 percent of its adepts went to the stake, and only 53 percent were imprisoned. Never deeply rooted in Languedoc, Waldensianism, which taught doctrines that were not as alien to Catholic Christianity as were those of Catharism but which had more staying power in Europe as a whole, elicited an intermediate response. Waldensians were slightly more likely to be burned than were Cathars (7.8 percent vs. 6.4 percent), but they were less likely to be imprisoned (40 percent vs. 52.9 percent), with those who did experience this fate spending less time in the inquisitorial jails than Cathars did.[62]

In this essay I have touched on only a few aspects of the material in Gui's register. I have said nothing about the temporal and geographical variation in patterns of persecution. Nor, apart from considering how sex and type of heresy influenced sentencing, have I dealt with the difficult problem of how the inquisitors decided that some individuals were more worthy than others of harsh treatment. These are questions that will have to await future exploration of the *Liber sententiarum*. Gui's register is one of the oldest and best-known sources for the medieval inquisition. I hope I have demonstrated that we have not exhausted all that it can teach us about medieval heretics and inquisitors.

---

62. Readers with a statistical background may at this point wonder why I have not performed a chi-square test on these data. I did not do so because of the fact that in Gui's register a single individual could receive more than one sentence. To perform a chi-square test on a cross-tabulation in which individuals appeared more than once would be extremely misleading.

Toward a New Periodization of Ecclesiastical History: Demography, Society, and Religion in Medieval Verona

Maureen C. Miller

How historians divide the past into periods and characterize these discrete units is constantly changing as we bring new questions to our
sources. Certainly, developments in social and economic history since the
Second World War have radically altered our understanding of the Middle Ages and significantly modified periodization.[1] While C. W. Previté-
Orton's *Outlines of Medieval History* (1924) had the "revival" of Western Europe beginning in the wake of the Gregorian Reform (late eleventh
century), the latest edition (1990) of C. Warren Hollister's *Medieval
Europe: A Short History* locates it in commercial expansion beginning in
the tenth century.[2] Medieval ecclesiastical history, however, has
remained remarkably impervious to such revisions. While many excellent
new studies of the medieval church have appeared,[3] the traditional peri-

1. The work of David Herlihy contributed significantly to this revolution, incorpo-
rating the history of women and the family into the mainstream of medieval studies
and underscoring the influence of demography on medieval social and economic structures. His emphasis on demographic change has strongly influenced my own approach
to medieval ecclesiastical history.

2. C. W. Previté-Orton, *Outlines of Medieval History* (Cambridge: Cambridge
University Press, 1924), esp. 220–21, on the effects of the Gregorian Reform, followed
by a chapter entitled "The Revival of Secular Civilization" (222–29); C. Warren Hollister, *Medieval Europe: A Short History*, 6th ed. (New York: McGraw-Hill, 1990),
142–45. Hollister still describes the High Middle Ages as beginning ca. 1050 and end-
ing ca. 1300, but he acknowledges that other historians would begin them in 950 or
1000 and begins his own description of this period in the tenth- and eleventh-century
"Commercial Revolution."

3. The works of American historians such as Barbara H. Rosenwein, *Rhinoceros
Bound: Cluny in the Tenth Century* (Philadelphia: University of Pennsylvania Press,

odization of ecclesiastical history remains largely unchanged. Clearly, its revision is too large and complex an endeavor to accomplish in this essay. But I aim here to make at least a contribution toward that goal by reconsidering a pivotal era in ecclesiastical history: the eleventh and twelfth centuries.[4]

This period is traditionally characterized as the Age of Gregorian Reform. It is but one summit of reform in the traditional narrative of medieval and early modern church history, which carves the ecclesiastical past into moral valleys and peaks. The Carolingian reforms, for example, rescued the early medieval church from disorganization and abuses, only to have the invasions of the tenth century prematurely upset the church's "normative" development toward hierarchy. The Gregorian Reform rectified the abuses of the tenth century and prepared the way for the high point of medieval ecclesiastical development in the pontificate of Innocent III. The decline of the late Middle Ages then necessitated the Catholic Reform of the sixteenth and seventeenth centuries. This traditional narrative is highly teleological: it orders the entire development of the church into periods defined by the degree of "progress" toward the modern, papal-dominated, structure of the Catholic Church. Its use of "reform" as an organizing principle is also highly value-laden, obliging the ecclesiastical historian to measure the success of individuals and institutions in conforming to Christian ideals.

Several scholars have noted the deficiencies and limitations of the Age of Gregorian Reform in characterizing ecclesiastical change in the eleventh and twelfth centuries.[5] The rubric attributes the reform to Pope

1982), and *To Be the Neighbor of Saint Peter: The Social Meaning of Cluny's Property, 909–1049* (Ithaca: Cornell University Press, 1989); and Constance Brittain Bouchard, *Sword, Mitre, and Cloister: Nobility and the Church in Burgundy, 980–1198* (Ithaca: Cornell University Press, 1987) are good examples, as are the articles by R. I. Moore, "Family, Community and Cult on the Eve of the Gregorian Reform," *Transactions of the Royal Historical Society*, ser. 5, 30 (1980): 49–69 and "New Sects and Secret Meetings: Association and Authority in the Eleventh and Twelfth Centuries," *Studies in Church History* 23 (1986): 47–68.

4. This article summarizes some of the main points of my book, *The Formation of a Medieval Church: Ecclesiastical Change in Verona, 950–1150* (Ithaca: Cornell University Press, 1993).

5. The best critique of the traditional conceptualization is Ovidio Capitani, "Esiste un'«età gregoriana»?" *Rivista di storia e letteratura religiosa* 1 (1965): 454–81. Another is John Gilchrist, "Was There a Gregorian Reform Movement in the Eleventh Century?" *Canadian Catholic Historical Association, Study Sessions* 37 (1970): 1–10.

Gregory VII, although clearly it began well before his pontificate.[6] The narrative of the Gregorian Reform also tends to be overwhelmed by Gregory's political struggle with Emperor Henry IV over investiture, minimizing the significance of changes on the local level. Despite these and other difficulties, no new characterization has supplanted the Age of Gregorian Reform.[7]

My primary aim here is to offer a new outline of ecclesiastical change in these crucial centuries. In my view, the most important period of change in the history of the medieval church began in the mid–tenth and ended in the mid–twelfth century. This period is defined by institutional expansion.[8] The building of new churches quickened after the mid–tenth century as invasions ceased and Europe's population began to expand.[9] The increase in the number of new churches peaked in the first half of the twelfth century and then declined as the expansion of settlement slowed and competition for economic resources (especially tithes) increased. More than the building of new churches, however, occurred over these two centuries: immense growth sparked innovations affecting all aspects of ecclesiastical life.

My periodization is based on a detailed study of all aspects of ecclesiastical life in one diocese—Verona, Italy—in the early and central Middle

6. Uta-Renate Blumenthal, *The Investiture Crisis: Church and Monarchy from the Ninth to the Twelfth Century* (Philadelphia: University of Pennsylvania Press, 1988), 50–58, 64–79.

7. Colin Morris, in a recent synthesis, uses "the Papal Reform and the Conflict with Empire (ca. 1046–1122)" instead of the "Age of Gregorian Reform." As his nomenclature indicates, he downplays the reforming role of Gregory, but otherwise his narrative, chronology, and point of view (crediting the papacy with reform) differ little from the traditional approach. See Colin Morris, *The Papal Monarchy: The Western Church from 1050 to 1250* (Oxford: Clarendon, 1989), 79–133.

8. See Miller, *Formation*, 22–40 (on the definition of this period through institutional growth), and pages 185–87 on the data base of Veronese ecclesiastical institutions upon which it is based. This rapid increase in the founding of new churches from 950 to 1150 is not related to the great expansion of church landholdings in the eighth and ninth centuries demonstrated in David Herlihy's "Church Property on the European Continent, 901–1200" (*Speculum* 36 [1961]: 81–99). The chronological disjuncture between these two different expansions cautions against assuming direct causal linkages between wealth and institutional development. The expansion of population and settlement, not landholding, was behind the dramatic increase in church building from the mid–tenth to the mid–twelfth centuries.

9. David Herlihy, "The Agrarian Revolution in Southern France and Italy, 801–1150," *Speculum* 33 (1958): 30; David Herlihy, "Demography," in *Dictionary of the Middle Ages,* 13 vols., ed. Joseph R. Strayer (New York: Charles Scribner's Sons, 1982–89), 4:139–40.

Ages. The experience of this local church in the Age of Gregorian Reform was more complex and more significant than this designation implies. This church changed over the eleventh and twelfth centuries in the following ways: (1) there was a dramatic increase in the number of ecclesiastical institutions that comprised the church; (2) new institutional forms developed within the church for all sectors of Christian society—secular clergy, laypersons, and religious; and (3) a new, more inclusive spirituality emerged, which called on all persons to imitate Christ as closely as possible. These changes constitute a creative response to new demographic, social, economic, and political conditions in Western Europe.

Before considering each of these changes in greater detail, I must offer several observations about my evidence and aims. The bulk of my evidence is from one northern Italian city, and, while it is obviously impossible to find one diocese representative of all Western Europe, Verona does share important characteristics with many other local churches. The early medieval development of Verona's church follows a pattern common to the sees of continental Europe, which received Christianity in the centuries of Rome's imperial twilight.[10] Socially and economically, Verona was quite broadly typical of medieval European cities: it was a medium-sized urban center (20,000–25,000 inhabitants in the thirteenth century), which experienced strong, but not exceptional, economic growth in the central Middle Ages.[11] Some may object that Verona's political allegiance to the German Empire makes it a poor example of ecclesiastical development in the eleventh and twelfth centuries. Two observations may allay this concern. First, given the diversity of political conditions in Western Europe and the wide variety of responses to papal initiatives in this period,[12] a region recognizing the emperor is no less rep-

---

10. The local church emerged in the third and fourth centuries amid persecution, gained new legitimacy and favored status by converting the Germanic chieftains who conquered the region, and in the eighth century was incorporated into the Carolingian Empire and enjoyed the ecclesiastical and cultural revival that Charlemagne fostered.

11. See David Herlihy, "The Population of Verona in the First Century of Venetian Rule," in *Renaissance Venice*, ed. J. R. Hale (London: Faber & Faber, 1974), 95. Exceptionally large and prosperous cities in the Middle Ages were Paris (at least 210,000 inhabitants in 1328), Venice and Milan (each perhaps as large as 180,000), and Florence (about 120,000 inhabitants in 1338). Cities of Verona's size were more numerous (Herlihy, "Demography," 4:141).

12. *Studi Gregoriani* 13 (1989), the proceedings of a 1985 conference on "La Riforma Gregoriana e l'Europe," contains essays on the reception of the reform move-

resentative than one allied with the papacy.[13] Sees in a huge part of Western Europe, from the North Sea to the Adriatic, recognized the emperor as their overlord and a majority (three-quarters) of these sees, like Verona, remained loyal to their Salian lords during the investiture controversy.[14] Second, my own research has shown that political allegiances are not reliable indicators of reform or ecclesiastical vitality. There was reform and innovation in the Veronese church in the eleventh and twelfth centuries despite its firm loyalty to the emperor.[15] More critical to ecclesiastical change in this period were demographic growth and economic development; considering Verona's social and economic profile, this suggests that many aspects of its ecclesiastical development may be more widely shared.

Finally, it is not my aim in suggesting this new periodization and characterization to dismiss the importance of the changes that constituted the eleventh-century reform movement. The actions and ideas of Pope Gregory VII and other reformers were highly significant, but so, too, were those of many Christians, clerical and lay, in local communities throughout Western Europe. Also important were forces such as demographic growth and economic development, which influenced the thoughts and actions of individuals. My aim, unabashedly *annaliste,* is to present a capacious view of change and its causes, not to eliminate one group of historical actors in order to promote another.

The most fundamental change in the church from the mid–tenth century to the mid–twelfth century was its rapid expansion. The Veronese diocese in the year 1000 included 130 churches, chapels, and monasteries;

---

ment in Spain, France, northern Italy, Scandinavia, and the Anglo-Norman lands. See Antonio García y García, "Reforma gregoriana e idea de la 'Militia sancti Petri' en los reinos ibéricos"; Jean Gaudemet, "Grégoire VII et la France"; Giuseppe Fornasari, "La riforma gregoriana nel 'Regnum Italiae'"; and H. E. J. Cowdrey, "The Gregorian Reform in the Anglo-Norman Lands and in Scandinavia." All of these essays, save Cowdrey's, rely on papal evidence (largely Gregory's letters) rather than local sources in gauging reform and, nevertheless, show great variation across Europe.

13. Traditional church history has tended to treat those areas of Europe "allied" with the papacy during the investiture conflict as "normal" and those areas loyal to the emperor as disobedient or schismatic. This was, of course, the view of Gregory VII himself. Historians, needless to say, should be wary of its implications.

14. Herbert Zielinski, *Der Reichsepiskopat in spätottonischer und salischer Zeit. Teil I* (Stuttgart: Franz Steiner Verlag, 1984), 183, 296–99.

15. See Miller, *Formation,* 50–62, on the reform of the secular clergy in Verona.

only 150 years later, it included nearly twice that number (254).[16] This growth was largely in local, parochial churches (*plebes cum capellis*) where secular clerics offered the sacraments to the faithful.[17] A growing population and the expansion of settlement caused this multiplication of ecclesiastical institutions.[18] The effects of this increase were serious and far-reaching. The increase in the number of ecclesiastical institutions resulted in a growing demand for clergy, which in turn overtaxed the early medieval institutions for training priests. The reform councils' exhortations against ordaining underaged clerics connect this demand for priests to the dissatisfaction with the state of the clergy fueling the eleventh-century reform movement.[19] The multiplication of new churches also revealed the inadequacies of diocesan organization and prompted a long and sometimes bitter struggle on the part of bishops to get control of the ecclesiastical institutions within their dioceses. This struggle was most intense in Verona in the 1130s and 1140s, when Bishop Tebaldus used a combination of charismatic leadership, legal maneuvering at the papal court, and feudal violence to establish episcopal authority.[20]

---

16. These statistics derive from a special data base I have compiled on Veronese ecclesiastical institutions across the entire Middle Ages (see Miller, *Formation*, 185–87).

17. At the millennium, roughly half (56.4 percent) of the diocese's churches were in the countryside; by 1150, a much larger proportion (67 percent) were located outside the urban center. Of the 88 rural churches (institutions for the religious life here excluded) appearing from 1000 to 1150, 33 were baptismal churches (*plebes*) and 24 were the only churches in their communities. Of the 15 new churches in the city and suburbs, 9 became parishes.

18. Miller, *Formation*, 32–40.

19. Miller, *Formation*, 50–51. The Council of Rouen, in 1074, for example, restated the minimum canonical age for ordination to the priesthood as 30 years but allowed that this requirement might be waived in cases of urgent need. Even then, however, bishops were exhorted not to ordain anyone under the age of 25 (*Sacrorum conciliorum nova et amplissima collectio*, ed. J. D. Mansi, 53 vols. [Florence and Venice: Antonius Zata, 1759–98], vol. 20, col. 400). Similar injunctions were issued by the Roman Council of 1059 and the Council of Melfi in 1090 (*Sacrorum*, vol. 19, col. 915; vol. 20, col. 723). Ratherius of Verona also complained of clerics "hastening illegally to Holy Orders" before they were prepared intellectually or spiritually for priestly duties (Ratherius of Verona, "Urkunden und Akten zur Geschichte Rathers in Verona," ed. Fritz Weigle, *Quellen und Forschungen aus italienischen Archiven und Bibliotheken* 29 [1938–39]: 26–27).

20. Miller, *Formation*, 122–38, 163–74. Other diocesans used similar tactics. See Lucio Casto, "Il fondamento patrimoniale della potenza vescovile di Asti," *Bollettino storico-bibliografico subalpino* 73 (1975): 34–35; and Augusto Vasina, "Le pievi dell'area Ravennate prima e dopo il Mille," in *Le istituzioni ecclesiastiche della*

Qualitative changes accompanied the quantitative increase in ecclesiastical institutions within the diocese: new types of institutions emerged. This new variety in ecclesiastical institutions responded to the needs, both temporal and spiritual, of different groups within Christian society.

The new institutions of *scole* and congregations emerged for the secular clergy. From the late tenth century, centers for the formation and training of the clergy, called *scole* or *scholae,* emerged at urban and rural churches. They developed first at churches with close ties to the bishop. Three *scole* emerged in the tenth century and nine more over the course of the eleventh.[21] In the twelfth century, congregations for both urban and rural clerics were formed.[22] These controlled clerical appointments and gained a role in the election of the bishop.[23] They also provided assistance to ailing members, funeral expenses, and prayers for the departed.[24] These new institutions responded to the growing needs of

«*societas christiana*» *dei secoli XI–XII: Diocesi, pievi, e parrocchie,* Atti della sesta Settimana internazionale di studio, Milano, 1–7 settembre 1974, Miscellanea del Centro di studi medioevali, no. 8 (Milan: Vita e Pensiero, 1977), 607–27.

21. *Archivio Segreto Vaticano* (hereafter *ASV*), Fondo Veneto, nos. 6533, 6534; *Archivio di Stato di Verona* (hereafter *ASVR),* Santo Stefano, no. 2; *Codice diplomatico veronese,* ed. Vittorio Fainelli, 2 vols. (Venice: Deputazione di storia patria per le Venezie, 1940–63) (hereafter *CDV*), vol. 2, nos. 220, 247. On the ties of San Pietro in Castello, Santo Stefano, and San Lorenzo in Sezano to the bishops of Verona, see *Verona e il suo territorio,* 7 vols. (Verona: Istituto per gli studi storici veronesi, 1960–69) 2:9, 20, 70. *Scole* founded in the eleventh century are Santa Maria Consolatrice (1021), Santa Maria Novella (1035), San Giusto (1035), San Floriano in Valpantena (1054), Sante Maria, Agata, e Cecilia (1055), Santa Maria della Fratta (1061), Santa Maria in Cerea (1061), Sant'Anastasia (1082), and San Siro (1083). See *Archivio Capitolare di Verona* (hereafter *ACV*), I–5–1v (calp. mp n4); *ASVR,* Sant' Anastasia, no. 4; Orfanotrofio Femminile, no. 20; Santa Maria in Organo, no. 28; Ospitale Civico, no. 47; *ACV,* III–6–3r (AC 60 m4 n12); *ASVR,* Santa Maria in Organo, no. 52; and *Biblioteca Civica* (hereafter *BC*), Mss. Lodovico Perini, busta 22, Padri Dominicani.

22. The urban congregation first appears in a document of 1102 (*ASVR,* Clero Intrinseco, reg. 13 [Ist. Ant. Reg. I], fol. 1070). The earliest evidence of the existence of a congregation for rural clergy comes in a papal bull of 1185 (G. B. Biancolini, *Notizie storiche delle chiese di Verona,* 8 vols. [Verona: A. Scolari, 1749–71] 4:545–47). On the contemporaneous emergence of other clerical congregations, see Antonio Rigon, *Clero e città: ēFratalea cappellanorumś, parroci, cura d'anime in Padova dal XII al XV secolo* (Padua: Istituto per la storia ecclesiastica padovana, 1988), esp. 21–22.

23. For an example of the congregation's election and investiture of a priest in an urban church, see *ASVR,* Clero Intrinseco, reg. 12 (Ist. Ant. Reg. II), fol. 103. The 1185 bull cited above (note 22) reveals that the cathedral canons, the urban congregation, and the rural congregation each had a vote in electing the bishop.

24. Giulio Sancassani, "Aspetti giuridici nella vita ecclesiastica della città," in *Chiese e monasteri a Verona,* ed. Giorgio Borelli (Verona: Banca Popolare di Verona, 1980), 202–4.

training clerics and improving the moral and intellectual preparation of the clergy for service in their churches. The congregations also gave the clergy a greater role in the administration of the diocese.

In addition, new institutions emerged in this period for the laity. A Veronese document of 1131 reveals the city's first lay confraternity, the *convivium* of the urban church of Santa Felicità. These laypersons worked, in their own words, "for the honor and aid of the church of Santa Felicità." The organization had a *gastaldus* and seems to have been composed of artisans from the neighborhood around the church.[25] Lay persons also founded several leper hospitals outside Verona's walls in the twelfth century. The earliest, Santa Croce, emerged in the fourth decade of the century[26] and had a strong confraternal character.[27] Both the officials who ran the hospital and the lepers themselves were called "brothers" and "sisters."[28] Although a priest witnessed several documents, laypersons clearly administered the institution: they bought and sold lands on its behalf, served as directors, treasurers, warehouse keepers, and key bearers.[29] *Convivia* and hospitals allowed laypersons to participate more actively in their local churches and to follow Christ through a more direct, personal involvement in charitable activity.

Finally, new kinds of institutions arose for religious life in the eleventh and twelfth centuries. "Reformed" Benedictine congregations—such as the Vallombrosians and Camaldoli—adopted new institutional ties and systems of authority. Some, like the many varieties of regular canons, abandoned the Benedictine rule altogether. In Verona, a community of

---

25. *ASV*, Fondo Veneto, no. 6896. Lester K. Little's *Liberty, Charity, Fraternity: Lay Religious Confraternities at Bergamo in the Age of the Commune*, Smith College Studies in History, no. 51 (Bergamo and Northampton, Mass.: Pierluigi Lubrina Editore and Smith College, 1988), 36–39; and André Vauchez's, *Les laïcs au moyen âge: Pratiques et expériences religieuses* (Paris: CERF, 1987), 116, also place the emergence of lay confraternities in this period.

26. Bishop Tebaldus consecrated the church and leper hospital of Santa Croce on 6 April 1141 (*ASVR*, S. Silvestro, no. 5 app.) For other contemporary examples, see Pierre De Spiegeler, *Les hôpitaux et l'assistance à Liège (X^e–XVe siècles)* (Paris: "Les Belles Lettres," 1987), 57–60, 105–10.

27. Giles Gerard Meersseman considered the development of hospitals as part of a multifaceted confraternal movement (*Ordo fraternitatis*, 3 vols. [Rome: Herder, 1977], 1:136–49).

28. *ASVR*, Istituto Esposti, nos. 5, 6, 9, 1 app.

29. Not until the end of the twelfth century does a cleric act in any official capacity on behalf of the institution. For examples of the lay officials directing Santa Croce, see *ASVR*, Ospitale Civico, no. 75; and Istituto Esposti, nos. 7, 9, 12, 17, 1 app.

regular canons following the rule of St. Augustine and the institutes of Santa Maria in Porto was formed at San Giorgio in Braida in the early twelfth century.[30] In contrast to the religious life defined by the Benedictine rule, these canons devoted themselves more to charitable work in the world than to study and liturgy.[31]

The character of these new institutions reveals a fundamental shift in spirituality. In the early Middle Ages, Benedictine monasticism—its life of prayer, humility, obedience, and withdrawal from the world—was considered the fullest expression of Christian virtue. The limited resources of early medieval communities allowed only a few to devote themselves to this ideal, and very few were thought capable of achieving it. In the eleventh and twelfth centuries, however, the definition of the ideal Christian life changed, opening its pursuit to most believers.

This changed definition and its inclusivity are most evident in the emergence of the regular canons and leper hospitals. Although the new canons retained a strong life of communal prayer based on the offices, they emphasized acts of charity in the world. In his prologue to the institutes of Santa Maria in Porto—those followed by the Veronese regular canons—St. Peter of Onesti described exactly what the apostolic life of the canons should be. He called his followers to abandon the business of the world, the "negotia saeculi." But Peter's idea of abandoning the world is markedly different from the Benedictine notion. He continued,

> Therefore let them love fasting, let them comfort the poor, let them gather in guests, let them clothe the naked, let them visit the sick, let them bury the dead, let them serve the oppressed, let them console the sorrowful, let them weep with the weeping, rejoice with the joyful, let them not forsake charity, if possible let them have peace with all, let them fear the day of judgment, let them desire eternal life above all, let them put their hope in God, let them put nothing before the love of Christ, let them obey the orders of their prelates in all things, let them comply with their own bishop in all things according to the

---

30. *ASV*, Fondo Veneto, no. 6886; *Regesta pontificum romanorum. Italia pontificia*, ed. Paul F. Kehr, 10 vols. (Berlin: Weidmannos, 1906–), 7.1:264.

31. See the edition of the institutes of Porto in L. Holstenius, *Codex regularum monasticarum et canonicarum*, 6 vols. (Augustae Vindelicorum: I. A. and F. A. Veith, 1759), 2:143.

canonical institutes, and, finally, let them devote work to spiritual teachings, readings, psalms, hymns, canticles and let them persevere unfailingly in the exercise of all good works.[32]

The very order of these exhortations is revealing. The liturgical life—spiritual doctrines, psalms, hymns—is last, even after obedience to the bishop and other prelates. Highest on Peter's list of apostolic callings are fasting, caring for the poor, clothing the naked, and visiting the sick. These acts of charity are ranked even before the general exhortations to seek eternal life and put Christ before all. Indeed, the canons' idea of abandoning the world was rooted in concerns about the world and its problems.

This pursuit of Christ in the world is also obvious in the leper hospital of Santa Croce. For the lay brothers and sisters who founded and administered the hospital, acts of mercy to the least fortunate among them constituted a Christ-like life. The fact that the lepers themselves were called brothers and sisters suggests something more radical. Not only was caring for the poor and sick a way of following Christ, so too was *being* poor and sick. By the end of the twelfth century, the terms used to describe the relationship between the caretakers and the infirm at Santa Croce increasingly emphasized the latter definition. A document of 2 November 1199 called the lay caretakers *conversi*.[33] This implies that the lepers were the true *religiosi* of Santa Croce. Just as the lay *conversi* of Benedictine monasteries hoped to share in the spiritual benefits of the monks by supporting their religious lives, so these laypersons hoped to share the spiritual benefits of the poor lepers by supporting them.

Each of these three major changes—the rapid increase in the number of ecclesiastical institutions, the new variety of institutional forms, and changes in spirituality—is related to "reform." The multiplication of churches was one of the key factors behind this eleventh-century move-

---

32. "Ament praeterea jejunium, pauperes recreent, hospites colligant, nudos vestiant, infirmos visitent, mortuos sepeliant, tribulantibus subserviant, dolentes consolentur, cum flentibus fleant, cum gaudentibus gaudeant, charitatem non derelinquant, pacem, si fieri potest, cum omnibus habeant; diem judicii timeant, vitam aeternam per omnia concupiscant, spem suam Deo committant, amori Christi nihil praeponant, Praelatorum suorum imperiis per cuncta obediant, proprio Episcopo in omnibus secundum Canonum institutionem obtemperent, postremo spiritualibus doctrinis operam tribuant, lectionibus, Psalmis, Hymnis, canticis et ceterorum bonorum operum exercitiis jugiter insistant" (Holstenius, *Codex*, 2:143).

33. *ASVR*, Istituto Esposti, no. 32.

ment. Some of the new institutional types—such as the Vallombrosian congregation and regular canonries—were self-consciously founded to effect reform. The new spirituality was also strongly associated with institutions working for reform and, in its inclusiveness, reflected the broad popular appeal of the reform movement.

But to subsume all these changes under the rubric "Gregorian Reform" would be grossly inaccurate. New churches were built because old communities grew and new communities were established. New institutional forms responded to new social and economic conditions and to new understandings of the gospel—not chiefly to institutional or moral decay. It would also be inaccurate to characterize the new spirituality as primarily a reaction against, or an indictment of, earlier understandings of Christian imperatives.

Given the disjuncture between these broad patterns of ecclesiastical change in the eleventh and twelfth centuries and the traditional characterization, why have historians retained the "Age of Gregorian Reform"? What purposes does this characterization serve? First, the preference to see this period in terms of reform is part of a long tradition, alluded to earlier, of viewing the development of Christianity as a continuous interplay of sin and virtue, of cycles of decadence and reform. For many believers this is clearly a very comforting and inspiring view of the Christian past, and it accords well with classical notions of the didactic and moral purposes of history. Second, the invocation of "Gregorian" as well as "reform" is also meaningful: this characterization exalts the place of the papacy in ecclesiastical history, attributing moral virtue and redemptive action to those at the top of the institutional hierarchy. Finally, the usual recitation of the reform movement, which stresses the conflict between Pope Gregory VII and Emperor Henry IV over lay investiture, also produces a narrative emphasizing the unity of the church in the face of corrupt lay society. This polarized narrative structure, whether employed to describe conditions in the eleventh century or the present, ignores substantial differences and divisions within the church and does not accurately portray the factions engaged in struggle.[34] It is, I suggest, a simplifying fiction, which defines the church as those who support the papacy and assigns a particular role to the laity (exemplified at Canossa).

My own characterization—which highlights the expansion of pastoral care, the diversification of ecclesiastical institutions, and the emergence

---

34. See I. S. Robinson, "'Periculosus homo': Pope Gregory VII and Episcopal Authority," *Viator* 9 (1978): 103–31, for a good corrective to this tendency.

of a more inclusive spirituality—does not, obviously, promote these purposes. It emphasizes intensity and novelty of institutional change rather than moral improvement. This view considers the contributions of the unempowered as well as the empowered, and of social, economic, and political conditions as well as human actions, while acknowledging divisions within the church and embracing complexity. It yields a more accurate and a more positive assessment of the medieval church in the eleventh and twelfth centuries.

This characterization is more positive in that it reveals a complex institution successfully meeting the challenge of new demographic, economic, social, political, and religious conditions with tremendous creativity. This framework holds as much promise for great narrative history as the old popes vs. emperors schema, but it more accurately reflects the confluence of changes in the church. Reform is part of this transformation but only one part.

The implications of this new periodization and characterization are, of course, worth pondering. If one accepts that the medieval church was radically transformed in the period 950 to 1150, how should we characterize and conceptualize its development before and after? I suggest that the early medieval church was not just an underdeveloped version of the church that emerged by 1150 but an institution very different in its institutions, organization, and values. Recent work in Carolingian studies already points in this direction,[35] but the topic deserves serious consideration and research. Second, it seems to me that the thirteenth century, usually seen as the pinnacle of medieval ecclesiastical evolution, is better characterized as a highly creative, but ultimately troubled, development of the patterns established by the mid–twelfth century. Many scholars have already questioned the novelty of developments usually associated with the thirteenth-century church,[36] and others are now emphasizing the oppressive character of the age of Innocent III.[37] In sum, reconsidering the periodization of medieval ecclesiastical history opens marvelous new areas of inquiry and may better integrate the history of the church into the social, economic, and political development of Western Europe.

---

35. Richard E. Sullivan, "The Carolingian Age: Reflections on Its Place in the History of the Middle Ages," *Speculum* 64 (1989): 286–97.

36. Lester K. Little, *Liberty, Charity, Fraternity* (Northampton, Mass. and Bergamo: Pierluigi Lubrina, 1988), 39, 57; *La povertà del secolo XII e Francesco d'Assisi* (Assisi: Società internazionale di studi francescani, 1975).

37. R. I. Moore, *The Formation of a Persecuting Society* (Oxford: Basil Blackwell, 1987), 8–11.

When Heaven Came down to Earth:
The Family of St. Martial of Limoges
and the "Terrors of the Year 1000"

Daniel F. Callahan

In his rich and wide-ranging 1990 American Historical Association presidential address David Herlihy explored some of the meanings of "family" in the Middle Ages and the reality that underlies the concept.[1] One aspect not considered was the idea of the *familiae* of the saints and their importance in understanding the religious life of the early Middle Ages.[2] Standard lexicons of medieval usages (Du Cange, Niermeyer, and the *Thesaurus Linguae Latinae*), offer a number of definitions of *family* as applied to the saints, for example, the monks or religious of a house dedicated to that individual.[3] Another definition, for the early Middle Ages, is the totality of devotees who recognize the figure as a heavenly patron or advocate.[4] It is this last meaning that will be used to consider one such "family," that of St. Martial of Limoges in the tenth and eleventh centuries.

An earlier version of this essay was delivered at the 1992 meeting of the American Historical Association in a session dedicated to the memory of David Herlihy. I wish to express my gratitude to Professors Barbara Kreutz and Francis Hartigan for their helpful comments.

1. D. Herlihy, "Family," *American Historical Review* 96, no. 1 (1991): 1–16.
2. For a useful bibliography on early medieval hagiography, see S. Wilson, ed., *Saints and Their Cults* (Cambridge, 1983), 309–417.
3. "*Familia*" in *Glossarium Mediae et Infimae Latinitatis*, ed. C. DuCange, vol. 3 (1883–87), 409–10; J. F. Niermeyer, *Mediae Latinitatis Lexicon Minus*, vol. 1 (Leiden, 1960ff.) fasc. 5, pp. 407–8; *Thesaurus Linguae Latinae*, vol. 6 (Leipzig, 1912–26), cols. 234–46.
4. On the power of the saints for their devotees in this period, see H. Fichtenau, *Living in the Tenth Century*, trans. P. Geary (Chicago, 1991), esp. 309, 325; on the place of the monastic *familia*, see 121–23; for a valuable examination of the importance of family in this century, see part two (entitled "Familia"), 81–132.

The cult of this saint spread widely in Aquitaine in the early eleventh century as the monks of Limoges sought to increase the size of his family by presenting him as a direct apostle of Christ, who sent him from Jerusalem to Gaul.[5] Having successfully carried out his task of evangelization and then died, he continued in heaven to intercede for his people and await the Last Judgment, when, seated on his apostolic throne, he must present all the people of Gaul to Christ. The image of the apostolic throne and Martial's role at the Last Judgment require attention because of what they tell us about the millennial fears of this period and the role of such anxiety in expanding the size and influence of the holy families.

For the past century the so-called terrors of the year 1000 have been dismissed by most historians as nonexistent or, at most, the product of feverish imaginations such as that evident in the writings of Ralph Glaber.[6] Recently, however, a reevaluation has begun. Richard Landes, in his 1984 Princeton doctoral dissertation on the early career of the eleventh-century historian Ademar of Chabannes, presented some highly suggestive material.[7] More recently Johannes Fried has given us a valuable gathering of examples of millenial fears in many parts of Western Europe, and Henry Mayr-Harting has indicated in his two-volume feast on Ottonian book illumination that the reality of the heightened apocalyptic fears of the time cannot be dismissed.[8] In addition, in a number of articles and papers during the past decade, I have suggested that these

---

5. The literature on this growth is voluminous. See the following three pieces for more bibliographical data: J. Grier, "*Ecce sanctum quem deus elegit Marcialem apostolum:* Adémar de Chabannes and the Tropes for the Feast of Saint Martial," in *Beyond the Moon: Festschrift Luther Dittmer*, ed. B. Gillingham and P. Merkey, Wissenschaftliche Abhandlungen, no. 53 (Ottowa, 1990), 28–74; R. Landes, "Paix de Dieu, culte des reliques et communautés hérétiques en Aquitaine en l'an mil," *Annales* 46, no. 1 (1991): 573–93; and D. Callahan, "The Problem of the 'Filioque' and the Letter from the Pilgrim Monks of the Mount of Olives to Pope Leo III and Charlemagne: Is the Letter Another Forgery by Adémar of Chabannes?" *Revue Bénédictine* 102 (1992): 75–134.

6. The historiography on the "terrors" is immense. See the bibliographical notes supplied by H. Schwartz in *Century's End: A Cultural History of the Fin de Siècle from the 990s to the 1990s* (New York, 1990), esp. the notes for pp. 1–37. See also D. Milo, "L'an mil: Un problème d'historiographie moderne," *History and Theory* 27 (1988): 261–81.

7. R. Landes, "The Making of a Medieval Historian: Ademar of Chabannes and Aquitaine at the Turn of the Millennium," Ph.D diss., Princeton University, 1984. A substantially revised version is forthcoming from Harvard University Press.

8. J. Fried, "Endzeiterwartung um die Jahrtausendwende," *Deutsches Archiv für Erforschung des Mittelalters* 45 (1989): 385–473; H. Mayr-Harting, *Ottonian Book Illumination. Part Two: Books* (London, 1991), 45–48.

intense apocalyptic fears of the years 950 to 1050, this cardinal, or pivotal, century for western man, play a central role in the formulation of
the Peace of God, the appearance of popular heresy in the West, the rise
of anti-Judaism, the growing preoccupation with Jerusalem, the ascen-
dence to its peak of the popularity of the cult of St. Michael the
Archangel, the reversal in polarity of western spirituality, and the very
rise of the West itself.[9] At the heart of the reevaluation of the reality of
the "terrors" are the writings of Ademar of Chabannes on St. Martial
and the family of this saint of Limoges.

The cult of Martial centered on a third-century bishop who according
to Gregory of Tours was sent to Limoges from Rome at the same time as
Denis was sent to Paris, Sernin to Toulouse, and Trophime to Arles.[10]
Gradually devotion to Martial grew at the place of his burial, and by the
ninth century a flourishing community of religious was found there. A
Carolingian *vita* pushed Martial back to the first century and made him
a disciple of St. Peter.[11] In the latter part of the tenth or very early
eleventh century a new and much longer *vita* appeared, supposedly written by his disciple Aurelian, which made Martial a close disciple of Christ
himself, who sent him as a companion of St. Peter to the West and gave
him charge over all Aquitaine.[12] One of the features of this *vita* is the
depiction of people coming from all parts of Aquitaine, and beyond, to
Limoges four times a year to worship with their patriarch.[13] This practice
they continued even after his death, we are told, but thenceforth they

9. D. Callahan, "The Peace of God and the Cult of the Saints in Aquitaine in the
Tenth and Eleventh Centuries," in *The Peace of God: Social Violence and Religious
Response in France around the Year 1000*, ed. T. Head and R. Landes (Ithaca, N.Y.,
1992), 165–83; D. Callahan, "Adémar of Chabannes, Apocalypticism and the Peace
Council of Limoges of 1031," *Revue Bénédictine* 101 (1991): 32–49; D. Callahan,
"The Manichaeans and the Antichrist in the Writings of Ademar of Chabannes: 'The
Terrors of the Year 1000' and the Origins of Popular Heresy in the Medieval West,"
forthcoming in *Studies in Medieval and Renaissance History*; D. Callahan, "Ademar
of Chabannes, Millennial Fears and the Development of Western Anti-Judaism,"
Journal of Ecclesiastical History 46, no. 1 (1995): 19–35; D. Callahan, "The Cult of
St. Michael the Archangel and 'The Terrors of the Year 1000,'" paper delivered at the
1991 meeting of the Medieval Academy of America; D. Callahan, "Jerusalem in the
Monastic Imaginations of the Early Eleventh Century," forthcoming in *Haskins Society Journal*; D. Callahan, "Jerusalem and the Cross in the Writings of Ademar of Chabannes," forthcoming.

10. Gregory of Tours, *History of the Franks*, 1:30.

11. C. Bellet, *L'ancienne vie de saint Martial et la prose rythmée* (Paris, 1897),
43–50.

12. L. Surius, *De Probatis Sanctorum Vitis*, vol. 6 (Cologne, 1618), 365–74.

13. See especially ibid., chap. 16, p. 370, but also chap. 23, p. 373.

sought his intervention in heaven so that he might work miracles for his family of adherents.[14]

During the 1020s, when a great new basilica was being constructed at the monastery of Saint-Martial to bear witness to the growing prestige of the saint and provide for the increasing size of his *familia,* the monks sought to raise more revenue and spread the cult more widely. By the end of that decade a new liturgy celebrated Martial as an apostle and the Aurelian *vita* had been reworked to make him the heavenly spokesman for all of Gaul.[15] The individual responsible for many of these changes and the impresario of the expansion was Ademar of Chabannes.

Liturgist, artist, musician, historian, and general master of the monastic scriptorium, Ademar had come to Limoges from his own monastery of Saint-Cybard of Angoulême.[16] In a long letter he describes his pride in the celebration of the new apostolic liturgy in 1029 on the first anniversary of the dedication of the new basilica. At this moment of supreme triumph for all the alterations undertaken by the monks of Saint-Martial, and especially for those initiated by Ademar himself, a churchman from northern Italy, Benedict of Chiusa, appeared in the basilica to challenge the novelties and threaten to report these new blasphemies to the Pope.[17] The monks were clearly chastened. Ademar, returning to Angoulême in disgrace, would spend the next three years writing in defense of the changes, concocting false documents and altering manuscripts to support his case.[18]

Included in this material are his sermons found in (BN), Ms. Lat.

---

14. See especially ibid., chap. 27, p. 374.

15. On the changes, see D. Callahan, "The Sermons of Adémar of Chabannes and the Cult of St. Martial of Limoges," *Revue Bénédictine* 86 (1976): 255–63.

16. On the life of Ademar, in addition to the dissertation by Landes, see the highly readable piece by R. L. Wolff, "How the News Was Brought from Byzantium to Angoulême, or, the Pursuit of a Hare in an Ox Cart," in *Byzantine and Modern Greek Studies* 4 (1978): 139–89.

17. Ademar of Chabannes, "Epistola de Apostolatu Sancti Martialis," Patrologia latina, (hereafter PL) 141: 89–112.

18. The manuscripts of this monk, over 1,000 folios, a large percentage of which are his own compositions (many from the last years of his life), have attracted the attention of many scholars in the past century. On the forgeries, see, most recently, H. Schneider, "Ademar von Chabannes und Pseudoisidor—der 'Mythomane' und der Erzfälscher," in *Fälschungen im Mittelalter: Internationaler Kongress der Monumenta Germaniae Historica, Munchen, 16–19. September 1986, II, Gefälschte Rechtstexte: Der bestrafte Fälscher,* Monumenta Germaniae Historica, Schriften 33 (Hanover, 1988), 129–50; and D. Callahan, "Portrait of the Artist as a Medieval Forger: Ademar of Chabannes and His Insertions into Bede's *Expositio Actuum Apostolorum, Analecta Bollandiana* 111 (1993): 385–400.

2469, which from this point I shall call the Paris manuscript, and (DN), Ms. Lat. 1664, henceforth referred to as the Berlin manuscript. The sermons in these two manuscripts, most still unpublished, will here supply most of the data for Ademar's depiction of the apostolic throne of Martial in heaven as evidence of intense apocalyptic fears immediately prior to 1033, the millennial anniversary of Christ's resurrection.[19]

The idea that the apostles have thrones in heaven and will participate in the Last Judgment is based on Matthew 19:28, "And Jesus said to them, 'I solemnly tell you that in the new creation, when the Man sits on his glorious throne, you who have followed me will also sit on twelve thrones judging the twelve tribes of Israel," and Luke 22:29–30, "And I confer on you a kingship such as my Father has conferred on me, that you may eat and drink at my table in my kingdom and sit upon thrones as the judges of the twelve tribes of Israel."[20] Another prominent image of thrones in heaven is found in the Book of Revelation in which 24 elders, or ancients, sit in the divine presence. This image appears 12 times in that work's description of heaven.[21]

In a recent book, Margaret Barker, commenting on throne imagery in the early church, sees this idea as "the most fertile source of inspiration for the expression of early Christian thought."[22] When one recalls the importance of apocalyptic expectations in the first two centuries of the Christian era, it is difficult to disagree. The prominence of this image, however, also enables us to gauge the degree of apocalyptic fears in later periods.[23]

Again and again in the sermons the monk of Angoulême proclaims

19. Michael Frassetto and I are editing these sermons for publication in two volumes in the *opera* of Ademar for the Corpus Christianorum.

20. The scriptural passages are drawn from the *Anchor Bible*, ed. W. F. Albright and D. N. Freedman (New York, 1964ff.).

21. Book of Revelation, 4:4, 10; 5:5, 6, 8, 11, 14; 7:11, 13; 11:16; 14:3; 19:4. On the elders, see A. Feuillet, "The Twenty-Four Elders of the Apocalypse," in his *Johannine Studies* (Staten Island, N.Y., 1965), 183–214, esp. 183.

22. M. Barker, *The Gate of Heaven: The History and Symbolism of the Temple in Jerusalem* (London, 1991), 133. See especially chapter 4, "The Throne."

23. This is particularly true for visual representations. The many brilliantly illustrated manuscripts of Beatus of Liebana's commentary on the Book of Revelation and comparable works, such as the Bamberg Apocalypse done around the year 1000, merit much further attention from this perspective. For a valuable survey of these manuscripts, with an extensive bibliography for each, see R. K. Emmerson and S. Lewis, "Census and Bibliography of Medieval Manuscripts Containing Apocalypse Illustrations, ca. 800–1500 (Part I)," *Traditio* 40 (1984): 337–79.

that Martial has an apostolic throne in heaven and will preside over Gaul, especially Aquitaine, at the Last Judgment.[24] In one sermon in the Paris manuscript Ademar states that on the last day the saints of Aquitaine will be resurrected and that at that time Martial will sit in judgment with Christ.[25] In another piece he reminds the people of Aquitaine that the apostle had freed their ancestors from service to the devil. Thereafter they served their apostolic savior who will present his people to God on the day of judgment.[26] A third sermon has him presenting Aquitaine because it is the fruit of his labor.[27]

One of the principal problems Ademar must address is that Christ promised only the 12 apostles the apostolic thrones. A repeated theme, not surprisingly, in many of the pieces is that there is need for more than 12.[28] Since the 12 will judge the 12 tribes, additional apostolic judges are needed for the remainder. In a sermon in the Paris manuscript he attacks those who say only 12 will judge by citing St. Paul as another apostle and

---

24. The passages in the sermons that will be examined echo in part what is found in his letter on the apostolicity of Martial. Here addressing the saint, he states that the apostle will present all of Gaul to Christ on the Judgment Day (PL 141:106C).

25. BN, Ms. Lat. 2469, 19v: "Sic in die ultimo sanctorum multitudo ex Aquitania et Gallia orta, ibique sepulta, ibique resurrectura, illi palmam gratiae, caput gloriae post Christum referet, quem primum suae salutis cognovit praedicatorem quemque posteri praedicatores Aquitaniae et Galliae secuti, et usque in finem secuturi sunt in augmentatione filiorum Dei. Quamcumque enim provintiarum quisque apostolorum primus praedicare coepit, in regeneratione cum sederit Christus in sede maiestatis suae, super eam provintiam erit, quia in ea et pro ea remunerationem gloriae et palmam honoris a rege salvatore nostro Deo percipiet."

26. Ibid., 36v: "Nam et lex Aquitanis maxime perpetua constare semper solita est, ut Marciali singuli pro capite suo dent redemptionem, ut avertatur ab eis ira Dei. Quippe cum per eum ipsa regio tirannidem mortis evasit, et libertatem perpetuae vitae invenit, recte a servitute diaboli libera necesse est, post Deum serviat proprio principi, a quo presentanda est Deo in die iudicii, cuius patrocinio est protegenda sub umbra alarum misericordiae Christi."

27. Ibid., 25v: "Venerabilis profecto haec est domus Dei, inquam, ille Marcialis qui Domini apostolus egregius est tumulariam cernitur habere sepulturam, expectans ibi regenerationem futuram quando sedebit filius hominis in sede maiestatis suae, quando qui eum secuti sunt sedebunt super sedes XII, iudicantes XII tribus Israel. Quando non solum XII tribus Israel, sed etiam omnes gentes orbis terrarum iudicabuntur, quando non soli XII viri, sed etiam quique perfecti sancti de mundo iudicabunt. Quando idem discipulus Domini Marcialis, cum ceteris discipulis Domini gloriosus apparebit, quando in illo eximio apostolorum choro, unus ex illis ille gloriosus apostolus iudiciariam sedem optinebit. Quando ille portans manipulum suum, Aquitaniam provintiam fructum laborum suorum, in conspectu summi iudicis praesentabit, offerans oblata Christo super quae principatum adquirit ab illo."

28. See, e.g., ibid., 5v–6r, 8r, 25v, 61r.

also Martial as judge over Gaul.[29] In the Berlin manuscript he summarizes his position by stating that there are more than 12 apostles. Therefore, most certainly, if there are other apostles beyond the 12, Martial, the first doctor of *Gallia,* is without doubt one of them. The logic of the need for more than 12 apostles to judge allows him to make the case for the apostolicity of the patron saint of Limoges.[30]

The fact that the Book of Revelation contains much on the 24 thrones of the elders in heaven is also, not surprisingly, used by the monk of Angoulême to his advantage. Following the position of Bede in his commentary on the Book of Revelation, a work Ademar copied earlier in the Berlin manuscript, he presents the 24 as judges, an interpretation not supported by the imagery in the scriptural work itself.[31] In one sermon he states that only a schismatic would deny that there are 24 seats before the

---

29. Ibid., 33v: "Erunt ne soli duodecim apostoli iudicantes annon? Qui speculantes id solum evangelicum de XII sedibus in Mattheo et in Luca de XII tribubus Israel, si dixerint soli duodecim erunt, cum Dominus non adiuxent solos XII, sed vos qui secuti estis me sedebitis super sedes XII, ictum excipient huius modi. Ergo quia soli duodecim iudicabunt, solae duodecim tribus non etiam omnes orbis gentes iudicabuntur. Sed nec Paulus iudex erit, qui plus aliis omnibus apostolis laboravit." He goes on to demonstrate the necessity of more than 12 apostolic judges: "Ergo quia plus erunt quam XII iudices, necesse est fateamini plures esse apostolos quam XII qui cum ipsis XII caeteras gentes iudicabunt, quando Dominus veniet ad iuditium cum senibus populi sui. Profiteamini necessario Marcialem esse apostolum, qui super Galliarum gentibus quibus delegatus est ad praedicandum in apostolatus sorte, iudicandi optinebit potestatem."

30. DS, Ms. Lat. 1664, 71v: "Et sicut XII apostoli dicti sunt sessuri super XII sedes in regeneratione, ita XII tribus Israel dictae sunt iudicandae ab eis. Sed sicut non solum illae XII tribus, sed etiam omnes gentes iudicabuntur, ita non solum XII, sed etiam alii apostoli iudicabunt cum sanctis perfectis. Ideo hoc memoramus, ut de Marciale nullus schisma, nullus tumultus, nulla contentio neque dissensio sit inter vos, quem absque dubio apostolum Christi per omnia scimus, credimus et confitemur, fructumque apostolatus eius Aquitaniam totam videmus. . . . Certissime itaque tenete, quia si alii quidam sunt apostoli praeter XII, ergo Marcialis, doctor primus Galliae, absque dubio apostolus est. Si vero nulli alii sunt apostoli nisi tantum XII, ergo Paulus qui plus omnibus laboravit apostolus non est, quod dictu nefas est, ergo Lucas de LXX duobus mentitus est, quod cogitare mortiferum est."

31. For Bede's commentary, see PL 93:143 (Rev. 4:4): "Et in circuitu sedis sedilia viginti quatuor etc. Ecclesiam quam propter societatem fidei in una sede viderat, eamdem per geminum testamentum de patriarchis et apostolis generatam, in viginti quatuor sedilibus cernit, sedentem autem propter judiciariam ejus in Christo dignitatem. Sedebunt enim et judicabunt universa membra, sed in uno et per unum caput. Nam quomodo poterunt sancti in judicio sedere, stantes ad dexteram Judicis? Possunt etiam viginti quatuor seniores in illis intelligi, qui perfectionem operis, quae senario numero commendatur, clara Evangelii praedicatione consummant. Nam quater seni viginti quatuor faciunt." On the prevalence in the early Middle Ages of the interpretation of the 24 as judges, see Feuillet, "The Twenty-Four Elders," 194.

throne of God and that there are only 12 thrones for the apostles.[32] Elsewhere he presents Martial as one of the 24, one who came to Gaul having been taught as a youth directly by Christ but possessing the heart of
an elder. Ademar cites the scriptural passage in Isaiah 3:14 predicting
that the Lord will come for judging with the elders of his people as a
means of emphasizing the judging capacity of the elders but also as a way
of giving further importance to the apostle of Gaul.[33]

The discrepancy between 12 and 24 thrones is resolved in several
places in the sermons in the Berlin manuscript by citing Augustine's *City
of God*.[34] Ademar paraphrases book 20, chapter 5, by saying that in the
12 seats not 12 men but a great number of perfect individuals is signified,
since the number 12 is symbolic, a perfect number.[35] This evocation of
symbolism allows Ademar to escape the problem of 12 versus 24. Moreover, it gave him the apparent support of the weightiest of the church
fathers. There will be more than 12 judges and more than 12 apostles.

Again in the Berlin manuscript, after citing the same passage of Augustine, Ademar indicates that the 24 are composed of two groups of 12

32. BN, Ms. Lat. 2469, 33r: "Sic quoque Marcialis licet sit episcopus quia cate-
dram Lemovicensem tenuerit, quamlibet sit confessor quia in pace migraverit, eo quod
tamen a Domino praedicare missus sit, quodque ab eo potestatem ligandi et solvendi
acceperit, quis umquam scismaticus eum praesumit negare apostolum? Nisi ille qui
XXIIII sedes ante sedem Dei a Johanne descriptas, evacuare contendit, ut solummodo
duodecim thronos ad duodecim apostolos esse praeparatos fateatur, et hac occasione
deceptus solos XII esse, mentiatur apostolos?"

33. Ibid., 72r: "In illo [Martial] quippe vivens sedem habuit episcopalem, in hoc
iam spiritu reddito sedem habet quietem. In illo Dominum ad se venientem sicut
promissum fuerat expectavit, et expectatum praesentem habuit, in hoc diem illum
expectat quando Dominus eum resurgere, et secum consedere ad iudicandum faciet.
Sicut scriptum est, 'Dominus veniet ad iudicium, cum senibus populi sui.' Qui enim
primus Galliae Dominum missus a Christo Jesu et beato Petro praedicavit, quomodo
per Marcialem illa gentilitas non est populus Domini factus? Unde et princeps et pro-
todux sive primus pastor et doctor Aquitaniae, ille senili Dominum corde secutus, a
veteribus dictus est. Est itaque ipse unus de senibus populi Dei, cum quibus veniet rex
regum ad iudicandum. Nam si XXIIII senes super thronos in circuitu sedis Dei esse
sedentes describuntur, patet quia non soli XII apostoli ad iudicandum sedebunt. Unde
Dominus XII praedicens sessuros super XII thronos, nullam aliarum gentium inti-
mavit diversitatem iudicandum praeter XII tribus Israel, tribum Levi, tribum Efraim et
tribum Manasse, quae integrae tribus sunt exceptis duodecim tribubus praetermit-
tens."

34. See, e.g., DS, Ms. Lat. 1664, 94v, 102v–103r, 111r. See also BN, Ms. Lat.
2469, 72r, 33r–v.

35. DS, Ms. Lat. 1664, 94v: "Nec solum populus Israel, sed et caeterae gentes iudicabuntur. Ergo sicut in quinque virginibus innumerabiles virgines significantur, sic in
XII sedibus non XII homines sed magnus numerus perfectorum signatur, quia
numerus duodenarius perfectum numerum signat."

each, who represent all the *perfecti* of the Old and New Testaments.[36] He returns to this idea of the symbolic nature of the thrones later in the same manuscript when he states that the thrones themselves are not wooden or golden or made of any earthly material but are nothing other than the power of God conferred on the apostles.[37] In writing in this fashion he is able to deemphasize the consideration of number and focus on the power conferred by God on the judges, among whom is quite obviously the father of the church of Gaul.

In one of the early sermons in the Paris manuscript Ademar emphasized the connection between the thrones and the proximity of the Last Judgment. Those attacking the apostolicity of Martial are called members of the Antichrist. Their presence bears witness to the nearness of the Last Judgment. Men are not to be afraid of these attackers, but fear only God "since the hour of his judgment is coming."[38]

The proximity is presented much more dramatically toward the end of both the Berlin and the Paris manuscripts. In the former he writes in a commentary on the Lord's Prayer, "Know, brethren, that already have passed very bad tribulations and now they are very serious, as you see, since everywhere there is fear, everywhere wickedness and pride, the sword, pestilence, terrors from heaven and great signs."[39] He goes on to recount the death of a cleric in Angoulême and the subject of the eulogy he preached at the man's funeral, "The Terror of the Coming Judgment" (*De terrore venturi iuditii*).

In the Paris manuscript one way he conveys his sense of the imminence of the Last Judgment is through the vivid descriptions of the fire sickness

---

36. Ibid., 102v: "Et sicut in XII apostolos intelligimus omnes perfecti Novi Testamenti, ita in XXIIII seniores perspicimus omnes perfectos Veteris et Novi Testamenti, qui ante Deum gloriam maiorem habebunt. . . ."

37. Ibid., 111r: "Illud sublime altare Dei, quod est in conspectu divinae maiestatis Patris, non est corporale altare, non de terra, non de aliqua materia, sicut sunt altaria in terris, sicut illae XXIIII sedes seniorum sive XII sedes apostolorum non sunt ligneae vel aureae vel alicuius materiae terrenae, sed illae sedes non sunt aliud nisi potestas a Deo collata apostolis."

38. BN, Ms. Lat. 2469, 8r: Ademar here attacks those individuals who deny Martial is an apostle and has a throne. As the sermon will later make clear, he is attacking Benedict of Chiusa and associating Benedict with the Antichrist. Ademar tells the supporters of Martial, "Ne ergo timeamus eos, Deum solum timeamus et demus illi honorem, quia venit hora iudicii eius." I examine the issue of the awareness of the presence of the Antichrist in this period in the article on heresy mentioned in note 9.

39. DS, Ms. Lat. 1664, 113v: "Scitote, fratres, quia iam transierunt pessimae tribulationes, et modo pessimae sunt sicut videtis, quia ubique est timor, ubique iniquitas et superbia, gladius, fames, pestilentia, terrores de caelo et signa magna."

that struck so often in Aquitaine and elsewhere in the West in the century between 950 and 1050.[40] This illness, which we now know was ergotism, or St. Anthony's fire, was caused by a fungus on improperly dried rye grain. When ingested it produced psychotropic effects, causing the victim to think that his limbs or whole body were on fire.[41] Ademar and many fellow clerics saw the illness as a punishment from God on those who disturbed the Christian order, the Peace of God, and who thus were in league with the Antichrist.[42] The fire in this way became a powerful weapon in the spiritual warfare that also was manifested in the material order. In one of the sermons, in which he emphasized the heavenly origin of the fire, he quotes Psalm 17:9, "Fire from His face burned, coals were enkindled by Him," and Psalm 82:15–16, "As fire which burns wood and as flames burning mountains, You pursue them with Your tempest and shall trouble them in Your wrath." It was Martial who sought mercy for the suffering of his people and caused God to relent on this occasion.[43]

The last sermon in this manuscript is the one that most forcefully and successfully uses the image of fire sent from God. It achieves its impact by presenting a number of examples, primarily drawn from the Old Testament, of the power of the divine fire. The final image, taken from the Book of Revelation, presents the effects of an interdict placed on the churches of Limoges and Angoulême because of violations of the Peace of God. Commenting on the silence in the churches, Ademar says, "We see now to be fulfilled what John said in the Book of Revelation, 'A silence was made in heaven'" (Rev. 8:1).[44] This silence occurs at the opening of the seventh seal. The Book of Revelation continues, "And another angel

---

40. On the prevalence of ergotism in the West during this period, see the comments of Robert Gottfried in two articles in the *Dictionary of the Middle Ages*, ed. J. Strayer, "Famine in Western Europe," (New York, 1985), 5:5–6; and "Plagues, European," (New York, 1987), 9:676.

41. For a recent study of the seriousness and prevalence of this problem, see M. K. Matossian, *Poisons of the Past: Molds, Epidemics, and History* (New Haven, 1989), chaps. 2, 3, esp. 9–14.

42. For more details on the interrelationship of the fire sickness and the Peace of God for Ademar, see D. Callahan, "Adémar de Chabannes et la paix de Dieu," *Annales du Midi* 89 (1977): 21–43.

43. BN, Ms. Lat. 2469, 87r, published in part in L. Delisle, "Notice sur les manuscrits originaux d'Adémar de Chabannes," *Notices et extraits des manuscrits de la Bibliothèque nationale* 25 (1896): 290.

44. BN, Ms. Lat. 2469, 96r–97r, in Delisle, *Notices*, 295. The whole sermon is included on pages 293–96 and should be read in its entirety to get the full apocalyptic impact.

came and stood before the altar. He had a golden censer and he was given abundant incense to add to the prayers of the holy ones on the golden altar before the throne. . . . And the angel took the censer, and filled it from the coals on the altar and hurled them onto the earth" (Rev. 8:3–5). The apocalyptic origins of the fire sickness are never more apparent in these sermons. As one finds throughout them, however, Ademar presents a picture of the loss of a boundary between the spiritual and material orders, heaven coming down to earth during his lifetime.

The actions of the monk of Angoulême during the last two years of his life also bear witness to his sense of the proximity of the Last Judgment. He was one of the many whom Ralph Glaber describes as leaving the West in 1032–3 in order to bear witness to the last days in Jerusalem.[45] His preoccupation with both the earthly and the heavenly Jerusalem, the *visio pacis,* is evident in many of his writings and is especially apparent in the presentation of the connection between Jerusalem and Limoges, a joining achieved through the activity of Martial, who was the disciple of Christ in the Holy City and the bringer of apostolic Christianity to the New Jerusalem of the West.[46] The early 1030s witnessed a reversal, a *reditus* to complete the *exitus,* for Martial, with his disciple Ademar, returns to Jerusalem to participate in the Last Judgment.

The longing of the monk of Angoulême to achieve union with the Christ who is about to come is most strikingly seen in a prayer he wrote late in his life, very likely just before he left the West. It is a brief piece that has not previously been identified as being in the hand of the monk of Angoulême, but it is found appended to several short notices on Martial written by Ademar in a manuscript that today is in the Firestone Library at Princeton University.[47] The tight, hurried handwriting is the same as that found in Ademar's last known work, the Berlin manuscript.

In this prayer he is responding to the injunction in the epilogue to the Book of Revelation, "'I, Jesus, have sent my angel to you with this testimony for the churches. I am the root and the offspring of David, the

45. Rodulfi Glabri, *Historiarum Libri Quinque,* ed. and trans. J. France (Oxford, 1989), esp. iv, 6 (18), 198–99, and iv, 6 (21), 204–5.

46. On the connection between Jerusalem and Limoges, see my comments in "Sermons," 284–85, 291–92. See also my forthcoming article "Jerusalem and the Cross in the Writings of Ademar of Chabannes."

47. On this manuscript, Princeton Garrett 115, see A. Betgé-Brézetz, "Note sur un manuscrit d'Adhémar de Chabannes," *Bulletin de la Société archéologique et historique du Limousin* 106 (1979): 60–64. I wish to thank Richard Landes for calling the material to my attention and express my gratitude to Michael Frassetto for confirming our identification of Ademar's script.

bright morning star.' The Spirit and the Bride say, 'Come.' And let him who hears say, 'Come'" (Rev. 22:16–17). The epilogue later continues, "He who testifies to these things says, 'Yes, I am coming soon.' Amen, come, Lord Jesus" (Rev. 22:20). Ademar's prayer is his response to the request, "And let him who hears say, 'Come.'" On one level it is a trope on the offeratory prayer of the Mass, "Come, O Sanctifier, Almighty and Eternal God, and bless this sacrifice prepared for the glory of your holy name"; but, more importantly, on the apocalyptic level it is a clear response to the request in the Book of Revelation.[48] The prayer states:

> Come, therefore, invisible Lord, and bless this sacrifice prepared for you. Come, ineffable one, who blessed Abraham, Isaac and Jacob. Come; bless the holocaust because it was prepared for you. Come, admirable piety, confirm this work which you did among us. Come; grant your clemency. Come; confirm your priests. Come, eternal King, come and guard your kingdom, our sacrifice, our priesthood. Come, Lord ruler, come; remove the people from error. Come, Lord Saviour of the world, come; save the sailors; heal the sick. Come, most pious Father, come and recall the captives; make pilgrims return to their fatherland. Come, who for us placed your hands on the cross. Come; guard the penitent. Come, who from the cross promised paradise to the thief. Come; preserve your priests and the integrity of virgins which you guarded from the beginning. Come; free your servants and handmaids from the snares of our enemies. Come, Lord, who on the third day arose from the dead. Come and hear the holy prayers of your saints for us. Come, who ascended to heaven and walked over the wings of the winds. Come, who aroused Lazarus after three days. Come and show what hands you heal; cure where there is sickness; recall what is in doubt and confirm and conserve by perseverance what is whole in the faith. Come that whenever we take this holocaust, it may be a renewal for us by you in the kingdom of heaven. Come; we unworthy invite you to bless this sacrifice. Come; we invite you, oh Lord, that by your body and blood our hearts may rejoice. Come, oh Lord, that in your glory by your praise by that prayer our minds may exult with all the angels, archangels and with your saints. Come, oh

---

48. It should be noted that when a High Mass is celebrated, this prayer occurs just before the incensing of the altar, an earthly activity that parallels the incensing of the heavenly altar by the angel at the opening of the seventh seal.

Lord, if we are unworthy, may the paternal Lord lack anger toward us that we may not die before you are merciful, we ask through Christ.[49]

The incessant plea of "come," invoked 29 times, is Ademar's response to the request at the end of the Book of Revelation. It is an especially appropriate one from an individual about to journey to Jerusalem at that particular time to await the answer. The prayer, moreover, was a fitting way for a monastic historian to conclude his writing career by responding to the epilogue of the first work seeking to explain the Christian meaning of history.

Although heaven did not come down to earth in 1033 in the way he expected, Ademar himself did meet his maker with his own death the very next year, apparently in Jerusalem.[50] Here, as he indicates in the earlier letter on the apostolicity of Martial, he would have ascended the Mount of Olives and joined that portion of the followers of St. Martial that had found its eternal reward.[51] May he have met the vision of peace that he believed the family of St. Martial will forever enjoy.

Appendix

The following prayer is found in a Latin manuscript in the Manuscripts Division, Department of Rare Books and Special Collections, Princeton University Libraries, Garrett MS 115, fol. 57v.

"Oremus, vere dignum, veni, igitur, domine invisibilis, et benedic sacrificium preparatum tibi. Veni, ineffabilis, qui benedixisti Abraham, Isaac et Jacob. Veni; benedic olochaustum quia tibi preparatum est. Veni, admirabilis pietas, confirma hoc opus quod operatus es in nobis. Veni; larga clementia tua. Veni; confirma sacerdotes tuos. Veni, aeterne rex, veni et custodi regnum tuum, sacrificium nostrum, sacerdotium nostrum,

---

49. See the appendix, below, for the Latin text.

50. Ademar's death in 1034 is recorded in a note by the early-thirteenth-century librarian of Saint-Martial Bernard Itier in *Chronicon Bernardi Iterii Armarii Sancti Martialis*, ed. H. Duplès-Agier, *Chroniques de Saint-Martial* (Paris, 1874), 47: "Anno gracie mxxxiiii, obiit Ademarus monacus, qui jussit fieri vitam sancti Marcialis cum litteris aureis, et multos alios libros, et in Jherusalem migravit ad Christum."

51. Ademar, "Epistola," PL 141:105: In this portion of the letter in which he considers Martial's presence at the ascension of the Lord on the Mount of Olives, Ademar states, "Ego enim vivens cum Christo, ego, qui nunquam moriar, ego, qui mortem non gustabo in aeternum, utpote credens in Christum, super montem excelsum ascendens. . . ."

Veni, domine dominator, veni; corripe gentes ab errore. Veni, domine salvator mundi, veni; salva navigantes; sana aegrotos. Veni, piissime pater, veni et revoca captivos; reverti fac peregrinos ad patriam suam. Veni, qui pro nobis manus in cruce posuisti. Veni; custodi penitentes. Veni, qui latroni de cruce paradisum promisisti. Veni; conserva sacerdotes tuos et integritatem virginum quam custodisti ab initio. Veni; libera famulos et famulas tuas de faucibus inimicorum nostrorum. Veni, domine, qui tercia die resurrexisti a mortuis. Veni et exaudi orationes pro nobis sanctas sanctorum tuorum. Veni, qui ad caelos ascendisti super pennas ventorum ambulasti. Veni, qui Lazarum quam triduanum resuscitasti. Veni et ostende quas medicas manus; quod infirmum est cura; et quod dubium revoca; et quod integrum fide perseverantia confirma et conserva. Veni ut quandocumque sumpserimus olochaustum, a te nobis reparetur in regno caelorum. Veni; invitamus te ad hoc sacrificium benedicendum indigni. Veni; invitamus te, domine, ut de corpore et sanguine tuo corda nostra laetificentur. Veni, domine, ut de tua gloria de tua laude de ista oratione mentes nostrae exultent cum omnibus angelis et archangelis et sanctis tuis. Veni, domine, et si sumus indigni, nobis, domine paterno, iras caris, ne moriamur prius quam misereraris, rogamus per Christum."

Patrimony and Clientage in the Florentine Countryside: The Formation of the Estate of the Cathedral Chapter, 950–1200

George Dameron

The archives of Florence are among the richest and most varied in Europe.[1] As the fifteenth century continues to draw the attention of scholars the world over, the eleventh and twelfth centuries still remain largely unexplored. In this essay, I propose to contribute to an understanding of those early centuries by exploring a perennial issue in Florentine historiography: the social, political, economic, and ecclesiastical ties linking the city and its surrounding countryside (the *contado*).[2] Some historians have theorized that before the thirteenth century urban influence in the countryside was negligible and insignificant. According to this hypothesis, there were few urban landlords in the countryside and few economic and social connections between city and *contado* before 1200. When compared to the history of other north Tuscan communes like Arezzo and Lucca, according to this line of thinking, the development of Florence seems to have been exceptional.[3] This essay will evaluate this

---

1. I was fortunate to have had the privilege of completing my dissertation in 1983 under the direction of David Herlihy, to whom this essay is dedicated. I wish to thank William Bowsky and Carol Lansing for their comments on earlier drafts of this essay.

2. For recent contributions to the exploration of this issue in Italy as a whole, see the essays in *City and Countryside in Late Medieval and Renaissance Italy: Essays Presented to Philip Jones*, ed. Trevor Dean and Chris Wickham (London and Ronceverte, 1990).

3. Chris Wickham, *The Mountains and the City: The Tuscan Appennines in the Early Middle Ages* (Oxford, 1988), 219, 353–54. This observation is based on the study of Poggialvento by Elio Conti (*La formazione della struttura agraria moderna nel contado fiorentino. Parte 1: La campagna nell'età precomunale*, vol. 1 [Rome 1965], esp. 162–80). Poggialvento is located southwest of Florence in the Pesa River valley.

hypothesis by examining the influence of a single urban lord in the Florentine countryside before 1200, the cathedral chapter. When combined with other recent research on ecclesiastical lords, this case study demonstrates that the economic, social, political, and religious links between the city and its *contado* before the thirteenth century were actually more significant and extensive than many historians have assumed. A key component linking city and countryside appears to have been the close relationship that existed before 1115 between the Countesses Beatrice and Matilda of Tuscany (1052–1115) and the cathedral chapter. The observations made in this essay underscore the need for further research on the political economy of eleventh-century Florence.

The nature of the relationship between the city elite and residents in the countryside has been a subject of dispute among Florentine medieval historians for several generations. For example, scholars have argued about whether the relationship between the city and the countryside before 1300 was conflictual or cooperative. On one hand, some historians have argued that the city-state was the product of the conquest of the *contado* by the city in the twelfth and thirteenth centuries, the final result of military conquest and the acquisition of rural property by the urban bourgeoisie. Before the middle of the thirteenth century, according to this view, the rural feudal nobility dominated the countryside, and the relationship between Florence and its hinterland was basically antagonistic. By 1300, however, rural property had passed into the possession of the urban bourgeoisie. Historians associated with this perspective include Robert Davidsohn, Romolo Caggese, and Gioacchino Volpe.[4]

In his justly celebrated local study of Poggialvento in the Val di Pesa, Elio Conti concluded that there were few urban landlords in that region of the countryside in the eleventh century.[5] If Poggialvento was broadly representative of the *contado* as a whole, there must have been little urban influence and few urban landlords in the hinterland before the thirteenth century.

---

4. See Gaetano Salvemini, *Magnati e popolani in Firenze dal 1280 al 1295* (Florence, 1899; rpt., Milan, 1960), 38, 53, 146, 173; Romolo Caggese, *Classi e comuni rurali nel medioevo italiano*, 2 vols. (Florence, 1907–8); Robert Davidsohn, *Storia di Firenze II. Guelfi e Ghibellini. Parte II: L'Egemonia guelfa e la vittoria del popolo*, vol. 3, trans. Giovanni Battista Klein (Florence, 1977), 538–59; and Gioacchino Volpe, *Medioevo Italiano* (Florence, 1961).

5. Conti, *La formazione della struttura agraria*, 162–80.

Arriving at very different conclusions, other historians (most notably Johann Plesner and Enrico Fiumi) have suggested that there existed great continuity and little conflict between city and countryside. On the basis of two case studies on Giogole and Passignano, Plesner argued that many city dwellers who came to dominate the countryside in the late thirteenth century were actually descendants of rural immigrants to Florence. These families never severed their connections to their rural estates. Fiumi argued that immigration of the rural *borghesia* into the city accounted for Florentine prosperity before the demographic collapse of the fourteenth century.[6] The debate over city-country relations is an important one, as it is directly relevant to the study of the origins of the territorial state. If there was indeed marked discontinuity between city and countryside before the thirteenth century, as Caggese and others have argued, the rise of Florence to economic and political mastery of Tuscany was unusually rapid.[7]

The study of church property—a field pioneered by David Herlihy, Philip Jones, and Cinzio Violante several decades ago—affords us a way of assessing the historical relationship between city and countryside.[8] I will examine one particular ecclesiastical landlord and institution, the cathedral chapter, and I will focus not only on property holding but on the connections between an urban institutional patron and its rural clien-

---

6. Johan Plesner, *L'émigration de la campagne à la ville libre de Florence au XIIIe siècle* (Florence, 1979; first published Copenhagen, 1934), chaps. 4, 5. See also Enrico Fiumi, "Sui rapporti economici tra città e contado nell'età comunale," *Archivio Storico Italiano* 114 (1956): 18–68. Fiumi agreed with Plesner on many key points but emphasized that rural emigrants to the city came from the rural *borghesia* rather than from the rural nobility ("Fioritura e decadenza dell'economia fiorentina," *Archivio Storico Italiano* 115 [1957]: 419–34). See also Enrico Fiumi, "Fioritura e decadenza," *Archivio Storico Italiano* 116 (1958): 499–505; 117 (1959): 484–501. Renzo Nelli's local study of Monte di Croce, *Signoria ecclesiastica e proprietà cittadina: Monte di Croce tra XIII e XIV secolo* (Comune di Pontassieve, 1985), underscores the continuity of urban influence at Monte di Croce in the thirteenth and fourteenth centuries. Relations between the bishop and local tenants were not normally antagonistic (32, 39–48, 55–58, 103–19).

7. For brief remarks on this issue, see Wickham, *The Mountains and the City*, 353–54.

8. For examples of their work on church property, see P. J. Jones, "An Italian Estate, 900–1200," *Economic History Review*, 2d ser., 7 (1954): 18–32; David Herlihy, "Church Property on the European Continent, 701–1200," *Speculum* 36 (1961), 81–105; David Herlihy, *Medieval and Renaissance Pistoia: The Social History of an Italian Town* (New Haven, 1967); and Cinzio Violante, *La società milanese nell'età precomunale* (Bari, 1974).

tele.[9] The study of patronage networks allows the historian to explore the nature of social, economic, and cultural relations linking city and countryside before 1200. There are numerous studies of clientage in Florence in the fifteenth century, but there are very few published studies of patronage for an earlier period.[10] Furthermore, there exists no systematic and complete analysis of the chapter patrimony, although several scholars have already written extensively about chapter properties.[11] We are fortunate, however, to have at our disposal a published cartulary of 193 documents relating to the cathedral chapter dating from 852 to 1149.[12] The number compares favorably with other collections for the same period. For the eleventh century alone there are 131 charters, more than the number available for the monastery of Strumi in the Casentino but less than that associated with eleventh-century Camaldoli.[13] For the sec-

---

9. For the purposes of this essay, I define patronage as the granting of protection, aid, access to political networks, and economic favors by one individual or group (patrons) to another individual or group (clients), in exchange for the support and loyalty of the latter. Patrons normally command more resources (political and economic) than do their clients. For this definition, I am indebted to the recent work of Carol Lansing and Ron Weissmann. See Carol Lansing, *The Florentine Magnates: Lineage and Faction in a Medieval Commune* (Princeton, 1991), 172–76; and Ronald Weissman, "Taking Patronage Seriously: Mediterranean Values and Renaissance Society," in *Patronage, Art, and Society in Renaissance Italy*, ed. F. W. Kent and P. Simons (Oxford, 1987), 25–45, esp. 25–26.

10. For the fifteenth century, see Dale Kent, *The Rise of the Medici: Faction in Florence, 1426–1434* (Oxford, 1978), esp. 25–29. For the fourteenth century, see Charles de la Roncière, "A Monastic Clientele? The Abbey of Settimo, Its Neighbors and Its Tenants (1280–1340)," in *City and Countryside*, 55–67; and "Fidélités, patronages, clientèles dans le contado florentin au xive siècle," *Ricerche Storiche* 15, no. 1 (1985): 35–60. For investigations of the problem in Florence and Tuscany before the fourteenth century, see Lansing, *The Florentine Magnates*; George Dameron, *Episcopal Power and Florentine Society, 1000–1320* (Cambridge, Mass., 1991); and Wickham, *The Mountains and the City*.

11. For the economic history of the cathedral chapter, see Robert Davidsohn, *Storia di Firenze. I: Le origini*, trans. Giovanni Battista Klein (Florence, 1977); Elena Rotelli, "La Proprietà del capitolo della cattedrale fiorentina dalle origini agli inizi del XIV secolo," in *La Chiesa in campagna: Saggi di storia dei patrimoni ecclesiastici nella Toscana settentrionale, sec. XIII–XIV*, ed. Domenico Maselli (Pistoia, 1988), 13–33; Dameron, *Episcopal Power*, 49–50, 95, 97, 115, 118, 121, 123, 148; Yoram Milo, *Tuscany and the Dynamics of Church Reform in the Eleventh Century* (Ann Arbor, 1979); and the various articles by B. Quilici cited in Dameron, *Episcopal Power*, 269–70.

12. Renato Piattoli, *Le carte della canonica della cattedrale di Firenze (723–1149)* (Rome, 1938) (hereafter cited as Piattoli, followed by the number of the document [*pergamena*] in the collection).

13. Wickham, *The Mountains and the City*, 155.

ond half of the twelfth century there are an additional 119 documents in the Archivio del Capitolo Fiorentino.[14]

One path by which we may explore patronage in the eleventh and twelfth centuries is to study the process of gift giving. By examining the patterns of gift giving (donations) to the cathedral chapter by rural donors, we can assess the nature of the complex dialectical relationship between urban patrons and their clients in the *contado*. In this essay, we will identify the location and nature of chapter holdings, the type of gifts given to the chapter, the identity of the donors and their motivations, and the favors, or countergifts the donors expected to receive from the chapter in exchange.[15] Several recent studies of this phenomenon have explored the motivations of the donors to ecclesiastical institutions, but they have given little attention to the religious and economic strategies or interests of the ecclesiastical institutions receiving those gifts.[16] Gift giving was not a one-way street; gifts were often solicited as well as freely given.

The cathedral chapter was one of the few urban lords in the eleventh century with a presence in the *contado*. Scrutiny of the lists of possessions and properties of the cathedral chapter in five imperial, episcopal, and papal privileges reveals that between 983 and 1102 the chapter gradually but inexorably accumulated property and rights in the following areas: the city of Florence (including the churches of Sant'Andrea, Santa Maria Novella, San Procolo, San Pietro Gatuari, and Sant'Ambrogio), the southwestern and northeastern Mugello, or Sieve River valley, north of the city (in the *pivieri* of Vaglia, Petroio, Cercina, San Cassiano, San Lorenzo, San Gavino Adimari, and San Giovanni Maggiore), the Arno plain west of the city (specifically the *pivieri* of Sesto, Pane, Brozzi, Careggi, Campi, and Signa), and four *pivieri* south and east of the city (Giogole, Ripoli, Campoli, and Impruneta).[17] Gifts, relinquishments of

---

14. Archivio del Capitolo Fiorentino, *Carte Strozziane* (hereafter cited as ACF CS, followed by the number of each *pergamena* assigned to it by Carlo Strozzi).

15. For a useful discussion of gift-countergift exchange, see A. J. Gurevich, *Categories of Medieval Culture*, trans. G. L. Campbell (London, 1985), 222–24; Wickham, *The Mountains and the City*, 195–96; and Duane Oshcim, *An Italian Lordship: The Bishopric of Lucca in the Late Middle Ages* (Berkeley and Los Angeles, 1977), 23–24.

16. See, for example, Maureen Miller, "Donors, Their Gifts, and Religious Innovation in Medieval Verona," *Speculum* 66, no. 1 (1991): 27–42; Wickham, *The Mountains and the City*, 180–220.

17. The *piviere* is principal unit of ecclesiastical organization, composed of the *pieve* (parish churches with baptismal fonts) and its several subordinate parishes with-

chapter property (*refutationes*), purchase, and land swaps (*permutationes*) were the means by which this accumulation and recovery of estates occurred.[18] The evidence suggests that the canons, and particularly the estate manager (the *proposto*), encouraged (if not solicited) local residents to give gifts in particular zones of the *contado* to create a clear economic and social presence for themselves in those areas. They later strengthened their presence by consolidating scattered properties.

As was true for the chapter of Lucca, the patrimony of the Florentine chapter consisted of landed estates (*curtes*), landed holdings sufficient to support a household (*sortes*), castles (*castelli*), oratories, churches with baptismal fonts (*pievi*) and their associated tithes, miscellaneous parcels of land, and vineyards.[19] Tithes were a principal source of income.[20] They frequently appeared in several of the inventories of chapter property included in imperial and papal documents. Rents were almost exclusively in money and apparently yielded only nominal returns. The bulk of the rents came from the leasing of land in or near the city, where the economy was more monetized than in the countryside.[21] Another source of income was the collection of public taxes and rights formerly in the possession of the German emperors. The chapter had complete or partial

---

out fonts. The five imperial and papal privileges are Piattoli 18, 39, 54, 91, and 154. For reference maps to locate the places mentioned in this essay, see the maps accompanying *Rationes Decimarum Italiae: Tuscia*, vol. 1: *La decima degli anni 1274–1280*, ed. P. Guidi, Studi e Testi, no. 58 (Vatican City, 1932); and vol. 2: *Le decime degli anni 1295–1304*, ed. M. Giusti and P. Guidi, Studi e Testi, no. 98 (Vatican City, 1942).

18. For example, the chapter acquired property in seven important *pievi*: Signa, in 964, 990, 1034, 1050, and 1092 (Piattoli 14, 20, 34, 51, and 145, respectively); Sesto, in 1025, 1089, and 1180 (Piattoli 31, 136, and ACF CS 250, respectively); San Martino a Brozzi, in 1046 and 1058 (Piattoli 48, 61); Cercina, in 1020, 1050, and 1180 (Piattoli 28, 52, and ACF CS 250, respectively); Giogole, in 1040, 1083, 1088, and 1180 (Piattoli 42, 109, 131, and ACF CS 250, respectively); San Gavino Adimari, in 1058, 1061, 1066, and 1079 (Piattoli 60, 63, 72, and 100, respectively); and Santa Maria Impruneta, in 1040 and 1180 (Piattoli 42, ACF CS 250).

19. Jones, "An Italian Estate," 19–20.

20. For examples of charters that mention the rights of the chapter to collect tithes, see Piattoli 14, 38, 91, 124, 152, 177.

21. The dates of chapter leases (*libelli*) before 1200 are the following: 934 (Piattoli 10), 955 (12), 966 (15), 1025 (31), 1065 (69), 1066 (70), 1066 (71), 1072 (82), 1078 (98), 1079 (102), 1081 (104), 1082 (106), 1082 (107), 1083 (108), 1084 (111), 1084 (114), 1086 (123), 1087 (126), 1089 (137), 1089 (138), 1098 (150), 1111 (157), 1114 (160), 1115 (161), 1115 (162), 1120 (163), 1125 (170), 1128 (178), 1128 (179), 1129 (181), 1159 (ACF CS 175), 1160 (ACF CS 176), 1183 (ACF CS 125), and 1199 (ACF CS 349).

ownership of several *castelli,* including those of Scarabone, Sommaia, Bossolo, Campiano, and Molezzano. It had the privilege of collecting public taxes like the *datium* at Molezzano, and it could claim rights of hospitality (*albergaria*) at Campiano.[22] As was true throughout Tuscany, the "classical" manor had disintegrated by 1200. However, unlike the estate of the chapter of Lucca, labor dues survived in a very limited way into the early thirteenth century.[23]

The influence exercised by the cathedral chapter did not, however, exclusively depend on the amount of tithes, rents, and religious fees it could collect. It also derived from the importance and number of friends, kinsmen, dependents, and allies it could rally in a particular region. The goal was not necessarily to accumulate wealth; it was to widen the net of social networks over which the chapter had influence.[24] The influence and power exercised over rural communities by the cathedral chapter derived primarily from the possession of patronage rights in certain *pivieri.* During the two centuries covered by this study, the chapter possessed patronage rights to several *pievi* and churches, including those of Signa, Cercina, Quinto, San Severo a Legri, San Martino (Impruneta), Santa Maria di Campiano (Mugello), Sant'Andrea di Novoli, San Michele di Gangalandi (near Signa), Santa Croce e San Niccolò Bibbiano (Mugello), and San Cristoforo a Viciano (Giogole), several churches in the city (San Pietro Gatuari, Santa Maria Novella, and Sant'Ambrogio), and numerous churches in the Mugello (unnamed in the sources).[25]

---

22. A thirteenth-century charter reveals that the chapter was still collecting the former imperial *datia* and *accatta* in the Mugello as late as 1262 (ACF CS 14). Hospitality rights (*albergaria*) are attested in Piattoli 151. The chapter acquired rights in the following *castelli*: Bossolo, in 1038 (Piattoli 41), unnamed *castelli* given by Geremia di Ildebrando sometime before 1062 (Piattoli 68), Scarabone, sometime before 1076 (Piattoli 91), Campiano, in 1078 and 1097 (Piattoli 95, 147), and Molezzano, before 1102 (Piattoli 154). Bossolo was back in episcopal possession by 1127 (Dameron, *Episcopal Lordship*, 208 9). Scarabone (Val di Carza, near Vaglia), Campiano (Val di Sieve), and Molezzano (northeast Mugello) were all in the Mugello. When one adds the total number of *castelli* under the partial or total *dominium* of the bishop and chapter before 1200, one realizes that these two church lords controlled or exercised substantial rights in an extensive number of *castelli* throughout the Mugello.

23. For labor services listed in 1201 at Cintoia (near Settimo) and Solicciano, see ACF CS 862. At Solicciano (near Settimo) the lease of two *staia* of a former demesne (*donicatum*) required labor services. For a comparison with the cathedral chapter of Lucca, see Jones, "An Italian Estate," 25.

24. See Gurevich, *Categories of Medieval Culture,* 247; and Barbara Rosenwein, *To Be the Neighbor of St. Peter: The Social Meaning of Cluny's Property, 909–1049* (Ithaca, N.Y., 1989), 4.

25. Piattoli 14, 18, 38, 90, 91, 100, 109, 124, 151, 152, 154, 177.

Patronage rights in rural *pievi* associated with St. John and the payment of modest rents by rural tenants on the feast days of the patron saints of the cathedral chapter helped forge a sacramental, social, and economic interdependence between the city and countryside. Ties linking city and hinterland extended from the city (the cathedral chapter) into the countryside (the tenants, rural clergy, and donors). Donors, leaseholders (*libellarii*), and archpriests (*pievani*) of rural parishes (*pievi*) under chapter jurisdiction looked inward to the urban cathedral chapter. They paid rents, venerated saints, requested prayers to be said on their behalf by the canons, sought election to clerical office, and forged political connections with the Countesses Beatrice and Matilda through a liaison with the chapter.[26] Members of the cathedral chapter looked outward into the countryside to draw income (tithes and rents), receive gifts of rural property, appoint local clerical officials to administer the sacraments, and promote the interests of their kinsmen.

In the second half of the eleventh century managers of chapter lands (specifically the *proposto*) inaugurated some very modest efforts to consolidate dispersed holdings by way of commutations and purchases.[27] Though scattered over wide areas of the countryside, there is evidence of property consolidation in parts of the Mugello, in the region around Sesto in the Valdarno Fiorentino, and in the area west of the city walls.[28] As was common elsewhere (such as in Rome and Arezzo), consolidation increased the political, social, and economic influence an ecclesiastical lord could exercise in a particular area.[29] This concentration and consol-

---

26. A standard recent study of the Tuscan marquis is Mario Nobili's essay, "Le famiglie marchionali nella Tuscia," in *I Ceti dirigenti in Toscana nell'età precomunale* (Pisa, 1981), 79–105.

27. Piattoli 118 and 119. One example is the purchase of land at Noceta in 1085: "Tamen decernimus terra petia ipsa, cui de duabus partibus est fini terra pred(ic)te canonice, de tertia parte est fini terra Ughizionis comitis, de quarta parte est fini terra que vocatur Berenzanica" (Piattoli 118, p. 295).

28. Chapter estates at Lucca were not normally consolidated (Jones, "An Italian Estate," 19). Relative to the location of gifts of property to the Florentine cathedral chapter, those of the Lucchese chapter appear to have been more scattered and dispersed.

29. In Rome, church lords grouped properties around patron churches (like Santa Maria Nova) to increase the number of faithful under their control and to enhance the quality of administration and management. See Étienne Hubert, *Éspace urbain et habitat à Rome du Xe siècle à la fin du XIII siècle* (Rome, 1990), 275–81. For consolidation of ecclesiastical estates at Arezzo, see Giovanni Cherubini, "Aspetti della proprietà fondiaria nell'Aretino durante il XIII secolo," *Archivio Storico Italiano* 121 (1963): 3–40, esp. 7–9.

idation made it easier for chapter officials to communicate with tenants and collect rents. Property consolidation protected chapter property from usurpation and alienation, since scattered pieces were much more easily appropriated than were large tracts. For instance, the chapter acquired property in seven grants (*finitiones*) around the beginning of the twelfth century in locations where the chapter had already established a foothold (such as at Signa, Campiano, and Cintoia). In 1121, the chapter and the monastery of San Miniato al Monte exchanged property for their mutual benefit, and the alienations at Signa in 1199 were designed to build and consolidate holdings offered to the chapter two centuries before.[30] Two of the three purchases of property before 1200 (all associated with Noceta) originated at the end of the eleventh century and involved parcels bordering chapter property on two of its contiguous sides.[31] Three of the four exchanges of property (*chartae commutationis*) also came at the end of the eleventh or early twelfth centuries.[32]

Some recent historians have questioned whether ecclesiastical institutions actually exercised effective control over the property given to them as gifts.[33] Indeed, evidence from the sources relating to the estate of the cathedral chapter reveals that property rights were fragile and often subject to dispute. For example, in 1078, Count Gherardo del fu conte Ildebrando gave to the chapter his portion of the *dominium* of the lands and churches of the landed estate (*curtis*) at Campiano. In 1097, Count Guido del conte Guido relinquished his hospitality rights (*albergaria*)

---

30. These alienations to the chapter included a landed holding (*sortis*) at Cintoia near Settimo in 1057 (Piattoli 59); *sortes* at Limite (near Signa) and Sala (Brozzi) in 1079 (Piattoli 101); partial rights to a *castello* at Campiano and the local church of Santa Maria in 1097 (Piattoli 147); land at Careggi near other possessions of the cathedral in 1112 (Piattoli 158); and properties at Signa in 1199 (ACF CC 603). The exchange with San Miniato is found in Piattoli 164.

31. Two of the purchases of parcels of land at Noceta in 1085 were made for 6 and 3 *soldi*, respectively (Piattoli 118, 119). The cathedral chapter of Lucca made most of its purchases in the twelfth century, especially between 1160 and 1180 (Jones, "An Italian Estate," 29). The bishops of Florence and Lucca also purchased extensively in the twelfth and thirteenth centuries (Jones, "An Italian Estate," 30; Dameron, *Episcopal Lordship*, 212).

32. For example, in 1090 and 1095, Rozo, archpriest and property manager (*proposto*), arranged to exchange property with the monastery of Santa Maria di Mantignano and San Lorenzo (Piattoli 143, 146). The properties the chapter acquired were near chapter possessions at Cintoia and in the *piviere* of Santo Stefano in Pane.

33. Rosenwein, *To Be the Neighbor of St. Peter*, xii; John Howe, "'Monasteria Semper Libera': Cluniac-Type Monastic Liberties in Some Eleventh Century Central Italian Monasteries," *Catholic Historical Review* 78, no. 1 (1992): 19–34.

there, along with his rights to the *curtis, castello,* and church of Santa Maria di Campiano. However, only in 1100 did the holder of a fief from Count Guido renounce his claim to properties at Campiano, and it was 1122 before a certain Bonifazio di Tegrimo gave up his rights at Campiano to the Marquis Conrad.[34] The marquis, in turn, restored those possessions (*terras et res*) to the archpresbyter and estate manager of the cathedral chapter.[35] It should not surprise us, therefore, that in Tuscany before 1200, just as in legal disputes today, the dissonance between what the written record allowed and how people behaved was often very great. Several estates and properties were often the subject of dispute between the chapter and local lords before 1150. Proper rights of dominion often had to be sorted out by public or papal courts. At least three of these proceedings took place in 1100, 1122, and 1183.[36] Such conflicts should not, however, lead us to downplay the economic importance of landed estates or call into question the degree of effective control exercised by the chapter over its possessions. Indeed, they underscore their very importance. At the heart of eight conflicts involving the cathedral chapter were tangible economic interests: landed holdings (*sortes*), wood, tithes, and annual payments or rents.[37]

Echoing trends throughout Europe, the number of gifts given the chapter gradually increased during the eleventh century. Most gifts came into the chapter's possession after the middle of the eleventh century, especially between 1071 and 1090 (16). This is a pattern replicated elsewhere, as it coincided with the quickening of the reform movement and the restoration of church property by the laity.[38] To the east and south of

---

34. Piattoli 95, 147, 151, 152, 167.

35. "Ad hec ipse marchio recordatus est quod sic esset, et fecit vocare Bonifatium, ut de predictis terris et rebus legaliter satisfaceret. Tunc Bonifatius in manu predicti marchionis predictas terras et res omni modo reflutauit et se nullo mo ulterius intromisurum promisit. Et ad hec ipse marchio per fustem, quem sua tenebat manu, reinuestiuit predictum Iohannem archpresbiterum atque prepositum, vice prefate ecclesie, de omnibus predictis terris et rebu . . ." (Piattoli 167, p. 404). There was also a controversy in the twelfth century between the cathedral canons and a monastery over the donation of property in the Mugello made by Geremia di Ildebrando in the eleventh century (Piattoli, app. 2, pp. 462–63).

36. For such challenges, see Piattoli 152, 167; and ACF CS 49.

37. The dates of these disputes were 1061, 1077, 1100, 1122, the mid–twelfth century, and 1183 (Piattoli 62, 65, 66, 94, 152, 167, app. 2 [p. 462], and ACF CS 49, respectively).

38. Donations or gifts to the chapter were distributed in the following way: 960–70, three gifts (Piattoli 13, 14, and 17, respectively); 971–80, no gifts; 981–90, one gift (Piattoli 20); 991–1000, two gifts (Piattoli 21, 24); 1001–10, no gifts; 1011–20, one gift (Piat-

Florence, the monasteries of Camaldoli (in the Casentino) and Passignano (Val di Pesa) also received most of their gifts in the last quarter of the century. If we compare the cathedral chapter with these other institutions, we discover that the total number of gifts given to the cathedral chapter was rather low.[39] It would appear that donors preferred other ecclesiastical institutions to the cathedral chapter. However, we should approach these figures with some caution. There was no necessary correlation between the number and the importance of gifts to the institution receiving them. A few donations of large or strategically located properties were often preferable to the acquisition of many gifts of small dispersed parcels. The figures associated with the cathedral chapter, however, compare favorably with those of the bishopric of Florence for the same period. There is documentation for 16 gifts to the bishopric during the half-century between 1026 and 1075, and there is evidence for another 16 for the period between 1076 and 1125. After 1125, however, donors in the Diocese of Florence preferred to make donations to the bishopric rather than to the cathedral chapter. Whereas we have 3 gifts recorded as having been made to the chapter between 1125 and 1199, we have a record of 72 gifts to the bishopric. Much of the gift giving to the bishop involved property in the Val di Pesa and the Mugello. In 1199, several individuals transferred property at Signa to the cathedral chapter, the most significant series of gifts in the twelfth century.[40]

Most donors came from the upper and middle strata of society in both city and countryside, and their reasons for giving were very diverse. Donors to the chapter included bishops, notaries, members of the rural

---

toli 28); 1021–30, one gift (Piattoli 30); 1031–40, four gifts (Piattoli 34, app. 1, 41, 42); 1041–50, three gifts (Piattoli 48, 51, 52); 1051–60, two gifts (Piattoli 60, 61); 1061–70, three gifts (Piattoli 63, 72, 76a); 1071–80, seven gifts (Piattoli 81, 88, 90, 92, 93, 95, 100); 1081–90, nine gifts (Piattoli 109, 112, 121, 122, 124, 127, 131, 136, 139); 1091–1100, three gifts (Piattoli 145, 148, 151); 1101–10, no gifts; and 1111–20, one gift (Piattoli 159); 1121–30, one gift (Piattoli 177). There were only two more series of gifts in 1180 (ACF CS 250) and in 1195 (ACF CS 225). For comparison with the number of donations to churches in Europe as a whole, see Colin Morris, *The Papal Monarchy: The Western Church from 1050 to 1250* (Oxford, 1989), 61.

39. In the case of Camaldoli, there were 16 gifts and 12 sales between 1030 and 1070. In the 1070s, the number of gifts rose to 10; in the 1080s, there were 29 gifts and 18 sales (Wickham, *The Mountains and the City*, 192). Between 1071 and 1100, the monastery of Passignano received a total of 36 gifts (Conti, *La formazione*, 160).

40. Dameron, *Episcopal Power*, 211–12; Piattoli 177; ACF CS 250, 225, 603. For comparison with gifts to the Lucchese bishop at the same time, see Osheim, *An Italian Lordship*, 22–23.

aristocracy, clerics, and medium-sized landowners with enough property to give the chapter at least one landed estate (*curtis*) or one family holding (*sortis*). As was true of donors to ecclesiastical institutions at Verona, those giving to the Florentine cathedral chapter were from a diverse group. Of the 44 documents detailing gifts between 962 and 1195, 6 recorded gifts by bishops.[41] There were also 7 gifts made by clerics and their families. Probably among these grants were transfers of previously usurped chapter property. There were 2 gifts by notaries, 4 by widows (one of whom was a member of a prominent family), and 4 by rural aristocrats in the Mugello.[42] The reasons for giving were spiritual, economic, social, political, or strategic, or any combination of these. The most obvious motive (and the one stated clearly in the documents) was spiritual. A gift of land to the chapter usually required a countergift in return (prayers). A donor usually obligated the canons to offer prayers to the patron saints of the chapter (St. John and Zanobi) on behalf of himself or herself and his or her kin. For example, in 1070, the cleric Florenzo del fu Florenzo (called Rustico) and Bonina del fu Florenzo bought a third of a *sortis* at Novoli (near Campoli) for 10 *soldi*. In 1085, Florenzo and another cleric bought one sixth of a third part of a *sortis* at Novoli for 6 *soldi*. Two years later, Florenzo donated to the cathedral chapter all his rights in the church of Sant'Andrea a Novoli for the souls of his wife, himself, and his son.[43]

Donors often reserved the right to take the gift back if the spiritual integrity of the institution receiving the gift was called into question. For example, in 1050, the widow Tetberga del fu Azzo donated a plot of land (*sortis*) at Cercina to the chapter, declaring that her descendants could give the property to another ecclesiastical institution if Bishop Gerardo

41. Bishops Raimbaldo and Podo gave two key gifts to the chapter in the tenth century: usufrucht to the *pieve* of Signa (with its income), and the small abbey (*badiola*) of Sant'Andrea in Florence, respectively (Piattoli 14 and 24).

42. For bishops, see Piattoli 14, 24, 41, 112, 139, and 159; clerics, Piattoli 42, 81, 88, 124, and 136; notaries, Piattoli 60 and 72; widows, Piattoli 52, 61 (same person as 52), 122, and 145; and for aristocrats, Piattoli 68 (the gift of Geremia di Ildebrando), 95, 145, and 151. The widow Tetberga (former wife of Rodolfo del fu Atto) gave substantial gifts to the chapter: a *sortis* at Arneto (Piattoli 52) in 1050, and three *sortes* within the *piviere* of San Martino a Brozzi (Piattoli 61) in 1058. The most important gifts were those given by the bishops and members of the rural aristocracy in the Mugello. For a comparison with gifts given to the church at Verona, see Miller, "Donors, Their Gifts, and Religious Innovation," 27–42.

43. Piattoli 78, 120, and 124.

alienated any of it.[44] Such restrictions by donors are excellent examples of how donors exerted pressure on ecclesiastical institutions to end clerical absenteeism and the alienation of church property. It is also noteworthy that many of these principal donations to the chapter involved property in *pivieri* already consecrated to saints closely associated with Florence. This was particularly true of the cult of St. John, to whom the urban *pieve* was consecrated. The bishop gave usufructory rights to the *pieve* of San Giovanni e Lorenzo a Signa in 964, and the extensive possessions within the *pieve* of San Giovanni Maggiore in the Mugello came into chapter possession sometime before 1062. Some gifts were formalistic transfers in which the donor still possessed the usufructory rights to the property. In exchange for title to the property, the cathedral chapter was obligated to protect it. For example, in 1072, the chapter estate manager (*proposto*) leased property at Colonnata, Fulignano, and Lame for four *denari* to two priests, Guinizo del fu Guinizo and Gherardo del fu Pietro. Previously these same two priests, along with Giovanni del fu Stefano, had donated property to the chapter. In 1084, these three men and a certain Pietro del fu Sizo rented more land, which they had donated to the chapter just one day before. Because rents were not onerous and because the leasing of this property virtually conferred ownership, it is probable that these gifts were attempts to protect usufructory rights.[45] In another example, Gerardo del fu conte Ildebrando gave a third part of the *castello* of Campiano and other possessions to the chapter in 1078, but he retained the usufructory rights for himself and his male descendants.[46]

Donors who gave gifts of property to the cathedral chapter in one location were often able to lease chapter property elsewhere. In exchange for a gift, they were able to lease chapter property where it might have suited their interests better. For example, in 1079, Florenzo and Leone del fu Florenzo, Ugo del fu Raineri, and Berardo del fu Orso relinquished possession of three landed holdings (*sortes*) at Cammori, Sala,

---

44. Piattoli 52. In 1047, the notary Alberto del fu Eriberto donated one-third of a *sortis* to the *pieve* of San Piero a Sieve to establish a chapter there: "Et si forsitans usque ad ipso constituto canonici non abuerint ad ipsa ecclesia et plebe, quod ibidem regulariter non uiuant, tunc ipsa portiionem de suprascripta sorte et res deueniad et reuertat ad proprietatem et potestatem de canonica de domui Sancti Iohanni, sita in ciuitate Florentiia, ubi modo donnus Rollandus prepositus preesse uidetur, et de canonici qui ibidem regulariter uivunt" (Piattoli 50, p. 135).

45. Piattoli 82 and 111. For the example of the priest Gerardo, who leased the property he had given to the chapter in 1089, see Piattoli 136 and 137.

46. Piattoli 95 and 96.

and Limite. Four years later Florenzo del fu Florenzo leased land from the chapter at Panche on the road from Florence to Sesto. In another example, Giovanni del fu Bonizo bought two properties at Osce and Sorbo in 1074 for 10 *soldi* from Adamo del fu Giovanni. One parcel bordered the land of a cleric whose kinsmen had important ties to the cathedral chapter, Fusco del Florenzo.[47] Another parcel bordered property belonging to the chapter itself. In 1079, this same Giovanni del fu Bonizo donated property in the Mugello to a church that was within the patrimony of the chapter, San Niccolò and Santa Croce a Bibbiano. Three years later he leased a parcel of land at the Porta San Pancrazio near Florence for 10 *denari* from the cathedral chapter. Occasionally, as clients of the cathedral chapter, donors like Giovanni del fu Bonizo were obligated to serve as witnesses in cases involving their patron. In 1083, Giovanni del fu Bonizo acted as a witness for the archpriest of the cathedral chapter at Bivigliano in the Mugello when Imilia del fu Pietro promised never again to damage its interests.[48] Apparently, Giovanni del fu Bonizo had benefited from chapter patronage. In exchange for his donations and his service as a witness in legal disputes, he was able to lease valuable property belonging to the chapter on the edge of the city.

Several major donors made core gifts of landed property in certain key regions of the Arno Valley and the central Mugello, which significantly enhanced the presence of the chapter in those locations.[49] These gifts began in the late tenth century. When the bishop made donations to the cathedral chapter, he strengthened and consolidated his political, liturgical, and economic ties to the chapter. In 964, Bishop Raimbaldo granted the usufruct of the *pieve* of San Lorenzo e Giovanni at Signa in exchange for prayers for the souls of past and future bishops.[50] His primary motive

---

47. It is unclear whether this Fusco (Florenzo) del fu Florenzo was the prosperous cleric who had supported Bishop Pietro Mezzabarba and had given a valuable gift to San Miniato al Monte (Davidsohn, *Storia di Firenze*, 1:360). He could have been his son.

48. Piattoli 85, 86, 100, 106, 113. Patrons often required their clients to serve as witnesses in official documents. See, for example, Wickham's discussion of this phenomenon in *The Mountains and the City* (258).

49. For the Valdarno, I single out the gift of Teuzo del fu Lepizo in 1034 (Piattoli 34). Between 1050 and 1062, Geremia di Ildebrando made an important bequest of property in the Mugello (Piattoli 68).

50. "Et ideoque ego in Dei nomine manifestu sum ego Rainbaldus sancte Florentine ecclesie episcopus, quia pro remedio anime b(one) m(emorie) anticessoris meis et anime mee seu et pro remedium anime de sucessoribus meis per hanc cartul(am) offersionis nomine ad usufructuandum dare et offerere adque tradere preuidi in canonica

appears to have been a spiritual one. However, his aims also included political and economic concerns. Like the urban *pieve* entrusted to the chapter canons, the *pieve* at Signa was consecrated to St. John. In 967, an imperial official placed Signa under imperial protection, strengthening the bonds between Otto I and the two principal ecclesiastical instititutions of Florence. Located near Settimo and Mantignano in the Arno Valley west of Florence, Signa was an outpost of urban ecclesiastical influence in a region increasingly dominated by the aristocratic rural lineage of Cadolo, the Cadolingi.[51] Imperial protection of the canons' possession of Signa was a gesture of support for a valuable ecclesiastical ally. There is no record of other gifts to the cathedral chapter of property at Signa until 1034.

The episcopal gift of Signa to the chapter in 964 was the first of a series of conscious actions taken by the bishops of Florence and Fiesole to extend an urban ecclesiastical presence into the *contado*. The motives were at least twofold: to integrate the liturgical and sacramental life of certain areas of the countryside into the sphere of influence of the principal urban ecclesiastical institutions, and to reclaim tithes and *pievi* from the upwardly mobile rural aristocracy. A second significant action initiated by a bishop of Florence to expand his influence was the founding of the basilica of San Miniato in 1024. Like his predecessor, Bishop Raimbaldo, Bishop Hildebrand attempted to bring into the sway of an urban ecclesiastical institution and its saint the rural churches consecrated to that same saint. Composed of properties that included some of the estates contested by the Cadolingi and Guidi, San Miniato al Monte became the episcopal proprietary monastery and the center of a revived cult of St. Minias.[52] We find the same process at work in the Diocese of Fiesole: an episcopally sponsored transfer of relics, followed by the foundation and endowment of a monastery. In 1027, Bishop Jacopo established and endowed the monastery of San Bartolomeo Apostoli to rescue his church from negligent squalor, transferring the remains of the martyr St. Romolo and other companions to a new location. Changing the patron

---

de ecclesia uestra Sancti Ioh(annis) bactista, id est eccl(esia), quod est plebem nostra, Sancti Laurentii et Sancti Ioh(annis) batiste cum curte et casis omnibus illis, qui est posita in loco Exinea" (Piattoli 14, p. 41).

51. Piattoli 17; Rosana Pescaglini Monti, "I Conti Cadolingi," in *I Ceti dirigenti in Toscana nell'età precomunale* 194–96, 204 (Pisa, 1981).

52. Dameron, *Episcopal Power*, 24–37; Dameron, "The Cult of St. Minias and the Struggle for Power in the Diocese of Florence, 1011–24," *The Journal of Medieval History* 13 (June 1987): 125–41.

saint of the monastery from St. Peter to St. Bartholomew the Apostle, Bishop Jacopo endowed the institution with properties in the city and at Careggi (northwest of Florence).[53] In 1028, he founded and endowed the monastery of San Godenzo in the Mugello, located in the Diocese of Fiesole. The continuity of policy between the donation of 964 and the foundation of San Godenzo is evident in the fact that the two documents used the same introductory passage (*arenga*).[54]

The bishop's gift of the *pieve* of Signa firmly established a strong presence for the chapter in this zone of the Arno Valley west of the city. In 1034, the chapter received another very important gift located in the same area. The donor was a large landholder named Teuzo del fu Lepizo, who required prayers for himself and his wife. Along with the church of San Michele a Lecore, he bequeathed an oratory dedicated to St. Michael, and landed holdings and vineyards at Lecore, Olmetolo, Arena, Piano, and Signa.[55] This region around Gangalandi was extremely important to both the chapter and the commune of Florence, even at that early date. According to Davidsohn, Florentine strategic concerns and chapter complaints over the seizure of tithes by local counts brought about a confluence of interests between the city, the Countess Matilda (1076–1115), and the cathedral chapter. The tithes were associated with the churches of San Martino and San Michele in Gangalandi (and probably other churches as well), over which the chapter had claimed jurisdiction. The counts who appropriated them were kinsmen of the Alberti, traditional enemies of the Countess Matilda. The conflict between the chapter and the relatives of the Count Adimaro was rooted in a dispute over the patrimony of their kinsman Bernardo, a former archdeacon of the chapter. These nobles possessed the *castello* of Gangalandi, which dominated the Arno River near Signa.[56] Challenges to urban ecclesiasti-

---

53. Fiesole, Archivio Arcivescovile di Fiesole *Vescovado* II.B.2 (*Cartulario*, 1028 6 kalends March). The text is published in F. Ughelli, *Italia Sacra*, vol. 3 (Venice, 1718), cols. 224ff.

54. Archivio Arcivescovile di Fiesole *Vescovado* II.B.2 (Cartulario, 1028 6 kalends March), also published in Ughelli, *Italia Sacra*, vol. 3, cols. 227ff. For a discussion of the *arenga*, see Piattoli, p. 41n.

55. Piattoli 34, confirmed and protected by Bishop Atto in 1036 (Piattoli 38).

56. Pietro Santini, "Studi sull'antica costituzione del comune di Firenze," *Archivio Storico Italiano* 25 (1900): 41–43; Davidsohn, *Storia di Firenze*, 1:535–37; Fiumi, "Fioritura e decadenza dell'economia fiorentina," 402. Davidsohn claimed that the *castello* belonged to the Adimari. However, Fiumi convincingly disproved that assertion, demonstrating that these *conti da Gangalandi* were kinsmen of the Alberti and ancestors of a future Florentine magnate lineage, the Gangalandi.

cal rights and conflicting claims to property in the region apparently led to Florentine military intervention. In one of the first major Florentine military actions of the twelfth century, the Florentines attacked Monte Gualandi near Signa. Like the attack on Monte di Croce several decades later, the attack took place to preserve urban influence near Signa, not to establish it.

After the destruction of Monte Gualandi in 1107 by the Florentines, the kinsmen of the local count Adimaro relinquished to the churches of Gangalandi the free men, unfree men (*servi*), and tithes that most likely had been at the center of the conflict. The archdeacon of the cathedral chapter served as a witness. Apparently, the relatives of Count Adimaro had held some of those tithes and properties on a long-term lease from the bishop of Pistoia.[57] Ironically, the estate manager of the chapter (Giovanni) later gave the disputed lands and *castelli* to Ubaldino di Adimaro in 1124 in exchange for two large tracts (*moggi*) of land at Gonfolina near Gangalandi and for 10 Lucchese *denari*. It is probable that this property became an important part of the patrimony of the Gangalandi, later declared magnates at the end of the thirteenth century.[58]

By giving gifts to their patron, the cathedral chapter, donors apparently were able to establish connections with the political circles associated with the Countesses Beatrice (1052–76) and Matilda. The events near Signa and Gangalandi described above reveal that the cathedral chapter and the Countess Matilda shared common interests. Following the death of Emperor Henry III in 1056, imperial influence in Florence waned as the power of the marquis increased. In this context, political ties between the office of the marquis and the cathedral chapter apparently grew stronger.[59] Circumstantial evidence suggests that the Count-

---

57. "Ideoque omnem pravum usum, quem parentes nostri aut nos vel nostri homines tam serui quam liberi imposuimus ecclesie Sancti Martini atque Sancti Angeli, vel si earum bona siue decimationem, quam ab episcopo Pistoriense per libellum acquisitam pred(ic)te ecclesie Sancti Martini concessimus, aut alias decimationes tam de luco de monte Pulitano aut aliunde aliquo modo abstulimus, aut liberos homines, qui super predia pred(ic)tarum ecclesiarum habitabant, aut eorum famulos tam pro nobis quam pro heredibus nostris omnino refutamus" (Piattoli 156, p. 379). See also page 380 for mention of the archdeacon.

58. Piattoli 168. E. Rotelli incorrectly identified this lineage with the Adimari ("La proprietà del Capitolo," 18 and 19).

59. The marquis Boniface, Countess Beatrice, and Countess Matilda all attempted to expand their public authority over northern Italy. Countess Beatrice and her second husband Godfrey were able after the death of the emperor in 1056 to reestablish a

esses Beatrice and Matilda encouraged and possibly solicited well-heeled members of their entourage in the Florentine countryside to transfer property in the Mugello to the chapter in the decades after the middle of the eleventh century.[60] One example is very instructive. The cathedral chapter had possessed interests in the Mugello at least from the mid–tenth century. In 987, in Florence, Count Ildebrando and the imperial official Leo extended the imperial ban over the possessions of the chapter, which were confirmed by Otto II.[61] Sometime after 1050, but before 1062, Geremia di Ildebrando, possibly the descendant of this same Count Ildebrando, donated to the cathedral chapter certain estates (*curtes*), *castelli,* and churches in the *pivieri* of San Giovanni Maggiore, San Lorenzo, and San Cassiano. These possessions were located between the Sieve and the ridges of the Appenines. This substantial donation was one of the most important gifts of property to the chapter in the Mugello. It helped attract other gifts of property in this section of the Mugello for the remainder of the eleventh century, specifically in rural *pievi* consecrated to the dominant urban saints.[62] We cannot discount the possibility that some of these gifts were actually restitutions of church property appropriated earlier by the local aristocracy.

Further evidence of close connections between Countess Beatrice, the

---

political base in Florence. After the death of Godfrey in 1069, and that of Beatrice in 1076, Countess Matilda dominated northern and central Italian politics until her own death in 1115. She supported reform efforts in Florence. For general background, see Davidsohn, *Storia di Firenze,* 1:300–2; Milo, *Tuscany and the Dynamics of Reform,* 150–52; and Wickham, *The Mountains and the City,* 110.

60. For a description of the collusion between the marquises, the countesses, the bishopric, and the chapter see Dameron, *Episcopal Power,* 65–67; and Davidsohn, *Storia di Firenzi,* 1:329–31, 398–401. Matilda was also a principal donor to the bishopric of Lucca, which she considered a valuable ally (Osheim, *An Italian Lordship,* 22).

61. Piattoli 19. It leased a *sortis* in the Mugello at Lutiano in the *pieve* of Borgo San Lorenzo in 934 (Piattoli 10).

62. Among chapter possessions confirmed by Alexander II in 1062 were "curtes et ecclesias atque castella in territorio plebium Sancti Iohannis Maioris et Sancti Laurentii et Sancti Cassiani a finibus iugi alpium Mucillensium atque in fluuvium Seue que Hieremias filius Ildebrandi pro sua filiique sui anima per cartulam offersionis prelibate contulit canonice" (Piattoli 68, pp. 183–84). Geremia's original donation charter was lost, but it was probably made between 1050 and 1062. For a discussion of the dating and identification of these properties with present-day Piazzano, see Piattoli, p. 462. The chapter also received the *castello* of Scarabone (Val di Sieve), property (a *mansus*) at Lonciano on Monte Morello, and possessions in Fiesole before 1076 (Piattoli 91, 154). For information on the buildup of the episcopal estate in this region of the Mugello in the eleventh and twelfth centuries, see Dameron, *Episcopal Power,* 57–60, 77–79.

chapter, and the lineage of Count Ildebrando is found in a 1061 document. Rodolfo di Geremia was probably the son of Geremia di Ildebrando and the nephew of Gherardo del fu conte Gherardo (see below). In 1061, he was a witness in the *castello* of Borgo San Lorenzo in the Mugello when Countess Beatrice ruled in favor of the chapter in a dispute with the chapter of San Lorenzo. This conflict concerned certain properties in the *campus Regis,* a region located between the walls of Florence and the Mugnone River to the west of the city. She extended her official protection over the possessions of the chapter.[63] As clients of the countess, Geremia and his kinsmen made important donations to the cathedral chapter and served as witnesses in legal proceedings over which she presided.

There is more evidence for the existence of close connections between the cathedral chapter and Countess Matilda. In the *piviere* of San Giovanni a Petroio, Gherardo del fu conte Ildebrando, son of the count and possibly the brother of Geremia, transferred a third of the *castello* of Campiano and its accompanying possessions and income (including dependent churches and peasants) to the chapter in 1078. That same day he received it back in usufruct for himself and his male descendants for an annual rent of 12 Lucchese *denari.*[64] The Guidi lineage possessed rights in the *castello* and had a proprietary church at Campiano, indicating that perhaps Gherardo was restoring ecclesiastical property that had been previously taken. If Gherardo was a protégé of the Guidi, he might have made this gift to solidify the alliance between the Guidi and the countess. It is also possible he was seeking her protection from Guidi usurpations by donating to her "favorite charity." In 1097 and 1099, the chapter acquired extensive possessions from the Guidi themselves, by now close political associates of Countess Matilda and anti-imperial partisans.[65] Countess Matilda formally placed the properties under her protection. The actual proprietary rights, however, remained continually under dispute. The interests of the chapter in the *castello* and estate (*curtis*) of Campiano were still challenged in 1122 by two men (as we have previously seen), including a vassal of the Guidi named Guido del fu

---

63. Piattoli 66.
64. Piattoli 95 and 96.
65. Piattoli 147 and 151. For the Guidi, see Milo Yoram, "Political Opportunism in Guidi Tuscan Policy," in *I Ceti dirigenti in Toscana nell'età precomunale* (Pisa, 1981), 209–22, esp. 215. See the map following the article for the location of Guidi property.

previously seen), including a vassal of the Guidi named Guido del fu Bonifazio. The dispute was adjudicated by Marquis Conrad in 1122.[66]

There were other gifts to the chapter in this period made by several local landholders, who also possibly sought to curry favor with the countesses after the middle of the eleventh century. A circle of friends and kinsmen made a number of donations to the chapter in the northwestern area of the Mugello, in the *piviere* of San Gavino Adimari. The reasons for the gift giving appear to have been both spiritual and political. In 1058, the chapter received an offering of six pieces of land from two sets of brothers and two other individuals. One of the donors was a notary.[67] In 1061, Pietro del fu Vitale gave to the church of Santa Maria e Santa Croce a Bibbiano two pieces of land and a vineyard located near a church in the *piviere* of San Gavino Adimari. The charter described this church as being dependent on the cathedral chapter. The location of the gift indicates that the chapter estate manager wanted to bring together the cathedral chapter holdings at Bibbiano. Pietro offered the gift to the church in exchange for prayers for himself and two of those involved in the 1058 donation: Everardo and Sizo del fu Rolando. Among the witnesses were the same Alberico, Grifo, and Uberto del fu Lamberto who were involved in the 1058 donation.[68] In 1066, Gherardo di Pietro and his brother Pietro, a notary, gave two more gifts (including land and vineyards at Ircli and Tirlaccio) in the same *piviere* to the chapter. The ostensible reason for this gift was to assure that prayers would be said for the souls of the daughter of Pietro and the son of their friend Sizo.[69] However, there were perhaps other reasons as well. The absence of imperial pressures after the death of Henry III in 1056 had possibly convinced many members of the rural elite (like upwardly mobile notaries) to align their interests more closely with those of the marquis. The noble Cadolingi patrilineage also had properties in this area, as well as extensive possessions in the general vicinity.[70] It is possible that these small landholders sought the protection of Countess Beatrice in their relations with the Cadolingi.

After the middle of the twelfth century, the economic evolution of the estate of the chapter underwent dramatic changes. The number of dona-

---

66. Piattoli 152, 167.
67. Piattoli 60. The notary was Pietro di Giovanni (Piattoli, p. 161), whose brother Sichelmo also was a donor.
68. Piattoli 63.
69. Piattoli 72. In 1079, Giovanni del fu Bonizo gave a gift of extensive property holdings to Santa Croce and San Niccolò a Bibbiano. Those properties were located at Ircli, Rio di Monte, and Cerreto (Piattoli 100).
70. R. Pescaglini Monti, "I conti Cadolingi," in *I Ceti dirigenti*, 200.

tions to the cathedral chapter dropped significantly after the death of Countess Matilda in 1115, further evidence of the importance of the special relationship between the cathedral chapter and the countess. There was really only one set of significant documented donations in the twelfth century, and it dates from the end of the century. We have seen that gift giving to the bishopric, however, increased after the beginning of the twelfth century. Rural donors, especially in the Mugello and Val di Pesa, were shifting their largess away from the cathedral chapter to the bishopric. The bishopric had benefited from the legacy of the last Cadolingi count, who died in 1113. Its increased wealth and influence with the new urban consulate probably made the bishopric a more attractive patron to potential donors in the countryside. For these reasons, the bishopric experienced a significant increase in the number of its gifts after 1125.[71]

For the first time, we see rents in kind appear on the lists of rental dues in the twelfth century. This was not an unusual development, as sources associated with the bishopric of Florence and the cathedral chapter of Lucca also reveal.[72] We encounter detailed record keeping at this time. Inventories of chapter properties at Cintoia (1158 and 1201), Quinto (1201), San Jacobo of Florence (1201), and Solicciano (1201) appear in our sources. The prebend of the estate manager was inventoried as well in 1201.[73] Like other lords throughout Tuscany, the cathedral chapter imposed servile oaths of fidelity on its dependents to require them to pay their rents.[74] The fact that so many of these lists consisted of mixed payments (money, labor dues, capons, and so on) reveals that there had occurred some degree of property consolidation before 1200. Changes in the administration of chapter property, exacerbated no doubt by population pressures, apparently elicited the first documented evidence we have

---

71. For twelfth-century donations to the cathedral chapter, see Piattoli 159; and ACF CS 250 and 225. For the number of gifts to the bishops, see Dameron, *Episcopal Power*, 211. For an overview of the development of episcopal property holding in the twelfth century, see Dameron, *Episcopal Power*, 77.

72. Jones, "An Italian Estate," 27; Dameron, *Episcopal Power*, 101–3, 113–17, 133, 134, 137, 189.

73. ACF CS 657, 862, 869, 863. ACF CS 675, the inventory of the prebend of the *proposto*, listed 13 separate parcels of land. Two parcels were located at San Bartolo a Cintoia (near Settimo), and another (a *donicatum*, or the remains of a former manorial reserve) bordered the church of San Jacobo in Florence. The tenth was at Noceta (a site near Florence, which has probably disappeared and which I cannot locate). The rents required payments in grain and money. The creation of inventories like these was a common policy throughout Europe and Tuscany at this time (Jones, "An Italian Estate," 28; Dameron, *Episcopal Power*, 135–36).

74. ACF CS 864. For a fuller discussion of this process and a bibliography, see Dameron, *Episcopal Power*, 132–34.

of resistance to the lordship of the cathedral chapter at the end of the twelfth century. In 1183, the consulate intervened to oblige more than 20 dependents (*coloni et homines*) to meet their yearly obligations (*consueta et servitia*).[75] Further disruptions elsewhere required the intervention of the Florentine consuls in 1204. The estate manager (*proposto*) successfully petitioned the consuls to force dependents living at Coldaia (*pieve* of San Piero a Sieve in the Mugello), Sesto, and Lonciano to restore to the chapter the land and possessions (*terras et possessiones*) they were withholding.[76]

In conclusion, we have seen that before 1150 the canons of the cathedral chapter of Florence wielded influence in several key areas of the *contado,* particularly in the Valdarno Fiorentino and in the Mugello. They did so by acquiring property and ecclesiastical patronage rights and by fostering the development of a rural clientele. The countesses encouraged, and perhaps solicited, their own clients to patronize the cathedral chapter. The bishops and members of the rural aristocracy favored the cathedral chapter with certain key or core gifts in the tenth and eleventh centuries. Spiritual and economic considerations were principal motivations of the donors, but political concerns also appear to have been particularly important. Some of these gifts of land and jurisdictional rights served as "seed gifts" or "magnets" to attract donations from less powerful men and women who possessed land in the immediate vicinity of those core grants. Cathedral chapter officials brought together dispersed holdings, reclaimed lost properties, and often challenged claims of the rural aristocracy. When supplemented with recent research that has traced the extensive development of episcopal holdings in the Val di Pesa, the Mugello, the Valdelsa, the Valdarno, and in the lower Valdisieve, this study of the cathedral chapter demonstrates that there was a considerable amount of urban influence (by way of urban church lords) in several regions of the Florentine countryside before 1200. Whether rural clients of the cathedral chapter were paying their rents or tithes, soliciting prayers from the canons for their kinsmen, venerating St. John, or receiv-

---

75. ACF CS 49. The document is reproduced in Pietro Santini, *Documenti dell'Antica Costituzione del Comune di Firenze,* vol. 1 (Florence, 1895), 224–25.

76. "Certum est Clanni prepositum canonice Florentine nomine et vice dicte canonice questum fore apud predictam curiam de filiis Dosci et de Orlandino et Peruczo de Coldoria, qui inferunt ei iniuriam et molestiam in terris et possessionibus et hominubus ad dictam canonicam pertinentibus" (Santini, *Documenti,* 230). "Data fuit hec possessio in predicta curia a predicto iudice, et consule confirmata, anno domini mcciiij, iij nonas novembris, indictione viij. Nuntius huius possessionis dande fuit Lombardus nuntius eiusdem curie" (231).

ing sacraments from the chapter-elected local archpriest, they were living lives that were shaped by the interests of urban dwellers and the cults of urban saints. In exchange for their gifts, their local support, and their service as witnesses in legal disputes, clients of the cathedral chapter could expect protection for their properties and access to the circles of power (specifically those of the marquis and countesses). The economic and political connections between local landholders, the countesses, and ecclesiastical lords before 1200 deserve more study and research.

Combined with the local studies of Giogole and Passignano done by Johan Plesner, the study of Florentine ecclesiastical lordships supports the hypothesis that there existed more coherence and continuity between city and countryside before 1200 than many historians of the Arno city have assumed. This was particularly true in the Mugello and the principal river valleys. Florentine military operations in the twelfth century near Signa and Monte di Croce apparently took place not to establish urban influence but to preserve it. To ascertain the actual extent of urban property holding and influence in these zones before 1200, we will need more local studies like those of Plesner, Conti, and Nelli. However, we know enough now about urban presence in the countryside before the thirteenth century to observe that the integration of city and countryside in the thirteenth and early fourteenth centuries did not occur suddenly and rapidly. After 1200, there occurred substantial challenges to urban (particularly ecclesiastical) influence in the countryside, most importantly by the rural communes.[77] Nevertheless, despite these challenges, the long-standing presence of urban ecclesiastical lords and their patronage networks in the countryside before 1200 laid the foundation for the slow but inexorable strengthening of the ties between city and country in the thirteenth and fourteenth centuries as the population expanded. Without their urban presence in the countryside, which reached back to the eleventh century, the Florentines would not have had the resources during the lifetime of Giovanni Villani to sustain one of the richest and most populous cities in Europe. Without such long-standing ties linking city and countryside, the successful creation of a strong Florentine territorial state by the early fifteenth century would have been greatly impeded. The roots of the Renaissance territorial state indeed take us back to the eleventh and twelfth centuries.

---

77. For a detailed assessment of the developments after 1150, see Dameron, *Episcopal Power*, chap. 3, 93–140.

A Trecento Bishop as Seen by Quattrocento Florentines: Sant' Andrea Corsini, His "Life," and the Battle of Anghiari

Giovanni Ciappelli

Saints' lives are complex documents that have been used by scholars for various purposes. As is well known, historians have recently rediscovered these sources for the analysis of local history. One of the recent tendencies of this historiography has been the analysis of "civic religion," that is, the relation between social institutions and local politics, on the one hand, and the cult of a saint (usually the patron saint) on the other.[1]

From this point of view, the considerable corpus of Florentine hagiographical texts of the late Middle Ages has only been used partially for a study of their contexts.[2] Among these is a relatively late *Vita,* that of S.

This essay develops several themes that I addressed in David Herlihy's graduate seminar at Brown University, 1986–87. This problem will be expanded in my volume that will present a new edition of Saint Andrea's life.

1. For the recent bibliography see A. Benvenuti Papi, "San Zanobi: Membri episcopale, tradizioni civiche e dignità familiari," in his *Pastori di popolo. Storie e leggende di vescovo e di città nell'Italia medievale* (Florence, 1988), 127–76, 159, n.6. On the term "Civic Christianity," first used by Herlihy, see A. M. Orselli, *L'immaginario religioso della città medievale* (Ravenna, 1985), 362.

2. Given its importance for the spiritual and cultural atmosphere of the Gregorian Reform, the *Vita* of San Giovanni Gualberto has claimed the attention of scholars. See A. Degl'Innocenti, "Le vite antiche di Giovanni Gualberto: Cronologia e modelli agiografici, *Studi medievali,* 3d ser., 25 (1984): 31–91; and the essays of G. Miccoli and S. Boesch Gajano of 1960 and 1964 cited there (31, n.1). Anna Benvenuti Papi has been particularly involved in the study of other Tuscan and Florentine saints. In addition to her essay on San Zanobi, see her work on Umiliana de' Cerchi, Verdiana da Castelfiorentino, and Margherita da Cortona (reprinted in A. Benvenuti Papi, *"In castro poenitentiae." Santità e società femminile nell'Italia medievale* [Rome, 1990], 59–98; 141–168; 263–303).

Andrea Corsini, written toward the middle of the fifteenth century.[3] Belonging to an important patrician family, which counted among its members an archbishop of Florence in the first half of the Quattrocento, Andrea was a Carmelite and bishop of Fiesole between 1350 and 1374. His sanctity is tied to a posthumous event: the miracle of the battle of Anghiari (1440), in which the saint guided the Florentine troops to victory over Filippo Maria Visconti.

In this essay I will seek to analyze this source to extract from it the mentality and a sense of the society in which it was conceived. Bringing together other contemporary sources, I will give attention to the emergence of his cult in the Quattrocento and to the mechanisms of its construction, illustrated by its relation to popular imagination and the intervention of political and religious powers.

Born at the beginning of the fifteenth century, Andrea was one of 12 children of Nicolò Corsini, a merchant and member of an eminent Florentine family of the period. The Corsini were destined to become one of the major families of Florence during the course of the century. Surviving the chain of bankruptcies of the 1340s and the crises that followed,[4] they were able to remain powerful throughout much of Florentine history.[5] At the beginning of the Trecento their family could already claim among its ranks several priors of the city and a *gonfaloniere* of justice.[6] The family played on a strategy of diversification; alongside their tradition of commercial activities the young of the family sought careers in law and in the church.[7]

We know little for certain of the Andrea's biography before 1338, when a document certifies his presence in the friary of the Carmine.[8] In the succeeding years, before Clement VI nominated him as bishop of Fiesole in October 1349, he assumed various tasks in the Carmelite order (rising to the post of *provinciale* of Tuscany in 1348).[9] One known fact of his episcopacy is his residency in Florence thanks to a 1227–28 concession of Gregory IX to the Florentines, which required the bishops of

---

3. See note 18.

4. See A. Petrucci, ed., *Il libro di ricordanze dei Corsini* (Rome, 1965), XI.

5. See R. B. Litchfield, *Emergence of a Bureaucracy: The Florentine Patricians, 1530–1790* (Princeton, 1986), 42, 53, 170, 207, 333.

6. Petrucci, *Il libro di ricordanze dei Corsini*, X–XI.

7. Ibid., XI–XII.

8. P. Caioli, *S. Andrea Corsini carmelitano vescovo di Fiesole (1301–1374)* (Florence, 1929), 224.

9. L. Saggi, "Andrea Corsini, santo," in *Dizionario biografico degli italiani*, vol. 3 (Rome, 1961), 89.

Fiesole to reside in Florence.[10] But as far as his role as bishop goes, notwithstanding several biographies, much needs to be verified, given that the work now available is only of partial value. Only three recent studies specifically concern Andrea Corsini: a 1929 monograph by a Carmelite father and two essays by clerics largely based on the first.[11] The author of the 1929 book, Paolo Caioli, wrote a long biography that made use of documents and presented a appendix of several archival transcriptions, which gives on first impression the sense of a historically founded work. Caioli, however, mixed information drawn from the documents with episodes taken directly from hagiography. The result is disconcerting; the fruits of painstaking erudition are placed on the same plane as hagiography and legends, which he accepted tout court as historical facts. The two essays, both of 1961, written in a more rigorous period and context of criticism, face the *Vita* in a more objective manner.[12] Yet in several instances the authors continue to gather elements present in the hagiographical source without criticism,[13] and neither delves substantially into original research.

One of the few certainties regarding Andrea Corsini's life is the date of his death, 6 January 1374. He was buried at Fiesole, but 27 days afterward the Carmelite friars of Florence stole his body during the night and buried him in their church, where he lies today.[14] His brother Matteo noted it in his *ricordanze,* specifying that at the moment of translation, the body was "intact, without any corruption and without a stench."[15]

Andrea's administration of his bishopric evidently seemed pious enough to his contemporaries to warrant the respect of sanctity. One of

10. On the transfer of the bishop of Fiesole's residence to Florence, see R. Davidsohn, *Storia di Firenze,* vol. 2 (Florence, 1972–73), 133–37.

11. The essays are Caioli, *S. Andrea Corsini*; Saggi, "Andrea Corsini"; and F. Caraffa, "Andrea Corsini, vescovo di Fiesole, santo," in *Bibliotheca Sanctorum,* vol. 1 (Rome, 1961), cols. 1158–67. Saggi is also a Carmelite, Monseigneur Caraffa is editorial director of *Bibliotheca Sanctorum.*

12. In particular, see Saggi, who stresses the inconsistencies of Caioli's work.

13. One example is Corsini's supposed peace mission to Bologna, which Caraffa treats as fact but Saggi doubts. Moreover, Caraffa believes that a *Vita* written by Coluccio Salutati was the model for the present *Vita.* On the other hand, Saggi did not check various episodes of Andrea's episcopate, as related in the *Vita.* See "De Sancto Andrea Corsino, episcopo faesulano, ordinis carmelitarum," in *Acta Sanctorum,* 3d ed., vol. 3 (Paris, 1863), 677, par. 8; "Vita. Auctore Petro Andree de Castaneis" [henceforth *Vita*], ibid., 686, par. 35; Caraffa, "Andrea Corsini," col. 1162; Saggi, "Andrea Corsini," 89–90; Caioli, "S. Andrea Corsini," 123–24, and 119–20.

14. See Saggi, "Andrea Corsini," 91.

15. Petrucci, *Il libro di ricordanze dei Corsini,* 94.

the first references to his sanctity appears in *Catalogum sanctorum carmelitarum* from the end of the fourteenth century.[16] Apart from this source, which also contains information on his episcopate, his death, and his miracles, along with a transcription of his burial inscription (made in 1385), the first true *Vita* was written after 1440 and is attributed to the Carmelite Pietro di Andrea del Castagni,[17] who was called to preach on Corsini immediately after the battle of Anghiari.[18]

The attribution of this *Vita* is in doubt, supported only by an ambiguous affirmation within the text.[19] The only criterion for the date of the *Vita* comes from an analysis of its internal elements: an obvious *post quem* is given by the battle of Anghiari (1440), since the *Vita* describes a miracle connected with that event. And, since the ceremonial form of thanks for the miracle of Anghiari that it describes changed in 1466, the *Vita* must have been written before that date.[20] The Bollandists even thought that the *Vita* may have been written by Coluccio Salutati,[21] but

---

16. See Saggi, "Andrea Corsini," 90, 92.

17. The manuscript is conserved in the Biblioteca Vaticana (*Vat. Lat.*, 3813, ff. 28v–47v), published for the first time together with the acts of canonization by the Carmelite Domenico di Gesù in 1638, nine years after Andrea became a saint ("Vita beati Andreae de Corsinis," in *Acta canonizationis Sancti Andreae Corsini* [Paris, 1638], 171–244). Domenico di Gesù, however, did not publish the *Vita* directly from the manuscript but used a copy furnished by a French Carmelite. The Bollandists reprinted that edition, only adding an introduction ("De Sancto Andrea Corsino," 676–92). A comparison with the manuscript shows not only modifications such as improvements in the Latin but also the substance of the text (see Saggi, "Andrea Corsini," 90). For now, the *Vita* in the *Acta Sanctorum* remains the most recent edition (cf. *Bibliotheca Hagiographica Latina Antiquae et Mediae Aetatis*, 2 vols. (Bruxelles, 1898–1901) [anast. reprint 1949; new suppl., ed. by H. Fros, 1986]: 1:74, n.445). Beyond the *Vita* attributed to Del Castagno, there exists another anonymous *Vita*, which was published together with the first by the Bollandists ("Alia vita incerto auctore," in "De Sancto Andrea Corsino," 688–92). This second *Vita* is largely a summary of the first one.

18. *Vita*, 686, pars. 35–36.

19. The Bollandists cite the opinion of Domenico di Gesù, who maintains that a passage in the *Vita* expresses modesty and in effect desires to indicate the author's name ("De Sancto Andrea Corsino," 676, par. 7). But this is difficult to justify since in other places the author refers to himself in the first person singular: (*Vita*, pars. 35, 36, 44, and 46). Such observations are found also in Saggi, "Andrea Corsini," 90. The attribution is also taken as given, without considering these contradictions, in the recent biographical note of R. Zaccaria ("Del Castagno, Piero," in *Dizionario biografico degli italiani*, vol. 36, [Rome, 1988], 446–47), which has the merit of adding many new biographical elements.

20. "De Sancto Andrea Corsino," 677, par. 7; and G. Richa, *Notizie istoriche delle chiese fiorentine*, vol. 10 (Florence, 1754–62), 81.

21. "De Sancto Andrea Corsino," 677, par. 8; see also n.13.

this seems truly a fantasy defied by the tone and style of the work. On the other hand, according to the recent research of Luisa Miglio,[22] it might be justifiable to attribute the tombstone inscription (1385) to Salutati, whose text is cited in the *Vita* and could have served to enrich the hagiography.

In conclusion, we are not certain who the author of this source may have been. Moreover, given that the last miracles may have been added later,[23] more than one author might have written it. If we disregard these doubts and lacunae, we can say with great probability that the *Vita* was conceived in the ambience of the Carmelites. In character with this kind of source, its purpose was celebratory and moralistic, going beyond biographical facts.

Despite the fact that the *Vita* was written relatively late for its genre, and despite the nearness in time between the text and its subject (the saint), most of it is far from being historically demonstrated. Apart from the date of death, the episode of the translation of his corpse (confirmed by other sources), and the reference to the battle of Anghiari, little else appears accurate. For example, the name of his mother, the form of his episcopal nomination, the date of the beginning of his episcopate, and the episodes connected to his supposed sojourn as a student in France are all inventions.[24] Indeed, a good part of the rest appears as a cornucopia of *topoi* from traditional hagiography.[25]

But, apart from this blind following of hagiographic sources, it is useful to pose a series of questions: to what extent does the *Vita* derive from the hagiographer's desire to produce an image of pure sanctity? Or, to what extent does it come from an oral tradition and reflect what people wished to hear about the saint? What lines of argument were followed in the trial of his confirmation of sainthood? Here, to grasp its entirety, we must entertain the major posthumous event in the life of Andrea Corsini, his intervention in the battle of Anghiari.

The principal reason not only why Andrea was canonized but why he rose to the same level as other traditional patron saints of the city is the episode of 1440. Until that date Andrea was not a particularly important saint. In the absence of official canonization, he was no more than a

---

22. L. Miglio, "Un nome per tre epitaffi: Coluccio Salutati e gli elogi funebri dei Corsini," *Italia medievale e umanistica*, 26 (1983): 361–74.

23. "De Sancto Andrea Corsino," 677, par. 8.

24. Saggi, "Andrea Corsini," 91.

25. These will be examined in detail in my critical edition of his *Vita*.

beato (blessed one). But what happened next was crucial for his celestial career. By chance another source other than the *Vita* survives, which sheds further light on the episode. This is a diary containing annotations on the prophecies of Andrea, written, as far as we can tell, by the protagonist of the event himself, the young man to whom Andrea appeared.

The annotations on these visions are contained in a diary compiled by a young Florentine, Giovanni Dazzi.[26] We do not possess the original manuscript, but we draw our information from two copies: an almost contemporary copy by Sandro di Piero di Lotteringo[27] and a seventeenth-century manuscript whose copyist must have seen the original in the library of Bernado Mazzinghi.[28] In the diary, which begins with the usual invocation for Florentine *ricordanze* of the period,[29] the young man describes his experience beginning with his first "encounters" with the future saint. On 21 April 1440 (about two months before the battle) Giovanni, who was praying alone in the church of the Carmine, saw the blessed one emerge from his grave and kneel at the foot of the crucifix.

---

26. We owe the attribution of the name to D. M. Manni, *Osservazioni istoriche sopra i sigilli antichi*, vol. 11 (Florence, 1739–82), 135, when referring to the seal of the Dazzi family. However, it remains unclear why Manni's Dazzi is named Giovanni di Dino, while the author of the manuscript is called Giovanni di Andrea (unless Dino is taken as the diminutive of Andrea) and his family name is not specified.

27. Biblioteca Riccardiana di Firenze, *Riccardiano*, 2729, fols. 11r–14r. From the codex, formerly, O.III.XVIII, Lama has transcribed the diary in its entirety (G. Lami, *Catalogus Codicorum Manoscriptorum qui in Bibliotheca Riccardiana Florentiae adservantur* [Liburni, 1756], 213–15). Also, Richa (*Notizie istoriche*, 10:72–80) reproduces Lami's transcription. Sandro di Piero di Lotteringo's copy, taken from the Strozziano transcription, contains, in addition, the dates for nearly all of the events announced in the prophecies. While the Strozziano copyist seems to have used the original manuscript, the Riccardiano copyist seems either not to have known how to interpret it correctly or to have used a defective copy, since it contains clear errors in meaning lacking in the seventeenth-century copy. For the following citations we will use the Lami edition.

28. Cf. Biblioteca Nazionale Centrale di Firenze (henceforth: BNCF), *Magliabechiano*, cl. XXXVIII, 116 (formerly *Strozziano*, f., 1024, with an earlier classification "FH" used by Manni [cf. note 26]). It is a miscellaneous volume containing notes on Andrea Corsini, also cited by Caioli. The transcription of Dazzi's diary goes from fol. 44r to fol. 47v.

29. "In the name of God the Father and Lord, and of the Glorious Madonna Saint Mary, and of the glorious Messer Santo Andrea, bishop of Fiesole and Florentine citizen, and of the house of the Corsini, and generally of the entire celestial court of Paradise, who have given me grace that I might write in honor of the holy Faith of Christ. I Giovanni d'Andrea. . . . make remembrance of that which I have received from Beato Andrea, and what, when, and why, or in what country, beginning today on the thirtieth of April 1440, as it is the truth" (Lami, *Catalogus*, 213).

Accompanied by another monk,[30] Andrea prayed and wept. When the young man asked him what he was doing, the blessed one responded: "You know, that I pray for this city, which is in great trouble, but in the end it will achieve victory. Tell what you have seen to the Eight, and then to the friars." Thus, Andrea gave the young Dazzi information to use as proof of his vision: "Give them this sign: say that I was facing the outside and now I am facing the choir." The young man decided to say nothing about this to anyone, but in a few days fell ill and became paralyzed in the legs. His friends carried him to the church of the Carmine, where he told the story to the superior and suddenly was healed. Then, on 29 April, he went to the Eight (actually the Ten of the Balía),[31] who followed him to the church and checked the position of the saint's body in his grave. The day after, the blessed one again appeared to Giovanni inside the church, and it happened again five days later. Andrea predicted to the young Dazzi that the Florentines "will be out of this [trouble] entirely by June 1440." A week later, Giovanni again met the blessed one in the piazza in front of the church "with a great multitude of armed men." Giovanni asked what this signified, and Andrea responded, "they have come to guard the city." Dazzi followed him, while in the piazza della Signoria they were joined by St. John the Baptist and in the piazza of S. Reparata (today the piazza del Duomo) they met St. Peter and San Zanobi, who were leaving the cathedral. "And I asked: 'What is the meaning of this armed body of men?' He responded: 'They are going to put an end to this trouble.'" Two weeks later the saint ordered the city to organize a procession and show his body to the people. According to Dazzi, the Pope did not want to grant permission for this, and only upon the insistence of the blessed one, and Dazzi to the Signoria, which in turn solicited the Pope, did he consent.

On 6 June, Andrea predicted two victories: one in Lombardy on 19 June and the other at Anghiari on the twenty-ninth. The first battle indeed happened, but the victory was not yet decisive.[32] On the twenty-fourth, Andrea declared again that "a great victory would come," which the Eight would know of before it left, that is, before it left office. The prophecy was realized, unlike the other prophecies Giovanni asserted

---

30. Probably Angelino, another Carmelite *beato* (cf. Richa, *Notizie istoriche,* 10:72).

31. See the *Provvisione* of 13 June 1466 (see n. 64), which mentions the Dieci.

32. See D. Buoninsegni, *Storie della città di Firenze dall'anno 1410 al 1460* (Florence, 1637), 75; Sozomeno of Pistoia, *Chronicon Universale,* ed. G. Zaccagnini, *Rerum Italicarum Scriptores,* n.s., 16.1 (Città di Castello, 1908).

had been revealed to him by the blessed one concerning the destiny of Florence and Italy in the years to come.[33]

We can see Andrea's involvement in the battle of Anghiari from several points of view. In the first place, as Anna Benvenuti Papi has maintained, it was principally a "hagiographical operation."[34] In the episode one can discern above all an attempt on the part of the bishopric to restore its sacred character. One of its principal promoters was certainly Lodovico Scarampi, archbishop of Florence just before the battle of Anghiari, who in 1439 had organized the solemn translation of the relics of the ancient bishop and patron of Florence, San Zanobi,[35] and who had even participated as a military leader at the triumph of the Florentine and papal forces against the Milanese at Anghiari, even though he was now no longer dressed as an archbishop.[36]

For a long time the venerable patron saints of many Italian city-states were ancient bishops, who, after the success of episcopal authority, substituted ancient martyrs or saints in the role of protector of the city from external threats, a power attributed in classical times to the tomb of the hero.[37] But if the ancient patron-bishop was no longer deemed capable of responding to this need, it would be necessary to find another. At this moment, when the city was fighting a difficult war, an occasion for filling the role was offered by the presence of the blessed Andrea Corsini: a bishop with unmistakable odor of sanctity, he was a Florentine citizen whose body already rested within the city walls. An intervention such as the one attributed to Andrea by the young Dazzi was the only link needed to promote him to the rank of saint.

Naturally, the operation could be remunerative also for the future saint's family, the Corsini, who, while still important within the Florentine oligarchy, were undergoing a relative decline in political life.[38] In addition, the desire of the Carmelite order to obtain an official saint played an important role.[39]

33. Lami, *Catalogus*, 215.
34. Benvenuti Papi, "San Zanobi," 153.
35. Ibid., 127, 149.
36. Bartolomeo Zabarella had followed him as archbishop. See R. Bizzocchi, *Chiesa e potere nella Toscana del Quattrocento* (Bologna, 1987), 208.
37. Cf. S. Bertelli, *Il potere oligarchico nello stato-città medievale* (Florence, 1978), 152.
38. Benvenuti Papi, "San Zanobi," 148, 153.
39. As Anna Benvenuti Papi has suggested, it would be valuable to analyze the influence of the rules of the mendicant orders on Quattrocento Florentine models of sanctity (Corsini, Dalle Celle, Dominici, Antonino, etc.).

However, we must remember that such operations should not be seen as coming solely from above. The political-institutional context is obviously important, but episodes such as the miracle of Anghiari also express other values. In its "coda,"[40] the *Vita* describes 10 miracles, all but 2 concern healing by the saint: an intervention in favor of a priest opposed by his parishioners and the punishment of a skeptic. Rather than lacking specificity, as is often the case in these narratives, these incidents are placed in precise urban settings, showing characteristics that are distinct from the other miracles contained in the *Vita*. The 8 miracles of this sort occur between 1439 and 1440. According to the *Vita*'s author, all were certified by a notary.[41] All occurred around the grave of Andrea in the church of the Carmine, and most concerned parishioners of San Frediano. The fantasies and inaccuracies found in the *Vita* might also lead a reader to consider this notarial intervention in the sacred sphere as a last attempt to augment the credibility of the narrative, which would have been entrusted to the faithful. The fact is that, of the two notaries cited as having redacted the described episodes, the books (*imbreviature*) of one do not survive.[42] For the other they correspond almost exactly (with several errors in the interpretation of the text) to what is reported in the *Vita*.[43] Obviously, the notary was not present at the miracle (that would have been treated with suspicion); rather he was the functionary who confirmed the *publicam fidem* of the episodes that their protagonists related. This shows the relationship between the Florentines and the notary (who was called even in cases with only a strictly religious connection). It also shows their relationship with faith itself and the social context in which it was manifested.

These notarial acts express the fulfillment of a series of needs. (On the basis of the second notarial act, we can assume that the first one corresponds with the narrative in the *Vita*.) The first of these needs is confined to the ecclesiastical world, certifying the veracity of the miracle to confirm a burgeoning cult and for later use in the canonization of the saint. In the dynamic of the miracles, the narrative, however, expresses

40. *Vita*, 687–88, pars. 37–46 (which could also be a later addition).

41. *Vita*, 688, pars. 44 and 46.

42. The notary is Domenico di Amedeo di Francesco (o Franceschi), several of whose *imbreviature* appear among those of Bartolomeo di Lorenzo di Iacopo Adami (Archivio di Stato di Firenze [henceforth ASF], *Notarile antecosimiano*, 81 [formerly A 81]), but not for the year that interests us, 1439).

43. ASF, *Notarile antecosimiano*, 16201 [formerly P 128], ser Paolo di ser Lorenzo Paoli, fol. 50.

other needs of the laity, who were either its protagonists or gave testimony: the need for those who had witnessed the miracle not to be considered daydreamers (confirming the incredulity even in this type of society, which also resonates in the story of the skeptic who is punished);[44] the need on the part of the laity to confirm the dignity of the saint in whom they already believe (certainly also tied to the clergy's interests);[45] and the need on the part of the community of the faithful to have a saint who was a "neighbor," who was venerated in the church of their community, and who belonged to that community historically.

In the dynamic of miracles, other phenomena are expressed—for example, the influence of preaching (also beyond the city walls of Florence) on the diffusion of these forms of devotion. Two of the miraculous cures came from the Florentine *contado* (Prato and Capalle), and both were moved to visit the church of the Carmine in Florence by sermons that described the saint's virtues.[46] It would be possible to cite further examples: starting with these testimonies one could attempt to follow the ways in which the cult was diffused and its connections with the laity. By establishing a comparison with other hagiographical stories it would also be interesting to discover at what times the miraculously healed sought the intervention of a notary (where, how, and why) and to try to make broader generalizations than is possible from this small sample. In the economy of our discourse, the miracles of 1439–40 help to classify Dazzi's vision of the battle of Anghiari as well as the later promotion of the citizen saint, Andrea Corsini.

The vision of Dazzi has two elements in common with the notarized episodes, the place where miracles are performed and the origins of the protagonist. At this time at least in the parish of San Frediano, it was certainly an expression of an already existing devotion.[47] Unlike the other miracles the vision lacks testimony, and it is placed on a higher plane—not having received individual grace but announcing a collective one. Evidently at the moment when the episode occurred the time was ripe, not only at the political-institutional level but also in terms of the collective consciousness, for Corsini's promotion. And the vision of the young

---

44. *Vita*, 687, par. 42.

45. Also present at the redaction of the notarial act by Paoli is the Carmelite friar Filippo di Tommaso, to whom the woman who was the object of a miracle first turned. Perhaps it was this friar who suggested that a notary record the act.

46. ASF, *Notarile antecosimiano*, 16201, fol. 50; *Vita*, 688, pars. 45 and 46.

47. In the miracles of 1439, artisans and their wives or widows are often present and almost all belong to the parish of San Frediano (cf. *Vita*, 687–88, pars. 39–43).

Dazzi expressed it well in a fashion that articulated certain forms of consciousness. Certainly, this does not mean that Dazzi's vision is the only
way to imagine a citizen-saint within an entire city or a group of people.
But, undoubtedly it reflects one possibility, sufficiently diffused to sanction such a phenomenon in a public manner, as we will see.

In Dazzi's account the saint is so much the *urbis custos,* that he can
observe the armed troops around the city and where he meets his colleagues in this role, St. John the Baptist, Bishop Zanobi, and St. Peter.
Before this date, the cult of the apostle is not present in these Florentine
civic traditions, but the reason St. Peter is placed here is his tie to the
battle of Anghiari. The Florentines won the battle on 29 June, that is,
on the feast day of Saints Peter and Paul, and, as has been emphasized,
"segments of time were sacred to certain powers." Not only is every
day of the year associated with a saint, but when the causes of fortunate events for the commune are searched, it was usually a saint's day
that won the palm.[48] Thus, Dazzi recognized the role of Peter as patron
and protector at the moment when his name was tied to the Florentine
victory.

There are many precedents for celebrating a saint because an important victory occurred on that patron's feast day. The Florentine victory
over the Aretines at Campaldino in 1289 caused the Florentines to celebrate the feast of San Barnaba. For the same reason the feast of St.
Augustine began to be celebrated publicly in Santo Spirito after the victory at Mantua against Gian Galeazzo in 1397.[49] But there is a precedent
also for the specific role played by Andrea in this miracle. Because of his
name, St. Victor was chosen from among the four saints honored in the
church on the day of the Florentine victory over the Pisans at Cascina
(1364). It is this episode that furnished the closest model for Dazzi's
vision. On this occasion the blessed Paula, a Camaldolese nun, was
brought "in spirit" to the door of San Frediano[50] when the Florentine
troops were leaving for battle; she witnessed St. John the Baptist blessing
the troops.[51]

---

48. R. C. Trexler, "Ritual Behavior in Renaissance Florence: the Setting,"
Medievalia et Humanistica, n.s., 4 (1973): 134.
49. U. Dorini, "Il culto delle memorie patrie nella Repubblica di Firenze,"
Rassegna nazionale, 179 (1911): 15, 18.
50. Perhaps this coincidence of many episodes of mysticism in the same parish is
no accident.
51. Dorini, "Il culto delle memorie patrie," 15–16.

If we return from Dazzi's vision to the account of the battle, we find another strange coincidence. By an unknown witness Andrea is seen riding with his hand on a "baculum," which could be the pastoral rod but here has the function of the baton of war, which he uses to lead his troops against the enemy.[52] This behavior cannot be ascribed to his role as a bishop, given that Andrea was not a "war bishop," as certain "count-bishops" of the preceding period were. But two points are relevant here. On one side of the episode at Anghiari we find the presence of another militant prelate, the former bishop Ludovico Scarampi, whose "ideological" role in this affair has already been noted (and who may have had some direct responsibility for the elaboration of these ideas) and whose mere presence in the battle might have stimulated the fantasies of the presumed witnesses.[53] On the other side there is another precedent for the episode, this time drawn from Milanese history. A century earlier, in 1339, St. Ambrose had been the protagonist of the battle of Parabiago, where Luchino Visconti defeated Lodrisio. Ambrose has been portrayed "on horseback" with his hand on a *scutica* or *flagellum,* caught in the heat of battle, his white robe blowing in the wind.[54]

Probably the Florentines, just at the moment when they were confronting yet again their ancient and hated enemy, felt the need to juxtapose their bishop-saint to the Milanese one and assign to Andrea a similar attitude.[55] Why was the role not assigned to Zanobi, who corresponds more closely with Ambrose? An answer might be that Zanobi, even though he was the patron of the episcopal see, was seen as a communal patron relatively late, since he belonged to the Girolami family, which was considered even at the end of the Trecento to be "entirely Ghibelline."[56] Florence needed a new patron, a new bishop, closer to the Florentines than was Zanobi, both in time and in politics.

---

52. Cf. *Vita,* 686, par. 34: "Several devout ones either engaged in battle or nearby confessed to have seen in the air a bishop dressed in white on horseback with a baton in his hand, leading an infinite number of armed men against our enemies . . ."

53. See nn. 37–38.

54. Bertelli, *Il potere oligarchico,* 152. On a still more ancient tradition of a saint with nonmilitary attributes who on horseback leads troops against the enemy, see F. Cardini, *Alle radici della cavalleria medievale* (Florence, 1981), 308–9.

55. After all, Andrea was their citizen, even if he had been bishop of Fiesole. But Fiesole, the first diocese, represented somehow the ancient spirit of Florence.

56. Trexler, *Public Life in Renaissance Florence* (New York, 1980), 1–2; A. Molho and F. Sznura, eds. *Alle bocche della piazza. Diario di anonimo fiorentino (1382–1401),* (Florence, 1986), 140 (a. 1392).

It is clear that the civil as well as the religious powers had every opportunity to take advantage of this episode. We must not forget that even the informal recognition by the Pope of Andrea's sanctity, which he admitted in the victory celebration with a specific reference to Andrea's prophecy, was strongly influenced by the fact that Filippo Maria Visconti was not only the enemy of Florence but also of the Papal States.[57] But it would be anachronistic to see in the behavior of the past only that which is congruent with our attitudes today. At least, we should not think of Andrea's prophecy about Anghiari as simply a ploy orchestrated on high. We must conclude that this episode expresses needs and projections authentically belonging to the contemporary Florentine imagination. Thus, if we wish to obtain a full vision of the episode, both levels must be seen as closely linked.

To give an idea of what a similar episode could represent—beyond the expression of diffused consciousness—as the product of the mixture of civic and religious values, of preoccupations from above as well as from below, it is useful to note the official consequences of the event.

Eight days after the battle, with a text clearly spelling out their motivations,[58] the colleges and the lords decided to make offerings to the churches of San Pier Maggiore and San Paolo every twenty-ninth of June in memory of the grace they had received for the victory of Anghiari. At communal expense, they decided to dress 20 poor to march in a procession on that day from the piazza dei Signori to San Pier Maggiore, to listen to mass, and to wear white for eight days afterward. Fifteen days later, they decided also to bless the commune of Anghiari, in memory of the victory,[59] by granting them exemptions from every form of tax and *gabelle*[60] for 10 years and instituting there a fair on the twenty-ninth of June. No mention, however, was made of Andrea Corsini.

---

57. Eugenio IV was allied with Venice, Florence, Genoa, René of Anjou, and Francesco Sforza against Filippo Maria Visconti and Alfonso d'Aragona. Cf. *Vita*, 685, par. 33 (". . . the plundering enemy of the Church and the Florentines").

58. ASF, *Provvisioni (registri)*, 131, fols. 126r–127r (6 July 1440): "no iunii proximi preteriti, videlicet die solemnitatis beatissimorum Apostolorum Petri et Pauli. . . . Dei benignitate, orationibus ipsibus principibus apostolorum, virtutibus et opera tam commissariorum quam militum nostrorum et Ecclesie, hostes . . . omnes devicti sunt . . . providerunt . . ." (fol. 126r).

59. ASF, *Provvisioni (registri)*, 131, fols. 132v–134r (21 July 1440).

60. The following payments were, however, excluded from the exemptions: the "cavalcate" and military supply; the gate *gabelles*; the rectors' salaries; the offering of wax for the feast of San Giovanni; maintenance of roofs, wells, and ovens; the breaking of ground for new barracks in Anghiari; that which was owed for the Catasto, and the salt *gabelle*.

Only two weeks later (a month after the battle), "iustis causis moti," as the Signoria affirmed following the reports of Tuccio di Marabottino Manetti and Orsino di Lanfredino Lanfredini, the Signoria decided that along with the Six of the Mercanzia and the captains of the guilds, they should come to the church of the Carmine to make an offering every year on the second Sunday of June.[61]

The celebrations for the twenty-ninth of June before the church of San Pier Maggiore were never interrupted during the Republican period, and were preserved for a long time afterward. They became the occasion for the celebration of a *palio* (horserace).[62] On the other hand, the procession in honor of Andrea Corsini was occurring irregularly as early as 1458 and ended definitively in 1461.[63] However, in June 1466, two months before the antimedicean conspiracy of Dietisalvi Neroni, the traditional celebration in honor of Andrea Corsini was temporarily revived, though in modified form; the offering was made at the church of San Pier Maggiore in a fashion that would benefit the friars of the Carmine as well.[64]

What had happened? On the one hand, in February 1461, the Signoria was constrained from taking part in any celebrations, which had become a burden on the state and posed a more than negligible expense. Of the roughly 60 festivals and more than 80 solemn offerings reported by a special commission elected for this purpose,[65] only 31 festivals remained, and the offerings were cut in half. Of those tied to important events for the history of the city, only San Barnaba, Sts. Peter and Paul, St. Anna, St. Victor, S. Reparata, and S. Diongi were allowed to remain.[66] After this date, the offering to the Carmine disappeared forever (it was already missing on the list redacted by this special commission). On the other hand, despite the fact that one of their members had been archbishop of Florence between 1411 and 1435, participation in politics by the Corsini family had been on the decline. Yet they appear to have

---

61. ASF, *Provvisioni (registri)*, 131, fol. 147 (4 August 1440).

62. Dorini, "Il culto delle memorie patrie," 18.

63. We cite from the Strozziano apograph, which was used also by Caioli (p. xxiii). See BNCF, *Magliabechiano*, cl. XXXVIII, 116, fol. 88.

64. ASF, *Provvisioni (registri)*, 157, fols. 63v–65v (13 June 1466). The provision has also been transcribed by Caioli (*S. Andrea Corsini*, 253–58).

65. Dorini, "Il culto delle memorie patrie," 21–22; ASF, *Signori e collegi (speciale autorità)*, 32, fols. 161r–163r (29 October 1460); *Provvisioni (registri)*, 151, fols. 355v–357r (6 February 1460–61).

66. Dorini, "Il culto delle memorie patrie," 21–22.

enjoyed a relative improvement in their political lot during this period.[67] Moreover, in the years following the provision of 1461, the Carmelites (who missed both the economic benefit and the honor that they had derived from the ceremony) almost surely exerted pressure to receive some compensation for their absence on this list of official celebrations.

It thus does not appear to be an accident that on the occasion of Paul II's ascension to the papacy, on October of that year, the Signoria sent instructions to their ambassadors at the Holy See with a note regarding "the friars and friary of the Carmine" with "the desire of canonizing a bishop of Fiesole for whom there is great devotion . . . and thus beseech your Sanctity to fulfill their desire."[68]

While we cannot check the letters of the Signori for the following six weeks,[69] in the same period various other letters deal with this subject. In December 1465, there was one letter to the Pope and another to various cardinals.[70] The second mentioned a gathering of the faithful around the grave of Andrea, the miracles attributed to him, and even the recognition given to them by Eugene IV. Similar letters were sent on 15 February 1465–66[71] and 9 May 1466,[72] and we know of still others that were written in November to the cardinal of Rouen and in June 1467 to the Pope and the College of Cardinals.[73] It is interesting to note that instructions analogous to those of 1464 were given to Matteo Palmieri, an ambassador to the papacy, on 6 June 1466, a week before the last of the cited provisions was promulgated, and to ambassadors Lorenzo Ridolfi and Giovanni Canigiani on 3 September 1466.[74] Meanwhile, the Corsini

---

67. Benvenuti Papi, "Pastori di popolo," 148, 153. After three *gonfalonieri* of Justice (1408, 1412, 1417), the Corsini had others, in 1445, 1467, and 1491 (cf. ASF, *Manoscritti*, 248 [*Priorista Mariani*, vol. 1], fols. 211v–214r.

68. ASF, *Legazioni e commissarie*, 15, fols. 125r–128r: 127r.

69. The register containing them no longer survives, while *filza* 44 in the fund *Signori, Missive, I Cancelleria* ends on 15 September 1464, and note 45 begins on 20 April 1465.

70. To the cardinals of Avignon, Spoleto, Nice, Rouen, Teano, Pavia, to the Florentines Antonio degli Agli, future bishop of Fiesole, and to Leonardo Dati, general of the Dominican order (ASF, *Signori, Missive, I Cancelleria*, 45, fols. 47, 49r).

71. To the Pope and the same group of clerics (ASF, *Signori, Missive, I Cancelleria*, 45, fol. 58).

72. To the Pope and the College of Cardinals and to the three cardinals charged with the canonization proceedings (ASF, *Signori, Missive, I Cancelleria*, 45, fols. 73–75).

73. Ibid., fols. 114r, 162v.

74. BNCF, *Magliabechiano*, cl. XXXVIII, 116, fol. 112v.

298 Portraits of Medieval and Renaissance Living

received two important appointments in a short span of time: one was elected to the Balìa in September 1466, and another was elected *gonfaloniere* of Justice for the last two months of 1467.[75]

Apart from the rhetoric, that which is affirmed in several of the letters to cardinals is also significant: "Daily people gather continually at the place where the relics of his corpse are buried"; and "Nothing satisfies the desires of our people: it is incredible to say how many solicitations we receive."[76] Certainly, Andrea had not yet been canonized, and in the spirit of the provision of 1461 the offerings to the Carmine had to be interrupted, from which time it lacked public honors for several years. But, it is significant that the Florentine government, after years of neglect, suddenly experienced an overflow of civic spirit centered around the figure of Andrea Corsini when a series of factors converged,[77] among which was certainly that of popular devotion and the consciousness of the luster that would come to the city through the recognition of a new citizen-saint. Quickly the Florentine government satisfied at least the most immediate desires of the Carmelites with the correction of the provision of 1440.[78] But for the rest it would take a long time, and it was not enough that the affair should be remembered again with the succession of Paul II.[79] It would take a different dynastic, political, and diplomatic context, and a major appearance of the Corsini family at the papal Curia, to finalize the issue of his sainthood, but before that occurred a century and a half would pass.[80]

---

75. BNCF, Conventi soppressi, C.4.895 (S. Maria Novella), fol. 191v (Priorista Petriboni); and N. Rubinstein, The Government of Florence under the Medici, 1434 to 1494 (Oxford, 1966), 293.

76. ASF, *Signori, Missive, I Cancelleria*, 45, fols. 49r, 73.

77. These included renewed pressure from the Carmelites and the presence of possibly a more powerful Corsini family in Florentine public life.

78. See n. 64.

79. Caioli, *S. Andrea Corsini*, 175–76.

80. Andrea Corsini was canonized by Urban VIII in 1629. Clement VIII had already begun the process of canonization, requested, above all, by Henry IV of France, the husband of Maria de' Medici, and by Ferdinando I de' Medici, grand duke of Tuscany, but the process was interrupted by the death of the Pope in 1605. It was pursued by Paul V but was again interrupted by his death in 1621. After Gregory XV, Pope for only two years, Urban VIII (1623) was again met with requests from Maria de' Medici, now queen of France, Ferdinando II, grand duke of Tuscany, and other high prelates of the Corsini family (Caioli, *S. Andrea Corsini*, 177–78).

Part 3
Power and Patronage in the Middle Ages and the Renaissance: Social History in Town and Countryside

Was There a Medieval Middle Class? *Mediocres* (*mediani, medii*) in the Middle Ages

Giles Constable

It is often said that there were no social classes and no class consciousness in the Middle Ages. "Any attempt to divide people of these older societies into classes," wrote Peter Munz, "let alone to ascribe class consciousness to them, is not to understand them as they understood themselves."[1] By

---

A version of this essay was published as an appendix to my *Three Studies in Medieval Religious and Social Thought* (Cambridge, 1995), 342–60. For help in writing it I am indebted particularly to Paul Meyvaert and Walter Simons. The following abbreviations will be used.

Büchner	Rudolf Büchner, *Die Rechtsquellen* (*Beiheft* to Wattenbach-Levison [see below]; Weimar, 1953).
CC	*Corpus Christianorum.*
CC:CM	*Corpus Christianorum: Continuatio mediaeualis.*
MGH	*Monumenta Germaniae historica.*
PG	*Patrologia graeca.*
PL	*Patrologia latina.*
Wattenbach-Holtzmann	Wilhelm Wattenbach, *Deutschlands Geschichts-quellen im Mittelalter. Deutsche Kaiserzeit,* ed. Robert Holtzmann (Tübingen, 1948).
Wattenbach-Levison	Wilhelm Wattenbach, *Deutschlands Geschichts-quellen im Mittelalter. Vorzeit und Karolinger,* ed. Wilhelm Levison (Weimar, 1952–73).

1. Peter Munz, "History and Sociology," in *Gesellschaft-Kultur-Literatur . . . Beiträge Luitpold Wallach gewidmet,* ed. Karl Bosl, Monographien zur Geschichte des Mittelalters, no. 11 (Stuttgart, 1975), 15. On the inadequacy of the concept of class in the Middle Ages, see Alexander Murray, *Reason and Society in the Middle Ages* (Oxford, 1978), 14–17; and Jacques Heers, *Le Moyen, une imposture* (Paris, 1992), 182–211, esp. 183, 211. On the lack of a term for class, see J. Batany, "Le vocabulaire des catégories sociales chez quelques moralistes français vers 1200," in *Ordres et classes. Colloque d'histoire sociale, Saint-Cloud, 24–25 mai 1967,* ed. D. Roche and C. E. Labrousse, Congrès et Colloques, no. 12 (Paris and The Hague, 1973), 61–62; and J. Batany, P. Contamine, B. Guenée, and J. Le Goff, "Plan pour l'étude historique du vocabulaire social de l'Occident médiéval," *Ordres et classes,* 87.

definition, therefore, no middle class existed in the sense that it is understood today, when 80 percent of the people in industrialized societies are said to see themselves as members of the middle class. Yet the term *class* was occasionally used in a social sense in the Middle Ages, as when William of Tyre, referring to 1153–54, said that "In these dangerous times many from other peoples, both nobles and men of the second class [*secunde classis*] came together";[2] and there were many references to people called *mediocres,* or more rarely *mediani* or *medii.* In the tripartite divisions of society in the Middle Ages, some categories were seen as in the middle between two others, either above and below or, as it was sometimes put, on the left and right or between first and third. It is the purpose of this essay to study these people and the categories to which they belonged.[3]

The term *mediocris* was used in various types of works in late antiquity. In the Theodosian Code it appeared in edicts and decrees dealing with taxes and had a primarily economic meaning. The *mediocres* were contrasted with the *potiores* in 324, with the *ditiores* and *infimi* in 328, and with the *opulentes* in 400 and 405. In 417, tax relief on abandoned lands was granted only on lands "of which the lords do not exist or are *mediocres* in poverty and are shown to have only those lands."[4] People of middling fortune were distinguished from the more noble in the Code of Justinian and a free man of middling place (*mediocris loci ingenuus*) from the lord of an estate.[5] These texts show that for lawyers and administrators in the fourth and fifth centuries *mediocris* was a recognized term for a person who was relatively far down, but well above the bottom of, the social and economic scale.

2. William of Tyre, *Chronicon,* XVIII, 5, in CC:CM, LXIIIA, 816.

3. *Mediocris* is translated here as "middling," *nobilis* as "noble," *ignobilis* as "non-noble," *pauper* as "poor" (see n. 48), *infimus* as "low," and *imus* as "humble." In Byzantine society, according to Alexander Kazhdan in *The Oxford Dictionary of Byzantium* (New York and Oxford, 1991), I, 468, "a third category of men of moderate means [*mesoi*]" was occasionally introduced between the "great" and "small" or the "powerful" and "poor." *Mediocritas mea* was used as a *Selbstverkleinerungsformel,* between *maiestas tua* and *parvitas mea,* in late antiquity and the early Middle Ages. See Ernst Robert Curtius, *Europäische Literatur und lateinisches Mittelalter* (Bonn, 1948), 92; and Tore Janson, *Latin Prose Prefaces,* Acta Universitatis Stockholmiensis: Studia Latina Stockholmiensia, no. 1, 13 (Stockholm, 1964), 125. Louis the Pious referred to himself as *nostra mediocritas* in MGH: *Capitularia,* I, 303, no. 150.

4. *Codex Theodosianus,* XI, 1, 27 (400 [405]); XI, 16, 3 (324); XI, 16, 4 (328); and XIII, 11, 15 (417); ed. Paul Krüger and Theodor Mommsen (Berlin, 1954), I.2, 577, 598, 769; trans. Clyde Pharr (Princeton, 1952), 294, 306, 404.

5. *Codex Justinianus,* II, 19, 11; XI, 54, 1, 1; and XII, 45, 1, 1, ed. Paul Krüger (Berlin, 1954), 109, 444, 478.

Among the Germans the *mediocres* seem to have had a somewhat higher status, though it is hard to be sure. In the laws of the Alemanni and Burgundians, according to Edgar McNeal, the *mediocres* and *mediani* were a class of landlords who usually held grants of land from the king,[6] and Heinrich Brunner studied their position on the basis of the differing wergilds found in the Germanic law codes.[7] There are references in the laws of the Visigoths, which date between the fifth and seventh centuries, to middling and first people and to laymen *sive sit nobilis, sive mediocrior vilisque persona,* where it is uncertain whether two ranks of nobles and low *mediocres* are intended or three ranks of nobles, more middling, and low.[8] In the early sixth-century laws of the Burgundians a middling person, free middling people, or "someone from the *mediocris populus*" ranked below the noble *optimates* and above the minor or inferior people,[9] and in the *Pactus Alamannorum,* which is now usually dated in the seventh century, the *medianus* ranked between the first, or *meliorissimus,* and the *minofledus.*[10] The term *mediocris,* or *medianus,* was not used in the Saxon or other Germanic law codes, where the upper ranks were called *nobiles* or *edhilingui,* the middle group *ingenui, ingenuiles, liberi,* or *frilingi,* and the lower ranks *liti, lazzi,* or *serviles.* Fleckenstein suggested that the free middle group was composed of low nobles, who were distinguished from the upper nobles by wealth and favor but not by law,[11] but the differences in punishments and wergilds

---

6. Edgar H. McNeal, *Minores and Mediocres in the Germanic Tribal Laws* (Columbus, 1905), esp. 124.

7. Heinrich Brunner, *Deutsche Rechtsgeschichte,* I, 2d ed., Systematisches Handbuch der deutschen Rechtswissenschaft, II, 1, 1 (Leipzig, 1906), 343.

8. *Lex Visigothorum,* IX, 2, 8; and XII, 2, 15, in *MGH: Leges nat. Germ.,* I.1, 371–72, 423. See also Büchner, 6–9.

9. *Leges Burgundionum,* II, 2; XXVI, 1–3; and CI, 1, in *MGH: Leges nat. Germ.,* I.2, 42, 63, 114, trans. Katherine Fischer Drew (Philadelphia, 1972), 23, 41, 85. See also Büchner, 10–12.

10. *Pactus Alamannorum,* Frag. 2, 36–38; Frag. 3, 21; and Frag. 5, 16, in *MGH: Leges nat. Germ.,* V.1, 23, 25, 32. Cf. the use of *medianus* (as contrasted with *summus* or *optimus*) for a horse and an ox in the *Leges Alamannorum,* A 63.2 and 71.2, B 70.4 and 78.2, in *MGH: Leges nat. Germ.,* 132, 137. See Büchner, 29–33, on the various dates proposed for the *Pactus.* On the *mediani* in Alamanic law, see Eberhard Otto, *Adel und Freiheit im deutschen Staat des frühen Mittelalters,* Neue deutsche Forschungen, Abteilung mittelalterliche Geschichte, no. 2 (Berlin, 1937), 151–55; and Josef Fleckenstein, "Die Entstehung des niederen Adels und das Rittertum," in his *Herrschaft und Stand* (Göttingen, 1977), 21.

11. Martin Linzel, "Die Stände der deutschen Volksrechte, hauptsächlich der Lex Saxonum" (1933), reprinted in his *Ausgewählte Schriften* (Berlin, 1961), 313; and Fleckenstein, "Entstehung," 21.

show that there were some clear legal distinctions between the three ranks.

The category *mediocris* was used more loosely in other late antique sources. Tertullian apparently had in mind both social and economic factors when he wrote that many women "who were both noble by family and blessed with property" married non-noble and middling men.[12] Julius Firmicus Maternus included several references to *mediocres* in his astrological work *Matheseos,* including one in which they were described as "middling in life and patrimony and behavior" and another in which they were defined as those "who neither abound in means nor are depressed by the lack of necessities, but to whom increases of means are granted with the passage of time."[13] This suggests that he regarded the *mediocres* as upwardly mobile people whose circumstances were improving. Dracontius, writing in Carthage in the late fifth century, however, ranked the *mediocris pauper* (which may mean either the moderately poor or the poor middling person) among the oppressed.[14] It is sometimes hard to tell whether *mediocris* referred to social status, economic resources, or physical stature, or whether it was a personal name, as in the case of John *mediocris,* the sixth-century bishop of Naples.[15]

Augustine included the *mediocres* with the common men, artisans, poor men, and beggars who, he said, together with great rich men, senators, and outstanding women, renounced their property during the persecutions.[16] *Divites pauperes mediocres* appear in the list of "all men to be saved" (1 Timothy 2:4) in the *Enchiridion,* which was reproduced in the *Chapters of St. Augustine* attributed to Johannes Maxentius.[17] Quodvultdeus, who was bishop of Carthage from 437 to 453, said that kings,

12. Tertullian, *Ad uxorem,* II, 8, 4, in CC, I, 392–93.

13. Julius Firmicus Maternus, *Matheseos,* III, 10, 8; III, 10, 10; III, 13, 10; and IV, 14, 17; ed. W. Kroll and F. Skutsch (Stuttgart, 1968), I, 173, 190, 230; trans. Jean Rhys Bram (Park Ridge, N.J., 1975), 107, 114, 132.

14. Dracontius, *Romulea,* V, 201, in MGH: *Auctores antiquissimi,* XIV, 145.

15. *Gesta episcoporum Neapolitanorum,* I, 16, in MGH: *Scriptores rerum Langobardicarum et Italicarum,* 410, and *Catalogus episcoporum Neapolitanorum,* in MGH: *Scriptores rerum Langobardicarum et Italicarum,* 436.

16. Augustine, *Sermones post Maurinos reperti,* ed. Germain Morin, Miscellanea Agostiniana, no. 1 (Rome, 1930), 85 (Denis XVII, 4). See also page 632 (Morin XI, 11), where Augustine referred to *homines mediocres et angusti.*

17. Augustine, *Enchiridion,* XXVII, 103, in CC, XLVI, 105; and pseudo-Johannes Maxentius, *Capitula sancti Augustini,* 18, in CC, LXXXVA, 270–71. The phrase, which is without punctuation or conjunctions, may mean either rich, poor, and middling men or rich men and poor middling men.

middling men, and poor men came together at Christ's table.[18] Julian of
Eclanum contrasted *mediocres* with rich men and included them with the
poor in his commentaries on Joel 1:5 and Amos 9:14,[19] and Leo I wrote
that "In the distribution of alms not only the rich and those with abundant supplies but also the middling people and poor should have their
shares."[20] Bishop Germanus of Auxerre, when he was traveling, "sub-
mitted to the hospitality of middling people," according to his *Life* by
Constantius, which was written about 480.[21]

Augustine also used *mediocris* in a moral sense in *Against Julian,*
where he described those who were in the middle between people who
were gentle by nature and those who were vengeful.[22] The later concept
of the *mediocriter boni* and *mali* who were punished in purgatory was
influenced by Augustine's description in the *Enchiridion* of the sacrifices
offered for the dead, which, he said, were actions of thanks for the very
good, propitiary offerings for the not very good (or not very bad in some
versions), and of no use to the very bad.[23] This passage, with "not very
bad," was included in the *Decretum* of Gratian, and was commented
upon by several Decretists, of whom some added a fourth category of not
very, or *mediocriter,* good, and in time the categories of moderately bad
and moderately good merged into a single moral middle category
between the good and the bad.[24]

18. Quodvultdeus of Carthage, *Liber promissionum*, III, 39, in CC, LX, 186.

19. Julian of Eclanum, *In Iohel*, I, 5; and *In Amos*, II, 14, in CC, LXXXVIII, 230, 329.

20. Leo I, *Tractatus 44*, in CC, CXXXVIIIA, 260.

21. Constantius, *Vita Germani episcopi Autissiodorensis*, 11, in *MGH: Scriptores rerum Merov.*, VII.1, 258. In the *Vita Bibiani vel Viviani episcopi Santonensis*, 4, in *MGH: Scriptores rerum Merov.*, III, 96, the author, writing in the late eighth or early ninth century (see p. 92), said that the Goths in around 460 desired the property of the *nobiles* of Saintes after they took the wealth of the *mediocres personae*. On this passage, see Walter Goffart, *Barbarians and Romans* A.D. *418–584* (Princeton, 1980), 96–97, who translated *nobiles* as "the well born" and *mediocres* as "ordinary men."

22. Augustine, *Contra Julianum*, IV, 16, in PL, XLIV, 745.

23. Augustine, *Enchiridion*, 110, in PL, XL, 283 (which has *non valde mali*) and CC, XLVI, 109 (which has *non valde boni* but no discussion of the variant).

24. Gratian, *Decretum*, C.XIII, q.2, c.23 (with *non valde mali*), ed. Emil Friedberg (Leipzig, 1879), 728. On the use of this text by the Decretists and its importance for the doctrine of purgatory, see Jacques Le Goff, *La naissance du purgatoire* (Paris, 1981), 307, and the unpublished paper by P. V. Aimone, "Il purgatorio nella Decre-tistica," presented at the Ninth International Congress of Medieval Canon Law, in Munich, 13–18 July 1992, with references (mostly from manuscripts) to Huguccio, the *Summa Lipsiensis*, Alanus Anglicus, Laurentius Hispanus, Johannes Teutonicus, and others who used the idea of *mediocriter boni* and *mediocriter mali*.

A middle category of people is also found in philosophical works. Calcidius, who wrote his commentary on the *Timaeus* in the late fourth or early fifth century, expounded Plato's distinction between soldiers, on one side, and artisans and husbandmen, on the other, into three types of men who rule, act, and are ruled and whom he located respectively in the highest, middle, and lowest places and compared to the head, chest, and lower parts of the body and to the faculties of reason, energy, and cupidity.[25] Denis the pseudo-Areopagite, writing probably about 500, said in the *Celestial Hierarchy* that each hierarchy had first, middle, and last orders, and in the *Ecclesiastical Hierarchy* he defined the three types of orders as one that is segregated by sacred functions and consecrations (the clergy); a middle (*mesos*) order, "which rejoices at the sight of some sacred things" (the laity); and the highest order of monks.[26] Calcidius and Denis were not widely read in the early Middle Ages, but later they influenced the concept of a middle category of people found in the works of philosophers and theologians like Thomas Aquinas.[27]

There are a number of references to *mediocres* in the letters written by Cassiodorus in the early sixth century. Theodoric wrote to Pope Agapitus, for instance, that the Senate should not receive *mediocres* but only *probati*. Athalaric contrasted the middling men with the *primarii* or *primates* above and the *rustici* below and decreed that the orders should live together equitably, saying, "Do not burden the *mediocres* lest the

---

25. *Timaeus a Calcidio translatus commentarioque instructus*, ed. J. H. Waszink, Corpus platonicum Medii Aevi: Plato latinus, no. 4 (London and Leiden, 1962), 8 (*Timaeus* 17c), 246–47 (*Commentarius Calcidii*, 232–33). See also Paul Edward Dutton, "*Illustre civitatis et populi exemplum*: Plato's *Timaeus* and the Transmission from Calcidius to the End of the Twelfth Century of a Tripartite Scheme of Society," *Mediaeval Studies*, 45 (1983): esp. 84–85.

26. Denis the pseudo-Areopagite, *De caelesti hierarchia*, IV, ed. Balthasar Corderius (Venice, 1754), I, 38 (= *PG*, III, 194A), ed. René Roques, Günter Heil, and Maurice de Gandillac, Sources chrétiennes, no. 58 (Paris, 1958), 98; and *De ecclesiastica hierarchia*, VI, ed. Corderius, 249–50 (= *PG*, III, 531C), and the notes on p. 254. The quotation is taken from the Latin version. In the Greek the middle order is described as theoretical and as a participant in some sacred things. I am indebted to Glen W. Bowersock for help on this point. See David Luscombe, "Conceptions of Hierarchy before the Thirteenth Century," in *Soziale Ordnungen im Selbstverständnis des Mittelalters*, Miscellanea Mediaevalia, no. 12.1 (Berlin and New York, 1979), esp. 1–3 on Denis.

27. Luscombe, "Conceptions of Hierarchy," 4–19, esp. 17–18 on the middle class; and Dutton, "Plato's *Timaeus*," 82–83, on the revival of interest in Calcidius in the twelfth century.

potiores may deservedly oppress you."[28] In these texts the *mediocres* seem to be a defined category between the upper ranks of society and agricultural workers. Cassiodorus also used the term in a moral sense in his *Exposition on the Psalms,* where he said that the garment in Psalm 103:6 covered "not only middling men but . . . also those saintly and most eminent men" and that the trees in Psalm 103:16 were the people who came to church: "They indicate the middling men." The mountains in Psalm 148:9 stood for *homines sublimes,* the hills for "middling men dealing with impartiality" [*mediocres aequalitate tractantes*], and the trees, cedars, beasts, cattle, serpents, and birds for other categories of men.[29] Here, as in some of the letters and in the edict of Athalaric, the *mediocres* were associated with equity and fair treatment, which suggests that they were liable to oppression.

In the sixth, seventh, and eighth centuries the category of *mediocres* appears in various sources. Gregory of Tours said that Abbot Aredius, who as a boy was one of the *aulici palatini* in the household of King Theodobert, indicating that he was certainly of high birth, "came from not middling . . . parents but was fully free" [*non mediocribus . . . ortus parentibus, sed valde ingenuus*].[30] Some *mediocres* in sixth-century Gaul were therefore apparently not fully free, but they were not necessarily poor. The church of Cahors was endowed by many nobles and middling people during the episcopate of Desiderius, who was bishop from 630 to 655 but whose *Life* was not written probably until the ninth century.[31] Aldhelm, who became abbot of Malmesbury in 675 and bishop of Sherborne in 705, wrote in *On Virginity* that the clemency of Christ took care of the *mediocres* and the contrite.[32] And in Bede's *Ecclesiastical History* the *mediocres* were associated with (both "not only . . .

28. Cassiodorus, *Variae,* I, 41 (Theodoric in 507–9); VII, 14; VIII, 19 (Athalaric in 527–28); VIII, 31 (Athalaric in 527); IX, 2 (Athalaric in ca. 527); and XII, 22 (537–38), in CC, XCVI, 45, 274, 324, 337, 347, 490.

29. Cassiodorus, *Expositio Psalmarum, In Ps.,* CIII, 6 and 16, and CXLVIII, 10, in CC, XCVIII, 927, 932, 1318.

30. Gregory of Tours, *Historia Francorum,* X, 29, in *MGH: Scriptores rerum Merov.,* I, 440. See the translations by O. M. Dalton (Oxford, 1927), II, 465, who said "of free birth, sprung from parents of no mean station," and the notes on pp. 600–601; and by Lewis Thorpe (Harmondsworth, 1974), 589: "of free birth, being descended from quite important people."

31. *Vita sancti Desiderii episcopi Caturcensis,* 28, in *MGH: Scriptores rerum Merov.,* IV, 585. The distinction between kings and middling men in the anonymous early seventh-century *Testimonia divinae scripturae,* 26, in CC, CVIIID, 83, which was formerly attributed to Isidore of Seville, may derive from Augustine.

32. Aldhelm, *De virginitate,* 48, in *MGH: Auctores antiquissimi,* XV, 296.

but also" and "together with") bishops, great men (*maiores*), nobles, and kings and princes.[33] The clergy or order of continent men, Bede said in his treatise *On the Temple,* were in the middle between the orders of the married laity and virgin monks and nuns.[34]

It became more frequent in the lives of saints written at this time to specify their modest or middling origins, in contrast to the preceding period, when the noble families of saints were emphasized.[35] Venantius Fortunatus, who lived in the second half of the sixth century, wrote that Bishop Marcellus of Paris was "middling in parents and lofty in way of life," and the parents of St. Richarius, whose *Life* dates from the second half of the eighth century, were said to have been *mediocres pauperes* and not to have been noble as a result of wealth or highly placed family.[36] Abbot Anso of Lobbes, who died in 800, wrote in the *Life* of his predecessor, Erminon, who died in 737, that he came "not from lowly parents but from middling people of the Franks, and although he was noble in family he was more noble in mind."[37] *Mediocris* here was the opposite of *infimus* and was not incompatible with *nobilis.* The seventh-century abbot Frodobert of Celle was said, in his *Life,* which was written by Adso of Montierender in the tenth century, to have "sprung from middling parents but shone from the incomparable brightness of his mind."[38]

33. Bede, *Historia ecclesiastica*, III, 25 and 27, and IV, 23, ed. Bertram Colgrave and R. A. B. Mynors, Oxford Medieval Texts (Oxford, 1969), 296, 306–8, 312, 408.

34. Bede, *De templo*, I, in CC, CXIXA, 162–63.

35. See Joseph-Claude Poulin, *L'idéal de sainteté dans l'Aquitaine carolingienne d'après les sources hagiographiques (750–950)*, Travaux du laboratoire d'histoire religieuse de l'Université Laval, no. 1 (Quebec, 1975), 45–46; Martin Heinzelmann, "Sanctitas und 'Tugendadel'. Zu Konzeptionen von 'Heiligkeit' im 5. und 10. Jahrhundert," *Francia* 5 (1977): 741–52; and Réginald Grégoire, *Manuale di agiologia*, Bibliotheca Montisfani, no. 12 (Fabriano, 1987), 298–301. André Vauchez, *La sainteté en Occident aux derniers siècles du moyen âge* (Bibliothèque des Écoles françaises d'Athènes et de Rome, no. 241 [Rome, 1981], 204–5), stressed the association of sanctity and nobility in the early Middle Ages, but noted "un léger abaissement du niveau social des saints" in the Carolingian world.

36. Venantius Fortunatus, *Vita sancti Marcelli*, IV, 13, in *MGH: Auctores antiquissimi*, IV.2, 50; and *Vita Richarii sacerdotis Centulensis primigenia*, 4, in *MGH: Scriptores rerum Merov.*, VII, 446 (443 on the date).

37. Anso of Lobbes, *Vita sancti Erminonis episcopi*, 1, in *MGH: Scriptores rerum Merov.*, VI, 462. See also Léon Van der Essen, *Étude critique et littéraire sur les Vitae des saints mérovingiens de l'ancienne Belgique* (Louvain and Paris, 1907), 74; and Wattenbach-Levison, 167. On the hagiographical formula *nobilis origine . . . sed nobilior virtute*, see Poulin, *Idéal*, 45; Heinzelmann, "Sanctitas," 746; and Vauchez, *Sainteté*, 205.

38. Adso of Montierender, *Vita Frodoberti abbatis Cellensis*, 1, in *MGH: Scriptores rerum Merov.*, V, 74 (69 on date).

An interesting insight into the meaning of *mediocris* in the ninth century is given in the commentary on the *Ars maior* of Donatus by the Irish grammarian Murethach (Muridac), who taught at Auxerre before 840 and who said that the comparative (*mediocrior*) and superlative (*mediocrissimus*) of *mediocris* were not used "because a man is called middling who takes his place (*subsistit*) neither from a proud family nor from a lowly one, just as a certain wise man said, 'There go noble and non-noble and middling girls.' For if it should receive a comparative, *mediocris* would no longer exist."[39] For Murethach, therefore, *mediocris* was a term that derived its meaning from the extremes to which it was related.

In Carolingian legislation *mediocris* appears to have referred to anyone whose socioeconomic position was, as Murethach put it, between high and low. Charlemagne decreed in the capitulary on his estates, which dates from between 770 and 800, that the mayors should be selected not from more powerful men (*potentiores homines*) but from *mediocres* who were *fideles*.[40] In the capitulary on bishops, which probably dates from 792, he distinguished between the bishops, abbots, and abbesses who could contribute a pound of silver and the *mediocres, minores,* and *pauperes* who could contribute, respectively, half a pound, five shillings, and only alms; among the counts he distinguished between the *fortiores* who gave one pound and the *mediocres* who gave half a pound.[41] Archbishop Rihcolf of Mainz established in 810, apparently with reference to breaches of fasting, that greater men (*maiores*) should pay a shilling a day, middling men six pennies, and poor men according to their means.[42] Lothar, in a decree of 825 concerning the obligation of free men to perform military service, made special provisions for *mediocres liberi,* presumably free middling men, who were unable to serve themselves, and also for those who were too poor either to serve or to support someone else.[43]

Although these texts were concerned with administrative, military,

---

39. Muridac (Murethach), *In Donati artem maiorem,* II, in *CC:CM,* XL, 74. See also Louis Holtz, *Donat et la tradition de l'enseignement grammatical,* Documents, études et répertoires publiés par l'Institut de Recherche et d'Histoire des Textes (Paris, 1981), 439.

40. *MGH: Capitularia,* I, 88, no. 32.60. This raises the question, which also applies to the Salzburg notice of ca. 790 cited in n. 50, below, of whether some *mediocres* were not *fideles.*

41. Ibid., I, 52, no. 21.

42. Ibid., I, 249, no. 127.

43. Ibid., I, 329–30, no. 165.1.

and religious matters, the position of the *mediocres* was often defined primarily in economic terms. Lupus of Ferrières in about 843 divided people into *dives, mediocris,* and *pauper,* and Anastasius *Bibliothecarius,* writing in the 870s, referred to *primori, mediocres,* and *exigui* in a passage concerning imperial financial exactions in Constantinople.[44] Hincmar apparently had in mind social status, and perhaps also age, in addition to economic circumstances, when he wrote in *On the Order of the Palace,* which dates from 882, about distressed people, "and especially widows and orphans, both *seniores* and *mediocres,* each one according to their poverty and quality."[45] There are two references to noble, middling, and low in the *Deeds of Charlemagne,* by Notker *Balbulus* of St. Gall, who also described a protest made to the emperor "by some of the *mediocres.*"[46] Flodoard of Reims, whose *Annals* cover the years 919 to 966, described under the year 920 a man named Hagano whom Charles the Simple made *potens ex mediocribus,* and these words were repeated in the 990s by Richer, who also referred to someone else as "from the middling men."[47] Here the contrast seems to have been between *potens* and *mediocris,* which may have been the equivalent of *pauper* and have referred primarily to a weak and unprotected status.[48] Ratherius of Verona clearly had economic resources in mind, however, when he

---

44. Lupus of Ferrières, *Epistola* 31, ed. Léon Levillain, Classiques de l'histoire de France au moyen âge, nos. 10, 16 (Paris, 1927–35), I, 142; and Anastasius Bibliothecarius, *Historia tripertita,* in Theophanes Confessor, *Chronographia,* ed. C. de Boor (Leipzig, 1885), II, 326. See also Wattenbach-Levison, 465–66.

45. Hincmar of Reims, *De ordine palatii,* 25, ed. Thomas Gross and Rudolf Schieffer in *MGH: Fontes iuris germanici antiqui,* no. 3 (Hanover, 1980), 78 (10 on the date).

46. Notker Balbulus, *Gesta Karoli imperatoris,* I, 1 and 3, and II, 12, ed. Hans F. Haefele, in *MGH: Scriptores rerum Germanicarum,* n.s., no. 12 (Berlin, 1959), 2, 4, 71. See also Wattenbach-Levison, 277–80.

47. Flodoard, *Annales,* ed. Philippe Lauer, Collection de textes pour servir à l'étude et à l'enseignement de l'histoire, no. 39 (Paris, 1905), 2; and Richer of Reims, *Historia,* I, 9 and 15, ed. Robert Latouche, Classiques de l'histoire de France au moyen âge, nos. 12, 17 (Paris, 1930–37), I, 24, 38. On Hagano, see Robert Parisot, *Le royaume de Lorraine sous les Carolingiens (843–923)* (Paris, 1898), 628–31; and Jane Martindale, "The French Aristocracy in the Early Middle Ages," *Past and Present* 75 (1977): 6, 23.

48. See Karl Bosl, "Potens und Pauper. Begriffsgeschichtliche Studien zur gesellschaftlichen Differenzierung im frühen Mittelalter und zum Pauperismus des Hochmittelalters" (1963), reprinted in his *Frühformen der Gesellschaft im mittelalterlichen Europa* (Munich, 1964), 106–34. Bosl argued in this influential article that *pauper* in the early Middle Ages meant "weak" and "defenseless" rather than economically poor.

included *divites, mediocres,* and *pauperes* in a list of "all Christians, all the baptized, every order, condition, sex, age, and profession."[49]

In some parts of the Carolingian empire the *mediocres* seem to have constituted an established social and legal category. One of the brief notices from Salzburg in about 790 referred to "the names and fields of faithful men both nobles and *mediocres.*"[50] According to an agreement between the bishop of Constance and the abbot of St. Gall in 854, "What is just should be established in the presence of the first men and the middling men of the province."[51] There are several references to *mediocres* in the St. Gall formularies, including one to a meeting of chief men and middling men in about 900; another in a letter of 964 concerning the distribution of charity, which was to be given, among others, to both middling and great men; and another to a monk who belonged to the middling people by birth (*mediocribus apud nos natalibus*) but to the best by his way of life, showing that in this area *mediocris* depended on family.[52] A tripartite division of society, with no explicit mention of *mediocres,* is found in the *History* of Nithard of St. Riquier, which dates from the mid–ninth century, and a century later in the *Saxon Deeds,* by Widukind, who said that "The Saxon people, not counting the servile condition, are until now divided by a tripartite custom and law."[53] Both middling and noble freemen were raised and instructed in the household of Bishop Ulric of Augsburg, who died in 973, and a century later King Rudolf was elected, according to Bruno of Merseburg, by the greater and middling men who came together from all over Saxony.[54]

49. Ratherius of Verona, *Praeloquia,* VI, 20, in CC:CM, XLVIA, 187.

50. Willibald Hauthaler, *Salzburger Urkundenbuch,* vol. 1, *Traditionscodices* (Salzburg, 1910), 36 (Breves notitiae, 14).

51. Hermann Wartmann, *Urkundenbuch der Abtei Sanct Gallen* (St. Gallen, 1882), 3:687.

52. *Formulae Sangallensis,* Misc. 9 and Coll. 24 and 25, in *MGH: Formulae,* 383 (379 on date), 410, 411; see also p. 398 (*primis, mediis, extremis*). See also Otto, *Adel und Freiheit,* 151–55, on references to *mediocres* in these and other sources from St. Gall, which was in ancient Alamannia.

53. Nithard of St. Riquier, *Historiarum libri IIII,* IV, 2, ed. Ernst Müller, in *MGH: Scriptores rerum Germ.* [44] (Hanover and Leipzig, 1907), 41; and Widukind of Corvey, *Rerum gestarum Saxonicarum libri III,* I, 14, ed. K. A. Kehr, in *MGH: Scriptores rerum Germ.* [60] (Hanover and Leipzig, 1904), 20. See also Wattenbach-Levison, 353–59; and Wattenbach-Holtzmann, 25–34 (on these works); and Otto, *Adel und Freiheit,* 45.

54. Gerhard, *Vita sancti Oudalrici episcopi,* 3, in *MGH: Scriptores* in fol., IV, 390 (see Wattenbach-Holtzmann, 256–59); and Bruno of Merseburg, *De bello saxonico,* 93, ed. Wilhelm Wattenbach, in *MGH: Scriptores rerum Germ.* [15] (Hanover and Leipzig, 1880), 69. See also Ekkehard IV, *Casus sancti Galli,* 10, in *MGH: Scriptores* in fol., II, 122, who said that Abbot Ekkehard II instructed both *mediocres* and *nobiles.*

Mediocris was also a recognized social status in northern Italy, southern France, and northwestern Spain from the ninth until at least the twelfth centuries. The injunction in Charles the Bald's privilege for Farfa in 875 that disputes should be settled "not by law but by more noble and truthful men" was changed by Berengar I in 920 to "by middling people and by more noble and truthful men,"[55] which suggests that society was divided into *nobiles, mediocres,* and *viles.* In the *Liber tramitis* of Farfa, which derived from the customs at Cluny in the first half of the eleventh century, the section on "What should be done for dead laymen" presumably referred to nobles or magnates, since the ceremonies involved all the monks, and the customary specified that "If one of the middling men should die, let as many go as the prior will order."[56] At Fruttuaria, of which the customs also derived from Cluny by way of Dijon and date probably from the late eleventh century, the category of *mediocris* appeared even among the monks, since in the chapter "On the Chanting of Nocturns" the responsibilities were divided, first between the *pueri, iuuenes et novicii,* and *maiores,* who may have been the same as the *seniores.* The *iuuenes* were then further divided into two groups of *iuuenes minores,* who chanted with the novices, and *iuuenes maiores,* who chanted with the *mediocres seniores,* who were mentioned three times in this chapter.[57] It is unclear exactly what the term *mediocris* meant here. It is not found elsewhere in the customary and probably referred to a particular group of *seniores* who participated in nocturns.

The viscount of Béziers and Agde called on *mediocres* and *minores* as well as great men and nobles to give evidence at an inquest in 897, and

55. Arthur Giry, Maurice Prou, and Georges Tessier, *Recueil des actes de Charles II le Chauve,* Chartes et diplômes relatifs à l'histoire de France (Paris, 1943–55), II, 395, no. 401; and L. Schiaparelli, *I diplomi di Berengario I,* Fonti per la storia d'Italia, no. 35 (Rome, 1903), 325, no. 124.

56. *Liber tramitis aevi Odilonis abbatis,* 206, ed. Peter Dinter, Corpus consuetudinum monasticarum, no. 10 (Siegburg, 1980), 284–85. See also Joachim Wollasch, "Zur Datierung des Liber tramitis aus Farfa anhand von Personen und Personengruppen," in *Person und Gemeinschaft im Mittelalter. Karl Schmid zum fünfundsechzigsten Geburtstag* (Sigmaringen, 1988), 237–55, who dated the two recensions 1027–33 and 1033–40.

57. *Consuetudines Fructuarienses-Sanblasianae,* IIIb, III, 794, ed. L.G. Spätling and Peter Dinter, Corpus consuetudinum monasticarum, no. 12.1–2 (Siegburg, 1985–87), II, 140. See also Maria Lahaye-Geusen, *Das Opfer der Kinder. Ein Beitrag zur Liturgie- und Sozialgeschichte des Mönchtums im Hohen Mittelalter,* Münsteraner theologische Abhandlungen, no. 13 (Altenberge, 1991), 114–15, who said that the *mediocres seniores* were "die weniger wichtigen älteren Konventsmitglieder" and may indicate "das Vorhandensein einen adligen 'Mittelschicht' innerhalb des Konventes."

two unpublished documents from southwestern France, including one from Cuxa in 1009, referred respectively to *maiores, mediocres,* or *minores* and to a *magna, mediocris,* or *parva persona.*[58] Gerald of Aurillac called himself "an Aquitanian and a middling person" in his *Life* by Odo of Cluny, though he was described elsewhere in the work as *potens et dives* and as distinguished by *carnis nobilitas,* and Ralph Glaber referred at least four times in his *Histories* to great men or magnates, middling men, and little or lowly people.[59] He described the participants in the pilgrimages to Jerusalem, for instance, as "the order of inferior people, then the middling people, after them some very great kings and counts, marquesses and bishops, and lastly, what had never occurred [before], many noble women with poorer ones." This seems to come close to the modern division into upper, middle, and lower classes, and it is also striking for its explicit recognition of the presence of women.

According to a charter of about 1100, Bishop Isarn of Grenoble brought together nobles, middling, and poor men from distant lands "because he found few inhabitants in this bishopric . . . and the said bishop gave these men fortified places [*castra*] to inhabit and lands to work, in which places and lands the said bishop kept authority and services."[60] Ekkehard of Aura, who died in 1125, said that after the conquest of England in 1066 the nobles were killed and the bishops exiled and that William "subjugated the middling men to his soldiers in servitude."[61] This suggests that Ekkehard regarded the *mediocres* as free but

---

58. Claude DeVic and Joseph Vaissete, *Histoire générale de Languedoc* (Paris, 1730–45), 2:33, no. 18, ed. Auguste Molinier (Toulouse, 1872–1904), 5:94; and Elisabeth Magnou-Nortier, *La société laïque et l'église dans la province ecclésiastique de Narbonne (zone cispyrénéenne) de la fin du VIIIe à la fin du XIe siècle,* Publications de l'Université de Toulouse-Le Mirail, no. A 20 (Toulouse, 1974), 242, n. 167, see also p. 253 on the division into *majores* and *minores,* which is found in a document of 1057 in J. B. Rouquette, *Cartulaire de Béziers (Livre Noir)* (Paris and Montpellier, 1918–22), 86, n. 70.

59. Odo of Cluny, *Vita Geraldi,* I, 1, 29, in *PL,* CXXXIII, 639B, 642D, 659C; Ralph Glaber, *Historiarum libri quinque,* IV, 5, 14, 17; IV, 6, 18; and V, 1, 16, ed. Maurice Prou, Collection de textes pour servir à l'étude et à l'enseignement de l'histoire, no. 1 (Paris, 1886), 103, 105, 106, 127; and ed. John France, Oxford Medieval Texts (Oxford, 1989), 194, 198, 200, 238. On the passages from the *Life* of Gerald of Aurillac, see Arsenio Frugoni, "Incontro con Cluny," in *Spiritualità cluniacense* Convegni del Centro di studi sulla spiritualità medievale, no. 2 (Todi, 1960), 23; Martindale, "French Aristocracy," 22; and Vauchez, *Sainteté,* 205, n. 59.

60. Jules Marion, *Cartulaires de l'église cathédrale de Grenoble,* Collection de documents inédits sur l'histoire de France (Paris, 1869), 93, no. B, 16.

61. Ekkehard of Aura, *Chronicon,* s.a. 1066, in *MGH: Scriptores* in fol., VI, 199.

susceptible to servitude. Two interpolations, made probably in the second half of the twelfth century, into Ademar of Chabannes's account of early eleventh-century expeditions to the Holy Land changed "many princes" to "noble, middling, and poor men" and added "an infinite multitude of middling, poor, and rich men."[62] Bishop Peter of Vic in 1174 decreed that anyone who failed to use his new currency would be fined 10 shillings if he were a *probus homo,* 5 shillings if *mediocris,* and 2 shillings if *de villanis* who came from outside, or *de extraneis,* and that if he were *de minoribus* he would draw water on market days and be put in the pillory on other days.[63] The specificity of the punishments indicates that the distinctions between these ranks were generally recognized in Catalonia in the twelfth century.

Several scholars have remarked upon the role of the *mediocres* or middle ranks in the developing feudal society of the tenth, eleventh, and twelfth centuries.[64] According to Alexander Murray, "The term was not unknown in the central Carolingian period. But examples thicken conspicuously from the late tenth century, leaving the impression that some, at least, of the big mass of dark-age *pauperes* had begun to lift themselves from that category."[65] The number of references to *mediocres* in the early Middle Ages suggests, however, that the development may have been in both directions, or even the other way; some middling people probably lost status, as Ekkehard of Aura said of post-Conquest England, during the feudal age.

In religious writings and saints' *Lives* the term was still used in a relatively loose way. Atto of Vercelli said that "One should behave differ-

---

62. Ademar of Chabannes, *Chronicon,* III, 68, ed. Jules Chavanon, Collection de textes pour servir à l'étude et à l'enseignement de l'histoire, no. 20 (Paris, 1897), 194, nn. m, n. These additions are found in MS Paris, Bibl. nat., Latin 5926, on which see Ademar, *Chronicon,* xx–xxi.

63. Jaime Villanueva, *Viage literario à las iglesias de España* (Valencia and Madrid, 1803–52), 6:241–43. See, on this document, Jaime Lluis y Navas Brusi, "Le droit monétaire dans la région de Vich pendant la reconquête espagnole," *Revue numismatique,* 5th ser., 18 (1956): 222; and Thomas N. Bisson, *Conservation of Coinage: Monetary Exploitation and its Restraint in France, Catalonia, and Aragon (c. A.D. 1000–c. 1225)* (Oxford, 1979), 78–79, to which I am indebted for identifying the punishments of the *minores.*

64. In addition to Magnou-Nortier, *Société,* see P. Van Luyn, "Les milites dans la France du XIe siècle," *Le Moyen Age* 77 (1971): 5–51, 193–238, esp. 225 on *media nobilitas;* Jean Flori, "Chevaliers et chevalerie au XIe siècle en France et dans l'Empire germanique," *Le Moyen Age* 81 (1976): 125–36, esp. 131; and Martindale, "French Aristocracy," 5–45, esp. 6, 13, 22–23.

65. Murray, *Reason and Society,* 96.

ently with powerful men of the world, with middling men, and with humble men," and Odo of Cluny divided the world, though united by a single faith, into three grades of first, middle, and third.[66] Abbo of Fleury, who died in 1004, described the clerical order as in the middle between the lay and monastic orders.[67] In the *Book of the Miracles of St. Faith*, a man was said to enjoy "the sufficiency of a middling life" according to the position of that place.[68] Bishop Notger of Liège, who died in 1008, was venerable to the powerful and amiable to the *mediocres*,[69] and similar terms were used in the late-eleventh-century *Life* of Walter of Pontoise, who knew how to rule rich, middling, and poor men in such a way that "The rich and middling men venerated him as a superior but the poor men considered him a poor man like themselves."[70] In the continuation of Sigebert's *Deeds of the Abbots of Gembloux,* written by Godescalc in the 1130s, Abbot Liethard raised "many nobles and middling men by his admonition and praiseworthy familiarity."[71]

The term *mediocris* in these works seems, like the modern use of *middle class,* to refer not to a legally defined social group but to a broad category of people who were neither at the top nor at the bottom of society. In treatises on letter writing, people were commonly classified as high or superior, middle or equal, and low or humble.[72] The *dictator* Paul of Camaldoli, who worked in northern Italy probably in the third quarter of the twelfth century, wrote in his discussion of the order of names in the salutations to letters that

66. Atto of Vercelli, *Expositio in epistolas Pauli: Epistola ad Colossenses*, 4, in *PL*, CXXXIV, 639D; and Odo of Cluny, *Occupatio*, VI, 771–74, ed. Anton Swoboda (Leipzig, 1900), 141.

67. Abbo of Fleury, *Apologeticus*, in *PL*, CXXXIX, 464B–65A. See also Marco Mostert, *The Political Theology of Abbo of Fleury*, Medieval Studies and Sources, no. 2 (Hilversum, 1987), 49.

68. *Liber miraculorum sancte Fidis*, IV, 6, ed. A. Bouillet, Collection de textes pour servir à l'étude et à l'enseignement de l'histoire, no. 21 (Paris, 1897), 183–84

69. Anselm of Liège, *Gesta episcoporum Tungrensium, Traiectensium et Leodiensium*, II, 30, in *MGH: Scriptores* in fol., VII, 206.

70. *Vita sancti Gauterii*, in J. Depoin, *Cartulaire de l'abbaye de Saint-Martin de Pontoise* (Pontoise, 1895–1909), 188. See also *Fundatio monasterii Comburgensis*, 3, in *MGH: Scriptores* in fol., XV.2, 1031, referring to "both men and women, rich and middling."

71. Godescalc, *Continuatio gestarum abbatum Gemblacensium*, 59, in *MGH: Scriptores* in fol., VIII, 545.

72. Heinz-Jürgen Beyer, "Die Frühphase der 'Ars dictandi,'" *Studi medievali*, 3d ser., 18.2 (1977), 19–43 (585–609 of entire volume), esp. the chart on 27 (593); and Giles Constable, "The Structure of Medieval Society According to the *Dictatores* of the Twelfth Century," in *Law, Church, and Society: Essays in Honor of Stephan Kuttner,*

A good *dictator* should know in advance the designated order of persons so that he may better fit the manner of speaking to their greatness and quality. For to exalted persons and in great causes the splendor of the words and the greatness of the deeds should be displayed in a manner fitting the material. To middling people [*mediocres personae*], however, suitable things can be said temperately. A weak person, however, should have fewer words the lower he is and use no long sentences, so that his brevity or that of his interlocutor generates no obscurity and is not deprived of vigor in joining words to matter. By keeping these qualities well, we shall legitimately fulfill the triple manner of speaking which many call humble, middling [*medium*], and grandiloquent.[73]

Theologians and commentators in the eleventh and twelfth centuries used the middle category both for the clergy and for certain types of Christians, like the *mediocriter boni* and *mediocriter mali* found in the works of the canonists. Clerics "should be middling [*medii*] between God and men," according to Anselm of Laon, who also said that the virgins, whom he equated with Daniel and monks, occupied the highest grade. The continent (Noah and the clerics) were in the middle, and the married (Job and the laity) were at the bottom.[74] Gerhoh of Reichersberg in his commentary on Psalm 64:1 equated the *mediocres* with active men, who were represented by Peter, and the *perfecti* with contemplatives, whose representative was John, and in a vision of Elizabeth of Schönau the rectors took a middle way between those of the continent and the married.[75] For Bernard of Clairvaux, "The beginning of wisdom [is] the fear of God; the middle, hope; and love, the fullness," and he equated each grade,

ed. Kenneth Pennington and Robert Somerville (Philadelphia, 1977), 253–67, esp. 260–62 on the middle order. The present essay is the fulfillment of the plan expressed in the final note of this work to gather the various references to *mediocres* in medieval sources.

73. MS Paris, Bibl. nat., Latin 7517, fol. 55ᵛ, cited in Constable, "Structure," 259, 266.

74. Anselm of Laon, *Epistola ad H. abbatem s. Laurentii Leodiensis*, in *PL*, CLXII, 1590B; and Franz Bliemetzrieder, *Anselms von Laon systematische Sentenzen*, Beiträge zur Geschichte der Philosophie des Mittelalters, no. 18.2–3 (Münster i. W., 1919), 135.

75. Gerhoh of Reichersberg, *Comm. in Psalmos*, VI, in *PL*, CXCIV, 13CD; and Elizabeth of Schönau, *Liber viarum Dei*, V, in *Die Visionen der hl. Elisabeth und die Schriften der Aebte Ekbert und Emecho von Schönau*, ed. F. W. E. Roth (Brünn, 1884), 90 (= *PL*, CXCV, 167A).

respectively, with beginners, learners, and the perfect.[76] A German sermon, which may have derived from Bernard, described the three orders as *süne, schaelkch,* and *mitlüte,* who served, respectively, out of love, fear, and hope;[77] and in a Bernardine text on the cross, which has also been attributed to Hugh of St. Victor, the three types of men were called carnal, animal, and spiritual, whose respective crosses were abstinence, fear of God (like some monks "who lead a middling life"), and love.[78] Alcher of Clairvaux, in the *Book of the Spirit and the Soul,* said that the three types of people in the city of God were wise men, soldiers, and artisans, whom he ranked respectively as superior, middle, and low.[79]

Mediocris was still used in a strictly economic sense by some writers, like Stephen of Fougères, who divided people into rich, poor, and middling in the *Life* of Abbot Geoffrey of Savigny, which was written after 1170.[80] For others it was a social term and was used primarily in contrast to noble and humble or sometimes poor or of small fortune. Monasteries for "many virgins, both of noble and of middle (*medii*) and of low birth," were founded by Abbot Theoger of St. George in the Black Forest, who became bishop of Metz and whose *Life* was written in 1138–46.[81] Herbord of Michelsberg, the biographer of Bishop Otto of Bamberg, compared the conversion of Poland downward from the princes to the middling people and the entire nation with the upward spread of Christianity in the early church, when "The religion of the Christian faith, beginning with the common crowd and low people, progressed to middling people and also involved the greatest princes of this world." At Otto's death, Herbord wrote, "The entire city wept, young men and virgins, old men

76. Bernard of Clairvaux, *In natali sancti Andreae sermo I,* 5, ed. Jean Leclercq et al., *S. Bernardi opera* (Rome, 1957–77), 5:430 (= *PL,* CLXXXIII, 506D).

77. Anton Schönbach, *Altdeutsche Predigten* (Graz, 1886–91), 2:92.

78. H.-M. Rochais, *Enquête sur les sermons divers et les sentences de saint Bernard* (= *Analecta sacri ordinis Cisterciensis,* no. 18.3–4 (Rome, 1962), 90–92.

79. Alcher of Clairvaux, *Liber de spiritu et anima,* 36, in *PL,* XL, 808 (among the works of Augustine). On *mediocres* in the work of Ralph of Flaix, writing about 1150, who divided the faithful into the robust who possessed nothing and the weak who enjoyed worldly things, see Beryl Smalley, "Ralph of Flaix on Leviticus," *Recherches de théologie ancienne et médiévale* 35 (1968): 70. The Cistercian Henry of Marcy, who became cardinal-bishop of Albano in 1179, divided people spiritually into *infimae, mediocres,* and *summae* in *Tractatus de peregrinante civitate Dei,* XIII, in *PL,* CCIV, 357A.

80. *Vita B. Gaufridi Saviniacensis,* 5 and 12, ed. E. P. Sauvage, in *Vitae BB. Vitalis et Gaufridi primi et secundi abbatum Saviniacensium in Normannia* (= *Analecta Bollandiana,* 1:357–90) (Brussels, 1882), 44, 51.

81. *Vita Theogeri,* I, 25, in *MGH: Scriptores* in fol., XII, 459.

with adolescents, every order wept, every religion wept, rich and poor, nobles, middling men, with the crowd of peasants."[82]

Landric of Nevers helped *nobiles et mediocres* who were on their way to Rome; a monk of Gottweig had a vision of the *principes et mediocres* in hell; many *nobiles et mediocres et fortunae minores* made grants to the abbey of Zwiefalten; and Conrad of Eberbach referred to "an innumerable multitude" of *nobiles, mediocres,* and *pauperes* in the first book of his *Great Origins of Cîteaux,* which dates from about 1190.[83] John of Gembloux contrasted the rich and powerful *potentes* with "the other men, that is, the middling men and the poor."[84] And Andrew the Chaplain in his treatise on love classified both men and women as plebeian, noble, and more noble, reserving the most noble for the clergy, and said that everyone should marry within his or her own order: "I firmly assert that no man should transgress the boundaries of his order but should seek the proper love of a proper woman within his order and ask for the middling love of a middling woman [*et mediocris personae mediocrem postulare amorem*], and thus each order is preserved inviolate."[85]

Mediocris here meant modest or humble, since the people Andrew had in mind were between his other orders but were not necessarily poor in an economic sense. The same is true of John of Condé, in a poem on the evil customs of the world, in which, after discussing the cleric and the knight, he asked, "Et que fet li peuples moyens?"[86] The twelfth-century hermit Wulfric of Haselbury was said in his *Life* by John of Ford to have

---

82. Herbord of Michelsberg, *Dialogus de Ottone episcopo Bambergensi,* I, 41, and III, 3, ed. Philipp Jaffé, *Monumenta Bambergensia,* Bibliotheca rerum Germanicarum, no. 5 (Berlin, 1869), 740, 793. This work was composed in 1159–60.

83. *Histoire des comtes de Nevers,* in CC:CM, XLII, 237; *Vita Altmanni episcopi Pataviensis,* 37, in MGH: Scriptores in fol., XII, 240; Ortlieb of Zwiefalten, *Chronicon,* I, 20, in *MGH: Scriptores* in fol., X, 84; Conrad of Eberbach, *Exordium magnum Cisterciense,* I, 21, ed. Bruno Griesser, Series scriptorum s. ordinis Cisterciensis, no. 2 (Rome, 1961), 79 (= PL, CLXXXV, 1012B). See also the references to *medii* in the variants to Peter the Chanter (attr.), *De oratione et speciebus illius,* ed. Richard Trexler, in *The Christian at Prayer: An Illustrated Prayer Manual Attributed to Peter the Chanter (d. 1197)* (Binghamton, 1987), 253; and to *mediocres* in the description by Rodrigo Jiménez de Rada in *Historia de rebus Hispaniae,* III, 8, in CC:CM, LXXII, 86, of an army in the late seventh century as being divided into great, middling, and young men.

84. John of Gembloux's letter to Guibert of Gembloux in 1177–80, in CC:CM, LXVIA, 331.

85. Andrew the Chaplain, *De amore libri tres,* VI, B, ed. E. Trojel (Munich, 1964), 51. The Latin passage is in brackets, indicating that it is missing in one manuscript.

86. Aug. Scheler, *Dits et contes de Baudouin de Condé et de son fils Jean de Condé,* III; *Jean de Condé,* II (Brussels, 1867), 225. See also Batany, "Vocabulaire," 66.

come "from the middling people of the English [*de mediocri Anglorum gente*]"; Arnulf of Villers, who was born about 1180, "took his origin from middling parents"; and St. Edmund of Abingdon's parents were described as "of middling fortune," where *mediocris* meant either that they were between "the armigerous class of feudal tenants" and "the servile class," according to Edmund's modern biographer, or that they had a fair or average fortune.[87] The Cistercian Beatrice of Tienen, who died in 1268, said that she came "from middling parents" and that "Her father, named Bartholomew, indeed shone moderately [*mediocriter*] among his people by his worldly honesty but appeared much more brightly in the eyes of divine majesty by his pious works and assiduous persistence in divine acts."[88] Bartholomew's profession is uncertain—he may have been a butcher or a builder—but he certainly was not poor, since he founded three Cistercian monasteries.[89]

Some interesting references to urban *mediocres* come from England in the thirteenth and fourteenth centuries. Thirteen sworn *mediocres homines* of the borough of Scarborough are found in the roll of the eyre for 1259–60, and *mediocres* appear in many sources concerning King's Lynn.[90] These *mediocres* may be the same as the "secondary people" at

---

87. John of Ford, *Vita beati Wulfrici*, 1, ed. Maurice Bell, Somerset Record Society, no. 47 (n.p., 1933), 13; *Vita Arnulfi conversi*, 4, in *Acta Sanctorum*, 3d ed., 30 June, VII, 559; and Matthew Paris, *Vita sancti Edmundi*, 1, in C. H. Lawrence, *St. Edmund of Abingdon* (Oxford, 1960), 222. On Edmund, see Lawrence, *St. Edmund*, 108; and Murray, *Reason and Society*, 408, who pointed out the implication of Edmund's name "Rich." On the *Life* of Arnulf, see Simone Roisin, *L'hagiographie cistercienne dans le diocèse de Liège au XIIIe siècle*, Université de Louvain, Recueil de travaux d'histoire et de philologie, 3d ser., no. 27 (Louvain and Brussels, 1947), 32–34, 82, n. 6, citing two other saints with *mediocribus parentibus*, which was clearly a hagiographical topos at this time. On the social origins of saints in the late Middle Ages, see Murray, *Reason and Society*, 337–41, 405–12; Vauchez, *Sainteté*, 204–23, 324–26 (tables on 216, 325); and Donald Weinstein and Rudolph Bell, *Saints and Society: The Two Worlds of Western Christendom, 1000–1700* (Chicago and London, 1982), 194–219 (table on 197).

88. L. Reypens, *Vita Beatricis. De Autobiografie van de z. Beatrijs van Tienen O. Cist. 1200–1268*, Studiën en tekstuitgaven van Ons geestelijk erf, no. 15 (Antwerp, 1964), 17.

89. Reypens, *Vita Beatricis*, 201–3; Roger De Ganck, "The Three Foundations of Bartholomew of Tienen," *Cîteaux. Commentarii Cistercienses* 37 (1986): 54.

90. *Three Yorkshire Assize Roles for the Reigns of King John and King Henry III*, ed. Charles Travis Clay, Yorkshire Archaeological Society, Record Series, no. 44, for 1910 (Leeds, 1911), 120; and E. F. Jacob, *Studies in the Period of Baronial Reform and Rebellion, 1258–1267*, Oxford Studies in Social and Legal History, no. 8 (Oxford, 1925), 119–20, 136, n. 5. On the *mediocres* at King's Lynn in the fourteenth and fifteenth centuries, see Alice Green, *Town Life in the Fifteenth Century* (London, 1894), 2:402–26, esp. 407–9.

Lincoln, where the inquiries concerning tallage assessment in 1274 were addressed separately to the *magni, secundarii,* and *minores,* and as the "middle people" at Norwich, where the chapter in the customary dealing with tallage referred to the *medius populus civitatis illius et pauperes.*[91] Most important is the passage concerning the Mise of Amiens of 1264 in the *Book on Ancient Laws,* or *Chronicles of the Mayors and Sheriffs of London,* by Arnold Fitz-Thedmar, who died in 1275 and described the rejection of King Louis's award by the men of London, the barons of the Cinque Ports, and "almost the entire body of the middle people of the kingdom of England," where *communa mediocris populi* may have, as E. F. Jacob said, "rather more technical a meaning than has commonly been supposed."[92]

The thirteenth-century theologians and canonists used *medii* more strictly in the sense of "middle." Hostiensis described the secular clergy as "in the middle . . . as it were the center" between the active life of the laity and the contemplative life of religious men and women, and said that "This mixed type, leading a mixed life, requires a mixed knowledge."[93] Bonaventura, in the Vatican version of his commentary on the Hexaemeron, also called the order of prelates mixed because it included both action and contemplation and said that "according to this process, it is placed in the middle" and that "The second order is clerical, both active and contemplative, which should both foster and contemplate, as they are in the middle [*medii*] between God and the people." In the Siena version the order of prelates was called highest in the order of ascents and middle, between the actives and contemplatives, in the order of disciplines, and later the clerical order was again called *medius.*[94] Thomas Aquinas used the idea of a middle group in his discussion of "Whether there are many orders in one hierarchy," which depended heavily on

---

91. Jacob, *Studies,* 136.

92. Arnold Fitz-Thedmar, *De antiquis legibus liber: Cronica maiorum et vicecomitum Londiniarum,* ed. Thomas Stapleton, Camden Society, no. 34 (London, 1846), 61; and Jacob, *Studies,* 134, 137. See, however, F. M. Powicke, *King Henry III and the Lord Edward,* vol. 2 (Oxford, 1947), 447, n. 3, who translated *omnis communa mediocris populi* as "the whole body of the lesser folk" and questioned Jacob's interpretation.

93. Henry of Segusia (Hostiensis), *Summa aurea,* proem., 10 (Venice, 1586), cols. 6–7.

94. Bonaventura, *In Hexaemeron* (Vatican version), XXII, 16 and 19, in *S. Bonaventurae . . . opera omnia* (Quaracchi, 1891), 5:440; and (Siena version) IV, 3, 16–17, and 19, ed. Ferdinand Delorme, Bibliotheca franciscana scholastica Medii Aevi, no. 8 (Quaracchi, 1934), 255.

Denis the pseudo-Areopagite. "Three different orders, high, middle, and low, are distinguished in every hierarchy," Thomas said, "in accordance with the various offices and activities of the angels." Just as any perfect multitude has a beginning, a middle, and an end, so in towns there are the *supremi* or *optimates,* the *infimi* or *vilis populus,* and the *medii* or *populus honorabilis,* each of which is distinguished by its respective offices and activities.[95]

John of Jandun, in his *Exposition on the Third Book of* [Aristotle's] *"De anima,"* defined a social hierarchy in intellectual terms, going from concrete and specific at the bottom to abstract and general at the top. The lowest category included not only "common men and ignorant peasants" but also merchants, craftsmen, and lawyers, who used only sense and imagination and knew only sensual, common, and specific things (*sensibilia, communia, propria*). The highest category consisted of metaphysicians and other outstanding or well-known men (*praecipues seu maxime noti*) who rose above the senses to the essences of abstract forms and distinguished qualities like goodness and evil. Between these upper and lower categories came two categories of *mediocres,* of which one was closer to the bottom and included mathematicians, who considered numbers, sizes, *perfectabilia,* and sensual things. The upper category of *mediocres* were more perfect, John wrote, because "by their good thinking they elicit unsubstantial properties from sensual things and discuss great uncertainties concerning natural things." These grades, he concluded, are the virtues by which men are diversified.[96]

The Brothers of the Common Life were described as a *genus medium* and *status tertius* and their way of life as a *via media* between the cloister and the world.[97] John XXII, in a letter written in 1318, distinguished between good and bad Beguines and praised "the other women of praiseworthy status . . . some of illustrious, some of noble, others of middling, and others of humble status and family."[98] This letter was cited in a

---

95. Thomas Aquinas, *Summa theologica,* I, 108, 2, concl. (Turin, 1938), 1:682. See also David Luscombe, "Thomas Aquinas and Conceptions of Hierarchy in the Thirteenth Century," in *Thomas von Aquin,* Miscellanea mediaevalia, no. 19 (Berlin and New York, 1988), 261–77, esp. 273.

96. MS Rome, Biblioteca Vaticana, Vat. lat. 760, ff. 99^v–100^r, cited by Murray, *Reason and Society,* 469–70, with a translation and commentary (pp. 268–69), saying that this fourfold scheme was "based on an obscure passage in Averroës."

97. Kaspar Elm, "Die Bruderschaft vom gemeinsamen Leben," *Ons geestelijk erf* 59 (1985): esp. 481–82.

98. Alexander Patschovsky, "Strassburger Beginenverfolgungen im 14. Jahrhundert," *Deutsches Archiv* 30 (1974): 150.

memorial presented in 1328 to the delegates of the bishop of Tournai on behalf of the beguinage of St. Elizabeth at Ghent, which was founded by the sisters Joanna and Margaret, countesses of Flanders and Hainault, on account of the number of women who could not find husbands and for the sake of the daughters of honest men, "both nobles and *mediocres,*" who wanted to live chastely but were unable to enter religious houses owing to their numbers or to their parents' poverty.[99] *Mediocris* here has been translated as "ignoble" and "of ordinary or common birth,"[100] but in the light of its use by John XXII and other contemporaries it probably referred to a somewhat higher category of people who were neither nobles nor commoners.

These texts show, therefore, that, although there was no single middle class in the Middle Ages, there were many middle classes, some of which came close in their nature to the way that the middle class is seen today. The term *mediocris* was sometimes used in the sense of "modest" or "humble" for anyone who was neither noble nor rich, but it usually referred to a middle category in a tripartite division of people. Some of the *mediocres* were between those who were above and below them in a hierarchical structure defined in terms of legal status, wealth, social rank, power, intellect, morality, behavior, or way of life. The status of *mediocris,* unlike some other medieval types of social differentiation, was rarely used as a category of self-definition. Gerald of Aurillac's description of himself as a *mediocris* was probably an expression of modesty. Nor was it marked, except in a few cases, mostly from late antiquity, by an awareness of the possibility of change or movement, as it were, toward one of the extremes between which it existed. Denis the pseudo-Areopagite called laymen the middle order because they rejoiced in the sight of, or participated in, some sacred things. Anselm of Laon and Bonaventura, on the other hand, said that the clergy were in the middle (*medii*) between God and man. For Bede, Anselm of Laon, and Elizabeth of Schönau the continent clerics were between the married people of the lay order and

---

99. Jean Béthune, *Cartulaire du Béguinage de Sainte-Elisabeth à Gand* (Bruges, 1883), 74, no. 106.

100. Ernest W. McDonnell, *The Beguines and Beghards in Medieval Culture* (New Brunswick, 1954), 83; Walter Simons, "The Beguine Movement in the Southern Low Countries: A Reassessment," *Bulletin de l'Institut historique belge de Rome* 59 (1989): 75, n. 38; and Walter Simons, "Een zeker bestaan: De Zuidnederlandse begijnen en de *Frauenfrage,* 13de–18de eeuw," *Tijdschrift voor sociale geschiedenis* 17 (1991): 125 ("van gewone afkomst").

the virgins of the monastic order. The author of the Pontigny commentary on the Rule of Benedict described the life of laymen as inferior, of clerics as middling, and of priests as superior, and then added that monks were at the top.[101] For Hostiensis and Bonaventura, the clergy were in the middle because they led a mixed life of action and contemplation. To see either the laity or the clergy, let alone some of the other groups that have been mentioned in this paper, as a middle class is a long way from modern social thinking, but the pattern of thought that saw some groups of society as between other groups, combined with the tendency to define society in socioeconomic terms, helped to prepare the way for the later emergence of the modern concept of the middle class.

---

101. MS Auxerre, Bibl. mun., 50, f. 103[r]. I am indebted to C. H. Talbot for a transcript of this manuscript.

Poverty, Payments, and Fiscal Policies in English Provincial Towns

Lorraine Attreed

In 1419, the mayor of Exeter ordered a half-gallon of wine while accounting for the money his city owed the Crown.[1] Like all officers of medieval English boroughs, Exeter's chief magistrate needed to fortify himself against the central government's growing demands for urban contributions. These demands were particularly heavy during Henry V's reign and remained so for several decades, coinciding with an extended period of both agrarian and urban economic contraction affecting most of postplague Europe.[2] This was the age in which town complaints about poverty became commonplace and when kings unstable on their thrones responded to them to bolster both reigns and receivers' rolls. From 1434, the Crown remitted portions of lay subsidies, waived ancient fee-farm payments, and refrained from asking beleaguered towns for loans. Yet, because these three kinds of payment constituted a major part of Crown income, monarchs had to weigh urban complaints against government solvency. Taxes, farms, and loans helped pay for military campaigns, royal household expenses, and personal annuities for servants loyal to the Crown. Any town's contribution to the central administration formed only a small portion of total Crown revenue, yet raising the payments caused boroughs considerable grief. The following examination of urban fiscal policies reveals the financial claims made upon borough bud-

---

1. Devon Record Office (DRO), Receivers' Roll, 7–8 Henry V. He ordered a pottle, equal to a half-gallon, but, because the number of officials present at the accounting was not noted, how much wine each man drank remains unknown.

2. For a general discussion, see N. J. G. Pounds, *An Economic History of Medieval Europe* (New York, 1974), esp. chaps. 6, 10. A. J. Pollard, *North-eastern England during the Wars of the Roses: Lay Society, War, and Politics 1450–1500* (Oxford, 1990), 43–52, 71–73, examines the crisis in the context of regional economies, with extensive references.

gets, assesses urban complaints about poverty, shows the strategies of civic officials when under economic stress, and illuminates larger problems of late medieval monarchs' relations with their urban subjects.

Three provincial towns provide the records, the geographical contrasts, and the differing rates of development that make such comparisons possible. Late medieval Norwich was a large and generally prosperous borough with a population of between 8,000 and 9,000 in the aftermath of the plague. If tax records can be trusted, this East Anglian cloth center had developed into the largest and wealthiest provincial town in England by the early sixteenth century, replacing York (our second example) as the leading provincial city.[3] Between 1400 and 1550, the northern center experienced declining population and overseas trade, shrinking in inhabitants from 12,000 to 8,000.[4] Not only did cloth manufacture move from city to countryside, but the nature of York's participation in overseas trade also changed after 1440. Although all areas suffered from exclusion by the Hansa merchants from the Baltic markets, London and the towns of the south were in a much stronger position to dominate new sources of commerce with the Low Countries. As the fifteenth century progressed, financing for large-scale trading ventures became increasingly difficult to find, and high overhead costs resulting from an elaborate civic structure have been blamed for exacerbating the problem of local finances.[5] This essay will pay particular attention to York's cries of poverty to discern whether they should be taken more seriously than those of boroughs such as the third example, Exeter. This southwestern port possessed a sturdier economy in the plague's aftermath; its population grew from about 3,000 in 1377 to 8,000 in the 1520s and drew its wealth from a lively cloth industry and commercial exchange. Such growth nonetheless failed to dissuade its officers from

---

3. Charles Phythian-Adams, *Desolation of a City: Coventry and the Urban Crisis of the Late Middle Ages* (Cambridge, 1979), 12. J. F. Pound, "The Social and Trade Structure of Norwich 1525–1575," *Past and Present* 34 (1966): 49, suggests that Norwich's population was over 12,000 in 1525. Mary D. Lobel, *Historic Towns Atlas*, vol. 1 (Oxford, 1969), 18, n.47, revises this figure to 9,200.

4. R. E. Glasscock, "English *circa* 1334," in *A New Historical Geography of England before 1600*, ed. H. C. Darby (Cambridge, 1976), 184, table 4.3; Alan R. H. Baker, "Changes in the Later Middle Ages," in *A New Historical Geography*, 243, table 5.1; David Palliser, "York under the Tudors," in *Perspectives in English Urban History*, ed. Alan Everitt (London, 1973), 59.

5. Pollard, *North-eastern England*, 71–73.

worrying about town finances and the fate of the poor.[6] The complaints and pleas of all three towns must be carefully assessed in light of the financial records that have survived in both local and royal archives.

The local records can be used to establish the boroughs' domestic budgets: the receipts and expenses pertaining to internal administration and government.[7] Receipts were derived from trade-related activities such as tolls and market fees, as well as rents, fines, and freemen's entry payments. These receipts often possess a slightly fictitious quality, as the amount included both payments already made and those that were expected to be made on later accounts. Expenses consisted of wages for civic officials, retainer fees for lawyers and patrons, and payments for repair of public works. A balanced budget indicated accounting success; significant excess was rare, and far more common were deficit entries either carried over to the following fiscal year or personally covered by the receivers or chamberlains unfortunate enough to be in charge that year. Tables 1–3 present the data from the seven reigns studied. Receipts (however fictitious) and expenses are averaged for the time periods indicated, and expenses are expressed as a percentage of receipts in order to discern indebtedness. York's 17 surviving chamberlains' accounts are tantalizing in their fragmentary state, with enough remaining to indicate that the northern city faced financial difficulties of a more threatening nature than did either Norwich or Exeter. Those two boroughs managed to stay within their local budgets, which felt the worst strain as a result of expensive royal visits and patronage costs. Structural changes in trade and industry in the northeast prevented York from knowing such financial security. Deficits carried over from previous fiscal years haunted

---

6. W. G. Hoskins, "English Provincial Towns in the Early Sixteenth Century," in *Provincial England: Essays in Social and Economic History* (London: Macmillan, 1963), 72; Hoskins, *Two Thousand Years in Exeter* (Exeter: James Townsend and Sons, 1960), 51. Despite Exeter's growth and development, at the end of the fifteenth century the trustees of a former mayor's estate were convinced that the opposite was true and gave the city a manor and lands for the relief of poor inhabitants burdened by fee farms, tallages, and other royal demands (DRO, Documents D267, 282, 283; W. G. Hoskins and H. P. R. Finberg, *Devonshire Studies* [London, 1952], 234–41).

7. For the 133-year period spanning the years 1377 to 1509 (the reigns of Richard II through Henry VII), Exeter has 121 Receivers' Rolls surviving; Norwich has 105 accounts (a mixture of treasurers' rolls, chamberlains' rolls, chamberlains' account books, and apprenticeship indentures, only 67 of which contain totals for both receipts and expenses); and York has 17 chamberlains' rolls. The York material through 1500 has been published in R. B. Dobson, ed., *York City Chamberlains' Account Rolls 1396–1500*, Surtees Society, vol. 192 (Gateshead, 1980).

York's chamberlains, already challenged by expenses that exceeded receipts. Although none of this material tells us much about the nature of wealth in the community, nor how much additional money could be potentially raised if assessment methods changed, York's persistent problems indicate that borough's difficulty in contributing more money no matter how unbalanced the budget or frustrated the chamberlains. By 1484, the mayor and council were forced to elect four men rather than three to share the burdens of that office, and many freemen chose to pay fines of 5 to 10 pounds rather than take up such an arduous task.[8]

TABLE 1.   Exeter Finances, 1377–1509 (domestic budget)

	Average Receipt per Annum	Average Expense per Annum	Expense as Percentage of Receipt
Richard II 1377–99	£130 17s.	£ 98 9s.	75%
Henry IV 1399–1413	£145 2s.	£135 10s.	93%
Henry V 1413–22	£146 16s.	£115 1s.	78%
Henry VI 1422–61	£130 13s.	£ 94 3s.	72%
Edward IV[a] 1461–83	£142 16s.	£117 7s.	82%
Richard III[b] 1483–84	£157 10s.	£153 8s.	97%
1484–85	£249 4s.	£253 4s.	102%
Henry VII 1485–1509	£187 13s.	£170	91%

Source: Devon Record Office, Receivers' Rolls (121 surviving for period).
[a]Uncollectible rents first began to be recorded on the rolls during Edward IV's reign. They ranged from £4 to £6 per annum between the 1460s and the early years of the sixteenth century.
[b]Because the accounts of these two rolls differ so widely, both are presented here.

8. Lorraine Attreed, ed., *The York House Books 1461–1490* (London, 1991), 300; Dobson, *Chamberlains' Accounts,* xxxvii–xxxix (and see p. xxv for comments on the

But no medieval town existed in a vacuum, for the Crown expected a variety of payments from its boroughs, forcing them to raise money in excess of that consumed by local expenses. The most regular payment made to the royal government was a town's fee farm, the fixed payment made annually by the royal sheriff or the town's own officers, demanded by the king in recognition of a borough's favored status. Such farms resulted from the proceeds of fairs, rents, and tolls and provided the royal government with about £2,500 *per annum,* 90 percent of which was alienated to royal pensioners, ecclesiastical foundations or used to repay

TABLE 2.   Norwich Finances, 1378–1504 (domestic budget)

	Average Receipt per Annum	Average Expense per Annum	Expense as Percentage of Receipt
Richard II 1377–99	£199 18s.	£120 3s.	60%
Henry IV 1399–1413	£185 14s.	£148 9s.	80%
Henry V 1413–22	£176 1s.	£138 15s.	79%
Henry VI 1422–61	£214 2s.	£164 8s.	77%
Edward IV 1461–83	£146 6s.	£134 3s.	92%
Henry VII[a] 1485–1509	£168 13s.	£118 5s.	70%

Source. Norfolk and Norwich Record Office, Treasurers' and Chamberlains' Rolls (105 surviving for the period, 67 with both receipts and expenses listed).
[a]Accounts for the reign of Richard III are fragmentary. The first complete return of Henry VII's reign is for the year 1488–89.

fictitious nature of such accounts). Although York's chamberlains had to make up corporate overruns out of their own purses, not all civic officials had this responsibility. Worcester in the sixteenth and seventeenth centuries experienced no decrease in enthusiasm for officeholding, not least because its servants were not expected to make up deficits out of personal resources (Alan D. Dyer, *The City of Worcester in the Sixteenth Century* [Leicester, 1973], 196–97).

Crown lenders.[9] Fee-farm amounts were set early in the towns' histories, sometimes in the twelfth century, and tied to trade and revenue levels of those years. Many civic officials of the fourteenth and fifteenth centuries

TABLE 3.   York Finances, 1396–1509 (domestic budget)

	Total Receipts	Net Expenses[a]	Net Expenses as Percentage of Receipts
1396–97	—	£408 12s. 9.5d.[b]	—
1433–34	£235 4s. 4d.	—	—
1442–43	£230 7s. 1.5d.	£178 19s. 2d.	78%
1445–46	£237 1s. 8d.	£230 2s. 5.5d.	97%
1449–50	£202 10s. 9d.	—	—
1453–54	£204 11s. 4d.	£224 19s. 9d.	110%
1454–55[c]	£203 2s. 5.5d.	£220 12s. 1d.	109%
1462–63	£195 2s. 5d.	£196 3s. 2.5d.	101%
1468–69	£254 16s. 10.5d.	£198 6s. 7.5d.	78%
1470–71	£343 4s. 11d.	£234 17s. 8d.	68%
1475–76	£182 18s. 5.5d.	£247 3s. 7d.	135%
1478–79[d]	£237 16s. 3.5d.	£249 13s. 8d.[c]	105%
1486–87	£219 10s. 7d.	£301 15s. 5d.	137%
1499–1500	£232 1s. 4d.	£188 1s. 1d.	81%
1501–2	£272 17s. 0d.	£210 15s. 6d.	77%
1506–7	£217 3s. 0d.	£221 6s. 4.5d.	102%
1508–9[f]	£199 7s. 4.5d.	£189 1s. 7.5d.	95%

Sources: (1396–1500) R. B. Dobson, ed., *York City Chamberlains' Account Rolls, 1396–1500*, Surtees Society, vol. 192 (Gateshead, 1980), app. 2; (1501–9), York City Archives, C5:1, C5:2, C5:3.

[a]Excludes deficits carried over from the previous account (*superplusagium*). Such deficits ranged from £23 in 1475–76 to over £506 in 1486–87.

[b]Only gross total expenses are included in this account.

[c]For the reign of Henry VI (1422–61), covered by these six accounts, average annual receipts were about £219 and average net expenses £214, consuming 98 percent of receipts.

[d]For the reign of Edward IV (1461–83), covered by these five accounts, average annual receipts were about £243, average net expenses £225, consuming 93 percent of receipts.

[e]Account fragmentary, partial expenses only.

[f]For the reign of Henry VII (1485–1509), covered by these five accounts, average annual receipts were about £228 and average net expenses £222, consuming 97 percent of receipts.

9. Susan Reynolds, *An Introduction to the History of English Medieval Towns* (Oxford, 1977), 198; Thomas Madox, *Firma Burgi* (London, 1726), 18, 263; William Hudson and John C. Tingey, eds., *The Records of the City of Norwich*, 2 vols. (London and Norwich, 1906, 1910), 1:42, 2:74–75.

bitterly complained that their towns no longer reached such levels of commerce and begged the Crown to ease their burdens.[10] Trade-based revenues were also difficult to collect and pay to the royal government when the Crown seized borough liberties in punishment for local unrest and violence, which was Norwich's particular problem during the 1430s and 1440s.[11]

Irregular payments due the Crown included the lay subsidy (fifteenths and tenths) granted by Parliament and loans to the king. The lay subsidy, for towns the tenth part of the value of movable property, was originally assessed anew at each grant, until it was fixed in 1334 on the basis of a composition between royal commissioners and the communities that paid it.[12] Each subsidy contributed just over £37,000 to Crown finances and made heavy demands upon urban resources: York, for example, contributed £162 for each lay subsidy levied, the rate fixed in its days of

---

10. York's civic officials made this complaint in 1482, noting that towns that once paid tolls for trade with York no longer did so, having received waivers from the royal government. Hansa merchants able to trade freely in England (a favor not returned to English merchants acting abroad) were also noted (Attreed, *York House Books*, 270–71).

11. Hudson and Tingey, *Records of the City of Norwich*, 1:342–43. Fee-farm and other payments to the Crown were not interrupted when the king first seized the city's liberties in 1437–38; however, the city did not make its customary payments during the 1443–47 seizure and accumulated a debt of over £440, as well as a fine of 1,000 marks. The fee-farm debt was eventually canceled in 1452 after Norwich brought its case to the court of the Exchequer. For the documents of these financial problems at the Crown level, see Public Record Office (PRO), Council and Privy Seal records E.28/71, E.28/72; King's Remembrancer Memoranda Rolls E.159/220, Brevia directa, Trinity 22 Henry VI, rot.12v; E.159/221, Brevia directa, Trinity 23 Henry VI, rot.1v; Lord Treasurer's Remembrancer Memoranda Rolls, E.368/216, Precepta, Michaelmas 22 Henry VI; E.368/224, Communa, Michaelmas, rot.23; and King's Bench *Coram Rege* rolls, KB.27/746, rex 29, ff.175–76. Local documentation of the seizure of the liberties and its financial cost to the city includes Norfolk and Norwich Record Office (NNRO), 9-d; 17-b, Book of Pleas, ff.16v–20v, 81v–85v. Henry VI's examination of the records of Norwich's behavior during the first seizure is noted in Nicholas H. Nicolas, ed., *Proceedings and Ordinances of the Privy Council of England*, 7 vols. (London, 1834–37), 5:242–43.

12. Frederick C. Dietz, *English Government Finance 1485–1558*, University of Illinois Studies in the Social Sciences, vol. 9 (Urbana, 1920), 13; Robin E. Glasscock, ed., *The Lay Subsidy of 1334*, British Academy Records of Social and Economic History, n.s., vol. 2 (London, 1975), xvi, 49, 192, 227, 357; J. F. Hadwin, "The Medieval Lay Subsidies and Economic History," *Economic History Review*, 2d ser., 36 (1983): 214; R. S. Schofield, "Parliamentary Lay Taxation 1485–1547," Ph.D. diss., University of Cambridge, 1963, 7–8.

fourteenth-century prosperity and in excess of its fee farm of £160.[13] The
number of subsidies levied varied according to the military and other
emergencies the Crown presented to the Commons, with Henry V man-
aging to extract just over one levy for each year of his reign. His successor was forced to respond to widespread pleas of poverty, at first
(1433–44) returning a total of £4,000 from each levy and by 1445 excus-
ing destitute areas of £6,000 per subsidy.[14] The collection of an established and agreed-upon sum according to a time-honored system proved
easy to accept. Poll taxes and other extraordinary subsidies sometimes
provoked hostile reactions, but violence is not generally associated with
the fifteenths and tenths. How hard local collectors pressed their friends
and neighbors for payment is impossible to determine; unpaid by the central government, these servants received wine and payment of one mark
from Exeter's council, and a reward of two marks from Norwich, doubtless in addition to bribes advanced by inhabitants.[15] Payment of the subsidies was stretched out over several terms, but in general 80 percent of
the money was collected a year after most fifteenths and tenths were
granted.[16]

Alternatives to the fifteenth and tenth proved difficult to initiate and
unprofitable to collect. Evasion as well as violent resistance marked the
notorious poll taxes of the 1370s and 1381. In 1377, York paid £120,
which at a *per capita* rate of 4d. indicates at least 7,200 taxable residents.

---

13. York's share constituted a princely .4 percent of the total (£37,429 18s.) the
king received from each subsidy.

14. John Strachey, ed., *Rotuli Parliamentorum* [*Rot. Parl.*], 6 vols. (London,
1767–77), 6:535–40; *Calendar of the Fine Rolls [Cal. Fine Rolls], 1430–37* (London,
1936), 185–88; *Cal. Fine Rolls, 1445–52* (London, 1939), 30–33. In 1433, York
received a rebate of £16 19s. 7 ¾d., and Norwich £9 18s. ¾d. In 1445, the figures
were £25 9s. 5½d., and £14 17s. 1d., respectively.

15. Schofield, "Parliamentary Lay Taxation," 102–3, 469; W. A. Morris and J. R.
Strayer, eds., *Fiscal Administration*, vol. 2 of *The English Government at Work,
1327–1336* (Cambridge, Mass., 1947), 36; DRO, Receivers' Rolls, 5–6 Henry IV, 1–2
Henry VI; NNRO, 7-c, Treasurers' Rolls, 3–4, 6–9 Henry V, 1–2 and 8–9 Henry VI;
18-a, Chamberlains' Account Book, 1384–1448, 5–6 Henry V, ff.122–23. The collectors were empowered to distrain property if citizens did not contribute, and municipal
sheriffs could imprison the recalcitrant (Schofield, "Parliamentary Lay Taxation,"
102–3; *Calendar of Close Rolls, 1422–29* [London, 1933], 51–52).

16. PRO, E.179/217/61 (33 Henry VI). A study of Exchequer Receipt Rolls, records
of daily payments to the Crown, reveals that tiny amounts of the levies continued to
trickle into the central government 15 to 24 months after they were first granted. For
an example of lingering collection, see E.401/760 *sub* 4 February 1439 (17 Henry VI):
10s. 1.5d. from York as part of the second half of the tenth levied 15 Henry VI.

Three years later, the tripled rate encouraged evasion of over 44 percent. Evasion also ate into the fiscal resources of Norwich and Exeter, although on a smaller scale.[17] Henry IV revitalized feudal aids for the marriage of his daughter, to which York (the only city mentioned in the writ) seems to have contributed 10s.[18] Taxes on income levied in 1436 and 1450 netted the Crown £5,000 and £6,000, respectively, and were composed of individual citizens' payments rather than corporate contributions.[19] Edward IV and Henry VII also tried imaginative combinations of land and income taxes and gained from Parliament special subsidies, as well as fifteenths and tenths, especially for measures of defense. Henry VII enjoyed such a combination in 1489–90 to support 10,000 archers for a Breton campaign: movables and income from property were taxed, but the final sums are unclear. The total fell below expectations, necessitating a "normal" fifteenth and tenth the following year.[20] Boroughs complained loudest when new combinations of taxes were attempted, underlining the overwhelming advantages of the fifteenth and tenth, "the moost easy, redy and prone payment of any charge to be born within this Realme."[21]

Loans constituted one of the most unpredictable drains upon urban resources. Towns found it as difficult to refuse to lend money to a

---

17. R. B. Dobson, ed., *The Peasants' Revolt of 1381* (London, 1970), 55–57; Edward Miller, "Medieval York," *The Victoria History of the Counties of England: A History of Yorkshire, The City of York*, ed. P. M. Tillott (London, 1961), 66; PRO, E.179/149/62, E.179/159/34, E.179/217/13, 15, 16; N. Bartlett, ed., "Lay Poll Tax Returns for the City of York in 1381," *Transactions of the East Riding Antiquarian Society* 30 (1953), n.p.; J. I. Leggett, "The 1377 Poll Tax Return for the City of York," *Yorkshire Archaeological Journal* 43 (1971): 128–46.

18. *Cal. Fine Rolls, 1399–1405* (London, 1931), 147–49; PRO, E.372/248 (3–4 Henry IV).

19. T. B. Pugh and C. D. Ross, "The English Baronage and the Income Tax of 1436," *Bulletin of the Institute of Historical Research* 26 (1953): 1–28; Roger Virgoe, "The Parliamentary Subsidy of 1450," *Bulletin of the Institute of Historical Research* 55 (1982): 124–38. Persons with incomes over £200 per annum contributed 2s. to the pound. Norwich citizens paid £55 15s., and York paid £47 13s. 6d. See also PRO, E.179/238/78, E.179/159/83, E.179/217/56.

20. Margery M. Rowe, ed., *Tudor Exeter: Tax Assessments, 1489–1595*, Devon and Cornwall Record Society, n.s., vol. 22 (Torquay, 1977), vii–viii; Schofield, "Parliamentary Lay Taxation," 4, 166–80. The subsidy granted eight years later for defense against Perkin Warbeck and the Scots sparked violent reactions from the west country, where growing wealth was penalized by an unstable monarchy threatened by the invasion and unable to wait for its money (Ian Arthurson, "1497 and the Western Rising," Ph.D. diss., University of Keele, 1981, 504–19).

21. *Rot. Parl.*, 6:151.

monarch as it was to refuse troops, whether the occasion was the French threat to Gascony, a royal marriage, or a spurious attack on Calais.[22] Lending was not a problem that affected only the elite social leaders of a town. In 1409, Norwich lent 500 marks to the king, 60 percent of which was raised out of common funds. The remainder had to be assessed by a general levy that affected all but the poorest citizens.[23] However, loans were negotiable to a greater extent than were the lay subsidies. Monarchs commissioned men of standing and wealth in each county to persuade others, usually towns, to provide support. Boroughs conferred among themselves as well, as in 1475 when Norwich sent a representative to Bury St. Edmunds to determine how much other burgesses were prepared to lend the king.[24] When the amount was decided, the money could flow from chamberlains' surpluses, general levies, or the personal generosity of aldermen and other civic officials interested in advertising their wealth and increasing their local stature.[25]

Methods of repayment depended upon the nature of the need, the intended relationship between lender and Crown, and the reign in which the loan was made. A study of London corporate loans from 1400 to 1450 reveals that the city lent money out of a sense of duty and in response to the king's necessity, eschewing interest payments in the hope that the loans would be viewed "as oil to lubricate the machinery of royal favor and privilege."[26] Lancastrian monarchs took seriously their promises to repay, often providing lenders with tallies of assignment on the wool subsidy, the customs from a nearby port, or on the lay subsidy next levied on the community that offered the money. Throughout his reign, Henry IV awarded corporate and individual lenders the right to export wool without paying duty, a method of repayment convenient only to those who participated in the trade.[27] Repayment plans exem-

22. G. L. Harriss, "Aids, Loans and Benevolences," *Historical Journal* 6 (1963): 4, 8, 16.

23. Francis Blomefield, *A Topographical History of the County of Norfolk*, 2d ed., 11 vols. (London, 1805–10), 3:125.

24. NNRO, 18-a, Chamberlains' Account Book, 1470–90, f.75v. In 1481, city representatives went to Lynn for advice on appropriate lending (NNRO, 18-a, Chamberlain's Account Book, 1479–88, f.20v).

25. DRO, Receivers' Roll, 1–2 Henry V; NNRO, 16-d, Assembly Book I, f.19; *Records of the City of Norwich*, 2:48–49.

26. Caroline Barron, "The Government of London and Its Relations with the Crown, 1400–1450," Ph.D. diss., University of London, 1970, 423, 440, 451–52.

27. Barron, "Government," 21; *Cal. Patent Rolls, 1399–1401* (London, 1903), 251, 353–55; *Cal. Patent Rolls, 1401–1405* (London, 1905), 403, 416–17; PRO, E.404/2/261.

plified the truism that it takes money to make money. During reigns with frequent tax levies, subjects lent frequently, for repayment could be made from the next fifteenth and tenth. At the end of Henry VI's reign, for example, when Parliament granted few taxes, individuals and boroughs were more reluctant to lend because reimbursement could not be so easily guaranteed, especially in a contracting economy.[28] Although Norwich took second place only to Bristol as the leading lender to the Crown, the East Anglian center advanced only £28 per annum during Henry VI's reign, and York (in fourth place among urban lenders) only £17 per annum, so uncertain were their officials as to benefits and repayment plans.[29]

The system did not always work smoothly. In 1436, Norwich lent the Crown £100, which failed to be covered as promised by the fifteenth from the county of Essex. Four years later, the citizens were forced to sue in Exchequer for recovery, because they planned to give the sum to the duke of Gloucester who was coming to visit.[30] The use of jewels as sureties caused problems as well. Henry V pledged swords, crowns, and ornaments to raise money from boroughs, whose officers were burdened with the safekeeping of these objects and the dilemma of whether to sell them if the king defaulted. In 1415, Henry pledged a tabernacle of jeweled silver gilt, raising a total of 860 marks, 100 of which came from Exeter. Civic officials shared the care of the item with Devon abbeys and members of the gentry, and had to answer in the Exchequer for it, at a cost of 3s. 4d for each trip. Although licensed to dispose of the tabernacle if the king did not repay the loans, the caretakers did not do so, and in 1422 carriage of the jewel back to London cost Exeter officials an extra 20d.[31] Norwich officials shared this reluctance to sell one of Henry

28. Ralph A. Griffiths, *The Reign of Henry VI* (Berkeley and Los Angeles, 1981), 109. See E.401/780. York's loan of 100 marks made on 26 October 1442 was covered by the second half of the lay tax from the East Riding, paid into the receipt of the Exchequer the following day.

29. This analysis excludes London, upon whose officers Henry came frequently to rely, as well as upon the wealthy staplers of Calais (Anthony Steel, *Receipt of the Exchequer, 1377–1485* [Cambridge, 1954], 196–97, 261–66, 344–52; Griffiths, *Henry VI*, 119, 393).

30. PRO, E.401/748, *sub* 3 May 1436; NNRO, 16-d, Assembly Book I, f.14 (October 1440). Gloucester did not appear, but the duke of Norfolk took his place and, when he asked for a loan on behalf of the Crown, Norwich told him it was too poor to lend *(Records of the City of Norwich, 1:283).*

31. DRO, Receivers' Rolls, 5–6, 7–8 Henry V, 1–2 Henry VI; Thomas Rymer, ed., *Foedera, Conventiones, Letterae . . .* , 3d ed., 10 vols. (The Hague, 1739–45), 9:285; *Cal. Patent Rolls, 1413–16* (London, 1910), 354; Richard A. Newhall, *The English Conquest of Normandy, 1416–1424* (New Haven, 1924), 147 n.13.

V's gold coronets. In 1417–18, they sent a representative to the Exchequer to sue for the money due them. When this failed, in 1420, the jewel itself was taken south, but again the city (along with Lynn, which shared responsibility) could not exchange it for the money due. In 1424, Norwich officials began a suit in the Exchequer and approached urban patrons Sir Thomas Erpingham and the bishop of Norwich, but five years later they had succeeded only in redeeming the circlet for 60 percent less than their advance.[32]

Despite these bad experiences, almost totally confined to the reign of Henry V, Ricardian and Lancastrian borrowing fulfilled an immediate need and adequately secured repayment. Loan demands were never cheerfully welcomed by boroughs, but town officials calculated such outlays to be shrewd investments. Anxious for increases in chartered privileges, Norwich lent the royal government an average of £33 per annum during Richard II's reign, £90 per annum under Henry IV, and more than £100 per annum to Henry V (see table 4). Cries of poverty lay in the future: in 1397, when a few citizens rashly promised the king a corporate loan of 500 marks, the city hoped the king would accept less yet found the money when asked. A town aspiring to county status could do no less, one reason why Norwich advanced 1,000 marks to Henry IV soon after his accession.[33] Direct benefits such as the acquisition of municipal offices and trading privileges also persuaded York to lend money during this period: Richard II received two loans of £200 each in addition to gifts and hospitality during royal visits, and more than £1,300 was granted to Henry IV within the first five years of his reign.[34] When at all possible, town governments tried to respond positively to the king's call for funds. In many cases, the loans acted as another form of urban patronage, more effective than gifts of wine or small pensions in con-

32. NNRO, 18-a, Chamberlains' Account Book, 1384–1448, ff.122–23; 7-c, Treasurers' Accounts, 7–8, 8–9 Henry V. A crafty individual could turn possession of royal jewels to his own advantage (see K. B. McFarlane, "At the Deathbed of Cardinal Beaufort," in *Studies in Medieval History presented to F. M. Powicke*, ed. R. W. Hunt, W. A. Pantin, R. W. Southern [Oxford, 1948], 412, 416, 418).

33. *Records of the City of Norwich*, 2:40, 45; Rymer, *Foedera*, 8:9–12; *Cal. Patent Rolls, 1396–99* (London, 1909), 180–81; Blomefield, *History of Norfolk*, 3:119.

34. Rymer, *Foedera*, 8:152; *Cal. Patent Rolls, 1396–99*, 363–64, 368; *Cal. Patent Rolls, 1399–1401*, 353. In addition to 1,500 marks given by the city upon his landing at Ravenspur, Henry IV gained from York 500 marks for a Welsh campaign in 1403, and £200 pledged by six individuals in 1404 (Nicolas, *Proceedings Privy Council*, 1:200–203; Miller, "Medieval York," 67).

TABLE 4. Urban Loans, 1377–1509

	Exeter	Norwich	York
Richard II			
1378		£191	
1385		150 m.	
1386		£100	£200
1397		500 m.	£200
Henry IV			
1400			1,500 m.[a]
1402		1,000 m.	
1403			500 m.
1404			£200[b]
1409		500 m.	
1412		400 m.	
Henry V			
1415	100 m.	500 m.	
1417		1,000 m.	£654[c]
Henry VI			
1430		£94 12s.	£162[b]
1434		£200	
1435		£200	
1436	200 m.	£300	£331 17s. 8d.
1437		£100	
1446		£38	100 m.
1452		100 m.	
1454		£100	£100
Edward IV:			
1481		£200	
1482		50 m.	

Source: L. C. Attreed, "The English Royal Government and Its Relations with the Boroughs of Norwich, York, Exeter and Nottingham, 1377–1509," Ph.D. diss., Harvard University, 1984, chap. 10.
[a]Half given before Henry IV's accession.
[b]Raised by individuals, not corporately.
[c]Total for Henry V's entire reign.

vincing the monarch to extend his favor and grant a desired charter or privilege. Lending money may also have helped many subjects feel a part of the government and its actions, a welcome impression as Crown machinery began to take on the forms of bureaucracy and fall out of touch with local conditions and needs.

Borrowing patterns changed under the Yorkist monarchs, affecting boroughs' responses to demands. By modifying both the reasons given for advances and the ways in which the money was collected, the Yorkists discovered that funds did not always have to be repaid. The urban protestations of poverty that convinced a weaker predecessor had less effect upon the propagator of benevolences.[35] Edward IV was quick to remind his subjects that "by the lawe we may call and lawfully compelle [you] to go with us . . . into any place of this land for the defens of the same against outward enemyes" and that the loans he called benevolences were defined as little more than the equivalent of such personal service and were no more likely to be repaid. Whether through commissioners or more effectively during personal visits, the king reminded urban subjects in particular how he was sparing them the inconvenience of personal military service, only asking for what they "list give of their free will."[36] Fortunately for town governments, the Yorkists and the first Tudor found it more profitable to approach wealthy individuals rather than reluctant city councils, a move that does much to confirm the veracity of urban pleas of corporate poverty, particularly in the north. Thus, York was corporately responsible for no loan during Edward IV's reign and Norwich for less than £250.[37]

By combining the financial data for the three boroughs, we can gain insight into the nature of economic pressure brought to bear by the royal government, quite apart from the towns' domestic budgets and the monies raised to stay within town walls. In table 5, data on loans, subsi-

---

35. See PRO, E.28/47, for one such plea of poverty, made by Norwich in 1426 on the grounds that all its wealth lay in the cloth seized by Dutch merchants abroad.

36. Nicolas, *Proceedings Privy Council*, 5:418–21; Harriss, "Aids, Loans and Benevolences," 10. The reluctant were forced to give an increased amount. That benevolences were defined in this way can be seen in York, where in 1481 troops for a Scottish expedition were described as a benevolence (Robert Davies, ed., *York Records: Extracts from the Municipal Records of the City of York* [London, 1843; Dursley, England: Gloucester Reprints, 1976], 115–16).

37. NNRO, 16-d, Assembly Book I, ff.111, 112v, 114. Not all loans went unpaid by Yorkists. In 1474, Edward IV directed sheriffs in York and Norwich to proclaim that he was willing to repay any creditor who presented a tally made before 1470 (*Cal. Close Rolls, 1468–76* [London, 1953], no. 1212).

TABLE 5. Total Crown Demands (Pipe Roll information plus lay subsidy and loan data)

	Average Payments Due Crown per Annum	Crown Demands as Percentage of Local Receipts	Crown Demands as Percentage of Net Local Expenses
Norwich			
Richard II			
1377–99	£246	123%	205%
Henry IV			
1399–1413	£299	161%	201%
Henry V			
1413–22	£329	187%	237%
Henry VI[a]			
1422–61	£202	95%	123%
Edward IV			
1461–83	£177	120%	132%
Henry VII			
1485–1509	£159	94%	134%
Exeter			
Richard II	£68	52%	69%
Henry IV	£68	47%	50%
Henry V	£92	63%	80%
Henry VI	£65	50%	69%
Edward IV	£56	39%	47%
Henry VII	£56	30%	33%
York			
Richard II	£278	—[b]	68%[c]
Henry IV	£347	—[b]	—[b]
Henry V	£391	—[b]	—[b]
Henry VI	£252	115%	118%
Edward IV	£234	96%	107%
Henry VII	£281	123%	125%

Source: Public Record Office, Exchequer documents, especially E.372 series; and see previous tables.
[a]Based on normal demands, excluding arrears of waived fee farm.
[b]Insufficient local financial data.
[c]Based on gross total expenses.

dies, fee farms, and the many small rents and payments demanded by the Crown are averaged for each year of the pertinent royal reigns. This sum is then compared to the local receipts and net expenses set forth in tables 1–3 and expressed as a percentage. Some years were undoubtedly harder than others, as civic officials struggled not only to collect the tolls and rents that paid local salaries and repaired defenses, but such sums might be amassed two and three times over when kings sought financial expressions of support and loyalty. Nevertheless, the data reveal that royal expectations of Exeter were controlled and reasonable, befitting a small town with modest growth during these centuries. The annual payments expected of Norwich and York are significantly higher, and table 6 indicates the differences in how well the two boroughs handled the burden. The same Pipe Rolls that set forth urban debts of the fee farm, small rents, and escheats also note whether the sheriffs paid the entire debt at the time of accounting. Norwich sheriffs were able to pay all but the smallest amounts of their debts to the Crown; York had a harder time, especially in the years of heavy lay subsidies. Once again, the northern city's cries of poverty appear to be grounded in truth.

Nevertheless, it would be unwise to rely totally upon imperfect statistics to decide which boroughs were actually experiencing hardship and which ones exaggerated their financial difficulties. Cries of poverty expressed more than simple economic stress. Social historians have begun to trace pervasive changes in medieval concepts of poverty and the

TABLE 6.   Percentage of Debts on Pipe Rolls Unpaid to Crown at Time of Remittance

	Norwich[a]	York
Richard II	3.0%	0.0%
Henry IV	7.0%	9.0%
Henry V	0.0%	34.0%
Henry VI	7.0%[b]	10.0%
Edward IV and		
Richard III	0.0%	1.0%
Henry VII	1.6%	22.0%

Source: Public Record Office, E.372 series.
[a]Exeter omitted because details of borough finances are silently subsumed under Devonshire.
[b]Based on normal demands and payments, excluding those for the fee farm (later waived) and penalty payments imposed while city liberties were in the king's hands, 1443–47.

poor, noticing that during the fourteenth and fifteenth centuries attitudes toward the destitute hardened, which led to the fear and loathing lying behind sixteenth-century legislation against vagabonds and beggers.[38] Further study is needed to determine what factors contributed to these changes in attitude: real fiscal hardship; the deleterious financial effects arising from internal violence and the national unrest of the Wars of the Roses; civic officials' fear of failing to safeguard their towns from plunging into poverty if expenses got out of hand; and uncertainty concerning the balance between corporate responsibility for the poor and private benevolence expressed in wills and bequests. Until these factors can be weighed, we can only conclude that officials' stereotypical claims of poverty expressed fears about the financial, social, and psychological state of town life, fears no less real for being impossible to quantify.

But civic officials were not paralyzed by their fears. What they could not accomplish or control themselves could be passed to urban patrons, members of the nobility who often held important positions in royal government and were thought to have influence with the king. Some lived in the countryside surrounding the town and knew of urban problems first-hand; others resided in Westminster and relied upon the occasional visit to catch up on borough affairs and enjoy the ceremonial welcomes and gifts so flattering to aristocratic egos. For all the complaints about tight budgets, town officials tried to reward their "good lords" and interest them in a borough's well-being. The gifts were fairly modest; wine, fish, local fruit and game generated expenses under 10 percent of annual receipt levels in those years not marked by costly royal visits (see table 7). Of equal or greater value was the ceremony extended to visiting nobles, no less important for being on a much smaller scale than that provided visiting royalty at great cost to local receipts.[39] I have explored on other

---

38. Michel Mollat, *The Poor in the Middle Ages*, trans. Arthur Goldhammer (New Haven and London, 1986), esp. pt. 4: "Paupers and Beggars: Alarming Presences (Mid-Fourteenth to Early Sixteenth Century)," 191–293. Miri Rubin, *Charity and Community in Medieval Cambridge* (Cambridge, 1987), studies changing forms of charitable giving and the role of hospitals in the later Middle Ages. My article, "Preparation for Death in Sixteenth-Century Northern England," *Sixteenth-Century Journal* 13 (1982): 37–66, focuses on sixteenth-century charitable behavior, showing through the use of wills that bequests to the poor occupied the minds of individual testators and that private charity was an important aspect of medieval and early modern culture.

39. See Exeter's account for 1483–84 (Richard III's visit); and York's accounts for 1396–97 (Richard II's visit), 1478–79 (Edward IV's visit), and 1486–87 (Henry VII's visit), tables 1, 3, 7.

TABLE 7. Local Gift and Patronage Expenses

	Average Gift Expenses per Account	Gifts as Percentage of Receipts
Norwich		
Richard II	£15 5s.	7.6%
Henry IV	£15 11s.	8.4%
Henry V	£11 17s.	6.7%
Henry VI	£8 13s.	4.0%
Edward IV	£11 13s.	7.9%
Henry VII[a]	£ 6 1s.	3.6%
Exeter		
Richard II	£5 13s.	4.3%
Henry IV	£10 13s.	7.3%
Henry V	£12 7s.	8.4%
Henry VI	£10 5s.	7.9%
Edward IV	£10 8s.	7.3%
Richard III		
1483–84[b]	£16 12s.	10.5%
1484–85	£27 11s.	11.1%
Henry VII	£7 17s.	4.2%

	Gift Expenses	Gifts as Percentage of Receipts
York		
1396–97[b]	£243 11s. 11d.	59.6%[c]
1433–34	£5 11s. 1d.	2.4%
1442–43	£7 3s. 11d.	3.1%
1445–46	£8 4s. 4d.	3.4%
1449–50	£7 7s. 1d.	3.6%
1453–54	£8 12s. 11d.	4.2%
1454–55	£9 0s. 7d.	4.4%
1462–63	£8 19s. 5d.	4.6%
1468–69	£3 2s. 8d.	1.2%
1470–71[d]	£1 2s. 0d.	0.3%
1475–76	£3 4s. 1d.	1.7%
1478–79[b]	£38 2s. 11d.	16.0%
1486–87[b]	£36 2s. 9d.	16.4%
1499–1500[d]	£1 1s. 8d.	0.5%
1501–2	£4 19s. 0d.	1.8%
1506–7	£4 8s. 10d.	2.0%
1508–9	17s. 4d.	0.4%

Sources: See tables 1–3.
[a]Gift and patronage expenses for the reign of Richard III average £1 per annum in Norwich.
[b]Years of royal visits to city.
[c]Receipts not provided; expenses used as basis of calculation.
[d]Incomplete figures in this account.

occasions the nobles' roles in helping towns gain administrative, constitutional, and judicial privileges; here, I will note the major ways in which towns approached members of the aristocracy to persuade them to assist in trade and commerce, sources of wealth for towns in balancing internal and external budgets.[40]

However well intended or surfeited with wine and fish, a town's good lords could not create trade where none existed. But they could use their contacts with the royal government to solve specific problems and bring trade-related profits a town's way. A valuable contact for the city of Norwich was the Lancastrian retainer Sir Thomas Erpingham. A Norfolk man with a house in the city, Erpingham had close ties with John of Gaunt, and his royal son and grandson, which eased the city through the confusing years of transition to the Lancastrian regime.[41] Sir Thomas helped Norwich gain its 1404 charter of incorporation (refused by Richard II) and, after a decade of dispute over what its clauses meant, joined in interpreting its trading privileges and rights of municipal election. Known as the Composition of 1415, this agreement allowed Norwich to deal with the competition city merchants experienced from foreign traders, interpreting the liberties to restrict foreign mercantile activity, hiring practices, and participation in local government.[42] A shrewd assessor of political realities, Erpingham turned his attention and that of Norwich to the Prince of Wales from 1409 to 1411, when Henry IV was ill and the young man held power.[43] This shift gained Norwich the ulnage and survey of worsted cloth in the city and county, at the cost

40. See my "Arbitration and the Growth of Urban Liberties in Late Medieval England," *Journal of British Studies* 31 (1992): 205–35; and "The Politics of Welcome—Ceremonies and Constitutional Development in Later Medieval English Towns," *City and Spectacle in Medieval Europe*, ed. Barbara Hanawalt and Kathryn L. Reyerson (Minneapolis, 1994), 208–31.

41. Simon Walker, *The Lancastrian Affinity 1361–1399* (Oxford, 1990), 37 n.127, 92 n.64, 193–94, 200–201, 269; J. H. Druery, "The Erpingham House, St. Martin's at Palace, Norwich," *Norfolk and Norwich Archaeological Society* [*Norfolk Archaeology*] 6 (1864): 144, 147; Trevor John, "Sir Thomas Erpingham, East Anglian Society and the Dynastic Revolution of 1399," *Norfolk Archaeology* 35 (1970): 96–97; *Cal. Patent Rolls, 1381–85* (London, 1897), 557.

42. Hudson and Tingey, *Records of the City of Norwich*, 1:29, 106; *Calendar of the Charter Rolls*, vol. 6, *1427–1516* (London, 1927), 30; Philippa C. Maddern, *Violence and Social Order: East Anglia 1422–1442* (Oxford, 1992), 179–80. The Composition was predominantly concerned with election procedures and the duties of civic officers, but it touched on foreign merchants as well.

43. John, "Sir Thomas," 106; Hudson and Tingey, *Records of Norwich*, 2:56; Blomefield, *History of the County of Norfolk*, 3:125.

of more than £36 in legal fees and gifts to government clerks and Erpingham himself.[44] Worsted production had been an expanding industry in the area since the early fourteenth century; civic control over its measurement standards and sales brought in small amounts of money (under £10 per annum), which was used for wall repair, while preserving the city's reputation for quality cloth bought by locals and foreigners alike.[45]

But wine and processions could not create goodwill in local lords in all cases. Norwich's profitable partnership with Erpingham was supplanted in the mid–fifteenth century by more hostile relations with William de la Pole, duke of Suffolk, whose interference in civic elections and destruction of local mills lost the city its liberties and damaged trade and commerce.[46] Exeter had a similarly mixed experience with its local "good lords," caught as it was for much of the fifteenth century amid the rivalries between the Courtenay earls of Devon and the Bonville family. Both Courtenays and Bonvilles retained Exeter citizens and civic officials as counsellors and advisors. Exeter's relations with the Courtenays date from the 1240s, when the family's blockage of the River Exe and domination of local trade and customs at the nearby port of Topsham set the tone for the abrasive and abusive relations between Courtenays and city. The Bonvilles were not influential enough with the royal government to win their urban clients trade concessions at the Courtenays' expense. Worse luck for the city, neither family showed Exeter particular favor in

44. Hudson and Tingey, *Records of Norwich*, 2:55–57.

45. Norwich stressed the effect on sales that any decline in quality could cause: "[Cloths were being] fraudulently made by certain workmen to the scandal of the merchants of the city and the surrounding county and the loss of the lords, gentry, and others who used to buy them and the merchants who used to cross with them to Flanders, Seland, and divers other places beyond the seas" (*Calendar of the Patent Rolls, 1408–13* [London, 1909], 194–95; Strachey, *Rot Parl.*, 3:637). Ulnage (or alnage) accounts are notoriously difficult to work with, their farmed payments discouraging conclusions about contributions of cloth production to local or national revenue. See E. M. Carus-Wilson, "The Aulnage Accounts: A Criticism," *Economic History Review* 2 (1929): 114, 122; Herbert Heaton, *The Yorkshire Woollen and Worsted Industries*, 2d ed. (Oxford, 1965), 69, 85, 127; and A. R. Bridbury, *Medieval English Clothmaking: An Economic Survey* (London, 1982), 47–53, 59. Ulnage payments covered royal defense costs, contributed to annuities for royal pensioners, and reimbursed those who had made voluntary or involuntary loans to the Crown.

46. Maddern, *Violence and Social Order*, 194–96, examines the background to the events of the 1440s and Suffolk's participation.

the 1440s when called upon to arbitrate a dispute between the town and episcopal authorities over jurisdiction near the cathedral.[47]

Of all provincial cities, York possessed the best relations with its good lord, Richard, duke of Gloucester, a local patron who (once he became king) did not forget the "little people" who had made it all possible. Considering York's financial difficulties, it is not surprising to find its officials persistently pressuring Richard, as Edward IV's brother, to do something about the state of its commerce. Richard was one of several people asked to persuade the king to aid York's communications with the Low Countries by the establishment of a separate northern trading organization under its own governor. Sadly for York, the king merely issued a proclamation urging fair treatment in trade.[48] Richard was more successful in his campaigns against that bane of water-borne trade, fishgarths. These wicker or wooden baskets or traps collected large amounts of fish for their owners (local lords and religious houses for the most part) but impeded traffic on the river and decreased the number of fish that could be caught with a modest hook and line. Richard promised the civic officials his aid in destroying such traps, following his visit to York in 1476, and wrote on the city's behalf to his own tenants. Traps placed by the Duchy of Lancaster's tenants of Gowdall on the Aire proved particularly difficult to abolish. The city council sent a letter the following year to the king noting the great loss the Crown suffered when local economies were cheated of their deserved wealth, prompting Edward IV to put his younger brother in charge of investigating the problem. Richard was commanded to "take a view and oversight of the fishgarths and weirs" when next he came home to Yorkshire and to direct the destruction of likely impediments to urban trade.[49] In the spring of 1479, civic officials spent more than £21 (or 9 percent of total receipts) inspecting the rivers, identifying offending traps, and sending messengers to Richard and to local nobleman Henry Percy, earl of Northumberland, for their assistance.[50] Despite Richard's diligence, not to mention the 1475 act of Parliament banning fishgarths in northern rivers, the problem was not easily or quickly solved. In 1482, a riot broke out in Snaith over

---

47. See Attreed, "Arbitration"; and chapter 8 of my Ph.D. thesis, "The English Royal Government and Its Relations with the Boroughs of Norwich, York, Exeter and Nottingham, 1377–1509," Harvard University, 1984.

48. Miller, "Medieval York," 103–4.

49. Attreed, *York House Books*, 9–10, 129–30.

50. Dobson, *Chamberlains' Accounts*, 163–64.

the destruction of a fishgarth, and two summers later a party of civic officials examining northern rivers discovered numerous traps operated by the major bishops, abbots, and nobles of the region.[51] Even worse, the Crown owned a few fishgarths itself in rivers in the Duchy of Lancaster, a conflict of interest that embarrassed Richard after his accession to the throne in 1483.[52] By no means a petty annoyance of small importance, the problem of the fishgarths was symptomatic of the northeast's disturbing economic problems and of the lengths to which an ambitious local lord would go to help the area and himself.

Generous quantities of wine, fish, bread, and exotic game made their way to Richard and his family in recognition of his help and of a relationship that grew more special upon his coronation. Soon after that ceremony, the royal family visited York on their tour around the country, tarrying long enough for their young son to be invested as Prince of Wales in York Minster. In a special ceremony held before his departure, Richard gave the city what everyone at that point thought was a great boon: the dismissal of tolls and other charges imposed on merchants entering the city, thereby encouraging the free passage of trade and commerce.[53] Richard's entourage was a day's ride down the road before anyone remembered that the sums involved composed the city's fee-farm payment, and York's officials sought reassurances that they would indeed be excused from making that payment to the Crown. The Exchequer continued to expect the fee farm, however, and neither Richard nor his successor, Henry VII, was able to satisfy the demands of either the royal bureaucracy or the city. Thus, a good lord's probably sincere grant resulted in decades of petitions, costs, and frustrations for an already financially stressed borough.[54]

---

51. Attreed, *York House Books*, 269, 318–20.

52. Attreed, *York House Books*, 307; for other references to fishgarths, see 116, 311–12.

53. Attreed, *York House Books*, 729.

54. For details, see my articles, "The King's Interest—York's Fee Farm and the Central Government," *Northern History* 17 (1981): 24–43; and "Medieval Bureaucracy in Fifteenth-Century York," *York Historian* 6 (1985): 24–31; as well as the introduction to my *York House Books*, xxi–xxii It is possible that Richard had no intention of acting on his promise to York and never told the Exchequer to excuse the city. But even before leaving the city Richard took the trouble to change the source of an annuity provided to Sir John Savage, an important supporter in the Welsh marches. Savage had until then derived his annuity from York's fee farm (Rosemary Horrox and P. W. Hammond, eds., *British Library Harleian MS.433*, 4 vols. [Upminster and London, 1979–83], 2:18). York was no less important a source of support than Savage, and it is unlikely that Richard intended to confuse or offend either one.

The reticence of financial records kept by both royal and urban governments inhibits the formation of radical conclusions and reveals the limitations of statistics derived from fragmentary archives created for purposes other than our own. Even the most complete accounts and balanced entries rarely are accompanied by insights into the full financial picture of town wealth. Medieval historians may be doomed never to know urban officials' thoughts on the ease or difficulty with which they raised money, much less the exact reason why Exeter's mayor felt the need for a half-gallon of wine while making his accounts. At the very least, the comparative method attempted in this study maximizes the sheer number of financial records examined, but it also allows more accurate analysis. The contrasting pace and direction of economic growth in the three towns warns against formulating broad generalizations about urban development in postplague England. Towns such as York, which had once been provincial capitals with lively economies, experienced change for the worse as commercial and industrial patterns shifted. New centers such as Norwich already knew financial fortune, while Exeter's economic boom lay ahead. Likewise, all urban complaints about the difficulties of paying local and royal debts cannot be accepted as either fictive or accurate in the face of such comparisons. Urban officials may have shared a language of complaint, but they did not share all the same experiences and challenges.

The differences in growth and decline that are the rewards of comparative history for modern historians served only to confuse medieval monarchs and their governments. Although kings tried to speak helpfully and sympathetically to town needs, their actions were not always based on timely understanding of systemic problems. Perhaps it was too much to ask a Lancastrian or Yorkist government to remember that York's economy was stretched thin while Exeter's finances could withstand heavier demands. Even if such precision were possible, extraordinary need such as that defined by Henry V tended to ignore individual differences while maximizing national demands. That so much of what Agincourt's hero as well as less martial kings required could be raised hints at the unknown, and essentially unquantifiable, side of medieval economic history.

To that end, it is as incumbent upon us as it was to medieval citizens to realize that a town's true wealth lay in its contacts as much as in its cash reserves. A royal visit, during which problems and needs could be directly discussed with the monarch, occurred rarely. More conveniently at hand were local nobles and royal officers who were able to spend more time on site and accurately direct the administrative machinery to ameliorate town troubles. The comparative method, this time focusing on their patrons, again makes clear the vast differences towns experienced. York's battered economy received much attention from a prince well placed to create beneficial change; Norwich suffered the uncertainty of an unpredictable, almost irrational foe; and Exeter's patrons represented the best and worst of friendship in high places. Although any analysis must ultimately conclude that patrons nice or nasty had only a slight effect on the long-term nature of urban economy, we should not denigrate the towns' perceptions of their royal contacts. However straitened the budget, urban officials directed timely gifts to visitors and potential friends. Everyone knew that fiscal health was tied to commercial and administrative benefits by living bonds. Henry VI recognized this fact in 1449, when, in granting the city of York various privileges and monetary concessions, he concluded that the borough's poverty was caused in part by the fact that it "has not been relieved for [a] long time by the king's presence, courts, councils or parliament."[55] Rather than urging civic officials to avoid such costly outlay, Henry understood that the initial expense of hospitality and spectacle, enjoyed by king, nobles, and citizens alike, could reap long-term financial benefits resulting from trade increases and better understanding of the nature of town resources. When that happened, the mayor of Exeter and leaders of other towns could make their accounts and pass the wine with pleasure rather than as painkiller.

55. *Calendar of Patent Rolls, 1446–52* (London, 1909), 221.

Municipal Finances in Medieval Castile: Palencia at the Middle of the Fifteenth Century

María Jesús Fuente

At the 1962 Conference on Urban Finances and Accountancy, held in Blankenberge, Belgium, Marinette Bruwier pointed out that, although historians had done much work on the medieval city over the last hundred years, they had neglected its financial history.[1]

Since then things have changed. Two years after the Conference of Blankenberge, another conference that dealt with taxation in the Middle Ages took place in Spa, also in Belgium.[2] Early in the 1970s, Jean Favier published a documentary history of public finances in the later Middle Ages.[3] William Bowsky came out with a monograph on medieval Siena[4] and shortly afterward Anthony Molho wrote another one on medieval Florence,[5] the city that was later studied by David Herlihy and Christiane Klapisch-Zuber.[6] Following the path opened by Françoise Humbert's study of the finances of Dijon,[7] several French

---

1. *Finances et comptabilité urbaines du XIIIe au XVIe siècle*, Colloque International (Blankenberge, 1962). Bruxelles, Pro Civitate, Collection Histoire, in 8°, n.7, 1964, 21.

2. *L'Impôt dans le cadre de la ville et de l'Etat*, Colloque International (Spa, 1964). Bruxelles, Pro Civitate, Collection Histoire, in 8°, n.13, 1966.

3. J. Favier, *Finance et fiscalité au Bas Moyen Age* (Paris. 1971).

4. W. M. Bowsky, *The Finance of the Commune of Siena: 1287–1355* (Oxford, 1970).

5. A. Molho, *Florentine Public Finances in the Early Renaissance, 1400–1433* (Cambridge, Mass., 1971).

6. D. Herlihy and C. Klapisch-Zuber, *Les toscans et leurs familles. Une étude du catasto florentin de 1427* (Paris, 1978).

7. F. Humbert, *Les finances municipales de Dijon du milieu du XIV siècle à 1477* (Paris, 1961).

doctoral theses,[8] some of which have been published, analyzed urban finance in medieval France.[9] And the Centre National de la Recherche Scientifique devoted one of its conferences to the subject of fiscal issues in medieval and early modern Europe.[10]

Although these historians have studied different places and employed different methods, they have all agreed on one point: fiscal problems were at the heart of many conflicts and revolts during the Middle Ages. In virtually every uprising fiscal problems were among the most serious causes.

At the crux of these conflicts were two issues—what would be taxed and who would pay taxes. As a rule, historians have found, the lower classes preferred direct taxation,[11] especially if it was progressive, whereas the upper classes preferred indirect taxation. Indirect taxation was growing as the economy evolved. Merchants and craftsmen were more and more obliged to pay taxes, and land was no longer the only tax base. Historians have also found that, since the noblemen, knights, and squires enjoyed privileges that enabled them to avoid paying direct taxes, the taxpayers tried to find ways to make these privileged persons bear a part of the fiscal burden.

Whether these findings hold true for Spain is hard to say because historians have not devoted much attention to urban finance in medieval Spain. M. A. Ladero[12] has studied the fiscal policy of the kingdom of Castile. Some scholars have written chapters on municipal economy in monographs about Castilian cities.[13] Others have researched a particular

---

8. A. Droguet, *Les finances municipales de Marseille dans le second moitié du XIVe siècle*, th. Ec. Nat. des Ch., dactyl., 1975; A. Guerreau, *Une ville et ses finances, Mâcon (1350–1550)*, th. Ec. Nat. des Ch., dactyl., 1971.

9. A. Rigaudière, *Saint-Flour ville d'Auvergne au Bas Moyen Age. Etude d'histoire administrative et financière* (Paris, 1982); S. Curveiller, *Dunkerque ville et port de Flandre à la fin du Moyen Age* (Lille, 1989).

10. J. Ph. Genet, *Genèse de l'état moderne Prélèvement et Redistribution, Actes du Colloque de Fontevraud 1984* (Paris, 1987).

11. D. Herlihy, "Direct and Indirect Taxation in Tuscan Urban Finance, ca. 1200–1400," *Finances et comptabilité urbaines du XIIIe au XVIe siècle*, Colloque International (Blankenberge, 1962), 388 ff.; R. Cazelles, "Les variations du prélèvement et de la répartition selon les équipes au pouvoir," in *Genèse de l'Etat Moderne*, 205–6.

12. M. A. Ladero, *La Hacienda Real de Castilla en el siglo XV* (La Laguna, 1973); *El siglo XV en Castilla. Fuentes de renta y política fiscal* (Barcelona, 1982).

13. J. M. Monsalvo, *El sistema político concejil. El ejemplo del señorío medieval de Alba de Tormes y su concejo de villa y tierra* (Salamanca, 1988); J. C. Martín Cea, *El mundo rural castellano a fines de la Edad Media* (Valladolid, 1991).

aspect of the municipal economy, like the sources of income (*communs* or censuses of city property),[14] and others have edited fiscal accounts of Spanish cities.[15] But only in Murcia has medieval finance been studied in depth.[16]

One reason for the lack of studies is the scarcity of documentation. In very few Castilian cities have the fiscal records survived. One exception is Palencia, a medium-sized Castilian city, which has preserved a good series of the accounts of the *mayordomo,* the municipal official in charge of finance. The series, which starts at 1432, allows us to study municipal finance in the late Middle Ages and in particular to trace the shift from direct to indirect taxation.

Examining the series, we can see at once the significant difference between the sources of income of the first half of the fifteenth century and the second half. Before 1448, the income came from direct taxation. Afterward this form of taxation produced little or no revenue. To account for the change I intend to look closely at the records of the middle of the century and in particular at two very revealing documents, one from 1448 and the other from 1452.[17]

The following analysis focuses on the relationship between fiscal policy and political conflict in medieval Palencia, where, as elsewhere, these policies were at the heart of local uprisings. The story raises several questions. Who led the revolt? And why? Who opposed it? And why? How

---

14. J. A. Pardos, "La renta de alcabala vieja, portazgo y barra . . . del concejo de Burgos durante el siglo XV (1429–1503)," in *Historia de la Hacienda española, edades antigua y medieval, en homenaje a D. Luis García de Valdeavellano, Actas del III Symposium de Historia de la Administración* (Madrid, 1974).

15. J. L. Martín and A. García, *Cuentas municipales de Gata (1520–1524)* (Salamanca, 1972). A. Collantes de Terán, *Inventario de los papeles del mayordomazgo del siglo XV,* vol. 1: *1401–16* (Seville, 1972); vol. 2: *1417–31* (Seville, 1980).

16. D. Menjot, *Fiscalidad y sociedad. Los murcianos y el impuesto en la Baja Edad Media* (Murcia, 1986); Mā. Belén Piqueras, *Fiscalidad real y concejil en el reinado de Enrique IV: el ejemplo de Murcia (1462–1474)* (Cádiz, 1988); F. Chacón, "Una contribución al estudio de las economías municipales en Castilla. La coyuntura económica concejil murciana en el periodo 1496–1517," *Miscelánea Medieval Murciana* (1977); M. LL. Martínez Carrillo, "Servicios castellanos y política municipal. Aspectos fiscales de la reforma concejil murciana de 1399," *Miscelánea Medieval Murciana,* vol. 5 (1980); A. L. Molina, "Repercusiones de la guerra castellano-aragonesa en la economía murciana," *Miscelánea Medieval Murciana,* vol. 3 (1977); J. Torres Fontes, "La hacienda concejil murciana en el siglo XIV," *AHDE,* 26 (1956): 741–57.

17. The one of 1448 is in the Municipal Archive of Palencia, document without number. The one of 1452 is in the Archive of the Cathedral of Palencia, catalogued 2.2.17.

was it resolved? Who gained, and who lost? The answers to these questions can tell us much about municipal finance in medieval Castile—and, as developments were in some ways different in Palencia than in other cities, in medieval Europe as well.

The Urban Conflict in 1448

The first of the two above-mentioned documents is a judgment dated May 20, 1448, that was supposed to resolve a conflict over tax policy in Palencia. It was handed down by a prominent noblewoman of the city, Doña Ynes Enrriques, widow of the lord of Almaçan. The documents do not mention why she was asked to be the arbitrator, but it was probably because she was a member of one of the most important families of Palencia.

Two sides had appeared before her. On one side were the representatives of the taxpayers (*comun, boni homini, çibdadanos,* and *pecheros*). On the other were the representatives of the nontaxpayers (*caballeros, escuderos,* and *exentos*).[18] Both groups were asking for changes in the way taxes were collected in the city.

The taxpayers made seven requests, as follows.

First, to give half of the money produced by the confraternities to the city, and with it to pay *pedido* and *prestido,* the taxes that the king sometimes demanded from the taxpayers. In years in which the king did not ask for taxes, they asked that the money be used for other purposes.

Second, to charge *imposición,* an indirect tax on consumption, on the wine barrels sold in the city (35 *maravedíes* for each barrel), in order to contribute to the royal taxes (*pedido* and *prestido*).

Third, to use the money collected from the *imposiciones* and the rents of the city property to pay the royal taxes and the seigneurial taxes, in particular the *martiniega,* the domanial tax that received its name from St. Martin and was due on November 11, the saint's day. Also, they asked that the accounts be supervised by *diputados de la comunidat,* representatives of the taxpayers.[19]

---

18. The Spanish documents mention *pecheros* and *exentos,* referring to taxpayers and nontaxpayers. Since there is no English word for *exentos,* I will use the Spanish word to describe citizens with privileges of exemption.

19. Control of the accounts and fiscality was a goal of citizens with lower rents in several medieval cities. See A. Rigaudière, op. cit., 1:167; Ph. Wolff, "Réflexions sur l'histoire médiévale de Carcassonne," *Actes des XLIe et XXIVe Congrès de la Féderations historique du Languedoc méditerranéen et du Roussillon et de la Féd. des*

Fourth, to resort to direct taxation only when the money collected by other means was insufficient. If more money was needed to pay the royal *pedido,* then the taxpayers would be obliged to contribute.

Fifth, if there was not enough money to pay the *martiniega* of the bishop, everybody, including the exempted, knights, and squires, would have to pay according to his means. There were to be no exemptions other than those for craftsmen deemed essential to the city (blacksmiths or cask makers, for example).[20]

Sixth, exemption was to be confined to those who had been exempted for at least 10 years.

The last request was intended to exempt new people who came to live in the city from all taxes.

In response to the taxpayers, the knights, squires, and *exentos* presented seven alternate requests to Doña Ines.

First, they asked that only one-third of the rents or income of the confraternities be earmarked for the city and that this money be used to pay not only the royal *pedidos* and *emprestidos* but also the *martiniega* of the bishop. Two-thirds of this money would go for the royal taxes and one-third for the seigneurial tax. The reasons will be explained later.

Second, they accepted the *imposición* of the wine barrels, but demanded a smaller amount for each barrel (20 *maravedíes*). The money thus collected would be distributed in the same manner as the rent from the confraternities: two-thirds for *pedidos* and *emprestidos* and one-third for the *martiniega.*

Third, they wanted the tax on wine and must to be controlled not only by representatives of the *comun,* but also by representatives of knights and squires.

Fourth, they did not have objections to the fourth petition of the taxpayers, in which the taxpayers had agreed to pay if extra money was needed to give the king the money required for the *pedido.*

Fifth, they agreed to contribute if the city needed more money to pay the *martiniega* of the lord, but they disagreed with the method. They

Soc.ac. et sav. Langu., Pyr., Gasc. tenus à Carcassonne les 17–19 mai 1968 (Carcassonne, 1970), 135–46; and J. Combes, "Finances municipales et oppositions sociales à Montpellier au commencement du XIVe siècle," *Actes du XLIVe Congrès de la Féderation historique du Languedoc méditerranéen et du Roussillon tenu à Privas les 22–23 mai 1971* (Montpellier, 1972), 99–120.

20. María J. Fuente, *La ciudad de Palencia en el siglo XV. Aportación al estudio de las ciudades castellanas en la Baja Edad Media* (Madrid, 1989), 217.

wanted to pay *comunmente*—all citizens paying the same amount—and not *en mas cuantia*—paying more because it was done proportionally. For that they asked that two or three representatives of their group be called as witnesses when the taxes were being imposed.

Sixth, they asked that those who were exempt from paying the *pedido* be allowed to continue not paying it and that this exemption be extended to their wives and children.

Finally, they did not want exemptions for the new citizens.

The petitions of both groups reveal much about the fiscal and economic organization of the city and the interests that underlay the taxpayers' desire to change the way the money was collected.

Each group wanted changes in the method of collecting money for the city. The exempted preferred to give a third of the rent of the confraternities to the city, rather than the half requested by the taxpayers, because they (the *exentos*) were the members of the richest confraternities. In their view, this was an indirect way of paying money to the city. The same thing happened with the *imposición* on the barrels. The wine would be introduced in the city mostly by the richest, who were most of the *exentos,* which was why they wanted a lower tax per barrel.

Although both groups wanted changes in the use of the money, they did not agree on how to spend it. Since the privileged did not pay royal taxes, but did pay seigneurial taxes, they wanted the money received from the confraternities and the *imposición* of the barrels to be used to pay one-third of the *martiniega* of the bishop. The *exentos* agreed to pay a direct tax if the city did not collect enough money for the *martiniega,* but they probably believed that additional funds would rarely be needed. If by any chance they did have to pay, they did not want a proportional assessment, as the taxpayers had requested, but wanted everyone to pay an equal amount. Finally, those with privileges did not want to exempt new citizens because they believed that the additional contributions of new taxpayers would lessen the burden for everyone.

Doña Ynes Enrriques's judgment tried to provide a compromise.[21] She accepted the first petition of the taxpayers and decided that half of the rents of the confraternities should go toward the income of the city. However, she went along with the *exentos'* request that this money should be spent so that two-thirds would pay royal taxes and one-third the lord tax. Her response to the second petition was similar. She

---

21. It is not possible to know if she decided or if some lawyer did the work for her. Even if she decided herself, she probably solicited some help.

accepted the taxpayers' request that there be a tax on barrels of wine that entered the city, but the amount would be the one proposed by the exempted: 20 *maravedíes.*

Doña Ynes looked for a compromise in the case of other petitions as well. She required the *exentos* to pay the tax, if necessary, for the *martiniega,* but she exempted them from other taxes. She allowed them to keep their privileges if they could prove that they had had tax exemptions for five years. She gave both groups the power to decide what to do about the newcomers. New citizens could be exempted from the *pedido* or the *prestido* if the taxpayers wanted, and they could be required to pay the *martiniega* if this was the will of the exempted.

The noblewoman's judgment also held that the group of people receiving the rents of the city must contain members of both factions. When there was no difference between the petitions of the two groups, as was true when the taxpayers agreed to levy a direct tax if that became necessary to pay royal taxes, she let things stand as they were.

Doña Ynes ordered that her decision be implemented as of June 10, 1448. In effect, the *cargo,* or account of income, of the economic year 1448–49[22] results directly from the recommendations of this document.[23] The main income came from half of the rents of the confraternities and the collection of royal taxes. The amount was 94,906 *maravedíes,* which were used to pay the royal taxes (72,304.5 *maravedíes*), along with other expenditures mentioned in the *data,* or account of expenditures, of the *mayordomo,* Diego, Ferrandes de Flores.[24]

The account of the following year shows more specifically how Doña Ynes's resolution was implemented. Following the petition of the privileged, the money collected from the rents of the confraternities was distributed as follows: two-thirds for the *pedido* and one-third for the *martiniega* (half to pay the share of the taxpayers and the other half the share of the *exentos*). The money collected from the *imposiciones* was distributed the same way: two-thirds for the *pedido,* one-sixth for the *martiniega* of the taxpayers, and one-sixth for the *martiniega* of the *exentos.*

In 1450–51, a new source of income appeared: rents of town lots. Though they were not mentioned in Doña Ynes's decision, they became

22. The municipal and economic year started in Palencia on the first Sunday of March.

23. Municipal Archive of Palencia, Books of Account of the *mayordomo* or treasurer, 1448–49.

24. This *data* was only one of the expenditures of the *comun,* or taxpayers, because it covers only two-thirds of the half of the rents of the confraternities.

another source of income. City property, confraternities, *imposiciones,* and town lots were thus the four sources of income from which city officials got the money necessary to pay municipal expenses.

The Judgment of the Bishop and Lord of the City (1452)

The success of Doña Ynes's resolution was short-lived. By 1452, the conflict was still unresolved. Not only did the same problems exist, but there was displeasure with Doña Ynes's decision. Why were the citizens dissatisfied with the first judgment? Were some more unhappy than others? In what ways did they show their lack of satisfaction?

The judgment of 1452 suggests answers. That year, four *amigos árbitros* (arbitrators), the same noblewoman (Doña Ynes Enrriques), and the three highest authorities of the cathedral (the bishop, the dean, and the arcediano de Carrión),[25] dictated a decision aimed at finally resolving the disputes between the taxpayers and the *exentos.*

These disputes had various causes. The main continuing source of conflict was over the distribution and method of collecting taxes, as well as over the *imposiciones,* the confraternities, the town lots, the custody of the gates and towers, and the exemptions.

Two confraternities, in part, brought the underlying conflict into the public arena. One was made up of taxpayers and named *cofradía del Cuerpo de Dios* (confraternity of the Body of God), and another was called St. Antón of the Squires (this one was recently organized, probably in response to the influence of the confraternity of the taxpayers).

The confraternity of the *Cuerpo de Dios,* which grew rapidly between 1446 and 1452, caused many of the city's troubles during these years. Some said that it was more of a *liga e monipodio* (confederation of people) than a properly constituted confraternity because it was the cause of the "pleitos e debates e contiendas e costas e muertes" (trials and debates and confrontations and costs and deaths) that had occurred in the city and supposedly were continuing.

The problems, a kind of urban revolt, had not only a social but an economic cost. As a result of the tumult, some properties were not well tended, and many fields were not being worked. This neglect caused enough economic damage to create a fear that people would abandon the city. This fear led the citizens to request the mediation of the four arbi-

---

25. This *arcediano* was one of the four canon dignities of the cathedral of Palencia.

trators, whom they asked for "orden que oviesen de tener e guardar e regla commo oviesen de bevir" (orders to be kept and observed and rules to dictate how they should live).

The judgment of the four arbitrators had several provisions. One ordered the dissolution of the two confraternities mentioned above.[26] Another asked the mayors and aldermen to assume responsibility for the keys to the gates and towers of the city and to entrust them to faithful citizens. The most important provisions concerned the finances of the city and will be analyzed in detail.

The first provision concerned with finances ordered that all the revenues collected by the Council (*Concejo*)—from the confraternities, the town lots, the *imposiciones,* and the city property—should be kept together and used to pay the seigneurial and royal taxes and other expenditures of the city. The revenues should be received by the mayors, the aldermen, the mayor of accounts, the accountant, and the court clerk. To avoid corruption their management would be supervised by the representatives of the taxpayers (*diputados del comun*).

The *imposiciones* became one form of the income, but the arbitrators decided that the barrels of wine would not be taxed as they entered the city. The wood that the citizens needed, charged with an *imposición* during 1452, would no longer be taxed either. To make up for the loss of revenue, the arbitrators called for two new *imposiciones,* one called *fieldad,* a sort of sales tax, the other *corta del pescado,* a tax on the sale of fish. Both were to be paid by customers.

Another provision dealt with exemptions. Some citizens were exempted by mayors and aldermen, while others had acquired the privilege by virtue of being knights, squires, or members of the nobility (*hidalgos*). The exemptions granted by the municipal officers were almost abolished because their power was narrowed to exempt only newcomers who came to serve the city.

As for the knights, squires, and nobility, the arbitrators pointed out that they contributed to the municipal treasury in different ways. They were members of confraternities, half of whose rents were already taken. Also they were the owners of the largest flocks and household looms, both of which were indirectly taxed with the *imposiciones.* As the arbitrators considered that these *exentos* were contributing enough, they did

---

26. The confraternity of the *Cuerpo de Dios* sold some of its property, i.e., the wax, but the confraternity was not dissolved. Some years later there was news of it in the Books of Account of the *mayordomo.*

not ask them for any other tax except those supporting defense and public works. In return the *exentos* accepted the provision that all the income of the city would be kept together and from it the municipal authorities would pay the taxes for the king and the lord and the other expenditures.

The four arbitrators, especially the bishop, left one of the most important issues for the end. The lord of the city declared that the citizens had done many illegal things during the past six years; as a result he had started a proceeding before the Pope. According to the lord, the citizens had wrongfully placed a census on the town lots, imposed indirect taxes on some products, and taken half of the rents of the confraternities. In other words, the citizens had done everything the taxpayers asked in order to avoid direct taxation. This was illegal because the citizens needed the approval of the lord, according to the *Fuero,* or law of the city. However, the bishop did not ask them to revert to the previous arrangement. Instead, since the city did not have subject villages or vassals of any kind to help it lighten the burden of fiscal charges, and since the taxpayers were so heavily taxed that the city might lose population, the lord decided to give a gift to the city. He transferred his ownership of the town lots, which henceforth would be administered by the municipal authorities. With these measures the bishop was accepting de iure what the citizens had already done de facto—raising city income by levying *imposiciones,* renting the town lots, and obliging the confraternities to contribute half of their rents.

The Result of the Conflict

The judgment of the four arbitrators ended a time of troubles and initiated a period of peace. It also brought substantial economic, social, and jurisdictional changes to the city.

There was, first, a change in the way municipal finances were handled. In 1448, the citizens and Doña Ynes followed the medieval practice of requesting a particular revenue for a particular expenditure.[27] In 1452, the bishop and the other arbitrators rejected this method and decided that all the incomes would be kept together.

The sources of income would be the four mentioned above: income of

---

27. B. Chevalier, "Fiscalité municipale et fiscalité d'Etat en France du XIVe à la fin du XVIe siècle. Deux systèmes liés et concurrents," in *Genèse de l'état moderne Prélèvement et Redistribution, Actes du Colloque de Fontevraud 1984,* 139.

the confraternities, census of town lots, rents from city property, and taxes on products. The amount collected from these sources remained more or less constant during these years.

Of the three new sources of income, only the *imposiciones* can be considered an indirect tax. The revenues from the town lots and confraternity properties were not taxes, though they were a means of forcing the richest and most privileged citizens to contribute to the municipal treasury.

How did these changes affect the different social groups of the city? At first glance, it looks as if the winners were the taxpayers and the losers were the *exentos,* who had to accept what the lord, pushed by the taxpayers, asked of them. However, research based on other Castilian and European cities shows that the taxpayers were not a homogeneous group, and in consequence we have to look more carefully at this group to see if all the members, or only some, derived benefits from the changes. Let us look at the taxpayers who were especially active in the revolt of those years.

In the judgment of 1452, there is a list of 29 men of the *comun* who watched the lord render his decision and were probably active participants in the controversy. Among these men were Diego Ferrandes de Flores, sometime treasurer of the City Hall;[28] Sancho Garcia Cubero, representative of the *comun* in the year in which the *diputados,* or representatives, were named and renter of *imposiciones* and town lots for several years; Ferrand Martines de Villabermudo, sometime municipal official (alderman and representative); Pero Garcia Carpenter, collector of the *martiniega forana* (the seigneurial tax paid by foreigners with properties in Palencia) in 1452–53; Toribio Ferrnandes de Santoyo, envoy representative of the city to the royal court at Valladolid, in 1449; Diego Lopes, municipal official in 1451; Alvar Ferrnandes de Çisneros, sent by the city in 1454 to solve a problem in the *chancelleria,* or institution of royal justice; Juan Rodrigues Segoviano, another treasurer in 1450–51; and Pero Ferrnandes de Calabaçanos, renter of several city properties.

As this list shows, the protagonists in the conflict were not anonymous people of the *comun* but, on the contrary, taxpayers of importance in the political, social, and economic life of the city. They were municipal

---

28. He appears to be the *mayordomo,* or treasurer, in at least three years, 1450–51, 1454–55, and 1457–58.

officials, representatives of the city, renters of city property, and in all likelihood the richest taxpayers.[29]

Hence, in Palencia the wealthiest spearheaded the fight against other citizens who had equal wealth but possessed privileges enabling them to avoid payment of taxes. In other cities, where everyone paid taxes or where the tax rate was progressive or proportional, the situation was different; there the *comun* fought to get direct taxation because this form of taxation benefited the people with lower rents. But in the case of Palencia, where there was a significant group of *exentos,* the burden fell upon the biggest taxpayers, who not only paid directly but were forced from time to time to lend money to municipal officials.[30]

Who paid according to the new system? Though it is impossible to be precise about how much people paid in indirect taxes, it is possible to estimate how much each group paid to the city. From the confraternities came the highest sums. The city had 65 confraternities, some of professionals, some pious,[31] some of taxpayers, and some of *exentos.* Almost all had properties that produced income. It is likely that the richest confraternities, the ones with the highest revenues, were those of the richest men of the city, probably noblemen, knights, squires, or others privileged with exemptions. From these confraternities came a good part of the money that flowed into the municipal coffers.

Imposiciones were taxes on everyone, rich and poor, but at the beginning the richest probably paid the most. In the first year for which data about *imposiciones* are available, 1449, the city taxed several goods: sheep, three kinds of cloth, two types of wood, water, dung piles, wine caves, and some properties around the city called *exidos.* It also taxed activities such as dyeing and tanning. These taxes on goods and activities (12 in total) seem to have been imposed as a means of extracting money from the city's artisans and the foreign merchants.

Much the same was true in the case of the census of town lots. Citizens who rented them not only had to pay the census but had to build on the

---

29. It is well known that treasurers were always wealthy citizens because sometimes cities had to borrow money from them.

30. On the role of loans in municipal finances, see A. Molho, op. cit., 60ff.; W. A. Bowsky, op. cit., 166ff.; J. Favier, op. cit., 279ff.; A. Rigaudière, op. cit., 898ff.; and F. Humbert, op. cit., 165.

31. Municipal Archive of Palencia, Book of Accounts of the *mayordomo,* lists the confraternities and their rents from 1449. The number of confraternities was 65, but it was increased to 66 in 1466, when, after a terrible plague, the citizens created the confraternity of St. Sebastian.

lot. To pay the census and build on a lot required the sort of financial resources that were available only to the wealthiest citizens.

Did the new fiscal policy help low-income people? Probably not, but it did not hurt them either. They did not have to contribute, or at least they did not pay much through confraternities or town lots. Though they did pay through the *imposiciones,* the amounts were probably small, some *maravedíes* for the few head of sheep they owned and some for the water, wood, and dung piles. This contribution helped them to avoid direct taxation, though, if this form of taxation had been imposed in a proportional way, as the taxpayers proposed, the poor would not have had to pay much anyway.

Finally, the conflict had consequences for the jurisdiction of the bishop. He had to accept that the taxpayers had violated customary law (the *fuero* and the customs of the city), and he had to accede to their petitions. By so doing he lost part of his power over the citizens and at the same time part of his income. Why did the bishop behave this way? In the document it says that he did it to help the citizens by lightening their burden ("para aliviamiento e ayuda"). If this is so, the citizens must have been both overwhelmed and fed up with the old fiscal policies. Otherwise the lord would not have been so responsive to their petitions, and he would not have approved the new economic order.

Conclusion

This conflict brings to light an unusual way of facing the problems of raising and spending public money in a medieval city.[32] Unlike other cities, where residents fought for direct taxation to force the rich to pay more,[33] and unlike cities where citizens fought for indirect taxation as the main source of municipal income,[34] Palencia found a way to acquire its income from different sources, one of them indirect taxation, and thus avoid direct taxes.

Palencia also does not follow the pattern of European cities that needed a new basis of taxation to shift the burden from landowners to

32. A. Rigaudière, op. cit., 2:939.
33. D. Herlihy, op. cit.
34. B. Palacios and M. I. Falcón, "Las haciendas municipales de Zaragoza, a mediados del siglo XV (1440–1472)," in *Historia de la hacienda española (épocas antigua y medieval)* (Madrid, 1982), 565ff.

merchants and artisans.[35] This may be because some of the protesters were themselves merchants and craftsmen and because landowners continued to be taxed, if not for cultivating the land then for raising the sheep, which were indirectly taxed in the *imposiciones*.

Though the promoters were the largest taxpayers, they did not wish to harm low-income people by imposing taxes on many consumption items. Indeed, the change did not much affect the poor, but it did affect the wealthy, who were now obliged to contribute through other means than indirect taxation. This could be one reason why the *comun* helped the protesters in this conflict.

Another reason could be that the fight was not only against the *exentos* but also against the jurisdiction of the lord, who had to accept de iure a de facto situation. This could have happened because the ones who posed the conflict had economic power and, in consequence, political power, too. This issue of the control of the lord over municipal finances has been studied in some German cities, where this control was not important,[36] because the elites, what M. Maschke calls the "social shells," who controlled incomes and expenditures, were the ones who really had the power. Like the German cities, Palencia was a city in which the control of urban finance was held by those "social shells," the wealthiest taxpayers, the urban oligarchy, who used their economic and political power to impose their will on other groups in the city.

---

35. A. M. Arnould, "L'Impôt dans l'histoire des peuples," *L'Impôt dans le cadre de la ville et de l'Etat*, Colloque International (Spa, 1964), 18.

36. M. Maschke, *Finances et comptabilité urbaines du XIIIᵉ au XVIᵉ siècle*. Colloque International (Blankenberge, 1962), 339, a discussion of the paper of F. Blockmans, "Le contrôle pas le Prince des comptes urbains en Flandre et en Brabant, au Moyen Age."

Religious Diversity and Communal Politics in Thirteenth-Century Italy

James M. Powell

Canon 13 of the Fourth Lateran Council (1215) opened with the words:[1]

> Lest too great a diversity of religions lead to serious confusion in the church of God, we firmly forbid anyone in the future to found a new religion, but, whoever desires to be converted to religion should take up one already approved.

The concern expressed in this canon referred specifically to the rapid growth of new religious orders in the latter part of the twelfth century and in the years immediately preceding the council. Traditionally, historians have focused their discussion of its meaning on the growth of the mendicant orders.[2] Since the publication of Herbert Grundmann's important work in the 1930s on religious movements, there has been significant emphasis on the ties between the mendicants and the develop-

I would like to thank the members of the Quodlibet Society at Cornell University for the opportunity to present this paper and to hear their comments. A special thanks to Professor James John for his careful reading of the revised version and his many helpful suggestions.

1. *Conciliorum Oecumenicorum Decreta*, 3d ed. (Bologna, 1973), 242: "Ne nimia religionum diversitas gravem in ecclesia Dei confusionem inducat, firmiter prohibemus, ne quis de caetero novam religionem inveniat, sed quicumque voluerit ad religionem converti, unam de approbatis assumat."

2. James M. Powell, "The Papacy and the Early Franciscans," *Franciscan Studies*, 36 (1976): 248–62, provides further discussion and notes (see esp. 248–53). See also Michele Maccarrone, "Riforme e innovazioni di Innocenzo III nella vita religiosa," *Studi su Innocenzo III* (Padua, 1972), 70–156. I do not believe, however, that Innocent actively formulated a policy opposed to the recognition of new religious orders prior to the Council. Rather, Canon 13 was most likely the result of opposition to his policies, which, though cautious, continued to remain open to experiment.

ment of forms of life based on the *vita apostolica* during the eleventh and twelfth centuries.[3] More recently, scholars have recognized that the relationship between monastic reforms and the increasing popularity of the *vita apostolica* among the laity reflected a major development in medieval spirituality.[4] The history of religious confraternities has also attracted considerable attention. The pioneering work of Gioacchino Volpe and Gennaro Monti produced rich results in the scholarship of Gilles Gerard Meersseman, Cinzio Violante, Paolo Sambin, Raoul Manselli, and Giorgio Cracco.[5] In the last two decades, numerous English-speaking scholars have published studies in the field, related especially to developments in the fourteenth, fifteenth, and sixteenth centuries.[6] None of these scholars has, however, to my knowledge, linked

3. Herbert Grundmann, *Religiöse Bewegungen im Mittelalter: Untersuchungen über die geschichtlichen Zusammenhange zwischen der Ketzerei, den Bettelorden und der religiösen Frauenbewegung im 12. und 13. Jahrhundert und über die geschichtlichen Grundlagen der deutschen Mystik* (Berlin, 1935; rpt., Vaduz, 1965), 127–35. See also John Moorman, *A History of the Franciscan Order* (Oxford, 1968); and M. H. Vicaire, *St. Dominic and His Times* (New York, 1964), esp. x–xi, 72–79.

4. Jill Raitt, ed. *Christian Spirituality: High Middle Ages and Reformation* (New York, 1987), 1–11; Henrietta Leyser, *Hermits and the New Monasticism* (New York, 1984); C. H. Lawrence, *Medieval Monasticism: Forms of Religious Life in Western Europe in the Middle Ages*, 2d ed. (London, 1990), 111–273.

5. Gioacchino Volpe, *Movimenti religiosi e sette ereticali nella società medievale* (Florence, 1961). Volpe's work was first published in 1922. See also Gennaro M. Monti, *Le confraternite medievali dell'alta e media Italia*, 2 vols. (Venice, 1927); and Gilles G. Meersseman, *Ordo Fraternitatis: Confraternite e Pietà dei laici nel medioevo*, 3 vols. (Rome, 1977). Cinzio Violante, *La pataria milanese e la riforma ecclesiastica* (Rome, 1955), is a groundbreaking work in the field; cf. Raoul Manselli, *Studi sulle eresie del secolo XII* (Rome, 1953). For Paolo Sambin and the historians influenced by his work, see Robert Brentano, "Italian Ecclesiastical History: The Sambin Revolution," *Medievalia et Humanistica* 14 (1986): 189–97. See also Paolo Sambin, *L'ordinamento parrocchiale à Padova nel medioevo* (Padua, 1941); Giorgio Cracco, *Realtà e carisma nell'Europa del Mille* (Turin, 1971); and Giuseppina de Sandre Gaspartini, *Statuti di confraternite religiose di Padova nel medioevo* (Padua, 1974). Roberto Rusconi has also made important contributions in several collections of essays he has edited: *L'attesa della fine: Crisi della società, profezia ed apocalisse in Italia al tempo del scisma d'occidente* (Rome, 1979); and *Predicazione e vita religiosa nella società italiana: Da Carlo Magno alla controriforma* (Turin, 1981).

6. Ronald Weissman, *Ritual Brotherhood in Renaissance Florence* (New York, 1982), 43–105; James R. Banker, *Death in the Community: Memorialization and Confraternities in an Italian Commune in the Late Middle Ages* (Athens, 1988), esp. his historiographical essay, 1–14; Christopher F. Black, *Italian Confraternities in the Sixteenth Century* (New York, 1989), 23–57; James M. Powell, *Albertanus of Brescia: The Pursuit of Happiness in the Early Thirteenth Century* (Philadelphia, 1992), 90–106; Lester Little, *Liberty, Charity, Fraternity: Lay Religious Confraternities at Bergamo in the Age of the Commune* (Bergamo, 1988), 13–15, 29–55.

the concerns over religious diversity expressed at the council to the proliferation of rules for lay or mixed religious associations. Nor has anyone
examined the impact of this religious diversity on the development of secular society. Some recent work has focused on the impact of religion on
politics. A notable example is Richard Trexler's study of public life in
Renaissance Florence, which has studied various kinds of ritual as an
expression of religious and political identity.[7] The focus of this essay is,
however, on the impact of religious diversity as reflected in the rules of
various kinds of associations on the statutes of the thirteenth-century
communes of northern Italy.

It represents an effort to trace the roots of social and political debates
that have long been associated with the fourteenth and fifteenth centuries
to the religious differences that had increasingly troubled the church and
society in the twelfth and thirteenth centuries, especially as these differences were reflected in various forms of religious rules. The experience of
the prelates of the Fourth Lateran Council with such groups as the
Waldensians and Humiliati undoubtedly brought the problem to the
fore. Possibly, this canon reflects a certain dissatisfaction with the direction of papal policy toward such groups during the pontificate of Innocent III. Brenda Bolton has sketched the issues faced by the papacy
regarding recognition of new religious groups in the late twelfth and
early thirteenth centuries, demonstrating how the decisions of Innocent
III put it at the center of the controversy over these complex issues, particularly because of the fear of heresy.[8] The experience of the Order of
Grandmont may suggest other reasons for the concerns of the hierarchy.
As Jean Becquet has made clear, the internal conflicts of the Order of
Grandmont reflected fundamental differences over the nature of authority within religious communities as well as a dispute between clerics and
lay brothers over control of the goods of the order and the interpretation
of the rule established by their founder, Stephen of Muret.[9] That rule
raised constitutional problems that seriously undermined the intention of

---

7. Richard Trexler, *Renaissance Florence: The Public Life of a Complex Society*
(New York, 1980), 1–128.

8. Brenda Bolton, "Innocent III's Treatment of the Humiliati," *Popular Belief and
Practice*, ed. G. J. Cuming and Derek Baker, 73–82. Studies in Church History, no. 8
(Cambridge, 1972).

9. Jean Becquet, "La première crise de l'ordre de Grandmont," *Bulletin de la
société historique et archéologique du Limousin* 87(1958–60), 283–324; James M.
Powell, *Anatomy of a Crusade* (Philadelphia, 1986), 36–37.

Stephen to found an order committed to poverty.[10] We do not have to look very far to see that disputes over rules were quite common within communities as well as with external critics. The cases of the Gilbertines and the Premonstratensians, both founded in the twelfth century and involving considerable departures from earlier monastic experience, provoked considerable criticism.[11] At the heart of these disputes lay the willingness of the twelfth-century religious to experiment. Although some of their efforts may impress us as reasonable and not very radical, that was hardly the view of their contemporaries. Even those, like James of Vitry, who were quite sympathetic to experimentation—James was the biographer of Mary of Oignies and close to the Beguines in Liege—were sometimes moved to criticize novelty, including that of the much-admired Francis of Assisi.[12] But Giles Constable has suggested that many put a positive construction on these developments, seeing increasing diversity as a sign of the flowering of religion.[13] Nevertheless, there can be little doubt that the position reflected in Canon 13 represented a considered view of many influential prelates.

What issues especially aroused these concerns about new religious orders? The Fourth Lateran Council made it clear that the major factor was the tendency of these rules to disregard monastic stability. Canon 13 is a restatement of that monastic tradition enshrined in the Benedictine rule that required a monk to belong to one house and to remain there under the rule of the abbot. It also established that no abbot should preside over several monasteries. In the view of the proponents of Canon 13, it was the abandonment or modification of these provisions that lay at the root of the internal divisiveness that had beset the church. Canon 13 was not merely an effort to turn back the clock; it was an effort to block what many prelates regarded as an unhealthy diversity, which was causing "serious confusion" in the church of God. In fact, however, the promulgation of Canon 13 had little permanent effect in stemming the tide. It may have led St. Dominic to adopt the Augustinian rule as the guide for the Order of Preachers, though the Dominicans soon filled that vacuum

---

10. Ibid., 36.

11. Lawrence, *Medieval Monasticism*, 170–72, and 224–27.

12. James M. Powell, "The Papacy and the Early Franciscans," *Franciscan Studies* 36 (1976): 248–62.

13. Giles Constable, "The Diversity of Religious Life and the Acceptance of Social Pluralism in the Twelfth Century," in *History, Society and the Churches: Essays in Honour of Owen Chadwick*, ed. Derek Beales and Geoffrey Best (Cambridge, 1985), 29–47.

with a rich body of statutes, but it only slightly impeded the progress of St. Francis of Assisi in his effort to innovate. Later founders easily circumvented its provisions, and it had little or no impact on the later constitutional development of religious orders.[14]

What is evident, however, is that Canon 13 did express the fears of many in the hierarchy regarding the recent direction of the church. Moreover, I would argue that these concerns were directed not merely at the proliferation of monastic rules but at that of the rules of the Order of Penance, of confraternities founded for specific religious purposes, and of some of those that brought together members of particular professions. Recent studies suggesting a growth of opposition to such groups in the thirteenth century support this line of thought.[15] Evidence of this concern is found in the *Summa Aurea* of the canonist Henry of Segusio, better known as Hostiensis, in a passage dealing with the larger meaning of religions that makes clear his own effort to support an interpretation of Canon 13 that applied to the growth of confraternities.[16] The proliferation of diverse forms of religious rules for mixed clerical and lay congregations as well as for the laity created the kinds of problems experienced by the early Humiliati. The work of Meersseman, though chiefly focused on the prehistory and subsequent development of the Third Orders, has made it clear that the number and variety of such groups offers a rich field for further investigation.

The history of confraternities in the church reaches back to its very early days, but little is known of them for many centuries. There were various forms of association as early as the Carolingian period. Some were episcopal; others were connected to monasteries. Many were associations of clergy. For example, those formed for the rural clergy provided a needed support system in a period when the strength of the church in rural areas was lacking.[17] Association for a particular purpose, such as care of the sick or of travelers, was fairly common. Other groups

14. Powell, "The Papacy and the Early Franciscans," 248–52.
15. Jacques Chiffoleau, "Entre le religieux et le politique: Les Confréries de Saint-Esprit en Provence et en Comtat Venaissin à la fin du moyen âge," in *Le mouvement confraternel au moyen âge: France, Italie, Suisse: Actes de la table ronde organisée par l'Université de Lausanne* (Geneva, 1987), 9–40, esp. 12–13.
16. Gilles G. Meersseman, *Dossier de l'ordre de la pénitence au XIIIe siècle* (Fribourg, Switzerland, 1961), has printed the excerpt from the *Summa Aurea* on p. 308. On this point, see also Andre Vauchez, *Les laics au moyen âge* (Paris, 1987), 101.
17. See Gilles G. Meersseman, "Confraternite laicali rurali," *Ordo Fraternitatis* 1: 35–67; and Meersseman, "Confraternite del clero rurale," 113–36.

met the needs of mixed groups of clergy and laity. Such groups were founded for a variety of purposes, chiefly charitable. Other associations were composed of specific professions, like the Fraternity of Masters and Scholars at Bologna. At Valenciennes, Meersseman shows how the merchants organized a confraternity. At Barbastro, concern about the Saracens led to the organization of a knightly association. Some groups were concerned chiefly to promote a particular form of devotion. The most famous example is that of the Rosary Confraternity, which belongs to the late thirteenth century and flourished for centuries thereafter.[18] By the twelfth century, more and more confraternities were founded with a view toward promoting works of penance.[19] The relation between these groups and innovation in new monastic forms was especially close, though concern about the taint of heresy seems to have made the Franciscans cautious in establishing a Third Order before the advent of the Franciscan Pope, Nicholas IV.[20] Meersseman has collected numerous rules of these groups in his *Dossier de l'ordre de la pénitence* and a supplement published as the "Premier Auctarium de l'ordre de pénitence."[21] The study of these rules suggests a society that perceived in them the fulfillment of an essential social need for structure that was not being met in existing political institutions. These religious rules provided a freedom for experimentation that was not yet possible in the communes, where factional divisions probably frustrated such initiatives. It is also clear that by the late twelfth century a culture of rules had developed that went far beyond the religious associations that had given it its earliest impetus.

Writing in the first half of the thirteenth century, Albertanus of Brescia, a *causidicus,* or legal counsellor, practicing in his native city, left a series of sermons and treatises that enable us to view the development of this culture of rules in specific terms.[22] Albertanus was a layman. He was

---

18. Gilles Meersseman, "Confraternite ospedaliere," *Ordo Fraternitatis* 1:137–49. See also, in the same volume, "Confraternite miste e corporazioni chiericali," 1:150–87; and "Corporazioni devote e milizie religiose," 1:188–216. For the confraternity of the rosary, see "Le origini della confraternità del rosario e della sua iconografia in Italia," 2:1170–1232.

19. Meersseman, *Dossier,* 9–38.

20. James M. Powell, *Albertanus of Brescia: The Pursuit of Happiness in the Early Thirteenth Century* (Philadelphia, 1986), 91; Moorman, *History of the Franciscan Order,* 218–19.

21. *Dossier,* see note 16, above. See also Meersseman's "Premier auctarium de l'ordre de la pénitence au XIIIe siècle: Le manuel des pénitents de Brescia," *Revue d'histoire écclésiastique* 62 (1967): 5–48.

22. The following discussion is based on my *Albertanus of Brescia.*

the author of three treatises and five sermons written between 1238 and 1250. In his first treatise, composed as he languished in prison in Cremona following his capture in 1238 by Frederick II, he established his vision of a society in which the concept of a religious rule served as a model for social organization. The title of his treatise, "De amore et dilectione Dei et proximi et aliarum rerum et de forma vite," is based on the Augustinian rule. The phrase "de forma vite" also refers specifically to the religious life. The treatise itself advances the idea of a rule as a fundamental key to social cohesion. The views of Albertanus were informed in part by his profound knowledge of the letters of Seneca, which was drawn in turn from his study of a Brescian manuscript of those letters annotated in his own hand. While in Genoa in 1243, as an adviser to his fellow Brescian, Manuel di Maggi, the podestà, he delivered a sermon to a group of judges and *causidici*. In his second treatise, "De doctrina dicendi et tacendi," dated 1245, Albertanus further developed his views on the structure of society and the role of professionals in its operation. In 1246, he wrote the *Liber consolationis et consilii,* an attack on the vendetta, which became his most popular work and was later adapted by Geoffrey Chaucer from a French version for his "Tale of Melibee." About this same time, Albertanus was active in a confraternity composed of fellow *causidici*. His four sermons, delivered to his Brescian colleagues in the Franciscan church of San Giorgio Martire in 1250, show that he had thought long and deeply about the place of professional confraternities in communal society. His sermons form a commentary on the rule of his confraternity and reveal how he regarded that rule not merely in religious but in broadly social terms, which found expression in his concern for the poor. Taking as his theme the biblical concept of liberating the poor from the powerful, Albertanus set forth a program for his fellow professionals. His concern was not merely with alms but with legal assistance. The *causidici* were to play their part by righting the wrongs done to the weak and the poor. He also viewed the confraternity as a foundation for a more socially cohesive society. He not only opposed the destructive force of violence but also attempted to explain its causes in terms of the inequities existing in his society, a theme that had already found expression in his *Liber consolationis et consilii.* In his explanation of the causes of the vendetta, he stressed differences of wealth and status as causes of violence.[23] He was also aware

---

23. Ibid., 107–20.

that diversity of religious views had an impact on the public life of the commune. For example, he was critical at one point of those who refused to take oaths, though he later relented in this matter. He also singled out as heretics those who refused to bear arms, despite the fact that similar views were found in the orthodox rules of the Order of Penance.[24] Likewise, his position on the use of food and clothing differed from the provisions normally found in these rules. Albertanus reflects the way in which religious diversity created divisions within early-thirteenth-century confraternity life.[25]

The central importance of rules in thirteenth-century Italy is amply demonstrated by the large number still in existence.[26] Many show close relationships to one another and considerable borrowing, indicative of their common models. Virtually all provide evidence that they were drafted by members of the clergy, though that was probably not the case for a rule from Bergamo recently edited by Lester Little.[27] The content of these rules shows a high degree of similarity, but at the same time there is considerable diversity. As the role of the mendicants in the composition of such rules increased in the course of the thirteenth century, the amount of borrowing also appears to have become greater. Application of Canon 13 to the proliferation of these rules may have led to a tightening of controls over these groups and toward the foundation of the Third Orders under the direction of the mendicants and other orders later in the century. Yet, even after this process was underway, there continued to be a considerable diversity in these rules and concern about the dangers inherent in associations of the laity on the part of ecclesiastical authorities.

---

24. Ibid., 64.

25. See, for example, ibid., 103, 118; Albertanus Brixiensis, *Sermones Quattuor* (Lonato, 1955), 50–51; and also his *De amore et dilectione Dei et proximi et aliarum rerum et de forma vitae: an edition*, ed. Sharon Hiltz, Ph.D. diss., University of Pennsylvania, 1980, 215.

26. On the number of such rules, see the discussion in Black, *Italian Confraternities*, 23–57.

27. Little, *Liberty, Charity, Fraternity*, 123. The compiler of the rule of San Michele of the White Well was the notary Paxino Razini de Poltriniano: "Quod consortium cum omnibus et singulis statutis et capitulis eiusdem venerabilis pater dominus Guiscardus, divina clemencia episcopus, sub anno currente Domini MoCCo septuagesimo secundo quintedecime indictionis, undecimo octobris, in episcopali palatio Pergami, in presencia domini Guiscardi Ceruonum, Suardi de Robertis et Petralli de Rivola, Testium rogatorum, auctoritate sua solemniter per cartam rogatam Paxinum de Poltriniano notarium" (125).

Even those that passed muster with the papacy contained provisions that aroused opposition at the time.[28]

The prohibition of taking oaths was among the most common provisions found in rules of the Order of Penance. The statute of the Humiliati approved by Pope Innocent III in 1201 contains the following injunction.[29]

> In addition, "before all else, brethren, refuse to swear an oath of any kind neither by heaven, nor by earth. Let your speech be: Yes, yes, No, no, so that you do not incur judgment," as the Blessed Apostle James has said.

A statute of a fraternity from 1215, the year of the Lateran Council, simply advises that all should abstain from oaths.[30] A similar prohibition of solemn oaths, but with exceptions in certain cases, may be found in the abridged version of the rule of the "Third Order" of St. Francis promulgated in 1289 by Pope Nicholas IV.[31] The political ramifications of this prohibition of oaths are obvious. The communes were sworn associations. While it is not clear that this fact provoked opposition from those who were committed to the rules of the Order of Penance, it is certain that the communes viewed the rejection of oath taking as a threat to their unity. Efforts were made to modify or eliminate the provision against oath taking from some rules. The rule of the Militia of Jesus Christ, drawn up by the Dominican Barthelemy of Vicenza and approved by Pope Gregory IX in 1235, contained no prohibition regarding the swearing of oaths.[32] Neither did the rule of the Militia of the Virgin, written by

---

28. A good example is the *Propositum* of the Humiliati, approved by Innocent III in 1201. The position taken regarding oaths was more stringent than that found in later approved rules (Meersseman, *Dossier*, 277).

29. Ibid., 277: "Insuper, 'ante omnia, fratres, nolite iurare, neque per celum, neque per terram. Sit autem sermo vester: Est, est, Non, non, ut non in iudicium incidatis,' sicut ait beatus Iacobus apostolus. (James, 5, 12)." See also Albertanus Brixiensis, "De Doctrina loquendi et tacendi," in Thor Sundby, *Della vita e delle opere di Brunetto Latini* (Florence, 1884), 475–509, esp. 485; and Albertanus, *De Amore*, 221–23. But see also his sermons, *Sermones Quattuor* (Lonato, 1955), 48, for a later modification of his view.

30. Meersseman, *Dossier*, 89.

31. Meersseman, "Auctarium," 38: "A juramentis autem solempnibus omnes abstineant, nisi necessitate cogente. . . ."

32. Meersseman, *Dossier*, 290–95.

the Franciscan Rufino Gurgone in 1261.[33] These rules, to which we shall
return shortly, were specifically aimed at the knightly class in the cities.

Another issue that has recently received considerable attention from
historians involves sumptuary regulations. Such statutes are quite common. A rule dated about 1215 states simply that:[34]

> Men who belong to the fraternity should dress in humble clothing
> without color, whose price per ell should not exceed six solidi of
> Ravenna. Cloaks should be closed, not open like those of secular per-
> sons.
>
> Sisters should dress in the same humble clothing and should have a
> small linen cloak without trim. Both brothers and sisters should have
> only lamb furs.

The rule of the Humiliati, approved by Pope Innocent III, orders that
"clothing should neither be too fancy nor too abject and should not be
discarded too quickly, but should be such that nothing irreligious can be
found in them, because neither dirty ones nor those too exquisitly clean
befit a Christian."[35] The rules of the Militias make more detailed provision for dress according to rank, in keeping with the different grades of
membership in their associations.[36] The abridged *regula bullata* of the
Franciscan Third Order provides that:[37]

---

33. Ibid., 290–95.

34. Ibid., 93–96: "Viri qui fraternitatis fuerint, de panno humili sine colore induantur, cuius brachium VI solidorum ravennatum pretium non excedat. Chlamydes
habeant integras, non apertas, ut seculares. Sorores vero eiusdem humilitatis panno
induantur et habeant palludellum lineum sine crispaturas. Tam fratres quam sorores
pelles habeant agninas tantum." The "Memoriale" also forbids attendance at spectacles and plays and sets out rules on abstinence. These regulations are found almost
verbatim in the rule of the Franciscan Third Order promulgated by Pope Nicholas IV
in 1289. See Robert M. Stewart, "*De Illis Qui Faciunt Penitentiam:*" *The Rule of the
Secular Franciscan Order: Origins, Development, Interpretation* (Rome, 1991),
226–27. I have followed the translation made by Stewart here and elsewhere in this
essay with a few modifications.

35. Meersseman, *Dossier*, 281: "Vestimenta vero nec nimium nitida nec plurimum
debent esse abiecta, sed talia in quibus nihil irreligiosum possit notari, quia nec effec-
tate sordes, nec exquisite munditie conveniunt christiano."

36. Ibid., 293, 298. The regulations regarding the clothing of *milites* are especially
detailed in the "Règle de la Milice de la Vierge" of Rufino Gurgone, O.F.M., from
1261.

37. For the Latin text, see Meersseman, "Auctarium," 38.

The brethren of this fraternity should usually be dressed in inexpensive clothing, of a color not completely white or black, unless they are dispensed temporarily in the matter of price by the visitors on the advice of the minister for a legitimate and obvious reason. Cloaks as well as furred coats should be without an opening at the neck, divided or in one piece, and not opened but pinned shut as becomes modesty, and let the sleeves be closed. The aforesaid brothers and sisters should have furs only from lambs, purses of leather, with thongs made simply without any silk. Other ornaments should be set aside according to the salutary counsel of St. Peter, Prince of the Apostles.

The same statutes forbid "immodest banquets or spectacles."[38] Other provisions sometimes found in these rules forbid gambling, especially playing with dice, blasphemy, and usury.[39] Abstention from meat, a common feature of all monastic rules, figures prominently in these as well.[40] The religious concerns behind this legislation are quite evident. Not only is there an often-expressed desire to separate the members from the world but also a wish to discourage the kind of social differentiation associated with clothing. The Order of Penance aimed at reducing social differences among the members, a policy that met with little clerical opposition.[41] Only in the case of the Militias do we find social distinctions in clothing enacted into the rules.[42] In the other rules, dispensations are permitted but clearly discouraged.[43] Rank is denied its privileges, though probably only after considerable internal debate. Likewise, the difference between the sexes was lessened to some degree, though few rules go so far as those of the Congregation of Mercy at Bergamo in 1265, which declared that "all persons of this congregation, both men

38. Ibid., 38: ". . . inhonesta convivia vel spectacula." Albertanus, *Sermones Quattuor*, 37–39, has an interesting discussion of banquets.

39. See Meersseman, *Dossier*, 279, on usury. See Little, *Liberty*, 146, on usury, gambling, barratry, and heretics; 132 on blasphemy; and 153 on gambling, etc., as on 146. Regulation of gambling is also common in Brescia, *Statuti di Brescia del secolo XIII*, cols. 179–80; 185, 229.

40. Meersseman, *Dossier*, 287. In the *propositum* of poor Catholics, there is a provision for abstention from fish on certain vigils as well (see 293, 299, for the knightly confraternities). See also Stewart, *De Illis Qui Faciunt Penitentiam*, 189.

41. This is evident from its retention in many of the rules drawn up by mendicants, though there was a tendency to mitigate the rule for some groups (Stewart, *De Illis Qui Faciunt Penitentiam*, 188).

42. Meersseman, *Dossier*, 293, 298.

43. Stewart, *De Illis Qui Faciunt Penitentiam*, 188.

and women, are participants and associates in the love of Jesus Christ in all the masses, prayers, preaching and all spiritual actions, all the alms and visitations of the sick and imprisoned . . . and all the good things that, with the Lord's aid, are done or may be done in this congregation . . . ."[44] It is not difficult to see in these rules elements that reflect ongoing social concerns. The need to participate effectively in a community carried with it a sense of responsibility to others that focused at least some attention on the problems of the larger society.

This sense of responsibility is well illustrated in the case of poverty. Obviously, this issue is directly related to the sumptuary provisions just discussed. Such legislation sprang from a view that Christians should restrict their consumption in order to provide for the needs of the poor. In a *Propositum* of Penitents directed by Poor Catholics, dated 1212 and approved by Innocent III, there is an extensive discussion of works of piety, with emphasis on the poor.[45]

And because six works of piety are profitable for salvation, they have proposed for the sake of God to serve the poor. One of them desires to construct on his own inheritance a house in which one side should have suitable provision for religious men and the other for women, and next to it also a hospital in which the weary may be refreshed and the poor find happiness, the sick may be restored to health, infants deserted by their mothers may be nourished, and women in labor may be sustained until they give birth and can go away; and with the

---

44. "Quinto ordinamus quod omnes persone huius congregationis tam viri quam mulieres in caritate Iesu Christi sint participes et consortes omnium missarum, orationum et predicationum ac omnium spirtualium actionum, omnium elemosinarum et visitationum infirmorum ac incarceratorum, omnium sepulturarum et omnium misericordiarum ac omnium bonorum que Domino adiuvante fiunt et in posterum fient in ista congregatione tam in vita quam in morte, ita ut etiam post mortem valeant et suffragentur eis bona et elimosine congregationis sancte Misericordie" (Little, *Liberty*, 117).

45. Meersseman, *Dossier*, 287: "Et quoniam sex opera pietatis proficiunt ad salutem, proposuerunt pro deo pauperibus deservire, quorum quidam in hereditate propria vult domum construere, in qua ex una parte viris et ex alia mulieribus religiosis mansio competens habeatur, et iuxta illam nichilominus xenodochium, in quo reficiantur fessi et pauperes recreentur, iuventur infirmi et nutriantur infantes a matribus derelicti, et mulieres laborantes in partu, donec abire valeant, sustententur in eo, ac iuxta possibilitatem domus ipsius adveniente hieme, prebeantur pauperibus indumenta, pannos quoque ad quinquaginta lectus de suis rebus ministrabit ibidem, et ecclesiam, ubi fratres domus ipsius possint, construi faciet, quae in signum subiectionis apostolice sedis reddet unum bisantium annuatim."

approach of winter, depending on the means available, clothing may be offered to the poor, and the house will supply extra sheets there for fifty beds from its resources. And he will also build a church where the brothers of the house can pray, and which will pay an annual rent of one bezant to the Holy See as a sign of dependence.

The rule of the Militia of Jesus Christ committed its members to free miserable persons from oppression.[46] This statement echoes those found in the writings of Albertanus of Brescia from a period just after this rule was promulgated in 1235.[47] The problem of poverty weighed much on people's minds at this time. Urban poverty had become an increasingly prominent feature of Italian civic life from at least the early twelfth century. Perhaps even earlier, probably related to increasing population pressures, poverty had emerged as a central concern among both religious and laity. In a society that was becoming more and more urban, it was no longer possible to deal with poverty along traditional lines rooted in the notion that societies were essentially unchanging. The measures cited above and the approaches recommended by Albertanus of Brescia are part of a broadly based recognition that effective organized action to liberate the poor from the dominance of the powerful was essential. The solutions to social problems that were meant to work in a static society were making way for more dynamic approaches. These recognized that poverty was not merely a more or less permanent condition of the social order but a product of changes that were taking place in the structure of society. The rules of confraternities reflected these changes in various ways, even as they maintained viewpoints that were essentially based on the older vision of society. Just as we have seen differences among these rules on other topics, there were differences regarding poverty. Some made no mention of the poor in specific terms. Others make a general provision. The abridged rule, for example, ordered the members to give the "usual" money to the treasurer for distribution to the poor and infirm according to the advice of the minister.[48] In some rules, emphasis was on the care of members rather than the poor in general. The rule of San Pancrazio, Bergamo, dated 1292, speaks of distributing the goods of the

---

46. Meersseman, *Dossier*, 292.

47. Powell, *Albertanus of Brescia*, 95–96, 113–14.

48. Meersseman, "Auctarium," 39: "Unusquisque autem usualem denarium massario tribuat, qui pecuniam coligat [*sic!*] et eam de consilio ministrorum inter fratres paupertate gravatos et precipue infirmantes. . . ."

association for the use of the poor.[49] From the writings of Albertanus, it is also evident that there were fears about the dangers of sedition or riot among the poor.[50] A division of the poor into those who were deserving and those who were dangerous, also evident in his writings, may well have reflected a reluctance on the part of some to embrace programs aimed at meeting the needs of the able-bodied poor.[51] This may account for some of the differences among the rules that seem to have been the object of revision by the mendicants. The rules of confraternities represented a first stage along a road in which civic action would play a greater role, though without supplanting the Christian view of poverty as an opportunity to express one's love for God through love for others.

A more divisive issue was the refusal, found in various rules, of members to bear arms. This provision, though controversial, was by no means limited to such heretical groups as the Waldensians, who refused to shed blood. Many committed to the Order of Penance shared this view. A statute attributed to an order of penitents about 1215 contained the following: "Members may not receive or carry mortal arms with them against anyone."[52] This provision was repeated in the *Memoriale* of 1228, confirmed by Pope Gregory IX.[53] Very likely, St. Francis of Assisi was influenced by these ideas. The dream that led him to abandon his participation in the papally directed military venture of Walter of Brienne against Markward of Anweiler in southern Italy in 1202 seems to suggest that bearing arms had become repugnant to him. Elsewhere, I have discussed this issue in relation to his sermon to the crusaders at Damietta in 1219.[54] In his *De Amore,* Albertanus defended the notion of just war and self-defense, alluding to the maxim, "All laws and rights proclaim the right to oppose force with force."[55] He was closely aligned with the thinking of those communal authorities who took exception to those refusing to bear arms. On the other hand, the writing and approval of rules for the various Militias may have been part of an effort to counter-

49. Little, *Liberty,* 162: ". . . et ea distribuendum in usu pauperum. . . ."

50. Powell, *Albertanus of Brescia,* 112–14.

51. Ibid., 113–15.

52. "Arma mortalia contra quempiam non accipiant vel secum deferant" (Meersseman, *Dossier,* 89).

53. Ibid., 101, but cf. Stewart, *De Illis Qui Faciunt Penitentiam,* 229.

54. Powell, "Francesco d'Assisi e la Quinta Crociata: Una Missione di Pace," *Schede Medievali* 4 (1983): 68–77; Powell, *Anatomy of a Crusade,* 158–60.

55. Powell, *Albertanus of Brescia,* 48; Albertanus, *De Amore,* 207. "Et in tantum tibi vim vi repellere licet quod si aliter periculum vitare non poteris, hominem occidisti, per leges et iura nullo modo puniaris."

act this opposition by validating the use of arms in defense of the church and for just cause. These rules contained a positive assessment of the role of arms, especially in defense of the poor, churches, and other worthy causes. The members of these militias had a role in defending the faith against heresy and protecting ecclesiastical liberty. As the rules stated:[56]

> Likewise let him prudently consider the use of arms, and so use them in licit ways, with the advice of the Apostolic See or the bishop required if there is any doubt that they are drawn illicitly.

Papal approval of such seemingly opposed approaches to the issue of arms bearing should evoke little surprise. In fact, if we look more closely, we may find that the apparent inconsistency is not as great as it appears. Both approaches aim at imposing limits on the use of arms.

The participation of so many individuals, both lay and clerical, in these confraternities also makes them important for an understanding of the development of medieval constitutional thought. More attention needs to be paid to them, alongside communal institutions, as schools for political participation. Experimentation in rules, quite evident in what we have been discussing, is also reflected in the development of constitutional structures of confraternites in ways that parallel contemporary political concerns. Efforts were made to ensure that offices would not become the monopoly of a few and that dishonesty in the handling of funds and endowments of the group should be prevented. Shared responsibility and frequent consultation were important principles of fraternal government. (We might also note that there is no evidence that women were excluded from elections, if they were admitted to membership. They were also elected to offices, though most probably with supervision only over other women.) Without belaboring the importance of confraternity rules for the development of medieval constitutionalism, this argument does support the conclusion that the culture of rules played a meaningful role in communal society.[57]

---

56. "Alias autem usum armorum sibi prudenter attendat, et sic eis utantur in licitis, quod ad illicita non trahantur, sedis apostolice vel diocesani consilio, si aliquid dubium emerserit, requisito" (Meersseman, *Dossier*, 293).

57. Little, *Liberty*, 118–19. This section of the rule of the Congregation of Mercy in Bergamo illustrates the importance of constitutional forms in the development of the rules of confraternities.

I would like to conclude by looking at some urban statutes from the thirteenth century. My effort is to show that the culture of rules was not limited merely to the sphere of religious rules. Secular society was open to influences from those who participated in the confraternities. In fact, many of the same individuals played a role in public life. At the same time, however, it is evident that the influence of these rules on secular law was limited. Beyond question, proponents of the incorporation of moral and sumptuary laws in secular statutes faced some opposition. But much the same could also be said for opposition to the incorporation of laws against heretics under pressure from the hierarchy and the papacy.

Considerable scholarly attention has been devoted to discussion of such developments as the inclusion of the legislation of Frederick II against heresy or of similar enactments in city statutes, often at the behest of the papacy.[58] These inclusions aroused controversy and opposition in some communes. The basis for the inclusion of this legislation in urban statutes was in Roman law. The Code of Justinian had brought heresy under secular jurisdiction. On this basis, Frederick enacted his laws against heresy at his imperial coronation in 1220 and again for Lombardy in 1224. The statutes of Ferrara, dated 1287, contain both letters of Pope Innocent IV and the laws of Frederick II.[59] The condemnation of heresy in the statutes of Treviso, however, makes no mention of the imperial laws.[60]

Moreover, the papal campaign against heretics was also a factor in internal political conflicts. Accusations of heresy were brought against political enemies. In Brescia, for example, the linking of one party to heretics was sufficient to induce a political crisis in which important local leaders were accused of heresy. Pope Honorius III cautioned the bishop to investigate carefully before proceeding. As a result, the accusations seem to have been dropped. Some of those who had been accused later

---

58. For this legislation, see Giovanni de Vergottini, *Studi sulla legislazione imperiale di Federico II in Italia. Le leggi di 1220* (Bologna, 1952); and Hermann Dilcher, *Die sizilische Gesetzgebung Kaiser Friedrichs II: Quellen der Constitutionen von Melfi und ihrer Novellen* (Cologne, 1975), 72.

59. *Statuta Ferrariae, Anno MCCLXXXVII*, transcription, introduction, and glossary by William Montorsi (Ferrara, 1955), 349–55. See also *Statuti di Brescia, Historiae Patriae Monumenta* (hereafter HPM), 16:125–27.

60. *Gli Statuti del comune di Treviso sec. XIII–XIV*, ed. Bianca Betto (Rome, 1984), 573–75; *Lo statuto caminese Trevigiano del 1283–1284*, ed. Bianca Betto (Venice, 1977), 100. The wording of the title of this statute seems clearly to indicate the influence of the Order of Penance: "Mercati et corporazioni. Giocatori d'azzardo ed eretici."

became leaders of the opposition to Frederick II in the city and supporters of the papacy.[61] In the writings of Albertanus, opposition to heresy
occupies a prominent place. He particularly singles out their opposition
to oaths and the death penalty for condemnation, even though, as we
have shown, these same positions were to be found in the approved rules
of the Order of Penance. His views may well suggest that communal leaders, anxious to avoid the taint of heresy, were trying to steer a course in
which they resisted some popular religious views as well as opposing the
inclusion of Frederick II's laws against heresy in their own statutes.[62]

In the case of sumptuary law, however, the existence of Roman legal
precedents may have led historians to neglect possible links between
these laws and the sumptuary provisions found in rules of confraternities.
In his article on sumptuary laws and prostitution in medieval Italy, James
A. Brundage cites a series of Roman laws ranging from the Lex Oppia in
215 B.C. to the Lex Aemilia Sumptuaria in 115 B.C., as well as biblical and
medieval precedents, including the *Decretum* of Gratian, which dealt
with female adornment in one canon, as precedents.[63] He notes, however, that sumptuary laws only became common in urban statutes after
1300. He does not examine possible precedents for statutes in the rules of
confraternities. The evidence is, however, very suggestive. The feature
that occurs most commonly in both sources in the thirteenth century is
the regulation of gambling, but regulations regarding usury, blasphemy,
and restrictions on clothing are also found.[64] There may well have been
reluctance or even opposition to the inclusion of statutes regulating food
and dress, as there was to the bearing of arms and the taking of oaths.

We also know that thirteenth-century communal statutes were sometimes influenced by such groups as the mendicants, who figure prominently as beneficiaries of communal largess in some statutes.[65] Their con-

---

61. Powell, *Albertanus of Brescia*, 29–31.

62. Ibid., 100–101, 118; *Sermones quattuor: Edizione curate sui codici bresciani*,
ed. Marta Ferrari (Lonato, 1955), 63.

63. James A. Brundage, "Sumptuary Laws and Prostitution in Late Medieval
Italy," *Journal of Medieval History* 13 (1987): 343–55, esp. 343–45.

64. *Gli statuti del comune di Treviso (sec. XIII–XIV)*, 367 for usury; 369 for
women's dress; 571–72 on blasphemy. *Statuta Civitatis Aquarum* (Acqui, 1618)
treats gambling, blasphemy, and usury (62). See *Gli Statuti di Genola*, ed. Rinaldo
Comba (Turin, 1970), 82–83 on gambling; and *Statuta Ferrariae*, 273–74, also on
gambling.

65. In Brescia, the commune donated funds for the construction of the church of
San Francesco. More common is the provision for alms to religious, as found in the
Statuti di Brescia, HPM, 16:105; the *Statuta Civitatis Aquarum*, 104–5; and the

cern with usury, which certainly has its roots in the same sources as do our confraternity rules, may explain why as much emphasis was placed on it as on laws against gambling and blasphemy.[66] However, the widespread inclusion of laws on these matters suggests pressure from many groups, representing a consensus among the politically active classes in the cities.[67] These were the same parties who participated in the confraternities. They were both men and women of the middle class, with some from the upper class. When we look specifically at regulations regarding dress, there is some evidence that, as early as the thirteenth century, rules against female adornment did influence urban statutes.[68] However, Brundage is quite right in maintaining that provisions of this kind were uncommon. There are, of course, many possible explanations for this fact. For one thing, the problem may not yet have been of sufficient magnitude to require communal legislation. On the other hand, the considerable opposition to such legislation noted later may already have been present and impeded its inclusion in statutes. This may have been the reason why one of the earliest statutes framed its regulations as a kind of relief to husbands and families.[69] Finally, the content of dress regulations found in confraternity rules differed from those in urban statutes by prescribing only simple clothing, sometimes a kind of habit, for both men and women and emphasizing cheapness rather than an extensive list of prohibited articles. The tendency toward more specific regulation is, however, already evident.[70] Perhaps what we are witnessing is part of a gradual growth of detailed regulation in the thirteenth and fourteenth centuries. We should also note that dress regulation in confraternity rules normally applied to all members, male and female. The stress on women's dress in urban statutes suggests that religious motivations may have broken down in the face of economic motives. We should not, how-

---

Statuta Ferrariae, 94–95. The important role of the mendicants in the Alleluia of 1233 has recently been discussed at length by Augustine Thompson, *Revival Preachers and Politics in Thirteenth Century Italy: The Great Devotion of 1233* (Oxford, 1992). He provides valuable information regarding their revision of urban statutes, adding yet another dimension to that presented here.

66. Little, *Religious Poverty and the Profit Economy* (Ithaca, N.Y., 1978), 181–83.

67. One of the best examples I have found is in the *Statuta Civitatis Aquarum* (61–62), where the law takes up genuflection to the host at mass and the separation of the sexes in church. Did women perhaps influence this law? The details regarding the place reserved for women suggest that there was a specific reason for the statute.

68. *Gli Statuti del comune di Treviso*, 369.

69. Ibid.

70. Meersseman, "Auctarium," 38; Meersseman, *Dossier*, 93–95, 281, 286, 289.

ever, allow these differences and the absence of such regulation in urban statutes in the thirteenth century to distract us from one feature that all of this legislation had in common. In its confraternal setting, it was based on a desire to ensure a certain order and equality in society. Essentially, it emerged from a view that saw the economy in static terms. Justice could be achieved only through restraint of excess, through fasting and abstinence, for example, while sharing one's excess with the poor.[71] Excessive consumption was a social sin that had its roots in economic ideas that predated Christianity. Christianity had taken these ideas for its own, and they would remain popular well into the modern period. They had been at the heart of the monastic economy. Thus, their increasing popularity in a period of burgeoning population and growing urban poverty should not surprise us. Their supporters, however, did not have a monopoly on the solutions to these problems. There were also those who saw the need and possibility for a broad transformation of society, who looked on profit in a new way. They took comfort in a society that was increasingly prosperous. They wanted to enjoy the wealth that the urban economies generated. As Hans Baron has pointed out, the writings of Albertanus contain a vigorous defense of the profit economy.[72] Similar views have been traced in the writings of the mendicants by Lester Little.[73] They are merely another example of the change we have been trying to describe.

The thirteenth century marked a critical point in the transition from a static to a dynamic conception of society. Both views have continued to exist and compete in modern times. They formed alternative visions that helped to shape the political agenda of the Italian communes in the thirteenth century and continued to play a significant role in the Renaissance. Older views, which have employed a secular/religious dichotomy to explain the dynamics of the birth of modern societies, are inadequate to deal with the complex interactions outlined here. If the division of religious and secular is to provide a basis for a fuller understanding of the late medieval period, it must be put into a context that recognizes that thirteenth-century people were able to make such a distinction while moving between two worlds and drawing experience from both.

---

71. Carolyn Walker Bynum, "Fast, Feast, and Flesh: The Religious Significance of Food to Medieval Women," *Representations* 11 (1985): 1–25.

72. Hans Baron, "Franciscan Poverty and Civic Wealth in Humanistic Thought," *Speculum* 13(1938): 1–37, esp. 3.

73. Little, *Religious Poverty and the Profit Economy*, 200–217.

Inventing Braudel's Mountains: The Florentine Alps after the Black Death

Samuel K. Cohn Jr.

A remarkable feature of David Herlihy's work is the variety of tools he brought to the study of the Middle Ages: economics, philology, numismatics, agronomy, urban studies, quantification, demography, and family sociology. Although his magnum opus, *Les Toscans et leurs familles,*[1] integrated all of these approaches, the student can map out in retrospect a methodological progression in the expansion of his historical curiosity from one theme to the next.[2] When I trained at the University of Wisconsin-Madison, demographic analyses were at the cutting edge of medieval studies and of Herlihy's interests. Here, in his memory, I return to those methods I learnt as his student and to sources on taxation I then pushed aside in the rush to finish a dissertation.

The relationship between city and countryside has been central to Italian historiography during the twentieth century.[3] To date, historians have framed this relationship as though the countryside (*contado*) were a

I completed this essay in December 1992; since then I have benefited from a year's leave of absence from teaching funded by the National Endowment for the Humanities and the Villa I Tatti (Florence, Italy), which I spent in the Archivio di Stato continuing research on the Florentine mountains and the territorial state. For the present essay, I wish to thank Gene Brucker, William Bowsky, and Anthony Molho for their comments and criticisms.

1. Herlihy and Christiane Klapisch-Zuber, *Les Toscans et leurs familles: Une étude du catasto florentin de 1427* (Paris, 1978).

2. See my "David Herlihy—Il ricordo di uno studente," *Archivio Storico Italiano* 152 (1994): 192–201; and "David Herlihy: A Student's View," *The History Teacher* 27, no. 1 (1993): 53–61.

3. The literature on the relation between city and countryside is vast. For Florence, see the summaries of these debates in Anthony Molho, *Florentine Public Finances in the Early Renaissance 1400–1433* (Cambridge, Mass., 1971), 23–25; and George Dameron, *Episcopal Power and Florentine Society, 1000–1320* (Cambridge, Mass., 1991), 7–11.

single unit and its relation to the city a simple binary opposition. Tax surveys, or *estimi,* for the Florentine contado known as the Capi della
famiglia (the heads of family) allow a regional investigation into demographic and fiscal differences of Florence's hinterland after the Black
Death. Did the commune of Florence treat all areas of the contado
alike—suburban parishes, plains, mountains, and territories recently
annexed into its traditional contado?

Elio Conti has described the evolution of the Capi della famiglia as the
preparatory studies for the Catasto of 1427.[4] Indeed, the Florentine government and the syndics of the rural parishes and communes progres-
sively refined the information over the 50-year period covered by these
tax records. The first records labeled as the Capi della Famiglia (1364)
differed little from earlier hearth-tax surveys common to Florence and
other city-states of Italy dating back to the thirteenth century. By its last
redaction (1412–14) most aspects of the Renaissance *catasti* had become
present: all household members were listed, their ages given, and their
property holdings, obligations, and debts individually described and esti-
mated in value.

As early as its second redaction (1371) the Capi survey began to
include information on peasant migration. Before 1427, the Florentine
state did not assess the individual but instead the *popolo,* or commune. It
then became the duty of the local officials of the rural communities to distribute the imposed communal tax burden among their residents.[5] For
this purpose, evidence of demographic change was as important as the
evaluation of property holdings. As a result, the Capi divided rural populations into four categories—"stanti" (those who had remained in the
community since the last redaction), "venuti" and "tornati" (those who
had returned or immigrated), "usciti" (those who had left), and "morti"
(those who had died).[6] With the shift in assessment from the community
to the individual in 1427, the importance of such information disap-

---

4. Elio Conti, *I Catasti agrari della repubblica fiorentina e il Catasto particellare
toscano (secoli XIV–XIX)* (Rome, 1966), 19.

5. On the Estimi as communally based assessments, see Bernardino Barbadoro, *Le
finanze della repubblica fiorentina: Imposte diretta e debito pubblico fino alla isti-
tuzione del Monte* (Florence, 1929); and Enrico Fiumo, "Sui rapporti economici tra
città e contado nell'età comunale," *Archivio Storico Italiano* 114 (1956): 25–28.

6. In some communities, other categories are found as well: noblemen were taxed
separately and at different rates, as were those who held property in the community
but who neither lived there nor were citizens of Florence.

peared. With it went the opportunity to examine that most elusive of demographic parameters for any period of history—migration.

These tax records fill hundreds of volumes, often of 1,000 folios apiece, and span the later Trecento and the early Quattrocento—1364–65, 1371–73, 1383–84, 1393–94, 1401–2, and 1412–14. To make inroads into it I have begun by sampling 19 communities in the Quarter of Santa Maria Novella. These cut two geographical trajectories. One runs from outside the city walls at San Lorenzo and Santa Lucia Ognissanti fuori le mura through the rich plains of the Valdarno Inferiore and the Bisenzio into the city of Prato. The other starts in the highlands north of the Mugello bordering the state of Bologna and crosses the mountains called the Alpi degli Ubaldini (and after the Florentine conquest in 1373 the Alpi Fiorentine) extending into the Mugello northwest of Scarperia and then across the highlands of Prato near the border of Pistoia.

A first quantitative look at these records raises questions about late medieval and early modern mountain communities—generalizations in some instances that go back as far as the early-fourteenth-century Bolognese agronomist Pietro de' Crescenzi.[7] But any historical analysis of "mountain civilization" must begin with Fernand Braudel, for whom altitude more than nationality distinguished social traits in premodern Europe.[8] For Braudel, mountain communities were poor, self-sufficient, and egalitarian, without sharp contrasts in the distribution of wealth. They were the backward and patriarchal refuge of outlaws, harboring "rough men, clumsy, stocky, and close-fisted."[9] Along with other niceties of urban culture, religion was here slow to penetrate: "A world of sorcerers, witchcraft, primitive magic, and black masses were the flowerings of an ancient cultural subconscious."[10]

Braudel supported these static characterizations with testimony taken from the late Middle Ages through the nineteenth century. He nonetheless called for a historical analysis claiming that "the contrast between

7. David Herlihy, *Medieval and Renaissance Pistoia: The Social History of an Italian Town, 1200–1430* (New Haven, 1967), 35.

8. Fernand Braudel, *The Mediterranean and the Mediterranean World in the Age of Philip II*, 2 vols. trans. Sîan Reynolds (New York, 1966 [Paris, 1949]). For a survey of trends in the historiography of mountains from Vidal de la Blache's "possibilisme" to Braudel, see Pier Paolo Viazzo, *Upland Communities: Environment, Population and Social Structure in the Alps since the Sixteenth Century* (Cambridge, 1989), esp., introduction.

9. Braudel, *The Mediterranean*, 1:46.

10. Ibid., 1:37.

plain and mountain is also a question of historical period."[11] This historical analysis, however, was confined to a single paragraph, which speculated that the earliest prebiblical, even prehistoric, civilizations may have arisen in the mountains and then spread irreversibly to the plains.[12]

Since Braudel's *Mediterranean,* others have been more historically minded in their treatment of Tuscan mountaineers. From a close study of archival sources and property relations, Elio Conti updated Braudel's shift of civilization from mountains to plains. Conti found the plains still "scarcely populated" from the tenth through the twelfth centuries, while "in the hills life flourished with a pace that it would never again realize."[13] More recently, Chris Wickham underscored Conti's chronological findings, adding that "economic integration was far less in earlier periods [the ninth through the twelfth centuries] and as a consequence, the economic contrasts between mountains and plains were less as well."[14] Furthermore, for the territory just east of Wickham's Garfagnana, David Herlihy has shown the mountains' historical malleability. Their social characteristics were not fixed by a one-time transition. After the Black Death and through the fifteenth century, the mountains of Pistoia flourished economically and demographically relative to the lower hills, which earlier had been the cradle of rural wealth and population.[15]

The historian most conversant with medieval and early modern mountain communities in Tuscany is Giovanni Cherubini. His panoramic surveys of mountain ecology and society extend from Monte Amiata in the southernmost corner of Tuscany to the mountains of Romagna, the southern watershed of the Po Valley. While Cherubini's conclusions preserve the Braudelian paradigm of mountain life, his descriptions betray

---

11. Ibid., 1:53.

12. Ibid., 1:51–53. Recent research, however, seriously contests these assumptions about ancient and prehistoric topography, finding almost the opposite population trends. In the prehistoric and ancient period the Mediterranean mountains were far less populated relative to the plains than they were after the year 1000. See J. R. McNeill, *The Mountains of the Mediterranean World: An Environmental History* (Cambridge, 1992), chap. 3, "The Deep History of Mediterranean Landscapes;" and Brent D. Shaw, "Bandit Highlands and Lowland Peace: The Mountains of Isauria-Cilicia," *Journal of the Social and Economic History of the Orient* 33 (1990): 199–233, 237–70.

13. Elio Conti, *La formazione della struttura agraria moderna nel contado fiorentino,* vol. 1: *Le campagne nell'età comunale* (Rome, 1965), 211.

14. Chris Wickham, *The Mountains and the City: The Tuscan Appennines in the Early Middle Ages* (Oxford, 1988), 6.

15. Herlihy, *Pistoia,* 50–51.

the strains and contradictions inherent in these generalizations. For instance, his analysis of the Catasto of 1428–29 has shown wide discrepancies in the social structure across the Florentine Apennines from the "dry mountains" of the Casentino in the southeast, where the poor[16] constituted 88.4 percent of taxpayers, to the Pistoiese mountains in the northwest, where its percentage fell by nearly half (46.2 percent), and those of middling wealth—the "*mediani*"—approached the poor in number (40.8 percent). But he dismissed these variations to shore up Braudelian generalizations of mountain equality in poverty, arguing that "the presence of a few conspicuously wealthy individuals does not change the overall picture, in which mountain egalitarianism is distinguished from the proletariatized peasants of the hills and plains."[17] Yet, he never supplied the figures to compare this "mountain egalitarianism" with holdings from parishes in the hills and plains.

When Cherubini later turned south to the mountains of Monte Amiata and the alluvial plains of the Maremma, his data further weakened the Braudelian paradigm. Because of problems of drainage, marshlands, and malaria, the plains remained well into the seventeenth century the depressed periphery, while villages on the high slopes of Amiata possessed the highest population densities and the greatest sources of wealth. Yet, despite the rich commentary of contemporaries such as Pope Pius II and the figures supplied by the survey of 1640, Cherubini did not question his earlier conclusions drawn from the north about mountain poverty, equality, and backwardness.[18]

True, none of the historians of Tuscany cited above has explored the full range of mountain traits on which Braudel generalized. No one has

---

16. Giovanni Cherubini utilizes the categories of property holding devised by Elio Conti from the 1427 Catasto assessments (Conti, *La formazione*, vol. 2, pt. 2, Monografie e Tavole Statistiche (secoli XV–XIX), 243–45). Conti defines the poor as property holders whose taxable wealth was between 1 and 50 florins, as opposed to the *miserabili* who had no taxable wealth.

17. Giovanni Cherubini, "La società dell'Appennino settentrionale (secoli XIII–XV)," in *Signori, contadini, borghesi: Ricerche sulla società italiana del basso medioevo* (Florence, 1974), 130–31. For similar conclusions, see his earlier "Qualche considerazione sulle campagne dell'Italia centro-settentrionale tra l'XI e il XV secolo," in *Signori, contadini, borghesi*, 51–119.

18. Cherubini, "Risorse, paesaggio ed utilizzazzione agricola del territorio della toscana sud-occidentale nei secoli XIV–XV," in *Civiltà ed economia agricola in Toscana nei secc. XIII–XV: Problemi della vita delle campagne nel tardo medioevo (Pistoia, 21–24 aprile, 1977* (Pistoia, 1981), 91–115.

studied criminal records systematically to test whether mountain violence or its control differed in kind or quantity from violence in the plains.[19] Nor have historians explored the supposed "backwardness" of Italian highlanders' religiosity and folklore before the apostolic visitations of the late sixteenth century.[20] The state archives of Florence and Bologna—the records of the Capitano, Podestà, and the Notarile—allow us to query such notions. But in this essay I will not be so ambitious. I will draw on only one survey of the Capi della famiglia—that of 1393–94—to investigate a matter of central importance to historians of Tuscany:[21] was the social structure of the mountains distinctive in terms of wealth and its distribution? Such an inquiry must go beyond the tax records of the mountains and compare them to villages further down the valleys.

In evaluating these surveys, the historian is faced straight away with a thorny problem of classification. What constitutes a mountain village? While geographers and historians usually take the figure of 500 meters in altitude to demarcate a mountain settlement and 200 meters for "the hills," Braudel has rightly questioned this arbitrary standard. In zones such as Colorado or the Alto Adige, 500 meters constitute the lowlands. To avoid the relativity of geographical location, Braudel, however, falls into the trap of tautology: instead of a quantitative threshold, he defines mountain communities by those very characteristics he finds to constitute "mountain civilization."

Defining the "mountains" north of Florence is less problematic than is a global definition. The near-sea-level cities of the Arno Basin—Florence and Prato (50 and 61 meters, respectively)—are the points of departure, and thus 500 meters can be adopted to demarcate the mountains. Nonetheless, how do we classify a village such as Santa Maria Morello,

---

19. Such may have been one objective of Arturo Palmieri's *La montagna bolognese del Medio Evo* (Bologna, 1929), but the work fails to study the criminal sources systematically; they are instead consulted haphazardly and are used only evocatively, as though they were another literary source.

20. See the recent excellent essay by Susanna Peyrouel Rambaldi, "Podestà e inquisitori nella montagna modenese: Riorganizzazione inquisitoriale e resistenze locali (1570–1590)," *Società e storia* 14, no. 52 (1991): 297–328.

21. For this study, I have determined the tax rate by linking the Lira, or final tax per household derived by Florentine officials in 1394 (Archivio di Stato Firenze [ASF], Estimo no. 286), with the surveys conducted a year earlier by local officials of the individual parishes and communes (ASF, Estimo nos. 218–20). With regard to the number of villages assessed (*allibrati*), this survey was the most complete of all the Capi records, at least for the Quarter of Santa Maria Novella.

with its parish church in a valley at 314 meters but whose lands extended up mountain slopes to the peaks of Monte Morello, at 1,000 meters?[22]

One way around the problem of definition is to rely on what contemporaries called the mountains, or "le alpi." For the most part, this approach has been taken here. Seven of the nine mountain villages included in this study are drawn from a zone that tax officials and notaries called the "Alpes Florentinum." Still, how does one classify a village such as Schignano in the district of Prato whose parish church lay at 460 meters and whose lands climbed the slopes of the Poggio di Javello (984 meters), but which contemporaries did not call "alpium" or "pie'alpi?" Here, the historian might turn to notarial descriptions of land conveyances or the Estimi of 1401–2, which first itemized and described the property holdings of Florentine villagers. If patterns of cultivation resembled those of the so-called "alpi"—woodlands, chestnuts, and a mix of grazing and grains—then I classified the village among the mountain communes. Such is, in fact, the case with two villages—Schignano and Morello—that lay much closer to Florence and its valley commerce than did the Florentine Alps.

In terms of wealth and its distribution, were the mountains in 1393 distinguishable from parishes and communes in the valleys and hills? A first glance at table 1 suggests that the Florentine contado northeast of the city does not support the most basic of Braudel's generalizations— mountain poverty and egalitarianism. The wealthiest parish found in this study was the small mountain hamlet of Morello. The average family property value was more than 241 lire and 446 lire if only property holders are considered—a sum that would have purchased a well-furnished farm (*podere*) at the end of the Trecento.[23] Further, if merchant residents of urban Prato are not included, the wealthiest "contadino" found in this

---

22. I have taken the altitudes of villages from *Annuario Generale dei comuni e delle frazione d'Italia: Edizione 1980/1985* (Milan, 1980), which measured the village altitude at the parish church or market square, usually the lowest place in a mountain village. Cherubini ("San Godenzo nei suoi statuti quattrocenteschi," in *Fra Tevere, Arno e Appennino: Valli, communità, signori* [Florence, 1992], 145–65) and others have recognized as mountain villages such communes as San Godenzio, at an altitude of only 404 meters but with lands that climb the slopes of the Alpi di San Benedetto to peaks well over 1,000 meters.

23. See, for instance, the notarial books of the Mazzetti family, who worked the villages from the city walls of Florence west through the Arno Valley parishes of Quarto, Quinto, and Sesto into the hills of Calenzano (ASF, Notarile antecosiamo [NAC], M352, M353, M355, M356, M357, M358, M359). Their records survive from 1348 to 1426 with only a few lacunae.

TABLE 1. Distribution of Wealth, 1393

Village	Mean Estimo (>0)	Number of Families	SD	Mean Estimo (all)	SD	Percent Nullateneni
I. Suburban parishes						
1. S. Lucia Og. *f.m.*	439.16	7	484.53	78.82	257.33	82.05
2. S. Lorenzo *f.m.*	294.23	19	309.26	116.46	240.36	60.42
3. S. M. Nuovoli	124.63	12	62.91	59.82	76.50	52.00
4. S. M. Quarto	152.69	13	81.61	53.65	87.64	64.86
II. Plains and hills						
5. S. MRT Campi	75.63	24	63.88	31.29	55.30	58.62
6. S. M. Padule	25.00	1	0	1.92	6.93	92.31
7. S. MRT Sesto	83.73	66	99.91	46.44	85.12	44.54
8. Castelnovo (PR)	265.67	15	152.21	99.63	159.00	62.50
9. S. Giusto (PR)	96.46	15	97.15	24.95	64.29	74.14
III. Mountains						
10. Schignano (PR)	25.00	8	5.35	13.33	13.45	46.67
11. S. M. Morello	445.70	13	520.44	241.42	439.07	45.83
12. Montecuccoli	115.71	58	114.95	73.75	107.23	36.26
13. Mangona	31.36	44	24.95	12.00	21.66	61.74
14. Montecarelli	23.64	28	13.67	12.04	15.35	49.09
15. S. M. Casaglia	23.61	31	17.26	17.85	18.13	24.39
16. S. MRT Castro	113.47	36	99.08	69.24	95.07	38.98
17. S. M. Bordignano	136.51	63	97.27	104.88	102.96	23.17
18. S. PL Castiglione	65.83	6	53.14	56.43	54.52	14.29
IV. The city—Prato						
Porta S. Trinita	576.48	82	790.08	283.06	623.02	50.90
Total	186.27	541	382.17	92.20	284.44	50.50

f.m. (*fuori le mura* [outside walls])

study also resided there. This villager, Bartolo di Baroco di Bartolo, listed as 104 years old,[24] the head of a complex family with four married couples and 17 family members stretched over four generations, did not possess a family name; nor was he a nobleman (otherwise he would have been taxed as such); nor did he happen to be a Florentine citizen with a country residence.[25]

Morello was not the only mountain village to house wealthy peasants. One of the highest communes of the "alpi fiorentine," Montecuccoli (633 meters) along the crest of the Monti di Calvana, was home to 3 families, each of whose taxable wealth exceeded 500 lire. They were among the 15 wealthiest found for the country samples.[26] In fact, more of these wealthiest families came from Montecuccoli than any other village except Morello.[27] Perhaps, then, it was not by chance that when the late-fourteenth-century storyteller Franco Sacchetti satirized a wealthy peasant he chose a highlander, even if a well-to-do "secondo uomini d'alpe," indeed, one living in the Bolognese Alps bordering the alpi fiorentine.[28] As Chris-

---

24. Unfortunately Bartolo's age was not stated in the redaction of 1371 (Estimo no. 215, 69r), but in the 10 years since the previous tax redaction in 1383 (Estimo no. 217, 877r), he had aged mightily. His age had jumped by 24 years, thus not only showing the problems of age calculation for peasants but also suggesting their veneration of the elderly.

25. Of course, citizen-farmers did dot the Florentine countryside, playing important roles in local politics, business, and society. In the notarial records of Ser Antonio di Giusto, who worked the Alpine villages north and east of Scarperia, the Florentine citizen Pellegrinus f.q. Ubaldini de Catanis appears often in this notary's transactions as the patron of the local baptismal church of San Silvestro, a dealer in real estate, a *mundualdus* to women's notarial acts, and a witness to a myriad of village transactions. Indeed, many of Ser Antonio's acts were drawn up in the rural palace of this Florentine magnate. Despite his residence in Scarperia, like much less important rural citizens of Florence, Pellegrinus took advantage of his citizenship—the right to pay the less onerous forced loans (*prestanze*) to the city and thereby to avoid the direct taxes (*estimi*) imposed on the countryside. Indeed, the largest category of petitions made to the officials of the Estimo from 1355 to the inauguration of the Catasto came from such alleged citizen countrymen. They claimed to have paid or to be entitled to pay the urban *prestanze;* thus, they were Florentine citizens, not "allibrati," in the contado's Estimo (see ASF, Estimo nos. 73, 74, 79).

26. ASF, Estimo no. 219, 848r-v.

27. This tally does not include the urban population of Prato (the Porta di Santa Trinita).

28. Franco Sacchetti, *Il Trecentonovelle*, ed. Antonio Lanza (Florence, 1984), CLXXIII, 383–86. This story contradicts Braudel's notion of a separate mountain culture cut off from the city and emeshed in "sorcerers, witchcraft, primitive magic, and black masses." Though duped by the "buffone" Gonnella, this wealthy mountain family turned to the services of what they gathered was a university-trained "medico" to cure their goiter.

tian Bec has pointed out, this story stands in isolation from the stereo-typical impoverished peasant of late medieval and Renaissance stories.[29] Similarly, Giovanni di Pagolo Morelli introduced his family diary by waxing rhapsodically on the beauty, nobility, and "grande abbandon-danza" of the Mugello highlands stretching from Uccellatoio beneath the peaks of Monte Morello to the "giorgo dell'Alpe degli Ubaldini."[30]

Yet, mindful of Cherubini's caveat, we must ask whether individuals such as the ancient paterfamilias Bartolo were not "conspicuous" excep-tions "that fail to modify the overall pattern of mountain egalitarian-ism"? When we move down the social ladder another rung to those who possessed property valued at more than 50 florins—Conti's "medianti," or middling sort—again the alpine villages are well represented. The parish of Santa Maria Bordignano, north of Firenzuola along the border of Bologna, here leads the list. Indeed, these more fortunate "middling" peasants were scattered equally through the lowlands and the mountains; in both zones, they comprised 6 percent of the families.

As these statistics make clear, the majority of peasants found in the samples from 1393 were either poor (with property values between 1 and 50 florins) or propertyless. Thus, despite a handful of wealthy and mid-dling families, the mountain communities may have still been peopled by peasants with small plots in contrast to what Cherubini calls "the prole-tariatized peasants" of the lower valleys.[31] On first impression, the dis-tribution of wealth found in the Capi of 1393 appears to support this generalization. Santa Maria Padule, as its name suggests, lay in the marshlands of the Arno Valley near Sesto and was by far the poorest community in this sample. All those who had remained since the previous tax survey a decade earlier (1383) were propertyless. Moreover, the rate of out-migration was higher there than anywhere else. Yet the property-less "*nullatenenti*" and "*miserabili*" also filled the surveys of mountain

---

29. See Christian Bec, "La paysan dans la nouvelle toscane (1350–1530)," in *Civiltà ed economia agricola in Toscana*, 31–32: "La première caractéristique qui frappe les conteurs . . . est la pauvreté du monde paysan . . . qui se traduit dans le vêtement, les intérieurs des maisons campagnardes, ou l'alimentation."

30. Giovanni di Pagolo Morelli, *Ricordi*, ed. Vittore Branca (Florence, 1956), 90–103.

31. On this point, Braudel and Cherubini appear to disagree. Both stressed "moun-tain egalitarianism." However, for Cherubini it was the equality of the poor but prop-ertied peasants, while for Braudel the mountains harbored the most destitute and des-perate elements of the Mediterranean. (See Braudel, *The Mediterranean*, 1.30: "Can we define the mountains as the poorest regions of the Mediterranean, its proletarian reserves? On the whole this is true.")

parishes, constituting substantial portions of their populations (table 1, col. 7). The wealthy village of Morello hardly displayed "mountain egalitarianism"; alongside Bartolo di Baroco, 46 percent of the population was propertyless. Further north and higher up, Montecarelli's propertyless exceeded 49 percent, and in the larger commune of nearby Mangona its proportion reached 62 percent.

Indeed, whether they were located in the mountains or the plains does not appear to have affected the average wealth of these 18 villages scattered through the Florentine territory of Santa Maria Novella. To judge the importance of where peasants resided for determining their property value, I have regressed their taxable wealth against a number of independent variables readily figured from the documents—distance of the village from Florence, if the village lay in the newly annexed district of Prato (1351), if it lay in the mountains, family size, family structure (the extent to which families were extended collaterally or generationally), if its head was aged (over 60), if he or she were infirm or handicapped, and if a family had a woman as its head (table 2). Even though the adjusted R^2 of this regression model is weak (.0897), the effects of certain factors on a family's taxable wealth are significant—family size and complexity and age of the household head.[32] At the same time, the fact of living in the mountains, hills, or plains played no role whatsoever in determining wealth.

In addition, standard deviations of the wealth found for these villages can serve to assess the distribution of wealth (table 1). Once again, the data do not reflect "mountain egalitarianism." Instead, the distribution of wealth correlates with the average assessment of wealth. The most egalitarian of the villages was the most impoverished—the lowland, marsh-ridden parish of Santa Maria Padule—while the differences between rich and poor were the most extreme in the privileged mountain parish of Morello. But the distribution of wealth was more or less similar for the other villages, especially when compared to the vast inequalities of the city, here seen in the tax assessments of Prato's "Porta di Santa Trinita." When aggregated, the differences in average wealth and its dis-

---

32. On the complex and nonlinear relations between family size, family complexity, and wealth, see Christiane Klapisch-Zuber and Michel Demonet, "A Correspondence Analysis of a XVth Century Census: The Florentine Catasto of 1427," *Journal of European Economic History* 4 (1975): 415–28; and Christiane Klapisch-Zuber and Michel Demonet, "'A uno pane e uno vino': La famille rurale toscane au début du XVe siècle," *Annales: ESC* 27 (1972): 873–901.

tribution (the standard deviation) between the mountains and the low-lands were decidedly insignificant. Those from the plains possessed 57.08 lire of taxable wealth with a standard deviation of 138.08 as opposed to 58.40 lire with a standard deviation of 131.39 in the mountains.[33]

Can other characteristics distinguish the mountains from the plains at the end of the fourteenth century? Does a comparison of household structures, for instance, lend credence to claims that a stricter sense of

TABLE 2.   Regression of Property Values, Estimo of 1393–94

Source	SS	df	MS		
Model	1561288.29	8	195161.036		
Residual	14315155.2	832	17205.7154		
Total	15876554.5	840	18900.5279		
Variable	Coefficient	SE	t	Prob > $|t|$	Beta
Wealth					
Size[a]	16.74009	1.973134	8.484	0.000	.2966024
Dist1[b]	−.1669715	.2477549	−0.674	0.501	−.0387036
Senex[c]	25.05472	9.59942	2.610	0.009	.0880887
Comx[d]	−30.39369	9.548142	−3.183	0.002	−.1089486
Hcap[e]	−19.86763	14.13954	−1.405	0.160	−.0521082
Female[f]	24.88006	23.34071	1.066	0.287	.0398853
Moun[g]	13.79581	16.1993	0.852	0.395	.0501912
Prato[h]	−14.22133	14.61229	−0.973	0.331	−.03379
Cons[i]	20.59476	19.19088	1.073	0.284	

Number of obs   =   841
F (8, 832)   =   11.34
Prob > F =   0.0000
R^2 =   0.0983
Adj R^2 =   0.0897
Root MSE   =   131.17

[a]Family size.
[b]Distance squared from Florence.
[c]If household head is 60 or older.
[d]Complex family structure.
[e]Handicapped family head.
[f]Female household head.
[g]Mountain village.
[h]Territory of Prato.
[i]Constant.

33. A t-test shows that the difference in the means of wealth between the mountains and the lowlands has a probability of less than 12 percent (observations equal 926, $t = -0.15$ at 924 degrees of freedom).

patriarchy reigned in the highlands? As we saw earlier, Morello's 104-year-old patriarch commanded not only the largest resources of any peasant found in this study, but he headed a complex family of 17 persons extended over four generations—a near impossibility for the preindustrial household according to Peter Laslett and his school.[34] Indeed, households of 10 or more were extremely rare (28 representing less than 3 percent of all the families in which household members were individuated),[35] but the majority of these (15) came from the mountains. The tiny village of San Martino del Castro just under the Futa Pass supplied more than one-sixth of them (5), and the largest family surveyed as a single unit (21 members) came from the mountain commune of Mangona.[36] The highest average household sizes also come from the mountains. Among "the stanti," Castro led the list with close to six members (5.76), while the impoverished marshlands of Padule sank to the bottom (2.83; see table 3).

Despite these facts, household size does not invariably distinguish the mountains from the plains. The communes of Montecuccoli and Montecarelli—two of the highest villages in the "alpi florentine"—ranked next to Padule in possessing the lowest average household sizes (3.32 and 3.31, respectively). On the other hand, the Arno Valley parishes of Santa Maria Nuovoli and Santa Maria a Quarto in Florence's immediate hinterland, as well as San Giorgio Castelnuovo (40 m) and San Giusto (47 m) in the district of Prato all comprised average households of five members or more and possessed some of the largest families found for these villages.

Nor do clear patterns emerge from the percentages of families with either generational and collateral extensions (married brothers or cousins and their families living in the same household or being taxed as a single family unit). While impoverished Padule possessed no complex families, the greatest proportion of them came from the alluvial plains of San Giusto. Family structure also varied for the mountain communes, from

---

34. *Household and Family in Past Time*, ed. by Peter Laslett and Richard Wall (Cambridge, 1972).

35. By 1393, the rectors of the parishes would almost invariably list family members individually with their ages for the "stanti" and the "venuti," while the "usciti" were listed only by the name of the household head or by vague phrases such as "the heirs of the former . . ." or "with his wife and children." The one exception to this rule is the listing of "usciti" for the parish of Santa Maria a Nuovoli.

36. ASF, Estimo no. 219, 868v.

TABLE 3. Family Size and Net Migration, 1393

Village	"Stanti" Households	Family Size	"Venuti" Households	Family Size	"Usciti" Households	Net Migration (households)	Net "Stanti"
I. Suburban Parishes							
1. S. Lucia	31	3.81	8	4.75	8	0	0.00
2. S. Lorenzo	31	4.55	17	3.59	9	8	0.26
3. S. M. Nuovoli	13	5.23	12	6.67	8	4	0.31
4. S. M. Quarto	21	5.00	16	4.19	12	4	0.19
II. Plains and Hills							
5. S. MRT Campi	42	4.50	16	4.25	15	1	0.02
6. S. M. Padule	6	2.83	7	5.43	15	-8	-1.33
7. S. MRT Sesto	100	4.78	19	3.79	27	-8	-0.08
8. Castelnovo (PR)	23	5.57	17	3.82	19	-2	-0.09
9. S. Giusto (PR)	37	5.03	21	5.24	29	-8	-0.22
III. Mountains							
10. Schignano (PR)	12	4.17	3	2.00	3	0	0.00
11. S. M. Morello	18	5.11	6	5.17	13	-7	-0.39
12. Montecuccoli	82	3.32	9	2.33	9	0	0.00
13. Mangona	107	4.07	8	3.00	47	-39	-0.36
14. Montecarelli	42	3.31	13	2.69	30	-17	-0.40
15. S. M. Casagli	41	5.07	0	0.00	13	-13	-0.32
16. S. MRT Castro	59	5.76	0	0.00	17	-17	-0.29
17. S. M. Bordignano	82	4.20	0	0.00	16	-16	-0.20
18. S. PL Castiglione	7	4.57	0	0.00	6	-6	-0.86
IV. The City—Prato							
Porta S. Trinita	146	4.22	21	2.86	32	-11	-0.08
Total	900	4.40	193	4.02	328	-135	-0.15

Montecarelli, with a little over 5 percent of its households extended, to Castro, with a quarter of its families either stem or joint.

Finally, the notion that the mountains were patriarchal strongholds is tempered by the extent to which mountain women were household heads. While a comparison of patriarchy in the mountains and plains will have to await the study of other sources, these data are suggestive. Female heads, invariably widows or spinsters, did not always rule in the absence of other males, and several governed families of five or more members.[37] In the small mountain hamlet of San Paolo di Castiglione, the local officials violated the Estimo statute by recognizing a married woman as the head of a household she shared with her husband, perhaps because she was identified as the heir of their 25 lire of taxable property.[38] The mountain parishes of Bordignano and Santa Maria Casaglia, moreover, had the highest percentages of families with women as household heads—13.27 and 15.38, respectively. These were the only villages where the percentage of female "capi" exceeded that found for the urban population of the Porta di Santa Trinità (10.05 percent). By contrast, households led by women are completely absent from Padule as well as from the much larger and more prosperous baptismal parish of San Martino a Campi, and in alluvial San Giusto only 1 family out of 87 was listed under a woman's name.

More than any of the traits thus far surveyed, patterns of migration distinguished the mountains from the plains in 1393. As Cherubini asserted (without the support of statistics), the mountains were "the great belchers of population."[39] With the exception of impoverished Padule, villages in the lowlands either remained stable or gained in population at the end of the Trecento (1383–93), while the mountain districts

37. A widow from Santa Maria Nuovoli whose husband had recently died headed a family of seven, which included her 15-year-old son (Estimo no. 219, 591r). Similarly, a widow from Nuovoli headed a seven-member family. In the parish of Quarto, a 40-year-old widow headed a household of five, although the eldest son was only 2 (Estimo no. 219, 544v). And a 50-year-old widow from the Apennines village of Bordignano headed a family of five (Estimo no. 218, 288v).

38. Estimo no. 219, 298r. For the Estimo law, see Estimo no. 73, 3r: "Quod nulla uxore alicuius vivente viro potuerit vel possit . . . referri vel allibrari in dicto nuovo extimo . . ."

39. See "Conclusion," *Strutture familiari, epidemie, migrazioni nell'Italia medioevale*, ed. Rinaldo Comba, Gabriella Piccini, and Giuliano Pinto (Naples, 1984), 539.

spewed forth their human resources (table 3). Only in Montecuccoli did newcomers balance those who left a mountain community. By contrast, nearby Montecarelli lost over one-third of its residents, and the village of San Paolo Castiglione, seven miles northeast of Firenzuola along the Bolognese border,[40] lost about as many families as remained from the last Estimo a decade earlier.

As suggested above, the Capi's categorization of rural taxpayers into "stanti", "venuti" (or "tornati"), and "usciti" allows us to go beyond net migration for individual villages to estimate the distances and types of migration between rural communities, urban centers, and foreign territories. Foregoing a detailed comparison of such networks of human exchange, a few observations are pertinent. The figures on movements to and from the mountains do bear out at least one of Braudel's claims. In pursuit of new rents or *mezzadria* (sharecropping) contracts,[41] peasants in the plains, particularly those with little or no landed property, moved short distances, often from one adjacent parish to the next and over distances separated at times by only a few farms.[42] By contrast, the movement of highlanders could cover impressive distances. Not only were they more likely to migrate beyond the borders of the Florentine state to mountain communities in Bologna, but they moved into the territories of Imola, Modena, Pisa, Siena, and Grosseto—the latter probably through the ties of transhumance, the winter pasturing of their flocks in the Maremma.[43]

But can we honor the claims of Braudel, Cherubini, Fiumi, and others that the highlanders moved inexorably downward into the plains and cities, seeking opportunity and refuge from their primitive and harsh way

---

40. This village is most likely the one Repetti, in *Dizionario storico della Toscana*, vol. 1 (Florence, 1833–45), 590, identifies as Castiglioncello di Firenzuola, located 7 miles northeast of Firenzuola, then on the border of the granduchy and the Romagna Imolese; its parish in the eighteenth century was called SS. Giovanni e Paolo, and it appears on recent *carte militari* as Castiglioncello.

41. See the notarial records of the Mazzetti family for the area between the city walls and Calenzano.

42. On migration and the *mezzadria* system, see Herlihy and Klapisch-Zuber, *Les Toscans et leurs familles*, 315ff.

43. On transhumance between the Maremma and the Florentine Apennines, see Cherubini, "Paesaggio agrario, insediamenti e attività silvo-pastorali sulla montagna tosco-romagnola alla fine del Medioevo," in *Fra Tevere, Arno e Appennino*, 49–53; and Cherubini, *Una comunità dell'appennino dal XIII al XV secolo: Montecoronaro dalla signoria dell'abbazia del Trivio al Dominio di Firenze* (Florence, 1972), 50–53.

of life?[44] As Niccolò Rodolico and others have shown, the time for such a migratory attraction would certainly have been the period after the Black Death through the early Quattrocento, when labor shortages and lower guild matriculation fees opened new opportunities for those from the countryside.[45] Yet the evidence from the Capi of 1393 does not bear out these assumptions. Of those highlanders whose destinations the local syndics of the commune knew, only 3 percent moved to the plains, and only slightly more found their way to Florence (7 percent; see table 4). Immigrants to Florence in the decade 1383–93, moreover, were neither the wealthy found by Johann Plesner for late-thirteenth-century Passignano[46] nor the brawny ("il braccio più forte") soon to become revolutionary Ciompi in Rodolico's version of Florentine immigration after the Black Death.[47] As can be best seen through these records, the city-bound, not only from the mountains but across the contado at the end of the Trecento, did not migrate as nuclear or extended families at all but, for the most part, were single women seeking urban employment as domestic servants (*fante*).[48]

TABLE 4. Migration of the Highlanders

	"Venuti"	"Usciti"	Total
Unknown[a]	3	25	28
Plains	1	4	5
Hills	3	5	8
Florence	1	9	10
Mountain	24	51	75
Beyond	6	60	66
Total	38	154	192

[a]Or untraceable by the tax authorities.

44. Braudel, *The Mediterranean*, 1:44, 47; Cherubini, "Conclusione," 539; Enrico Fiumi, "Sui rapporti economici tra citta e contado nell'età comunale," *Archivio Storico Italiano* (*ASI*) 114 (1956): 68.
45. Rodolico, *La democrazia fiorentina*, 1–45; Charles M. de la Roncière, *Prix et salaires à Florence au XIVe siècle (1280–1380)* (Rome, 1987).
46. Johann Plesner, *L'émigration de la campagne à la ville libre de Florence au 13e siècle* (Copenhagen, 1934).
47. Rodolico, *La democrazia fiorentina*, 44–45.
48. In the mountain commune of Mangona, four left for Florence to become domestic servants. All were women who appear to have migrated alone. One was an unmarried girl whose father had recently died, two were widows, and the fourth was a married woman whose husband remained behind in the village. On country women who came to the city as domestic servants, see Klapisch-Zuber, "Women Servants in Florence during the Fourteenth and Fifteenth Centuries," in *Women and Work in Preindustrial Europe*, ed. Barbara A. Hanawalt (Bloomington, 1986), 56–80.

Nor do the migratory patterns of these highlanders underscore a glacial, unremitting slide of these supposedly primitive people down the slopes toward the beacons of urban civilization. They appear not to have been eager at all to leave behind their mountain ways and the accompanying harsh conditions imposed by weather or terrain. When they moved, they left for other mountain villages (40 percent of the known cases), and most often they crossed the border into the foreign districts of Bologna, Pistoia, Imola, Lucca, Modena, or even Siena (46 percent). Unfortunately, either because they did not know or did not need to, the officials often failed to specify these foreign villages of destination; usually they merely signaled them with phrases such as "quello di Pistoia" or "nel contado di Bologna." But, when the rectors did specify the foreign destination, almost invariably it was a mountain village—Quinzano (622 m), Castel dell'Alpi (694 m), Sant'Andrea in the Val di Sambro (589 m), San Damiano (691 m), Baragazza (675 m), Qualto (762 m), Bruscoli (765 m), and Pietramala (851 m, then within the confines of the Bolognese state). As these altitudes suggest, often the mountaineers' movement was, instead of downward, upward from the lower "alpi fiorentine" to the higher Bolognese Alps.

If not by the economic explanation of mountain people moving down to greener pastures opened by the great mortalities of the second half of the Trecento, how then should we account for the mountains' "vomiting" of their human resources? In contrast to the celebrated thesis of Johann Plesner,[49] the Capi do reveal that poverty, as Herlihy and Klapisch-Zuber have noted, was the "motor" of peasant migration[50]—both "venuti" and "usciti" were worse off than those who "stayed." Yet, if poverty were the only explanation, mountains and plains should have shown little difference in the quantity or character of migration. As we have shown, wealth did not markedly distinguish the one from the other at the end of the Trecento. Nor were the propertyless the only ones "to go off begging [*andarsene acattando*]." Later, in the survey of 1401–2, in

49. The Plesner thesis lives on despite the devastating criticism marshalled early on by Gino Luzzato, "L'inurbamento delle popolazioni rurali in Italia nei secoli XII e XIII," in *Studi di storia e diritto in onore di Enrico Besta*, vol. 2 (Milan, 1939), 183–203; and later, on other grounds, by Conti, *La formazione*, 1:49. Other historians, such as Fiumi, "Fioritura e decadenza dell'economia fiorentina (part 1)," *ASI*, 115 (1957): 429–34, have criticized Plesner's definition of nobility but have continued to shore up his assumptions about the character of rural migration.
50. Herlihy and Klapisch-Zuber, *Les Toscans et leurs familles*, 318.

which local officials were required to itemize villagers' properties, abandoned *poderi* can be found listed with their assessed taxes alongside the names of mountaineers who had left their real estate for foreign places to beg or wander "per lo mondo." In one such case, the rural rector from the alpine village of Castro di San Martino attached his laconic comment: "eviction; abandoned farm; no one to work it, because no one wishes to pay the Estimo."[51] In other instances, the mountain rectors and syndics ended their reports with pleas, unlike any found in the lower valleys, for reducing their collective payments in consideration of the expenses of war, the inability to harvest crops because of military invasion, and the burdens from other taxes.[52]

Beyond these occasional marginal notes, the quantification of tax rates from these records points to a characteristic that, more than any other social fact thus far gleaned from the records, distinguished the mountains from the lowlands at the end of the fourteenth century. As Bernardino Barbadoro discovered against the claims of earlier historians from the seventeenth through the early twentieth centuries, the late medieval Estimi of Florence did not fix a standard ratio between property value and the tax to be paid.[53] Instead, city officials set a communal tax for a rural district. Then syndics of the rural communities, aided by locally elected tax officials, would divide this levy among their neighbors as they saw fit, basing their decisions on property assessments, the number of able-bodied men, and other considerations not so easily uncovered in the archival records. Such divisions did not always meet with the approval of the community, and on occasion the petitions to the tax board of the Estimo back in Florence amounted to legalized tax revolts.[54]

51. Estimo no. 225 (1412), 359r, the village of Castro di S. Martino.

52. See, for instance, the plea from the men of Mangona claiming that their Estimo should be reduced because they had been levied for yearly expenses to provide food and munitions and to repair the Florentine fortifications, "la roccha di Manghone" (Estimo no. 219, 874r), and the plea from the Castro S. Martino, whose failure to harvest their grain or draw "a drop of wine" they blamed on their "sterile and bad" soil and because of the war "with the Count" (Estimo no. 218, 285r).

53. Barbadoro, *Le finanze*, 78–80.

54. Thus, after the Estimo of 1355, the parish of Sant' Andrea Legnaia in the southern suburbs of Florence claimed that its locally elected officials were corrupt and had used their positions to lower their share of the tax burden. In response, Florentine officials ordered a new election and a revised Estimo, whereupon the assessments imposed on the earlier officials, who proved to be the richest members of the parish, increased substantially (Estimo no. 73, 114r–115r).

Probit analysis juxtaposes the variables distance, wealth, sex of household head, family size, and residence in the mountains as the determinants of out-migration (see table 5). Here, far beyond the other factors, the tax rate was the cause of families leaving their villages in the mountains as well as in the plains. Indeed, this model flies in the face of Braudel and others who have assumed that poverty and the inclement conditions of mountain life were the forces that moved migrants from their homesteads in the countryside. Once these variables are interrelated, despite higher rates of migration from the mountains, alpine residence in and of itself played no role in out-migration; indeed, after the above-mentioned variables have been factored, the mountaineers proved more intent on staying on their farms than were those farther down the valleys.[55]

As the above discussion should suggest, those in power in the city of Florence did not look upon the contado as an undifferentiated mass to be treated by a unified standard policy, as modern discussions of fiscal policy and the relationship between city and countryside generally assume.

TABLE 5.   Probit Analysis of Out-Migration

Variable	Coefficient	SE	t	Prob > |t|	Mean
Out					.2394822
Dist[a]	.0045209	.0024049	1.880	0.060	34.52589
Prato[b]	.2645089	.121007	2.186	0.029	.1326861
Sex[c]	.0878873	.1739791	0.505	0.614	1.057443
Tax rate	10.32075	1.135006	9.093	0.000	.0191462
Fsize[d]	−.0311645	.0216927	−1.437	0.151	4.27445
Wealth[e]	−.0016964	.0006579	−2.578	0.010	50.40561
Moun	−.4329393	.1576457	−2.746	0.006	.5226537
Cons	−.8033016	.2304088	−3.486	0.001	1

Probit Estimates   Number of obs = 1236
                                    $\chi^2 (7)$ = 108.98
Log Likelihood = −625.90641   Prob > χ^2 = 0.0000
[a]Distance squared.
[b]Territory of Prato.
[c]Female household head.
[d]Average family size in village.
[e]Average wealth in village.

55. Both residence in the "mountain" villages and the "alps" varied negatively with out-migration, e.g., deterred movement out of one's homestead. For the "alps" it was in fact a significant variable.

Table 6 shows the variation in tax rates from village to village. Of course, fluctuations or differences in the tax rate could be offset by under- or overestimations of the property value. Thus, as the Kents have shown for the urban *gonfalone* of Leon Rosso during the fifteenth century, patronage and corruption continued to play an important role in tax assessment even after the Catasto reforms of 1427 established standardized rules for assessments and exemptions.[56]

TABLE 6.   Tax Rates for Propertied Peasants, 1393–94

Village	Tax Rate	Families
I. Suburban parishes		
1. S. Lucia Og. f.m.	0.00366	7
2. S. Lorenzo f.m.	0.00906	19
3. S. M. Nuovoli	0.00745	11
4. S. M. Quarto	0.00845	12
II. Plains and hills		
5. S. MRT Campi	0.02392	24
6. S. M. Padule	0.01800	1
7. S. MRT Sesto	0.02067	67
8. Castelnovo (PR)	0.00948	15
9. S. Giusto (PR)	0.01985	14
III. Mountains		
10. Schignano (PR)	0.07514	7
11. S. M. Morello	0.00692	13
12. Montecuccoli	0.01805	57
13. Mangona	0.10750	43
14. Montecarelli	0.05690	27
15. S. M. Casagli	0.05394	32
16. S. MRT Castro	0.01196	35
17. S. M. Bordignano	0.00647	61
18. S. PL Castiglione	0.01226	5
IV. The city—Prato		
Porta S. Trinita	0.01397	86
Total	0.02640	541

56. D. V. Kent and F. W. Kent, *Neighbours and Neighbourhood in Renaissance Florence: The District of the Red Lion in the Fifteenth Century* (Locust Valley, N.Y., 1982), 24–36; Paula Clarke, *The Soderini and the Medici: Power and Patronage in Fifteenth-Century Florence* (Oxford, 1991), 35ff. After the return of the Medici in 1434, the objective forms devised in 1427 were largely abandoned. See Elio Conti, *L'im-*

Nonetheless, the discrepancies in the tax rates of villages sampled for this study are extraordinary. The suburban communities adjacent to Florence's city walls, which housed artisans and workers as well as peasants whose social composition was similar to that of peasants residing in peripheral parishes within Florence's city walls, paid the lowest rates. The average tax of those with property from Santa Lucia Ognissanti fuori le mura amounted to only 0.366 percent of their assessed worth. Those further away in the alpi fiorentine invariably paid more. Highlanders from Montecarelli and Santa Maria Casaglia were required to hand over 15 times more than the suburban rate to the Florentine Commune (5 percent of their property value). For the mountain village of Schignano in the district of Prato, the rate increased to 7.5 percent—8 times the rate imposed on peasants from Prato's lowland village of San Giorgio Castelnuovo and 20 times the suburban rate of Santa Lucia "outside the walls."

In the alpi fiorentine, the rates could climb even higher. The peasants from the large commune of Mangona were assessed 11 percent, not of their yearly income but of their property value.[57] Such a rate constituted a drastic inequality vis-à-vis the lowlands. It was 12.7 times that owed by peasants in the parish of Quarto, where sharecropping and urban investment in land had become widespread,[58] and a staggering 29.4 times that owed by the privileged contadini residing in the Florentine suburbs. In 1395, when the Estimo Straordinario was levied at a rate of one florin on the lire, it meant that Mangona had to hand over 44 percent of its landed wealth to the Florentine state in that year alone, and matters would only

---

posta diretta a Firenze nel Quattrocento (1427–1494) (Rome, 1984); Elio Conti, *Ricordi fiscali di Matteo Palmieri (1427–1474)* (Rome, 1983); and Lauro Martines, "Forced Loans: Political and Social Strain in Quattrocento Florence," *Journal of Modern History* 60, no. 2 (1988): 304.

57. The actual sum depended on the tax coefficient, which varied from 10 soldi to 1.5 florins. In the 1390s, the coefficient was climbing steadily from 12 soldi at the beginning of the decade to 1 florin on the assessed lira, or almost eight times that rate by 1395. See ASF, Camera Del Comune: Provveditori e Massai, Entrata e Uscita, no. 12, (1395), 205r.

58. For 1427, see Herlihy and Klapisch-Zuber, *Les Toscans et leurs familles,* 268–72. For the late Trecento, the notarial books from the Mazzetti family, who worked heavily within the parish of Quarto and its surroundings, are filled with mezzadria contacts and other land rents in which urban investors leased farms and smaller plots to peasants. By contrast, not a single mezzadria contract appears in the 560 acts recorded by the notary Ser Antonio di Giusto, who served the villages in the highlands around Scarperia and Barberino between 1428 and 1435.

have worsened with Florence's war with Milan and deepening fiscal crises at the end of the century.[59]

But once again a single mountain pattern cannot be seen in these data. The wealthy mountain hamlet of Morello was assessed at one of the lowest rates (0.692 percent), substantially below that of the lowland parishes of Sesto, Padule, Campi, and San Giusto. Did distance count more than altitude? Even if it did, this fact alone cannot explain all the variance. Witness Santa Maria Bordignano, the most distant of these parishes, a mountain hamlet nestled high in the valleys separating the territories of Florence and Bologna: its rate was the second lowest among the villages (0.647 percent). In this case, however, a clue is supplied by the marginal pleas that accompanied this parish's tax records. The local officials claimed that their villagers paid a double tax; that they ("noi huomini predetti habitanti nel detto popolo") possessed the major part of their lands in the territory of Bologna, where they were also "*allibrati.*"[60] The tax officials must have sympathized. They may have also been sensitive to the military importance of these border villages, especially given the growing threats from the Bolognese, the incursions of the feudal forces of the Ubaldini, and the invading troops from Milan. Finally, Santa Maria Bordignano and Morello were the two wealthiest parishes according to their property assessments, and wealth and the tax rate seem to have been negatively correlated across the villages sampled in this study. That is, even apart from the enormous tax advantages granted to Florentine citizens, the Florentine tax appears to have been steeply regressive; the richer the peasant household, the lower its tax rate.

Castro di San Martino, near the Futa Pass, was another mountain village not burdened as heavily as others in the Florentine Alps. The residents of this village were mostly *fictaiuoli* (leaseholders) of the feudal Ubaldini family, which waged open warfare against the Florentine state periodically throughout the fourteenth and early fifteenth centuries.[61]

---

59. On the complexities of tax coefficients and varying rates applied to the coefficient, see Giovanni Ciappelli, "Il Cittadino fiorentino e il fisco alla fine del Trecento e nel corso del Quattrocento: Uno studio di due casi," *Società e storia* 12 (1989): 823–72.

60. Estimo no. 219, 296r.

61. See, for instance, the chronicles of Matteo Villani, *Cronache storiche di Giovanni, Matteo e Filippo Villani*, ed. Francesco Dragomanni, vols. 5, 6 (Milan, 1848), rubr. xxiii, xxv, lxxxi, lxxxviii, cviii; and *Cronaca fiorentina di Marchionne de Coppo Stefani*, ed. N. Rodolico, in *Rerum Italicarum Scriptores* 30, pt. 1 (Città di Castello, 1903), rubr. 256, 351, 490, 548, 549, 611, 639, 641, 739.

What then can explain their tax breaks relative to the rates of their mountain neighbors? Were Castro's lower Estimi a ploy on the part of the Florentine state to prise these peasants' loyalties from their feudal lords? Or could they have resulted from Florentine mercy on this village, which had pleaded vigorously in the margins of its tax returns that it had been badly damaged by invading troops and crop failures?[62] Unfortunately, the tax records here remain silent.

Could the number of able-bodied men—an assessment of a family's potential labor power—have affected tax rates, and will it thereby help in explaining the discrepancies? Indeed, the Estimo was more than a property tax; it was also a head tax on adult males.[63] As for the later Catasti, tax officials mindful of the labor potential of the household took note of handicaps, old age, and infirmities that might reduce a family's earnings. These matters can readily be detected in inequalities in the rate for those who possessed no property—the *nullatenenti*. The average tax burden varied from one village to the next, following roughly the inequalities of the tax rates for those with assessed property. But the amount of the tax could also vary radically from one *nullatenente* to the next within the same parish, ranging from as little as no tax at all for those deemed the truly *miserabile*[64] to more than one lira—a tax usually charged to those with substantial furnishings, animals, and landed properties.[65]

Still other factors may have affected tax rates—family size, family structure, age of the household head, whether a village lay outside the original contado of Florence in the newly acquired district of Prato,[66] and

---

62. The local officials of Castro attached a note to their returns telling the Florentine authorities that they did not know how to distribute the Estimo because of poverty and crop failures resulting from war with the "conte" (Estimo no. 218, 285r).

63. Later these two components of the contado tax would be separated in the Catasti of the Quattrocento.

64. Total exemption for contadini from the Estimo was extremely rare. Even those called "miserabili" usually paid a small sum of 4 or 5 soldi, and the tax officials claimed some fee even from elderly widows who lived alone, possessed no property, and appeared to be on their deathbeds—who at any rate died before paying their "lira."

65. In one case, a family of six from the villa of San Giusto in the alluvial plains of the Bisenzio had recently sold all its lands, remaining propertyless, and yet their earlier "imposte"—one of the highest in the village, 4 lire, 17 soldi—remained (Estimo no. 218, 976r).

66. Florence began to tax Prato as a part of the Florentine contado in the Estimo of 1355, almost immediately after its political incorporation into the Florentine

whether the family head was female.[67] Regression analysis allows us to test and go beyond the impressions cast by the data in tabular form. It provides a means for determining the effect of such factors on an independent variable, in this case the tax rate (see table 7).

TABLE 7.   Regression of Tax Rates, Estimo of 1393–94

Source	SS	df	MS		
Model	.1728996	9	.019211067		
Residual	.573283527	435	.001317893		
Total	.746183127	444	.001680593		
Variable	Coefficient	SE	t	Prob > |t|	Beta
Tax Ratio					
Wealth	−.000071	.0000104	−6.813	0.000	−.3020953
Size[a]	.002245	.0006657	3.373	0.001	.1547792
Dist1[b]	−.0005502	.0000836	−6.586	0.000	−.4504218
Senex[c]	.0021525	.0036461	0.590	0.555	.0255964
Cmpx[d]	.0042274	.003762	1.124	0.262	.0497386
Hcap[e]	.0183416	.0061974	2.960	0.003	.1426816
Female[f]	−.0094785	.0095393	−0.994	0.321	−.0479562
Moun[g]	.0480802	.0058348	8.240	0.000	.5685184
Prato[h]	.0069843	.0065747	1.062	0.289	.0465086
Cons[i]	.0109119	.007689	1.419	0.157	

Number of obs   =   445
F (9, 435)   =   14.58
Prob > F   =   0.0000
R^2 =   0.2317
Adj R^2 =   0.2158
Root MSE   =   .0363
[a]Family size.
[b]Distance squared from Florence.
[c]If household head is 60 or older.
[d]Complex family structure.
[e]Handicapped family head.
[f]Female household head.
[g]Mountain village.
[h]Territory of Prato.
[i]Constant.

state. This did not happen with neighboring Pistoia and its territory, which at the same time (1351) became a subject town of Florence. 67. In the later Catasto, female heads were exempt from the head tax.

67. In the later Catasto, female heads were exempt from the head tax.

A number of these factors are highly significant (well under the conventional 0.05 confidence level). Indeed, as speculated earlier from table 2, Florence's tax on its countryside was regressive; the wealthier the rural property holder, the lower the tax rate. Family size was also significant; as one might expect with a tax that evaluated potential agricultural labor power, the larger the family, the more the household owed. As earlier surmised, distance played a significant role in Florentine tax policy; the further the village was from the city, the more disadvantaged the taxpayer. But, unlike the impressions cast earlier by the village tallies summarized in table 6, it is now possible to say that distance did not cancel out the effect of altitude, even though highland villages were generally the most distant from the center, Florence. Indeed, residence in the highlands played a greater role in determining the tax rate than did distance or any other variable.[68]

But as we have said, unlike the later Catasti, the Capi fused the head tax with property assessments. Could a higher percentage of males, particularly able-bodied ones between the ages of 13 and 70,[69] have contributed to the drastic tax imbalance? After all, the harsh conditions of mountain life and patterns of migration may well have sent women down the slopes in search of employment as domestics. Indeed, although the rural holdings of Bernardo Machiavelli (the father of Niccolò) lay south of the city, near San Casciano, one of his domestic servants was an eight-year-old girl from the Commune of Mangona, high in the alpi fiorentine, whom he fed, clothed, and dowered after a 10-year period of service.[70] A statistical analysis, however, does not confirm that these tax discrepancies arose from such migratory facts. When the head tax for these males is subtracted from the total assessment, the differential in tax rates widens; Mangona's rate jumps to 35.3 times that required of Santa Lucia's more privileged suburbanites. Moreover, when the calculated property tax, instead of the total tax rate, is regressed as the dependent

---

68. See table 6, Beta-coefficient for the mountains = +.5573.

69. The guidelines counting those responsible for the head tax in the Capi were more stringent than those later levied by the Catasti. Instead of able-bodied males between the ages of 18 and 60 (Otto Karmin, *La Legge del Catasto Fiorentino del 1427* [Florence, 1906], 28–29), the Capi charged all males who were not servants, blind, or mad between the ages of 13 and 70 (Estimo no. 79, Deliberation of 1414, n.p.).

70. Bernardo Machiavelli, *Libro di Ricordi,* ed. Cesare Olschki (Florence, 1954), 167.

variable, the model remains essentially the same: more than any other factor the fact of residing in the mountains determined a higher tax rate.[71] Similarly, the regression of taxes charged to those without any taxable wealth—the *nullatenenti* and *miserabili*—shows a significant bias against the mountaineers in Florentine tax policy. While, as we should expect, labor power measured by family size was more critical in determining the tax on the have-nots than it was on those with property, residence in the mountains once again was the most powerful factor in determining a family's tax (Beta = .282; see table 8).

Florence placed this unequal burden on its mountaineers, moreover, just when the *contado* and the subject towns in general were being forced to bear the brunt of Florence's rapidly increasing indebtedness.[72] Why did the city oligarchy at the end of the fourteenth century decide to hit its highland peasants so brutally, forcing many to leave their lands along or near to the sensitive and troubled border with the state of Bologna? Thus far my research through the *Consulte e Pratiche,* the *Provvisioni,* and the *Libri fabrarum* has turned up few motives for this bias in tax policy.[73] But the context of labor shortages and urban investment in agriculture suggests an answer.

From the Catasto of 1427, Herlihy and Klapisch-Zuber have shown that urban investment in land, and in particular the labor-intensive farms of the *mezzadria* system, were concentrated in the valleys and low hills close to Florence.[74] Earlier, Herlihy argued that the wave of urban investment quickened after the Black Death and continued through the Quattrocento.[75] Later, in "The Problem of the 'Return to the Land,'" he changed his mind.[76] But in the same volume Christiane Klapisch-Zuber

71. The adjusted R^2 for the calculated property tax equals .2028 as against .2158 for the total tax rate, and the weight (Beta coefficient) of the mountains is .557 as opposed to .569.

72. See Marvin Becker, "Economic Change and the Emerging Florentine Territorial State," *Studies in the Renaissance* 13 (1986): 7–39: Becker, *Florence in Transition* (Baltimore, 1966–68); and Molho, *Florentine Public Finances,* 22–45.

73. I wish to thank Gene Brucker for this judgement.

74. Herlihy and Klapisch-Zuber, *Les Toscans et leurs familles,* 268–72.

75. Herlihy, "Santa Maria Impruneta: A Rural Commune in the late Middle Ages," in *Florentine Studies,* ed. N. Rubinstein (London, 1968), 242–76.

76. Herlihy, "The Problem of the 'Return to the Land' in Tuscan Economic History of the Fourteenth and Fifteenth Centuries," in *Civiltà ed economia agricola in Toscana nei secc. XIII–XV,* 401–21, where he has argued not from direct evidence but from fluctuations in the total returns from the rural Estimi that "investments either grew or declined in phase with the long-term economic cycle of prosperity and decline" (416).

TABLE 8.   Regression of Taxes on the *Nullatenenti*

Source	SS	df	MS			
Model	10012126.9	9	1112458.55			
Residual	38481585.5	533	72198.0967			
Total	48493712.5	542	89471.7942			
Variable	Coefficient	SE	t	Prob > |t|	Beta	
Tax						
Heads[a]	71.77799	18.92969	3.792	0.000	.1925746	
Size[b]	34.00815	5.908879	5.755	0.000	.2799266	
Dist1[c]	−1.30907	1.096892	−1.193	0.233	−.0941067	
Senex[d]	59.88856	25.15718	2.381	0.018	.0975962	
Cmpx[e]	−47.77158	24.75958	−1.929	0.054	−.078588	
Hcap[f]	2.498543	38.37953	0.065	0.948	.0028017	
Female[g]	−31.56781	70.35718	−0.449	0.654	−.0189111	
Moun[h]	168.4868	48.01574	3.509	0.000	.2818944	
Prato[i]	31.65798	36.68122	0.863	0.388	.0352821	
Cons[j]	28.96749	52.01746	0.557	0.578		

Number of obs   =   543
F (9, 533)   =   15.41
Prob > F   =   0.0000
R^2 =   0.2065
Adj R^2 =   0.1931
Root MSE   =   68.70
[a]Number of men age 14–70.
[b]Family size.
[c]Distance squared from Florence.
[d]If household head is 60 or older.
[e]Complex family structure.
[f]Handicapped family head.
[g]Female household head.
[h]Mountain village.
[i]Territory of Prato.
[j]Constant.

with compelling evidence continued to support Herlihy's earlier position: the *mezzadria* fueled by urban investments, spread in times of trouble and particularly after the Black Death.[77] The vast quantities of notarial acts left by the Mazzetti family, who worked the Arno Valley villages stretching from the city walls through the parishes of Nuovoli, Castello, Quarto, Quinto, Sesto, Campi, and into the hills of Calenzano, allow the historian to chronicle the ebb and flow of this investment history before

77. Klapisch-Zuber, "Mezzadria e insediamenti rurali alla fine del medio evo," in *Civiltà ed economia agricola in Toscana nei secc. XIII–XV*, 154.

the Catasto of 1427. In their protocols alone as many as 10,000 acts survive between 1348 and 1426.

A comparison of land transactions from 1371 to 1401 with the acts from the mountain notary Ser Antonio di Giusto, who regularly redacted business in the alpi fiorentine, is instructive. In the land market of the nearby Arno Valley parishes, the presence of the city is overwhelming. In 82 sales, urban buyers constituted the majority (58 percent) and were present either as buyers or sellers in 85 percent of these conveyances.[78] When the size of these properties is considered, the role of the urban investor looms considerably larger. While rural residents swapped among themselves strips of land measuring less than 10 *stiori* (about three acres), those from the city bought estates (*poderi*) with buildings, animals, and other furnishings and lands often measuring well over 100 *stiori* and often valued in the hundreds of florins. By the second half of the fourteenth century, not only old oligarchic families such as the Strozzi, who had owned land in these communities for centuries, but artisans and small provisioners—druggists, goldsmiths, cobblers, butchers, vintners, coppersmiths, bakers, bowl makers, wheelwrights, belt makers, and even disenfranchised workers (several doublet makers and a wool shearer)—bought and sold landed properties in these rural parishes of the Arno Valley.[79] Successive acts can be found in which urban investors bought lands from resident peasants whom they immediately turned into sharecroppers by leasing the same lands to them under the conditions of the *mezzadria*.[80] By contrast, the sales redacted by Ser Antonio for the "alps" and hills around Barberino and Scarperia were overwhelmingly transactions between highlanders. A little over 10 percent of these buyers and sellers were citizens of Florence. Indeed, the percentage of urban investors becomes negligible if Pellegrinus f.q. Ubaldini de Cattanis is discounted, who appeared in Ser Antonio's witness lists to have resided year-round in his palace at Barberino.[81]

This widely differentiated fabric of urban landholding and urban interests in the countryside surrounding Florence leads us to speculate about the reasons for the sharp differences in tax rates between moun-

---

78. ASF, Not. antecos. no. 13,521 (M352 [1370–1401]).

79. Not. antecos. no. 13,521, 40r, 185r, 204v; ibid., 125r, 163r, 188r; ibid., 186r; ibid., 54r, 146r, 154v, 169r, 227v, 231r; ibid., 130v; ibid., 106r; ibid., 226r; ibid., 155r, 193v; ibid., 169r; ibid., 61v, 69v, 70v; ibid., 130r.

80. See, for instance, ibid., 187r, n.p., 1397.ix.9, and n.p., 1398.vi.29.

81. ASF, Not. antecos. no. 792.

tains and plains. Historians since Nicola Ottokar have stressed the importance of patronage for understanding Florentine politics.[82] For the most part, these studies have concentrated on clientage within the city of Florence and have yet to investigate whether such ties offered political and fiscal advantages to those in the countryside.[83] Yet, as any reader of Florentine *ricordanze* knows, these tentacles of power extended further, literally to the ground, to those in villages where Florentine citizens concentrated their rural holdings and relied on the exploitation of the resident labor force. The diary of Bernardo Machiavelli mixed entries of his farmhands' economic dealings, marriages, and misfortunes with those of his own family.[84] And Giovanni di Pagolo Morelli's advice to his future progeny demanded regular visits and rigorous surveillance over one's rural holdings, to compare the work habits and production of one farm with another and to reward and punish accordingly.[85] It stands to reason that those villages where patricians such as the Machiavelli, the Morelli,[86] or the Corsini[87] held their estates would be the ones offered tax advantages at the expense of others further removed whose surplus hardly affected Florentine private interests. As Marvin Becker and Anthony Molho have shown, Florentine citizens faced a rapidly increas-

---

82. Nicola Ottokar, *Il Comune di Firenze alla fine del Dugento* (Florence, 1926). See also Nicolai Rubinstein, *The Government of Florence under the Medici, 1434–1494* (Oxford, 1965); Dale Kent, *The Rise of the Medici: Faction in Florence, 1426–1434* (Oxford, 1976); Kent and Kent, *Neighbours and Neighbourhood; Patronage, Art and Society in Renaissance Italy,* ed. F. W. Kent and Patricia Simons (Oxford, 1987); Anthony Molho, "Cosimo de'Medici: Pater Patriae or Padrino?" *Stanford Italian Review* (1979): 5–33; Roberto Bizzocchi, *Chiesa e potere nella Toscana del Quattrocento* (Bologna, 1987); and Gene Brucker, *Renaissance Florence,* 2d ed. (Berkeley, 1983).

83. That such ties did exist can be found in A. Lillie and F.W. Kent, "The Piovano Arlotto: New Documents," in *Florence and Italy: Renaissance Studies in Honour of Nicolai Rubinstein,* ed. by Peter Denley and Caroline Elam (London, 1988), 347–67; and F. W. Kent, *Bartolommeo Cederni and his friends: Letters to an Obscure Florentine* (Florence, 1991), 40–41.

84. Bernardo Machiavelli, *Libro di Ricordi,* ed. Cesare Olschki (Florence, 1954).

85. Morelli, *Ricordi,* 234.

86. Despite Giovanni's praise of the Mugello's nobility and vast resources, the Morelli chose to expand their rural holdings southward and much closer to the city after the Black Death. His uncle Bartolomeo purchased two poderi in the village of Ema, near Galluzzo (Morelli, *Ricordi,* 136).

87. *Il Libro di Ricordanze dei Corsini (1362–1457),* ed. Armando Petrucci (Rome, 1965). From the 1360s through the early fifteenth century the Corsini steadily expanded their rural holdings in roughly the same area as did the Machiavelli—in the Quarter of Santo Spirito around the market town of San Casciano.

ing public debt resulting largely from the expansive military budgets of the late fourteenth century. They nonetheless remained staunchly determined not to bring direct taxes upon themselves. As a consequence, Florentine oligarchs shifted the tax burden increasingly onto the shoulders of those in the contado. But heavy tax burdens in those lowland and hill villages near the city where Florentine citizens possessed their farms and profited from their sharecroppers' and other tenants' production and well-being likewise would have threatened the economic resources of these urban proprietors.

Such concerns over the economic fortune and security of rural holdings may have proved even more problematic in the late Trecento than they did earlier or later. How were these urban proprietors, whether wealthy patricians or small shopkeepers, to maintain their rural investments in the plains and nearby hills during this period of acute labor shortages that followed in the wake of pestilence and depopulation? The Capi della famiglia reveals one solution practiced at least since the 1370s: fiscal policy.[88] Radically inequitable tax rates forced highlanders more than others to forego their independence as small landowners and herders and perhaps might induce them to become dependent and propertyless sharecroppers in the rich alluvial plains of the Arno, the Bisenzio, and other nearby zones where urban investment and the *mezzadria* system flourished.

As the Capi della famiglia records reveal, the policy was only half a success. The highlanders were forced to flee their homesteads in greater numbers than any other taxpayers covered in this study. But, as against what the Florentine state might have planned and what later historians figuring the laws of economic advantage have argued, the highlanders did not head for the lower valleys, where taxes were only a fraction of what they were in the mountains. Instead, those highlanders who left their homesteads moved to other mountain villages, most often skipping across the border into the territories of Bologna, Pistoia, Imola, Modena, and Forlì, where they faced other taxes, to be sure, but perhaps no longer the heavy inequalities of the Florentine Estimo. At any rate, they certainly could thereby leave their heavy debts behind. Thus, the mountaineers protested with their feet, leaving farms uncultivated and diminishing the tax base upon which the government of Florence and its expansionary

---

88. A similar pattern of high tax rates for the mountaineers can be seen for the Estimo of 1371–72.

politics had become increasingly dependent. As the criminal records of the Capitano del Popolo attest,[89] mountain people, moreover, turned more directly against the state and the policies that had impoverished their villages. But this study of the Estimo of 1393 suggests that the state and not geography generated these Braudelian traits of mountain poverty and hostility to the city's "civilization."

Were the Florentines so foolish as not to recognize that their tax strategies might be backfiring? Indeed, once war with Milan, joined by Bologna, helped to fuel local uprisings across the Florentine Alps at the beginning of the fifteenth century,[90] shifts in official Florentine sentiment can be detected in the brief notes on the deliberations found in the *Libri fabrarum* and the *Provvisioni*. As early as 1364,[91] but increasingly after 1385, the Florentine ruling councils began trying to entice Florentine agricultural laborers back to the territory of Florence, offering them tax exemptions and moratoria on debts.[92] In these sources, the ruling elite of Florence began to recognize that their lands in the *alpi fiorentine* had become deserted. In 1391, "considerantes novitas exortas in alpibus et poderibus Florentinorum," the Council of the People granted a cancellation of all debts owed to Florence by those highlanders who would return to their homelands in the contado of Florence within one year.[93] In 1402, they reversed their tax policy again, with even better incentives, offering these mountaineers a sweeping three-year moratorium on all debts and taxes to the Commune of Florence.[94] The Florentine state repeated these desperate pleas for agricultural labor to return to the mountains through

---

89. The records of the Podestà and Capitano describe earlier rebellions against the Florentine state in the *alpi fiorentine*; see, for instance, the sentence of the Capitano del Popolo, no. 661, 42v–45r, on 17 September 1373.

90. See, for instance, the uprisings of *popoli* of the *alpi fiorentine* along the Bolognese border whose "rebelles" were sentenced by the *Capitano del Popolo*, no. 2207 (21.iv.–22.ix. 1403), 1r–2r, 3v–5r). For revolts at the same time across the alps of the Romagnola and Casentino, see Cherubini, *Communità dell'appennino*, 157–61.

91. ASF, Provvisioni, Registri, no. 52, 34v.

92. Provvisioni, no. 74, 204v, 11.xii.1385; Consulte e Pratiche, no. 25, 184v, 20.ii.1387, and 192v, 4.iii.1387. I wish to thank Gene Brucker for these references. In further research on the Provvisioni I have been able to find repeated attempts by the Florentine legislators to entice rural laborers to return or emigrate into the Florentine contado through the 1390s and early years of the fifteenth century.

93. *Libri fabarum*, no. 43, 232r, 1391.xii.4.

94. ASF, Provvisioni Duplicati, no. 72 (1402), 111v–113v (original numeration). For the disastrous effects of Florentine tax policy on the contado more generally at the end of the fourteenth century, see Molho, *Florentine Public Finances*, 28ff.

the early fifteenth century, and even beyond the tax reforms of 1427, extending the grace periods against the payment of all debts and taxes for as much as 20 years.[95] Again, the vicariate of Firenzuola and the alpi fiorentine figured prominently whenever these legislative decrees singled out specific places.

In sum, a quantitative analysis of the Capi della famiglia throws into question the Braudelian portrayal of mountain peoples in the Mediterranean. While these sources cannot test generalizations about mountain folklore, religion, and violence—the supposed "primitive" behavior of mountain people—they can challenge the structural characteristics that Braudel and others have asserted underlay such a character—mountain poverty and mountain egalitarianism. We have found that neither the levels of wealth nor its distribution distinguished the mountain villages of the northwestern quarter of Florence, Santa Maria Novella, from communities further down in the hills and in the lowlands of the Arno and the Bisenzio. On the other hand, the records from 1393 do underscore one of Braudel's generalizations—mass migration from the mountains. The direction of this movement, however, was not that claimed by Braudel and others—the inexorable, unrelenting flow of highlanders to the plains and cities. Although highlanders fled their homesteads, they migrated to other mountain villages, most often across the Florentine border. The reason for migration, moreover, was not the pull of a more pleasant, civilized life in the lowlands and the cities, away from the harsh conditions of their mountain villages, as historians have often reasoned.[96] Instead of exerting the "pull" of migration, the city—in this case Florence—was its "push." The fiscal policy of the Florentine government overburdened the mountaineers, forcing them to leave their lands. This policy, and not some racial or geographical determination of the mountains themselves, may have caused other social characteristics to follow—the hostility and violence of mountain people toward the state, its religious practices, and codes of behavior. As David Herlihy discovered for

---

95. See Provvisioni, no. 105, 215v–216r; no. 110, 70v–71r, 100v–101r; no. 112, 137v–140r, 143r; no. 117, 45v, 122v–23r; no. 118, 116v–117v. Again, I wish to thank Gene Brucker.

96. Recently, historians such as Rinaldo Comba have stressed factors such as taxation, which pushed the mountaineers from their homesteads ("Emigrare nel Medioevo: Aspetti economico-sociali della mobilità geografica nei secoli XI–XVI," in *Strutture familiari*, 63).

neighboring Pistoia, the mountains along the northern Florentine border had a more variegated and complex history than that of a steady movement of the highlanders to supposed greener pastures further down the slopes.

A Geography of the "Contadi" in Communal Italy

Giorgio Chittolini

The role played by cities in the organization of territories is well known. Historians often repeat the claim that "There is no 'territory' without a city."[1] This is certainly true for the cities of northern and central Italy when they carried out their "historical mission" of unifying and organizing territories and demonstrated that they were able to give shape to large, vigorous territorial organisms, or "contadi," that were in effect real city-states displaying remarkable cohesion and durability.[2] The great

---

1. T. Malmberg, *Human Territoriality: Survey of Behavioural Territories in Man with Preliminary Analysis and Discussion* (The Hague, Paris, and New York, 1980), cited in M. Roncayolo, "Territorio," in *Enciclopedia Einaudi*, vol. 14 (Turin, 1981), 236. See also W. Christaller, *Central Places in Southern Germany* (Englewood Cliffs, 1966); A. E. Smailes, *Urban Geography* (Padova, 1964); P. Claval, *La logique des villes. Essai d'urbanologie* (Paris, 1981); D. Herlihy, "Società e spazio nella città italiana del Medioevo," in *La storiografia urbanistica* (Lucca, 1977), 174–90, esp. 178 ff. A recent reexamination of the city/territory relationship, appears in a comprehensive analysis of "models of cities" throughout history in P. Rossi, ed., *Modelli di città. Funzioni e strutture politiche* (Turin, 1987), esp. 564–70. See also L. Gambi, "Le regioni italiane come problema storico," in *Orientamenti di una regione attraverso i secoli: scambi, rapporti, influssi storici sulla struttura dell'Umbria*, Atti del X Convegno di Studi Umbri (Perugia-Gubbio, 1978), 9–33; and P. Remy, *La ville. Phénomène économique* (Brussels, 1966).

2. On the "historical mission" of cities, see G. Volpe, *Medioevo italiano*, 2d ed. (Florence, 1961), 246. For a brief restatement and ample bibliography on territorial organization carried out by city-states, see G. Chittolini, "The Italian City-State and Its Territory," in *City States in Classical Antiquity and Medieval Italy*, ed. A. Molho, K. Raaflaub, and J. Emlen (Ann Arbor, 1991), 589–602. Other information, in addition to the fundamental works of N. Ottakar, G. De Vergottini, and E. Sestan, can be found in several recent publications: O. Capitani, "Città e comuni," in *Comuni e signorie: istituzioni, società e lotte per l'egemonia*, Storia d'Italia, ed. G. Galasso, vol. 4 (Turin, 1981), 5 ff.; A. I. Pini, "Dal comune città-stato al comune ente amministrative," in *Comuni e signorie: istituzioni, società e lotte per l'egemonia*, 451–587; R. Bordone, *La società urbana nell'Italia comunale (secoli XI–XIV)* (Torino, 1984); and

417

urban communes, almost all of which grew from ancient Roman towns and episcopal seats, as these were the only centers that could rightly be called cities, were able to impose themselves upon vast areas of the peninsula as the keystones of territorial organization that would give rise to wide systems of city-states.[3] This process was very different from that which took place during the same period beyond the Alps, in Europe, where the network of "urban" territories was much more splintered and weak and, most importantly, was submerged within the considerably wider framework of seignorial and princely domains.[4]

P. Cammarosano, "Città e campagna. Rapporti politici ed economici," in *Società e istituzioni dell'Italia comunale: L'esempio di Perugia (secoli XII–XV)* (Perugia, 1988), 303–49. Also important are the studies of P. Jones, especially "La storia economica. Dalla caduta dell'impero romano al secolo XIV," in *Storia d'Italia*, ed. R. Romano and C. Vivanti, vol. 2: *Dalla caduta dell'impero romano al secolo XVIII* (Turin, 1974), 1495–1540.

3. On the derivation of almost all the large communes of north-central Italy from ancient Roman municipal centers that became episcopates between late antiquity and the early Middle Ages, see E. Sestan, "La città comunale italiana dei secoli XI–XIII nelle sue note caratteristiche rispetto al movimento comunale europeo," in *Congrès international des Sciences Historiques (Stockholm, 21–28 August 1960), Rapports, II, Moyen Age* (Goteborg, Stockholm, and Uppsala, 1960), 91–120; A. Haverkamp, "Die Staedte im Herrschafts- und Sozialgefüge Reichsitalien," in *Stadt und Herrschaft: Roemische Kaiserzeit und Hohes Mittelalter*, ed. F. Vittinghoff, Historische Zeitschrift Beiheft, no. 7 (Munich, 1982), esp. 152–56, 170–71, 232–33. On the tradition of attributing to these centers the name of the city only, contrary to what took place in other European countries, see, in addition to the works cited above, E. Dupré Theseider, "Vescovi e città nell'Italia precomunale" in *Vescovi e diocesi in Italia nel Medioevo (secc. IX–XIII)* (Padua, 1964), 56–67; and G. Fasoli, "Storiografia urbanistica e discipline medievistiche," in *La storiografia urbanistica*, 155–66; for a recent discussion, see G. Kobler, "Zur Problematik von 'Civitas-Stadt' im Mittelalter," in *Lexikon des Mittelalters*, vol. 2 (Munich, 1983), 2113–14. See also G. Chittolini, "'Quasi-città'. Borghi e terre in area lombarda nel tardo Medioevo," *Società e storia* 13 no. 47 (1990), 3–26, esp. 6–7. For a more general discussion of the "institutional synthesis" of bishop and city in Italy, see G. Tabacco, *Egemonie sociali e strutture del potere nel Medioevo italiano*, 397–427.

4. In other European countries, as is well known, the name "city" was much more widespread, and the number of cities—or rather the number of centers defined as such—was in the end proportionally much greater. But their demographic and economic consistency was on average much more limited than it was in Italy, and, even for very large cities, their capacity for territorial expansion was much more limited (see note 9, below). On the "number of cities" and the density of the urban network in various areas of medieval Europe, see, in addition to E. Ennen, *Die Europaeische Stadt des Mittelalters* (Goettingen, 1972), information on the later period in J. De Vries, *European Urbanization, 1500–1800* (Cambridge, Mass., 1984). For the German area and Central Europe, see, in particular, H. Amman, "Wie grosse war die mittelalterliche Stadt?" in *Die Stadt des Mittelalter*, ed. C. Haase (Darmstadt, 1969),

However, this ability to organize territories was not equally strong among the different Italian regions. The situation in north-central Italy was much different from that in the south, from Lazio and the Abruzzi regions toward the south. The southern situation was a result of limited urban growth after the year 1000 and the profound crisis that affected ancient urbanism during the early Middle Ages, because of which many ancient cities either failed to survive or, if they did remain, were without any real urban substance.[5] Moreover, marked differences appeared among the various regions of north-central Italy. These differences sometimes seem to refer directly to the features of the ancient Roman division of districts—again, with various areas bearing different characteristics—and reflect the greater or lesser ability of early medieval cities to endure, in other words, the varying forces at work in the rise of the communes.

Thus, in the north, around a central nucleus, or Lombard core, which extended in part to northern Tuscany and was made up of extensive and cohesive contadi, there appeared a surrounding "periphery," comprising Veneto to the east and Piedmont to the west, where a system of large, strong, urban territories had not evolved. The territorial and urban network in the Romagnol-Umbrian-Marches region, which in antiquity had been characterized by a different process of urbanization that unfolded in ways unique to that area, presented yet a different physiognomy. Standing apart—and beyond the scope of this discussion—were the coastal zones and mountainous areas, where the influence of urban centers on

411–20. (For the French area, see J. Le Goff, "L'apogèe de la France urbaine," in *Histoire de la France urbaine*, vol. 2: *La ville médiévale des Carolingiens à la Renaissance* (Paris, 1980), 190–91, 401–3; and B. Chevalier, *Les bonnes villes de France du XIV au XVI siècle* (Paris, 1982), 37–41, 49–56, 61.

For a comparison with Italy, see M. Ginatempo and L. Sandri, "L'Italia delle città fra crisi e trasformazione," in M. Ginatempo and L. Sandri, *L'Italia delle città. Il popolamento urbano tra Medioevo e Rinascimento* (Florence, 1990), 195–98. For a comparison of the various capacities to organize territories between the Italian cities and cities beyond the Alps, and in relation to this, on the role of territorial unification and organization carried out by signori and principi, see, in reference to the German area, the recent "Settimana di studio" of the Istituto storico italo-germanico in Trento dedicated to *L'organizzazione del territorio in Italia e in Germania: secc. XIII–XIV*, ed. G. Chittolini and D. Willoweit (Bologna, 1993).

5. E. Sestan, *La città comunale italiana*, 180 ff.; G. Galasso, "Le città campane dell'Alto Medioevo," in G. Galasso, *Mezzogiorno medievale e moderno* (Torino, 1965), 63ff.; for a recent restatement, see M. Ginatempo and L. Sandri, *L'Italia delle città*, 43–44, 202–7, and passim.

the organization of the surrounding territory exerted itself in different forms, here less direct and intrusive.[6]

In the following pages I will investigate and summarize the different characteristics that define the territorial and urban districts in these regions of north-central Italy between the twelfth and fourteenth centuries. Throughout the discussion one must keep in mind—as a watermark underlying these pages—the old network of dioceses of late antiquity, which in turn was traced out upon the network of Roman municipal centers. Similarly, although we will not address it in this essay, the reader must bear in mind the events and transformations that took place in these areas during the early Middle Ages. In the second part of the essay I will examine the various capacities to survive demonstrated by the geography of urban territories between the Middle Ages and modern period.

---

6. In the coastal areas, apart from the changes provoked by the action of rivers and the sea, changes that sometimes notably altered ancient conditions (one readily thinks of what happened to Aquileia, Grado, Ravenna, Luni, etc.), the formation of dependent territories does not appear to be directly related to the dynamics of the development of urban centers. Cities such as Genoa, Venice, Pisa, and Ancona were characterized by a distinctly mercantile physiognomy. They were situated, geographically as otherwise, on the margins of the system of city-states in the Po Valley and were integrated within the system of Mediterranean and European commerce. During the communal period they pursued a foreign policy not so much of territorial conquest in their neighboring areas as of commercial agreements, of the confirmation of their mercantile and financial hegemonies, and of the creation of colonies and maritime bases in distant lands (spheres of influence, which became the "territories," so to speak, of those cities). For a discussion of some characteristics of the "coastal city" in relation to territory, see R. Caggese, *Classi e comuni rurali nel Medioevo italiano. Saggio di storia economica e giuridica*, vol. 1 (Florence, 1908), 9–12.

In the mountains, as a rule, cities as such did not have strong capacities to organize territories, since they and their districts were the sites of the success and expansion of other forces, either seignorial, of lay princes, or ecclesiastical. This was the case for cities of the western Alps in their relations with Savoy and other powers of the region. A similar situation held in the diocesan centers of Trento and Bressanone, which were both of episcopal principates. Moreover, on a lower level, there remained deeply rooted and active in the territory minor seignorial forces as well as other community forces such as federations based on *pieve*, valley, or peasant ties, all of which limited the ability of the city to expand. More information can be found in G. Veyret, "Les villes et les Alpes," in *Grandes villes et petites villes* (Paris, 1970), 541–47; G. Dematteis, "Le città alpine," in *Atti del XXI congresso geografico italiano*, vol. 2 (Novara, 1974), 7–107; J. P. Leguai, "Un réseau urbain médiéval: Les villes du comté, plus duché de Savoie," in *Les villes en Savoie et in Piémont au Moyen Age* (Chambery and Torino, 1979); P. G. Gerosa, "La città delle Alpi nella storiografia urbana recente," in *Le Alpi per l'Europa. Una proposta politica. Economia, territorio e società. Istituzioni, politica e società*, ed. E. Martinengo, papers presented at the second congress on "Le Alpi e l'Europa," Lugano, 14–16 March, 1985 (Milan, 1988), 139–60.

The Various Configurations of Urban Territories during the Communal Period

The Paduan-Veneto-Tuscan Core

The ability of cities to give life to extensive and cohesive territories is clearly evident in the Po Valley, that is, communal "Lombardy" (the area comprising the eastern zone of Piedmont, western Emilia, and western Veneto). Here urban centers, in relatively limited numbers, appeared able to impose their dominion over relatively vast and compact surrounding areas. Contained within an imaginary quadrilateral that extends about 45 or 50 square kilometers and has its vertices at Vercelli (to the northwest), Treviso (to the northeast), Asti (to the southeast), and Bologna (to the southwest), we find some 20 large urban communes, which built up equally vast city-states (namely, Novara, Milan, Como, Bergamo, Brescia, Piacenza, Parma, Reggio, Modena, Bologna, Mantova, Verona, Vicenza, and Padua).[7] Their contadi varied in size, ranging from the very large areas of Milan and Bologna (between 4,000 or 5,000 square kilometers) to much more limited areas such as that of Lodi, which was under 1,000 square kilometers. The average size, however, was 2,000 to 3,000 square kilometers, which represents an area much greater than that of the territories of the large European cities, where 1,000 square kilometers was surpassed only in very rare cases (such as Nuremberg and Zurich), and under exceptional conditions, and where some cities, although they were powerful and important centers, had territories of at most a few hundred square kilometers (more often only in the tens of kilometers).[8]

It was in the Po Valley region defined above that the conquest of the contado was carried out in its fullest form. Here there appeared with the greatest clarity that particular type of organization of territories based on a real system of vast city-states, without the presence of *superiores*, that is, the preeminent authority of princes and sovereigns. These territories

7. See map 1, which shows the distribution of diocesan seats ca. 600, in *Atlas zur Kirchengeschichte*, ed. H. Jedin, K. Scott Latourette, and J. Martin (Freiburg, 1987), 23.

8. Some of the information appears in L. Genicot, *Le XIIIe siècle européen* (Paris, 1968), 122–25. For an outline and bibliography on the German area, see G. Wunder, "Reichstaedte als landesherren," in *Zentralitat als Problem der mittelalterlichen Stadtgeschichsforschung*, ed. H. Meynen (Cologne and Vienna, 1979), 79–91; and P. Morow, "Cities and Citizenry as Factors of State Formation in the Roman-German Empire of the Late Middle Ages," *Theory and Society* 18 (1989): 638–39.

stretched across the landscape, one next to the other, without any serious problems of continuity and without the delicate and easily unraveled borders of seignorial territories or autonomous territories of "minor," not urban, centers.[9]

One should note that this outcome is the product, on one level, of the vigorous expansion of the communes, an expansion that in turn was based upon the ancient, vigorous network of Roman municipalities and original seats of dioceses. Even in antiquity this network was characterized by much regularity in its widely meshed design, in the balance between city and countryside, and in the strength of its framework because of the particular nature of the process of urbanization that took place during the Roman era.[10] This network lasted throughout the early Middle Ages without any deep lacerations or tears in its fabric, as it was strengthened by a strong, precocious establishment of dioceses.[11] Later, between the tenth and thirteenth centuries, on the well-known wave of great expansion, it was essentially reinstated in the same form.[12]

We find extensive contadi under the dominion of strong cities also in north-central Tuscany, another area marked by the presence of large cen-

---

9. For a recent comprehensive discussion of this, with information on the variations in diverse areas, see G. M. Varanini, "L'organizzazione del distretto cittadino nell'Italia padana (secoli XIII–XIV)," paper presented at the "Settimana di studio" on *L'organizzazione del territorio in Italia e in Germania* (see note 4, above), forthcoming. See also note 2, above, and notes 27 and 42, below.

10. E. Gabba, "Urbanizzazione e rinnovamento urbanistico nell'Italia centromeridionale del I secolo a. C.," *Studi classici e orientali* 21 (1973): 73–112; E. Gabba, "Considerazioni politiche ed economiche sullo sviluppo urbano in Italia nei secoli II e I a. C.," in *Hellenismus im Mittelitalien*, ed. P. Zanker, Abb. d. Ak. d. Wissenschaft in Goettingen (Goettingen, 1976), 317–26.

11. E. Sestan, *La città comunale italiana*, 180ff.; A. Haverkamp, "Die Städte im Herrschafts- und Sozialgefuege Reichsitalien," 154–55; M. Ginatempo, "Introduzione," in M. Ginatempo and L. Sandri, *L'Italia delle città*, 46. The changes pertain above all to the Apennine area, the lowest border along the river Po, and to the coastal area.

12. From a legal standpoint, in order to legitimize its authority in the territory, the municipal commune would declare itself heir to the ancient powers of the Carolingian count in its district. They would assert this in spite of the fragile and ephemeral nature of those comitial divisions as compared to the greater strength displayed by the older boundaries of diocese and municipality. See G. Sergi, "Introduzione," in J.-P. Poly and E. Bournazel, *Il mutamento feudale. Secoli X–XII* (Milan, 1990), 16. On the analogous weakness of the French counties as structures of district organization, as well as the much more marked seignorial fragmentation of the ancient *pagi*, see P. Feuchère, "Essai sur l'évolution territoriale des principautées françaises," *Le Moyen Age* 58 (1952): 85–117; and J. F. Lemarignier, *La France médiévale. Institutions et sociétés* (Paris, 1970), 122.

ters belonging to the old municipal and episcopal traditions, and thus able to bring about in a widespread and incisive manner the unification and organization of territories.[13] However, compared with Lombardy, this unification appeared to happen with much less systemization and with several *défaillances,* which resulted in less complete outcomes. Within the fabric of ancient municipal and ecclesiastical districts similar to that of the Po Valley there appeared several diocesan centers, such as Luni and Fiesole, which did not develop into city-states and left room for the expansion of other forces within their dioceses. Other centers, such as Volterra, and on a different level even Lucca and Siena, were unable to retain for their communal contadi the area of the old bishoprics.[14] Nor was the process of unification by the cities facilitated by the political history of the region, which was characterized in the central and late Middle Ages by a lengthy indetermination of political and territorial divisions that continued—much more so here than in Lombardy, where structures became disciplined and crystallized early on under the domination of the Visconti—up to the fourteenth and fifteenth centuries. There was greater instability here, as smaller territories emerged and poked holes in the fabric of the "urban" contadi. These minor territories, or "small" contadi, such as those that formed around San Gimignano, Pescia, Prato, Colle, and San Miniato, ranged in size between 100 and 150 square kilometers but showed much solidity by often remaining unchanged, century after century, before and after the Florentine conquest of the area.[15] This was the case even though the physiognomy of the region continued to be characterized mostly by large urban contadi such as that of Florence (which early on spread itself over the lands of the diocese of Fiesole and surpassed 3,500 square kilometers in the fourteenth century), of Pisa, a very large area although much less controlled (about 3,000 square kilo-

---

13. For the characteristics of this area, an area "of central hills and larger internal basins," which was more thickly urbanized and different from other parts of the region, see G. Pinto, *La Toscana nel tardo Medioevo. Ambiente, economia rurale, società* (Florence, 1982), 41ff.; and M. Ginatempo and L. Sandri, *L'Italia delle città,* 201.

14. For the early medieval and communal periods, see the still relevant work of F. Schneider, *Die Reichsverwaltung in Toscana von der Gruendung des Langobardenreiches bis zum Ausgang der Staufer (568–1268),* vol. 1 *Die Grundlagen* (Rome, 1914), translated into Italian as *L'ordinamento pubblico nella Toscana medievale,* ed. R. Barbolani di Montauto, with an introduction by E. Sestan (Florence, 1975).

15. See A. Zorzi, "La formazione del territorio fiorentino fra XII e XIV secolo," in the "Atti" of the "Settimana di studio," *L'organizzazione del territorio in Italia e in Germania.*

meters), or the contadi of Lucca and Pistoia (each a little less than 1,000 square kilometers).[16]

The Northern Peripheries and the Papal States

At the edges of this Paduan-Venetian-Tuscan "heartland" we find different features in the peripheral zone that borders the "communal" area to the north and in the area that extends to the southeast into the regions of Romagna, the Marches, and Umbria. In the north of the peninsula, to the east and west of the Po Valley, urban renewal during the age of communes, while vigorous, was not perhaps as unrestrained and ran up against the authorities of the princely territories that in part disciplined and controlled it. Moreover, the rebirth of the cities here did not develop from an automatic grafting onto the ancient Roman network. This was due not only to the fact that various ancient centers either had been lost (thanks to the disappearance of old diocesan centers and of *civitates,* or municipalities, before them) or did not develop adequately, and thus showed little capacity to produce well-knit, obedient contadi out of the older territories, but also because various new centers had taken hold and become successful.

This is evident in the northeastern Venetian areas, to the east and north of the territories of the cities of Vicenza, Padua, and Treviso.[17] Here, numerous centers fell into decay, especially in the coastal areas: from the most famous case of Aquileia, a metropolis and patriarchate, to the succeeding patriarchate of Grado also characterized by a very limited communal/urban development, and from the Roman city of Concordia, which became a diocese and remained so but without a large commune, to the Roman city and episcopal seat of Adria and the small and later

16. For Florence, see Zorzi, "La formazione del territorio fiorentino fra XII e XIV secolo." Maps of the territories of Pisa and Pistoia appear in O. Banti, *Jacopo d'Appiano. Economia e politica nel comune di Pisa al suo tramonto (1392–1399)* (Pisa, 1971), 125; and D. Herlihy, *Medieval and Renaissance Pistoia: The Social History of an Italian Town, 1200–1430* (New Haven and London, 1967) covers 2, 3.

17. See, in particular, S. Bartolami, "Frontiere politiche e frontiere religiose nell'Italia comunale: il caso delle Venezie," *Castrum 5* (1993). See also the works of A. Castagnetti especially his recent *Le città della marca veronese* (Verona, 1991); and *Città murate del Veneto,* ed. S. Bartolami (Milan, 1988), especially the article contained therein by S. Bartolami, "Città e 'terre murate' nel veneto medievale: le ragioni della storia e le ragioni di un libro," 13–22. On the ecclesiastical geography of the Venetian area, see D. Rando, *Le istituzioni ecclesiastiche veneziane nei secoli VI–XII. Il dinamismo di una chiesa di frontiera* (Trento, 1990), 15ff.

bishoprics of the lagoon zone around the future Venice, namely, Chioggia, Castello, Torcello, Iesolo, Cittanova, and Caorle. This crisis affected, though to a lesser degree, even Roman centers and bishoprics in the interior (where the mountainous and subalpine features of the territory seem to have slowed down any steady growth and large territorial developments). This was the case for the Roman municipality of Asolo; the Roman city and episcopal seat of Oderzo; the episcopate of Ceneda, a "town that was already the capital of a Lombard duchy but so marred by a chronic *debilitas loci* and by *raritas habitantium* that still in 1329 it feared the nightmare of the suppression of its episcopal seat and consequent religious union with Treviso"; and, lastly, "the mountainous bishoprics of Feltre and Belluno (recognized as *civitates* at the Peace of Constance in 1183) which around 1197 were temporarily forced to join together in order to survive."[18]

These centers did not succeed in becoming great urban communes able to extend their territorial control over the whole of their ancient districts, regardless of whether they were ecclesiastical and/or civil districts. Some, such as Oderzo and Ceneda, did manage to maintain a small territory of their own even when they were subjected to other cities or other lords. Others, such as Feltre and Belluno and in part Vicenza, were able to remain longer as autonomous communes but with much more reduced districts. Instead, these territories became, during the medieval and communal period, areas of expansion of other forces, at times not even forces represented by cities but by unusual figures for Italy, namely, princely bishops or lay lords who succeeded in creating strong seignorial structures. Other territories became the sites of expansion of other, stronger, nearby cities (communal Padua and communal and Caminese Treviso). Still other territories provided the space for the flourishing of numerous "minor" centers, many newly founded or the result of new growth in a geography of urban territories weaker than elsewhere (in the dioceses of Aquileia, Udine, and Cividale; Concordia, Pordenone, and Portoguaro; Ceneda and Conegliano; Vicenza and Bassano; and Adria and Rovigo). Compared to other centers (which developed by means of a more physiological growth even in the contadi of the great cities of west-central Veneto),[19] these centers possessed strong demographic consistency;

18. S. Bartolami, "Frontiere politiche e frontiere religiose."

19. For example, in the Paduan region, Monselice, Este, Montagnana, Piove, and Cittadella; in the Veronese region, Legnago and Cologna; and in the area of Treviso, Castelfranco and Mestre (see *Città murate del Veneto*).

remarkable political and administrative vitality; wide autonomies, during both the late communal and seignorial period and after the Venetian conquest; and the ability to cut out again new territories for themselves. Thus, this resulted in an unstable and unsettled political geography—a more fluid and shattered panorama of territories—of city contadi that were less strong and compact.

We can make a similar case for western Piedmont, the zone west of the Vercelli-Asti line, where the *civitates*-bishoprics showed an equal lack of energy and effort at expansion, and were not able to achieve the position of independence from other powers that characterized the Po Valley region. This is also due to the fact that from the time of the original communes onward they were more securely inserted within larger territorial structures and much earlier became part of princely states of the seignorial-feudal tradition, similar to those of central Europe (such as the *signorie* of the counts of Savoy and of the marquises of Monferrato and of Saluzzo).[20] Thus, their ability to expand territorially turned out to be fairly limited due to their weaker strength, to the presence of other local seignorial powers, and above all to the disciplining efforts of powers with great force and range who aspired to organize the entire region and who restricted and compressed the urban territories to fit their administrative framework. Moreover, strong new centers found room, correlatively, within the thinner process of urbanization (an often prominent phenomenon in late medieval Piedmont). These centers were significant because of their substantial dimensions (sometimes superior to those of the old "cities"), because of their economic strength, because of the urban functions they took on, and because of the territories that they created, even though they were restricted and incorporated within the political and administrative framework of *signorie,* as noted above (in addition to the particular case of Alexandria, we can mention Cuneo, Chieri, Pinerolo, Moncalieri, Savigliano, Mandovì, and Bra).[21]

---

20. See, for example, on the earlier period, G. Sergi, "Le città come luoghi di continuità di nozioni pubbliche del potere. Le aree delle marche di Ivrea e di Torino," in *Piemonte medievale. Forme di potere e della società. Studi per Giovanni Tabacco* (Torino, 1985), 5–27. On the processes of territorial organization around seignorial and feudal forces, see G. Sergi, "Dinastie e città del Regno italico nel secolo XI," in *L'evoluzione delle città italiane nell'XI secolo,* ed. R. Bordone and J. Jarnut (Bologna, 1988), 151–73. For Monferrato, see A. A. Settia, *Monferrato. Strutture di un territorio medievale* (Turin, 1983).

21. Recent discussions appear in the volume *I borghi nuovi. Secoli XII–XV,* Atti del IV Convegno internazionale di storia e archeologia, ed. R. Comba (Cuneo, 1992).

We also find a weak geography of contadi in other regions of central Italy that were part of the Papal States, for instance, in the Romagnol-Umbrian-Marches zone. Here there appeared a dense and viable urban network, which, as noted above, since its Roman origins had been characterized by a more tightly meshed framework and a greater number of cities. In spite of a strong flourishing of communes in this area, its network continued to be made up of smaller cities, less able to build large contadi and urban-centered territorial divisions and less capable of imposing themselves as structures of territorial organization.[22] For example, one can count about a dozen civitates indicated as such in all of the contemporary sources in the *Marchia anconitana,* that is, at least within the frontiers that defined the region between the end of the Middle Ages and the beginning of the modern era, an area of about 6,500 square kilometers. There were seven urban centers in the duchy of Urbino as it was configured toward the end of the fifteenth century, an area of about 2,500 to 2,700 square kilometers that extended to the northern part of the Marches region and shared some borders with Romagna, Umbria, and Tuscany.[23]

Thus, the dioceses of this area had proportionally reduced dimensions, of a few hundred square kilometers on average. But, more importantly, the contadi were not of a corresponding size because the territories that were politically dependent on the cities were much more limited and thus left room for other installations as well as other minor centers. These features were often fostered by the actions of the pontifical government intent on curbing unrestrained and overly large territorial expansion and concerned instead with supporting lesser autonomies in order to control the uneasy world of local forces, if not within the strong provincial forces

22. B. G. Zenobi, "I caratteri della distrettuazione di antico regime nella Marca pontificia," in *Scritti storici in memoria di Enzo Piscitelli,* ed. E. Paci (Padua, 1982), 61–106; Ph. Jansen, "Qu'est ce qu'une petite ville en Italie à l'époque médiévale? Les critères fournis par les Constitutions Egidiennes des Etats," in *Les petites villes du Moyen Age à nos jours,* ed. J.-P. Poussou and Ph. Loupès (Paris, 1987), 15–28; F. Bonasera, "Le città delle Marche elencate nelle *Constitutiones Aegidianae* (1357). Contributo alla geografia storica delle Marche," *Studia picena* 27 (1959): 93–104. Various discussions also appear in *Il picchio e il gallo. Temi e materiali per una storia delle Marche,* ed. S. Anselmi (Jesi, 1982).

23. F. Bonasera, "Le città delle Marche"; G. Chittolini, "Su alcuni aspetti dello stato di Federico," in *Federico di Montefeltro. Lo stato, le arti, la cultura,* ed. G. Cerboni Baiardi, G. Chittolini, and P. Floriani (Rome, 1986), 1: *Lo stato,* 61–66. On the ecclesiastical geography of the Urbino area, see G. Zarri, "Le istituzioni ecclesiastiche nel ducato di Urbino nell'età di Federico da Montefeltro," in *Federico di Montefeltro,* 124–39.

of the government then at least in a balanced and common dependence
upon the Papal See. Along with the civitates, we find *terrae magnae, terrae mediocres,* and simple *terrae parvae,* following the well-known distinctions and hierarchies of the *Constitutiones Aegidianae.* These were
lively, active centers, which had their own territories and repeated on a
smaller scale the model of city/contado relations. Also appearing in
strong relief on the map of the region were the *castra,* smaller centers,
sometimes with a small district containing a few *ville,* but substantial
organisms nevertheless. These were autonomous and well-defined units
(of greater substance than, for example, territorially homologous rural
communes of the Po Valley) of the same form as the *terra castellorum*
evoked by the jurist Bartolo da Sassoferato.

Thus, the panorama of territories, according to the lines that defined it
in the Roman era, in the Byzantine period, and then during the development of the communes, apart from the geographic and economic features
of the region, is characterized by small territories of varying natures even
if predominantly urban.[24] But the momentum here was refracted into a
series of microcities and microterritories. It is a picture that displays traits
similar to the regions conterminous with Romagna (in particular for the
on-average limited size of contadi) and with Umbria (which presented a
more varied alternation of large and small urban districts). These are
regions that, with the Marches, which we examined in greater detail
above, are related also by the original features of Roman urbanization
and by their common dependence on the papacy.[25]

The Communal "Contadi" and Administrative Divisions of
the Regional States during the Early Modern Period

The geography of urban territories that had formed in the communal
period displayed a high degree of continuity during the period of rede-

---

24. On the differences between Longobardia and Romania, see A. Castagnetti,
L'organizzazione del territorio rurale nel Medioevo (Bologna, 1982).

25. For Romagna, in addition to Castagnetti, *L'organizzazione del territorio,* see J.
Larner, *The Lords of Romagna: Romagnol Society and the Origins of the Signorie*
(Ithaca, N.Y., 1965). For Umbria, see H. Desplanques, *Campagnes ombriennes. Con-
tribution à l'étude des paysages ruraux en Italie centrale* (Paris, 1966), esp. 99–111;
and A. Bartoli Langeli, "L'organizzazione territoriale della Chiesa nell'Umbria," in
Orientamenti di una regione attraverso i secoli, 414–41. Concerning a large contado,
see A. Grohman, *Città e territorio tra Medioevo ed età moderna (Perugia, secc.
XIII–XVI),* 2 vols. (Perugia, 1981).

fining areas and boundaries that accompanied the building of regional states between the fourteenth and fifteenth centuries. During this period the fragmentation and instability inherited from the communal age were overcome by the creation of larger and more structured political and territorial divisions.

Within the heart of the system of free city-states in the Paduan-Veneto area (and, in part, in Tuscany), the coherence of the old contadi visibly influenced the dynamics of territorial formation during the fourteenth and fifteenth centuries and was reflected in the entire shape of the new states as well as the design of their borders. These new states were in fact nothing other than the aggregate of the old city-states, now under the signoria of a prince or dominant city. Similarly, the inherited past of the communal contadi left a profound impact on the internal "provincial" structure. The new government of signori and princes did not fundamentally change the nature of the older territorial system of districts within the matrix of communes.

At the margins of these regions away from the persisting urban framework, in other areas that we have seen where smaller, weaker, communal contadi lay among territories of a different nature within more fragmented and unstable divisions, the processes of formation of new, wider, and essentially regional states (in those places where these did take hold) appeared to take place on less certain bearings and following a more tormented line. Within the larger states that were already established and in the process of ordering their internal territory, such as the Papal States and the Savoy state, the old fragmentation had strong repercussions and left clear imprints upon the ongoing processes of administrative reorganization. It was this that determined the inconstancy and instability of administrative partitions, producing tormented and unstable geographical results, similar to those that were unfolding beyond the Alps in Europe.

The Endurance of the Contadi in the Regional States of the Paduan-Veneto-Tuscan Area

The strong capacity for endurance of the large districts molded by cities is very evident in the "Lombard" and Paduan areas. Because the creation of contadi—it is perhaps necessary to recall—was carried out in full during the height and later stages of the communal period, they had turned into territories of remarkable coherence and organic unity. The imposi-

tion of city authority upon these areas, the so-called conquest of the contado, had from the start been shaped in terms of a complete victory of
total dominion (by dint of regalia conceded or usurped from the
emperor) to the detriment of other possible competing rights (seignorial
rights or those belonging to lesser communities) upon a diocesan or
"municipal" territory that the city felt to be its own.[26] As the effective
conquest took hold it led to very wide control, which derived from the
systematically pursued elimination of indirect forms of government, from
the creation of a system of minor districts that were presided over by city
dwellers in the capacity of officials (as podestà and vicars), and from the
imposition over the entire territory of the rights and laws of the city as
well as its fiscal, administrative, and judicial arrangements (through
urban tribunals and local judges). Here, as elsewhere, the process took a
different shape than that found beyond the Alps.[27] Moreover, the unity
of the territory was strengthened, not simply by the extent of the city's
dominion and the way that it was imposed but by the fact that interests
common to the city and rich citizens found shape within it, and it was in
respect to these interests that the contado had been organized. The driving interests were thus political and economic control, both in the area of
mercantile and manufacturing policies, and, more importantly, in the
area of agriculture and landed property (since the contado was the natural area of expansion of urban landed-property interests, property was
carefully guarded and continually being increased).[28]

Thus, in the process of formation of the Milanese, Venetian, and (in part)
Florentine states, the coherence of the old urban contadi was well

---

26. This is quite different from the formation processes of other urban European
"territories" that took place as the product of a slow acquisition of individual and disparate "titles" of signoria. See, for example, for Germany, E. Isenmann, *Die deutsche
Stadt im Spatmittelalter, 1250–1500* (Stuttgart, 1988), 236–43.

27. On the situation of territories under urban dominion in Europe, or that which
has been generically defined the Umland or the Stadraum of the city, see, for example,
Zentralitat als Problem der mittelalterlichen Stadtegeschichsforschung, ed. H. Mey-
nen (Cologne and Vienna, 1979); M. Mitterauer, *Markt und Stadt im Mittelalter.
Beitrage zur historische Zentralitatsforschung* (Stuttgart, 1980); *Bevolkerung,
Wirtschaft und Gesellschaft: Stadt-Land-Beziehungen in Deutschland und Frank-
reich. 14. bis 19. Jahrhundert,* ed. N. Bulst and J. Hoock (Trier, 1983); *Stadtisches
Um- und Hinterland in vorindustrieller Zeit,* ed. H. K. Schulze (Cologne, 1985); E.
Isenmann, *Die deutsche Stadt,* 231–35; and "Città e campagne in Europa," special
issue of *Storia della città* 36 (1986).

28. See notes 2 and 30.

reflected in their whole design (since these states had been established as the ensemble of the older city territories), as, too, were the dynamics of their borders. In fact, in the Paduan and Lombard areas, between the end of the thirteenth and the first decades of the fifteenth centuries, the early hegemony of Milan and the Visconti did not prevent the political geography of the region from experiencing frequent and profound changes (i.e., acquisitions of territories, losses, and repeated divisions among the members of the family). These variations rendered the political border of the dominion unstable and fluid for over 150 years. Yet, even within this lively dynamic, the processes of composition and decomposition took place, as rule, by means of great blocks, each of which was made up of a city and its contado.

> The Visconti disarmed but did not dissolve the municipal institution. It always possessed the principal feature that distinguished the Italian city from transalpine ones, that is, an intimate union with its territory and the tenacious cohabitation of landowners who never wanted to relegate themselves to the countryside which nourished them, nor submerge themselves in the capital city that obliterated them. Every now and then inheritance or war or rebellion of the populace or the infidelity of condottieri broke apart the broad heritage of the Visconti. It was the cities that suffered this rupture, as stratified rocks that flaked away: Brescia, Verona, and Padua were at one time under the dominion of the Visconti, then the Scaligeri, now the Carraresi, now the Venetians. But it was only the banner and garrison that changed, little more than an altered alliance. The innermost municipal life was not disturbed nor shifted.[29]

In terms of internal arrangements, the old city-states in the Lombard and Veneto areas of the Po Valley that had been made subjects of princely regimes and "dominant" cities were naturally transformed into the provinces of new regional states. The urban centers that had dominated them naturally became the capitals of the provinces, and the old contadi, especially those located in the plain, remained their subjects, thanks to the vast competence that the municipal governments maintained in

---

29. C. Cattaneo, "La città considerata come principio ideale delle istorie italiane" (1858), reprinted in *Scritti storici e geografici,* ed. G. Salvemini and E. Sestan, vol. 2 (Florence, 1957), 381–47, 432.

administrative, jurisdictional, and fiscal matters.[30] The new administrative divisions were kept stable for a long time during the modern era, if with some slight internal and border adjustments. If some modifications did take place, they did not bring about radical movements. (These were simply a matter of reduced separation, concessions of privileges, or feudal concessions granted to lands of the plain, yet always within the geographical and administrative bounds of the province.) Similarly, erosions and breakups would now and then take place at the margins, in the areas near the alpine mountains or around lakes, in recognition of autonomies belonging to "valleys," mountainous, or lake districts.[31] Nevertheless, these were changes that did not seriously disturb an overall preeminence of the older city commune over most of its old contado, nor did they lead to the design of a new and different provincial geography. This took place, all the more in the area under the dominion of the Republic of Florence, where, although there remained an underlying division that largely reused the boundaries of the old city districts and recognized some old city-state prerogatives over their old contadi, from the beginning of the fifteenth century new minor jurisdictional, fiscal, and administrative divisions (*vicariati, capitanati*) were delineated. These were cut from within the old contadi and were largely autonomous from the older urban capitals but dependent directly on Florence. This, therefore, brought about a splitting of the old municipal districts and a weakening of the previous influence of the city. (This is similar to the situation discussed above in which the territorial organization had been since the time of origin less coherent, more uneven, and interposed among minor territories, yet here

---

30. G. Chittolini, "The Italian City-State and Its Territory," 598; G. M. Varanini, "Dal comune allo stato regionale," in *Il Medioevo. Popoli e strutture*, esp. 706–8, and bibliography.

31. For the Venetian area, see, for example, A. Ventura, *Nobilità e popolo nella società veneta del Quattrocento e Cinquecento*, 2d ed. (Milan, 1993), 111ff. For the Lombard area, see G. Chittolini, "Quasi-città"; G. Chittolini, "Le 'terre separate' nel ducato di Milano in età sforzesca," in *Milano nell'età di Ludovico il Moro*, Atti del convegno internazionale, (Milan, 1983), vol. I, 115–28; G. Chittolini, "Principe e comunità alpine in area lombarda alla fine del Medioevo," in *Le Alpi per l'Europa*, 219–36. On the characteristics of feudal lands, see G. Chittolini, "Feudalherren und ländliche Gesellschaft in Nord- und Mittelitalien (15.-17. Jahrhundert)," in *Klientelsysteme im Europa der Fruhen Neuzeit*, ed. A. Maczak (Munich, 1988), 243–60; G. Gullino, "I patrizi veneti di fronte alla proprietà feudale (secoli XVI–XVIII)," *Quaderni storici* 43 (1980), 162–93; and S. Zamperetti, *I piccoli principi. Signorie locali, feudi e comunità soggette nello Stato regionale veneto dall'espansione territoriale ai primi decenni del '600* (Treviso and Venice, 1991).

it is primarily the product of the very intrusive policies of the Florentine state in the Quattrocento that were taken up again later in the Cinquecento).[32]

In the Po Valley, however, there was considerable stability among territorial divisions brought about by the communes as well as much continuity of the old boundaries. In some cases this continuity was very strong. For example, the territory of Bologna, which measured about 3,200 square kilometers, remained unchanged from the communal period to the end of the ancien régime. Even the present Bolognese Province follows essentially unchanged the course of the older boundaries, with the later addition of the territory of Imola.[33] Likewise, the territory of Verona, after the famous definition completed by the magistrates of the commune in 1184, preserved an extraordinary constancy in both its size (about 3,000 square kilometers) and its borders up to the fall of the Republic and beyond.[34] And there are various other cases in which

---

32. E. Fasano Guarini, "Città soggette e contadi nel dominio fiorentino fra Quattro e Cinquecento: il caso pisano," in *Ricerche di storia moderna,* ed. M. Mirri, (Pisa, 1976), vol. 1, 1–94; G. Chittolini, *La formazione dello stato regionale e le istituzioni del contado* (Torino, 1979), 292–352. The weakness of the Tuscan provincial centers should probably be considered in relation to the steep fall in population in the fourteenth and fifteenth centuries and the new economic geography of the region. Certainly the political divisions imposed at the beginning of the Quattrocento left enduring traces on the administrative appearance of modern Tuscany. Particularly significant is the lack of the rise of any movement of Territories and Contadi, which we find in Lombardy and Veneto at the end of the Cinquecento. This absence was due to a reorganization of fiscal, jurisdictional, and administrative weight among the subject cities, already underway during the first decades of the Quattrocento.

33. See map (which shows the shape of the diocese and district "between the tenth and fourteenth centuries") in *Storia dell'Emilia Romagna,* ed. A. Berselli (Bologna, 1984), ccxi. See also the map of the current province, which shows Imola. For the outline of the district borders in the Trecento, see the map published in A. Sorbelli, *La signoria di Giovanni Visconti a Bologna e le sue relazioni con la Toscana* (Bologna, 1901). For the size of the territory, see K. J. Beloch, *Bevölkerungsgeschichte Italiens, II: Die Bevölkerung des Kirchenstaates, Toskanas und der Herzogtuemer am Po* (Berlin, 1939), 106.

34. See map (showing the borders during the communal period), in E. Rossini, *Storia di Verona* (Verona, 1975), 390–91, 423–24. The borders did not change in the Scaligeri, Visconti, and Venetian periods. For the territory's area during the Venetian era (3,022 square kilometers compared to 3,036 for the present province), see K. J. Beloch, *Bevoelkerungsgeschichte Italiens,* vol. 3: *Die Bevölkerung der Republik Venedig, des Herzogums Mailand, Piemonts, Genuas, Corsicas und Sardiniens. Die Gesamtbevölkerung Italiens* (Berlin, 1961), 118 (also for information on the small intervening border shiftings).

the borders of the current provinces follow for long stretches the traces of the old district divisions.

The Less Stable Political and Administrative Geographies of the "Peripheries"

Much more varied and unstable, however, was the situation of the other areas discussed above, where lively "nonurban" communities, and sometimes *signorie* and feudal lands, opposed cities that may have been strong but did not in general display great efforts at territorial expansion. These were the areas of the north that can be called "marginal" with respect to the core of city-states, as well as the Marches, Romagnol, and Umbrian areas of the Papal States. Fragmentation and instability were manifest not only in the processes of the formation of new states, where these did take place, but also in the defining of administrative divisions within regional states of either old or recent origin.

In several of these regions during the later Middle Ages processes of territorial unification took place on a relatively vast scale, processes that were analogous to those successfully carried out previously by the great communal and Tuscan cities between the twelfth and fourteenth centuries when they created their contadi. The state of Urbino offers an eloquent example, as it was slowly built up between the Trecento and Quattrocento under the signoria of the Montefeltro. The territory over which Federico eventually gained the title of duke in 1472 was about 2,800 square kilometers, corresponding in size to the contado of a Lombard city. Yet that dominion was the result of a laborious and uncertain process of conquest and unification that involved the separate acquisitions, carried out in different times, of many small "territories," that is, small cities with their little contadi, *terre* and *castra* with their districts, and lay and ecclesiastical signorie. And the fact that this process of territorial recomposition was carried out so late—when those small territories and districts of urban, *borghi,* or seignorial origins had long been defined—and only around the power of a *signore*—not around a great urban center—considerably influenced the shape of the state's formation, just as it left marks upon its internal appearance. In fact, when the Montefeltro signoria expanded its power, unable to draw upon the lines and structures of territorial unification naturally available to a large city commune due to its old tradition as the principal center of civil and ecclesiastical matters, the lordship had to orient itself in different directions at different times as it struggled to find unfailing orientations around which different territories would be able to join with it.[35] As a result it had often changed form and structure. And even after the signoria had found a central, supporting axis and, between the fifteenth and sixteenth centuries, firm and stable boundaries, the administrative divisions kept the signs of the variety and heterogeneity of the territories from which they were constituted as well as the appearance of an aggregate territory that was hardly cohesive and homogenous.

Similar events shaped the territorial formation and establishment of the marquisate of Monferrato, where, within a more fluid and blurred regional context, instability and border variations perhaps lasted longer. In the thirteenth and fourteenth centuries uncertainty surrounded the aggregation undertaken by the Aleramici and Paleologi of the many small territories into which the area had been fragmented. These territories were at times drawn to the marquises and at other times—as small tesserae composing a delicate, ephemeral mosaic—pushed toward nuclei of external aggregations in an evolutionary process that continued to be fluid and uncertain up to the early centuries of the modern era. The result was a disarticulated body and a fragile structure.

Original territorial fragmentation that had not been made compact through the actions of the city commune left its mark also in states that had been established for a long time and were, not by chance, of monarchic foundation. States such as Savoy and the Papal States between the later Middle Ages and the modern era gradually ordered and defined their administrative structures in response to the same needs for consolidation and internal reorganization that were being felt all over the peninsula. Even the presence of strong, vital cities did not necessarily lead to a geography of urban contadi. Cities possessed and preserved their own weight, sometimes an important one, but this was not a capacity for territorial organization, at least not "territorial" in the Italian sense. Thus, because they lacked the formative mold of large, unified, and ordered contadi in their interior, the provincial and administrative internal ordering of these states was very fragmented, and they experienced difficulty in organizing themselves according to provincial structures that were exten-

35. G. Franceschini, *I Montefeltro* (Milan, 1970), esp. 297–318; G. Franceschini, *Documenti e regesti per servire alla storia dello Stato d'Urbino e dei conti di Montefeltro*, vol. 1: *(1202–1375)*, vol. 2 *(1376–1404)* (Urbino, 1982).

sive enough (i.e., able to discipline the preexistent fragmentation) and substantial (such as those in the Po Valley, which grew naturally out of old city contadi).

For the Papal States during the early modern period, for example, one speaks of "regions that cannot be found," so long did their configuration remain undefined and mutable.[36] The old provinces of the state (Campagna and Marittima, Patrimonio, *Sabina,* the duchy of Spoleto, Umbria, the Marches of Ancona, Romagna, and other minor ones—even from its origin it had been an heterogeneous division) in fact ended up being eroded and dismembered by the separations and immunities of individual territories or of intermediate administrative districts. These districts, in turn, were without consistency because they lacked natural frontiers (and, precisely, historical borders) as well as centers that could be recognized as effectively preeminent and deserving the unquestioned rank and scope of capital. Instead, various popes often recognized the privileges of autonomous seignorial powers, as well as the aspirations to gain autonomy and increase in lands, as they were promoted to the rank of cities or were given privileges of exemption. The results were arbitrary joinings of heterogeneous territories in inevitably weak unions in which fiscal policies were structured differently from administrative and other matters. Similarly, "capital cities" were without any effective control over their immediate areas (in the manner of the cities of Po Valley over their old contadi) and lacked even the rank and functions of simple posts of magistracies and offices. Borders, too, were unstable and mutable, under which one can easily make out the older threads of urban/diocesan territories and those of the terre and castra. In his study of the Umbrian countryside, Henry Desplanques noted that "a visitor to the Apostolic See at the end of the sixteenth century described Umbria with the following words: Gubbio borders with Città del Castello, Perugia with Chiusi and Cortona, etc. As if under the Roman empire there are only cities."[37] In other words, it is the old administrative structure of the Roman municipality and diocese that continued to be felt as the supporting fabric of territorial organization, underlying the borders of the pontifical divisions.

---

36. R. Volpi, *Le regioni introvabili. Centralizzazione e regionalizzazione dello Stato pontificio* (Bologna, 1983), 35 ("per buona parte del Cinquecento la configurazione delle province—come del resto l'effettivo controllo che su di esse esercitano i legati—resta incerta e mutevole"). For the preceding period, see, above all, J. Guiraud, *L'etat pontifical après le Grand Schisme. Etude de géographie politique* (Paris, 1896).

37. H. Desplanques, *Campagnes Ombriennes,* 106.

Similarly, in Piedmont under the Savoy lordship the pattern of "provincial" partitions remained for a long time weak and unstable, nor did the cities have any importance in territorial government, as they were meshed within the administrative network of the overlord. This is valid both for the late medieval territorial divisions and for the "provinces" of the modern period.[38] (The number of provinces "on this side of the mountains" went from 6 in 1560, to 16 in 1619, 12 in 1622, 14 in 1723, and so on.)[39] Moreover, one can make out this original fragmentary nature in the provincial ordering of states, even those with a predominance of cities in their territories yet where the influence of the city was less intense.

Friuli during the entire period of Venetian domination kept its well-known administrative and jurisdictional fragmentation as characteristics unique to it compared to the rest of the Terraferma under this dominion. At the same time the Trevigiano region, a frontier area between the cities of the Veneto and the more fragmented western areas, also contained a much less ordered and disciplined contado than did other provinces of the Terraferma.[40] The ordering of the Lombard mountainous areas in the state of Milan, the Apennine areas of the Farnese state and those of the Estense state all present similar anomalies.[41] These are irregularities with regard to Italy as defined by its cities, but they are divisions and develop-

---

38. For the later medieval period, see G. Astuti, "Gli ordinamenti giuridici degli Stati sabaudi," in *Storia del Piemonte* (Rome, 1961), esp. 495–96 (also for the role of the cities); and A. Barbero and G. Castelnuovo, "Governare un ducato. L'amministrazione sabaudo nel tardo medioevo," *Società e storia* 15 (1992): 465–514.

39. Some information on the ecclesiastical geography of the state may be found in A. Erba, *La chiesa sabauda tra Cinque e Seicento* (Rome, 1979), 5 and passim. Also taken into consideration are the Italian dependencies of the county of Nizza, the valley of Aosta, and the marquisate of Monferrato.

40. For a discussion on the administrative arrangements of the Venetian state, see A. Tagliaferri, "Ordinamento amministrativo della Terraferma," in *Atti del Convegno 'Venezia e la Terraferma attraverso le relazioni dei rettori'* (Milan, 1981), 15–43. On Fruili, see P. Cammarosano, F. De Vitt, and D. Degrassi, *Il Medioevo*, ed. G. Miccoli, Storia della società friulana (Tavagnacco, 1988). On the Trevisan area, see G. Del Torre, *Il Trevigiano nei secoli XV e XVI. L'assetto amministrativo e il sistema fiscale* (Venice and Treviso, 1990), 23ff.

41. See, for example, G. Tocci, *Le terre traverse. Poteri e territori nei ducati di Parma e Piacenza tra sei e settecento* (Bologna, 1985). An emphasis on the "anomaly" of the Ligurian Apennines with respect to the territorial models of organization in the Po Valley can be found in O. Raggio, *Faide e parentela. Lo stato genovese visto dall Fontanabuona* (Torino, 1990); and E. Grendi, *Il Cervo e la Repubblica. Il modello ligure di antico regime* (Torino, 1993).

ments that are completely normal with regard to those beyond the Alps.[42]

One can note that the urban durability that is evident in the civil territorial divisions (for example, in the Paduan-Lombard area) may be compared with the ecclesiastical divisions in the late medieval and modern periods (and, moreover, these ecclesiastical areas had already provided the mold for the formation of contadi during the "communal" phase). Changes in the number and frontiers of the dioceses, all over urban Italy, were very infrequent during the entire stretch of time from the emergence of the communes to the end of the ancien régime and were even fewer than in south-central and southern Italy. These changes were all the more frequent where the urban mark was less strong (such as in Piedmont, in western Veneto, and partially in Tuscany), and much more difficult where an urban stamp was more enduring (such as in Lombardy).[43]

Thus, it is a geography, ecclesiastical as well as civil, that endured over the centuries, sometimes up to the end of the ancien régime.[44] The long duration of urban territories appears to be primarily the product of the robustness and capacity to endure that characterized the territorial reinforcement structured by the cities during communal Italy as well as the result of the endurance of the hierarchical relations between cities and territories that were established at that time.

---

42. X. de Planhol, *Géographie historique de la France* (Paris, 1988), 187ff; F. Uhlhorn and W. Schlesinger, *Die deutschen Territorien* (Stuttgart, 1984).

43. G. Chittolini, "Quasi-città." For Tuscany, see E. Fasano Guarini, "Nuove diocesi e nuove città nella Toscana del Cinque-Seicento," paper presented at the conference "Colle di Val d'Elsa: diocesi e città tra '500 e '600," held at Colle di Val d'Elsa, 22–24 October 1992, forthcoming.

44. On the different connotative features of cities during the early nineteenth century, see, for example, F. Sofia, "Per una definizione di Città nelle statistiche descrittive italiane nel periodo napoleonico," *Storia urbana* 30 (1985): 3ff.

The Imaginary Piazza: Tommaso Garzoni and the Late Italian Renaissance

John Martin

Status was a central preoccupation of Renaissance Italians. Together with the quest for fame, competition for greater social standing shaped much of the political life and, indeed, much of the cultural life of the peninsula from the age of the communes down to the period of the Counter Reformation. Although historians since Burckhardt have perhaps exaggerated the degree to which the scrambling for power and prestige was responsible for both the political and artistic creativity of the period, there can be no doubt that in the fourteenth, fifteenth, and sixteenth centuries many Italians—whether nobles or merchants, professionals or artists, humanists or artisans—were often motivated by a desire to improve their status. Key terms of the Renaissance vocabulary such as *fortuna* and *virtù* reveal the degree to which the shifting winds of fortune and a belief in the possibility of seizing the occasion or of shaping one's own destiny made themselves felt. Yet attitudes toward status were never consistent. In the early Renaissance, Dante had reproved those who held that wealth was the source of nobility, and Boccaccio suggested that the very best among us may be born into the most humble households. But this world gradually gave way to one in which birth and not virtue determined nobility. The change in climate was pervasive: the political and social history of the period makes it clear that there were fewer new men, fewer *cives novi,* in the late Renaissance than there had been at its beginning.[1]

---

1. Jacob Burckhardt, *The Civilization of the Renaissance in Italy,* 2 vols. (New York, 1958); see especially part 2 for the psychology of the search for fame and the development of the individual. Burckhardt's emphasis on the development of the indi-

In itself, however, this change in climate, which was linked both to the decline in social mobility and to the triumph of the court, tells us very little about the way in which Italians responded to (or how they perceived) the increasing rigidity of the social hierarchy in the late Renaissance. Granted, at the upper levels of Italian society, the status preoccupations of the wealthy—the aping of other European nobilities and the grasping after the concomitant trappings of the gentleman such as the hunt or heraldry—are among the more familiar characteristics of the social history of Italy in the sixteenth and seventeenth centuries. From the vantage point of the elites, individual men and women had come to be defined in terms of their social position rather than their abilities. But does this mean that those who did not belong to the landed classes were, as Eric Cochrane once observed, "relegated to positions of hopeless inferiority?"[2] Was the ideology of the court, which had begun to find expression in writers such as Ariosto and Castiglione, shared by other social groups in Italian society, or did artisans and merchants especially—for these had been the classes for whom the development of an aristocratic ethos was most prejudicial—have different perceptions of the social order?

---

vidual has been somewhat recast in more recent studies of the period. Lauro Martines's *Power and Imagination: City States in Renaissance Italy* (New York, 1979), for example, brings shifts in social mobility closer to the foreground. For the centrality of the dialectic of *fortuna* and *virtù* in the period, see the useful remarks of Quentin Skinner in his *The Foundations of Modern Political Thought*, vol. 1: *The Renaissance* (Cambridge, 1978), 88–101. On Dante's view of the nobility, see above all his third Canzone in the *Convivio* in Dante, *Opere*, ed. V. Branca et al., vol. 5 (Florence, 1954), 3–7. On Boccaccio, see especially the story of Griselda, in which the author asks, "che si potrà dir qui, se non che anche nelle povere case piovono dal cielo de' divini spiriti, come nelle reali di quegli che sarien piú degni di guardar porci che d'avere sopra uomini signoria?" (*Decameron*, ed. Cesare Segré [Milan, 1976], 669). On shifts in the concept of nobility in late medieval and early modern Italy in general, see Francesco Tateo, *Tradizione e realtà nell'umanesimo italiano* (Bari, 1967); and C. Donati, *L'idea di nobiltà in Italia (secoli XIV–XVIII)* (Bari, 1988).

2. Eric Cochrane, *The Late Italian Renaissance* (London, 1970), 57. On the emergence of an increasingly rigid social hierarchy, see H. G. Koenigsberger, "Republics and Courts in Italian and European Culture," *Past and Present* 83 (1979): 32–56; and Stuart Woolf, *A History of Italy, 1700–1860* (London, 1979), 21–23, as well as the works by Tateo and Donvito cited in the note above. While Peter Burke is correct to observe that "until more systematic studies have been made, any account of the Italian social hierarchy must remain impressionistic" (*Culture and Society in Renaissance Italy, 1420–1540* [New York, 1972], 244), see, for an important exception, David Herlihy and Christiane Klapisch-Zuber, *Tuscans and their Families: A Study of the Florentine Catasto of 1427* (New Haven and London, 1985), 122–26. The fundamental work for the development of an aristocratic ethos in Italy was, of course, Castiglione's *Il cortegiano*, first published in Venice in 1528. On the imitation of other European nobilities by the Italian aristocrats, see Eric Cochrane, *Florence in the Forgotten Centuries* (Chicago, 1973), 206–7.

One approach to the recovery of the perceptions of merchants and craftsmen lies in the analysis of books of trades. These works, popular throughout Europe in the late Middle Ages, became especially so in the sixteenth century. In part, as a genre, books of trades were a response to a growing demand for technical knowledge on the part of newly literate artisans and businessmen. But the special value of the works, to us as well as to the men and women of the Renaissance, lies in their explicit concern with the moral and political dilemma of the right ordering of society. In them, the author or authors grappled with problems of hierarchy. Accordingly, they often included in their overviews of occupations and professions not only those who practiced technical or skilled trades but also the elites of the society, secular and ecclesiastical lords as well as professionals and artists whose "occupations" were essential components of the social order.[3] Moreover, because of their broad readership, books of

<hr/>

3. The sixteenth century witnessed a profusion of texts on the crafts and other "occupations." In general such works have attracted the attention of historians of science (see Walter E. Houghton Jr., "The History of Trades: Its Relation to Seventeenth-Century Thought," *Journal of the History of Ideas* 2 (1941): 33–60; and Paolo Rossi, *I filosofi e le macchine 1400–1700* (Milan, 1980). But the works discussed by Houghton and Rossi clearly merge with others decidedly less technical in emphasis. Especially significant is Jost Amman and Hans Sach's *Eygentliche Beschreibung aller Stände auff Erden* (Frankfurt, 1568), a work that—deeply inspired by Luther—recognized a place in the social hierarchy for every calling. There was a contemporaneous Latin translation of this book by Hartmann Schopper, under the title Πανοπλία *omnium illiberalium mechanicarum aut sedentarium artium genera continens* (Frankfurt, 1568). But, while there is clearly some overlap between the moralizing works and the more technical treatises, the precise relation remains fuzzy. On the place of such writings within the context of late medieval and early modern literature, see Benjamin A. Rivkin, "Introduction" to the Dover facsimile edition of Amman and Sach's *Ständebuch* (New York, 1973), which places this book in the tradition of medieval encyclopedias and notes that the twelfth-century *Didascalicon* of Hugh of St. Victor, with its attention to the mechanical arts, was especially influential; Hellmut Lehman-Haupt's *The Book of Trades in the Iconography of Social Typology,* the first annual Bromsen Lecture, pamphlet of the Boston Public Library (Boston, 1976), which gives a brief outline of books of trades published from the fifteenth to the nineteenth century; and, finally, William Eamon, *Science and the Secrets of Nature in Medieval and Early Modern Culture* (Princeton: Princeton University Press, 1994), which, unfortunately, I have not been able to use in my study of Garzoni.

In Renaissance Italy, there were many such works. Extremely important was Polydore Vergil's *De inventoribus rerum,* which, first published in 1499, ran to more than 30 editions by the time of Vergil's death in 1555. Translated into Italian in 1543, it continued to be a "bestseller" throughout the latter half of the century, evidently with resonance among the popular as well as the elite classes. Though Vergil's work dealt with many issues other than crafts, it covered a wide variety of trades, from agriculture to glass making to architecture. See Denys Hay, *Polydore Vergil* (London, 1952), 52–78. In the late sixteenth century, a number of works appeared that attempted, trades are more likely than political treatises—the readership of which was decidedly more limited—to reveal the ways in which nonelite groups thought about the social and political order. These works, I argue, provide essential clues about early modern perceptions; they tell us something about the ways in which texts in early modern Italy provided a language or a set of categories through which readers (above all, merchants and artisans) could come to *envision their social universe*. And, as we shall see, the social categories such texts offered were often sharply at odds with the models of society that the more privileged orders hoped their subjects would adopt as their own.

Among Italian books of trades there is none that for sheer enormity and complexity can compare with Tommaso Garzoni's *La Piazza universale di tutte le professioni del mondo*, first published in Venice in 1585. This work of nearly 1,000 pages, with its 155 *discorsi* and discussions of over 400 professions or occupations, is a veritable quarry of information about the most varied social groups: from street singers to actors, and from humanists to bakers.[4] Moreover, this book certainly represents one of the more successful works within the genre. The erudite Girolamo Ghilini was entirely accurate in his mid-seventeenth-century observation that "as soon as the *Piazza* was taken off the press, it had everywhere the greatest appeal and approval."[5] For by the 1650s, some

---

much as Amman's and Sach's *Ständebuch* had done, to provide an overview of the professions: Leonardo Fioravanti's *Dello specchio di scientia universale* (1542), Gregorio Morelli's *Scala di tutte le scienze, et arti* (1568), and Tommaso Garzoni's *La piazza universale di tutte le professioni del mondo* (1585). Reflections on the crafts and trades had become part of the fashion of late Renaissance culture.

4. Tommaso Garzoni, a Lateran canon, was well known in the late sixteenth and early seventeenth centuries for a variety of works. He was born in the Romagna in 1549 and briefly studied law in Ferrara and Siena before taking vows. He died in 1589. Garzoni's writings include *Il teatro de' vari e diversi cervelli mondani* (Venice, 1583), *L'hospidale de' pazzi incurabili* (Venice, 1586), *La sinagoga de' gl'ignoranti* (Venice, 1589), and *Il serraglio de gli stupori del mondo* (Venice, 1604), as well as an edition of the works of Hugh of St. Victor. The best introdution to Garzoni is Paolo Cerchi, *Enciclopedismo e la politica della riscrittura: Tommaso Garzoni* (Pisa, 1980), but see also Benedetto Croce, "Pagine di Tommaso Garzoni, *La critica* 42 (1944): 251–59; and Ugo Tucci, "I mestieri nella *Piazza universale* del Garzoni," in *Studi in memoria di Luigi del Pane* (Bologna, 1982), 319–31. In my view, Cerchi's reading minimizes the paradoxical nature of Garzoni's text and exaggerates its efforts to repress the Erasminan elements in the popular writings of such figures as Doni, Lando, and Agrippa. Nonetheless, it should be noted that Swift's observation concerning Burton's *Melancholy*—"an infinite digression on an infinity of subjects"—applies to *La Piazza universale* as well. The current study examines a multidimensional work from only one angle: it makes no claim to be comprehensive.

5. Girolamo Ghilini, *Teatro d'huomini letterati*, vol. 1 (Venice, 1647), 217.

30 editions of this compendious work had been published.[6] Its popularity, moreover, may have even encouraged the German satirist Grimmelshausen to plunder it for its detailed descriptions of the low life.[7] Yet
not all opinion was favorable. After the first edition of the work, humanists protested that they had been omitted from the *professioni* Garzoni
described, and a seventeenth-century Spanish critic accused Garzoni of
promising more than he delivered.[8] What is certain, however, is that for
some 80 years the work was well known in Europe, provoking considerable discussion. Then, from the late seventeenth century on, Garzoni's
star is fallen—the man and his works become forgotten to all but a handful of erudites.

At first Garzoni's perceptions of the social world of his day appear
fully in keeping with the courtly and hierarchical values of the late
Renaissance. For although the piazza (the imaginary town square that
serves as the organizing principle of Garzoni's text) carries the reader
directly into the bustle of everyday life, it is a bustle that Garzoni orches-
trates and choreographs with the goal of preserving or even increasing
social distinctions. To take two extremes as examples, latrine cleaners are
relegated to the most distant corners of the piazza while *signori* are permitted to stroll at its very center.[9] The German publisher Merians, in his
expensive German edition of the work, captured this choreography with
a detailed engraving. At the center of an imaginary city rides a prince,
and around him in the distance are the various craftsmen and charlatans

---

6. I count 29 editions in all, including 1 Latin and 4 German translations and 4 editions of an adaption (a virtual but abridged translation) into Spanish.

7. J. J. C. von Grimmelshausen, *Simplicius Simplicissimus* (Nuremberg, 1688). On
Grimmelshausen's use of Garzoni—he plundered the German edition of 1619—see
Kenneth Nagus, *Grimmelshausen* (New York, 1974), 44.

8. After the first edition of his work, Garzoni was compelled to add a discorso on
humanists, and at the very beginning of this discorso he refers to the protests by the
members of this *professione* who had felt excluded: "Io pensava d'haver in questo mio
libro abbracciato, e compreso tutte le professioni" (Garzoni, *La Piazza universale di
tutte le professioni del mondo* [Venice: 1589], 956)—all my references to this work
will be to this, and not the first, edition. The Spanish critic was Baltasar Gracián in his
El Criticón (1651), cited in Tommaso Garzoni, *Opere*, ed. Paolo Cerchi (Naples,
1972), 505. See also Paul F. Grendler, "The Concept of Humanist in Cinquecento
Italy," in *Renaissance Studies in Honor of Hans Baron*, ed. A. Molho and J. A.
Tedeschi (Florence and DeKalb, 1971), 453–63.

9. On latrine cleaners (*curadestri*) and their place in the choreography of the
piazza, see Garzoni, *Piazza*, 847.

who populate the early modern city.[10] In this context, therefore, one might argue that Garzoni can be read as a kind of Galateo for the piazza, that he not only reflected the values of his time but that he also played a role in fashioning a hierarchical world.

There is much evidence for this. The *Piazza* begins, for example, with a dedication to Alfonso II, the duke of Ferrara, and the first three discourses focus on princes, magistrates, and ecclesiastics, groups traditionally placed at the summit of the social hierarchy. Moreover, his book is devoted as much to a discussion of the social practices of nobles, such as the hunt and dueling, from which mechanical men are excluded, as it is to urban trades.[11] But it is Garzoni's spirited diatribe against false nobles that provides the most support for maintaining the social hierarchy. The passage is contrived to keep the pretentious in their place. "This, my discorso," Garzoni proclaims at its very outset,

> will enlighten many *meccanici* who, nowadays, because they have four farthings in their purses and dress with stylish caps, obstinately love to be called *signori* and play the role of nobleman so openly that the whole city has nothing to speak of, if not of them—declaiming their grandfathers *facchini,* their fathers water porters, their brothers lowly night watchmen, their sisters whores, their mothers ruffians, and maintaining that all their ancestors were smeared with bacon fat, soiled with oil, bemudded with dung, tarred with pitch, beshitted with matter from the latrine, and decorated as chimney sweeps and slaters. . . . They will be enlightened, I say, because here one will see what constitutes true nobility, with so much authority and with the opinions of such worthy writers, that if they do not wish to persist with their noses buried in dung—in the stench of their own vileness—they will be forced to confess themselves plebians and not to have claimed their cottages for palaces, their slutty alleyways for *piazze,* their farms for cities, the view beyond their doors and walls for possessions and fields, woods for gardens, caverns for golden rooms, sheep and goats for pages, ploughing for knightly exercise, the mooing of the cows for the study of gentlemen, ditch digging for the efforts of a soldier, the lead-

10. Garzoni, *Piazza universale. Das ist: Allgemeiner Schawplatz Marckt und Zusammenkunfft Professionen Künften Gesschäfften Händeln und Handtwerken* (Frankfurt, 1659), frontispiece.

11. On hunters (*cacciatori*), see Garzoni, *Piazza,* 517–21; on champions in duels (*duellanti*), see 584–92.

ing of an ass or the carrying of a stretcher for the undertaking of an otherwise famous captain. The wretched really do not know what nobility is, but once they have been made sure of its essence, and once they have come to understand from how many sources it is derived, then they will better know their lowliness and ignobility.[12]

In this passage, which opens the *discorso* on nobles, Garzoni promises enlightenment, suggesting that the quixotic presumption of many is a consequence of their ignorance. With unbridled billingsgate, he mocks their pretensions. Garzoni suggests that social distinctions are needed, and he appears to develop a vision of Italian society in keeping with the refeudalization and the increasingly absolutist regimes of sixteenth-century Italy.

Garzoni's notion of hierarchy, moreover, serves not only to draw boundaries between lords and craftsmen but also to develop distinctions within the world of artisans. Yet, unlike many of his contemporaries, who made birth into a previously privileged family a prerequisite for nobility, Garzoni extends the notion of nobility to many of the crafts, to apothecaries, for example, and to watchmakers, tailors, printers, barbers, and furriers.[13] In doing so, he argues that the nobility of a craft is the consequence of many factors. The antiquity of an art might invest it with a certain *nobiltà,* but there are other criteria as well. It should be necessary, and it may even be ornamental. Another pivotal criterion for nobility is cleanliness, or rather a perception of cleanliness. He makes this explicit in the case of bookmen and barbers. Of the bookmen he notes, "there is nothing dirty at all about this;" and of the barbers he observes that their art is "clean and neat, having as its end and goal the cleanliness of the body."[14] But the principle becomes clearest in Garzoni's discussion of the vile arts. In any situation in which Garzoni perceives a material that is somehow foul or soils, even if the craft or art is ancient and necessary, he is likely to categorize it as vile. Of pork butchery, for example, Garzoni observes "it is also a dirty and vile trade, because its practitioners are always greasy like cooks, and between scullery boys and them one

---

12. Garzoni, *Piazza* (*nobilisti, overo gentilhuomini*), 167–68.

13. For apothecaries (*speciari*), see Garzoni, *Piazza,* 661–66; for watchmakers (*maestri d'horologi*), 622–25; tailors (*sartori*), 817–20; printers (*stampatori*), 833–35; barbers (*barbieri*), 855–57; furriers (*pelliciari*), 828–29.

14. On bookmen (*librari*), Garzoni, *Piazza,* 832; on barbers (*barbieri*), 856.

finds little or almost no difference."[15] Dyers, also practitioners of a vile art, "have their hands and faces all stained and soiled from their dyes."[16] Tanners, "known among the most vile, have a dirty, stinking trade, fetid beyond words."[17] And a similar principle seems to be at work for locksmiths, potters, linen workers, wool combers, rag venders, chimney sweeps and, not suprisingly, latrine cleaners.[18] The miller is the exception that proves the rule, for, "although his cap and frock coat are covered with flour, this makes little difference, since the dusting is white, and such that, if it is shaken out a bit, it quickly comes off."[19]

On one level, Garzoni's identification of the lowliest professions with filth and of nobility with cleanliness serves to heighten the awareness of boundaries within the social hierarchy. The *Piazza* seems to imply the existence of an underlying material principle in the shaping of a society of orders. And the material principle, by implication, acts to lock certain craftsmen into positions of inferior status. In this sense, Garzoni shares a preoccupation with cleanliness and hierarchy that was relatively widespread in early modern Italy. In his *Galateo,* for example, Monsignor Giovanni della Casa exorted his readers to wash their hands before eating and not to offer drink from a glass already used; in addition, he provided an etiquette for sneezing and for spitting—all matters of personal hygiene to us but primarily issues of social boundaries to sixteenth-century Italians.[20]

On another level, however, Garzoni's conception of the social world undermines the notion that material activity alone could determine status. In fact, his social vision would act to ennoble many of the crafts that the courts of Italy had come to denigrate. Certainly, to Garzoni, the vile appears to be the natural and unrefined, and, consequently, he vilifies the handlers of the products of nature—whether the flesh of animals or

---

15. Garzoni, *Piazza,* (*lardaruoli*), 822.
16. Garzoni, *Piazza* (*tintori*), 524.
17. Garzoni, *Piazza* (*maestri di corami*), 650.
18. On locksmiths, (*magnani*), see Garzoni, *Piazza,* 458; potters (*figuli, o vasari*), 465–66; linen workers (*linaruoli*) and wool combers (*scartegini*), 487; rag venders (*stracciaroli*), 917; chimney sweeps (*spazzacamini*), 844; latrine cleaners (*curadestri*), 847.
19. Garzoni, *Piazza* (*molinari*), 552.
20. Giovanni della Casa, *Galateo,* trans. Konrad Eisenbichler and Kenneth R. Bartlett (Ottawa, 1990); on this work, see Ruggiero Romano, "Intorno a talune opere de Monsignor Giovanni Della Casa," in Romano, *Tra due crisi: l'Italia del Renaissance* (Milan, 1971), esp. 170. Similar implications in the *Galateo* are explored by Norbert Elias, *The History of Manners,* trans. Edmund Jephcott (New York, 1978).

excrement. But the material distinction is not always determining. In fact, it is culture that plays the decisive role. To Garzoni, the possession of an intellective process—a skill, knowledge, technique, or theory—that shapes the environment is ennobling, even if the worker has direct contact with the natural. Thus, Garzoni is consistent when he praises gardeners—men who certainly have direct contact with nature. "Who can deny," Garzoni asks, "that, [although their art is vile in appearance], . . . they are celebrated both within and outside the Piazza?"[21] Similarly, following the Romans, and Varro in particular, he praises agriculture, noting the extensive knowledge the farmer must have in order to cultivate his fields, though he denigrates the peasant (*villano*) who "is sordid . . . and changes his shirt only when the snake changes his skin or the stag his horns, that is, only once a year."[22]

Clearly, therefore, Garzoni's categories are not naturally given; rather, they are socially constructed, and the crucial element that ennobles man is the use of his art, his wit, and his science. Even the use of one's hands is ennobling if it is seen as activity that is combined with the use of one's intellect. By drawing such distinctions, Garzoni enhanced the prestige of the elite crafts. He himself recognized that his inclusion of many of the most humble professions was bold, but he argued that such inclusiveness served a purpose, for, "although some are in themselves most vile, and infamous, nonetheless, they illustrate with their shame the more noble arts, as clouds cause the rays of the sun to appear more beautiful."[23] Garzoni not only ennobled the elite crafts, but he also gave them an elevated position within the social universe of artisans.

To the elite craftsmen of early modern Italy, therefore, Garzoni was doubtless appealing. His vision of the piazza enhanced their prestige both by associating them with the nobility and sharply distinguishing them from the vile arts. In this sense, Garzoni did not reflect but challenged the social arrangements of his time, for this was a period in which the overwhelming majority of the commercial and industrial arts were denigrated—even the term *meccanico* had come to be used as insult.[24] In par-

---

21. Garzoni, *Piazza* (*hortolani*), 894.

22. On Varro's praise of agriculture as a science, see Garzoni, *Piazza*, 505; on the disparagement of the *villani*, 510.

23. Garzoni, *Piazza*, 30.

24. "Ma percioché questa parola Mechaniche non verrà forse intesa da ciascheduno per lo suo vero significato, anzi troveransi di quelli chè stimeranno lei essere voce d'ingiuria (solendosi in molte parti d'Italia dire ad altrui Mechanico per ischerno et villania, et alcuni per essere chiamati Ingegnieri si prendono sdegno), non

ticular, manual work, which in the earlier Renaissance had at times been viewed as a mark of honor, was increasingly deprecated. In 1569, for example, an elaborate legal procedure was instituted in Venice to limit the rights of citizenship (a special status, which conferred both commercial and office-holding privileges) to those wealthy inhabitants of the city who had never worked with their hands.[25] The entreaty of a certain Sebastiano Masilio, the son of an apothecary, is illustrative. In his petition for citizenship before the *Avogaria di Comun,* he asserted, "I have always lived honorably and never practiced a mechanical art," and the judges of the *Avogaria* sought to make sure that not only he but also his father had never worked with his hands.[26] "In all well-ordered Republics," the Venetian political theorist Giovanni Maria Memmo observed at about the same time—and his views were widely shared by his contemporaries throughout Italy—"the plebes and the artisans have been excluded from the administration of the state, as they themselves are deprived of virtue . . . and in fact it is impossible that those who are occupied in the manual arts should be able to obtain any virtue."[27] Garzoni, quite clearly, offered an alternative perspective, one that, although it disenfranchised many artisans, simultaneously ennobled many others. To these latter craftsmen, he offered a language of pride and honor. He

---

sarà fuor di proposito ricordare che Mechanico è vocabolo honoratissimo," (*Le Mecaniche dell'illustrissimo sig. Guido Ubaldo de' Marchesi del Monte* [Venice, 1581], cited in Rossi, *I filosofi e le macchine,* 62).

25. On the esteem accorded manual labor in the fourteenth century, see Richard MacKenney, "Arti e stato a Venezia tra tardo Medio Evo e '600," *Studi veneziani,* n.s., 5 (1981), 129; and, on the active role of guildsmen in fourteenth-century Florentine politics—also a measure of the esteem they enjoyed—John Najemy, "Guild Republicanism in Trecento Florence: The Successes and Ultimate Failure of Corporate Politics," *American Historical Review* 84 (1979): 53–71. On the 1569 legislation in Venice, see especially Giuseppe Trebbi, "La cancelleria veneta nei secoli XVI e XVII," *Annali della Fondazioni Luigi Einaudi* 14 (Turin, 1980). Trebbi observes, "fin dagli anni settanta del Cinquecento, gli aspiranti al riconoscimento della cittadinanza originaria devono dimostrare che la loro famiglia sia astenuta, almeno da tre generazioni, dall'esercizio di 'arti mechaniche'" (70).

26. "et sempre son visuto honoratamente ne mai feci esertitio mechanico" (*Archivo di Stato di Venezia, Avogaria di Comun, cittadinaza originaria,* busta 365/5, petition of 12 April 1578).

27. Giovanni Maria Memmo, *Dialogho . . . nel quale dopo alcune filosofiche dispute, si forma un perfetto Prencipe, et una perfetta Republica, e parimente un Senatore, un soldato, et un mercante* (Venice, 1563), 92. Marino Berengo offers an excellent discussion of the growing class consciousness of the Italian nobility in the late sixteenth century in his *Nobili e mercanti nella Lucca del Cinquecento* (Turin, 1965), 254–63. He connects this consciousness to changes in the Italian economy and

gave them a sense of place and importance, and he even provided them with collective genealogies that celebrated the antiquity, usefulness, skill, and beauty of their trades.

But the power and the delightfulness of *La piazza universale* does not lie merely in the ennoblement of the elite crafts; it lies also in Garzoni's ability, through paradox and satire, to call the social arrangements of his day into question.[28] In Garzoni's lively prologue, cast in the form of a debate between Momo, the fault-finding god of mutterers and pedants, and Minerva, the goddess of wisdom, Momo objects that the work is too leveling. Garzoni, Momo asserts, "upsets the world and the elements with his countless complaints against the professors of the sciences and the trades." "The author," he continues, "makes fun of all conditions of men without regard more for this one than for that one."[29] While Minerva accurately counters that Garzoni does rank the *professioni,* my analysis of work confirms not only Minerva's but also Momo's point of view. The seventeenth-century poet Iacomo Cesato, moreover, noted that Garzoni's writings were most often in the possession of the "capricciosi" and that many judged his writings witty.[30] And the frontispiece of the 1659 German edition noted that the *Piazza* was "lustig zu lesen."[31] A first exploration of the work might suggest a ponderous seriousness, but Garzoni is constantly undermining the very structures he establishes.

The central organizing principle of the work—the use of the imaginary piazza as the *theatrum mundi*—is a signal that this is the case. To be sure, the first three discorsi are suggestive of a hierarchical principle. But the order in which Garzoni presents the other professions throughout the remainder of the work (and the balance of these overwhelms the first

---

observes that the stress on a nobility of wealth led to increasingly prejudicial views toward manual labor: "Nel diffuso declino delle attività mercantili, il volgersi del ceto nobiliare verso il godimento delle sue rendite patrimoniali e l'eslusivo monopolio degli *offici,* trovava il suo immediato riscontro nell'esclusione di ogni altro ceto dalla vita pubblica. La "viltà" del sedere al telaio o in piccola e media bottega assumeva cosí un significato nuovo, che al mondo comunale era rimasto sconosciuto" (257). On similar transformations in the Veneto, see Angelo Ventura, *Nobiltà e popolo nella società veneta del '400 e '500* (Bari, 1964).

28. For a different and decidedly lay current of social criticism and satire in Italian literature in the sixteenth century, see Paul Grendler, *Critics of the Italian World* (Madison, 1969).

29. Garzoni, *Piazza,* 1–2.

30. Iacomo Cesato, ed., *Rime piacevoli di sei begl'ingegni piene di fantasie, stravaganze, capricci, motti, sali, & argutie* (Vicenza, 1603), sig. a6.

31. Garzoni, *Piazza universale. Das ist: Allgemeiner Schawplatz,* title page.

three discourses) is seemingly random. As the literary scholar Paolo Cerchi has observed, "the apparently hierarchical design is quickly abandoned: from grammarians one passes to doctors of the law, then to calendar makers, surgeons, and pronosticators . . . and immediately after arithmeticians and other mathematicians come the butchers." Cerchi then adds, "if there is a logical order in the *Piazza, a me è sfuggito*" (it has escaped me).[32] But that is precisely Garzoni's point: the piazza was by its very nature open-ended and antihierarchical; it is the public stage par excellence that quite deliberately undermines courtly, absolutist claims that there is or should be a single, fixed ordering of the social world. Absolutist princes may have wished otherwise, but the public squares of Italian cities remained contested spaces.

Equally subversive of hierarchy is Garzoni's willingness to reprove all professions, from the most exalted or noble to the most humble or vile. Garzoni's world is woven with deceits, petty and grand. Deception is everywhere, from the tricks used by the charlatan to sell his potion, to the butcher who adds the weight of his thumb to his scales, to the merchant who, "with beautiful and mellifluous words," seeks to make his customers believe his goods to be other than they are.[33] It was to this aspect of the work that Momo objected in the prologue. And Minerva's defense, while justifying this approach, makes it clear that Garzoni spares no one. "He unveils the shortcomings of this profession and that one in order to eradicate vices and to help men by prudently revealing knowledge of evil to everyone."[34] Deceit and vice, therefore, are ubiquitous, and Garzoni's world, a social hierarchy, is not a moral one. To some degree, this vision is Augustinian. "God"—here Garzoni is citing Augustine—"made both the poor and the rich from the same soil."[35] But Garzoni's subversion of courtly values is not merely religious; it is also political. At the end of his discorso on magistrates, for example, he adopts the myth of Venetian stability and makes it clear that, in his mind, republican arrangements are superior to all others.[36]

---

32. Cerchi, *Enciclopedismo e la politica della riscrittura*, 58.
33. On the charlatans (*ceretani*), see Garzoni, *Piazza*, 741–49; on the butchers (*beccari*), 153; on the merchants (*mercanti*), 546.
34. Garzoni, *Piazza*, 7.
35. "Dominus de vno limo terrae fecit & pauperes, & diuites," Garzoni, *Piazza*, 32.
36. Garzoni, *Piazza*, 55. For the myth of Venice, Garzoni cites Cornelio Frangipane's celebrated oration to Doge Francesco Donà. On this oration, see Edward Muir, *Civic Ritual in Renaissance Venice* (Princeton, 1981), 14.

Ironically, the clearest evidence of Garzoni's refusal to allow the social hierarchy to stand on its own is his artful discorso on nobles. The discorso begins—as we have seen—with a spirited satire on those *meccanici* whose pretensions lead them to claim to be *nobili* or *gentilhuomini*. And, indeed, in this discussion, the "true" nobleman is enlisted, and perhaps even pleased when Garzoni turns to the discussions, ancient and modern, of those writers who had grappled with the issue of what constitutes nobility: birth, wealth, or virtue. But, although Garzoni himself appears to embrace the view that "the true and most perfect nobility" is a combination of lineage and virtue, there is, in fact, no synthesis.[37] The discorso overwhelms the reader with a broad range of often conflicting opinions taken from biblical, Greek, Latin, and Italian sources, though Bartolus, Plato, and Aristotle—each with a sense of the diversity of nobility—are given the greatest emphasis. The author recognizes that the discussion, with its long list of authorities, is dizzying and constitutes something of an intellectual labyrinth, but, despite his efforts, he seems unable to summarize. The glory of one's ancestors, one's own wisdom, knowledge, virtue, proximity to a prince, wealth, and military accomplishments are all sources of nobility.[38] And just as the sources vary so does the practice—Garzoni has but to contrast the gallantry and the ostentation of the Neapolitan and Milanese nobles with the austerity of the Venetian and the Genoese, and then the urban style of the Italian nobles with the rural occupations of the French, German, and British, to drive this point home. But Garzoni never allows his presentation to remain static. For nobles, even "true nobles," there is an underside. Military prowess, for example, with its traditional dependence on murder, shows Garzoni "that, throughout much of history, malice has been the source from which the bloodied stream of this nobility is derived." History has other lessons as well. "Almost all nobility," he reminds us, "is derived from persons who in the beginning were ignoble and vile." This was certainly the case with Agathocles the Sicilian, who was the son of a potter, and with the French monarch Hugh Capet, a butcher's son. Momentarily the discorso, in its relativism, seems to break down all distinctions between true and false nobility. Despite all the philosophical discussion on the subject—a preoccupation of much Counter Reformation literature—nobility is the claim of those who can make it and is neither absolute nor God-given.

---

37. Garzoni, *Piazza*, (*nobilisti, overo gentilhuomini*), 170.
38. Garzoni, *Piazza*, 172.

Nonetheless, he concludes as he began, railing against those *nobili moderni,* those pretentious men and women who, with a bit of property, some fancy stockings, and a change of hats, turn the world upside-down, "depicting themselves to the world as nobles and are called such by the mad crowd." But they are, Garzoni adds, with a final allusion to the authorities, "mera canaglia."[39] The reader, however, is less convinced, for Garzoni has rested even the category of true nobility on such conflicting foundations. The discorso is structured, therefore, as a paradox. Garzoni is certainly mocking the lower classes for their pretensions, but he mocks the pretensions of the upper class as well.

A final but perhaps equally powerful aspect of the work that demonstrates that Garzoni is by no means committed to a hierarchical ordering of his world is the *affection* of his language. The body of Garzoni's writings made it clear that the world was his subject and that his readings and interests carried him everywhere. But he did not treat all topics with the same enthusiasm. In fact, throughout *La Piazza universale,* he expresses the most affection for those groups in society that had no possibility of incorporation into the established social hierarchy. Like the mannerist painters of his time, Garzoni allows seemingly secondary motifs to become suddenly prominent.[40] Indeed, Garzoni's greatest fascination is for the rogues and ruffians, the charlatans and itinerant actors, the tricksters of his world. It is in his discussion of this genuinely popular world that the piazza comes to life.

The number of charlatans in his own time—so he tells us—had grown like weeds, "in such a way that in every city, in every land, in every piazza, one does not see anything but charlatans and mountebanks."[41] Moreover, Garzoni knows the deceits and tricks of this *mal'erba,* and he seems committed to putting the reader on notice about the types of mountebanks who are intent on taking money from the unsuspecting. Similarly, he writes of ruffians that the rogues are not victims of poverty but of sheer laziness. They lead lascivious lives, and Garzoni asserts his approval of the efforts of the authorities to control such vagabonds, in the case of Venice actually naming one of the better-known ruffians, a

---

39. On the diversity of noble styles of life, see Garzoni, *Piazza,* 176; on the underside of noble origins, 176; and on the pretensions of *nobili moderni,* 177.

40. On mannerism in this period, see Arnold Hauser, *Mannerism: The Crisis of the Renaissance and the Origin of Modern Art* (London, 1965). Paolo Cerchi has also compared Garzoni and the mannerists; see his introduction to *Le opere di Tommaso Garzoni.*

41. Garzoni, *Piazza (ceretani, o ciurmatori),* 742.

certain Zulfino, who, once his dissimulations had been uncovered, had been expelled from the city.[42]

Despite these pieties, this early modern underworld fascinates Garzoni. He discusses the *zergo* of its inhabitants ("a language that they have made up among themselves, which few outside their sect can understand") and describes the tricks by which some pretend to be lepers and others lords.[43] Once again, deceit is equalizing. But most striking to the reader is the sudden liveliness of the piazza. If we visit the piazza late in the evening with Garzoni, from ten until midnight, there are charlatans everywhere, and the square, whose life Garzoni otherwise struggles so hard to choreograph, remains characterized by the spontaneous and the unexpected. "In one corner of the piazza," he observes,

> you'll see a galant Fortunato spin yarns along with Fritata and entertain a crowd. . . . They make up stories, tales, and dialogues and unravel mysteries. They improvise songs, argue violently with one another, make up, and burst into laughter, argue again, then jump up onto their bench, interrogate each other, and finally pull out their pill box—which is, after all, the point of all this chatter. In another corner, Burattino yells out that it seems the executioner is about to hang him. With a porter's sack on his back and the cap of a scoundrel on his head, he calls out loudly for an audience. And the people come over, with the plebians pushing and the gentlemen making their way to the front; and he has hardly furnished his delightful, comic prologue before he begins a strange story about Padrone, but he breaks the arms, stunts the minds, and ruins the finances of all who gather about to listen to him. And if this one with pleasing gestures, sharp sayings, words spiced for others' ears, comic tales, the neck of a hanged man, a thief's mustache, and the voice of a monkey, the acts of a ruffian, gathers up a sizable crowd, another will drive him away with garbled speech, a Bolognese accent, fatuous talk, barber's tales, the flaunting of his doctoral privileges, the certificates of his lords, and his proclamation that he is a doctor without learning.[44]

---

42. Garzoni, *Piazza* (*guidoni, o furfanti, o calchi*), 580–81.

43. Garzoni, *Piazza*, 582.

44. Garzoni, *Piazza*, 745. For both the social and literary context of Garzoni's discussion of charlatans, see Piero Camporesi's introduction to his edition of the *Speculum cerretanorum*, in Piero Camporesi, ed., *Il libro dei vagabondi* (Turin, 1980), esp. xcv–cxli.

But others—and Garzoni's rich description continues—spring up to replace him. There is a Tuscan, a Milanese, and a Mantuan.[45] In every part of the piazza, there is a spontaneity that defies all hierarchy.

But how does one account for the success of the *Piazza universale?* In part, its popularity may have been the consequence of what Rosalie Colie has felicitously called the *paradoxia epidemica,* that profusion of paradox in the literature of the late Renaissance, a fashion that was itself largely the result of the profound upheaval in moral and political values that took place in the sixteenth century.[46] From the vantage point of the social historian, however, the success, and therefore the meaning, of Garzoni's work cannot be explained in purely literary terms. A work of literature, after all, does not respond merely to other works of literature; it can also respond to shifting social and political conditions. And when a work is both widely read and read in a well-defined period of time—Garzoni's *Piazza* meets both conditions—its value for the historian is immense. Moreover, in the case of Garzoni's work—with its stress on the ubiquity of deceit and pretense; in its passion for the spontaneous, popular and unincorpated world; and, above all, in its use of the piazza as the central metaphor for his reflections on the nature of social hierarchy—it becomes clear that at least some men and women in the late Renaissance had begun to call into question the increasingly hierarchical arrangements of their times. In the Italy of the late Renaissance, therefore, the society of orders was not without its critics. One book of trades is only a beginning, but its analysis is suggestive. For the history of the late Renaissance, it seems, books of trades hold the promise of illuminating broadly held assumptions about the social order, even of providing the foundations for an anthropology of popular attitudes toward politics and work—power and labor—in early modern Europe.

---

45. Garzoni, *Piazza,* 745–46.

46. Rosalie Colie, *Paradoxia Epidemica: The Renaissance Tradition of Paradox* (Princeton, 1966), esp. 33.

A Bibliography of David Herlihy's Works

The following bibliography includes Professor Herlihy's books, articles, edited volumes, source collections, and published lectures. It includes review essays but not reviews of individual books. It does not include encyclopedia entries. Translations are listed under the heading of the original publication in English. Reprintings have been noted whenever possible.

1951

1. "Battle against Bigotry: Father Peter C. Yorke and the American Protective Association in San Francisco, 1893–97." *Records of the American Catholic Historical Society of Philadelphia* 62 (1951): 95–120.

1954

2. "Pisan Coinage and the Monetary Development of Tuscany, 1150–1250." *American Numismatic Society. Museum Notes* 6 (1954): 143–68.
3. "Una nuova notizia sull'origine della *curia maris*." *Bollettino Storico Pisano* 22–23 (1953–54): 222–27.

1957

4. "Treasure Hoards in the Italian Economy, 960–1139." *Economic History Review* 10 (1957): 1–14. Reprinted in 52.

1958

5. *Pisa in the Early Renaissance: A Study of Urban Growth*. New Haven: Yale University Press; reprinted, Port Washington, N.Y.: Kennikat Press, 1973. Italian translation, *Pisa nel duecento. Vita economica e sociale d'una città nel medioevo*. Cultura e Storia Pisana, no. 3. Pisa: Nistri Lischi, 1974; 2d ed., 1990.
6. "The Agrarian Revolution in Southern France and Italy, 801–1150." *Speculum* 33 (1958): 23–41. Reprinted in 52.

1959

7. "The History of the Rural Seigneury in Italy, 751–1200." *Agricultural History* 33 (1959): 58–71. Reprinted in 52.

1960

8. "The Carolingian Mansus." *Economic History Review* 13 (1960): 79–89. Reprinted in 52.

1961

9. "Church Property on the European Continent, 701–1200." *Speculum* 36 (1961): 81–105. Reprinted in 52.

1962

10. "Land, Family and Women in Continental Europe, 701–1200." *Traditio* 18 (1962): 89–120. Reprinted in *Women in Medieval Society*, 13–46. Ed. Susan Mosher Stuard. Philadelphia: University of Pennsylvania Press, 1976. Reprinted in 52.

1964

11. "Direct and Indirect Taxation in Tuscan Urban Finance, ca. 1200–1400." *Finances et comptabilités urbaines du XVIIIe au XVIe siècle*, 385–405. Actes du Colloque International Blankenberge, 1962. Brussels: Centre Pro Civitate. Reprinted in 58.

1965

12. "Population, Plague and Social Change in Rural Pistoia, 1201–1430." *Economic History Review* 18 (1965): 225–44. Reprinted in 58.

1966

13. "Medieval Society: Peasant, Lord and Townsman." In *Great Problems in European Civilization*, 124–51. Ed. Kenneth M. Setton and Henry R. Winkler. 2d ed. Englewood Cliffs, N.J.: Prentice Hall.
14. "An Essay in Social History: The Society Which Gave Us Dante and Giotto." *Newsletter of Phi Sigma Theta* 37 (1966): 6ff.

1967

15. *Medieval and Renaissance Pistoia. The Social History of an Italian Town.* New Haven: Yale University Press. Italian translation, *Pistoia nel medioevo e nel rinascimento, 1200–1430.* Florence: Olschki, 1972.

1968

16. *Medieval Culture and Society*. New York: Harper & Row; and New York: Walker.
17. "Santa Maria Impruneta: A Rural Commune in the Late Middle Ages." In *Florentine Studies: Politics and Society in Renaissance Florence*, 242–76. Ed. Nicolai Rubinstein. London: Faber; Evanston, Ill.: Northwestern University Press. Reprinted in 58; Italian translation, "Santa Maria Impruneta: un comune rurale nel tardo Medioevo" in 76, 7–46.

1969

18. (With Robert S. Lopez and Vsevolod Slessarev, eds.) *Economy, Society, and Government in Medieval Italy: Essays in Memory of Robert L. Reynolds*. Kent, Ohio: Kent State University Press.
19. "Family Solidarity in Medieval Italian History." In *Economy, Society, and Government in Medieval Italy*, 173–84. Ed. David Herlihy, Robert S. Lopez, and Vsevolod Slessarev. Kent, Ohio: Kent State University Press. Reprinted in 52.
20. "Vieillir à Florence au Quattrocento." *Annales: Sociétés-Economies-Civilisations* 24 (1969): 1338–52. Reprinted in 58.

1970

21. "The Tuscan Town in the Quattrocento: A Demographic Profile." *Medievalia et Humanistica*, n.s. 1 (1970): 81–109. Reprinted in 58.
22. "Computerizing the Manuscript Census—A Comment." *Historical Methods Newsletter* 4 (1970): 10–11.

1971

23. *The History of Feudalism*. New York: Walker; reprinted, Atlantic Highlands, N.J.: Humanities Press; Sussex: Harvester Press, 1979.
24. *Women in Medieval Society*. The Smith History Lecture. Houston: University of St. Thomas. Reprinted in 52.
25. "Alienation in Medieval Culture and Society." In *Alienation: Concept, Term, and Meanings*, 125–40. Ed. Frank Johnson. New York: Seminar Press. Reprinted in 52.
26. "The Economy of Traditional Europe." *Journal of Economic History* 31 (1971): 153–64.
27. "Editing for the Computer—The Florentine Catasto of 1427." *American Council of Learned Societies Newsletter* 22, no. 2 (March 1971): 1–7.
28. "Yves Renouard and the Economic History of the Middle Ages." *American Historical Review* 76 (1971): 127–31.

1972

29. "Mapping Households in Medieval Italy." *Catholic Historical Review* 58 (1972): 1–24. Reprinted in 58.
30. "Marriage at Pistoia in the Fifteenth Century." *Bullettino Storico Pistoiese,* ser. 3, 7 (1972): 3–21. Reprinted in 58.
31. "Problems of Record Linkages in Tuscan Fiscal Documents of the Fifteenth Century." In *Identifying People in the Past,* 41–56. Ed. E. A. Wrigley. London: Arnold. Reprinted in 58.
32. "Quantification and the Middle Ages." In *The Dimensions of the Past. Materials, Problems, and Opportunities for Quantitative Work in History,* 13–51. Ed. Val R. Lorwin and Jacob M. Price. New Haven: Yale University Press.
33. "Raymond de Roover—Historian of Mercantile Capitalism." *Journal of European Economic History* 1 (1972): 755–62.
34. "Some Social and Psychological Roots of Violence in the Tuscan Cities." In *Violence and Civil Disorder in Italian Cities, 1200–1500,* 129–54. Ed. Lauro Martines. Berkeley and Los Angeles: University of California Press. Reprinted in 58.

1973

35. "Ecological Conditions and Demographic Change." In *One Thousand Years. Western Europe in the Middle Ages,* 3–43. Ed. Richard L. DeMolen. Boston: Houghton Mifflin.
36. "L'economia della città e del distretto di Lucca secondo le carte private nell'alto medioevo." In *Atti del V. Congresso internazionale di studi sull'alto medioevo,* 363–88. Spoleto: Centro di studi sull'alto medioevo. Reprinted in 52.
37. "The Population of Verona in the First Century of Venetian Rule." In *Renaissance Venice,* 91–120. Ed. J. R. Hale. London: Faber and Faber; Totowa, N.J.: Rowman and Littlefield. Reprinted in 58.
38. "Three Patterns of Social Mobility in Medieval Society." *Journal of Interdisciplinary History* 3 (1973): 623–47. Reprinted in 52.

1974

39. *The Family in Renaissance Florence.* Forums in History, FE 125. St. Charles, Mo.: Forum Press.
40. (With Mortimer Chambers, Raymond Grew, Theodore K. Rabb, and Isser Woloch.) *The Western Experience.* New York: Knopf. 2d ed., 1979; 3d ed., 1983; 4th ed., 1987; 5th ed., 1991; 6th ed., 1995.
41. "The Generation in Medieval History." *Viator* 5 (1974): 347–64. Reprinted in 52.

1975

42. "Life Expectancies for Women in Medieval Society." In *The Role of Women in the Middle Ages,* 1–22. Papers of the sixth annual conference of the Center for Medieval and Early Renaissance Studies, State University of New York at Binghamton, 6–7 May 1972. Ed. Rosemarie Thee Morewedge. Binghamton, N.Y.: State University of New York Press. Reprinted in 52.

1976

43. "Computer Assisted Analysis of the Statistical Documents of Medieval Society." *Medieval Studies: An Introduction,* 185–211. Ed. James M. Powell. Syracuse, N.Y.: Syracuse University Press. 2d ed., 1992.
44. "The Medieval Marriage Market." In *Medieval and Renaissance Studies 6. Proceedings of the Southeastern Institute of Medieval and Renaissance Studies, Summer, 1974,* 3–27. Ed. Dale B. J. Randall. Durham, N.C.: Duke University Press. Reprinted in 52.
45. "Società e spazio nella città italiana del Medio Evo." In *La storiografia urbanistica,* 174–90. Atti del primo Convegno internazionale di storia urbanistica, Lucca, 24–28 settembre 1975. Ed. Roberta Martinelli and Lucia Nuti. Lucca: CISCU. Reprinted in 58.

1977

46. (With Harry A. Miskimin and Abraham Udovitch.) *The Medieval City.* New Haven: Yale University Press.
47. "Deaths, Marriages, Births, and the Tuscan Economy (ca. 1300–1550)." In *Population Patterns in the Past,* 135–64. Ed. Ronald Demos Lee. New York: Academic Press. Reprinted in 58.
48. "The Distribution of Wealth in a Renaissance Community: Florence, 1427." In *Towns in Societies,* 131–57. Ed. Philip Abrams and E. A. Wrigley. Cambridge: Cambridge University Press.
49. "Family and Property in Renaissance Florence." In *The Medieval City,* 3–24. Ed. Harry A. Miskimin, David Herlihy, and Abraham Udovitch. New Haven: Yale University Press. Reprinted in 58.
50. (With Léopold Génicot, Robert-Henri Bautier, Augusto Campana, André Sempoux, and Jean François Lemarignier.) "Tavola Rotonda: Tipologia delle fonti." In *Fonti medioevali e problematica storiografica,* 63–83. Atti del Congresso internazionale tenuto in occasione del 90o anniversario della fondazione dell'Istituto Storico Italiano (1883–1973), Roma, 22–27 ottobre 1973. 2 vols. Rome: Istituto Storico Italiano per il Medio Evo, 1976–77.

1978

51. (With Christiane Klapisch-Zuber.) *Les Toscans et leurs familles. Une étude du Catasto florentin de 1427.* Paris: Fondation nationale des sciences poli-

tiques and Ecole des hautes études en sciences sociales. English translation, *Tuscans and their Families: A Study of the Florentine Catasto of 1427.* New Haven: Yale University Press, 1984; paper ed., 1989. Italian translation, *Toscani e le loro famiglie. Uno studio sul catasto fiorentino del 1427.* Bologna: Il Mulino, 1988.

52. *The Social History of Italy and Western Europe, 700–1200.* London: Variorum Reprints.

53. "Computation in History: Styles and Methods." *Computer* 11 (August 1978): 8–17.

54. "Medieval Children." In *Essays on Medieval Civilization. The Walter Prescott Webb Memorial Lectures,* 109–41. Ed. Bede Karl Lackner and Kenneth Roy Philip. Austin: University of Texas Press.

55. "The Natural History of Medieval Women." *Natural History* 87 (March 1978): 56–67.

56. "Le relazioni economiche di Firenze con le città soggette nel secolo XV." In *Egemonia fiorentina ed autonomie locali nella Toscana nord-occidentale del primo Rinascimento: vita, arte, cultura,* 79–109. Settimo Convegno internazionale del Centro italiano di studi di storia e d'arte, Pistoia, 18–25 settembre 1975. Pistoia: Centro italiano di studi di storia e d'arte; Bologna: Editografica.

1979

57. (With Christiane Klapisch-Zuber.) "Le cadastre florentin du XVe siècle et l'ordinateur." In *Fifth International Conference of Economic History. Cinquième Conférence internationale d'histoire économique, Leningrad 1970,* 8: 83–88. 8 vols. Ed. Herman Van der Wee, Vladimir A. Vinogradov, Grigorii G. Katovsky. Ecole des hautes études en sciences sociales, Congrès et colloques, no. 15. The Hague, Paris, and New York: Mouton, 1974–79.

1980

58. *Cities and Society in Medieval Italy.* London: Variorum Reprints.

1981

59. "Numerical and Formal Analysis in European History." *Journal of Interdisciplinary History* 12 (1981): 115–35.

60. "The Problem of the 'Return to the Land' in Tuscany." In *Civiltà ed economia agricola in Toscana nei secc. XIII–XV. Problemi della vita delle campagne nel tardo medioevo,* 401–16. Ottavo Convegno internazionale del Centro italiano di studi di storia e d'arte, Pistoia, 21–24 aprile 1977. Pistoia: Centro italiano di studi di storia e d'arte.

61. (With Christiane Klapisch-Zuber.) "Reflections and Responses." *Journal of Interdisciplinary History* 11 (1981): 503–6.

62. "Renaissance Florentine Historiography: Three Recent Studies." Review essay: G. Brucker, *The Civic World of Early Renaissance Florence;* F. W. Kent, *Household and Lineage in Renaissance Florence;* D. Kent, *The Rise of the Medici Faction in Florence, 1426–1434. Medievalia et Humanistica,* n.s., 10 (1981): 229–33.

1982

63. "Santa Caterina and San Bernardino: Their Teachings on the Family." In *Atti del simposio internazionale cateriniano-bernardiniano, Siena 17–20 aprile 1980,* 917–33. Ed. Domenico Maffei and Paulo Nardi. Siena: Accademia Senese degli Intronati.

1983

64. "The Making of the Medieval Family: Symmetry, Structure, Sentiment." *Journal of Family History* 8 (1983): 116–30.

1984

65. "The American Medievalist: A Social and Professional Profile." *Speculum* 58 (1983): 881–90.
66. "History and Culture of the Italian Middle Ages: Two Recent Studies." Review essay: M. Becker, *Medieval Italy;* W. Bowsky, *A Medieval Italian Commune. Medievalia et Humanistica,* n.s., 12 (1984): 235–38.
67. "Households in the Early Middle Ages: Symmetry and Sainthood." In *Households: Comparative and Historical Studies of the Domestic Group,* 383–406. Ed. Robert M. Netting, Richard R. Wilk, and Eric J. Arnould. Berkeley: University of California Press.

1985

68. "Avances recientes de la demografia historica y de la historia de la familia." In *La historiografía en Occidente desde 1945: actitudes, tendencias y problemas metodológicos,* 223–45. Actes de las III Conversaciones Internacionales de Historia, Universidad de Navarra, Pamplona, 5–7 aprile 1984. Ed. V. Vázquez de Prada, I. Olabarri, and A. Floristán Imízcoz. Pamplona: Ediciones Universidad de Navarra.
69. "Did Women Have a Renaissance? A Reconsideration." *Medievalia et Humanistica,* n.s., 13 (1985): 1–22.

1987

70. *Medieval Households.* Cambridge, Mass.: Harvard University Press. Italian translation, *La famiglia nel Medioevo.* Bari: Laterza, 1987; paper ed., 1989.

71. "The Family and Religious Ideologies in Medieval Europe." *Journal of Family History* 12 (1987): 3–17.
72. "The Florentine Merchant Family of the Middle Ages." In *Studi di storia economica toscana nel medioevo e nel rinascimento in memoria di Federigo Melis,* 179–201. Ed. Amleto Spicciani. Biblioteca del "Bollettino Storico Pisano," Collana Storica, 33. Pisa: Pacini.
73. "Outline of Population Developments in the Middle Ages." *Determinanten der Bevölkerungsentwicklung im Mittelalter,* 1–23. Ed. Bernd Herrmann and Rolf Sprandel. Weinheim: Acta Humaniora and VCH, 1987.
74. "El trabajo de la mujer en la sociedad medieval." Fundación Claudio Sánchez-Albornoz, *Memoria de Actividades, 1986–87,* 45–55. Avila: Gráficas Carlos Martin.
75. "Walls, Material and Moral." Review essay: J. Chapelot and R. Fossier, *The Village and House in the Middle Ages;* M. King, *Venetian Humanism in an Age of Patrician Domination. Medievalia et Humanistica,* n.s., 15 (1987): 207–10.

1988

76. (With Richard C. Trexler.) *L'Impruneta: una pieve, un santuario, un comune rurale.* Monte Oriolo, Impruneta and Florence: F. Papafava.
77. "Tuscan Names, 1200–1530 (The Josephine Waters Bennett Lecture)." *Renaissance Quarterly* 41 (1988): 561–82.

1990

78. *Opera Muliebria: Women and Work in Medieval Europe.* New York: McGraw Hill; Philadelphia: Temple University Press.
79. "Age, Property, and Career in Medieval Society." In *Aging and the Aged in Medieval Europe,* 143–58. Selected Papers from the Annual Conference of the Centre for Medieval Studies, University of Toronto, held 25–26 February and 11–12 November 1983. Ed. Michael M. Sheehan, CSB. Toronto: Pontifical Institute of Medieval Studies.
80. "Making Sense of Incest: Women and the Marriage Rules of the Early Middle Ages." In *Law, Custom, and the Social Fabric in Medieval Europe: Essays in Honor of Bryce Lyon,* 1–16. Ed. Bernard S. Bachrach and David Nicholas. Kalamazoo, Mich.: Western Michigan University.
81. "Women and the Sources of Medieval History: The Towns of Northern Italy." In *Medieval Women and the Sources of History,* 133–54. Ed. Joel T. Rosenthal. Athens, Ga.: University of Georgia Press.

1991

82. "The Rulers of Florence, 1282–1530." In *Athens and Rome, Florence and Venice: City-States in Classical Antiquity and Medieval Italy,* 197–221. Ed.

Anthony Molho, Kurt Raaflaub, and Julia Emlen. Stuttgart: Franz Steiner Verlag.

1992

83. "Black Death: Shock and Social Fissures." *The Maine Scholar* 5 (1992): 33–44.

Contributors

Samuel K. Cohn Jr. is Professor of Medieval History at the University of Glasgow.

Steven A. Epstein is Professor of History at the University of Colorado at Boulder.

David Herlihy was Barnaby Conrad and Mary Critchfield Keeney Professor at Brown University.

Christiane Klapisch-Zuber is a Professor at the Centre de Recherches Historiques at the Ecole des Hautes Etudes en Sciences Sociales.

Anthony Molho is Professor of History at Brown University. His coauthors are independent scholars in Florence.

Lisa M. Bitel is Assistant Professor of History and Women's Studies at the University of Kansas.

Barbara H. Rosenwein is Professor of History at Loyola University of Chicago.

Stephen D. White is Professor of History at Emory University.

Barbara M. Kreutz is Dean Emerita of the Graduate School of Arts and Sciences at Bryn Mawr College.

Stephen Weinberger is Robert Coleman Professor of History at Dickinson College.

Bruce L. Venarde is Visiting Assistant Professor of History at Tufts University.

James Given is Professor of History at the University of California at Irvine.

Maureen C. Miller is Associate Professor of History at Hamilton College.

Daniel F. Callahan is Professor of History at the University of Delaware.

George Dameron is Associate Professor of History at St. Michael's College.

Giovanni Ciappelli is a Professor of History at the Università degli Studi di Trento.

Giles Constable is Professor of History at the Institute for Advanced Studies.

Lorraine Attreed is Associate Professor of History at the College of the Holy Cross.

María Jesús Fuente is Professor of History at the Universidad Carlos III.

James M. Powell is Professor of History at Syracuse University.

Giorgio Chittolini is Professor of Medieval History at the Università Statale di Milano.

John Martin is Professor of History at Trinity University.

Index